FLORIDA REAL ESTATE Broker's Guide

Linda L. Crawford and Edward J. O'Donnell

President: Dr. Andrew Temte
Chief Learning Officer: Dr. Tim Smaby
Executive Director, Real Estate Education: Melissa Kleeman-Moy
Development Editor: Evonna Burr

FLORIDA REAL ESTATE BROKER'S GUIDE, FIFTH EDITION

Published by DF Institute, Inc., d/b/a Dearborn Real Estate Education
332 Front St. S., Suite 501
La Crosse, WI 54601

Printed in the United States of America
Second revision, January 2014
ISBN: 978-1-4277-4434-0 / 1-4277-4434-3
PPN: 1610-1305

CONTENTS

INTRODUCTION

Congratulations on taking the next step in your real estate career! Your decision to take the broker prelicense course indicates your commitment to increasing your professional competence.

This textbook follows the Florida Real Estate Commission (FREC) Course II syllabus and meets Florida's requirements for the 72-hour broker prelicense course. The material is designed to build on the knowledge licensees have obtained in education courses taken during their careers as sales associates.

The book is divided into four major sections.

Part I, "Getting Started in the Real Estate Brokerage Business," focuses on the important laws that regulate a broker's daily activities. Knowledge of these laws helps the licensee provide fair and honest service to consumers and reduces exposure to disciplinary action or civil damages. The material covers requirements for obtaining and maintaining a Florida real estate broker's license, the application and registration process, and the advantages and disadvantages of the different business entities that may be registered as brokerage firms. Escrow account management includes the time requirements for deposits, the procedures in case of disputes over the deposits, and the reconciliation requirements. Because the FREC periodically visits real estate offices to ensure compliance, a chapter covering office inspection and discipline is devoted to this. A chapter on owning and operating a brokerage firm covers budgeting for a new brokerage firm, accounting, tax requirements, and recruiting and training sales associates.

Part II, "Valuing Real Property," describes the process appraisers use to estimate a property's value. While brokers usually do not prepare appraisals in the normal course of their business, understanding the valuation process is critical in listing, marketing, and selling real property. Also critical is knowledge of laws and rules governing appraisal, set through the Appraiser Qualifications Board (AQB) and the Appraisal Standards Board (ASB). Licensees who list and sell real property must understand the steps involved in preparing a comparative market analysis, a subject covered in detail. Estimating the value of businesses also is included in this section.

Part III, "Listing and Selling Real Property," begins with a discussion of brokerage relationships with customers and principals. Contract law is described as it relates to a broker's listing and sales agreements. Because financing is the key to nearly every sale, licensees must understand the law as it relates to notes and mortgages, the different types of loan programs, and the qualification process. Every licensee must understand the duties required to close a transaction, as covered in this section. While licensees do not actually prepare closing statements, this section describes the process and contains three practical composite closing statement problems.

Part IV, "Specialties," provides an overview of several important subjects. The investment real estate chapter details the advantages and disadvantages of different types of income properties and provides you with an opportunity to practice financial analysis techniques. Brokers also must understand the laws regulating land planning and the comprehensive plan, as well as environmental issues affecting real estate transactions.

Managing investment property is another important brokerage specialty discussed in this section.

Understanding the vocabulary used in a profession is a key ingredient in mastering a subject area. This is particularly true in the real estate profession. Each chapter begins with key terms that are highlighted in bold print throughout the text, just before their definitions.

We also have included learning objectives at the beginning of each chapter. This is your guide to the most important points to be mastered in the text. End-of-chapter questions emphasize these concepts again.

Throughout the material, you will find important information such as legal references, examples, and case studies. These items were designed to help you better understand and apply each chapter's objectives.

The authors wish to express their appreciation to the following persons who were willing to provide their professional advice and the assistance necessary in the completion of this book.

Special thanks to those individuals who have thoughtfully and thoroughly reviewed previous editions of this text: Valleri J. Crabtree, JD, CLU, former Director of Instructor and Course Development, IFREC Real Estate Schools; Ron Guiberson, CRS, Bob Hogue School of Real Estate; Sandi M. Kellogg, Resource/Training Director, Coldwell Banker Ellison Realty, Inc.; Terence Nero, Real Estate Instructor, Gold Coast School of Real Estate; and Daniel J. Taddeo, Daniel Taddeo Real Estate School. Howard Stevens, Bob Hogue School of Real Estate, assisted with the development of Microsoft® PowerPoint® slides for this edition of the text. Howard also provided valuable suggestions for updating this edition of the text.

We would also like to thank the staff at Dearborn™ Real Estate Education, especially Evonna Burr, for their encouragement and professionalism.

We wish you well in your career as a Florida broker.

Linda L. Crawford
Edward J. O'Donnell
August 2013

PART ONE

GETTING STARTED IN THE REAL ESTATE BROKERAGE BUSINESS

CHAPTER

1 BECOMING A LICENSED REAL ESTATE BROKER

KEY TERMS

active license
address of record
broker associate
business broker
compensation
current mailing address
group license
involuntary inactive
license
moral turpitude
multiple licenses
mutual recognition agreements
nolo contendere
owner-developer
prima facie evidence
real estate services
real property
reciprocity
register
registration
resident
voluntary inactive
withhold adjudication

OVERVIEW

This chapter begins with an explanation of who must be licensed and the qualifications necessary for obtaining a Florida broker license. The prelicense education requirement and the various ways the experience requirement can be satisfied are detailed. Postlicensing and continuing education requirements also are presented, as are exemptions from the educational requirements. Finally, the chapter discusses how to obtain a broker's license through mutual recognition and contrasts real estate licensure and registration. It also covers license regulations in detail.

Once you have completed this chapter, you should be able to:

- explain the postlicensing and continuing education requirements for brokers;
- list exceptions to the broker prelicense course requirement;
- explain the three ways a broker applicant can satisfy the experience requirement;
- discuss the requirements for obtaining a broker license through mutual recognition;
- distinguish between voluntary and involuntary inactive statuses;
- distinguish between licensure and registration;
- distinguish between a group license and multiple licenses;

- understand the rules regarding change of address and residency; and
- identify practices exempt from licensure.

REAL ESTATE SERVICES

The Florida real estate license law identifies eight real estate-related activities referred to as *real estate services* that require a Florida real estate license. **Real estate services** include any real estate activity involving compensation for performing the service for another. To remember the eight services of real estate, use the memory crutch (mnemonic) acronym A BAR SALE, where the first letter of each service forms the memory aid.

TO REMEMBER: A BAR SALE

A	Advertise real estate services
B	Buy
A	Appraise
R	Rent or provide rental information or lists
S	Sell
A	Auction
L	Lease
E	Exchange

Real estate services are further defined in law to include the following activities in the sale, exchange, or lease of real property, including mineral rights, business enterprises, or business opportunities:

- Offer to, agree to, or attempt to perform real estate activities
- Advertise or otherwise indicate to the public that one is in the business of performing real estate services
- Direct or assist in the procurement of sellers, buyers, lessors, or lessees
- Negotiate or close a real estate transaction (*Note*: Case law has determined that the *intention* to close a real estate transaction is sufficient.)

Anyone who performs real estate services for another person for compensation of any type must be licensed, unless specifically exempted by law. **Compensation** is defined as anything of value or a valuable consideration, directly or indirectly paid, promised, or expected to be paid or received. Compensation includes money in the form of a salary, bonuses, commissions, and gratuities. Compensation is also things of value such as dinner, flowers, wine, gift certificates, event tickets, and so forth.

It is a violation of license law to share a commission with or to pay a fee or other compensation to an unlicensed person for the referral of real estate business clients, prospects, or customers. However, a Florida broker may pay a referral fee to a broker licensed in another state so long as the foreign broker does not violate Florida law.

LICENSE APPLICATION

A Social Security number is required to apply for a real estate license. In the Full Legal Name section of the license application, applicants must enter their name as it appears on their Social Security card. Florida law requires that an applicant's Social Security number be disclosed on all professional license applications. The Social Security number is used to determine whether applicants are in compliance with child support obligations.

A real estate license application is good for two years from the date the complete application is received by the DBPR.

GENERAL LICENSING PROVISIONS

Sales associates and broker associates are employed by and work under the direction and control of a broker or an owner-developer. Sales associates and broker associates are agents of their employer. An **owner-developer** is an unlicensed entity that sells, exchanges, or leases its own property. An example of an owner-developer is a real estate development company that owns land that it develops into subdivisions, and then builds and sells homes. An owner-developer's sales staff must hold active real estate licenses in order to be paid a commission or other compensation based on actual sales (that is, on a transactional basis). The sales staff is exempt from real estate licensure if paid strictly on a salaried basis.

A broker is a person who, for another and for compensation (or in anticipation of compensation), performs real estate services. Becoming a broker requires additional education, experience, and passing the broker license exam. While many sales associates want the prestige of a broker's license, they are not interested in opening their own real estate brokerage business. A **broker associate** is an individual who holds a broker's license but who chooses to register and work in real estate under the direction of another broker.

REQUIREMENTS FOR LICENSURE

An individual applying for a real estate sales associate or broker license must:

- be 18 years of age or older;
- have a high school diploma or its equivalent;
- possess a Social Security number;
- be honest, truthful, trustworthy, of good character, and have a good reputation for fair dealing; and
- be competent and qualified to make real estate transactions and conduct negotiations with safety to investors and others.

MORAL TURPITUDE

Moral turpitude is conduct contrary to honesty, good morals, justice, or accepted custom. Embezzlement and crimes of larceny, including writing bad checks, are generally considered moral turpitude. A real estate licensee pled guilty to leaving the scene of an accident with injuries. The courts ordered the licensee to pay monthly restitution to the victim. The victim requested in writing that the FREC not impose revocation so that the licensee could continue to pay restitution. The FREC imposed a six-month suspension, $2,500 fine, costs, and 12 months' probation, and ordered the licensee to attend a two-day FREC meeting.

Reference: DBPR Case Number 2009064637.

When completing an application for licensure, the applicant must disclose:

- if ever convicted or found guilty of a crime or ever entered a plea of **nolo contendere** (no contest); if under investigation for civil or criminal prosecution; or if any judgment or decree has been rendered wherein the charges involved **moral turpitude** or fraudulent or dishonest dealing (refer to text box, Moral Turpitude, on this page);
- if any name or alias other than the full legal name indicated on the application has ever been used, including a maiden name (*Note:* Full legal name is the name as it appears on the applicant's Social Security card);
- if ever denied licensure or had a license suspended or revoked by the real estate licensing agency of another state or nation;
- if ever denied registration or a license to practice any regulated profession, business, or vocation, or had a registration or license suspended or revoked in this or any other state or nation; and
- if ever guilty of any conduct or practice that would have been grounds for suspension or revocation under F.S. 475, had the applicant then been licensed to practice real estate in this state or elsewhere. This includes acting, or attempting to act, as a real estate sales associate or broker in violation of F.S. 475, during the year before the applicant filed an application, or until a valid license was issued, regardless of whether compensation was an issue.

Applicants guilty of these offenses will be considered qualified for registration only if passage of time, good behavior, or other sufficient reasons cause the Commission to believe that the interest and welfare of the general public will not be endangered.

Application Requirements

Broker and sales associate applicants must submit an application. The application is furnished by the Department of Business and Professional Regulation (DBPR) and may be downloaded from the Internet at the DBPR's Form Center. (See Web link on next page.) Applicants may download, print, and mail the application, or they may apply online.

BACKGROUND CHECK OF CRIMINAL HISTORY

On the license application, applicants are asked if they have ever been convicted of a crime, found guilty, or entered a plea of guilty or nolo contendere (no contest) to a criminal charge, even if the applicant received a withhold of adjudication.

When the court determines that a defendant is not likely to again engage in a criminal act and that the ends of justice and the welfare of society do not require the defendant to suffer the penalty imposed by law, the court may withhold adjudication of guilt, stay (stop) the imposition of the sentence, and place the defendant on probation. A withhold of adjudication must be disclosed on the application.

Nolo contendere is a plea of no contest entered in a criminal court of law. The defendant does not admit or deny the charges, though a fine or sentence may be imposed by the court.

WEB LINK

You can apply for a real estate license online at the DBPR's Form Center. The address is **http://www.myfloridalicense.com**. Select "Apply for/Update Licenses."

Applicants are cautioned to complete the application carefully, particularly with respect to past history concerning felonies, misdemeanors, and traffic offenses (other than parking, speeding, inspection, or traffic signal violations). When responding regarding past history (background questions on application), applicants who have been convicted of a crime, found guilty, or entered pleas of guilty or **nolo contendere** (no contest), even if court action (*adjudication*) was withheld, should attach full details of all cases with dates and outcomes, including any sentence and conditions imposed. Attach to the application important documentation such as copies of police records. Failure to truthfully disclose this information may result in denial of a real estate license. In cases where a license has already been issued, it may result in revocation of the license. An application number is assigned when an application is filed online. Applicants who responded "yes" to any background questions should mail applicable documentation with a cover letter indicating the application number.

Applicants must submit their fingerprints as part of the license application process. An applicant's fingerprints are scanned and electronically submitted to the Florida Department of Law Enforcement (FDLE) and to the Federal Bureau of Investigation (FBI). The purpose of the fingerprinting process is to determine whether an applicant has a criminal history. The DBPR has contracted with its test vendor, Pearson VUE, to provide fingerprinting services for real estate applicants. Fingerprints are scanned at Pearson VUE's test sites and other locations subcontracted by Pearson VUE. Once students have enrolled in the prelicense course for brokers and have made application for a license, they are encouraged to go ahead and complete the fingerprinting process. Students do *not* have to wait until the application is submitted and the course is completed before getting their fingerprints scanned. In fact getting fingerprints scanned early will allow the application to be approved sooner because the DBPR will not have to hold up the application approval pending the results from the criminal history check.

WEB LINK

To schedule a fingerprinting appointment, contact Pearson VUE at **www.pearsonvue.com**. Select "Book Digital Fingerprinting Appointments." Applicants choose a date and time and are asked to provide demographic information (gender, eye color, and so forth). Payment is due at the time of making the appointment.

For additional facts regarding the fingerprinting process and for instructions regarding how out-of-state applicants should submit fingerprint information, download and print DBPR's "Electronic Fingerprinting Frequently Asked Questions" at **http://www.asisvcs.com/publications/pdf/351024.pdf**.

The application fee must accompany the application. Checks and money orders are accepted for applications received by mail. Online applicants may charge the fee to a credit card. The notice of satisfactory completion of the prescribed course (grade report) must be presented to the examination site before taking the exam.

A 30-day period is allowed after receipt of the application to check for errors and omissions and to send the applicant a *notice of insufficiency* concerning any additional information required. An applicant's failure to supply additional information may not be grounds for denial of a license unless the applicant was notified within the 30-day period.

WEB LINK

To check the status of your application, use the DBPR Online Services at **www.myfloridalicense.com/**. Select "Verify a License" on the home page. Then select "View Application Status."

Any application for licensure that is not processed within the legislated time periods must be considered approved. An applicant must be informed of approval or denial of the application within 90 days after receipt of the last correctly submitted application. When the Commission denies an application, it sends a copy of the denial to the applicant, lists the reasons for the denial, and advises that there are 21 days from the date of the order to request a hearing in accordance with Chapter 120, F.S.

Nonresident Applicant Requirements

U.S. citizenship is *not* required of applicants. However, applicants must possess a Social Security number. Furthermore, applicants do not have to be residents of Florida.

Nonresident licensee requirements. A Florida real estate licensee who moves out of state and becomes a nonresident of Florida is required by law to notify the Commission within 60 days of the change in residency. A Florida resident licensee who fails to notify the Commission of becoming a nonresident may be issued a citation and fined $300. Nonresident licensees must satisfactorily complete the post-licensing and continuing education required of all Florida real estate licensees. Nonresident applicants and licensees must comply with all other F.S. 475 requirements and FREC rules.

Mutual recognition agreements. To date, the FREC has mutual recognition agreements with licensing authorities in eight states: Alabama, Arkansas, Connecticut, Georgia, Indiana, Mississippi, Nebraska, and Oklahoma. The intent of mutual recognition agreements is to recognize the education and experience of individuals licensed in another state or nation when the other jurisdiction has education and experience requirements comparable to Florida's requirements. The agreements apply exclusively to *nonresidents* who are licensed in other jurisdictions. A resident of Florida who is licensed in a mutual recognition state *cannot* apply for a Florida real estate license under mutual recognition.

MUTUAL RECOGNITION IS NOT RECIPROCITY

Reciprocity is an agreement between two states that allows a real estate licensee with a valid license in one of the states to practice real estate in both states. There is no reciprocity between Florida and any other state.

Florida instead has entered into contractual agreements with some other states known as **mutual recognition agreements**. Florida and another state enter into a contract to recognize each other's real estate license education and experience. Mutual recognition applicants must demonstrate knowledge of Florida's real estate laws by passing a license exam that consists of 40 questions concerning Florida-specific real estate law. After demonstrating knowledge of Florida license law, the applicant is issued a Florida real estate license. Only nonresidents of Florida may use education and experience obtained in a mutually recognized state to obtain a Florida real estate license.

If a holder of a real estate license from a state with which Florida has a mutual recognition agreement desires a Florida real estate license, the individual submits a Florida real estate license application. The applicant requests mutual recognition on the license application and indicates from which state mutual recognition is being requested. Mutual recognition eligibility requires that the applicant be a nonresident of Florida. An applicant applying for mutual recognition must obtain a *certificate of license history* from the Real Estate Commission in the state where the applicant is licensed. A certification of license history must contain the applicant's initial license exam information, current license status, the number of active months of licensure within the preceding five years, and whether any disciplinary action has been taken against the licensee. The certification is submitted with the application.

Real estate applicants approved for licensure under mutual recognition are exempt from the prelicense education course. However, the mutual recognition applicant must demonstrate mastery of Florida's real estate license law by passing a written Florida-specific real estate law license exam. The exam consists of 40 questions worth 1 point each. A grade of 30 points (75 percent) or higher is required to pass the exam. After demonstrating knowledge of Florida license law, the applicant is issued a Florida real estate license. Individuals who receive a Florida real estate license under mutual recognition must fulfill the same post-license and continuing education requirements as all other Florida real estate licensees.

Mutual recognition agreements also ensure that Florida licensees have equal opportunity for licensure in mutual recognition states. The agreements are state-specific, and what is required of Florida licensees varies among mutual recognition states depending on how another state's license law compares to Florida's license law. A Florida real estate licensee interested in obtaining a license from a mutual recognition state should contact the state's Real Estate Commission for information regarding application procedures.

REGULATIONS PERTAINING TO PRELICENSE COURSES

A student may not miss more than eight hours of instruction. An instructional hour is considered to be 50 minutes. (Section 475.17, F.S.)

A student may attend makeup classes to take the end-of-course exam or a makeup exam if absences were due to student or family illness, if done within 30 days of the regularly scheduled exam time, or later with Commission approval. Makeup classes must consist of the original course material that the student missed. (61J2-3.008, F.A.C.)

The school or institution provides each student passing the end-of-course exam with a FREC-prescribed grade report of successful completion of the course. The school must submit a roster notifying the Commission of the name of each student who has satisfactorily completed the education requirements. (Section 475.175, F.S.)

The student must pass the school-administered end-of-course exam with a grade of 70 or higher. (61J2-3.008, F.A.C.)

A student failing the end-of-course exam must wait at least 30 days from the date of the original examination to retest. Within one year of the original examination, a student may retest a maximum of one time. Otherwise, a student failing the end-of-course exam must repeat the course prior to being eligible to retake the end-of-course examination. Schools must administer a different form of the end-of-course exam to a student who is retaking the exam or repeating the course. (61J2-3.008, F.A.C.)

Students may choose to complete a distance-learning course and satisfactorily complete a timed, distance learning course examination. (Section 475.17, F.S.)

The prelicense course may be taken by correspondence or other suitable means by anyone who, because of individual physical hardship, cannot attend the course where it is regularly conducted or who does not have access to distance learning courses. (Section 475.17, F.S.)

Florida resident defined. For application and licensing purposes, FREC rules define a **resident** of Florida as a person who has resided in Florida continuously for a period of four calendar months or more within the preceding year, regardless of whether the person resided in a recreational vehicle, hotel, rental unit, or other temporary or permanent location. Any person who presently resides in Florida in any of the above-described accommodations with the intention of residing continuously in Florida for four months or longer, beginning on the date the person established the current period of residence, is also considered a legal Florida resident. This is the test used to determine whether an applicant for licensure qualifies as a nonresident under mutual recognition.

TIME LIMIT FOR PRELICENSE EDUCATION

If an applicant does not pass the state license exam within two years after the course completion date, the course completion expires and the applicant must again complete the prelicense education course. The completion date is the date the student passed the prelicense end-of-course exam.

Reference: Section 475.181(2), F.S

Education Requirement

Broker applicants must successfully complete the broker course (Course II) or an equivalent FREC-approved prelicense course. Course II consists of 69 hours of instruction and 3 hours for the end-of-course examination in the fundamentals of real estate appraising, investment, financing, and brokerage operations and management. FREC rules mandate the content of the state license examination. To the extent subject areas can reasonably be separated, 45 points are based on law, 40 points on principles and practices, and 15 points on real estate mathematics. The math questions consist of 8 points concerning HUD-1 closing statement calculations and 7 points of general math calculations. A passing score of at least 70 is required on the end-of-course exam.

Exceptions to the broker prelicense course requirement. Broker applicants who have received a four-year degree in real estate from an institution of higher education are exempt from the broker prelicense education course (Course II). Although active members in good standing with The Florida Bar are exempt from the sales associate course (Course I), they are *not* exempt from the broker prelicense course. (Refer to the text box, Summary of Education Exemptions, on page 13.)

Broker Experience Requirement

Broker applicants must fulfill an experience requirement in addition to the education requirement. A broker applicant fulfills the experience requirement by having held an active real estate license for at least 24 months during the five-year period preceding application to become a Florida real estate broker. A broker applicant can fulfill the experience requirement in one of three ways:

- The applicant has held an active sales associate license under one or more real estate brokers for at least 24 months during the five-year period preceding application to become a Florida real estate broker. The employment can be under a Florida real estate broker or a broker licensed in another state or in any foreign jurisdiction.
- The applicant held an active sales associate license while working as a salaried employee of a government agency and performing the duties authorized in Chapter 475, F.S., for at least 24 months during the five-year period preceding application to become a Florida real estate broker.
- The applicant held an active broker license in another state or in any foreign jurisdiction for at least 24 months during the five-year period preceding application to become a Florida real estate broker.

The experience cannot be earned by working for an owner-developer unless the owner-developer is a licensed broker who holds a current, valid, active real estate license. A broker applicant who holds a Florida real estate sales associate license must fulfill the 45-hour post-licensing education requirement before the initial sales associate license expires in order to be eligible to obtain a Florida broker license, even if the applicant is applying real estate experience from another state. If the broker applicant does not hold a Florida real estate sales associate license, the 45-hour sales associate post-licensing education requirement does not apply.

Florida Broker License Examination

When the application processing is complete and the applicant is considered qualified, the DBPR notifies the national testing vendor. The vendor then sends a notice informing the candidate of eligibility to take the state license examination.

Applicants schedule examination appointments directly through the testing vendor. License examinations for broker applicants are given at test sites located throughout Florida. The license exam may also be taken in any state where the test vendor has a test center.

The examination consists of multiple-choice questions and is administered as a computerized test. The license exam is offered in English and Spanish. Students who want the Spanish version must request the Spanish language exam when making the test reservation. The passing score on the license exam is a grade of 75 or higher.

Students' answers are graded at the test site. Students who pass the exam are given a "pass" notification at the test site. A real estate license is mailed to broker applicants who passed the exam. Active sales associates who pass the broker license exam and plan to continue working for the same employer as broker associates do not need to submit any paperwork—the DBPR records will be updated to indicate that the licensee has upgraded from a sales associate to a broker associate. Inactive licensees that pass the broker exam will receive a broker license but the status of the license will be inactive. Inactive licensees must submit form DBPR RE-10 to activate the broker license. There is no charge to change the license status from inactive to active status. (*Note:* There are additional legal requirements concerning broker offices that must be met before broker applicants may legally begin to operate, as discussed in chapter 2.)

Students who fail the license exam are given a failure notice at the test site. The failure notice includes a breakdown of the points scored in each major subject area. The notice also includes information about reviewing the exam, retaking the exam, and requesting a hearing to challenge the exam. Requests to review the exam must be received within 21 days after the release date on the original grade notification. Review appointments are scheduled with the test vendor. Students may only review the questions they answered incorrectly.

An applicant has the right to petition for a formal hearing before the Division of Administrative Hearings. A request for a hearing before an administrative law judge must be filed within 21 days from the date of the on-site grade notice, or 21 days from the date of the letter notifying the student of the DBPR evaluation decision regarding the student's challenges. The request for a hearing is filed with the Chief, Bureau of Education and Testing, DBPR.

SUMMARY OF EDUCATION EXEMPTIONS

	Prelicense Course I	Prelicense Course II	Post-License	Continuing Education
4-Year Real Estate Degree*	Exempt	Exempt	Exempt	Not Exempt
Florida-Licensed Attorney**	Exempt	Not Exempt	Not Exempt	Exempt

* Exempt from Prelicense Courses I and II but must pass license exam.

** Must be an active member of The Florida Bar. Exempt from Course I only. Must pass license exam.

WEB LINK

Download a copy of the Candidate Information Booklet at **http://www.myfloridalicense.com/dbpr/servop/testing/documents/RE.brokercib.pdf**. The Booklet includes important information regarding taking the state license exam.

POST-LICENSING EDUCATION

Broker licensees are required to successfully complete post-licensing education *before the first renewal* of their licenses. The course requirement is satisfied by completing one or more courses totaling 60 hours of 50 minutes each, including the end-of-course exam. To receive credit for the post-license course, students must earn a grade of at least 75 percent on the end-of-course exam. Licensees who fail the post-license end-of-course exam must wait at least 30 days from the date of the original examination to retake a different form of the end-of-course examination. (Alternatively, licensees who do not want to wait 30 days may choose to retake the course and, in such cases, take a different form of the end-of-course exam.)

Failure to complete the post-licensing education requirement will cause the initial license to become null and void. This requirement places the initial license in a conditional (probationary) status. However, brokers may request and receive a sales associate license if they complete 14 hours of continuing education within six months following expiration of the broker license and have complied with all requirements for renewal.

Individuals who have attained a four-year degree in real estate from an institution of higher education are exempt from the post-license education requirements. Florida-licensed attorneys who are also licensed real estate brokers must complete the post-licensing education requirement. (Refer to text box, Summary of Education Exemptions on this page.)

CONTINUING EDUCATION

After completing the post-license education requirement during the initial license period, active and inactive licensees must complete at least 14 hours of continuing education during every two-year license period after that. Three of the 14 hours must consist of core law

TIPS REGARDING BROKER POST-LICENSE EDUCATION

Students should *not* enroll in a post-license course until first becoming licensed. Caution—If you take your post-license course before becoming licensed as a broker, the course will not count.

Students are encouraged to take their post-license education soon after becoming licensed. Do not wait until the last minute. Plan to complete the course at least 30 days before the expiration date on your license. Licensees who fail the broker post-license end-of-course exam must wait at least 30 days from the date of the original examination to retake a different form of the end-of-course examination. Therefore, it is wise to allow yourself ample time so that if you need to retake the exam you can do so prior to the expiration date on your license. If you are taking the course by distance education, your school will need time to grade your exam and electronically submit the results to the state *before* your expiration date. You also need to allow for unexpected events such as computer problems, sickness, and emergencies.

which includes updates to applicable rules and statutes. A licensee who takes the three-hour core law course in each year of the renewal period receives six hours of credit toward the 14-hour continuing education requirement. The continuing education requirement may be satisfied by attending a classroom course, by completing an approved distance learning course, or by attending a Commission-approved education seminar or conference.

A licensee may substitute attendance at one legal agenda session of the FREC for three classroom hours of continuing education (CE) credit. A licensee may substitute three CE credits only one time per renewal cycle. To obtain the credit, the licensee must notify the DRE at least seven days in advance of the licensee's intent to attend the FREC's legal agenda session. A licensee may not earn CE credit for attending a legal agenda session if the licensee is a party to a disciplinary action slated for that FREC legal agenda.

Active members in good standing with The Florida Bar are exempt from the continuing education requirements for real estate licensees. (Refer to text box, Summary of Education Exemptions on page 13.)

An individual may not operate as a broker or sales associate without having a valid and current active license. Brokers may not employ, or continue to employ, a sales associate who does not hold a valid and current sales associate license. A licensee may *not* practice real estate following the expiration date of the license. A broker or sales associate who does so, even accidentally, commits an unlawful act.

LICENSE RENEWAL

The initial effective date of a real estate license is the date the applicant passed the license exam. All real estate licenses are issued with an expiration date of either March 31 or September 30. The expiration date (March 31 or September 30) that is assigned to a particular license is the date that will give the licensee as close to 24 months of licensure

RECOMMENDED PENALTIES

The penalty range for a first violation of practicing real estate without a valid and current license is a $250 to $2,500 administrative fine and suspension to revocation.

The penalty for subsequent violations is a $1,000 to $5,000 administrative fine and suspension to revocation.

Reference: 61J2-24.001, F.A.C.

as possible, without exceeding 24 months. License law mandates that the initial license period must provide at least 18 months of licensure but not more than 24 months.

For example, assume the initial effective date of a license is July 25, 2012. The license will expire on March 31, 2014 (approximately 20 months of licensure). Thereafter, every two years (biennially) on March 31, the real estate license expires and must be renewed.

License Renewal

Ninety days before the end of a license cycle, the DBPR sends a renewal notice to licensees. The DBPR either mails the notice to the licensee's last known address of record or it electronically sends the notice to the licensee's e-mail address of record. Brokers must complete their post-license education *before the first renewal* of their initial license. After the post-license education is satisfied and the initial license is renewed, licensees must complete 14 hours of continuing education during each renewal period.

To renew a real estate license, the licensee submits a renewal application and the biennial license fee. When a licensee signs and returns the renewal application, the licensee is attesting to have completed the education requirement. A late fee is charged if a license is renewed after the expiration date. If a licensee does not renew the license by the expiration date, the license reverts automatically to involuntary inactive status (discussed later in the chapter). An active licensee who fails to renew a license following expiration has 24 months in which to renew the license. A real estate licensee must *not* practice real estate following the expiration date of the license. It is also unlawful for a licensee holding a current *inactive* license to perform the services of real estate for compensation.

Armed Forces Exemption. A licensee in good standing who is a member of the U.S. Armed Forces is exempt from the renewal requirements during the licensee's period of active duty and six months after discharge from active duty. If the military duty is out of state, the exemption also applies to a licensed spouse. The Armed Forces exemption applies provided the licensee is not engaged in any real estate activity in the private sector for profit.

The DBPR may issue a temporary real estate license to the spouse of an active duty member of the Armed Forces who is assigned to duty in Florida. The spouse must hold a valid real estate license in another state or foreign jurisdiction. A temporary license expires six months after the date of issue and is not renewable.

Active versus Inactive Status

An **active license** is required to engage in real estate brokerage services. Licensees who choose not to engage in the real estate business may place their licenses on inactive status. There are two types of inactive status: (1) voluntary inactive and (2) involuntary inactive.

Inactive Status	
Voluntary inactive	The licensure status that results when a licensee has applied to the Department to be placed on inactive status and has paid the renewal fee prescribed by rule
Involuntary inactive	The licensure status that results when a license is not renewed at the end of the license period prescribed by the Department

Reference: Section 475.01, F.S

Voluntary inactive. A licensee who has qualified for a real estate license but who voluntarily chooses not to engage in the real estate business during a given period and requests such a change is placed on **voluntary inactive** status. A licensee cannot legally perform any real estate services for compensation while holding a voluntary inactive license. A licensee may change an active license to a voluntary inactive license status by submitting to the DBPR the proper form. The licensee pays no fee to change status other than the renewal fee at the beginning of each license renewal cycle. Such licensees hold current inactive licenses.

Voluntary inactive brokers who subsequently wish to activate their licenses may do so at any time simply by completing the proper form. Current voluntary inactive and active licenses may be renewed indefinitely. Voluntary inactive licensees must complete the continuing education requirement every two years and pay the appropriate fees to renew their inactive licenses. A license that is not renewed at the end of the license period reverts automatically to involuntary inactive status (except in the case of initial licenses when post-license education requirements have not been completed).

Involuntary inactive. If a licensee fails to renew an active or voluntary inactive license before the expiration date (other than the first renewal), the license reverts automatically to **involuntary inactive** status. An individual cannot legally perform real estate services after the license has expired. A license that has been on involuntary inactive status for more than two years automatically expires (becomes null and void) by operation of law without further FREC or DBPR action.

Ninety days before expiration of involuntary inactive licenses, the DBPR notifies licensees of this upcoming deadline. Once the two-year period of involuntary inactive status has lapsed, an individual who wants to reenter the real estate business must start the license process over again, beginning with Course I.

Involuntary inactive licensees may activate their licenses during the two-year period following expiration of a valid current license only after satisfactorily completing FREC-prescribed courses of instruction and paying the appropriate late fee. When a license has been involuntary inactive for:

- 12 months or less, licensees may satisfy the education requirement by completing 14 hours of FREC-approved continuing education; or
- more than 12 months but less than 24 months, licensees are required to complete 28 hours of a Commission-prescribed education course.

UNDERSTANDING THE TERMS LICENSURE AND REGISTRATION

Generally in order to perform services of real estate for compensation an individual must hold an active real estate license. To be licensed, an individual must demonstrate real estate knowledge and competency by providing proof of education, experience, passing a license examination, and so forth.

To register, it is necessary to submit to the DBPR certain information about a person or entity so that the information can be entered into the DBPR's computer database.

For example: Brokerage entities are registered with the DBPR; officers and directors of a brokerage corporation are registered with the DBPR under the brokerage entity; and sales associates and broker associates are registered under the name of the business brokerage/employer.

There is another situation that causes a license to be placed in involuntary inactive status. If a broker is disciplined and as a result the broker's license is suspended or revoked, the licenses of the sales associates who are registered under the broker will be automatically placed in involuntary inactive status. This is because a sales associate can only perform real estate services for compensation under the direction of the sales associate's employer. A sales associate's license is returned to active status as soon as a new broker employer is chosen and the information is filed with the DBPR.

Registration and Licensure

Registration is the process of submitting information to the DBPR that is entered into the Department's records. Information that is placed on record with the DBPR includes the name and address of each licensed broker and sales associate; the name and business address of each sales associate's employer; the sales associate's and broker's license status (active or inactive); and the person's involvement as an officer, director, or partner of a real estate business. Sales associates and broker associates licensed in Florida must be registered under their employing broker (or owner-developer, if applicable). Sales associates and broker associates may have only one registered employer at any given time. Florida licensees may also hold active licenses in other states. Individuals who do not intend to engage actively in the real estate business, such as a director of a real estate corporation, simply register this information with the DBPR so that the information can be entered into the database. However, an individual who wishes to actively engage in the real estate industry must be licensed and registered as active with the DBPR.

If a broker chooses to form a corporation (or other business structure) to broker real estate, the corporation must be registered with the DBPR and a registration fee paid. Brokers must renew the brokerage corporation's registration every two years, the same way brokers must renew their broker licenses. (Refer to the section titled, Real estate brokerage corporations, under Corporations in chapter 2 for additional information.) All real estate brokerage entities must be registered with the DBPR including, real estate brokerage partnerships, limited liability partnerships, corporations, and limited liability companies.

PRIMA FACIE EVIDENCE

Prima facie evidence is a legal term used to refer to evidence that is good and sufficient on its face (at first view) to establish a given fact or prove a case. Unless it is refuted by evidence to the contrary, prima facie evidence will prove a case (presumptive evidence).

A real estate license indicates the licensee's name, issue date, and expiration date, and it serves as prima facie evidence that the licensee holds a current and valid license. Furthermore, official Commission documents become prima facie evidence once they are signed by the FREC chairperson or the chairperson's designee and affixed with the Commission's seal.

Failure to ensure that a real estate brokerage business entity is registered properly with the DBPR, or failure to ensure that each general partner, officer, or director engaged in real estate brokerage activity is licensed properly, is punishable by a citation and a $500 fine.

A real estate broker must register any involvement the broker has in a real estate brokerage business. An active broker may serve in a nonbrokerage capacity as an officer or a director with one or more real estate corporations or as a partner in one or more real estate partnerships while maintaining an active license with another real estate brokerage firm. Such involvement is allowable; however, the DBPR must be informed of the broker's involvement with the various real estate entities and the information is registered into the DBPR/DRE database. To register such involvement, the broker completes the appropriate DBPR form. The form is used to provide information on the partners, managers, officers, and directors of a real estate business entity. Information required on the form includes the organization name, trade name (if applicable), and management information. Management information includes the name, office held, percentage of ownership, active or inactive license status, and residence address. The names of all licensed and unlicensed general partners, officers, and directors must be disclosed when registering or renewing a real estate business entity. If a general partner, officer, or a director is added or removed, the change must be submitted to the DBPR.

Owner-developers are not regulated by the DBPR. However, licensed real estate sales associates may be employed by an owner-developer. In such cases, the name and address of the owner-developer is registered with the DBPR. Once the owner-developer information is registered into the DBPR database, sales associates and broker associates may be registered under the owner-developer.

Licensure is obtained when an applicant passes the state license exam. Passing the license examination gives the applicant the right to request and be issued a real estate **license**. The license is a written document that serves as **prima facie evidence** (accepted at face value) that the licensee (holder) is duly licensed as of the effective date shown on the license. (Refer to the text box, Prima Facie Evidence on this page.)

Multiple Licenses

Multiple licenses are issued to a broker who qualifies as the broker for more than one business entity. For each business that a person is a broker, a separate broker license must be obtained. A broker who holds more than one Florida broker license is said to hold **multiple licenses**, which means that the individual legally acts as a broker for more than one brokerage firm. For example, Jane Doe is the broker for both Extra-Fine Real Estate Services and Midnight Realty, two separate brokerage entities. Jane needs multiple broker licenses to qualify both brokerage entities.

Because sales associates and broker associates may have only one registered employer at a time, sales associates and broker associates may *not* hold multiple licenses. A broker licensee, therefore, may *not* be licensed as a broker associate for one firm and at the same time be licensed as a broker with another firm.

Group License

A **group license** is sometimes issued to sales associates or broker associates who are registered under an owner-developer. An owner-developer may own properties in the names of various entities. If the entities are all connected so that ownership and control is with the same individual(s), sales associates and broker associates employed by the owner-developer may be issued a group license. In actual practice, the sales associate (or broker associate) is issued a sales associate license and no distinction regarding group license is made on the face of the license. For example, Joseph Jones is an owner-developer. He owns and controls two development companies, Happy Estates and Excellent Homes. If associate Alice is employed by Mr. Jones to sell properties for both development companies, she has a group license. Alice has one sales associate license and one employer (Mr. Jones).

Current Mailing Address

Licensees are responsible for notifying the DBPR in writing of their current mailing address, e-mail address, and place of practice. **Current mailing address** is the current residential address a licensee uses to receive mail through the U.S. Postal Service. A post office box is considered an acceptable mailing address. The DBPR sends official communication to a licensee at the last known mailing address or e-mail address, referred to by the DBPR as the **address of record**.

Licensees must notify the DBPR in writing within ten days of a change in current mailing address. Licensees who fail to timely notify the DBPR of a change of address are in violation of Florida Statute 455 and are subject to a citation and $500 fine. Florida licensees who move out of state must also comply with all nonresident requirements.

If a broker changes business address, the license ceases to be in effect until the DBPR is notified of the new business location and it is properly registered. No brokerage business may be conducted until the location is properly registered. The DBPR must be notified of the new office location within *ten days*. (*Note:* If the new business address is a new brokerage office location, the new location must be registered and the branch office fee paid. See Branch Offices in chapter 2.)

The broker must also submit the names of any sales associates who are no longer employed by the brokerage. The licenses of the sales associates who are no longer employed with the broker will be placed in involuntary inactive status. This notification also fulfills the change of address notification requirements for sales associates who remain employed by the brokerage. The DRE automatically updates the business address information for all of the firm's licensees. The licenses of sales associates working for the brokerage remain effective and in force.

Sales associates must be registered under their employing broker (or owner-developer). Therefore, sales associates who change employers may not work under the new broker (or owner-developer) until the FREC has been informed and the associate is registered under the new employer. Section 475.22 of the Florida Statutes imposes a ten-day time period for licensees to notify the Commission of their new employer.

INDIVIDUALS WHO ARE EXEMPT FROM A REAL ESTATE LICENSE

Individuals may buy, sell, exchange, or lease real property for themselves. Therefore, individuals and business entities are exempt from a real estate license in the following circumstances:

- Property owners do not need a real estate license to buy, sell, exchange, or lease their own real estate.
- Corporations, partnerships, trusts, and joint ventures may buy, sell, exchange, or lease their own property. Salaried employees of these business entities may buy, sell, exchange, or lease real property for their employer, provided the activity is incidental to their employment and they are not paid a commission or compensated on a transactional basis.
- Individuals who deal in personal property are exempt from obtaining real estate licenses. *Personal property* is defined as any tangible item that is not permanently attached to real property. Section 475.01, F.S., defines **real property** or "real estate" as any interest or estate in land and any interest in business enterprises or business opportunities, including any assignment, leasehold, subleasehold, or mineral right. (*Note:* Because the definition of real property includes any interest in business enterprises or business opportunities, individuals who specialize in the sale of businesses [known as **business brokers**] must hold Florida real estate licenses.)

Also exempt from real estate licensure are salaried employees:

- who work in an on-site rental office in a leasing capacity and who do not receive a commission;
- who are managers of condominiums or cooperative apartment complexes who rent individual units for periods no longer than one year and who are not paid a commission;
- of an owner-developer (real estate broker) provided they do not receive a commission;
- of a governmental agency who perform real estate services for the state or local government and who do not receive commission (*Note:* This exemption includes persons who appraise railroad property for tax purposes.); and
- of business entities who negotiate the sale or purchase of radio, television, or cable enterprises provided the sale does not involve real property. (*Note:* If the transaction involves the sale or lease of land, buildings, or other improvements to land, a real estate license must be retained for that portion of the transaction.)

Chapter 475 of the Florida Statutes exempts the following individuals from holding a real estate license:

- Persons who sell cemetery lots. (*Note:* This exemption exists because Chapter 475, F.S., excludes cemetery lots from the definition of real property.)
- Individuals who rent lots in a mobile home park or recreational travel park.
- Attorneys-at-law when acting within the scope of their professional duties in an attorney-client relationship. (*Note:* In Florida, holding a Florida Bar license does not entitle an attorney to compensation for performing real estate services.)
- Certified public accountants (CPAs) when performing accounting duties within the scope of their professional duties.
- A person who has been given a power of attorney (referred to as an attorney-in-fact) in order to sign contracts and conveyances on someone's behalf. (*Note:* A person cannot appoint another individual as an attorney-in-fact for the purpose of conducting real estate services for others.)
- Owners of a time-share periods for their own use and occupancy who later offer the time-share periods for resale.
- State-certified and licensed real estate appraisers who are licensed under Chapter 475, Part II, for the purpose of conducting appraisal services.
- Court-appointed individuals acting within the limitations of their duties.
- Hotel and motel clerks who rent lodging accommodations on behalf of the establishment.
- Federally regulated banks and dealers registered with the Securities and Exchange Commission (SEC) selling business enterprises to accredited investors.
- Apartment property owners or property management firms for the purpose of paying a finder's fee of not more than $50 to a tenant of the complex for a rental referral.

SUMMARY OF IMPORTANT POINTS

- Real estate services include any real estate activities involving compensation for performing the service for another. Compensation is anything of value paid or promised to be paid to an individual for performing services of real estate.
- An owner-developer is an unlicensed entity that sells, exchanges, or leases its own property. Sales staff must hold active real estate licenses to be paid commission. The sales staff is exempt from licensure if paid strictly on a salaried basis.
- A broker associate is an individual who meets the requirements of a broker but who chooses to work in real estate under the direction (employ) of another broker.
- Applicants must be at least 18 years of age and have earned a high school diploma or its equivalent. U.S citizenship is not required, and applicants do not have to be Florida residents. However, applicants must possess a Social Security number.
- Resident licensees who move out of the state must notify the Commission within 60 days of the change in residency.
- A resident of Florida is a person who has resided in Florida continuously for a period of four calendar months or more within the preceding year.

- Broker applicants must complete at least 24 months of experience during the five-year period preceding applicant to become a Florida license real estate broker.
- Sales associates must complete 45 hours of post-license education before the expiration of their initial license. Brokers must complete 60 hours of post-license education before the expiration of their initial license. Failure to do so will cause the license to become null and void.
- Fourteen hours of continuing education each license period is required for all real estate licensees following the initial license period.
- There are two types of inactive status: voluntary and involuntary. A licensee who has qualified for a real estate license but who voluntarily chooses not to engage in the real estate business may request voluntary inactive status. Involuntary inactive status occurs when a licensee fails to renew an active or voluntary inactive license before the expiration date.
- "Multiple licenses" refers to those cases in which a broker holds more than one broker's license.
- A group license is issued to a sales associate or a broker associate employed by an owner-developer (real estate developer) who owns properties in the name of various entities. A group license entitles the licensee to work in the various sales projects owned by the owner-developer.
- Licensees must notify the DBPR in writing within ten days of a change in mailing address.

FREC Disciplinary Guidelines

475.25(1)(g) Has license disciplined or acted against or an application denied by another jurisdiction.
First violation: $250 to $1,000 administrative fine and a 30-day suspension up to revocation
Subsequent violations: $1,000 to $5,000 administrative fine and suspension up to revocation

475.25(1)(m) Obtained a license by fraud, misrepresentation or concealment.
First violation: $250 to $1,000 administrative fine and a 30-day suspension up to revocation
Subsequent violations: $1,000 to $5,000 administrative fine and suspension up to revocation

475.25(2) License issued by error of the Commission. *Usual action:* Commission shall impose a penalty of revocation (*Note:* referred to as revocation or cancellation without prejudice.)

475.42(1)(a) Practice without a valid and current license.
First violation: $250 to $2,500 administrative fine and suspension up to revocation
Subsequent violations: $1,000 to $5,000 administrative fine and suspension up to revocation

475.42(1)(c) Broker employs a sales associate who is not the holder of a valid and current license.
First violation: $250 to $1,000 administrative fine and suspension up to revocation
Subsequent violations: $1,000 to $5,000 administrative fine and suspension up to revocation

475.25(1)(s) Has had a registration suspended, revoked or otherwise acted against in any jurisdiction.
First violation: $250 to $1,000 administrative fine and a 60-day suspension up to revocation
Subsequent violations: $1,000 to $5,000 administrative fine and suspension up to revocation

Reference: 61J2 24.001, F.A.C.

REVIEW QUESTIONS

1. Mississippi Fuel Company is a publicly traded company (listed on the NYSE) that purchases land and oil rights and drills for oil and gas. A member of the board of directors is responsible for negotiating the company's oil leases. The board member receives an annual salary and an end-of-the-year bonus. Which statement is TRUE of this situation?
   a. The board member must be a licensed real estate broker.
   b. The board member must be a licensed real estate sales associate.
   c. The corporation must be registered with the DBPR on behalf of the FREC because it is involved in real estate sales and lease negotiations.
   d. The board member does not need a real estate license as long as the salary and bonuses are not associated with any particular real estate transaction.

2. Which individual is NOT exempt from licensure?
   a. A person who appraises real estate for the county property appraiser's office
   b. Someone who lists and sells businesses
   c. An individual who rents mobile home lots in a mobile home park
   d. Someone who sells cemetery lots

3. A Florida-licensed real estate broker from Tallahassee decides to move to Alabama and open a real estate office there, so that he can be near his grandchildren. What must he do?
   a. Notify the DBPR of his change of business address within ten days after the change
   b. Notify the DBPR within 60 days of becoming a nonresident
   c. Notify the DBPR of the change in current mailing address within ten days after the change
   d. He must do all of the above.

4. A nonresident holds a Florida real estate broker's license. Which statement is TRUE?
   a. He is exempted from the broker post-license course because he is a nonresident.
   b. He must successfully complete 14 hours of continuing education every license period following the initial license period.
   c. He will be assessed a nonresident fee in addition to his renewal fee every license period.
   d. His license status is automatically changed to voluntary inactive status until he reestablishes Florida residency.

5. A broker has been licensed for ten years. If the broker does NOT renew his license by the end of the license period, the license will automatically
   a. expire.
   b. revert to voluntary inactive status.
   c. revert to involuntary inactive status.
   d. be canceled.

6. A developer purchased a tract of land and subdivided the property into individual lots. The developer hired his son, who was not licensed to sell the lots. The father agreed to pay his son a salary of $200 per week. After two weeks, the son had sold only two lots, so the father decided to add an incentive. The father promised his son that after every fifth lot was sold, he would give his son a lot free and clear. After one more week, the son had sold only one more lot. The son quit his job to go work for another developer who paid a higher weekly salary. Which statement applies to this arrangement?
   a. There is no violation of F.S. 475.
   b. The son alone has violated F.S. 475.
   c. Only the father has violated F.S. 475.
   d. Both the father and the son have violated F.S. 475.

7. A broker purchased a list of FHA foreclosure properties from an FHA employee. The broker agrees to pay the FHA employee a percentage of any commissions he earns from the sale of properties on the list. Which statement is TRUE?
   a. The broker may compensate the FHA employee because the FHA pays his salary.
   b. The fee paid to the FHA employee is a referral fee, which is legal under Florida real estate law.
   c. FHA foreclosure properties are not covered under Chapter 475, F.S.
   d. The broker has violated Chapter 475, F.S., by compensating an unlicensed person for performing services that require a real estate license.

8. Which broker applicant(s) is (are) exempt from the prelicense and post-license education requirements?
   a. Active member in good standing with The Florida Bar
   b. Individual who became licensed through mutual recognition
   c. Individual who received a four-year degree in real estate from an accredited institution of higher education
   d. All of these applicants are exempt.

9. Carla has had an inactive Georgia real estate license since 1980. She also has had an active New York real estate broker license since 1996. Carla now lives in Boca Raton, and she wants a Florida real estate broker's license. Which statement BEST describes Carla's situation?
   a. Carla may apply for mutual recognition.
   b. Carla has fulfilled the experience requirement because she has been licensed in Georgia since 1980.
   c. Carla must enroll in Course I.
   d. Carla must complete the broker prelicense course successfully.

10. Who must hold an active real estate license under Chapter 475, F.S.?
   a. Business brokers who negotiate leases on commercial property
   b. Property managers who pay $25 finders' fees to tenants who refer prospective renters
   c. Salaried employees of the owners of apartment complexes who rent units from on-site rental offices
   d. Salaried employees of corporations involved in buying and selling company-owned property

11. A broker hired a sales associate whose initial license expired on September 30 of this year. At the annual Thanksgiving dinner, the broker learns that the sales associate neglected to complete her post-license education. She reassures the broker that everything is OK because she renewed her license on time, and she promises to take the post-license course immediately. Based on this information, which statement(s) is (are) TRUE?
    a. The sales associate's license became null and void on October 1 of this year.
    b. The FREC can discipline the sale associate for practicing real estate without a valid real estate license.
    c. The broker can be disciplined for continuing to employ a sales associate who is not properly licensed.
    d. All of the above are true.

12. John holds a valid Florida real estate license. His wife is a corporal in the U.S. Army. She is assigned to duty in Saudi Arabia, so the couple moves overseas. Under these circumstances, which statement is TRUE of John's real estate license?
    a. John is exempt from all renewal requirements for up to six months after the couple return to the United States.
    b. John is exempt from all renewal requirements while his wife is on active duty and for six months after discharge from active duty provided the military duty is out of state.
    c. John is exempt from all renewal requirements, and he may perform real estate services in Saudi Arabia, provided he doesn't violate any laws of that nation.
    d. John is exempt from continuing education courses while living in Saudi Arabia, but he must continue to renew his real estate license every renewal cycle.

13. A broker has been licensed in Florida for 20 years. When he closes his office and purchases a new sailboat, with plans to retire, he decides to keep his real estate license. If the broker wants to occasionally perform real estate services for compensation, which option is BEST?
    a. Place his license in voluntary inactive status
    b. Place his license in involuntary inactive status
    c. Keep his broker license active and not inform the DBPR that he has closed his office
    d. Change to broker associate status under another broker

14. A broker owns and operates Root and Toot Realty in St. Petersburg. The broker also owns and operates Root Commercial Realty in Clearwater. Additionally the broker serves in a nonbrokerage capacity as vice president of another real estate company. Based on this information, which statement is TRUE?
    a. The broker must apply for and hold multiple licenses and have her nonbrokerage involvement registered by the qualifying broker.
    b. The broker must apply for a group license and register her nonbrokerage involvement.
    c. The broker is in violation of Chapter 475, F.S.
    d. The broker needs only one broker license, but must register both offices.

15. Which statement is TRUE regarding a broker who changes business address and does not notify the DBPR?
    a. The license ceases to be in effect until the broker notifies the DBPR of the new business address.
    b. The license is suspended until the broker notifies the DBPR of the new business address.
    c. The broker cannot conduct brokerage business; however, the broker's sales associates may continue to conduct new business under the broker.
    d. The broker may continue to conduct brokerage business without interruption as long as the broker notifies the DBPR within ten days of the change in business address.

INTERNET EXERCISE

To answer the questions below, you will need to use the Internet. Begin by going to the Division of Real Estate (DRE) Web site at: *www.myfloridalicense.com/dbpr/re/index.html.* At the DRE Web site, locate and select the link to go to "Statutes and Rules."

Select "Florida Administrative Code Chapter 61J2" to answer the following questions. The FREC's Citation Authority is located in Rule 61J2-24.002.

1. A nonresident who fails to file the required irrevocable consent form may be issued a citation and fined what amount?
2. A broker who fails to obtain a multiple permit may be issued a citation and fined what amount?
3. A licensee who fails to timely notify the DBPR of a change in current mailing address may be issued a citation and fined what amount?

CHAPTER 2

OPENING A REAL ESTATE OFFICE

KEY TERMS

Americans with Disabilities Act (ADA)
blind advertisements
corporation
corporation sole
fictitious name
general partnership
joint adventure
limited liability company
limited liability partnership
limited partnership
ostensible partnership
point of contact information
public accommodations
sole proprietorship
telemarketing
telephone solicitation
trade name

OVERVIEW

An active broker may choose to be the sole owner of a real estate business or form a business with others. Florida laws allow certain types of businesses to register as real estate brokerage entities. The type of business entity chosen has serious legal and tax implications. A broker should seek the advice of an attorney and an accountant.

This chapter describes the various types of business entities that may engage in real estate brokerage activities in Florida. Other issues that affect the creation of a real estate office, such as the statutory requirements for principal offices and branch offices and the registration of officers, directors, and sales associates, also are explained. Administrative rules governing signs, advertising, recordkeeping, and conduct are discussed as well. The chapter concludes with an explanation of important federal and state laws regulating accessibility to commercial facilities, nondiscriminatory advertising, and telemarketing.

Once you have completed this chapter, you should be able to:

- differentiate among the various types of businesses that may be registered as brokerage entities;
- explain the requirements associated with registering a trade name with the DBPR;
- explain the requirements for fictitious name registration;
- identify the requirements for a broker's office(s);

- explain what determines whether a temporary shelter must be registered as a branch office;
- list the requirements related to signs;
- describe the accessibility requirements outlined in the Americans with Disabilities Act as it applies to real estate offices;
- list the license law requirements related to advertising by real estate brokers;
- describe the requirements for rental lists;
- describe the Fair Housing Act requirements for advertising real estate; and
- list the Federal Communications Commission's do-not-call rules.

BUSINESS STRUCTURES THAT MAY BE REGISTERED AS BROKERAGE ENTITIES

A broker may choose from a variety of business entities. Sole proprietorships, partnerships (both general and limited), limited liability partnerships, corporations, and limited liability companies may be registered as real estate brokers and/or real estate brokerage entities.

Chapter 475.01, F.S., defines the term *broker* to include any person who is a general partner, officer, or a director of a partnership or corporation that acts as a real estate broker.

All real estate brokerage entities must register with the DBPR. Registration includes the names of every licensed and unlicensed general partner of a real estate brokerage general partnership or limited partnership and every officer and director of a real estate brokerage corporation. Every member of a member-managed real estate brokerage limited liability company must also register. A person licensed as a sales associate or broker associate may not register as a general partner, a member of a member-managed real estate limited liability company, a manager of a manager-managed real estate limited liability company, or an officer or director of a brokerage corporation.

Each business structure has unique features. Sole proprietorships are the simplest form of business organization. However, many brokers choose instead a business structure that reduces personal liability. Brokers should consult with legal advisors and tax advisors and consider carefully the liabilities and tax consequences of the various types of business entities before making this important decision.

Sole Proprietorship

A **sole proprietorship** is a business owned by one person. A real estate brokerage sole proprietorship exists when the broker is the only owner. It is easy to organize and flexible to operate. A sole proprietor who holds a current and valid broker's license may run a real estate brokerage business. Brokers may use their own name or a fictitious name as a trade name once it has been registered with the DBPR.

The broker-owner is entitled personally to all of the profits. Sole proprietors are personally liable for the business losses as well as the debts and *torts* (negligent acts arising from breach of duty created by law) of sales associates and others working for the broker when acting within the scope of their duties as either independent contractors or employees.

SOLE PROPRIETORSHIP AT A GLANCE

The broker:

- is the only (sole) owner
- is personally liable for business debts and torts
- must register sole proprietorship with the DBPR
- must register trade name (if applicable) with the DBPR

If the sole owner-broker should die or for some other reason be unable to run the business, it is unlikely that the business will survive. A sole proprietorship may be dissolved by ceasing business activities and notifying the DBPR, expiration of the broker license, court order, or death of the owner. When a broker considers this form of business structure, it is important that the broker consult an attorney and a tax accountant to plan for how the business will continue to operate if the sole owner becomes incapacitated.

If the broker chooses to do business under the broker's own name, the broker simply needs to have an active broker license in good standing. The broker must register the business address with the DBPR by completing the appropriate form. If the broker wants to operate under a trade name, it too must be registered with the DBPR. A **trade name** is a business name other than the legal name of the person doing business. A brokerage entity may be registered and operate under no more than one trade name. Chapter 475 (license law) does not require a sole proprietor to register a trade name with the Department of State. However, if another business entity has previously registered that name with the Department of State, the brokerage may not use the name.

General Partnership

A **general partnership** is an association of two or more persons for the purpose of jointly conducting a business. Each person is responsible for all the debts incurred in the conducting of that business; each has the power to bind the other or others in transactions; and each is entitled to receive a share of the profits in an amount agreed on by the parties. General partners are agents for each other. If one partner enters into an agreement, it binds the other partners to the agreement. Florida general partnerships are not subject to direct taxation. General partnerships feature *pass-through* treatment for federal income tax purposes. The partnership itself does not pay taxes, although it does file an information return, reporting the amount of income allocated (whether or not distributed) to each partner. General partners are personally responsible for paying taxes on their share of earnings.

A general partnership is created by a contract that may be written, oral, or implied from the conduct of the parties. Registration with the Department of State is voluntary. However, to conduct business, registration is prudent. To register, the partnership must submit to the Florida Department of State, a Partnership Registration, and a Statement of Partnership Authority.

GENERAL PARTNERSHIP AT A GLANCE

- Two or more persons are involved.
- A general partnership is created by contract (written, oral, or implied).
- All partners are personally liable.
- Each partner is responsible for all partnership debts.
- Each partner can bind the other partners in contracts.
- Each partner shares in profits and losses as agreed upon.

Real estate brokerage general partnerships. Brokers may choose to form a general partnership. Requirements regarding real estate brokerage general partnerships include the following:

- The partnership must register with the DBPR under the partnership name. To register a real estate brokerage general partnership, an Application for Real Estate Company License (DBPR form RE 7) is filed with the DBPR along with the required fee. (*Note:* DBPR form RE 7 is a general form for all types of business structures.) The partnership registration must be renewed every two years.
- Active Florida brokers, inactive Florida brokers, and unlicensed individuals may be partners in a real estate brokerage partnership. The name, Social Security number, and address of non-broker owners of the general partnership are listed on the application.
- At least one partner must be licensed as an active Florida broker (the qualifying broker). The qualifying broker is the individual who should complete and sign the application. Section three of the application designates the name and license number of the qualifying broker.
- Partners who will deal with the public and perform services of real estate must be licensed as active brokers. All brokers who are general partners must be listed on the application. The broker's name, license number, status (active or inactive) are entered on the form.
- Sales associates and broker associates may *not* be general partners in a real estate brokerage partnership.

Any change in a real estate brokerage general partnership's composition must be reported to the DBPR. For example, the DBPR must be notified to withdraw a party from the registration record as well as to add a partner to the record. To amend the composition of a brokerage entity, a corporation amendment package (used for all types of business entities) must be submitted to the DBPR. If the partnership has only one active broker (broker of record) and the broker dies, resigns, or is removed as a general partner, the broker must be replaced within 14 calendar days. No brokerage business may be conducted by the partnership or by a licensee registered with the partnership until a new active broker is identified and registered under the partnership. Failure to timely appoint another active broker will result in the automatic cancellation of the partnership registration, and the licenses of all people associated with the partnership will become involuntary inactive. If, on the other hand, the partnership has more than one active broker and one of the brokers dies or resigns, the partnership registration and the partners' and sales associates' licenses are not affected by the vacancy.

A general partnership can be dissolved because of the death, withdrawal, bankruptcy, or legal disability of any of the general partners. However, under Commission Rule 61J2-5.019(3), if two or more persons continue the business and at least one is an active broker with the partnership, the partnership continues. It is wise to seek legal counsel before forming a general partnership, including assistance with forming a partnership and help drawing up a partnership agreement.

If the partnership operates under a fictitious (trade) name, the name must be registered with the DBPR. Chapter 475, F.S., does not require fictitious (trade) names to be registered with the Department of State. However, if another entity has previously registered the same trade name with the Department of State, the applying business entity may not use that same trade name. When an application is submitted, the DBPR conducts a fictitious name search to verify whether another business entity is registered under that trade name. For additional information regarding registering trade names with the Department of State, Division of Corporations, refer to Trade Names, later in this chapter.

Ostensible partnership. If two parties are *not* partners, they must be careful not to give the impression they are. An **ostensible partnership** (or quasi-partnership) exists where there is no real partnership, but the parties act or do business in such a manner that the public, having no knowledge of the parties' private relations, reasonably would assume that a partnership exists. Ostensible partnerships are considered fraudulent and deceitful, and licensees who operate as ostensible partners are subject to discipline. Ostensible partners also may be liable for each other's debts and torts. Brokers sometimes share office space but conduct their businesses separately. If such is the case, they cannot operate under the same name or use their joint names or the same trade name. Brokers should indicate their true statuses by using separate telephone listings, letterheads, advertisements, and office signs. Advertisements reflecting that a properly registered broker is a franchisee do not fall under the definition of ostensible partnership. Real estate licensees who operate as ostensible partners may be subject to license suspension.

Limited Partnership

A **limited partnership** is created by a written instrument filed with the Florida Department of State. There must be one or more general partners and one or more limited partners to qualify under the law. The limited partners must make an investment of cash or of property, but not of services.

The liability of the general partner(s) is nearly the same as in a general partnership. Limited partners are not liable to creditors of the partnership unless the limited partners' take part in the control of the business. Limited partners are liable for losses only for any unpaid part of their pledged contribution, any assets of the partnership in their hands, and any distribution made to them while the limited partnership is insolvent.

To form a limited partnership, the Florida Revised Uniform Limited Partnership Act (Chapter 620, Part I, F.S.) requires that the partnership file a *certificate of limited partnership* with the Florida Department of State. An *affidavit of capital contributions* declaring the limited partners' capital contributions and the limited partners' anticipated contributions must accompany the certificate of limited partnership. The fee to file both the certificate of limited partnership and the affidavit of capital contributions is based on the total

LIMITED PARTNERSHIP AT A GLANCE

- At least one general partner and one limited partner are required.
- General partners are personally liable for business debts.
- Limited partners invest cash and may not participate in management.
- Limited partners have limited liability.
- A certificate of limited partnership must be filed with the Florida Department of State.
- The partnership name must identify entity as a limited partnership; for example, "Limited" or "Ltd."

amount of anticipated and actual contributed capital. The statute also requires limited partnerships to file periodic reports with the Florida Department of State.

The name of a limited partnership must contain the word *Limited* or its abbreviation *Ltd.* A limited partner's surname cannot appear in the partnership name unless the surname is identical to that of a general partner or the business has been carried on with the name before the new limited partner's inclusion. If the name provisions are violated or if a limited partner takes part in managing the business, the limited partner becomes liable as a general partner. If the limited partnership operates under a fictitious name, the name must be registered with the Florida Department of State, Division of Corporations (see Trade Names on page 38).

Real estate brokerage limited partnerships. Requirements regarding real estate brokerage limited partnerships include the following:

- The limited partnership must register with the DBPR under the limited partnership name. To register a real estate brokerage limited partnership, an Application for Real Estate Company License (DBPR form RE 7) is filed with the DBPR along with the required fee. The limited partnership registration must be renewed every two years.
- General partners who deal with the public and perform services of real estate must be licensed as active brokers. All general partners who expect to perform real estate brokerage services on behalf of the limited partnership must be licensed as active brokers.
- At least one general partner must be qualified and licensed as an active broker.
- All other general partners must register (names and addresses are disclosed) with the DBPR for identification purposes.
- Sales associates and broker associates may not be general partners in a real estate brokerage limited partnership; however, they may be limited partners. (Limited partners are regarded in the same light as stockholders in a corporation.)
- Limited partners are not required to register with the DBPR.

LIMITED LIABILITY PARTNERSHIP AT A GLANCE

- Limited liability for all
- File limited liability partnership with the Florida Department of State
- Name must identify entity as a limited liability partnership, for example, "Limited Liability Partnership" or "LLP"
- The broker must register:
  - brokerage limited liability partnership with the DBPR
  - all general partners with the DBPR
  - trade name with the DBPR and the Florida Department of State

Limited Liability Partnerships

A **limited liability partnership** is a separate legal entity that conducts business and can own property. The partners in a limited liability partnership enjoy protection from personal liability in much the same way as limited partners in a limited partnership. Limited liability partners are not liable for obligations or liabilities of the partnership arising from contract, errors or omissions, negligence, malpractice, or wrongful acts committed by another partner or by an employee, agent, or representative of the partnership. A limited liability partner is liable for any errors, omissions, negligence, malpractice, or wrongful acts committed by that partner, or any person under the partner's direct supervision and control in any activity in which the wrongful acts occurred, or for any debts for which the partner agreed in writing to be liable. The partners in a limited liability partnership are not subject to the limitations imposed on limited partners in a traditional limited partnership. Registered limited liability partnerships must file with the Florida Department of State according to Chapter 620, F.S. The name of a registered limited liability partnership must include the words *Registered Limited Liability Partnership*, or the abbreviation *L.L.P.*, or the designation *LLP* as the last words or letters of its name. LLPs may register as real estate brokerage entities.

Corporations

A **corporation** is an artificial person or legal entity created by law and consists of one or more persons. It is considered to have an existence of its own, separate from the individuals. If the corporation is organized under Florida statute, it is said to be a *domestic corporation*. A *foreign corporation* is organized under the laws of a state other than Florida, but it may conduct business in Florida if it first obtains a *certificate of authority* from the Florida Department of State. An *alien corporation* is authorized by a jurisdiction other than any of the United States, the District of Columbia, Puerto Rico, Guam, or any possession or territory of the United States to conduct business. A corporation has the legal capacity to contract and conduct its affairs under its *articles of incorporation*, which must be filed, along with its annual reports, with the Division of Corporations, Florida Department of State.

CORPORATIONS AT A GLANCE

- Limited liability for all
- File articles of incorporation with Florida Department of State
- The corporation name must identify the entity as a corporation, such as Corporation, Corp., Incorporated, Inc., Company, or Co.
- A corporation exists perpetually.
- Shares of stock represent ownership.
- An annual report must be filed with the Division of Corporations, Florida Department of State

The corporate structure provides several unique features, including limited liability, centralized management, continuity of life, and transferability:

- Liabilities a corporation incurs are obligations of the corporation—not of the individual owners. Because the business is regarded as a separate entity, the security for any obligations the corporation undertakes is limited to the corporate assets. The owners' personal assets are not subject to seizure to satisfy corporate debts unless the individuals bind themselves as guarantors of corporate debts and liabilities.
- A corporation's stockholders (owners) elect a board of directors. The directors elect the officers of the corporation, usually consisting of a president, vice president, secretary, and treasurer. The officers are responsible for managing the business operations. One individual may hold all of the offices of a corporation, and, in this situation, it would be a corporation of one.
- A corporation is considered to have perpetual existence; that is, an officer's or a director's death does not dissolve the company. A corporation files a *dissolution of corporation* with the Division of Corporations when it wants to end the business.
- Ownership in a corporation is transferred by the purchase and sale of stock.

A corporation's profits and losses accrue to the company. It is taxed on its income under corporate tax rules. Corporations distribute dividends to their stockholders. Corporation losses may not be deducted by the stockholders. However, corporations may carry the losses forward and apply them to the corporation's future earnings.

A *for-profit corporation* is created to conduct business in the broadest sense of the term. In Florida, for-profit corporations are organized under Chapter 607, F.S. A *not-for-profit corporation* is created for religious, charitable, or educational purposes. Generally, not-for-profit corporations are formed under Chapter 617, F.S., and organized substantially the same way as corporations for profit. Chapter 475, F.S., does not make a distinction between profit and not-for-profit corporations. However, any broker considering forming a not-for-profit corporation should consult the Florida Department of Revenue and the Internal Revenue Service (IRS) before proceeding.

Real estate brokerage corporations. In Florida, a corporation may be formed as a real estate brokerage firm after providing proof of legal corporate existence. Requirements regarding real estate brokerage corporations include the following:

- The corporation must register with the DBPR under the corporation name. Prior to submitting any paperwork to the DBPR, the corporation must first file articles of incorporation with the Florida Department of State. An existing corporation must be in good standing, meaning that the annual reports have been filed with the Division of Corporations. (Refer to Web link on the next page.) To register a real estate brokerage corporation, an Application for Real Estate Company License (DBPR form RE 7) is filed with the DBPR along with the required fee. (*Note:* DBPR form RE 7 is a general form for all types of business structures.) The corporation registration must be renewed every two years.
- At least one of the officers or directors must be licensed as an active broker (the *principal broker* or *qualifying broker*).
- Active Florida brokers, inactive Florida brokers, and unlicensed people may serve as officers and directors of a real estate brokerage; however, officers and directors who will deal with the public and perform services of real estate *must* be licensed as *active brokers*.
- All officers and directors who are not licensed must be registered with the DBPR for identification purposes; this is accomplished by submitting each individual's name, residence address, office held, and percentage of ownership when completing the management information section of the brokerage corporation application.
- Inactive brokers and unlicensed individuals may perform managerial functions for the brokerage corporation that do not involve real estate functions, such as administrative matters, bookkeeping, and accounting duties.
- Sales associates and broker associates may *not* be an officer or director in a real estate brokerage corporation. A sales associate or broker associate may be issued a citation and fined for serving as an officer or director of a brokerage corporation.
- Sales associates and broker associates may be shareholders of a real estate brokerage corporation.
- The licenses of sales associates, broker associates, and individual brokers are registered under the brokerage corporation (not with any individual broker of the brokerage corporation).

Any change in a real estate brokerage corporation's composition must be reported to the DBPR. For example, the DBPR must be notified to withdraw a party from the registration record as well as to add an officer or director to the record. If the only active broker of a brokerage corporation dies, resigns, or is removed from office, the vacancy must be filled within 14 calendar days. New brokerage business may not be performed by the corporation or by a licensee registered with the corporation until a new active broker is designated and registered. Failure to meet the 14-day deadline will result in the automatic cancellation of the brokerage firm's registration and the licenses of all its officers, directors, and sales associates will become involuntary inactive. If, on the other hand, the corporation has more than one active broker and one of the brokers dies or resigns, the corporate registration and the licenses of the officers, directors, and sales associates and broker associates are not affected by the vacancy. It is the responsibility of every active corporate officer and director to see that the corporation and all officers, directors, broker associates, and sales associates have current and appropriate registration and licenses.

WEB LINK

The DBPR visits the Division of Corporations Web site to check the names of the officers and directors of the corporation against the list of officers and directors on the application. The DBPR also verifies that the annual reports have been filed with the Florida Department of State. Before submitting the paperwork to the DBPR, check the public inquiry site at **http://www.sunbiz.org/.** Search by federal employer ID number (FEI) or by the name of the corporation.

S Corporations

Typically, real estate brokers who choose to incorporate are associated with closely held corporations owned by relatively few people, all or most of whom are involved directly in the corporation's business. As such, the businesses may qualify as S corporations. An eligible domestic corporation can avoid double taxation by electing to be treated as an S corporation under the rules of Subchapter S of the Internal Revenue Code. In this way, the S corporation passes income, loss deductions, and credits to its stockholders, to be included on their separate returns. Furthermore, individual stockholders may benefit from a reduction in their taxable income during a corporation's first years, when it may operate at a loss.

To qualify for S corporation status, a business must be a domestic corporation organized in the United States or originated under federal or state law. The business can issue only one class of stock. S corporations must have no more than 100 stockholders. A husband and wife count as a single shareholder without regard to how they hold their shares. The stockholders must be citizens or residents of the United States. Nonresident aliens cannot be stockholders. A corporation may become an S corporation by filing Form 2553, Election by a Small Business Corporation.

WEB LINK

Publication IRS Form 2553 Instructions explains the tests required to elect to be an S corporation. Go to **http://www.irs.gov/pub/irs-pdf/i2553.pdf.**

Limited Liability Company

Limited liability companies (LLCs) are another type of business entity that has grown in popularity. LLCs have been described as a hybrid between a partnership and a corporation. This is because an LLC provides its owners with protection from personal liability for business debts as do corporations, but the IRS does not tax the LLC in the same way it does not tax a partnership. LLCs, unlike corporations, are not double taxed.

LLCs also have certain advantages over S corporations. For example, an S corporation cannot have more than 100 stockholders; however, there is no limit to the number of owners (known as members) in an LLC. Both LLC members and S corporation stockholders may deduct business losses on their personal tax return. One disadvantage of LLCs is that the initial paperwork to set up a LLC is complex.

Articles of Organization or an application for authorization must be filed with the Florida Department of State along with the filing fee. The name of the limited liability company must end with the words limited liability company or limited company. It is acceptable to use the abbreviation LLC. (Also the word "limited" may be abbreviated as Ltd., and the word "company" may be abbreviated as Co.)

Limited liability companies may be registered as real estate brokerage entities. Brokers considering forming an LLC as a brokerage entity are cautioned to seek guidance from their legal consultants and tax consultants before proceeding.

There are two general classifications of LLCs:

1. **Member-managed LLC.** A member-managed LLC is run by the members (owners). Sales associates and broker associates *cannot* be members of a member-managed real estate brokerage LLC.
2. **Manager-managed LLC.** A manager-managed LLC is not managed by the members. Instead the members choose a manager to manage the LLC (similar to a director of a corporation). A member in a manager-managed LLC is an owner of the LLC (similar to a stockholder of a corporation). Sales associates and broker associates can be members of a manager-managed real estate brokerage LLC.

WEB LINK

Download helpful information regarding choosing a legal business structure at **www.floridatrend.com/small-business**.

OTHER BUSINESS FORMS THAT MAY NOT REGISTER

Several business forms are not allowed to register as real estate brokerage entities.

Corporation Sole

A **corporation sole** is an ecclesiastical or a church organization and should not be confused with a corporation for profit. It is normally headed by a bishop or another clerical official who has been empowered by a church to hold title to church property. However, the title descends to successors in office and not to heirs. A broker should exercise caution in dealing with a corporation sole. Before dealing with a corporation sole, a broker should obtain a written opinion from an attorney who has experience in such titles. A corporation sole *cannot* be registered as a real estate brokerage entity.

Joint Adventure

A **joint adventure** (or *joint venture*) is a temporary form of business arrangement often encountered in the real estate business. It has most of the features and creates most of the rights and liabilities of a partnership, except that the venture and the liabilities are confined to one business transaction, or a very limited number of business transactions. Two or more parties may decide to combine their efforts to complete a single business transaction or a fixed number of business transactions. No written agreements are required to form a joint venture.

Real estate brokers often combine their efforts in real estate transactions to create a joint venture. A joint venture, when composed of separate real estate brokers, can broker real property. In such a case, the joint venture would not be required to register with the DBPR because each of the individuals is registered and licensed. If two parties form a joint venture to provide real estate services for compensation, both parties must be licensed real estate brokers.

TRADE NAMES

A person may not operate as a broker under a trade name without causing the trade name to be noted in the records of the Commission and placed on the person's license, or so operate as a member of a partnership or as a corporation or as an officer or manager thereof, unless such partnership or corporation is the holder of a valid current registration.

Reference: Section 475.42, F.S.

Business Trust

A business trust is a form of business entity that may be created to engage in transactions involving its own real property. A business trust is formed by any number of persons who make an investment at a stipulated amount per unit. The monies collected in this manner are then used to buy, develop, and/or sell real estate. Title to real property acquired by a business trust is taken in the name of a trustee or group of trustees. A business trust *cannot* be registered with the DBPR as a real estate brokerage entity. However, any employee who buys or sells real property for a trust and is compensated on a transaction basis must be licensed.

Associations

A cooperative association is permitted to conduct commercial business and to convey, sell, or buy its own property, but it *cannot* be registered as a real estate brokerage entity.

Unincorporated associations are generally recognized as groups of people associated for some noncommercial common purpose. They are not regarded as partners and are not incorporated. An example would be a group of property owners in a subdivision who organize for such purposes as beautification, planning, maintenance, or even the performance of services such as garbage removal. Such associations can incur liabilities, and members are responsible for debts to creditors in the same manner as partners. For example, each member is liable for all the debts, but as to each other, the members are liable only for their individual proportionate share. Unincorporated associations sometimes buy or sell their own real property through a trustee or board of trustees. A real estate broker should exercise the same caution in dealing with an unincorporated association as when dealing with a corporation sole. Unincorporated associations *cannot* register as real estate brokerage entities.

TRADE NAMES

A **trade name** is a business name other than the legal name of the person doing business. The letters *T/A* are used to indicate "trading as." **Fictitious name** refers to the name registered with the Department of State. The letters *D/B/A* refer to "doing business as." Sole proprietors and business entities may choose to operate under these designations.

The Fictitious Name Act defines *fictitious name* as any name under which a person transacts business in the state of Florida, other than the person's legal name. Section 865.09, F.S., mandates that a person may not engage in business under a fictitious name unless the person first registers the name with the Division of Corporations of the Florida Department of State. The Division of Corporations is a filing agency that serves both as the statewide central custodian of business entity filings and annual reports and as the statewide central registration office for fictitious names. The Division of Corporations also is the resource for information regarding these records.

An *individual* broker or brokerage entity may use a trade name and applicable designation after the name is registered with the DBPR. Chapter 475 (license law) does not require a sole proprietor or brokerage entity to register a trade name with the Department of State. However, if another brokerage entity has previously registered that name with the Department of State, the brokerage may not use the name. If a brokerage corporation or partnership conducts business under a fictitious name, the business must comply with the Florida Fictitious Name Act and register the fictitious name with the Department of State. Partnerships, corporations, or other legal entities that have filed or registered with the Division of Corporations and that are in good standing with that Division are considered to have met the requirements for fictitious name registration, provided they do not transact business under any other name. Additionally, if an owner's first *and* last names are included in the business name, the business is exempt from filing a fictitious name. For example, Susan Brown's Real Estate Services need not register a fictitious name with the Division of Corporations; however, it must register with the DBPR.

A person registers by submitting an application for "Registration of Fictitious Name" with the Division of Corporations. The applicant must indicate the name to be registered, the business's mailing address, each owner's name and address, and the Federal Employer Identification (FEI) number. Registration under the Fictitious Name Act is for public notice *only* and does *not* give rise to a presumption of the registrant's rights to own or use the name registered, nor does it affect trademark, service mark, or corporate name rights previously acquired by others in the same or similar name. Furthermore, registration does not reserve a fictitious name against future use. A fictitious name registration is valid for five years. It expires on December 31 of the fifth year, but may be renewed for subsequent five-year periods.

WEB LINK

The Division of Corporations maintains an index of fictitious names. To search the index, go to **http://www.sunbiz.org/search.html** and click on the type of inquiry.

A fictitious name registered under the Fictitious Name Act may not contain the word *Corporation*, *Incorporated*, or *Company*, or the abbreviations *Corp.*, *Inc.*, or *Co.* unless the person or business for which the name is registered is incorporated or has obtained a *certificate of authority* to transact business in Florida pursuant to Chapter 607 or 617, F.S.

Broker associates and sales associates must have their real estate licenses issued in their legal names. They may not be licensed or registered under a trade name or a fictitious name. However, a broker associate or a sales associate is allowed to form a professional corporation, a limited liability company, or a professional limited liability company in the licensee's legal name. The broker can pay sales commissions to the professional corporation. A real estate sales associate or broker associate may form a professional corporation, limited liability company, or professional limited liability for income tax purposes only, and this is *not* to be confused with a brokerage business entity.

FOR MORE INFORMATION

A large selection of filing forms is available free of charge through the Department of State, Division of Corporations' Web pages. You may download the forms in Adobe's Acrobat PDF format by contacting *www.sunbiz.org.* Online filing is also available. To receive forms concerning S corporation requirements, contact IRS at (800) TAX-FORM or *www.irs.ustreas.gov.* to request publication 1120S, *Tax Information on S Corporations,* and Form 2553, *Election by a Small Business Corporation.*

In this case, the DBPR issues the real state license in the licensee's actual (legal) name and includes the entity designation on the face of the license. For example, Florida law requires that a professional corporation include the words "professional association" or the abbreviation "PA" in the name. Therefore, the sales associate license could state, for example, Jane Doe, PA. Florida law further mandates that a professional limited liability company include the words "professional limited company" or the abbreviation "PL" in the name. A sales associate license could state, for example, John Doe, PL. Florida law requires that a limited liability company include "limited liability company" or "limited company" or the abbreviation "LLC" or "LC" in the name. In such a case, a license could state, for example, Jane Doe, LLC.

Section 475.161, F.S. requires that such a professional entity must be made up of only one individual. Therefore a husband and wife sales team (both licensed real estate sales associates) would not be allowed to form a professional corporation. Each spouse would be required to each form a separate professional corporation. The sales associate or broker associate must first set up the professional entity through the Florida Division of Corporations and then register the information with the DBPR prior to doing business with the public. At this point, the broker can pay the PA (or other allowable professional entity) rather than the individual sales associate or broker associate.

Sales associates and broker associates must work under a broker or an owner-developer. Sales associates and broker associates are not allowed to register or be licensed as a general partner, member, manager, officer, or director of a real estate brokerage firm.

THE REAL ESTATE OFFICE

Choosing a location for your real estate office is one of the most important decisions you will make. The impression you make on the public begins at your front door. Your business projects its image through its advertising, the professionalism of the personnel, the quality of services provided, and the office and physical environment.

All active Florida real estate brokers are required to have an office and to register the office with the DBPR. (The DBPR charges a registration fee.) A broker's office must consist of at least one enclosed room in a building of stationary construction that will provide privacy to conduct negotiations and closings of real estate transactions.

CITATION AUTHORITY

475.22(1) and 61J2-10.022. Failed to maintain the required office as prescribed. *$500 citation*

475.22(1) and 61J2-10.024. Failed to maintain the required office entrance sign. *$100 citation*

475.22(2). Failed to register an out-of-state Florida broker's office. *$500 citation*

475.24, 61J2-8.003 and 61J2-10.023. Failed to register a location as a branch office. *$200 citation*

Reference: Rule 61J2-24.002, F.A.C

A broker's primary office is referred to as the *principal office*. The broker's books, records, and real estate transaction files are to be kept in the office. Florida law does not require the broker to have a telephone, desk, business checking account, or an escrow account. If local zoning permits, the broker's office may be in the broker's residence, provided the required sign (see Entrance Signs in this chapter) is displayed properly. A broker may have an office or offices in another state, provided the broker agrees in writing to cooperate with any investigation initiated under Chapter 475, F.S.

The amount (size) of office space should be based on the types of real estate services the business provides and the number of staff and sales associates it must house. If the broker plans to increase the size of the sales force as the business becomes established, the office space should be flexible enough to accommodate growth and change. Sales associates are *not* permitted to open offices of their own. They must be registered from and work out of an office maintained and registered in the name of their employer.

When choosing a business location, a broker also should take into account proximity to the customer base. The broker must analyze the marketplace to determine the location of one's target market and its relation to competing real estate businesses. Sales associates value being located close to their customer bases. The broker should give priority to good visibility, easy access from both sides of the street, efficient signage, and adequate parking. The broker should verify sign control regulations and zoning restrictions in advance and inquire about city and county occupation licenses.

Branch Offices

If a broker desires to conduct business from additional locations, the broker must register each additional location as a branch office and pay the appropriate registration fees. Thereafter, the broker must renew branch office registrations every two years.

The Florida Real Estate Commission may insist that a broker open and register a branch office whenever the FREC decides that the business conducted at a place other than the principal office is of such a nature that the public interest requires registration of a branch office. Further, any office will be considered a branch office if the advertising of a broker, who has a principal office elsewhere, is such that it leads the public to believe that the office of concern is owned or operated by the broker in question.

A *temporary shelter* in a subdivision being sold by a broker is not a branch office if the shelter is intended only for the protection of customers and sales associates. But if sales associates are assigned there, necessary sales supplies are on hand, and sale transactions are concluded there, then the temporary structure must be registered as a branch office. In short, the permanence, use, and character of activities customarily conducted at the office or shelter determine whether it must be registered.

Registrations issued to branch offices are *not* transferable. To illustrate, suppose a broker decides to close one branch office and open a new branch office at a different location. Even though these actions may take place at the same time, the registration of the closed office may not be transferred to another office. The new location must be registered and the fee paid. A broker may reopen a branch office in the same location during the same license period by requesting a reissue of the branch office license without paying an additional fee.

Entrance Signs

Active real estate brokers must display an official sign on either the exterior or interior of the entrance to their principal office and all branch offices. The sign(s) must be easily observed and read by anyone entering the office. The sign must contain the following information:

- Trade name (if one is used)
- Broker's name
- The words, "Licensed Real Estate Broker" or "Lic. Real Estate Broker"

Refer to the first example of an office sign. The registered trade name is Little Mo Realty, the broker's name is Murl H. Crawford, and the required wording "Licensed Real Estate Broker" appears on the sign.

Sole Proprietor with a Trade Name Sign

The names of sales associates and broker associates are *not* required on the entrance sign. However, if the associates' names appear on the sign, they must be placed below the name of the broker(s) and the appropriate title, sales associate or broker associate, must appear next to each associate's name. A line or observable space must separate the names of the real estate brokers from the names of the sales associates or broker associates (Refer to the previous example of an office sign.)

If the brokerage entity is a partnership, corporation, limited liability company (LLC), or limited liability partnership, the sign must contain the following information:

- Name of the firm or corporation (or trade name, if one is used)
- Name of at least one active broker
- The words "Licensed Real Estate Broker" or "Lic. Real Estate Broker"

Brokerage Corporation Sign

Americans with Disabilities Act (ADA)

Whether leasing or purchasing space, brokers must comply with federal and state laws regarding accessibility. Under Title III of the **Americans with Disabilities Act (ADA)**, places of public accommodation and commercial facilities must be accessible to persons with physical or mental disabilities. **Public accommodations** are facilities open to the public, including sales or rental establishments, service businesses, hotels, restaurants, movie theaters, auditoriums, and recreational centers. *Commercial facilities* include office buildings, factories, and warehouses. Real estate offices are considered both public accommodations and commercial facilities. ADA requirements also apply to private entities that own, lease, or operate commercial facilities, including real estate brokerage offices, even if the broker's office is located in a private residence. Buyers who purchase older homes with plans to turn the structures into offices may face costly unanticipated expenses to modify or upgrade the facility to ADA standards.

ADA governs employment practices regarding discrimination in hiring and reasonable accommodations in the workplace. Any alteration of an existing facility and all new public accommodations and commercial facilities must comply with the ADA's accessibility guidelines. When a broker leases commercial space, the lease agreement generally indicates who is responsible for the cost of any renovations required to comply with the ADA. Compliance includes removing barriers to walkways, parking lots, entrances, stairs, washrooms, water fountains, public telephones, elevators, electrical controls, and warning signals. The front door to every real estate office should be wide enough to accommodate a wheelchair. Sidewalks should have continuous common surfaces with no steps or sudden changes in level. A broker must install a ramp if needed to accommodate wheelchair access and must arrange room layouts to provide a place where people in wheelchairs can meet with sales associates. Accessible parking spaces must be marked clearly for use by disabled persons.

State law sets a minimum number of accessible parking spaces based on the total available parking, as well as the parking spaces' size and location. In addition to the ADA's accessibility guidelines, Section 316.1955, F.S., mandates the minimum dimensions of accessible parking spaces and requires that the spaces be located on the shortest safely accessible route from the parking spaces to the business entrance so that users will not have to walk or wheel behind parked vehicles.

Accessibility guidelines and specifications are available from local building inspectors and the Department of Justice. Local municipal or county governments are responsible for enforcing compliance with the codes. Before selecting an existing structure for a real estate office, a broker should contact the local building inspection department to request an inspection or hire a consultant to inspect the property to determine whether it complies with accessibility guidelines.

ADVERTISING AND SELF-PROMOTION

Anyone who advertises or represents that they are providing real estate services is acting as a real estate broker. Therefore, advertising is considered under Florida law to be a broker activity. All advertising must be in the name of the brokerage and under the supervision of the broker. Sales associates may not advertise real estate services in their own names. The broker is accountable for all advertising, regardless of who actually prepares the advertisement. Publication of false or misleading information by means of radio, television, or written matter for the purpose of inducing someone to buy, lease, rent, or acquire an interest in title to real property is illegal. If a sales associate prepares a misleading ad, both the broker and the sales associate can be disciplined. Advertising includes letterhead stationery and flyers, business cards, yard signs and billboards, newspaper and magazine ads, Internet, radio and television, promotional materials, and so forth.

All advertising must be worded so that reasonable people will know that they are dealing with a real estate licensee. A licensee may not advertise real estate services in such a way as to mislead the public that the offer is being made by a private individual rather than a real estate licensee. Advertisements must clearly reveal the licensed name of the brokerage firm. Advertisements that fail to disclose the license name of the brokerage firm are **blind advertisements**. For example, an advertisement that provides only a post office box number, telephone number, and/or street address is a blind ad and is prohibited.

A big part of a real estate associate's business is self-promotion—marketing the associate's services to the public. If a broker's sales associates create promotional materials, such as refrigerator magnets, calendars, and notepads, they must include the licensed name of the brokerage firm on them.

Licensees may insert their personal names in ads provided they include their last name as registered with the DBPR. Advertisements created by sales associates must be supervised directly by their broker. Sales associates and their brokers should review advertisements for accuracy and also make certain the ad is canceled when, due to sale or listing expiration, the property is no longer on the market. Licensees may indicate their nickname on business cards and in advertisements but only if their legal name as registered with the DBPR is also indicated (for example, Robert "Bob" Smith). Sales associates may indicate their after-hours phone number and/or address on their business cards provided the card also includes the name of the brokerage firm. FREC does not require that the brokerage firm's phone number or address be included in ads. It is a violation of FREC Rule 61J2-10.027 for a real estate broker or sales associate to use or display an identification or a designation of any association or organization having to do with real estate unless the licensee is entitled to use the identification or designation by means of membership, payment of dues, and so forth.

An important way to advertise real estate is with signage. For Sale signs serve three important functions: First, they let prospective buyers know that a property is for sale; second, For Sale signs generate more buyers who may purchase other properties listed with the broker; and third, For Sale signs generate new listings. Yard signs are a form of advertising and, therefore, must include the name of the brokerage firm.

Ultimately, a broker is responsible for an advertisement's quality, accuracy, and legality. All ads should be reviewed before publication, whether the company or individual sales associates submit and pay for them. Sale prices should be stated according to the terms authorized in the listing agreements. Brokers may not publish price information and price reductions without an owner's consent. It is important to avoid publishing any information that compromises the owner's negotiating position.

DISCIPLINARY GUIDELINES

475.25(1)(c). False, deceptive, or misleading advertising.

First Violation: $250 to $1,000 administrative fine and a 30-day to 90-day suspension

Subsequent Violations: $1,000 to $5,000 administrative fine and a 90-day suspension up to revocation

475.42(1)(n). Publication of false or misleading information; promotion of sales, leases, and rentals.

First Violation: $250 to $1,000 administrative fine and suspension up to revocation

Subsequent Violations: $1,000 to $5,000 administrative fine and suspension up to revocation

Reference: Rule 61J2-24.001, F.A.C.

Internet sites. When advertising on an Internet site, the name of the brokerage firm must appear adjacent to or immediately above or below the point of contact information. **Point of contact information** refers to any means by which to contact the brokerage firm or individual licensee, including mailing address(es), physical street address(es), e-mail address(es), telephone number(s), or facsimile (fax) telephone number(s). Brokers should keep Web site information up-to-date by removing sold or expired listings. The broker should also keep sales associate information current by removing information regarding sales associates who have left the brokerage and adding new sales associates.

The rules regarding advertising real property do not prevent real estate licensees from selling their own property. Real estate licensees who own property and are selling the property "by owner" may place their own classified advertisements. Licensees may include their personal contact information in the ads, such as the home phone number and street address of the property. It is not necessary for a licensee to indicate in the advertisement that the seller is a real estate licensee. However, because a licensee has superior knowledge and expertise in real estate, to reduce liability the "by owner" licensee-seller should disclose prior to entering into serious negotiations that the seller is a real estate licensee. Disclosure of this fact should also be documented in the sale contract. Such disclosure is mandated in the National Association of REALTORS® Standards of Practice. The NAR requires that member REALTORS® who advertise unlisted real property for sale or lease in which they have an ownership interest disclose their status as owners (or landlords) and as REALTORS®. Brokers should instruct their sales associates and broker associates who are considering selling property that they own "by owner" to consult with the broker and review the office policy manual. Some brokers expect the licensee to list the property through the brokerage office.

A broker should exercise caution when advertising financing terms concerning a listed property. Truth-in-Lending laws permit general expressions, such as "owner will finance," but specific financing information, such as "only $2,000 down," must be accompanied by specific information regarding the amount or percentage of down payment, the terms of repayment, and the annual percentage rate (APR).

Fair Housing Act

Under the Fair Housing Act, the protected classes are race, color, religion, sex, handicap, familial status, and national origin. No protection is given under the Fair Housing Act to individuals based on age, occupation, marital status, or sexual orientation. However, fair housing laws passed by state and local governments may expand the classes afforded fair housing protection in their jurisdiction.

Section 804(c) of the Fair Housing Act prohibits brokers from making, printing, and publishing advertisements that state a preference, limitation, or discrimination on the basis of race, color, religion, sex, handicap, familial status, or national origin. The prohibition applies to publishers, such as newspapers and directories, as well as to persons and entities that place real estate advertisements. It also applies to advertisements where the underlying properties may be exempt from the act's provisions, but where the advertisements themselves violate the act.

Race, color, national origin. Real estate advertisements should not include discriminatory preferences or limitations based on race, color, or national origin. Describing current or potential residents or neighborhoods in racial or ethnic terms, such as "nice Italian neighborhood" or "no Caucasians," is prohibited.

Religion. Advertisements should refrain from an explicit preference, limitation, or discrimination on the basis of religion, such as "Jewish home" or "no Christians." Furthermore, licensees should not use references to religious landmarks when giving driving directions to properties in advertisements. Using landmarks such as a reference to a mosque, church, or synagogue may indicate a religious preference, which would be a violation of the Fair Housing Act. Advertisements that use the legal name of an entity that contains a religious reference, such as Trinity Presbyterian Home, do not violate the act if the ads include disclaimers, such as "This Home does not discriminate on the basis of race, color, religion, national origin, sex, handicap, or familial status."

Sex. Advertisements for single-family dwellings or separate units in multifamily dwellings should not contain a preference, limitation, or discrimination based on sex. A phrase such as "female roommate wanted" is permissible only if it meets the requirements for the shared living exception. According to the assistant secretary for Fair Housing and Equal Opportunity, terms such as *master bedroom*, *mother-in-law suite*, and *bachelor apartment*, commonly used as physical descriptions of housing units, do not violate the act.

Handicap. Real estate advertisements should not contain explicit exclusions or limitations based on handicap, such as "no wheelchairs." Advertisements that describe the conduct required of residents, such as "nonsmoking," do not violate the act. Advertisements may describe accessibility features, such as "wheelchair ramp."

Familial status. *Familial status* refers to the presence of one or more children under the age of 18 who live with either a parent or guardian. Familial status also includes a woman who is pregnant. In effect, it means that the Fair Housing Act's protections extend to families with minor children. Unless a property qualifies as housing for older persons, all properties must be made available to families with children under the same terms and conditions as to anyone else. It is illegal to advertise properties as being for adults only or to indicate a preference for a certain number of children. The number of persons permitted to reside in a property must be based on objective factors such as sanitation or safety. Landlords cannot restrict the number of occupants to eliminate families with children.

DISCIPLINARY GUIDELINES

475.453. Broker or sales associate participates in any rental information transaction that fails to follow the guidelines adopted by the Commission and Chapter 475, F.S.

First Violation: $250 to $1,000 administrative fine and suspension

Subsequent Violations: $1,000 to $5,000 administrative fine and a 90-day suspension up to revocation

Reference: Rule 61J2-24.001, F.A.C.

Housing for older persons. Certain housing for older persons is exempt from the familial status protection under the Fair Housing Act, provided that:

- all units are occupied by persons 62 years of age or older; or
- at least 80 percent of the units are occupied by one or more persons 55 years of age or older and housing policies are published and followed that demonstrate an intent to be housing for persons 55 and older.

WEB LINK

To locate 55-and-older communities in a particular area, go to **http://fchr.state.fl.us**. Select "Directory of 55+ Housing Communities" from the menu.

If a group is not protected under the Fair Housing Act, discrimination against that group is not illegal. A landlord, for example, may place a newspaper advertisement stating that the landlord will rent residential property only to nonsmokers. The landlord's refusal to rent residential property to a potential tenant based solely on the fact that the prospect is a smoker is not a violation of the Fair Housing Act. Excluding nonprotected groups of people from renting property may be a poor business decision, but it is not a violation of the Fair Housing Act.

Fair housing poster. The Fair Housing Act requires the use of an equal opportunity poster. The poster features the equal housing logo and a statement pledging adherence to the Fair Housing Act. The poster (Figure 2.1) is available without charge from the Department of Housing and Urban Development (HUD). The poster must be displayed at real estate brokerage offices and other businesses involved in the housing industry. In the event a discrimination complaint is made against a broker, HUD considers failure to prominently display the equal housing opportunity poster in the broker's place of business as evidence of discrimination. HUD considers any charge of discrimination to be true unless disproved by evidence to the contrary. The burden of proof is placed on the broker to prove no discrimination has occurred in such cases. Additionally, it violates the Fair Housing Act and may expose a licensee to FREC disciplinary action. It is a broker's responsibility to provide training and supervision to ensure compliance with the law.

Advertising. All advertisements of real property must be accurate representations of the property. There is a difference between showcasing a property's features and misrepresenting the property. Truthful advertising is serious business. It is a second-degree misdemeanor to publish false or misleading information by means of radio, television, or written

FIGURE 2.1 ■ Equal Housing Opportunity Poster

U.S. Department of Housing and Urban Development

EQUAL HOUSING
OPPORTUNITY

We Do Business in Accordance With the Federal Fair Housing Law

(The Fair Housing Amendments Act of 1988)

It is Illegal to Discriminate Against Any Person Because of Race, Color, Religion, Sex, Handicap, Familial Status, or National Origin

- In the sale or rental of housing or residential lots
- In advertising the sale or rental of housing
- In the financing of housing
- In the provision of real estate brokerage services
- In the appraisal of housing
- Blockbusting is also illegal

Anyone who feels he or she has been discriminated against may file a complaint of housing discrimination:
1-800-669-9777 (Toll Free)
1-800-927-9275 (TDD)

U.S. Department of Housing and Urban Development
Assistant Secretary for Fair Housing and Equal Opportunity
Washington, D.C. 20410

Previous editions are obsolete

form HUD-928.1A (2/2003)

NOTICE

PURSUANT TO FLORIDA LAW: If the rental information provided under this contract is not current or accurate in any material aspect, you may demand within 30 days of this contract date a return of your full fee paid. If you do not obtain a rental you are entitled to receive a return of 75% of the fee paid, if you make demand within 30 days of this contract date.

Reference: 61J2-10.030, F.A.C.

material for the purpose of inducing another person to buy, lease, rent, or acquire an interest in real estate. A second-degree misdemeanor carries with it a criminal penalty of up to a $500 fine and 60 days in prison. If the individual has a Florida real estate license, the licensee also is subject to license suspension or revocation.

WEB LINK

Download "HUD's Advertising Guidance" at **http://www.hud.gov/offices/fheo/library/part109.pdf.**

Rental Information and Lists

Some real estate brokerage firms offer prospective tenants a list of properties available for rent. However, very few brokerage firms sell this information. Rental companies or anyone who advertises rental property information or lists in any manner is acting as a broker or a broker's representative and is subject to the laws regulating licensed occupations. Accordingly, any real estate licensee who furnishes rental information to a prospective tenant for a fee must provide the prospective tenant with a contract or receipt that contains a provision for repayment under specified conditions. It must state that a prospective tenant who does not obtain a rental is entitled to be repaid 75 percent of the fee if requested within 30 days of the contract/receipt date (see boxed text, Notice, on this page).

If the information provided to the prospective tenant is not current or is inaccurate in any material respect, the broker must repay 100 percent of the fee to the prospective tenant on demand. Any demand from the prospective tenant for the return of any part or all of the fee must be made within 30 days from the date the broker or sales associate contracted to provide services. Such demands may be made orally or in writing. The contract or receipt agreement must follow FREC guidelines, and the licensee must send a copy to the DBPR within 30 days of the first use.

Advertising rental property information or lists that are not current or are materially inaccurate is illegal. Any person who violates the requirements outlined above is guilty of a misdemeanor of the first degree, is subject to a fine of up to $1,000 and/or imprisonment of up to one year, and is subject to license suspension or revocation.

Telephone Solicitation

Telemarketing is the use of the telephone as a marketing tool to solicit services directly to the public. Telemarketing is regulated by state and federal law. The Telephone Consumer Protection Act of 1991 (TCPA) is a federal law concerning telephone solicitations. A **telephone solicitation** is defined as the initiation of a telephone call for the purpose of encouraging the purchase of, or investment in, property, goods, or services. The TCPA established a National Do Not Call Registry for consumers who wish to avoid telemarketing calls. Consumers at no charge may request to be on the list. Telemarketers must first search the national registry before making telemarketing calls. Calls are restricted to the hours of 8:00 AM to 9:00 PM.

The federal law covers both interstate (between states) and intrastate (within state) telemarketing calls. The law exempts (1) political solicitations; (2) telephone surveys (callers purporting to take a survey, but who also offer to sell goods or services, must comply with the do-not-call registry); and (3) charitable solicitations. Violators of the federal law may be fined up to $11,000 for each illegal call.

Florida's telemarketing law is administered through the Department of Agriculture and Consumer Services. Florida maintains a no sales solicitation calls registry for consumers at an initial charge of $10 ($5 each year thereafter). Florida has made its registry part of the national do-not-call registry. Violators of Florida's Telemarketing Act may be fined $10,000 per call.

A major difference between the state and federal telemarketing laws is that the Florida law exempts real estate licensees who solicit listings in response to a "For Sale" yard sign. However, the federal law does not exempt calls to for sale by owners (FSBOs). The Federal Communications Commission (FCC) recently ruled that under the federal law, real estate licensees may *not* call for sale by owners (FSBOs) and homeowners with expired listings to solicit for listings if the owners' names are listed on the National Do Not Call Registry, even if the homeowner's telephone number appears on a yard sign or in a newspaper ad. The federal law provides the following exceptions:

- Licensees representing a potential buyer may call the FSBO seller, but only if they have an actual buyer interested in the property and to negotiate a sale.
- A licensee may contact individuals with whom the licensee has had an established business relationship, even if the customer's number is on the national registry. For example, the company that previously listed a property may contact the former customer to solicit new business for up to 18 months after the business transaction has been concluded.
- Licensees may contact a customer for three months after a business inquiry or application (such as a customer who registered at an open house or a FSBO seller who requested information from a sales associate).

If a real estate licensee calls a FSBO or an expired listing under the exceptions listed above and the homeowner requests not to be called, the licensee must comply. Telemarketers must state their names, the business name, and the business telephone number. Telemarketers may not block their phone numbers.

Businesses that use telemarketing must develop and adhere to written procedures regarding the firms' calling policies. Businesses must advise and train their personnel and independent contractors engaged in telephone solicitation regarding do-not-call list maintenance and procedures. Furthermore, businesses may not use automatic telephone

CASE IN POINT

A corporation purchased a commercial property. The corporation executed a sale contract. The vice president signed a promissory note to the seller and directly under her signature wrote "Vice President" and the corporation's name.

When the note was not paid an action was brought to hold the vice president personally liable for the debt. The trial court and the 4th District Court of Appeals held that the vice president could be held personally liable because she did not sign using the words *as* vice president *for* the corporation.

Reference: *Florida Realtor.* Volume 72, Number 11, December 1997, p. 26.

dialing systems in such a way that two or more telephone lines of a multiple-line business are engaged simultaneously.

Real estate companies that wish to use telemarketing in their business strategy must obtain the list of phone numbers in the registry. The list is organized by area code and it is available from the Federal Trade Commission (FTC). There is no charge for the first five area codes. A fee is charged for additional area codes. Licensees must search the national registry at least quarterly and delete from their call lists the phone numbers of consumers who have registered. Consumers can file a complaint with the FCC against a telemarketer who violates the law.

Fax solicitations. FCC rules mandate that it is unlawful to send unsolicited advertisements to a residential or business fax machine without the recipient's prior express invitation or permission. The four requirements a sender must meet before sending an unsolicited advertising fax to a consumer are summarized below:

1. Sender must have an established business relationship with the recipient or written consent from the recipient prior to sending unsolicited advertising faxes.
2. Sender must have received the recipient's fax number voluntarily from the recipient in the context of the established business relationship.
3. Sender must clearly state on the first page of the advertisement that the recipient has the right to opt-out of receiving future unsolicited advertising faxes.
4. Sender must honor opt-outs received from recipients within 30 days of receipt.

WEB LINK

To learn more about the National Do Not Call Registry, visit the FCC Web site at **http://www.fcc.gov/encyclopedia/do-not-call-list**.

To find out more regarding Florida's do-not-call registry, visit the Florida Department of Agriculture and Consumer Services at **http://www.800helpfla.com/nosales.html.**

SUMMARY OF IMPORTANT POINTS

- Types of business entities that may register as a brokerage entity include the following: sole proprietorship, general partnership, limited partnership, limited liability partnership, corporation, and limited liability company.
- A *sole proprietorship* is a business owned by one person. A real estate brokerage sole proprietorship exists when the broker is the only owner. Sole proprietors are personally liable for the business losses as well as the debts and torts (negligent acts arising from breach of duty created by law) of sales associates and others working for the broker when acting within the scope of their duties.
- A *general partnership* is an association of two or more persons for the purpose of jointly conducting a business. General partners are agents for each other. If one partner enters into an agreement, it binds the other partners to the agreement. Florida general partnerships are not subject to direct taxation. General partnerships feature pass-through treatment for federal income tax purposes. At least one partner must be an active real estate broker in a general partnership real estate brokerage. Partners who will deal with the public and perform services of real estate must be licensed as active brokers.
- A *limited partnership* is composed of both general partners and limited partners. Limited partners invest cash and may not participate in management. Limited partners have limited liability. All general partners who expect to perform real estate brokerage services on behalf of the limited partnership must be licensed as active brokers. Sales associates and broker associates may not be general partners in a real estate brokerage limited partnership; however, they may be limited partners.
- A *corporation* is an artificial person or legal entity created by law, consisting of one or more individuals. At least one of the corporation's officers or directors must be licensed as an active broker. Active Florida brokers, inactive Florida brokers, and unlicensed people may serve as officers and directors of a real estate brokerage. However, officers and directors who deal with the public and perform services of real estate must be licensed as active brokers. Sales associates and broker associates may not be an officer or director in a real estate brokerage corporation. Sales associates and broker associates may be shareholders of a real estate brokerage corporation.
- An *ostensible partnership* (or quasi-partnership) exists where there is no real partnership, but the parties act or do business in such a manner that the public assumes that a partnership exists. Ostensible partnerships are considered fraudulent and deceitful, and any licensees who operate as ostensible partners are subject to discipline.
- A *trade name* is a business name other than the legal name of the person doing business. A broker or brokerage entity may use a trade name after the name is registered with the DBPR.
- *Fictitious name* refers to the name registered with the Department of State.
- To have an active status, a real estate broker is required to open an office and register it with the DBPR.
- If a broker desires to conduct business from additional locations, the broker must register each additional location as a branch office and pay the appropriate regis-

tration fees. Registrations issued to branch offices are not transferable to another location.

- The brokerage office sign must contain (1) the trade name (if applicable), (2) the broker's name, and (3) the words "Licensed (or Lic.) Real Estate Broker. If desired, the names of the sales associates and broker associates may be added below the broker's name(s), provided the appropriate title (sales associate or broker associate) appears after their name. A line or space must separate the broker's names from the associates' names.
- The Americans with Disabilities Act (ADA) prohibits discrimination in places of public accommodation and commercial facilities such as hotels and real estate offices.
- All advertising must be in the name of the brokerage and under the supervision of the broker. Licensees who include their personal name in advertisements must use their last name as registered with the DBPR. Blind advertising fails to disclose the license name of the brokerage firm and provides only a post office box number, telephone number, and/or street address.
- *Point of contact information* refers to the information provided on the Internet for contacting a brokerage firm or individual licensee, including mailing addresses, physical street addresses, e-mail addresses, telephone numbers, and FAX telephone numbers. The brokerage firm name must be above, below, or adjacent to point of contact information.
- Failing to provide accurate and current rental information for a fee is a first-degree misdemeanor. The penalty for a first-degree misdemeanor is a fine of not more than $1,000 and/or up to one year in jail.
- A *telephone solicitation* is a telephone call placed for the purpose of encouraging the purchase of, or investment in, property, goods, or services. Telemarketers (including real estate licensees) must search the National Do Not Call Registry before making telemarketing calls. Violators of the federal Telephone Consumer Protection Act may be fined up to $11,000 per call. The penalty for violating Florida's Telemarketing Act is $10,000 per call.

REVIEW QUESTIONS

1. A broker is considering various forms of business organizations for his new real estate brokerage. He wants protection from personal liability and favorable income tax treatment. Which business organization best fits his criteria?
   a. Limited partnership
   b. Corporation
   c. Corporation sole
   d. S corporation

2. Which business structure is NOT required to file with the Florida Department of State?
   a. Limited liability company
   b. S corporation
   c. General partnership
   d. Limited partnership

3. Which business name(s) is (are) required to be registered as a fictitious name with the Florida Department of State?
   a. Murl A. Howard, Licensed Real Estate Broker
   b. Robert Stoufer's Real Estate Services, Licensed Real Estate Broker
   c. Rebecca's Complete Real Estate Company
   d. All of the above are required to register a fictitious name with the Department of State.

4. Murl is forming his new real estate business, Little Mo Realty Company. He has already filed his articles of incorporation with the Florida Department of State. What other filing(s) is (are) required before Murl can begin operating his company?
   a. Murl must register the business entity and only the officers and directors who hold active broker licenses with the DBPR.
   b. Murl must register the names of only the licensed officers and directors with the DBPR.
   c. Murl must register the names of all the corporate owners with the DBPR, Division of Real Estate.
   d. Murl must register the corporation including the names of all the officers and directors with the DBPR.

5. Jack, Jill, and Heidi are active general partners in a partnership registered as a real estate brokerage entity. They have irreconcilable differences, and Jack withdraws as a general partner. Which statement is TRUE of this situation?
   a. The partnership registration is canceled automatically.
   b. The partnership registration and the partners' and sales associates' licenses are unaffected by the vacancy.
   c. Jill and Heidi must register the re-formed partnership within 14 calendar days and cannot engage in any new real estate business before doing so.
   d. Jill and Heidi must file the new organization with the Florida Department of State.

6. In a real estate brokerage operation, a licensed real estate sales associate may be a(n)
   a. limited partner.
   b. officer of a corporation.
   c. ostensible partner.
   d. general partner.

7. Murl and Mike are licensed brokers who each have their own real estate brokerage business. Murl specializes in marketing waterfront property. Mike specializes in acquiring property for the railroad industry. Murl and Mike make a verbal business agreement to combine their efforts to conduct a single business transaction. They want to find a site for East Coast Railways that is convenient to the Tampa Port Authority. Which statement is TRUE concerning this arrangement?
   a. Murl and Mike are required to register with the DBPR as a partnership.
   b. This arrangement creates an ostensible partnership.
   c. This arrangement is a joint venture, and as such Murl and Mike need not register the joint venture with the DBPR.
   d. Murl and Mike are in violation of Chapter 475.

8. A licensed real estate broker also has a small comic book business. On the weekends, he rents a booth at the Alachua County Flea Market, where he buys, sells, and trades comic books. He also displays photographs of his residential listings. Which statement is TRUE of this situation?
   a. The Commission likely would consider such activity to be deceptive advertising.
   b. He need not register his flea market location as a branch office.
   c. This ostensible business activity is illegal.
   d. Because he conducts business transactions at the site, he must register it as a branch office.

9. If a licensed, active real estate broker decides to operate her modest real estate business from her home, which statement is TRUE?
   a. As long as the broker operates independently as a sole proprietor, she need not register her home office.
   b. She must open a principal office in addition to maintaining her home office.
   c. The office portion of her home must be accessible to physically and mentally disabled buyers and sellers.
   d. Home offices are exempt from the entrance sign requirement if local zoning prohibits signs.

10. A broker of Little Mo Realty Company is ordering his exterior entrance sign for his principal office. Which instruction must he give the sign maker?
    a. Make the letters at least half an inch high.
    b. Include the words *Licensed Real Estate Company*.
    c. Include on the sign his first and last names, as registered with the Commission.
    d. List the names of his sales associates below his name.

11. Which statement is TRUE of a real estate office under the Americans with Disabilities Act?
    a. If the real estate office has fewer than 30 employees, it is exempt from ADA requirements.
    b. The office is considered to be both a commercial facility and a public accommodation and as such must be accessible to persons with physical or mental disabilities.
    c. A small real estate office is exempted from the accessibility requirements unless it employs an individual who needs special accommodations.
    d. One advantage of renting commercial space for a real estate office is that the landlord is responsible for any financial burden associated with the ADA.

12. A broker placed the following classified advertisement regarding one of his listings: "Gorgeous 3-bedroom, 2-and-a-half bath home with fireplace and pool. $116,900. Call Don at 555-8888." Which statement(s) is (are) TRUE of this advertisement?
    a. This is an example of a blind ad and is prohibited.
    b. Don must include the name of his real estate firm in the ad.
    c. If Don wants to include his name in the ad, he must use his last name, as registered with the DBPR, Division of Real Estate.
    d. All of the above are true.

13. Which statement(s) can be included in a classified advertisement?
    a. Close proximity to local junior college
    b. Wheelchair ramp accessible
    c. Nonsmoking female roommate wanted to share two-bedroom apartment
    d. All of the above can be included.

14. Which statement is TRUE of telephone solicitation for real estate services?
    a. Real estate licensees may not telephone potential buyers and sellers before 9:00 AM or after 8:00 PM.
    b. Brokers who use telemarketing must develop written procedures regarding their firms' telemarketing policies.
    c. Real estate licensees are exempt from the telemarketing laws.
    d. Real estate licensees may transmit to fax machines unsolicited advertisements featuring their listings.

15. Teresa purchased a rental list from a St. Petersburg brokerage company. She was looking for a two-bedroom apartment that would allow her to have a cat. Teresa found the perfect apartment from the list. The apartment description indicated that pets were allowed; however, the landlord stated that they were not. Which statement is TRUE of this situation?
    a. Teresa may demand from the brokerage company a refund of the entire fee she paid for the rental list, provided she makes her demand within 30 days of the contract date.
    b. Teresa must file a small claims case to be reimbursed the cost of the rental list.
    c. Teresa may demand from the brokerage company a refund of up to 75 percent of the fee she paid for the rental list, provided she makes her demand within 30 days of the contract date.
    d. The broker cannot be held liable in this case because the landlord can change the policy regarding pets at any time without notifying the broker.

CHAPTER 3

OWNING, MANAGING, AND SUPERVISING A REAL ESTATE OFFICE

KEY TERMS

accrual basis accounting
business plan
buyer's market
cash basis accounting
commission override
company dollar
Employer Identification Number (EIN)
fixed expense
franchise
graduated commission
hotelling
independent contractor
institutional advertising
lockbox
noncompete clause
seller's market
specific (product) advertising
transaction coordinator
variable expense

OVERVIEW

Opening a real estate brokerage firm requires a substantial investment of time and capital. The broker should develop a realistic business plan, project start-up costs, and estimate operating costs for at least six months. The broker must decide whether to remain independent or buy a franchise. The broker will also decide whether sales associates will be employees or independent contractors. The plan also must establish the sales associates' compensation. Other issues that must be addressed include how many employees and sales associates to employ and whether to hire a sales manager. The broker should develop a policy and procedures manual.

Once you have completed this chapter, you should be able to:

- list at least six categories of costs required when establishing a brokerage office;
- list the three factors a broker must consider when estimating income for the new firm;
- list the five factors a broker must consider when estimating expenses for the new firm;
- describe four advantages in purchasing a real estate franchise;
- describe four advantages in remaining an independent broker;

- describe the differences between cash basis accounting and accrual basis accounting;
- list the three major requirements for sales associates to qualify for independent contractor status;
- describe the different compensation plans for unlicensed and licensed personal assistants;
- list six sources for recruiting new sales associates;
- list the categories of potential employees protected under the equal employment opportunity laws;
- describe the five major compensation plans for sales associates; and
- list at least six major discussion topics for weekly sales meetings.

DEVELOPING A REALISTIC BUSINESS PLAN

Some brokers fail to set specific goals before starting their own firms. This can adversely affect the firm's success. The broker who prepares a business plan has already avoided a principal cause of business failure: poor planning. Firms that have been successful usually have strong foundations in business planning. The results show, not only in market share and profitability but also in customer satisfaction and the firms' reputations for ethical behavior.

A written **business plan** provides direction for an organization, as well as the steps involved in accomplishing its goals. By reviewing the plan continually, members of the organization understand their roles in its success and are more likely to work as a team to achieve the stated goals.

This chapter provides much of the information a broker needs to prepare a firm's business plan. The plan must analyze start-up capital requirements for budgeting and controlling operating expenses. The broker must decide whether to remain independent or join a franchise. Also, the broker must recruit, train, and retain qualified sales associates and employees. These tasks all should be included in the organization's business plan. See Figure 3.1 for a general guide for preparing a business plan.

WEB LINK

Go to the Small Business Administration's business plan page at **http://www.sba.gov/category/navigation-structure/starting-managing-business.**

CAPITAL AND START-UP COSTS

The typical broker candidate takes this course to enhance education and qualifications but intends to remain a broker associate in his or her present firm. Some candidates who have the required experience from another state prefer to start in Florida as a broker rather than as a sales associate. New brokers who open their own offices usually start small, perhaps even working from their homes. This chapter is designed for the broker who intends to open a firm or to become an officer or a partner in an existing firm.

Preparation of a business plan includes budgeting for start-up costs and expense reserves in the early months of operation. This process helps the broker understand how much money will be needed to open a business. Running out of money just before a com-

FIGURE 3.1 ■ General Guide for Preparing a Business Plan

Basic Information to Include in Your Business Plan

- **Why are you in business?**
  Tell what your company is, and what it's trying to do. This is often called a mission statement.

- **To whom will you be selling?**
  Give some customer demographic information, as well as estimating the size of your market. Tell how your customers make their buying decisions.

- **What will you be selling?**
  Describe your products/services, and how you expect to be positioned in the market.

- **What are the opportunities?**
  Tell about your market, including segments that are not being served, or the need for another firm to serve unfilled customer needs.

- **What are the challenges?**
  Describe problems such as market saturation with your product, business cycle turndowns, need for funding, or heavy price competition. List the nature of the competition and your primary competitors.

- **What will help overcome the hurdles?**
  Describe special qualifications, assets, and resources. List your key competitive capabilities.

- **What do you expect to happen in financial terms?**
  Provide profit and loss and cash-flow projections for the first three years of operations. Include all assumptions used in preparing the projections. Show important ratios that will help a prospective lender or investor understand your business.

- **How will you obtain the necessary funding?**
  Provide a personal financial statement as well as financing sources.

- **Who will help you accomplish your mission?**
  Give resumes for the key personnel. Include an organization chart.

- **Where will you do business?**
  Describe your company's facilities.

- **What will you do to achieve your objectives?**
  Include specific actions you'll take, and give a time line so that you can monitor your progress.

pany becomes profitable is not uncommon and often results from a failure to plan. Even if the new firm is small, with no sales associates or employees, start-up costs and expense reserves may be substantial.

A sample business plan executive summary is shown in Figure 3.2. A discussion of the financial part of the business plan is shown on the following pages.

FIGURE 3.2 ■ Sample Executive Summary Statement

Executive Summary
Julie's Realty, Inc.

Julie's Realty, Inc., is a medium-sized firm located in Avalon Beach, Florida, on a well-traveled main street. Its offices are well-appointed and suitable for the upscale clientele. Its principal market will be homes in higher price ranges. Its principal broker and sales associates are experienced, affluent, and personable.

Mission
Julie's Realty, Inc., is in business to provide the highest level of service to our customers. We will be the brokerage firm who most effectively markets luxury homes in the city of Avalon.

Services
Julie's Realty, Inc., offers homesellers a full range of counseling services, including the preparation of comparative market analyses, professional brochures, distinctive marketing programs, and discreet, effective negotiation. Julie's Realty offers buyers the considerable market and financial knowledge gained from years of experience.

Customers
Julie's Realty, Inc., customers are in the top 20 percent of the income group in this market area. Our income is generated not from a large number of transactions but from the sales of a small number of upscale homes. Our customers are less affected by real estate cycles, and buying power remains strong through most markets.

Competition
Our principal competition is two large franchise companies. While they have good sales associates and offer strong advertising, our deep community roots have allowed our market share to increase at an increasing rate for the past five years. A discount brokerage firm opened in the area three years ago, but we have felt no pricing pressures from our clients.

Management
Julie J. Flannery is the managing broker of the firm. She has extensive experience in the South Florida real estate industry. Ms. Flannery is deeply involved with the community, having served as Chairman of the United Way, the Chamber of Commerce, and as President of the Avalon Board of REALTORS®. Before opening Julie's Realty, Inc., Ms. Flannery was managing broker of one of South Florida's largest realty firms.

Personnel
Julie's Realty, Inc., has ten professional associates, all of whom hold a broker associate license. Eight are Graduates of the REALTORS® Institute (GRI designation), and all hold the Certified Residential Specialist designation. The staff has collectively 187 years of experience in the real estate brokerage field.
The support staff consists of a receptionist, executive secretary, three transaction coordinators, and four team leaders.

Initial Start-Up Costs

Some initial start-up costs include the following:

Attorney and accountant fees. The broker should budget for the legal and accounting fees associated with the creation of the legal entity, bookkeeping system, and the tax collection/payment systems.

Office setup and occupancy. The cash needed for office setup depends primarily on whether the broker intends to purchase or lease office space. Purchasing an office building usually takes a substantial cash down payment and closing costs, as well as funds to remodel the space. Usually, the broker buys a building that is too large, in order to allow for future growth, so the broker leases space to others until needed. The broker should consider the long-term economic benefits of purchasing a building. Rent payments tend to increase steadily, but a fixed-rate mortgage may provide real cost savings in the future. The other important consideration is the building's appreciation over time, which renting does not provide.

Most brokers initially rent their office space. Landlords generally require the first month's rent and a security deposit in advance, but this is much less money than a broker needs to purchase a building. Another advantage of renting is the flexibility it provides a broker who must move to larger quarters as the company grows.

Office equipment and furniture. The business plan helps the broker decide what to buy and how to pay for it. Attractive office space and quality furnishings help attract good sales associates. The broker on a tight budget often can find good-quality used furniture at excellent prices. The broker should not overlook the need to buy file cabinets, work tables, and accessories such as pictures and lamps when setting the budget. Necessary office equipment includes the telephone system, a computer, software, a printer, a copy machine, and a fax machine.

Signs and lockboxes. The broker may pay for signs and lockboxes (key safes attached to doorknobs or other fixtures on homes for sale) for the firm's listings, although many now require sales associates to buy or lease their own. If the broker provides the boxes, the start-up budget should cover at least three months of operation, even though, because of the expense, the boxes may be purchased as needed. Signs usually are sold with quantity discounts, often in lots of 25, 50, or 100 signs. Buying fewer than 25 signs usually is not cost-effective. Often national sign companies offer lower prices, but the broker should consider shipping costs when comparing prices with local companies.

National Association of REALTORS® (NAR), Board of REALTORS®, and Multiple Listing Service® (MLS) fees. The broker should include these fees in the budget. Competing in the residential market without access to the MLS is difficult. The Code of Ethics and professional standards required of REALTORS® is an important advantage of NAR membership. Finally, the education opportunities available through the local, state, and National Associations of REALTORS® provide another strong incentive to become a member.

Office supplies. The broker must budget for pens, paper, file folders, tape, scissors, staples, and numerous other office supplies.

Promotional materials. The broker must order letterhead paper, envelopes, business cards, listing and sales forms, promotional brochures, and other materials. Many printing companies found on the Internet offer very inexpensive print products.

Advertising, direct mail, and a grand opening. Although these are effective ways to announce a firm's opening, initial promotions can be very expensive, and the broker must choose them carefully.

ESTIMATING INCOME AND EXPENSES—FACTORS TO CONSIDER

When projecting income and expenses for a new firm, the broker should consider the scope of the firm's operations, office size, market conditions, the number and productivity of sales associates, income sources, and compensation plans.

Scope of company operations. The business plan should describe what types of services the firm will offer. Brokers who sell many categories of property understand that commission percentages differ for each service, so the mix of revenue sources may affect income projections.

The broker will have higher operating costs if the broker intends to operate in a wide geographic area. Expenses will be higher if branch offices are needed. Brokers who specialize in acreage or commercial properties may need to advertise in out-of-town newspapers. And if the firm offers property management with investment and residential sales, the broker must budget for more staff and equipment.

Market conditions. The business plan should describe the firm's market area. In larger cities, a new firm typically serves a smaller geographic area with many residents. In rural areas, small brokerage firms often market in adjacent counties. If the firm needs branch offices, that will increase its costs.

The broker also must evaluate the general market conditions in the area. If the market is strong, the broker may consider a more aggressive growth strategy. Sales associates should be trained to price listings competitively so that the broker does not pay to advertise listings that have little chance of selling.

Institutional advertising describes the firm, its personnel, and its services. Some brokers believe that this type of advertising is the most effective way to get listings. Others find that they get the most business from advertising specific properties for sale in newspapers or homes magazines.

The broker must consider economic conditions in the market area before making projections. A **buyer's market** generates more listings than can be expected to sell in a reasonable time, a feature of today's markets in Florida. Because brokers need more realistically priced listings to achieve the same level of sales, advertising, sign, and lockbox costs may be greater. In a **seller's market**, listings sell quickly, and many sellers market their own properties. This requires that the broker spend more on institutional advertising to attract listings.

Number and projected productivity of sales associates. Properly estimating the number of sales associates and their production level directly affects the overall financial estimate. New brokers tend to overestimate the number of sales associates who can be recruited, then underestimate the time it will take the new staff to become productive. Conservative estimates help avoid unpleasant surprises.

Income sources. When preparing the budget and financial statements, the broker should list income from commissions, property management fees, and referral fees separately. Residential property management fees can stabilize a firm's revenues because they continue in good times and bad.

Licensee/employee compensation. To recruit more sales associates, a broker might offer higher commission rates or provide extra services, such as personal assistants for a few hours per week. The broker must consider these factors when estimating expenses.

Fixed Expenses

Fixed expenses don't change proportionately with increases or decreases in income. These expenses include occupancy costs, salaries and other payroll costs, equipment rental and maintenance, furniture rental, business liability insurance, and property insurance.

Occupancy costs. Occupancy costs consist of rent or mortgage payments, utilities, janitorial service, building maintenance, and trash removal. While a mortgage payment is not strictly an operating expense, it must be shown in cash-flow projections. Occupancy expenses may vary somewhat depending on the number of persons in the firm, but they are considered fixed because most are based on contracts.

Many office buildings include utilities in the rent. More often, the broker pays for utilities separately. Air-conditioning consumes the most energy. The cost varies depending on power company rates, the building's insulation, and how the office is situated. If it is on the top floor or faces the west, it may cost more to cool. An interior office normally is insulated by other heated and cooled space and may experience lower rates.

Brokers must decide whether to have a bull pen design or have private offices. For comfort and efficiency, each sales associate should have a minimum of 100 square feet of space.

Sales associates can work in a "virtual" office, which is wherever they have access to a computer and telephone. Some brokers offer a higher commission split to associates who work from home because the broker isn't expected to provide office space. The sales associates share desks, known as **hotelling**, and the broker provides conference rooms for meeting customers. To comply with FREC requirements, the broker must be able to "adequately direct, control, and manage" the sales associates.

Payroll costs. Brokers estimate their own salary, as well as salaries for sales managers, secretaries, and clerical personnel. The broker should include employer's contributions for payroll taxes, medical insurance, and any other benefit plans.

Equipment costs and maintenance. The broker should include in the estimates the rental costs of any equipment, such as computers, copiers, telephones, fax machines, and postage meters.

Furniture rental. Some offices rent furniture instead of buying to conserve cash flow in the early years. The broker must weigh the short-term cash savings against the higher long-term costs.

Liability insurance. Several types of insurance protect the broker against claims, including coverage for accidents to the public, workers' compensation for employees, and errors and omissions insurance. Every broker should carry liability insurance.

Property insurance. The broker must buy insurance to protect against loss from fire, a windstorm, or another disaster that could destroy the company's furniture, equipment, and office improvements. The company would suffer further losses from business interruption.

Variable Expenses

Expenses that increase or decrease proportionate to income are called **variable expenses**. They include commissions, advertising, MLS® listing fees, telephone services, office supplies, and printing.

Commissions. Many brokers subtract their commissions expense directly from gross commissions income to get the **company dollar**—that is, the amount remaining for the company to pay other expenses and for the broker to make a profit. Commissions expense is tied directly to income because sales associates normally are compensated only when they generate income.

The percentage of the gross commission paid to sales associates may increase as an agent's production increases. When projecting this expense, the broker should base the estimate on the expected mix of sales associate commission rates.

Advertising. The primary types of brokerage advertising are specific and institutional. Traditionally, brokerage firms have spent most of their promotional dollars on advertising listings. An ad for a house is **specific (product) advertising. Institutional advertising** is designed to showcase the firm, and its services, management, and staff ("Jones Realty—22 years of service to the Miami area," for example). Because advertising represents a substantial percentage of a firm's expenses, the business plan should be quite detailed on how the funds are allocated. A strong marketing plan is well coordinated and consistent. The public should see the same image whether it is on TV, in the newspaper, or in a homes magazine.

MLS listing fees. Ordinarily, a firm pays listing fees to the Board of REALTORS® or to the company that operates the firm's computer service. The fees could be charged one time only, monthly, or quarterly. A fee commonly is charged for participation, access to the service, and each listing placed in the service.

Telephone. Telephone service can be a significant part of the firm's total expenses. The broker pays for each phone line into the office, for the switching equipment, and for the phones themselves.

Office supplies. The broker must buy the initial inventory of supplies to be used in the everyday operation of the company. Necessary items include staples, paper clips, file folders, paper, pens, markers, coffee, and light bulbs. While each item is inexpensive, the cumulative cost of office supplies can be very substantial over time.

Printing. Letterhead, envelopes, brochures, and forms are expensive. The company's business plan dictates whether the broker orders from a commercial printer or buys blank stock and prints the necessary stationery and brochures in-house. The broker also might include the design of the company's logo and advertising theme in this expense category (or it can be included in the advertising category).

FRANCHISE VS. INDEPENDENT FIRM

The new broker must decide whether to join a franchise or to remain independent.

Advantages of Purchasing a Franchise

Franchising has been a very successful part of American business. Real estate franchises offer brokers many advantages, such as:

- built-in referral networks, providing the names of new prospects moving into an area and offering income from other brokers for referrals they receive;
- formal training programs for sales associates with tested curriculums and trained instructors;
- national advertising, providing immediate name recognition and giving brokers market impact the moment they open their doors;
- advertising assistance that includes professionally designed logos, signs, and brochures (also, many franchises participate in regional cooperative advertising,

so many brokers can advertise their listings together to show a strong market presence); and

- management training programs that help brokers become more effective in planning and operating their firms.

Advantages of Remaining an Independent Broker

While recognizing the benefits in buying a franchise, many brokers remain independent because of lower start-up and monthly fees, more operating independence, and the ability to establish a local personality. Other advantages of remaining independent include:

- Franchises are expensive to buy. Many franchise companies require brokers to have substantial liquid assets and net worth, which may make the purchase more difficult for a new company.
- Independence means lower overhead. Most franchise companies charge a fee that ranges from four percent to eight percent or more of a firm's gross commissions income. Usually, the franchise company takes this fee off the top, before sales associates receive commissions, so sales associates often make less on each transaction.
- Increased operational freedom is a benefit of remaining independent. When a broker buys a franchise, the company places many restrictions on the broker's operations. Some brokers want to use their own creativity and advertising ideas and do not want to be tied to a regional advertising program.
- Local personality is easier to achieve as an independent than as a franchise. While it is true that the franchised real estate office is locally owned, the appearance is that it is part of a national firm. Some brokers believe that customers want to do business with a local company.

Whether the broker chooses to affiliate with a franchise or remain independent, the firm that is most likely to prosper is the one that gives the most ethical and effective service to its customers that prospers.

FINANCIAL MANAGEMENT AND TAX CONSIDERATIONS

Bookkeeping System (Cash vs. Accrual method)

Whether the broker uses the cash or accrual method of accounting depends on the firm's size, its structure, and how it uses its financial statements. (See Figure 3.6.)

Most small-business taxpayers use **cash basis accounting** primarily because it is simple. Income is taxable in the year received; expenses are deducted in the year paid. Usually, a firm's balance sheet shows no accounts receivable or accounts payable.

Accrual basis accounting attempts to match a firm's revenues and expenses. Income is recognized when all parties have accepted a contract. Expenses are booked for the period they benefited. Income is reduced for the period in which the contract falls through, if that happens.

FIGURE 3.3 ■ Budget for a New Brokerage Firm

Case Study—Julie's Realty, Inc.

When Julie Adams first opened her office, Julie's Realty, Inc., she prepared a startup budget. Her assumptions were as follows:

Number of sales associates to be recruited:	10
Office rent	$2,500 per month
Security deposit	One month's rent
Utility deposit	$500
Telephone installation	$400
Attorney and accountant fees	$1,000
Furniture and equipment:	
Desks	$3,000
Chairs	$1,500
Copy machine	$800
Computers	$2,500
Other	$1,500
License and Board of REALTOR® fees	$900
Supplies	$500
Printing	$1,000
Yard signs	$1,500
Insurance	$700
Exterior sign	$500

Other operating expenses (monthly)

Utilities	$500
Janitorial service (provided by landlord)	
Advertising	$1,200
Secretary wages (part-time)	$1,000
Payroll taxes	$100
Conventions and training seminars	$1,000
Telephone	$400
Printing	$100
Maintenance	$50
Licenses and dues	$100
Insurance	$60
Legal and accounting	$100

Using this information, prepare a start-up budget on Figure 3.4 and a monthly expenses worksheet on Figure 3.5.

FIGURE 3.4 ■ Budget for a New Brokerage Firm—Your Real Estate Office, Inc.

Sample Start-Up Cost Estimate

Number of sales associates: ________

Item	Amount
Attorney and accountant fees	$____________
Security deposit (lease) or down payment (bldg.)	____________
Rent for first month	____________
Decorating and renovation	____________
Utility deposit	____________
Telephone deposit and installation	____________
Furniture and equipment:	____________
Desks	____________
Chairs	____________
Copy machine	____________
Typewriters	____________
Computers	____________
Other	____________
License fees	____________
Board application, dues, and MLS® fees	____________
Supplies	____________
Postage	____________
Printing stationery, brochures	____________
Signs	____________
Insurance	____________
Exterior signs	____________
Franchise purchase	____________
New agent training	____________
Other: ______________________	____________
Contingency (10%)	____________
Total start-up costs	____________
Add six months operating expenses (from Figure 3.5)	____________
Minimum capital to open real estate office	$____________

FIGURE 3.5 ■ Estimated Monthly Expenses Worksheet

Your Real Estate Office, Inc.
Estimated Monthly Expenses

Occupancy	
• Rent	$__________
• Utilities	__________
• Janitorial	__________
Marketing	
• Advertising	$__________
• Signs	__________
• Brochures	__________
Human resources	
• Manager salary and benefits	$__________
• Secretary salary and benefits	__________
• Payroll taxes	__________
• Manager's expense	__________
• Conventions, seminars	__________
• Agent training and education	__________
Communications	
• Telephone	$__________
• Postage	__________
• Computer software	__________
Equipment and supplies	
• Office supplies	$__________
• Printing	__________
• Maintenance	__________
Other	
• Licenses and dues	$__________
• Insurance	__________
• Legal and accounting	__________
• Other __________	
• Contingencies (10%)	__________
Total Expense	$__________

FIGURE 3.6 ■ Cash Basis Versus Accrual Basis Accounting

Jane opened her real estate firm at the same time John opened his. Each firm had contracts with total commissions due in the amount of $100,000, of which $80,000 actually was closed at year end. Expenses totaled $70,000, although only $65,000 actually was paid at year end. Jane is on the cash basis system, and John uses accrual basis accounting. Their net incomes in the financial reports are as follows:

	Jane (cash basis)	John (accrual basis)
Gross income	$80,000	$100,000
Expenses	65,000	70,000
Net income	$15,000	$30,000

If John likes the accrual basis, he could use it for management reports during the year, then adjust those items at year end to get the benefits of both systems.

Financial Management

The broker should carefully review monthly, quarterly, and annual financial statements. A statement is usually more meaningful if compared to either the previous year's results or to this year's budget. When comparing the results to the budget, the broker should review the variance column and take corrective action if needed. This is called "management by exception."

Figure 3.7 shows the Profit and Loss for Julie's Realty, Inc., compared to the budget. As you can see, the gross income is lower than projected by $56,996, and net income is nearly $30,000 under what she had planned. Julie will have to see if there are any places to cut expenses.

- In reviewing the advertising, she sees that the secretary has allowed the sales associates to put in extra ads in the Sunday papers. That will have to be curtailed.
- Insurance premiums seem out of control, but there's not much to be done here except for making a note to adjust the budget.
- Utilities are high. Perhaps adding a programmable thermostat will provide cooling and heat when associates are in the office, then shut off in the evening.
- Telephone is higher than budgeted. Perhaps there are long distance calls being made that should be properly billed to the associates.

IRS Treatment Concerning Employees vs. Independent Contractors

The broker who opens a new real estate office should file Form SS-4 with the IRS to request an **Employer Identification Number (EIN)** that will be used on all tax returns and reports filed with the IRS. The broker also must apply for an account number with the Florida Department of Labor and Employment Security.

The nature of the independent contractor relationship. Most real estate brokerage firms treat their sales associates as **independent contractors.** If a broker meets all requirements, this results in substantial savings, primarily from the employer's share of Social Security taxes, Medicare taxes, workers' compensation insurance, unemployment taxes, and other

FIGURE 3.7 ■ Sample Profit and Loss Statement Compared to the Budget

Julie's Realty, Inc.
Profit & Loss—Budget vs. Actual
January through June, Current Year

	January–June	**Budget**	**$ Over Budget**	**% of Budget**
Income:				
Sales Commissions	$305,640	$360,000	($54,360)	84.9%
Property Management Fees	12,364	15,000	($2,636)	82.4%
TOTAL INCOME	318,004	375,000	($56,996)	84.8%
Commissions Paid to Sales Associates	174,902	206,250	$31,348	84.8%
Company Dollar	143,102	168,750	(25,648)	84.8%
Expenses:				
Advertising	7,564	6,000	($1,564)	126.1%
Insurance	820	360	($460)	227.8%
Legal and Accounting	725	600	($125)	120.8%
Licensing and Dues	610	600	($10)	101.7%
Maintenance	570	300	($270)	190.0%
Occupancy Costs:				
Rent	15,000	15,000	$0	100.0%
Utilities	4,230	3,000	($1,230)	141.0%
Personnel Costs:				
Salaries	6,900	6,000	($900)	115.0%
FICA and Unemployment Taxes	700	600	($100)	116.7%
Postage	2,000	2,000	0	100.0%
Printing	950	600	($350)	158.3%
Telephone	3,417	2,400	($1,017)	142.4%
Travel	4,000	6,000	$2,000	66.7%
TOTAL EXPENSES	$47,486	$43,460	(4,026)	109.3%
NET INCOME	$95,616	$125,290	($29,674)	76.3%

fringe benefits. The three major requirements a sales associate must meet to qualify for statutory independent contractor status follow:

1. The sales associate must hold a real estate license.
2. The sales associate's gross income must be based on production rather than on the number of hours worked.
3. The sales associate must work based on a written contract that states, among other things, that the sales associate is not considered an employee for federal tax purposes.

Factors that describe an employee relationship. In general, except for real estate licensees who meet the requirements, a worker who provides services for a broker is an employee if the broker can control what will be done and how it will be done in the following three areas:

1. **Behavioral control.** If a worker is told when, where, and how to work, what tools to use, and what sequence to follow, the worker is an employee. For example, if a broker requires a sales associate to take floor duty time or hold open houses, the sales associate is an employee.
2. **Financial Control.** If a broker reimburses a worker for expenses, pays the worker a salary or hourly rate, provides insurance or pensions, the worker is an employee.
3. **Type of Relationship.** If the worker is given benefits, or if the worker provides services that are a key aspect of the company's regular business activity, the worker is an employee.

These rules also apply to sales associates who employ personal assistants.

Reporting requirements for employees and independent contractors. A broker's basic responsibilities regarding taxes and reporting for employees and independent contractors include:

- recording the employees' names and Social Security numbers exactly as shown on their Social Security cards (or a penalty may be assessed);
- asking the employees to complete Form W-4, "Employee's Withholding Allowance Certificate" (If an employee does not do so, the broker may withhold tax as if the employee is single, with no withholding allowances. This form remains in effect until the employee submits a new one. An employee may claim fewer withholding allowances than entitled to claim.);
- withholding federal income tax based on Form W-4;
- withholding the employees' shares of Social Security and Medicare taxes;
- depositing the taxes withheld along with the employer's share of Social Security and Medicare taxes (The deposit due date depends on the amount withheld, and penalties can be substantial for late deposits.);
- depositing federal unemployment taxes each quarter if the undeposited amount exceeds $100;
- filing Form 941 within 30 days after the end of each calendar quarter showing the compensation paid and taxes due;
- filing the Unemployment Compensation Employer's Quarterly Report within 30 days after the end of each calendar quarter;
- by January 31, giving each employee Form W-2 and each independent contractor Form 1099-Misc, and filing with the IRS the annual federal unemployment tax return. 1099s must be sent to independent contractors (think: sales associates), landlords, persons who provide services, such as attorneys, CPAs, janitors, and so on. The earnings threshold is $600. Failure to report the 1099s carry heavy penalties; and
- by February 28, filing Forms W-2 and W-3 with the Social Security Administration and filing Form 1096 with the IRS.

STAFF AND SALES PERSONNEL

Great organizations have a common denominator: well-qualified, enthusiastic people who are motivated to work as a team. Putting the right people in the right positions is one of the most important broker functions. The positions the broker must fill include support staff and sales personnel.

Support Staff

The broker must select the necessary staff to support the sales personnel, including the following:

Receptionist/secretary. Customers and prospective sales associates form their first impressions of the company from the receptionist's greeting. The receptionist should be neat, personable, articulate, and helpful. A small firm may combine this position with that of secretary, bookkeeper, and personal assistant. The secretary's duties should be well defined regarding how much assistance to give the sales staff for typing, general mailings, preparation of brochures, and so on.

Bookkeeper. In a larger firm, or in an office with many property management units, the broker may need a bookkeeper to keep company records up to date. The broker is responsible for escrow and property management accounts, whether the broker or the bookkeeper does the daily posting. Blaming the bookkeeper for an error does not excuse the broker from disciplinary action from the FREC in case of an escrow shortage.

Support staff. Other employees of the firm include sales managers, personal assistants, and transaction coordinators. Sales managers usually are employed when a firm has ten or more sales associates. The sales manager may be compensated by salary, commission override, or some combination of the two.

Some brokers hire personal assistants to help sales associates measure homes, put up signs, complete market reports, and prepare brochures. Assistance might be offered on a rotating basis, with a sales associate paying an hourly fee for the help.

Transaction coordinators handle the administrative tasks involved with closings, including ordering title insurance, surveys, pest inspections, and so on. Many firms charge the buyer or seller a fee for this service in addition to the brokerage commission. The FREC requires that brokers inform the buyer or seller about any such fees at the beginning of the relationship.

Real Estate Sales Personnel

One of the broker's most challenging tasks is recruiting sales associates. Characteristics of good sales associates include honesty, empathy, self-esteem, motivation to succeed, and desire to provide good service. The good sales associate continues to seek professional knowledge in marketing, financing, construction, the economy, and the law. Brokers face tough competition to get the best sales associates. Sales associates usually join brokerage firms whose sales associates exhibit the same quality standards.

The business plan should set a goal for the number of associates to recruit. This number relates to budget requirements and the average company dollar each sales associate generates. For example, assuming a brokerage firm has projected total expenses of $100,000 annually (including the broker's salary and a fair profit) and the average sales associate is likely to generate $20,000 in company dollars, the broker must recruit five sales associates to achieve the goal.

If a broker has only enough office space for five sales associates, it is important that each sales associate produce at least the minimum $20,000 annually. When a sales associate does not produce at least the desk costs (total expenses divided by number of sales associates), the sales associate should be counseled. The broker may have to search for a replacement if the sales associate does not become more productive.

New licensees often attempt to work part time in real estate, at least until the income justifies working full time. Brokers who employ part-time sales associates usually experience problems because of the following:

- Part-time sales associates often are not available for sales meetings or training sessions; they usually work after office hours. This leads to sales associates who are not familiar with the office listings, new financing terms, or license law changes.
- Part-time sales associates rarely make enough in commissions to ever justify becoming full-time sales associates.
- Buyers and sellers who place their confidence in sales associates often are dissatisfied if the sales associate does not disclose that he or she works only part time.

Of course, in special situations part-time sales associates can be very productive. Therefore, the broker should consider what skills and contacts a person brings to the position.

Hiring a sales manager. When the office sales staff grows to more than ten associates, it may be time for the broker to consider hiring a sales manager. The manager's job is to recruit, train, and help the sales force. Many managers also are expected to be the office administrators. Managers sometimes are compensated with straight salaries, salaries plus bonuses, or salaries plus **commission overrides** (part of the commissions the company collects), depending on the gross commission income. Some are paid by commission override only.

FIGURE 3.8 ■ Minimum Monthly Transaction Formula

Calculation of Number of Monthly Transactions Required

Last year, Howard's brokerage office had 50 sales. The amount remaining after he paid commissions to sales associates was $67,500. Howard's current monthly expenses (including his salary) are $6,000, and he wants to make a minimum of $1,000 profit in addition to that. Assuming no change in the company dollar percentage, how many transactions must Howard have per month to pay all expenses, including his salary, and also give him a $1,000 per month profit on his investment?

Solution:

$$\frac{\text{Company dollar}}{\text{Number of transactions}} = \text{Average company dollar per transaction}$$

$$\frac{\$67{,}500}{50} = \$1{,}350 \text{ average company dollar per transaction}$$

$$\frac{\text{Amount needed for expenses + Profit}}{\text{Average company dollar}} = \text{Number of transactions required per month}$$

$$\frac{\$6{,}000 + \$1{,}000}{\$1{,}350} = 5.19 \text{ transactions required per month}$$

New sales associates often are paid lower commission splits until their production increases. This helps compensate the company for the additional training and assistance it provides. The broker might structure an override as a percentage of the company dollar on each transaction. An additional override/bonus may be available to the sales manager for each sales associate recruited.

For example, assume that owner Bob pays manager Fred a 7 percent override on the company dollar. New sales associate Sally, who gets a 50 percent split, makes gross commissions of $5,000. The company dollar is $2,500, so Fred makes $175 ($2,500 × .07). Experienced sales associate Judy, who gets a 70 percent split, makes gross commissions of $5,000. The company dollar is $1,500, so Fred makes $105. That works for Fred because Judy takes very little of his time, while he spends much more time with Sally.

Unlicensed personal assistants and clerical assistants. An important trend in Florida real estate practice has been the increased use of personal assistants. The real estate licensee who plans and delegates effectively can multiply efforts many times over by employing persons to do many of the day-to-day tasks that do not require a real estate license. Using a personal assistant allows the licensee to provide better service and expand customer base.

A licensee who employs an unlicensed personal assistant must be certain that the assistant does not go beyond what is allowed by law (see Figure 3.9). The broker is legally and financially responsible for the actions of personal assistants and should establish policies to ensure that the assistant does not violate the law.

Unlicensed personal assistants, because they receive salaries and may not be paid commissions, are under the licensee's or employer's control. They may not be classified as independent contractors.

Many sales associates prefer to use licensed personal assistants because they can do much more with respect to listings, sales, and personal contacts. Although sales associates may use licensed personal assistants, only brokers can pay them commissions. The brokers hold their licenses, and the FREC holds the brokers responsible for their actions. A broker must make clear to sales associates that licensed personal assistants are under the broker's legal control. The broker also may be legally and financially responsible for the actions of sales associates' employees.

The sales associates may be financially liable for the actions of their assistants. An accident on the job may make a licensee or employer liable to an assistant. And if the employee injures another person while running errands for the licensee, the licensee may be held liable to the injured party.

Occupational licenses. Most municipalities in Florida require that brokers maintain occupational licenses. Failure to register and pay for the license may result in substantial penalties. A recent change to the law exempts sales associates who work for the broker.

Recruitment and Selection

The broker must determine how many sales associates are needed to meet company goals and must calculate the most efficient and economic methods to recruit them.

Set recruiting goals. One of the most basic questions a broker must ask and answer is, "How many sales associates do I want on my staff?" Some brokers want as many as possible and will sacrifice quality standards in favor of numbers. Other brokers are satisfied to have smaller sales

FIGURE 3.9 ■ Legal Activities of an Unlicensed Personal Assistant

- Answer the phone and forward calls.
- Fill out and submit listings and changes to any multiple-listing service.
- Follow up on loan commitments after a contract has been negotiated and generally secure status reports on the loan progress.
- Assemble documents for closing.
- Secure documents (public information) from courthouse, utility district, and so on.
- Have keys made for company listings, order surveys, termite inspections, home inspections, and home warranties with the licensed employer's approval.
- Write ads for approval of licensee and supervising broker and place advertising (newspaper ads, update Web sites, etc.); prepare flyers and promotional information for approval by licensee and the supervising broker.
- Receive, record, and deposit earnest money, security deposits, and advance rents.
- Type contract forms for approval by licensee and supervising broker.
- Monitor licenses and personnel files.
- Compute commission checks.
- Place signs on property.
- Order items of repair as directed by the licensee.
- Prepare flyers and promotional information for approval by licensee and supervising broker.
- Act as a courier service to deliver documents and pick up keys.
- Place routine telephone calls on late rent payments.
- Schedule appointments for licensees to show *listed* property.
- Be at an open house:
  1. for security purposes, and/or
  2. to hand out materials (brochures).
- Answer questions concerning a listing from which the answer must be obtained from the licensed employer-approved printed information and is objective in nature (not subjective comments).
- Gather information for a comparative market analysis (CMA).
- Gather information for an appraisal.
- Hand out objective, written information on a listing or rental.

Legal Activities list was approved by the Florida Real Estate Commission on January 22, 1992, and was later updated.

staffs made up of highly trained, specially selected professionals. Whichever approach brokers take, they must be certain that the number of sales associates is manageable.

Sources for new sales associates. Because the transition from new licensee to seasoned professional takes a while, and a natural attrition of experienced sales associates occurs over time, brokers must prospect for good sales associates continually. They can use many sources to find the right personnel to staff their offices.

Advertising for new sales associates. Advertising can be very effective if the ad is designed and worded properly. A broker should target the ad to the widest possible group, and the advertising must not discriminate. An ad with wording similar to, "We have an opening on our professional staff for a sales associate" probably is more effective than "We need lots of sales associates." Brokers should consider running advertising in different sections of the newspaper to reach different interest groups. The business section, sports pages, comics, or TV pages often are more effective than classified advertising.

Career nights. Well-organized and well-presented career nights can be effective recruiting tools. Advertising and direct mail usually are the best ways to communicate a program to the public. The broker should select a central location, require reservations, plan refreshments, and compile handout literature. The broker should encourage attendees to arrange appointments for one-on-one career counseling sessions and should send all attendees a letter of thanks.

Prelicensing schools. Another source of new sales associates, sometimes operated by real estate companies specifically for this reason, is prelicensing schools. A school permit holder must carefully observe FREC Rule 61J2-17.015, which prohibits recruiting during classroom hours. Prelicensing schools often offer discounted tuition to attract larger numbers of prospects. If a school is operated professionally, students who pass the state exam may contact the real estate company about employment.

Other real estate firms. Recruiting experienced producers from other firms reduces the lengthy period required to bring new sales agents into production. Brokers find it easier if a prospective sales associate makes the first contact. This is more likely to happen if a broker operates a successful, respected firm that is home to other top producers. Many brokers refrain from making the first contact because of the ill will it breeds with brokers who lose their top producers.

Personal contacts. Sometimes the broker's own contacts are the best sources of sales associates. A pleasant waitress, an office supply sales associate, and acquaintances from a parents' meeting at school are all candidates. Even if a person decides not to follow up on the broker's invitation to join the firm, the contact may generate years of good will and additional real estate business.

Personal referrals from sales associates. Referrals from sales associates in the firm often are more effective than broker contacts. Many brokers offer a bonus or a commission override to sales associates to keep them focused on the need to staff the office with the best people.

Application Process

The broker must evaluate prospective employees and independent contractors with respect to their ability to do their jobs. The evaluation process includes completing an application form, verifying license status, checking references, and interviewing the applicant. Brokers must follow the requirements of the equal employment opportunity laws and the Americans with Disabilities Act (ADA).

Equal employment opportunity laws. Discriminating in employment is illegal if based on race, color, religion, sex, age, national origin, marital and family status, or disability. The broker must be certain that application forms do not contain questions that violate the law, and the broker must avoid asking such questions when conducting interviews. Examples of violations are questions about marriage plans, plans for having children, origin of a name, date of birth, feelings about working for someone younger or older, and availability to work Sundays.

ADA requirements regarding hiring personnel. Millions of Americans have disabilities of some type, and many have experienced discrimination in access to housing, commerce, and employment. The ADA legislation adopted in 1990 allows those citizens to participate in activities most people take for granted. While the law does not require preferential treatment for people with disabilities, it does prohibit discrimination in all employment practices such as hiring, firing, compensation, and training.

Under the law, an employer must make accommodations to allow disabled persons to do their jobs, provided the accommodations do not impose an undue hardship on the business. Such accommodations include providing large-print materials, arranging furniture to widen aisles, and raising desks to provide clearance for employees in wheelchairs. The employer also must establish application procedures related only to a person's ability to perform according to the job description.

Under the ADA, an employer may *not*:

- fire, or refuse to hire, persons associated with people with disabilities, or a person who works as a volunteer in community service activities for persons with disabilities;
- ask in person or on the application whether an applicant has a disability; however, employers may ask whether the applicant can do the job as described; or
- require a medical exam before extending an offer of employment, and then only if it is customary for all new employees to take medical exams. Drug testing is not considered a medical examination, and is permitted.

Application forms. The application is part of the employee's or sales associate's permanent records. The application may not contain questions that violate the equal opportunity employment laws. It may request only basic personal information, such as full name, address, telephone number, former employers, education, real estate license number, license status, and work experience related to the position. If the broker uses an application form for one applicant, it must be used for every applicant. Using the form selectively as a screening mechanism may lead to charges of discrimination.

Interview procedures. Many brokers prefer a two-interview process. The preliminary interview, usually brief, allows both the broker and the applicant to decide whether they want to continue the process. The broker may ask several open-ended questions to get the prospective sales associates talking about themselves, their likes and dislikes, and why they feel they would be good in the position.

When the broker believes that a person has the qualifications to be a good employee or sales associate, a second, more thorough, interview is scheduled. This gives the broker time to verify the applicant's license status and check the references.

Verifying license status. The broker should verify the applicant's license status and any prior disciplinary actions against the licensee by checking the DBPR database at *myfloridalicense.com*. The Division does not disclose pending investigations.

Checking references. As part of the application process, the broker should request references from the applicant from persons who know the applicant well and can testify as to personal character. The broker then should check with those persons and former employers. If the applicant currently works for another firm, the broker must be careful not to violate confidentiality by calling the other broker.

Every person applying for a job takes a very personal risk. The broker must be sensitive to this vulnerability. A thank-you letter and phone call to each unsuccessful applicant, while they may not carry the news the applicant wanted, are common courtesy. Failing to do so may leave the applicant with feelings of ill will toward the broker and the firm.

Employment Agreements

Tax considerations. The independent contractor agreement must specify that the sales associate will be treated as an independent contractor for federal income tax purposes and that the sales associate will be responsible for paying all taxes.

Noncompete clauses. Some employment and independent contractor agreements contain clauses that prohibit employees or sales associates from competing with the broker or working for any firm that competes with the broker after leaving the firm. The broker may believe that an employee or a sales associate will use or reveal to the competition certain trade secrets learned while working for the broker.

The broker should consider the difficulty in recruiting sales associates when they must agree to a **noncompete clause**. The inclusion of such a clause in a contract also may endanger the contract's independent contractor provisions.

Usually, the courts will not enforce broadly drawn noncompete covenants. A broker would have to show that a covenant is necessary to protect the business and the employer's good will and that the covenant does not impose an undue hardship on an employee. The broker should consult with an attorney about suggested wording of such covenants and their enforceability.

Hours and working conditions. The independent contractor agreement must not prescribe required working hours or establish vacation schedules. Independent contractors are accountable to the broker for the results of their work, not the hours or methods they use to achieve the results. The broker should include in the agreement a provision that sales associates will abide by the law and established codes of ethics.

Written acceptance of company policies. The employment agreement should include a statement that the independent contractor has read the firm's policies and procedures manual and agrees to abide by those provisions.

Compensation of Licensees

A wide range of compensation plans is available to sales associates. The broker must establish a plan that not only makes economic sense to the firm, but appears fair to sales associates. The competition for top producers has resulted in higher compensation programs for sales associates and lower profit margins for brokers. Plans include straight salary, fixed percentage commission split, commission split plus bonus, graduated commission based on production, and 100 percent commission with a management fee.

Straight salary. Some large commercial firms offer their producers straight salaries (plus bonuses, in many cases) to even out the peaks and valleys of having just a few large sales per year. Because the expense is fixed, the company may lose money in case of a market slowdown or a nonproductive sales associate. It also takes away the benefits of independent contractor status to the broker. Very few general real estate brokerage firms compensate by salary.

Fixed percentage commission split. The fixed commission plan stays at the same level throughout the year, regardless of the sales associate's production. Obviously, the plan's weakness is that it overcompensates the poor producers and undercompensates the superstars. The result of this plan is the loss of good producers, and few firms use it today.

Commission with bonus. This compensation plan is midway between a fixed commission plan and a graduated commission plan. The bonus often is paid at year end or even in successive quarters after year end. When compared with a graduated commission plan, this program has advantages for both the broker and the sales associate. The broker receives higher cash flows up front because part of the commission is paid later as a bonus. The sales associate gets lower commissions to start, but receives bonuses later, which may help smooth the income flows. The broker should consult with an attorney to ensure that the bonus does not invalidate independent contractor status.

Graduated commission. In a **graduated commission** program, the sales associate is compensated at a low rate until a certain level of production has been achieved. Subsequent commissions occur at higher rates that continue to rise as production increases to preset limits. This plan provides strong incentives to top producers and reduces the need for brokers to negotiate a different commission rate with each sales associate.

Obviously, this type of sliding scale offers many ways to compensate sales associates. Many firms pay sales associates based on gross commissions or on an office's share of the gross commissions.

One point of dissatisfaction exists among top producers. It is the policy of many brokers to reset the commission rate to its lowest level at the beginning of each year. If a sales associate worked up to a 70 percent rate last year and must start again at 50 percent this year, it may be perceived as the opportune time to leave the firm. Some offices use moving averages of production so that sales associates do not drop back to the lowest rate at the beginning of each year.

100 percent commission. Many independent brokers and several national franchise companies offer to pay from 95 percent to 100 percent of the gross commissions a company collects if the sales associates pay management or rental fees. A typical plan takes the desk costs plus the broker's profit and divides by the number of sales associates in the firm. The result is the management fee, which sales associates must pay at the beginning of the period regardless of whether they have produced a sale. Sales associates are expected to pay all expenses, including those often paid by the brokers in split commission firms (signs, lockboxes, advertising, postage, etc.).

Commission Reductions

Items like required fees and payments, franchise fees, signage fees, and other costs reduce the commission a sales associate receives. (See Figure 3.10 for an example.)

Required fees and payments. Required fees and payments include the following:

- management or rental payments in 100 percent plan offices; and
- errors and omissions insurance fees. An insurance company often charges this fee for each transaction. Normally, the broker splits the fee with the sales associate.

Franchise fees. Most franchise companies charge a percentage of the gross commission for each closing, which is taken off the top before the sales associate's split is calculated.

Sign fees. Many offices contract with sign companies to place real estate signs on and remove them from listed property.

The service is charged to each sales associate, either when the property is listed or when it is sold. Many sales associates must buy their own signs.

Other fees. Many brokers charge sales associates a percentage of the advertising costs of their listings. Sales associates usually pay listing charges, MLS listing fees, and other similar expenses.

FIGURE 3.10 ■ Sample of Office Charges to a Sales Associate

Your Real Estate Office, Inc.
1764 W. Orange Street
Sunnydale, FL 33473

INVOICE

To:
John Smith, GRI, CRS

500 N. Appleyard Drive

Sunnydale, FL 33475

INVOICE NO: 0451

DATE: April 3, 2013

	Description	Unit Price	Amount
12	24 x 30 yard signs (including shipping)	$32.94	$395.28
7	MLS listings added to system	17.49	122.43
1	Monthly MLS computer access fee	22.84	22.84
	Advertising—Sunnydale (see attached bill)	268.40	268.40
		TOTAL	$808.95

Please make certain your check is received in the office by April 10, 2013.
If you have any questions concerning this invoice, check with Mary Jones.

We appreciate the way you make Your Real Estate Office even better!

Training Sales Associates

Brokers are required by statute to adequately direct, control, and manage sales associates and broker associates in the firm. The first step for the broker is to develop a training program. A robust training program attracts good sales associates, increases production, builds loyalty to the company, and reduces turnover. The broker's training program may be structured to cover four major areas as follows:

1. **Company policies and procedures.** The policy manual is the best orientation course for new sales associates.
2. **Technical skills.** The training program should teach sales associates how to do their jobs. This means covering time management, goal setting, completing forms for listings and contracts, comparative market analysis, financing techniques, and closing costs. Until a sales associate can fill in forms and discuss costs, it is unlikely that he or she will risk talking to buyers or sellers!
3. **Listing skills.** The training program should help sales associates understand the importance of listings, how to prospect for listings, how to prepare listing presen-

tations, how to market listings, how to service listings, how to present offers to sellers, and how to get from contract to closing.

4. **Selling skills.** Finally, sales associates should be shown how to get appointments from phone calls, qualify buyers, show properties effectively, observe buying signs, and get contracts to the closing table.

Policy and Procedures Manual

Every real estate firm should develop a policy and procedures manual. The broker should recognize that people are more willing to abide by rules they help create. It follows that the broker should get the staff involved when writing the manual. Once the manual has been developed, communicated to, and understood by the staff, it will help prevent misunderstandings, promote fair play, and ensure that all members of the firm work toward common goals. Clear statements prohibiting discrimination and sexual harassment can be helpful when a broker defends against complaints of this nature. The policy manual also guides many of the broker's decisions with respect to the staff. The manual should define the company's purposes and function and should be as complete as possible. An example of suggested topics is shown in Table 3.1. All members of the firm should sign a statement saying that they understand the policy and agree to conform.

Statement of company's objectives. The manual should include a statement of the company's purpose, its business philosophy for providing professional service, and its adherence to a strong ethical code.

Define the company's function. This manual also should describe the types of properties the company lists and sells, its policy on property management, and the types of brokerage relationships it will take on.

Sales Manager Responsibilities

The sales manager is management's link to the sales staff. The manager is charged with supervising and controlling the sales staff and conducting company sales meetings.

Supervision and control of sales staff. Some of the manager's duties in this area include:

- monitoring sales activities and evaluating the performance of the company as a whole and of individual sales associates (Some sales managers give each sales associate a detailed activity report showing the performance for the month and year to date, comparing each sales associate's performance with the previous year and the sales associate's goals);
- ensuring compliance with office policy and procedures;
- helping sales associates solve problems;
- supervising advertising;
- scheduling floor duty for those sales associates requesting time;
- ensuring compliance with the law; and
- ensuring compliance with the NAR Code of Ethics if the broker is a member of a Board of REALTORS® or the National Association of REALTORS®.

TABLE 3.1 Subjects to Include in the Policy Manual

General:

- Antitrust policies
- Board of REALTORS® membership
- Brokerage relationships
- Commissions
  - Time of payment to sales associates
  - Offset for expenses
  - Schedule of rates charged
- Company history, philosophy, and goals
- Cooperation with other brokers
- Education
- Expenses
  - Paid by the company
  - Paid by the sales associate
- Office
  - Hours of operation
  - Housekeeping

Sales associates:

- Absence compensation to another sales associate
- Automobile insurance
- Business cards
- Caravan to company listings
- Confidentiality
- Dress code
- Electronic Communications
  - E-mail and the CAN-SPAM Act
  - Telephone solicitation and do-not-call laws
  - Internet advertising and the law
- Expenses
- Fair housing
- Floor time
- Independent contractor status
- Keys
- Listings
  - Files
  - Servicing suggestions
- MLS policies
- Newspaper advertising
- Personal assistants of sales associates
- Personal sales and purchases
- Referrals to out-of-town brokers
- Sales meetings
- Sexual harassment
- Signs and lockboxes
- Smoking
- Telephone
  - Answering
  - Long-distance calls
  - Personal calls

Employees:

- Contract files
- Hours
- Office appearance
- Secretary
- Supplies
- Telephone answering
- Time off

Sales meetings. All sales associates should be encouraged to attend weekly sales meetings, usually held in the company's staff meeting room. It is important that the meetings start and end on time. The program should be planned, have a definite agenda, and be presented in a way that respects the attendees' time. Some meeting topics include:

- announcements about sales and listings for the previous week;
- announcements about price changes or changes in terms;
- review of sales activity in the market;
- review of company goals for sales and productivity;
- recognition of the sales associates' accomplishments, such as course completion, designations received, community service, top producer, and top lister;
- communication between the sales team and management;

- discussion of recent law changes; and
- short training sessions on listing or sales ideas.

If a sales meeting is well presented, the sales associates will come away with a feeling of professional fulfillment and the knowledge that their time was well spent. Good meetings generate company loyalty and increased sales.

SUMMARY OF IMPORTANT POINTS

- Before opening a real estate office, a broker should prepare a business plan.
- The broker should decide whether the firm will be part of a national franchise or whether it will remain independent.
- The costs to open the company and the expenses for at least six months of operations are the minimum capital necessary to open the company's doors.
- Projecting income and expenses depends on the scope of the company's operations, its market area, economic conditions, and the number and productivity of its sales personnel.
- The broker must decide whether to pay taxes on an accrual basis or a cash basis.
- When using the accrual basis, income is recognized when earned, and expenses are booked in the period that is benefited.
- When using the cash basis, income is taxable in the year it is received, and expenses are deductible in the year they are paid.
- Most brokers treat their sales associates as independent contractors for tax purposes.
- Brokers do not pay employment taxes nor do they withhold income taxes for independent contractors.
- Brokers may not control the activities of independent contractors. The broker must understand the IRS reporting requirements to avoid penalties.
- The most important asset of the real estate office is its people.
- The broker must recruit good sales associates continually. Sources include advertising, career nights, prelicensing schools, other firms, and personal contacts.
- Whether hiring employees or independent contractors, the broker must be careful to follow all provisions of the fair employment laws and the Americans with Disabilities Act.
- A broker's desk cost is calculated by dividing the total expenses by the number of sales associates.
- The company dollar is calculated by deducting commissions paid from gross income.
- The average company dollar per transaction is calculated by dividing company dollar by the number of transactions.
- The number of transactions needed each month is calculated by dividing the monthly expenses plus profit by the average company dollar per transaction.
- Unlicensed personal assistants may not be paid commissions and must not perform selling activities.
- Licensed personal assistants may be paid for real estate selling activities only by the broker.
- The broker should develop a complete policy and procedures manual. Each sales associate should get a copy.

REVIEW QUESTIONS

1. The document that provides a company's mission statement and serves as the long-range blueprint for the company's operation is the
   a. budget.
   b. operating projections.
   c. sales manual.
   d. business plan.

2. The minimum amount of capital required to open a new brokerage firm is calculated by
   a. multiplying the company's expected market share by the projected commission rate and subtracting expenses.
   b. adding start-up costs to six months of projected operating expenses.
   c. multiplying the number of sales associates by their expected expenses and doubling it.
   d. adding start-up costs to the costs of renting or purchasing office space and multiplying by six.

3. Institutional advertising
   a. describes commercial property for sale.
   b. promotes a specific property the firm is offering for sale.
   c. tells about the firm, its personnel, and services.
   d. is normally used for to promote properties for rent.

4. The BEST example of a variable cost on a broker's income and expense statement is
   a. rent.
   b. commissions paid to sales associates.
   c. administrative salaries.
   d. utilities.

5. Startup costs for a new brokerage firm will be about $34,000. Monthly revenue for the first year is expected to be $15,000, and monthly expenses will be $12,000. What minimum amount of cash should the broker have available before starting up?
   a. $52,000
   b. $60,000
   c. $70,000
   d. $106,000

6. A broker's financial statements show $42,000 in cash and securities, $18,000 in commissions pending, $87,000 in furniture and equipment, $61,000 in accounts payable, and $86,000 in net worth. What type of accounting system does the broker use?
   a. Accrual basis
   b. Straight-line basis
   c. Cash basis
   d. Graduated commission basis

7. A broker plans to offer his sales associates a medical insurance plan for which he will contribute half the premium. Based on this information, which statement is TRUE?
   a. Florida's insurance laws prohibit such contributions.
   b. The IRS probably will classify his sales associates as employees.
   c. Insurance companies require that the employer pay the entire premium.
   d. He must include the entire premium as income on each sales associate's Form 1099-Misc.

8. Which is TRUE when a broker charges buyers and sellers transaction coordinator fees?
   a. Chapter 475 prohibits such charges.
   b. Legally, the charges may not be greater than the actual cost of providing the service.
   c. The broker must disclose the fees to the buyers and sellers before they enter into contracts.
   d. The charges violate the NAR Code of Ethics.

9. A broker projects office expenses to be $162,700 for the year. Her salary is included in the expense budget, but she wants to make at least $20,000 over and above that to compensate her for her investment. Her average sales associate produces $58,000 in gross commissions, and her sales associates average a 55 percent split. How many sales associates does the broker need to achieve her goal?
   a. Six
   b. Seven
   c. Eight
   d. Nine

10. A broker's financial statements for last year show that her office broke even. Her expenses were $120,000 for the year, and she had 94 transactions. If increased expenses will add $20,000 to last year's total, and if the average company dollar remains the same, how many transactions will the broker need to pay the expenses and make a $30,000 profit?
    a. 110
    b. 117
    c. 133
    d. 148

11. A broker has three employees and five independent contractors. What is the significance of January 31 regarding required reporting?
    a. She must send W-2 and W-3 forms to the Social Security Administration.
    b. She must send the new independent contractor agreement, signed by all sales associates, to the IRS.
    c. She must give each employee a W-2 form and each independent contractor a 1099-Misc. form, and she must file the annual federal unemployment tax return.
    d. She must have each sales associate sign a new W-4 form.

12. A sales associate employs a licensed personal assistant. He agrees to pay $6 per hour for administrative work, plus 25 percent of all commissions for work requiring a license. Based on this information, which statement is TRUE?
    a. This arrangement is legal if the sales associate withholds the required amounts for income taxes, Social Security, and Medicare.
    b. The sales associate may not pay the licensed assistant; the broker must make all payments.
    c. The sales associate may pay the hourly rate, and the broker must pay the commission split.
    d. The licensed personal assistant may not be paid any portion of the commissions the sales associate generates.

13. A brokerage firm had gross commission income of $3,000,200 on 354 sales last year. The broker pays the sales associates 55 percent. What is the broker's average company dollar per transaction?
    a. $3,189
    b. $3,235
    c. $3,397
    d. $3,814

14. A broker was interviewing a prospective employee. What question may he ask?
    a. "Are you Spanish, or is that your married name?"
    b. "Do you have a problem with working Sunday open houses?"
    c. "Are you happily married?"
    d. "Do you have an active real estate license?"

15. Which is a legal act of a private employer when in the process of interviewing a candidate for employment?
    a. Refuse to hire a person who works as a volunteer in community service activities for persons with disabilities.
    b. Require a medical exam before extending an offer of employment, regardless of whether it is customary for all new employees to take a medical exam.
    c. Provide an application for employment that includes a question about the applicant's race.
    d. Ask applicants who are disabled whether they are able to do the job as described.

CHAPTER

4

ESCROW MANAGEMENT

KEY TERMS

arbitration
commingling
commission notice
conflicting demands
conversion
declaratory judgment
deposit
escrow account
escrow disbursement order (EDO)
good faith
immediately
interpleader
lien notice
litigation
mediation
net proceeds
renewal commission
trust funds
trust liability

OVERVIEW

This chapter begins with a discussion of the requirements for establishing and maintaining an escrow (or trust) account. Rules regarding timely deposit of escrow funds and the requirements for maintaining interest-bearing escrow accounts are presented. Also, the procedure for completing the monthly reconciliation statement, including how to determine the broker's trust liability and reconciled bank balance, is detailed. The chapter concludes with a discussion of the escrow disbursement dispute process and an explanation of how to handle escrow issues involving special types of properties.

Once you have completed this chapter, you should be able to:

- define the term *escrow account;*
- define the terms *commingle* and *conversion;*
- describe the requirements for establishing an escrow account(s);
- describe the requirements for timely deposit of escrow funds;
- describe the procedure for handling postdated checks;
- describe the requirements for maintaining an interest-bearing escrow account;
- describe the procedure for disbursing funds from an interest-bearing escrow account;
- describe the requirements for maintaining escrow records;
- define the term *trust liability;*
- calculate the broker's trust liability;

- calculate the reconciled bank balance;
- prepare a monthly reconciliation statement;
- distinguish among the four settlement procedures; and
- recognize exceptions to the FREC's notification and settlement requirements.

ESTABLISHING ESCROW ACCOUNTS

In the course of business, a broker is entrusted with money, bank drafts, checks, documents, and other things of value. Florida laws and FREC rules are very explicit in requiring that all such property be accounted for. When a broker or sales associate receives any item of value from a customer or principal regarding a real estate transaction, the broker must deposit the item in an escrow account. An **escrow account** is an account for the deposit of money a disinterested third party (for example, the broker) holds in trust for others; hence the term **trust funds**. Escrow accounts hold other people's monies. Escrow accounts are also referred to as *trust accounts*. Trust funds include cash, checks, and money orders and items that can be converted into cash, such as deeds and personal property. In addition to earnest money deposits, brokers hold in trust for others money associated with leasing property such as rent deposits and security deposits. Brokers are not required to keep earnest money deposits separate from rental deposits. However, tracking trust funds is easier when separate escrow accounts are established for trust funds associated with sales and trust funds associated with rentals.

All funds entrusted to a broker on behalf of a principal or customer must be deposited in an escrow account. Florida license law defines a **deposit** as a sum of money, or its equivalent, delivered to a real estate licensee as earnest money, payment, or partial payment in connection with a real estate transaction. An earnest money deposit may be in the form of cash, currency, or any medium of exchange or securities that can be converted into money. Earnest money is also referred to as *good-faith deposits* or *binder deposits*.

Escrow funds cannot be commingled with the broker's personal funds or operating funds. **Commingling** funds is the illegal practice of mixing a buyer's, seller's, tenant's, or landlord's funds with the broker's own money or of mixing escrow money with the broker's personal or brokerage funds.

An escrow account, therefore, is associated with the type of monies held in the account. What makes an account an escrow account is that the account is used to hold funds belonging to anyone other than the broker. It is not mandatory to include the word *escrow* or *trust* in the account name. However, it is advisable to use the word *escrow* or *trust* in the account name to clearly indicate for IRS purposes that the funds in the account do not belong to the broker and therefore are not subject to seizure by the IRS. Such funds include earnest money tendered with respect to an offer to purchase real property, security deposits, and maintenance fees, as well as rental proceeds received from tenants. The types of monies that a broker may handle for others in the ordinary course of business include, but are not limited to:

- Sales deposits (earnest money)
- Property management (rent)
- Security deposits
- Pet deposits

- Maintenance deposits
- Money paid by sellers for marketing expenses not covered by broker

Timely Deposit of Funds

Florida real estate license law mandates the time frame for depositing escrow funds. Sales associates who receive a binder deposit from a customer or a principal must deliver it to their broker-employer no later than the *end of the next business day*. When a sales associate or an employee (such as a receptionist) of the brokerage company accepts funds on behalf of the brokerage company, the broker is accountable for those funds. Therefore, it is extremely important that brokers train their personnel regarding the importance of turning over all earnest money in a timely manner.

Brokers must place trust funds into an escrow account **immediately**, which means no later than the *end of the third business day* after their sales associate (or an employee of their brokerage company) has received it. The three-business-day period coincides with the day that the sales associate must turn over the deposit to the broker.

Assume a sales associate receives a deposit from a prospective buyer on a Wednesday (no legal holidays are involved):

- The sales associate has until the end of the next business day (Thursday) to deliver the deposit to the broker.
- The broker has until the end of the third business day (Monday) to deposit the funds. The three-business-day period for the broker to deposit the funds begins on the day the sales associate is required to deliver the funds to the broker. (In this example, the first day of the three-business-day period is Thursday.)

Now assume that the sales associate receives a deposit from a prospective buyer in the brokerage office on Wednesday (no legal holidays are involved) and the sales associate turns the check over to the broker that same day (Wednesday). When must the broker deposit the funds into the escrow account?

The day of receipt of the escrow deposit was Wednesday. The broker must deposit the funds by the end of business on the third business day after the brokerage received the funds. The three business days are Thursday, Friday, and Monday. So the fact that the sales associate delivered the escrow to the broker on Wednesday rather than waiting until Thursday made no difference regarding when the broker was required to deposit the funds. When computing the day for the broker to deposit the funds, the day the buyer (or lessee if this is a rent deposit) gives the funds to the brokerage is not counted in the broker's days. The first day of the three-business-day period always begins on the business day after the check is given to the brokerage. Keep in mind that a broker does not have to wait until the third business day to deposit the funds. The broker can make the deposit earlier. The broker can also receive the deposit directly without the involvement of a sales associate. The same rule applies in the case: The broker has until the end of the third business day to make the deposit.

If an escrow check is made out to the sales associate personally, the best course of action is to ask the prospective buyer to write a new check payable to the broker's escrow account. However, if this is not practical, the sales associate should immediately endorse the check and include the words, "For Deposit Only to the (name of the escrow account)" and turn it over to the broker.

DISCIPLINARY GUIDELINES

475.25(1)(k). Has failed, if a broker, to deposit any money in an escrow account immediately upon receipt until disbursement is properly authorized. Has failed, if a sales associate, to place any money to be escrowed with his registered employer. *First Violation*: $250 to $1,000 administrative fine and 30-day suspension to revocation. *Subsequent Violations*: $1,000 to $5,000 administrative fine and suspension to revocation.

Reference: Rule 61J2-24.001, F.A.C.

Postdated checks and insufficient funds. Occasionally a licensee may be given a postdated check (considered a promissory note) as an earnest money deposit. Although Florida statute (see F.S. 673) provides for checks and other negotiable instruments to be postdated, the broker should use extreme caution in handling such deposits. The seller's approval *must* be obtained before accepting the postdated check. The fact that the check is postdated should be noted on the purchase and sale contract. Once accepted, the broker should secure the instrument in a proper place, such as an office safe, until the date on the check becomes current, and then immediately deposit the check into the broker's escrow account. If the deposit is in the form of securities that the depositor intends to be converted into cash, the conversion should be made at the earliest practical time and the proceeds deposited immediately into the escrow account. A broker will not be held responsible for the nonpayment of an escrow check, *provided* the broker timely deposits the check into the escrow account and the broker's own culpable negligence did not cause the check not to be honored.

Acceptable depositories. Brokers may maintain either an interest-bearing or noninterest-bearing escrow account in a Florida commercial bank, credit union, or savings association. Some brokers do not want the responsibility and liability of maintaining an escrow account. Instead, they may choose to have a Florida-based title company that has trust powers to maintain the escrow funds, or alternatively, if designated in the sale contract, a Florida attorney may escrow the funds.

Title companies and attorney escrow accounts. Florida statutes and FREC rules do not require a broker to establish an escrow account. When a deposit is placed with a title company or with an attorney, the following procedure must be used:

- The real estate license who prepared or presented the sale contract must indicate on the purchase and sale agreement the title company's name (or attorney's name, if applicable), address, and telephone number.
- No later than ten business days after each deposit is due under the terms of the sale contract, the licensee's broker must request a written verification of receipt of the deposit. The broker's request to the title company (or to the attorney) must be in writing. If the deposit is held by a title company or by an attorney nominated in writing by the seller or the seller's agent, the verification is waived.
- No later than ten business days after the date the broker made the written request for verification of the deposit, the broker must provide the seller's broker with a copy of the written verification. If the title company (or attorney) failed to provide the broker with a written verification, this information must be given to the seller's broker no later than ten business days after the request for verifi-

FREC CITATION AUTHORITY

61J2-14.014(1). Failed to secure the written permission of all interest parties prior to placing trust funds in an interest-bearing escrow account. *$300 citation*

61J2-14.014(2). Failed to stop interest from accruing prior to disbursement. *$100 citation*

Reference: Rule 61J2-24.002, F.A.C.

cation of the deposit. If the seller is not represented by a broker, the licensee's broker must notify the seller directly.

Sometimes, the purchase and sale contract will require the buyer to make more than one earnest money deposit. For example, the contract may state that the buyer is to make a $5,000 earnest money deposit at the time the contract is accepted by the seller and then a second deposit of $15,000 30 days after the date the contract is signed by the seller. When the contract requires more than one earnest deposit, the procedure described above must be employed for every deposit specified in the purchase and sale agreement.

Real estate license law governs only broker's escrow accounts. A broker may be subject to administrative discipline for failing to follow the procedure described above. However, because real estate license law governs only broker escrow accounts, the FREC has no jurisdiction over the title company or the attorney that was used as an escrow agent. Brokers who choose to use a title company to escrow funds are cautioned to choose a reputable company with a proven track record. The broker is required under Chapter 475, F.S., to deliver the funds to the escrow agent within the same time frame required for depositing funds into a broker's escrow account. Therefore, the broker must deliver the funds to the escrow agent no later than the end of the third business day after the deposit was received by the brokerage.

Interest-Bearing Escrow Accounts

If the broker's escrow account is an interest-bearing account, the broker must get written permission from all parties before placing the funds in this type of account. The written authorization must specify who is entitled to the interest earned. The broker may receive the interest earned, but only if it is specifically agreed to by all parties. Rule 61J2-14.014 states that the written agreement must indicate consent to placing the escrow money into an interest-bearing escrow account, designate the party to receive the interest, and specify when the accrued interest is to be disbursed. Brokers must be able to document that written agreements exist regarding the placement of funds into an interest-bearing escrow account. The interest-bearing account must be an insured account in a depository located and doing business in Florida.

When it is time to disburse principal and/or interest to the designated party, the broker must first transfer the principal and interest to a non-interest-bearing escrow account. Alternatively, a broker may establish an individual interest-bearing escrow account for a specific transaction or sum of money and, on the agreed day of disbursement, close the account, with checks issued to the appropriate persons for the principal and interest. Cashier's checks may be used to disburse funds from an escrow account.

KEY CONCEPTS REGARDING ESCROW ACCOUNTS

- Broker may open an escrow account in a Florida bank, savings association, or credit union.
- Broker must be a signatory on the escrow account.
- Broker must review, sign, and date the monthly reconciliation statements.
- Broker must review the company's escrow accounting procedures.
- If the broker chooses not to open an escrow account, the funds may be held by a title company or in an attorney's trust account.
- Brokers must maintain records of real estate transactions for five years regardless of whether escrow funds were pledged (or two years after litigation if beyond the five-year period).

However, if the broker is the person designated to receive the interest, the principal portion is transferred to the non-interest-bearing escrow account for further disbursement to the designated party, and the interest is transferred directly to the broker's operating account. Interest accruing to the broker should not be allowed to accumulate from month to month in the escrow account. This is because the accrued interest is the broker's money and not the buyer's or the seller's funds. A broker designated to receive accrued interest must transfer the interest to the operating account on a monthly basis. Accumulated accrued interest that has not been timely transferred is considered to be an overage and a commingling of escrow funds with the broker's own funds.

Failure to stop interest from accruing before disbursement may result in a notice of noncompliance, provided it is the broker's first offense and the situation is corrected within 15 days; otherwise a citation may be issued. Failure to get written permission of all interest parties before placing trust funds into an interest-bearing escrow account may result in a citation.

Monies Paid in Advance for Performing Real Estate Services

Sometimes a broker will receive commission or partial compensation before completing the real estate service. When this occurs the broker is entrusted with funds that must be placed into the broker's escrow or trust account until the services are completed. Once the service is completed the broker has earned the compensation and may at that time transfer the funds into the broker's operating account. The Time-Share Act prohibits a real estate licensee from collecting an advance fee for the listing of a time-share unit.

Record Keeping

Brokers must keep business records, books, and accounts in compliance with Florida law and Commission rules and make them available for audit or spot checks by the DBPR at any reasonable time. Records must be preserved for at least *five years* from the date of any executed agreement, oral or written. FREC rule require brokers who receive escrow funds to retain deposit slips, bank statements, and all agreements between the parties to a transaction. Brokers must keep an accurate account of each deposit transaction and each separate bank account.

FREC rule stipulates that receipt of funds by a sales associate or an employee of the brokerage firm constitutes receipt by the broker. Because the broker is accountable for all funds that are turned over to the broker or anyone associated with the brokerage, it is critical that brokers maintain oversight regarding how funds are handled once they are collected and to make sure that escrow funds are always turned over to the broker in a timely manner. The DBPR auditor will check to make sure that all funds turned over to the brokerage company were deposited into the escrow account in a timely manner.

The broker must preserve at least one legible copy of all books, accounts, and records pertaining to the real estate brokerage business. Copies of real estate transactions must be preserved regardless of whether trust funds were involved. Brokers must retain records for at least five years:

- from the date of receipt of any money, funds, deposits, or checks entrusted to the broker; and
- from the date of any executed agreement, including buyer brokerage agreements, listing agreements, offers to purchase, rental property management agreements, rental or lease agreements, or any other written or verbal agreement that engages the services of the broker, even if no funds were entrusted to the broker.

If brokerage records have been the subject of litigation or have served as evidence for litigation, the relevant records must be retained for at least *two years* beyond the conclusion of the civil action or the conclusion of an appellate proceeding, but in no case, for less than five years.

Brokers who don't have sufficient office space to store five years' worth of business records may scan the records and preserve them on CD-ROM or other electronic storage. Brokers are not required to retain the original records as long as legible photocopies or electronic copies exist. Alternatively, a broker may maintain stored business records in a facility other than the broker's office, but the records must be readily available in case of an audit. Real estate brokers have been disciplined for failing to produce business records because of hurricane damage to the brokerage structure and because of alleged vandalism and theft. Therefore, it may be prudent to make electronic copies of business records and to store them in a secure off-site location.

Signatory on escrow account. FREC rules require the broker to be a signatory on all brokerage escrow accounts. The escrow accounts must be properly reconciled each month, and the broker must review, sign, and date the monthly reconciliations (see example of a Monthly Reconciliation Statement, Figure 4.1 on pages 95–97). The broker may designate another person, such as a bookkeeper, to sign checks on the account in the ordinary course of business. If a real estate brokerage has more than one licensed broker, one of the brokers may be designated as the signatory on the escrow account. In offices where someone other than the broker handles the day-to-day deposits and disbursements, such as the broker's bookkeeper or accountant, the broker must be able, if requested by the DBPR, to provide proof (copy of the bank's signature card) that the broker is a signatory on the escrow account. Brokers should use caution when delegating escrow responsibilities to another person. Florida law holds the broker accountable for reviewing the brokerage firm's escrow accounting procedures to ensure compliance with Florida license law. It is the broker who will be disciplined for violating any of the escrow requirements.

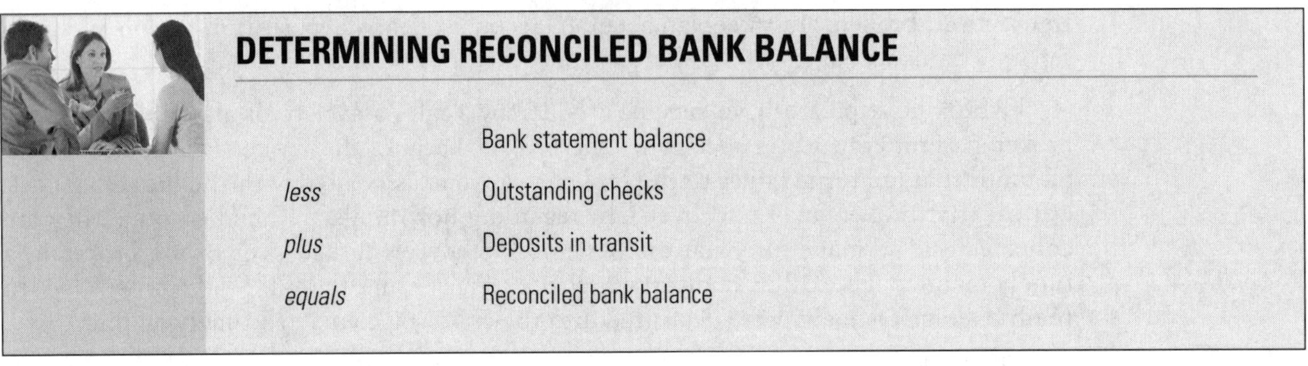

If a broker collects rents, security deposits, and other monies associated with property management services, the broker must follow escrow procedures. Brokers are not required to keep separate property management escrow funds from brokerage sales escrow funds, however, doing so is highly recommended. Brokers may open as many escrow accounts as necessary to conduct business. If a broker collects rent on behalf of the landlord and the rent payment is payable to the brokerage, the rent must be deposited into the broker's escrow account. After the funds have cleared the broker can disburse the rent to the landlord. If the landlord has given permission for the broker to deduct commission from the rent payments, the broker should transfer the commission to the broker's operating account and write a check from the escrow account payable to the landlord for the portion of rent belonging to the landlord.

Monthly Reconciliation Statement

At least monthly, a broker must prepare a written statement comparing the total trust liability with each trust account's reconciled bank balance. The minimum information the broker must include in the monthly reconciliation statement follows:

- date the reconciliation was conducted;
- date used to reconcile the balances;
- name of the bank or other authorized financial institution;
- name of the account;
- account number;
- account balance and date;
- outstanding checks identified by date and number;
- itemized list of the broker's trust liability;
- deposits in transit identified by date and amount; and
- any other items necessary to reconcile the bank account balance with the balance according to the broker's checkbook and other trust account books and records disclosing the funds' date of receipt and source.

The broker must review, sign, and date the monthly reconciliation statement. Figure 4.1 (pages 95–97) provides a sample statement.

To complete the monthly reconciliation, the broker begins by determining the trust liability. **Trust liability** is defined as the total sum of all deposits received, pending, and being held by the broker at any point in time. It is other people's monies placed with

FIGURE 4.1 ■ Sample Reconciliation Statement

Monthly Reconciliation Statement Real Estate Trust Account

FLORIDA ASSOCIATION OF REALTORS®

To be used in compliance with Chapter 61J2-14.012(2), Florida Administrative Code

1. **Trust Account Reconciliation Information**

Name of bank: XYZ Bank of Florida

Name of account: ABC Realty, Inc. Escrow Account

Account number: 12345

Reconciliation for the month of May, 2013. Date used for reconciliation: 5 / 30 / 13

Bank statement period 5 / 1 / 13 through 5 / 30 / 13.

Date reconciliation performed: 6 / 1 / 13

2. **Adjusted Account Balance**

Outstanding Checks

Date	Check #	Amount
5-15-13	1301	$ 500
5-24-13	1302	1,500
5-30-13	1303	2,000

Deposits Not Credited

Date	Amount
5-30-13	$ 10,000

Ending account balance (for statement period):		$ 57,000
Add deposits not credited:	+	$ 10,000
Subtract outstanding checks:	–	$ 4,000
Total (this is the Adjusted Account Balance as of date reconciliation performed):		$ 63,000

MSR-5 Rev. 4/04

Source: Florida REALTORS®. Reprinted with permission.

FIGURE 4.1 ■ Sample Reconciliation Statement (Continued)

3. **Itemized List of Broker's Trust Liability**

Client/Transaction Name:	*Reconciled Balance*
Smith/Jones	$ 10,000
Jackson/Brown	$ 12,000
Miller/Anderson	$ 30,000
Carter/Hess	$ 10,000
	$
	$
	$
	$
	$
	$
	$
	$
	$
	$
	$

Total of Broker's Trust Liability (Total of all deposits received, pending and being held by Broker as of the date reconciliation performed): $ 62,000

4. **Comparison of Reconciled Trust Account Balance with Broker's Trust Liability:**

Adjusted Account Balance (from paragraph 2) $ 63,000

Broker's Trust Liability (from paragraph 3) $ 62,000

If Adjusted Account Balance and Broker's Trust Liability agree, sign the Reconciliation Statement.

If Adjusted Account Balance and Broker's Trust Liability do not agree, complete the following to explain the difference. Then, sign the Reconciliation Statement.

(1) Shortages:
(Adjusted Account Balance is less than Broker's Trust Liability) **Total Shortage: $** __________

Reason for shortage (i.e., nsf, service charge, negative balance): __________

MSR-5 Rev. 4/04

FIGURE 4.1 ■ Sample Reconciliation Statement (Continued)

Corrective Action Taken: ______

(2) Overages:
(Adjusted Account Balance is more than Broker's Trust Liability) Total Overage: $ 1,000
Check only if applicable: ☑ Overage is due to deposit of Broker's own funds (not exceeding $5000 in property management escrow account and $1,000 in sales escrow account) into account for maintenance purposes in accordance with Rule 61J2-14.010(2).

Other Reason for Overage: ______

Corrective Action Taken: No corrective action needed

5. Signature

I, Martha Sammis, Broker, reviewed this monthly statement/reconciliation

on June 1, 2013.

Martha Sammis

Broker's signature (required on all Reconciliation Statements) the broker that correspond to specific real estate transactions—sales or property management. For sales escrow accounts, the trust liability includes all earnest money deposits. With respect to property management escrow accounts, the trust liability may include, for example, undisbursed rents, owner reserves, security deposits, and any other funds collected that would benefit the lessor or lessee—that is, the total monies the broker holds for others at the reconciliation cutoff date.

The broker determines the trust liability by summing the contract deposits (i.e., balances reflected for various transactions such as sales, rental proceeds, security deposits, and so forth). Brokers may use whatever method of recordkeeping they prefer. Some keep track of transactions manually, using ledger forms, while others use computer spreadsheet programs to generate lists of liabilities. Regardless of the method of accounting, information that must be recorded includes dates and amounts of deposits and dates and amounts of disbursements. This information is required for each escrow account the broker maintains, and each entry must be cross-referenced back to the transaction by party name or property address.

The broker then reconciles the bank balance. To do this, the broker begins with the monthly bank statement balance (or any interim statement received from the financial institution), then subtracts outstanding checks and adds all deposits in transit collected, but not yet reflected on the bank statement.

The broker's trust liability should equal the reconciled bank balance. If the trust liability and bank balance do not agree, the reconciliation must include an explanation of the shortage or overage and any corrective action the broker has taken to correct the difference. Whenever a trust bank account record reflects a service charge or fee for a nonsufficient-funds check, or whenever an account has a negative balance, the reconciliation must explain the returned check or negative balance and the corrective action taken. Ideally, the broker should arrange with the bank to have bank service charges debited from the broker's business operating account rather than the escrow account. If the broker receives notice from the financial institution that an escrow deposit check has been returned for nonsufficient funds, the broker should notify the principal immediately and seek the principal's instructions. The broker also should notify the check issuer.

The broker never should have a negative balance in an escrow account or in any individual account ledger. The negative balance indicates a shortage in the escrow account, which means the broker has spent other owners' funds to cover owners with negative balances. The broker may not spend funds on behalf of an individual owner when the funds in that owner's balance do not cover the expenditure. Such practice creates a shortage in the escrow account. Misappropriation of another's property exposes the broker to charges of conversion. **Conversion** is the unauthorized control and use of another person's personal property. The broker is not responsible for paying any check or draft unless it is unpaid due to the broker's culpable negligence and damage results to some party entitled to complain of such negligence.

Broker's money to maintain account. For the purpose of covering bank maintenance fees, check printing fees, and other bank business matters, the broker is allowed to place in the sales escrow account up to $1,000 of personal funds or brokerage funds. Brokers may keep up to $5,000 of their own monies in a property management escrow account. If a broker maintains sales escrow funds and property management escrow funds in a single escrow account, the amount of personal funds or brokerage funds in the account cannot exceed $5,000. Brokers must account for these funds in the monthly reconciliation statement, either in the trust liability section (including broker's name and the amount) or in the overage section. If the bank debits the account for service charges, the broker should reimburse the escrow account the service charge amounts when the $1,000 balance (or $5,000 balance) nears depletion.

Preparing a Monthly Reconciliation Statement—An Example

ABC Realty, Inc., maintains an escrow account at XYZ Bank of Florida. The account name is *ABC Realty, Inc., Escrow Account*, and the account number is 12345. ABC Realty's master trust liability ledger for the month of May 2013 is presented here:

ABC Realty, Inc.
Master Trust Liability
May 2013

Buyer	Seller	Date Deposit Received	Amount
Smith	Jones	5-3-13	$10,000
Jackson	Brown	5-4-13	$12,000
Miller	Anderson	5-10-13	$30,000
Carter	Hess	5-30-13	$10,000

ABC Realty's check register for the escrow account for the month of May 2013 reflects the disbursements shown below. As of June 1, 2013, the checks listed are the only outstanding checks:

ABC Realty, Inc.
Check Register for Escrow Account 12345
May 2013

Date of Check	Check Number	Payee	Amount
5-15-13	1301	Executive Title	$ 500
5-24-13	1302	J Smith, Esquire	$1,500
5-30-13	1303	Chicago Title	$2,000

The trust liability is calculated by summing all of the balances on the last day of the month (or some other date elected for the reconciliation). Four deposits were made during the month, totaling $62,000, which equals the broker's total trust liability.

The bank statement balance dated May 30, 2013, shows an ending account balance of $57,000 (refer to Figure 4.1 on page 95). The broker maintains $1,000 of personal funds in the escrow account to cover monthly service charges. The bank statement reflects all of the deposits made into the account during the month of May with the exception of the $10,000 deposit received on May 30, 2013. This deposit, considered to be a deposit in transit (i.e., the bank posted it after May 30), must be added to the bank statement balance to calculate the reconciled bank balance. Subtracting $4,000 in outstanding checks leaves an adjusted reconciled bank balance of $63,000.

$57,000 Bank statement balance – $4,000 Outstanding checks +
$10,000 Deposits in transit = $63,000 Reconciled bank balance

The $1,000 discrepancy is caused by the fact that the broker maintains $1,000 of personal funds in the account to keep the account open. The broker must note the $1,000 overage to maintain the account. (The notation is indicated on page 97 of Figure 4.1.) The final step is to prepare, sign, and date the monthly reconciliation statement.

Disciplinary Guidelines for Failing to Reconcile Escrow Accounts

Brokers who fail to reconcile their escrow accounts at least monthly are subject to a citation. Rule 61J2-24.002 provides that a broker may be issued a citation if the broker fails to properly reconcile an escrow account even though the account balances. Rule 61J2-24.002(cc) states that the broker is subject to a $500 citation. A citation may be issued only when the account balances. Any shortage, regardless of how small, results in a case against the broker. Cases are prosecuted through the Commission's regular disciplinary process.

ESCROW DISBURSEMENT DISPUTE PROCESS

When a broker assumes the responsibility of escrow agent in a real estate transaction, the deposit belongs to and is under the control of the depositor (for example, a prospective buyer) until another party (for example, the seller) acquires some interest or equity in the deposited funds. The broker must not deliver the deposit to the other party until the transaction is closed, except as otherwise directed and agreed to by all parties to the transaction. Section 475.25(1)(d), F.S., provides a dispute resolution process when a broker has good-faith doubt as to which person is entitled to the escrowed property, or if conflicting demands have been made for the escrowed property.

Conflicting demands occur when the buyer and seller make demands regarding the disbursing of escrowed property that are inconsistent and cannot be resolved. If a broker who maintains an escrow account receives conflicting demands on escrowed property, the broker must notify the FREC, in writing, within *15 business days* of receiving the conflicting demands unless specifically exempted (see below). Further, the broker must institute one of the four settlement (or escape) procedures (listed later in this chapter) within *30 business days* from the time the broker received the conflicting demands. For example, if a broker waits 10 business days to report the conflicting demands, the broker has just 20 business days remaining to implement one of the settlement procedures.

WEB LINK

Download the Notice of Escrow Dispute/Good Faith Doubt form at **http://www.myflorida.com/dbpr/re/documents/notice_escrow_dispute_rev.pdf.**

The four settlement procedures are as follows:

1. Mediation. If all parties give written consent, the dispute may be mediated. **Mediation** is an informal, nonadversarial process intended to reach a negotiated settlement. If the *nonbinding* mediation process is not successfully completed within 90 days following the party's last demand for the disputed funds, the licensee must employ one of the other three settlement procedures.

2. Arbitration. **Arbitration** is a process whereby, with the prior written consent of all parties to the dispute, the matter is submitted to a disinterested third party. Each side presents its case to a third party, who makes a *binding* judgment in favor of one side or the other. The parties must agree in advance to abide by the arbitrator's final decision.

3. Litigation. If the disputing parties cannot agree, a disputing party may file a lawsuit so that the matter can be resolved in a court of law. Such a legal process is referred to as **litigation**. The litigation can involve either of two court procedures:

- **Interpleader**. If the broker does not have a financial claim to the disputed escrow funds, the broker can deposit the funds with the court registry. The broker is then excused from the case, and the disputing parties argue their case in court. This court procedure is known as **interpleader**.
- **Declaratory judgment**. Brokers who believe they are entitled to a portion of the disputed funds can file a court action known as a **declaratory judgment**. In this court procedure, the judge declares each of the party's rights to the disputed escrow funds.

4. Escrow disbursement order (EDO). The broker may choose to request that the Commission issue an **escrow disbursement order (EDO)**, a determination of who is entitled to the disputed funds.

WEB LINK

To download the Request for Escrow Disbursement Order form, go to **http://www.myfloridalicense.com/dbpr/re/documents/RequestForEDORev0312.pdf.**

The FREC will not issue an EDO if the funds are held in an attorney's escrow account or are being held by a title company. An EDO procedure is only available if the funds are held in a brokerage escrow account. If the broker is informed in writing that the Commission will not issue an EDO, the broker must utilize one of the other settlement procedures. In such an instance, the broker must notify the Commission which settlement procedure will be used.

If the broker promptly employs one of the four settlement procedures and abides by the resulting order or judgment, a complaint may not be filed against the broker for failure to account for or deliver escrowed property (the broker has immunity from disciplinary action).

If a title company or an attorney is the escrow agent, the broker has no obligation to report an escrow dispute to the FREC or to institute a settlement procedure. Generally a title company or the attorney will not disburse funds without authorization from the parties to the transaction. Usually, if the parties cannot come to an agreement regarding the funds, the matter is submitted to a court of law for resolution.

TO REMEMBER

Four Escrow Settlement Procedures (MALE)

M	Mediation (nonbinding)
A	Arbitration (binding)
L	Litigation
E	Escrow Disbursement Order

KEY REPORTING DEADLINES FOR ESCROW ACCOUNTS

- Sales associates must deliver escrow deposits to their broker by the end of the **next business day.**
- Brokers must deposit escrow funds by the end of the **third business day**.
- Brokers must notify the FREC in writing of conflicting demands or of a good faith doubt within **15 business days**.
- Brokers must institute one of the settlement procedures within **30 business days** of receiving conflicting demands or of having a good faith doubt.
- If a broker requests an EDO and the escrow dispute is either settled or goes to court before the EDO is issued, the broker must notify the FREC within **ten business days.**

There are three exceptions to the notice and settlement procedures for sales escrow accounts:

1. Brokers who are entrusted with an earnest money deposit concerning a residential sale contract utilized by HUD in the sale of HUD-owned property are exempted from the notice and settlement procedures in Chapter 475, F.S. In such cases, the broker is required to follow HUD's Agreement to Abide, Broker Participation Requirements.
2. If a buyer of a residential condominium unit timely delivers to a licensee written notice of the buyer's intent to cancel the contract as authorized by the Condominium Act, the licensee may return the escrowed property to the purchaser without notifying the Commission or initiating any of the settlement procedures.
3. If a buyer of real property in good faith fails to satisfy the terms specified in the financing clause of a contract for sale and purchase, the licensee may return the escrowed funds to the purchaser without notifying the Commission or initiating any of the settlement procedures. (Although *not* required by law, licensees are cautioned that they may be exposing themselves to civil liability if they release escrowed funds prior to the parties agreeing as to who is entitled to the funds. The Florida REALTORS® has developed preprinted forms that can be used to obtain the written permission of all parties to release escrowed funds.)

Good-faith doubt. If a broker has a *good-faith doubt* as to which party should receive the escrowed property, the broker must notify the FREC, in writing, within *15 business days* after having such doubt and institute one of the settlement procedures within *30 business days* after having such doubt. The term **good faith** is used to describe a party's honest intent to transact business, free from any intent to defraud the other party, and generally speaking, each party's faithfulness to the duties or obligations set forth by contract. Therefore, if the broker doubts the parties' good faith, the law requires that the broker abide by the notice requirement and initiate one of the settlement procedures in a timely manner. Individuals must look to case law for interpretations of what specific circumstances constitute a good-faith doubt. Situations that *may* constitute good-faith doubt by the broker include:

- The transaction closing date has passed, and the broker has not received identical instructions from both the buyer and seller regarding how to disburse escrowed funds.
- The transaction closing date has not passed, but one or more parties have expressed the intention not to close and the broker has not received identical instructions from the buyer and seller regarding how to disburse escrowed funds.
- One party to a failed transaction does not respond to a broker's inquiry about escrow disbursement. In this situation, the broker may send a certified notice letter, return receipt requested, to that nonresponding party stating that a demand has been made on the escrowed funds and that failure to respond by a designated date will be regarded as authority for the broker to release the funds to the demanding party. (*Note:* Although *not* required by law, to limit the broker's potential liability, it is advisable before releasing the trust funds to secure the return receipt as proof the notice was delivered.)

Escrow Disbursement Dispute Process

When the DRE receives the broker's notice of conflicting demands or good-faith doubt, it assigns a case number. DRE personnel review the broker's notification and may request additional information from the broker regarding whether other escape procedures have been tried. Has the broker submitted the matter to arbitration or mediation? Has the broker sought adjudication by interpleader?

The file is monitored if the dispute is settled by arbitration, mediation, or interpleader or if it is determined that a dispute or good-faith doubt regarding the escrowed funds no longer exists. If the case involves issues that EDOs do not cover (for example, commission disputes), the DRE may direct the broker to institute another settlement procedure.

If review of the broker's notification indicates that the issuance of an EDO is the proper course of action, the DRE opens a case and sends a questionnaire to the broker, as well as to the parties to the transaction. A 21-day waiting period allows responses to the questionnaires. The legal section of the DRE reviews the case and makes a recommendation to the FREC and its legal counsel. When a case is closed because of issues that cannot be resolved, a letter is sent instructing the broker to proceed with arbitration or interpleader within the time frames outlined by law.

If the broker has requested an EDO and the dispute is settled or goes to court before the order is issued, the broker must notify the Commission within *ten business days* of the settlement or the decision to litigate the matter in court. Refer to Figure 4.2, Outline of Escrow Disbursement Dispute Process.

FIGURE 4.2 ■ Outline of Escrow Disbursement Dispute Process

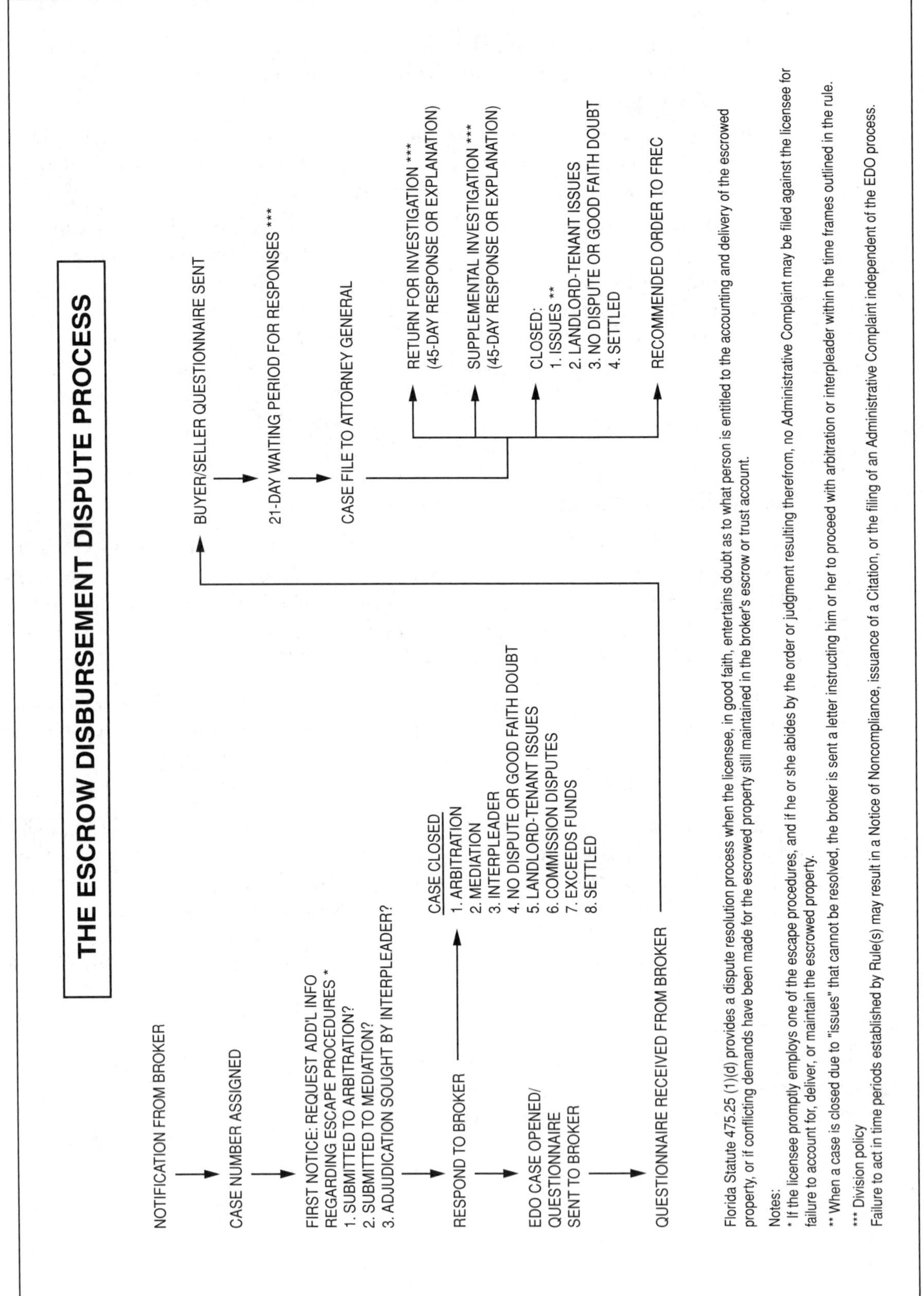

Reprinted with permission of the Department of Business and Professional Regulation, Division of Real Estate.

NOTIFICATION AND SETTLEMENT PROCEDURE REQUIREMENTS FOR SPECIAL TYPES OF PROPERTIES

Property Management Deposits and Advance Rent

The Florida Residential Landlord and Tenant Act relieves brokers of the duty to notify the FREC of disputes over security deposits and advance rent with regard to residential rental properties. Section 83.49(3)(d), F.S., provides that Florida real estate licensees holding security deposits and advance rent may disburse the funds without complying with the Commission's escrow dispute and notification procedures if the brokers have complied with all requirements set forth in Section 83.49, F.S.

If a tenant vacates the premises upon termination of the rental agreement and the landlord fails to make the proper claim on the security deposit, the broker can disburse the deposit to the tenant without obtaining the landlord's consent. If the landlord (or broker as the landlord's agent) makes a proper and timely claim on the security deposit and the tenant doesn't object to the claim properly, the broker may disburse the claimed amount to the landlord without obtaining the tenant's consent. If both parties claim the security deposit within the legislated time frame, the broker can hold the disputed amount in escrow until the parties settle the matter without having to notify the Commission. The broker must, however, keep proper records of the account. If desired, a broker may ask the FREC to issue an EDO in a landlord-tenant dispute. However, if an EDO is issued, the broker must disburse the funds as the EDO directs.

Condominium Unit Purchases

Chapter 718, F.S., establishes procedures for creating, selling, and operating condominiums. The law requires that the developer give a disclosure statement to buyers stating that the buyer may cancel the contract within *15 calendar days* of signing the contract or of receipt by the buyer of the condominium documents, whichever is later. A purchaser of an existing (resale) condominium unit has the right to cancel the contract within *3 business days* after the date of the execution of the contract and receipt by the buyer of the condo documents.

If a prospective buyer chooses to timely cancel the contract, a real estate licensee may return the escrowed binder deposit to the prospective purchaser without first securing the seller's permission, provided the licensee was notified in writing that the buyer is canceling the contract during the statutory time period for cancellation. Even if the seller objects, the Real Estate License Law states that the licensee may return the deposit to the purchaser without having to notify the Commission of conflicting demands.

Unclaimed Escrow Funds

The Department of Financial Services is the state depository for abandoned property. There is a five-year waiting period for turning over abandoned property. However, real estate brokers can petition to have the Department of Financial Services accept abandoned escrow funds sooner. Brokers who have searched diligently to locate the owners of escrowed funds may contact the Unclaimed Property Office, Department of Financial Services, for instructions on how to proceed.

CASE IN POINT

A licensee who filed for an escrow disbursement order two months late and failed to inform the FREC about how the money was disbursed was fined $1,250 and had to take a four-hour escrow management course.

A licensee who had an escrow account shortage due to bank charges and an overage due to failure to remove commission was fined $1,000 and had to take an escrow management course.

Source: *News and Report,* Florida Real Estate Commission.

WEB LINK

For information regarding unclaimed escrow funds, contact the Florida Department of Financial Services, 200 E. Gaines St., Tallahassee, FL 32399-0358, call 800-342-2762, or go to its Web site at **http://www.fldfs.com.**

BROKER'S COMMISSION

Antitrust Laws

The real estate industry is subject to state and federal antitrust laws. At the federal level, the Sherman, Clayton, and Federal Trade Commission acts deal with preserving competition and ensuring against restraint of trade. It is illegal for real estate brokers to conspire to fix commissions or fees for the services they perform. Local real estate boards and multiple listing services may not fix commission rates or splits between cooperating brokers. Brokers risk their assets and careers by attempting to get other brokers to charge a standard commission. Antitrust laws prohibit any action by a party to fix prices or inhibit competition by using unfair practices. Some of the prohibited actions include:

- conspiracy to set prices;
- splitting up competitive market areas;
- conspiring to boycott cut-rate brokers or otherwise interfering with their business; and
- requiring a minimum commission before allowing listings to be circulated in any service, such as through a multiple-listing service (MLS).

The amount of commission to be paid is negotiable, and it is arrived at by agreement between the broker and buyer or seller. If no specific agreement exists, a judicially determined commission will apply. Neither the FREC nor Florida law establishes or regulates the amount of commission paid. The sharing of brokerage compensation by a licensee with a party to the real estate transaction, with full disclosure to all interested parties, is allowed under Chapter 475, F.S.

Liens for Nonpayment of Commission

Residential property. A broker may place a lien on real property for nonpayment of commission *only* if the broker is expressly authorized to do so in a contractual agreement. Otherwise, when a buyer or seller refuses to pay a broker's commission after the commission has been earned, the broker would be required to take legal action to collect the monies due by filing a suit against the party for the amount due. The broker would have to obtain a civil judgment against the party who owed the commission. The FREC is authorized to suspend or revoke a real estate license for the unauthorized recording of a *lis pendens* or a lien or other instrument that affects the title of real property or that encumbers real property.

Commercial Real Estate Sales Commission Lien Act. Chapter 475, Part III, known as the Commercial Real Estate Sales Commission Lien Act, gives a broker lien rights for earned commission. This Act applies only to commercial property as defined in Chapter 475. The lien is only against the owner's net proceeds (personal property) from the sale and does not apply to the commercial real property. The owner's **net proceeds** are the gross sale proceeds less any existing liens of higher priority than the broker's lien and less the owner's closing costs for the sale transaction.

To establish a broker's lien rights, the broker must disclose to the owner (seller) at or before the time the owner executes the brokerage agreement for the listing (and subsequent sale) of commercial property, that Chapter 475, Part III, creates lien rights for commission earned by the broker. Commission includes any fee or other compensation that the owner agrees to pay the broker for licensed real estate services specified in the brokerage agreement. The disclosure must state that the Commercial Lien Act provides that when a broker has earned a commission under a brokerage agreement, the broker may claim a lien against the owner's net sales proceeds for the broker's unpaid commission.

If a dispute arises over unpaid commission, the broker must execute a notarized **commission notice** claiming the commission owed. The broker must, within 30 days after the commission is earned and at least one day before the closing, deliver a copy of a notarized commission notice to the property owner and to the closing agent. In the event the broker fails to timely deliver the commission notice because the owner entered into a contract for sale of the commercial real estate without the knowledge of the broker, the broker may enforce the lien provided a copy of the commission notice is delivered to the owner and the closing agent before the net proceeds are disbursed. If the closing agent has disbursed the funds prior to the broker delivering the notice, the lien may not be enforced.

The notarized commission notice must include the owner's name; a legal description of the property; the broker's name, address, telephone number, and license number; the effective date of the brokerage agreement; the amount of unpaid commission claimed by the broker; and that the broker is making a claim for commission in accordance with the brokerage agreement described in the notice. The notice must further state that if the owner disputes the claimed commission, the owner must notify the closing agent of the dispute within five calendar days after the closing. Otherwise, the owner will be deemed to have confirmed the commission owed and require the closing agent to pay the broker's commission from the owner's net proceeds. The broker must also include in the notice a statement that the notice may be recorded in the public records in the county where the commercial real estate is located. Once copies of the commission notice have been delivered to the owner and to the closing agent, the broker may proceed to have the notice recorded in the public records.

The lien against the owner's net proceeds takes priority as of the date of recording the commission notice. Priority of the lien does not relate back to the date of the brokerage agreement. The lien must be recorded at least 60 days to constitute constructive notice to a closing agent. The commission notice becomes effective once the deed transferring title from the owner to a bona fide purchaser is recorded. The commission notice expires one year after the date of recording, unless the owner remains obligated to pay the broker's commission and the broker records an extension notice within the last 60 days prior to

FIGURE 4.3 ■ Comparison of Commercial Sales Lien Act and Commercial Leasing Lien Act

	Sales Lien Act	Leasing Lien Act
Notarized disclosure at or before executing brokerage agreement	√	√
Lien belongs to the broker (not to broker's employee or independent contractor)	√	√
Lien priority is the date of recording the notice (not the date of executing the brokerage agreement)	√	√
Broker is obligated to record a satisfaction within seven calendar days after the commission is paid or the commission notice is discharged	√	√
Lien on net owner's proceeds at closing	√	
Notice must be delivered to closing agent prior to closing	√	
Commission notice expires one year after the date of recording	√	
Lien on interest in commercial property subject to a lease		√
Lien notice expires two years after the date of recording		√

the expiration date. The extension notice extends the expiration date one additional year. Successive extension notices may be recorded for as long as the owner remains obligated for the broker's commission. The broker is obligated to record a satisfaction within seven calendar days after the commission is paid or the commission notice is discharged.

A written contract for compensation between the buyer of commercial real estate and the broker is not a brokerage agreement with the owner. In such a case, the buyer's broker is not entitled to record a commission notice or to claim a lien against the owner's net proceeds. However, if an owner (seller) enters into a written contract for the sale of commercial real estate and the purchase and sale contract entitles the buyer's broker to receive compensation from the buyer under the terms of a buyer's broker's written contract with the buyer, the buyer's broker may give notice to the closing agent, the owner, and the buyer of the buyer broker's right to receive compensation.

Commercial Real Estate Leasing Commission Lien Act. Chapter 475, Part IV, known as the Commercial Real Estate Leasing Commission Lien Act, gives a broker lien rights for earned commission associated with a brokerage agreement to lease commercial real estate. If the landlord is the person obligated to pay the leasing commission, the broker's lien attaches to the landlord's interest in the commercial real estate. If the tenant is the person obligated to pay the leasing commission, the broker's lien attaches to the tenant's leasehold estate. A broker may initiate lien rights in the event the broker has earned a leasing commission under the terms of the brokerage agreement, including a renewal commission. A **renewal commission** is an additional commission under a brokerage agreement earned when a lease subject to the brokerage agreement is later renewed, or is later modified to expand the leased premises or extend the lease term.

A broker who has earned an unpaid leasing commission must file a **lien notice** within 90 days after the tenant takes possession of the leased premises (or 90 days after the broker performs additional services required for a renewal commission). The lien notice may be filed in the public records of the county in which the commercial property is located. The lien notice expires two years after the date of recording, unless the broker is claiming a commission earned under an automatic renewal provision in the brokerage agreement. In such instances, the lien notice expires ten years after the date of recording. The broker may extend the expiration date of a lien notice for an automatic renewal commission by recording an extension notice. A broker may enforce a lien notice for earned commission by filing a foreclosure suit in the same manner as if the lien notice were a mortgage recorded against the commercial real estate.

SUMMARY OF IMPORTANT POINTS

- An *escrow account* is an account for the deposit of money held by a third party in trust for another for safekeeping.
- *Escrow deposits* (or *trust funds*) include cash, checks, and money orders and items that can be converted into cash such as deeds and personal property. In addition to earnest money, deposits brokers hold in trust for others money associated with leasing property such as rent deposits and security deposits.
- *Commingle* is the illegal practice of mixing a buyer's, seller's, tenant's, or landlord's funds with the broker's own money or mixing escrow money with the broker's personal funds or brokerage funds.
- Sales associates must deliver binder deposits to their broker-employer no later than the end of the next business day.
- Brokers must deposit escrow funds into their escrow account immediately, which means no later than the end of the third business day after the brokerage received the funds.
- The seller's approval must be obtained before accepting the postdated check and the fact that the check is postdated should be noted on the contract.
- If the broker's escrow account is an interest-bearing account, the broker must get written permission from all parties before placing the funds into the account. The written authorization must specify who is entitled to the interest earned. The broker may receive the interest.
- Brokers may open escrow accounts in a bank, savings association, or credit union located in Florida. The broker must be a signatory on the escrow account. If the broker chooses not to open an escrow account, the funds may be held by a title company or in an attorney's trust account.
- Brokers must maintain records of real estate transactions for five years, regardless of whether escrow funds were pledged (or two years after litigation, if beyond the five-year period).
- Brokers are allowed to place up to $1,000 of personal or brokerage funds in a sales escrow account or up to $5,000 of personal or brokerage funds in a property management escrow account.
- At least monthly, a broker must prepare a written statement comparing the broker's total trust liability with each trust account's reconciled bank balance. The broker must review, sign, and date the monthly reconciliation statement.

- *Trust liability* is defined as the total sum of all deposits received, pending, and being held by the broker at any point in time. It is other people's monies placed with the broker that correspond to specific real estate transactions—sales or property management.
- The broker determines trust liability by summing the contract deposits (the balances reflected for various transactions such as sales, rental proceeds, security deposits, and so forth).
- The broker reconciles the bank balance, beginning with the monthly bank statement balance. The broker subtracts outstanding checks and adds all deposits in transit (deposits collected, but not yet reflected on the bank statement).
- The broker's trust liability should equal the reconciled bank balance. If the trust liability and the bank balance do not agree, the reconciliation must include an explanation of the shortage or overage and any corrective action the broker has taken to correct the difference.
- Brokers must notify the FREC in writing of conflicting demands or of a good-faith doubt within 15 business days. Brokers must institute one of the settlement procedures within 30 business days of receiving conflicting demands or of having a good-faith doubt. The four settlement procedures are (1) mediation, (2) arbitration, (3) litigation, and (4) escrow disbursement order.

REVIEW QUESTIONS

1. A broker maintains an interest-bearing escrow account. He secures written agreements from all parties to a transaction stating that he is to receive all accrued interest on escrowed funds for the benefit of the Association for Retarded Citizens. Each month when the broker prepares his reconciliation statement, he transfers the accrued interest into his operating account. Which statement is TRUE of this situation?
   a. The broker should transfer the accrued interest into a non-interest-bearing escrow account.
   b. The broker cannot disburse interest earned on escrowed funds to anyone other than the parties to the transaction.
   c. The broker can be charged with commingling escrow funds with his own business funds.
   d. The broker has withdrawn earned interest from the interest-bearing account properly and now may disburse a check from his operating account to the charitable organization.

2. A broker employs a bookkeeper, who is responsible for maintaining the brokerage's accounting ledgers. She also prepares and signs all checks disbursed from the broker's escrow and operating accounts. Which statement is TRUE of this situation?
   a. The bookkeeper may not prepare and sign commission checks unless she is a licensed real estate sales associate.
   b. The broker could be charged with culpable negligence for allowing his bookkeeper to withdraw funds from the escrow account.
   c. The broker does not need to sign the checks; however, he must be an authorized signatory on the account.
   d. The broker must countersign all checks disbursed from the escrow account.

3. A sales associate receives an earnest money deposit from a prospective buyer on Monday, late in the evening. She turns it over to the bookkeeper on Tuesday morning. Assuming no legal holidays are involved, when must the check be deposited in the broker's escrow account?
   a. The broker is in violation of Chapter 475, F.S., because he should have deposited the check into his escrow account immediately.
   b. The check must be deposited into the escrow account no later than the end of the business day on Thursday.
   c. The check must be deposited into the escrow account no later than the end of the business day on Wednesday.
   d. The check must be deposited into the escrow account no later than the end of the business day on Friday.

4. An investor made an offer on a sales associate's listing. The purchase and sale agreement indicated that the investor was depositing $5,000 as an earnest money deposit, payable to Bob Wilson, Attorney Trust Account. Which statement is TRUE of this situation?
   a. The earnest money deposit must be placed in an account the sales associate's broker maintains.
   b. Bob Wilson must have a real estate license to serve as escrow agent.
   c. The situation describes an acceptable arrangement for handling escrow funds.
   d. The broker must be a signatory on Bob Wilson's trust account.

5. Today is April 1. The sales associate has just received the investor's earnest money check dated April 7. Furthermore, the check is made payable to Bob Wilson, Attorney Trust Account. What is the BEST wording to include in the purchase and sale agreement?
   a. Receipt is hereby acknowledged of the sum of $5,000 dated April 7 payable to Bob Wilson, Attorney Trust Account (by check) as an earnest money deposit.
   b. Receipt is hereby acknowledged of the sum of $5,000 as an earnest money deposit.
   c. Receipt is hereby acknowledged of a promise to pledge $5,000 as an earnest money deposit on or before April 7.
   d. Receipt is hereby acknowledged of a check for $5,000 as an earnest money deposit to be held in escrow.

6. Which statement is FALSE regarding funds handled by a broker?
   a. A broker may delegate to a CPA the duty of preparing the monthly reconciliation statements for the broker's review and signature.
   b. Brokers who collect rent checks payable to the brokerage on behalf of the landlord may deposit the funds into the broker's operating account and then disburse a check from the operating account payable to the landlord.
   c. If a brokerage office has more than one broker registered under the brokerage, only one of the brokers must be a signatory on the escrow account.
   d. Real estate brokers are not required by law to maintain an escrow account.

7. A real estate broker may NOT set up an escrow account in which Florida-based institution?
   a. Credit union
   b. Securities firm
   c. Savings association
   d. Bank

8. During the last calendar month, a broker deposited four earnest money checks totaling $15,000. The escrow account ledger at the end of the last month reflects three outstanding checks totaling $10,000. (The account balance was zero at the beginning of the month.) What is the broker's trust liability for the month?
   a. $5,000
   b. $10,000
   c. $15,000
   d. $25,000

9. A broker's bank statement indicates an ending balance for the previous month of $15,000. $10,000 worth of deposits for the previous month remains in transit. $4,500 worth of checks for the previous month is outstanding. What is the reconciled bank balance for the month?
   a. $9,500
   b. $11,500
   c. $20,500
   d. $29,500

10. A broker has deposited $100 of her personal funds in her escrow account to cover monthly bank servicing fees. Which statement is TRUE of this situation?
   a. The broker is guilty of commingling.
   b. The broker must account for the $100 on her monthly reconciliation statement.
   c. The broker has an overage in her account of $100 and therefore is subject to a citation and fine of $200.
   d. The broker must transfer the $100 to her operating account.

11. A contract on a parcel of land falls through, and both the buyer and seller demand the earnest money deposit. What should the broker do?
   a. Notify the Commission within 30 business days that he has conflicting demands.
   b. Notify the Commission in writing within 15 business days of receiving the conflicting demands.
   c. Request an escrow disbursement order within 15 business days of the last demand.
   d. Notify the Commission in writing within 15 business days and request a declaratory judgment from the assistant attorney general's office within 30 business days.

12. A sales associate collects a binder deposit on Sunday afternoon. By the end of business on which day must the funds be deposited into the broker's escrow account?
   a. Monday
   b. Tuesday
   c. Wednesday
   d. Thursday

13. A tenant has vacated the premises at the end of her lease. The broker has inspected the property and found pet stains on the carpet. He assesses the cost to clean the carpet at $125. The broker gives the tenant proper notice of his intention to impose a claim against the security deposit. Which statement is TRUE of this situation?
   a. The broker must notify the FREC of conflicting demands immediately.
   b. The tenant must be given an opportunity to object properly to the claim against the security deposit.
   c. The broker should notify the Commission of the conflicting demands within 15 business days, then institute one of the settlement procedures within 30 days.
   d. The broker may immediately disburse the $375 balance to the tenant directly from the escrow account and transfer the $125 to his operating account to pay the carpet cleaning company.

14. In connection with sales escrow accounts, the Florida Real Estate Commission has rules and regulations that
    a. allow a broker to deposit up to $5,000 of personal funds in an escrow account as long as adequate records are kept.
    b. prohibit a broker from depositing more than $1,000 of personal funds in an escrow account.
    c. require the broker to disburse all accrued interest to the principal.
    d. require a broker to prepare escrow disbursement orders when making all disbursements from an escrow account.

CHAPTER

5 OFFICE INSPECTIONS AND THE DISCIPLINARY PROCESS

KEY TERMS

administrative complaint
citation
complainant
complaint
Division of Administrative Hearings (DOAH)
final order
first-degree misdemeanor
formal complaint
formal hearing
informal hearing
legally sufficient
notice of noncompliance
probable cause
recommended order
respondent
second-degree misdemeanor
stipulation
subpoena
summary suspension

OVERVIEW

This chapter begins with a discussion of how to prepare for an office inspection and audit of the broker's escrow (trust) account. The chapter also details the disciplinary process and concludes with an explanation of the Real Estate Recovery Fund.

Once you have completed this chapter, you should be able to:

- describe the office inspection process;
- describe the information and records that must be made available to the inspector during a routine office inspection and escrow account audit;
- explain the procedures involved in the reporting of violations, the investigation of complaints, and the conduct of hearings;
- describe the elements of a valid complaint;
- describe the composition of the probable cause panel;
- identify reasons why an application would be denied;
- recognize actions that would cause a licensee to be subject to suspension or revocation;
- distinguish between a first degree misdemeanor and a second degree misdemeanor;
- identify which violation of F.S. 475 is a misdemeanor of the first degree;

- identify individuals who would be eligible to seek reimbursement from the Real Estate Recovery Fund; and
- describe the monetary limits imposed by law on the Real Estate Recovery Fund.

DIVISION OF REAL ESTATE AUTHORITY AND RESPONSIBILITY

Chapter 475, F.S., provides for the regulation of real estate brokers, broker associates, sales associates, permitted instructors, and real estate schools. The Division of Real Estate, Department of Business and Professional Regulation, has the authority and responsibility to:

- routinely inspect and audit real estate schools and real estate brokerage businesses;
- investigate complaints; and
- monitor compliance with rules and statutes.

The DBPR is authorized to inspect and audit real estate brokers and brokerage offices at all reasonable hours to determine whether they comply with Chapters 475 and 455, F.S., and administrative rules promulgated under those chapters. The FREC is authorized to issue licenses and permits; determine the legal sufficiency of complaints; take disciplinary actions against real estate practitioners who violate laws or rules governing the profession; and deny, suspend, or revoke licenses and permits.

Office Inspections and Audits

The Florida Real Estate Commission delegates the inspection of real estate offices of those brokers who hold active licenses. The Investigation Section, under the direction of the DRE's Bureau Chief of Enforcement, routinely conducts office inspections and audits of the escrow accounts of real estate brokerage businesses, as authorized by Rule 61J2-14.012, F.A.C. The DRE also is authorized to make routine inspections of real estate proprietary schools.

The inspection process usually is initiated when the DRE sends a broker a letter informing the licensee of its intent to conduct a routine office inspection and review of the escrow account(s), if applicable. The letter outlines what types of records and information the investigator will review and what documents must be made available during the inspection. The broker and the investigator then agree on a date and time for the office visit.

During the office inspection, the investigator checks for compliance with the rules and statutes pertaining to both the brokerage office and signage. The investigator also inspects for current, valid licenses and compliance with the brokerage relationship disclosure requirements, as discussed below.

Minimum office requirements. The inspector verifies compliance with Sections 475.22 and 475.24, F.S., and Rules 61J2-10.022 and 10.023, F.A.C., concerning maintenance of an office and branch offices (see also chapter 2).

Office entrance sign. The investigator inspects the entrance sign for compliance with Section 475.22, F.S., governing the wording of real estate entrance signs (see also chapter 2).

Licenses. The inspector reviews copies of all licenses and registrations of the broker, brokerage entity, broker associates, sales associates, and branch offices. The investigator verifies whether all of the officers, directors, broker associates, and sales associates hold current and valid licenses pursuant to Rule 61J2-5.019, F.A.C.

Brokerage relationship disclosures. The inspector reviews brokerage relationship disclosures to verify compliance with the agency law (see also chapter 10).

Escrow accounts. A review of each escrow (trust) account includes inspection of all the records and transaction files associated with the account, including:

- monthly reconciliation statements (for the last 6 to 12 months);
- bank statements and canceled checks (for the last 6 to 12 months);
- checkbooks, deposit books, and bank deposit receipts;
- ledger books or computer records of sale and property management records;
- pending sale contracts (files);
- voided contracts and offers with escrow funds presently being held;
- any earnest money deposit disputes; and
- property management contracts, agreements, and leases (files).

The investigator also may require that the broker fax an up-to-date interim statement from the bank of all deposits and disbursements from the date of the last bank statement to the close of business the day before the audit. The investigator then completes an Office Inspection & Escrow/Trust Audit Form (see Figure 5.1) during the visit.

DISCIPLINARY PROCEDURE

The Division of Real Estate (DRE), Department of Business and Professional Regulation, is responsible for investigative matters related to real estate. This includes investigations to verify information provided by applicants and investigations of complaints against licensees. The Florida Real Estate Commission passes judgment on the DRE's investigations.

THE COMPLAINT PROCESS

Seven steps are involved in the process of dealing with complaints of alleged violations:

1. A complaint is filed
2. Investigation of the complaint
3. Probable cause determination
4. Formal complaint is issued if probable cause is found
5. Informal hearing or formal hearing is conducted
6. Final order is issued
7. Judicial review (appeal) of the final order

FIGURE 5.1 ■ Office Inspection & Escrow/Trust Account Audit Form

DEPARTMENT OF BUSINESS & PROFESSIONAL REGULATION

Division of Real Estate

OFFICE INSPECTION & ESCROW/TRUST ACCOUNT AUDIT FORM

DATE________________

NAME OF BROKER	NAME OF BROKER	
BROKER LICENSE #	BROKER LICENSE #	
NAME OF BROKER	NAME OF BROKER	
BROKER LICENSE #	BROKER LICENSE #	
NAME OF BROKERAGE	BROKERAGE LICENSE #	PHONE NUMBER
STREET ADDRESS CITY	COUNTY	ZIP

	YES	NO	REMARKS
OFFICE (RULE 61J2-10.022 & .023) ________	—	—	
REQUIRED OFFICE SIGN (RULE 61J2-10.024) ________	—	—	
AGENCY OR TRANSACTION BROKER DISCLOSURE (s.475.278, F.S.) ________	—	—	
MONTHLY RECONCILIATIONS (RULE 61J2-14.012) ________	—	—	
SALES: TOTAL TRUST LIABILITY ________			
RECON BANK BALANCE ________			
(SHORT/OVER) AMOUNT ________	—	—	
SECURITY DEPOSIT: TOTAL TRUST LIABILITY ________			
RECON BANK BALANCE ________			
(SHORT/OVER) AMOUNT ________	—	—	
RENTAL DISTRIBUTION: TOTAL TRUST LIABILITY ________			
RECON BANK BALANCE ________			
(SHORT/OVER) AMOUNT ________	—	—	

REMARKS:

I HEREBY CERTIFY THAT, TO THE BEST OF MY KNOWLEDGE, ALL RECORDS PERTAINING TO MY SALES ESCROW/TRUST ACCOUNT(S) AND MY RENTAL PROPERTY MANAGEMENT ACCOUNT(S) HAVE BEEN PROVIDED TO THE INVESTIGATOR . THE ABOVE VIOLATIONS WERE BROUGHT TO MY ATTENTION THIS DATE AND THROUGHLY EXPLAINED. I WILL TAKE CORRECTIVE ACTION WITHIN _____ DAYS AND PROVIDE DBPR WITH PHOTOS, SKETCHES AND DOCUMENTATION OF THE CORRECTIVE ACTION TAKEN.

(SIGNATURE OF BROKER) (DATE) (SIGNATURE OF INVESTIGATOR) (COMPUTER ID #) (DATE)

CITATION ISSUED YES NO #: ________________ COMPLAINT DOCKETED YES NO #:________________

NOTICE OF NON-COMPLIANCE YES______ NO_____

Pursuant to s. 455.225 (3), F.S., and s. 120.695, F.S. the Commission sets forth rules which are considered minor violations for which the DBPR shall provide a licensee with a notice of noncompliance. A violation of a rule is considered a minor violation if it does not result in economic or physical harm to a person or adversely affect the public health, safety, or welfare or create a significant threat of such harm. **The notice of noncompliance shall be issued only for an initial offense of a minor violation.**

VIOLATION:________________

CORRECTIVE ACTION:________________

WHITE COPY – FIELD OFFICE YELLOW COPY – LICENSEE

Reprinted with permission of the Division of Real Estate, DRE.

Step 1: Filing the Complaint

The complaint process begins when a **complaint** (an alleged violation of a law or rule) is filed with the DBPR.

Written complaints are reviewed initially to confirm jurisdiction and to determine a licensee's status. The complaint then is referred to the appropriate Division. Any complaint that is filed in writing and is legally sufficient will be investigated. A complaint is **legally sufficient** if it contains facts indicating that a violation of any of the following has occurred:

- Florida statute
- Any existing, legally enacted DBPR rule
- Any existing, legally enacted FREC rule

Anyone may file a complaint against a licensee, an applicant, or an unlicensed person for actions believed to violate Chapter 475, F.S. The alleged violation(s) need not pertain to a real estate transaction and need not have taken place in Florida. A Uniform Complaint Form is available from the DBPR (see web link below). Complaints that are not found to be legally sufficient are dismissed.

The DBPR may investigate an anonymous complaint or one made by a confidential informant if the complaint is in writing and is legally sufficient; if the alleged violation of law or rules is substantial; and if the Department has reason to believe, after preliminary inquiry, that the alleged violations in the complaint are true.

WEB LINK

You can download the "Uniform Complaint" Form DBPR-0070 and instructions at **http://www.myfloridalicense.com/dbpr/dbpr/le_portal/dbpr-0070-1.pdf**.

Step 2: Investigation

The DBPR may initiate an investigation on its own if it has reasonable cause to believe that a licensee has violated a Florida statute, DBPR rule, or FREC rule. Furthermore, the DBPR may conduct an investigation without notification to anyone subject to the investigation if the act under investigation is a criminal offense.

If the original **complainant** (person who files the complaint) withdraws the complaint or otherwise indicates a desire not to cause it to be investigated or prosecuted to completion, the Department may continue with the investigation and the Commission may take the appropriate final action on the complaint. Investigators, located in eight regional offices throughout Florida, are trained to conduct real estate and appraisal investigations. The DBPR, through the headquarters of the DRE, forwards legally sufficient complaints to the appropriate regional office.

When an investigation of a subject is undertaken, the DBPR will forward a copy of the complaint to the subject or the subject's attorney. The subject of the investigation may submit a written response to the complaint. The response must be considered by the probable cause panel. Once the fact gathering is completed, the DBPR prepares an investigative report and sends it to the DRE headquarters, along with a synopsis of findings, interviews, and applicable exhibits. The DRE forwards the report to the legal section for review and prosecution, as applicable. A complaint and all information obtained during any resulting investigation must be treated as confidential until ten days after probable cause has been found to exist or the subject of the investigation waives the privilege of confidentiality, whichever occurs first.

The DBPR is empowered to administer oaths; take depositions; and examine respondents, witnesses, and complainants. It can also issue subpoenas to obtain records, documents, or information that is material to the investigation. A Department investigator interviews the subject of the allegation(s), and if applicable, an audit is performed of any escrow account(s). Once the investigative process is completed, and provided the complaint is legally sufficient, the Department prepares a written investigate report that then is submitted to the probable cause panel.

The report consists of the investigative findings and contains recommendations regarding the existence of **probable cause** (reasonable grounds for prosecution) and a recommended course of action. If a licensee who is the subject of a consumer complaint is not found to be in violation of rule or statute, the case is submitted to the probable cause panel with a recommendation for dismissal.

Summary suspension. In rare situations, during the investigative process, the DBPR or the DRE may uncover something so serious that it cannot allow the licensee to continue to endanger the public welfare. For example, the investigator may discover that a broker has stolen thousands of dollars from the escrow account. In such extreme circumstances, the DBPR or the FREC may decide that the licensee cannot be allowed to continue to practice real estate during the normal disciplinary process. Such situations require emergency action. The DBPR Secretary (or a legally appointed designee) has the authority to issue a **summary suspension** (also referred to as an *emergency suspension order* or *final summary order*).

When it has been demonstrated that a summary suspension is necessary, due process does not require a hearing prior to the emergency suspension, provided a formal proceeding for suspension or revocation is promptly instituted.

Step 3: Probable Cause

Chapter 455, F.S., mandates that the determination as to whether probable cause exists is made by majority vote of a board's probable cause panel, or by the DBPR, if the profession does not have a board. The FREC *probable cause panel* is composed of two current members or one current and one former member of the FREC. The panel must include at least one professional member. If a former professional board member serves on the panel, the former Commissioner must currently hold an active real estate license. A consumer member, if available, may serve on the probable cause panel.

Probable cause proceedings are not open to the public, and the remaining FREC members are prohibited from attending. The segregation of the Commission members allows the probable cause panel to serve in a "grand jury" type of arrangement. Because the remaining Commissioners do not participate in the probable cause proceedings, they are able to maintain objectivity in the matter if it comes before the Commission in an informal hearing.

The probable cause panel's sole responsibility is to determine whether probable cause exists. The probable cause panel reviews the facts of the case and the staff attorney's report, which contains the investigative findings and the staff attorney's recommendations. After a complete review of the record, the probable cause panel, by majority vote, makes a determination as to whether **probable cause** (reasonable grounds for prosecution) exists. If the complaint information presented to the probable cause panel is not adequate in content, the panel may request, and the DBPR must provide, any available or necessary additional information. A request for additional information must be made within the time frame set forth in the statute.

The probable cause panel must make a decision within 30 days after receipt of the final investigative report, unless an extension is granted by the Secretary of the Department. If the panel fails to act within the statutory time limit (plus legal extensions), the Department may make a determination in the case.

If probable cause is found, the DBPR (or the FREC) must give timely written notice to a licensee's broker or employer when a formal complaint has been filed against a sales associate or a broker associate.

If the panel finds that probable cause does not exist, the DBPR is allowed ten days to override that decision and to file charges. Furthermore, if the Department finds that the panel was unwise in deciding that probable cause existed, it may choose not to prosecute a complaint. In such cases, the Department refers the matter to the FREC. The Commission may retain independent legal counsel, employ investigators, and continue the investigation if it deems necessary. If the panel finds that probable cause does not exist, it may simply dismiss the case, or it may dismiss the case with a *letter of guidance* to the subject. Once the probable cause proceeding has been concluded, the complainant and the subject of the investigation are sent written notification of the outcome.

Step 4: Formal Complaint

If probable cause is found to exist, the probable cause panel will direct the DBPR to file a formal complaint against the subject of the investigation (**respondent**). A **formal complaint,** also referred to as an **administrative complaint**, is an outline of allegations of facts and charges against the licensee. When an administrative complaint is mailed to a licensee, the licensee also receives an Election of Rights. The licensee is instructed to select one of three options in the Election of Rights and return the completed Election of Rights form to the DBPR on or before the 21st day after receipt of the administrative complaint. The licensee may choose to:

1. not dispute the allegations of fact and request an informal hearing;
2. dispute the allegations of fact and request a formal hearing; or
3. not dispute the allegations of fact and waive the right to be heard.

Sometimes a licensee-respondent and the licensee's attorney (if the licensee has legal counsel) will meet with a DRE attorney prior to a hearing to discuss a possible settlement and enter into a stipulation. A **stipulation** is an agreement as to the facts of the case and the penalty reached between the attorneys for the DRE and the licensee or licensee's attorney. To be effective, any agreed upon stipulation must be approved by the FREC. The licensee and the licensee's legal counsel, where there is one, are encouraged to appear before the FREC to defend the stipulation. The FREC will approve or deny the stipulation during a Commission meeting. If the FREC denies the stipulation, it usually provides guidance to the DRE attorney concerning additional penalties it believes appropriate in order for it to support a revised stipulation.

Occasionally the DBPR will issue a *nolle prosequi* (or nullification of the prosecution). If the prosecutor agrees, the case goes back to the probable cause panel to allow the prosecutor to withdraw the administrative complaint. A nolle prosequi, therefore, is a formal entry on the record that the prosecution declares it will not prosecute the case further. This procedure is used when the prosecution has erred in the drafting of the complaint, such as, the prosecutor made allegations that are incorrect, or the facts do not amount to violations of law. For example, a nolle prosequi might result if a licensee is issued an administrative complaint for not completing the required continuing education for a renewal cycle, however, the licensee has the school report indicating the licensee completed the required course with a passing grade.

Step 5: Case is Presented in Either an Informal Hearing or a Formal Hearing

If the licensee-respondent's case was not resolved with a stipulation, the respondent's case will either be heard by the FREC in an informal hearing or the case may be heard before an administrative law judge in a formal hearing. The licensee-respondent must admit to the alleged facts to be entitled to an informal hearing. If the licensee-respondent disputes the alleged facts that are made in the complaint, the licensee-respondent's case must be heard by an administrative law judge in a formal hearing. The licensee-respondent must be given at least 14 days notice of a hearing. The notice of the hearing informs the licensee-respondent of the time, place, and nature of the hearing. The notice also includes a statement regarding the legal authority and jurisdiction under which the hearing is being held.

An informal hearing is an expedited way of resolving the disciplinary case provided the licensee does not dispute the alleged facts stated in the complaint. During an **informal hearing**, normally held at a regular Commission meeting, the licensee-respondent is given an opportunity to explain the details of the case with supporting evidence and/or witnesses. Any Commissioners who served on the probable cause panel for the particular complaint may not participate in this informal hearing. If any party raises an issue of disputed fact during an informal hearing, the hearing is terminated and a formal hearing will be scheduled before an administrative law judge. The FREC will determine based on the admitted facts whether the licensee is guilty of the charges alleged in the complaint. If the licensee is found guilty of the charges, the FREC will determine which penalties are appropriate based on the details of the case, taking into consideration any *mitigating* circumstances (reasons to reduce the impact of the violation), and it will issue a final order. (Refer also to Step 6 on the next page.)

If the licensee-respondent requests a **formal hearing** or if the licensee-respondent disputes the allegations, the DBPR requests that the case be prosecuted under Chapter 120, F.S. Hearings under Chapter 120 are conducted by full-time Florida administrative law judges who are employed by the **Division of Administrative Hearings (DOAH)**. The DOAH may legally employ only those persons who have been members of The Florida Bar in good standing for the preceding five years. Administrative law judges are not subject to control, supervision, or direction by any party, commission, or department of state government. Once an administrative law judge is assigned, the DBPR may take no further action except as a litigating party.

The administrative law judge has the power to swear witnesses, to take their testimony under oath, and to issue subpoenas. A **subpoena** is a command to appear at a certain time and place to give testimony or to produce records. Failure to comply with a subpoena could result in a finding of contempt of court.

The administrative law judge prepares and submits to the DBPR and to all other parties a **recommended order** that includes the administrative law judge's findings and conclusions and the recommended penalty, if any, in accordance with the Commission's range of penalties as set forth in rule. Any party of record in the case may submit (within the statutory time limit) written exceptions to the administrative law judge's recommended order.

WEB LINK

To learn more about the formal hearing process, visit the Florida Division of Administrative Hearings Web site at: **http://www.doah.state.fl.us/ALJ/Rules/**. Select "Uniform Rules of Procedure."

Step 6: Final Order

The FREC (with the members who served on the probable cause panel excused) issues the final order in each disciplinary case. The **final order** is the FREC's final decision as to innocence or guilt and the determination of the appropriate penalty. The FREC issues a final order at the conclusion of an informal hearing. If the matter was heard by an administrative law judge in a formal hearing, the FREC must review and consider the administrative law judge's findings and recommended order before issuing its final order.

The respondent may appear in person or be represented by an attorney or both. Independent legal counsel represents the Commission in disciplinary proceedings. The Commission members who did not serve on the probable cause panel consider the administrative law judge's report and recommended order, plus any filed exceptions to the report and the accused party's final arguments, if any. After all final arguments are heard, the Commission members make a determination and issue the final order, concluding the quasi-judicial process.

The final order must be in writing. It must include the facts established during the proceeding and state each conclusion of law separately. A copy of the final order is mailed to each party in the case. The notice must inform the recipient of the appeal process. The final order becomes effective 30 days after it has been entered. A licensee has the right to practice real estate during the complaint process and up until the final order becomes effective.

The FREC is empowered to publish and disseminate its orders, but only after they have become final. Orders become final after the period reserved for appeal has expired or after a court has upheld the Commission's decision on appeal. The FREC is authorized to publish the names and addresses of any parties concerned in a final order.

Step 7: Judicial Review (Appeal)

The licensee-respondent may challenge the final order within 30 days by filing an appeal. The petition of judicial review (notice of appeal) must be filed with the DBPR and with the appropriate district court. The licensee may request a *stay of enforcement*. A stay of enforcement, if granted, stops the enforcement of a suspension or revocation in the final order pending the outcome of the appeal process. To obtain a stay of the final order, the district court of appeals must issue a *writ of supersedeas*. A writ of supersedeas is an order issued by a court containing a command to stay (stop), in this case, the DBPR from suspending or revoking a real estate license pending the outcome of the appeal process.

If the reviewing court finds that a material error in procedure by the FREC has affected the fairness of the hearing or the correctness of the action taken, the case will be sent back to the FREC for corrective action. Unless the court finds legitimate grounds to set

FIGURE 5.2 ■ The Complaint Process

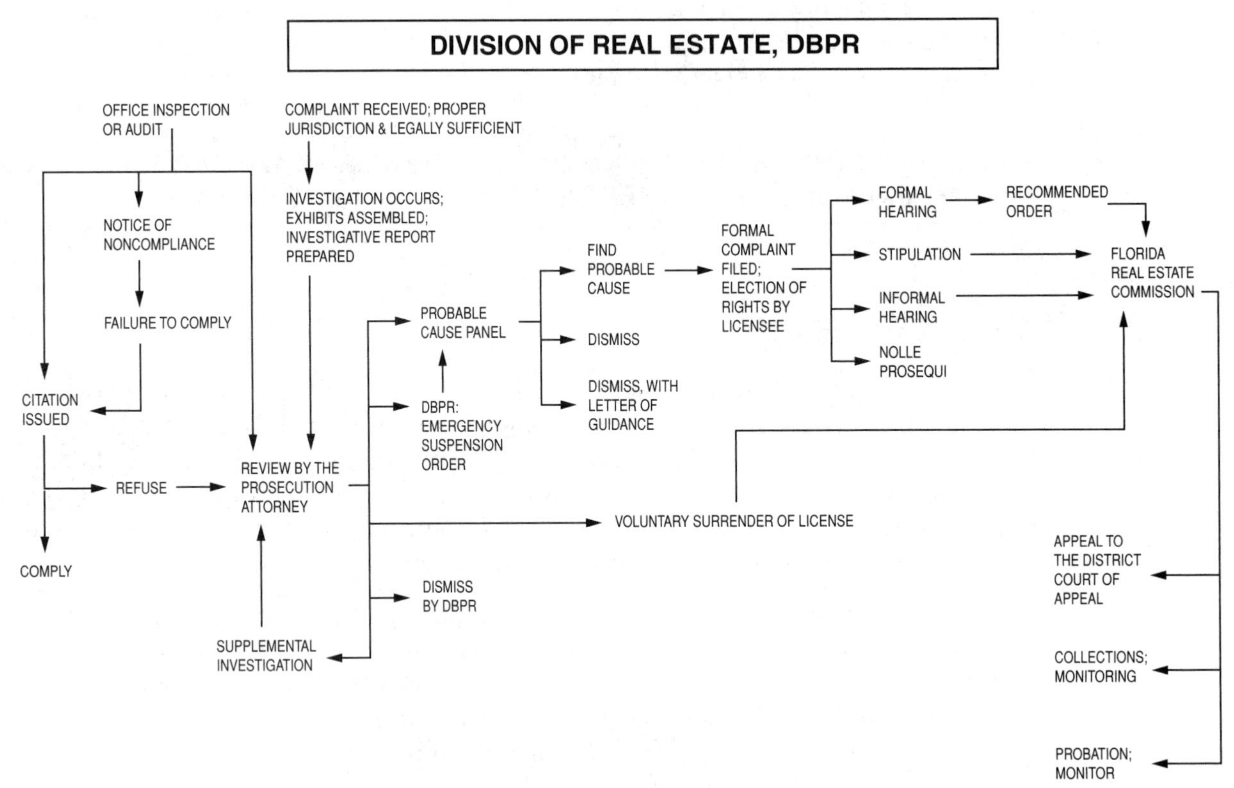

aside, modify, remand for further FREC proceeding, order additional action by the FREC, or order some auxiliary relief under Florida Statute 120.68, the court is required to affirm (support) the action taken by the Commission.

The DBPR is authorized to seek judicial review of any final order issued by the Commission. If a FREC final order is affirmed, reversed, or set aside, a mandate (copy) is filed with the Commission attesting to that event. The respondent's rights and privileges as a licensee are restored as of the date of filing, if the final order is reversed. Thereafter, the matters examined and the charges alleged cannot be reexamined in any other proceedings concerning the licensure of that person or party. When the inquiry or proceeding is in reference to an application to become licensed, the application is approved and processed. If a court reverses or sets aside a final order, the court may award attorney's fees and costs to the aggrieved prevailing party. The complaint process is diagrammed in Figure 5.2.

VIOLATIONS AND PENALTIES

The FREC is authorized to deny, suspend, or revoke licenses; to issue citations; and to otherwise discipline licensees. For the purpose of the following discussion, the term *license* includes the terms *registration*, *certification*, and *permit*. The grounds and penalties for these actions are listed in the following sections.

Grounds for Denial

Denial of an applicant's request for licensure keeps the applicant from becoming licensed to practice real estate in Florida. Several reasons for denial exist. Some denials result from errors made in the application process, or from failing the state licensing examination. When such instances occur, the applicant may correct or file a new application, or submit an application to retake the exam. Examples of grounds for license denial are:

- neglecting to answer all questions completely on the application;
- neglecting to forward the proper fees with the application request;
- neglecting to correct errors or omissions on applications returned; and
- failing to complete successfully the required end-of-course examination.

Other grounds for denial are more serious and result in an applicant being denied licensure. Examples of cause for license denial are that the applicant:

- lacked minimum qualifications;
- did not possess the character required by the provisions of Florida Statutes 455 and 475;
- did not possess the general competence to deal with the public or complaints against the applicant were received by the FREC or the DBPR;
- was guilty of acts that would have resulted in revocation or suspension of the license had the applicant already been licensed;
- acted in violation of any provision of F.S. 475.42 or was at the time subject to discipline under F.S. 475.25; and
- received assistance or cheated while taking a state license exam.

If the FREC denies an applicant on two occasions, the applicant may appeal to the Division of Administrative Hearings (DOAH). The DOAH makes a recommendation to the FREC, which may adopt or reject the DOAH recommendation. A judicial court may only vacate the order of the FREC if it denied the applicant due process or breached a mandate of law. A court of law cannot force the FREC to issue a license because Florida statutes reserved the power to grant or deny a real estate license to the FREC.

Grounds for Suspension

Suspension of an individual's license is a temporary penalty. The maximum period for which the FREC may suspend a license is ten years. Florida statutes refer to many acts that are illegal, any one of which may result in suspension. Each illegal act constitutes grounds for suspension or revocation of licensure, depending on the seriousness attached to the offense by the Commission. A second suspension for the same or a different violation may result in revocation of the license, registration, certification, or permit.

REVOCATION OR CANCELLATION WITHOUT PREJUDICE

A license may be revoked or canceled if it was issued through the mistake or inadvertence of the Commission. Such revocation or cancellation shall not prejudice any subsequent application for licensure filed by the person against whom such action was taken.

Reference: Section 475.25(2) F.S.

Grounds for Revocation

The most severe type of administrative penalty the FREC is authorized to impose is revocation of a license. Revocation of a license is permanent. When the FREC revokes a license, that licensee is put out of the real estate business. Exceptions to "permanent" occur when a licensee has filed for renewal but has not complied with the continuing or post-licensing education requirements prior to the expiration date or when an individual filed an application for licensure that contained false or fraudulent information. In such cases, the applicant may not reapply for a sales associate's license for five years unless the Commission specifies a lesser period of time in the final order based on mitigating factors presented by the licensee. At their discretion the FREC is empowered to revoke a licensee's license for any of the causes that constitute grounds for suspension or denial. Suspension or revocation plus a $5,000 fine is the minimum penalty for obtaining a license by fraud, misrepresentation, or concealment.

When a real estate broker's license is suspended or revoked, all licenses issued to sales associates and broker associates registered with the penalized broker are placed in *involuntary inactive status*. If the revoked or suspended broker is a partnership or corporation, affected sales associates, broker associates, partners, officers, and directors may request registration with a new employer or in the same partnership or corporation if it reorganizes to requalify under Florida statutes and FREC rules. The sales associates and broker associates are free to seek another employer and register as active under the new employer.

Types of Penalties

There are three types of penalties that may be imposed for violations of real estate license law: administrative, civil, and criminal.

1. Administrative penalties. The Commission may impose an administrative penalty for violations of the law or rules and regulations. Possible administrative penalties imposed by the FREC include denial of an application for a license; refusal to recertify a license for renewal; revocation of a license; suspension of a license for not more than ten years; a fine not to exceed $5,000 for each separate violation of Chapters 455 and 475, F.S.; and probation, reprimand, or other penalty (for example, publication of the disciplinary action taken against a licensee and the requirement to complete additional education).

The Commission may, in addition to other disciplinary penalties, place a licensee on probation. The FREC is empowered to set the time period and conditions of probation. Probationary conditions may include, for example, requiring the licensee to attend a prelicense

SUMMARY OF TYPES OF ADMINISTRATIVE PENALTIES

- **Denial** of license application (or refusal to renew a license)
- **Letter of reprimand** is a letter that is placed in the licensee's file describing a minor incidence of misconduct that resulted in no disciplinary action (also called a *letter of guidance*)
- **Notice of noncompliance** is a warning for a minor violation (an initial offense only) that allows a licensee 15 days to correct the minor infraction without consequence (nonresponse could result in disciplinary action)
- **Citation** concerns violations that are of no substantial threat to the public involving a fine that currently ranges from $100 to $500
- **Probation** allows the licensee to continue to practice real estate under the guidance of the FREC for a period of time while completing conditions specified by the FREC such as to complete education courses, attend FREC meetings, and satisfy all of the terms of the penalty
- **Fine** may be up to $5,000 for each violation of Chapter 455 and Chapter 475
- **Suspension** of license (for up to ten years)
- **Revocation** of license is permanent (with continuing education exception and license application exception)

or post-license course or another educational offering, to submit to and successfully complete the state-administered license examination, or to be subject to periodic inspections by a DBPR investigator.

The DBPR/DRE may issue a **notice of noncompliance** as a first response to a minor violation by a licensee. It must identify the specific statute(s) and rule(s) violated, provide information on how to comply, and state the time to comply. The Commission has established by rule minor violations that do not endanger the public health, safety, and welfare and that do not demonstrate a serious inability to practice the profession. Rule 61J2 24.003, F.A.C., lists the various violations for which a notice of noncompliance may be issued for a first-time offense, including, for example, a sales associate serving as an officer of a brokerage corporation. A notice of noncompliance may also be issued if a broker fails to register a trade name, does not have the proper office entrance sign, or neglects to sign the escrow account reconciliation in instances where the account balances. If the licensee fails to take action to correct the minor violation within 15 days after being notified, the licensee may be issued a citation. However, if the violation is not listed in the citation rule, the licensee may be subjected to other disciplinary penalties.

DBPR investigators-auditors have the authority to immediately issue citations in the field for minor violations discovered during an investigation or audit. **Citations** involve fines that currently range from $100 to $500 per offense and may include other assessments (for example, require educational course attendance). Several of the more common

LICENSE REISSUE

The Department shall reissue the license of a licensee against whom disciplinary action was taken upon certification by the Commission that the licensee has complied with all of the terms and conditions of the final order imposing discipline.

Section 475.25(3), F.S.

offenses cited include failure to timely notify the DBPR of a licensee's current mailing address or of a change in the current mailing address, failure to secure the written permission of all interested parties prior to placing trust funds into an interest bearing escrow account, and advertising in a manner in which a reasonable person would not know that one is dealing with a licensee or brokerage. A licensee receiving a citation has *30 days* to accept or reject the alleged violation(s), as specified in the citation. If the licensee does not dispute the matter, the citation penalty will become effective (a *final order*) and the case will be closed. If the licensee disputes the alleged violation(s), the licensee must file a written objection. The licensee will be allowed to state his or her case and, based on the merits, will have the case dismissed or carried forward to a formal hearing. If the licensee fails to pay the fine in a timely manner, the Commission will file an administrative complaint.

2. Civil penalties. Civil penalties may be enforced by the courts if a person has performed any real estate services without a license. The courts may rule that no sales commission is due.

3. Criminal penalties. A violation of Florida Statute 475 or any lawful order, rule, or regulation is legally a misdemeanor of the second degree (except as noted below). It may be punishable by a fine of not more than $500 and/or by imprisonment for not more than 60 days. A corporation may only be fined because a corporation cannot be imprisoned. All imprisonment penalties or fines, except administrative fines, must be obtained in a court of law because the Commission lacks the authority to assess such penalties. The FREC must report any criminal violation of Chapter 475, F.S., to the appropriate state's attorney's office.

First-degree criminal penalty. There is one violation of real estate license law that is a first-degree misdemeanor: failing to provide accurate and current rental information for a fee. The penalty for a **first-degree misdemeanor** is a fine of not more than $1,000 and/or up to one year in jail.

Other penalty actions. The assessing of one of the three types of penalties (administrative, civil, or criminal) does not prevent or affect the prosecution of any other proceeding. The same facts that are the basis for the prosecution of violations of real estate license law may prove to be an offense committed under other state statutes. Both violations may be charged, but the punishment (fine and/or sentence) cannot be greater than the highest prescribed in either statute. However, the Commission may, in addition to any other disciplinary action imposed, assess costs related to the investigation and prosecution of the case, excluding attorney's fees.

Unlicensed practice of real estate. The Secretary of the DBPR assigns a probable cause panel and a hearing officer to hear cases of unlicensed activity. The DBPR can issue fines of up to $5,000 per count to a person it finds guilty of unlicensed activity.

The DBPR may issue a cease and desist order to an unlicensed person who has violated F.S. 475, F.S. 455, or any other statute relating to the practice of real estate. The DBPR may also file a proceeding in the name of the state requesting the circuit court to issue an injunction or a *writ of mandamus* ordering the unlicensed activity to stop. If the person found guilty of unlicensed activity refuses to pay a fine issued by the DBPR, it may seek enforcement of the penalty through a civil court. The DBPR must refer any criminal matters to the State Attorney's Office. The state attorney may institute criminal prosecution against an unlicensed person. It is a felony of the third degree for a person to perform real estate services for compensation without a real estate license. The criminal penalty for a third-degree felony is a fine of not more than $5,000 and/or up to five years in jail.

FREC Disciplinary Guidelines

The Commission uses guidelines that apply to each specific ground for disciplinary action that it may impose. The purpose of these disciplinary guidelines is to give notice to licensees of the range of penalties that normally will be imposed for each count (offense) during a formal or informal hearing. A finding of *mitigating* (less severe) circumstances or *aggravating* (more severe) circumstances allows the Commission to impose a penalty other than those provided. The extent of a penalty, ranging from least to most severe, is reprimand to suspension and revocation or denial. Combinations of these and other penalties are allowed. Grounds and penalties are listed in Table 5.1 (later in this chapter) in numerical order by statute.

Real Estate Recovery Fund

The Florida Real Estate Recovery Fund's purpose is to reimburse any individual or business entity judged by a Florida court to have suffered monetary (compensatory) damages as a result of an act committed by a broker or sales associate who:

- was at the time the alleged act was committed, the holder of a current, valid, active real estate license issued under Chapter 475;
- was not the seller, buyer, landlord, or tenant in the transaction (except as noted below) nor an officer or director of a corporation, a member of a partnership, a member of a limited liability company, or a partner of a limited liability partnership which was the seller, buyer, landlord, or tenant in the transaction; and
- was acting solely in the capacity of a real estate licensee in the transaction.

Licensee as buyer or seller. A real estate licensee who was the buyer or seller (lessor or lessee) in a real estate transaction may also make a claim against the fund *provided* the licensee did *not* act in the capacity of a real estate agent. In other words, if a licensed person is the buyer or seller of real property and suffers monetary damages as a result of an act committed by another licensed broker or sales associate who did act in the capacity of an agent, the fact that the victim is licensed will not prevent the licensee from seeking reimbursement from the fund.

KEY CONCEPTS OF RECOVERY FUND

- Reimburses consumers who are financially injured by a licensee
- Licensee must hold active license at time of alleged act and acted in capacity of a real estate licensee in the transaction
- Spouse of the offending licensee (judgment debtor) is not eligible for reimbursement
- A civil suit was filed, a final judgment issued against licensee, and an attempt was made to collect on the judgment
- Claim must be made within two years of the alleged act or within two years of the discovery of the alleged act
- Maximum payment from one judgment (single transaction) is $50,000
- Maximum payment based on multiple judgments (more than one transaction) against a licensee is $150,000
- At time of payment from fund due to misconduct, license is automatically suspended until money plus interest is repaid to the fund
- Punitive damages and interest cannot be reimbursed from the fund
- A broker who complies with an escrow disbursement order and is later sued may be reimbursed from the fund without penalty

Claim resulting from an EDO. If a broker who complied with an escrow disbursement order is later required by a court of law to pay money damages as a result of legal actions taken by the buyer or the seller in the transaction, the FREC is authorized to order reimbursement to the broker for the amount of the judgment against the broker up to $50,000. No disciplinary action will be taken against a broker who had previously requested an EDO and followed its instructions. The broker's license will not be suspended and no repayment to the fund is required.

To be eligible for reimbursement, the broker must notify the FREC of the court case and the broker-defendant must diligently defend in court the disputed actions concerning the transaction. Furthermore, Florida Statute provides for the Commission to pay the broker-defendant's reasonable attorney's fees and court costs and, if the plaintiff (person who filed the lawsuit) prevails in court, the plaintiff's reasonable attorney's fees and court costs. In cases other than those regarding compliance with an EDO, court costs and attorney's fees may *not* be awarded. In all cases, punitive damages, treble (triple) damages, and interest may *not* be recovered from the fund.

A claim for recovery will not be considered unless a civil suit resulted in a final judgment against an *individual licensee* as defendant (not merely against real estate brokerage entity). A claimant must cause *a writ of execution* to be issued on the judgment, and the results (an asset search) must show that insufficient funds or property is available to satisfy the judgment. The claimant must also execute an affidavit showing that the final judgment is not on appeal or, if it was subject to an appeal, that the appellate proceedings have concluded and show the outcome of the appeal. Notice of the filing should be sent to the Commission or the Department of Legal Affairs by certified mail. The filing of a bankruptcy petition by a licensee does not relieve a claimant from the obligation to obtain a final judgment against the licensee in order to recover from the fund. The FREC may waive the requirement for a final judgment if a bankruptcy court obstructs obtaining such a judgment.

Time limit to file a claim. A claim must be made within two years of either the alleged violation or discovery of the alleged violation. However, in no case may a claim for recovery be made more than four years after the date of the alleged violation.

Monetary limits of claims. Payments for claims arising out of the same transaction are limited, in total, to $50,000 or the unsatisfied portion of a judgment claim, whichever is less, regardless of the number of claimants or parcels of real estate involved in the transaction. Payments for claims based on judgments against one broker or sales associate may not exceed, in total, $150,000.

A total of $1 million is the authorized limit for the fund at any one time. Funds are accumulated by charging each active and inactive licensee a fee when a new license is issued or an existing one is renewed. In addition, fines imposed by the FREC and collected by the DBPR are transferred into the fund under Section 475.482(4), F.S. The collection of these special fees stops when the limit is reached, and it begins again when the amount drops below $500,000. At that time, a $3.50 fee per year for brokers and $1.50 fee per year for sales associates is added to the license fee for both new and renewed licenses. The Chief Financial Officer makes all payments from the fund following receipt of a voucher signed by the DBPR Secretary.

Mandatory suspension. Suspension of a licensee's license is mandatory upon payment of any amount from the Real Estate Recovery Fund in settlement of a claim to satisfy a judgment against any licensee as described in 475.482(1), F.S. The license is automatically suspended on the date of payment from the recovery fund and will not be restored until the licensee has repaid the amount paid from the fund in full (plus interest).

Individuals who cannot make a claim. The following persons cannot make a claim for recovery from the fund:

- The spouse of the offending licensee (judgment debtor)
- A licensee who acted as a single agent or transaction broker in a real estate transaction that is the subject of the claim
- An individual whose claim is against a licensee who owned the property under contract, and the licensee was dealing for the licensee's own account (The licensee was not acting as a broker or sales associate.)
- A person who files a claim against a licensee who did not hold a valid and current license at the time of the transaction
- Individual who obtains a judgment against a real estate brokerage entity only rather than against a licensed individual

TABLE 5.1 ■ Disciplinary Guidelines: 61J2-24.001, F.A.C. (Effective date, February 2012)

	PENALTY RANGE	
Violation	**First Violation**	**Second and Subsequent Violations**
(a) Section 475.22, F.S. Broker fails to maintain office or sign at entrance of office	(a) Reprimand to $500 administrative fine	(a) 90-day suspension and $1,000 administrative fine
(b) Section 475.24, F.S. Failure to register a branch office	(b) Reprimand to $500 administrative fine	(b) 90-day suspension and $1,000 administrative fine
(c) Section 475.25(1)(b), F.S. Fraud, misrepresentation, and dishonest dealing	(c) $1,000 to $2,500 administrative fine and 30-day suspension to revocation	(c) $2,500 to $5,000 administrative fine and 6-month suspension to revocation
Concealment, false promises, false pretenses by trick, scheme or device	$1,000 to $2,500 administrative fine and 30-day suspension to revocation	$2,500 to $5,000 administrative fine and 6-month suspension to revocation
Culpable negligence or breach of trust	$1,000 to $2,500 administrative fine and 30-day suspension to revocation	$2,500 to $5,000 administrative fine and 6-month suspension to revocation
Violating a duty imposed by law or by the terms of a listing agreement; aided, assisted or conspired with another; or formed an intent, design or scheme to engage in such misconduct and committed an overt act in furtherance of such intent, design or scheme	$1,000 to $2,500 administrative fine and 30-day suspension to revocation	$2,500 to $5,000 administrative fine and 6-month suspension to revocation
(d) Section 475.25(1)(c), F.S. False, deceptive or misleading advertising	(d) $250 to $1,000 administrative fine and 30- to 90-day suspension	(d) $1,000 to $5,000 administrative fine and 90-day suspension to revocation
(e) Section 475.25(1)(d), F.S. Failed to account or deliver to any person as required by agreement or law, escrowed property	(e) $250 to $1,000 administrative fine and suspension to revocation	(e) $1,000 to $5,000 administrative fine and suspension to revocation
(f) Section 475.25(1)(e), F.S. Violated any rule or order or provision under Chapters 475 and 455, F.S.	(f) $250 to $1,000 administrative fine and suspension to revocation	(f) $1,000 to $5,000 administrative fine and suspension to revocation
(g) Section 475.25(1)(f), F.S. Convicted or found guilty of a crime related to real estate or involving moral turpitude or fraudulent or dishonest dealing	(g) $250 to $1,000 administrative fine and 30-day suspension to revocation	(g) $1,000 to $5,000 administrative fine and suspension to revocation
(h) Section 475.25(1)(g), F.S. Has license disciplined or acted against or an application denied by another jurisdiction	(h) $250 to $1,000 administrative fine and 30-day suspension to revocation	(h) $1,000 to $5,000 administrative fine and suspension to revocation
(i) Section 475.25(1)(h), F.S. Has shared a commission with or paid a fee to a person not properly licensed under Chapter 475, F.S.	(i) $250 to $1,000 administrative fine and 30-day suspension to revocation	(i) $1,000 to $5,000 administrative fine and suspension to revocation

TABLE 5.1 ■ Disciplinary Guidelines: 61J2-24.001, F.A.C. (Effective date, February 2012) (Continued)

	PENALTY RANGE	
Violation	**First Violation**	**Second and Subsequent Violations**
(j) Section 475.25(1)(i), F.S. Impairment by drunkenness, or use of drugs or temporary mental derangement	(j) Suspension for the period of incapacity	(j) Suspension for the period of incapacity
(k) Section 475.25(1)(j), F.S. Rendered an opinion that the title to property sold is good or merchantable when not based on opinion of a licensed attorney or has failed to advise prospective buyer to consult an attorney on the merchantability of title or to obtain title insurance	(k) $250 to $1,000 administrative fine and 30-day suspension to revocation	(k) $1,000 to $5,000 administrative fine and suspension to revocation
(l) Section 475.25(l)(k), F.S. Has failed, if a broker, to deposit any money in an escrow account immediately upon receipt until disbursement is properly authorized. Has failed, if a sales associate, to place any money to be escrowed with his registered employer	(l) $250 to $1,000 administrative fine and 30-day suspension to revocation	(l) $1,000 to $5,000 administrative fine and suspension to revocation
(m) Section 475.25(1)(l), F.S. Has made or filed a report or record which the licensee knows to be false or willfully failed to file a report or record or willfully impeded such filing as required by State or Federal Law	(m) $250 to $1,000 administrative fine and 30-day suspension to revocation	(m) $1,000 to $5,000 administrative fine and suspension to revocation
(n) Section 475.25(1)(m), F.S. Obtained a license by fraud, misrepresentation or concealment	(n) $250 to $1,000 administrative fine and 30-day suspension to revocation	(n) $1,000 to $5,000 administrative fine and suspension to revocation
(o) Section 475.25(1)(n), F.S. Confined in jail, prison or mental institution; or through mental disease can no longer practice with skill and safety	(o) $250 to $1,000 administrative fine and suspension to revocation	(o) $1,000 to $5,000 administrative fine and suspension to revocation
(p) Section 475.25(1)(o), F.S. Guilty for the second time of misconduct in the practice of real estate that demonstrates incompetent, dishonest or negligent dealings with investors	(p) $1,000 to $5,000 administrative fine and a 1 year suspension to revocation	
(q) Section 475.25(1)(p), F.S. Failed to give Commission 30-day written notice after a guilty or nolo contendere plea or convicted of any felony	(q) $500 to $1,000 administrative fine and suspension to revocation	(q) $1,000 to $5,000 administrative fine and suspension to revocation

TABLE 5.1 ■ Disciplinary Guidelines: 61J2-24.001, F.A.C. (Effective date, February 2012) (Continued)

	PENALTY RANGE	
Violation	**First Violation**	**Second and Subsequent Violations**
(r) Section 475.25(1)(r), F.S. Failed to follow the requirements of a written listing agreement	(r) $250 to $1,000 administrative fine and suspension to revocation	(r) $1,000 to $5,000 administrative fine and suspension to revocation
(s) Section 475.25(1)(s), F.S. Has had a registration suspended, revoked or otherwise acted against in any jurisdiction	(s) $250 to $1,000 administrative fine and 60-day suspension to revocation	(s) $1,000 to $5,000 administrative fine and suspension to revocation
(t) Section 475.25(1)(t), F.S. Violated the Uniform Standards of Professional Appraisal Practice as defined in Section 475.611, F.S.	(t) $250 to $1,000 administrative fine and 30-day suspension to revocation	(t) $1,000 to $5,000 administrative fine and suspension to revocation
(u) Section 475.25(1)(u), F.S. Has failed, if a broker, to direct, control, or manage a broker associate or sales associate employed by such broker	(u) $250 to $1,000 administrative fine and suspension to revocation	(u) $1,000 to $5,000 administrative fine and suspension to revocation
(v) Section 475.25(1)(v), F.S. Has failed, if a broker, to review the brokerage's trust accounting procedures in order to ensure compliance with this chapter	(v) $250 to $2,500 administrative fine and suspension to revocation	(v) $1,000 to $5,000 administrative fine and suspension to revocation
(w) Section 475.42(1)(a), F.S. Practice without a valid and current license	(w) $250 to $2,500 administrative fine and suspension to revocation	(w) $1,000 to $5,000 administrative fine and suspension to revocation
(x) Section 475.42(1)(b), F.S. Practicing beyond scope as a sales associate	(x) $250 to $1,000 administrative fine and suspension to revocation	(x) $1,000 to $5,000 administrative fine and suspension to revocation
(y) Section 475.42(1)(c), F.S. Broker employs a sales associate who is not the holder of a valid and current license	(y) $250 to $1,000 administrative fine and suspension to revocation	(y) $1,000 to $5,000 administrative fine and suspension to revocation
(z) Section 475.42(1)(d), F.S. A sales associate shall not collect any money in connection with any real estate brokerage transaction except in the name of the employer	(z) $250 to $1,000 administrative fine and suspension to revocation	(z) $1,000 to $5,000 administrative fine and suspension to revocation
(aa) Section 475.42(1)(g), F.S. Makes false affidavit or affirmation or false testimony before the Commission	(aa) $250 to $1,000 administrative fine and suspension to revocation	(aa) $1,000 to $5,000 administrative fine and suspension to revocation
(bb) Section 475.42(1)(h), F.S. Fails to comply with subpoena	(bb) $250 to $1,000 administrative fine and suspension	(bb) $1,000 to $5,000 administrative fine and suspension to revocation

TABLE 5.1 ■ Disciplinary Guidelines: 61J2-24.001, F.A.C. (Effective date, February 2012) (Continued)

Violation	PENALTY RANGE First Violation	Second and Subsequent Violations
(cc) Section 475.42(1)(i), F.S. Obstructs or hinders the enforcement of Chapter 475, F.S.	(cc) $250 to $1,000 administrative fine and suspension to revocation	(cc) $1,000 to $5,000 administrative fine and suspension to revocation
(dd) Section 475.42(1)(j), F.S. No broker or sales associate shall place upon the public records any false, void or unauthorized information that affects the title or encumbers any real property	(dd) $250 to $2,500 administrative fine and suspension to revocation	(dd) $1,000 to $5,000 administrative fine and suspension to revocation
(ee) Section 475.42(1)(k), F.S. Failed to register trade name with the Commission	(ee) $250 to $1,000 administrative fine	(ee) $1,000 to $5,000 administrative fine and suspension to revocation
(ff) Section 475.42(1)(l), F.S. No person shall knowingly conceal information relating to violations of Chapter 475, F.S.	(ff) $250 to $1,000 administrative fine and suspension	(ff) $1,000 to $5,000 administrative fine and suspension to revocation
(gg) Section 475.42(1)(m), F.S. Fails to have a current license as a broker or sales associate while listing or selling one or more timeshare periods per year	(gg) $250 to $1,000 administrative fine and suspension	(gg) $1,000 to $5,000 administrative fine and suspension to revocation
(hh) Section 475.42(1)(n), F.S. Licensee fails to disclose all material aspects of the resale of timeshare period or timeshare plan and the rights and obligations of both buyer or seller	(hh) $250 to $1,000 administrative fine and suspension	(hh) $1,000 to $5,000 administrative fine and suspension to revocation
(ii) Section 475.42(1)(o), F.S. Publication of false or misleading information; promotion of sales, leases and rentals	(ii) $250 to $1,000 administrative fine and suspension to revocation	(ii) $1,000 to $5,000 administrative fine and suspension to revocation
(jj) Section 475.451, F.S. School teaching real estate practice fails to obtain a permit from the department and does not abide by regulations of Chapter 475, F.S., and rules adopted by the Commission	(jj) $250 to $1,000 administrative fine and suspension	(jj) $1,000 to $5,000 administrative fine and suspension to revocation
(kk) Section 475.453, F.S. Broker or sales associate participates in any rental information transaction that fails to follow the guidelines adopted by the Commission and Chapter 475, F.S.	(kk) $250 to $1,000 administrative fine and suspension	(kk) $1,000 to $5,000 administrative fine and 90-day suspension to revocation

TABLE 5.1 ■ Disciplinary Guidelines: 61J2-24.001, F.A.C. (Effective date, February 2012) (Continued)

	PENALTY RANGE	
Violation	**First Violation**	**Second and Subsequent Violations**
(ll) Section 475.5015, F.S. Failure to keep and make available to the department such books, accounts, and records as will enable the department to determine whether the broker is in compliance with the provisions of this chapter	(ll) $250 to $1,000 administrative fine and suspension to revocation	(ll) $1,000 to $5,000 administrative fine and 90-day suspension to revocation
(mm) Section 455.227(1)(s), F.S. Failing to comply with the educational course requirements for domestic violence	(mm) $250 to $1,000 administrative fine and suspension to revocation	(mm) $1,000 to $5,000 administrative fine and suspension to revocation
(nn) Section 455.227(1)(t), F.S. Failing to report in writing to the Commission within 30 days after the licensee is convicted or found guilty of, or entered a plea of nolo contendere or guilty to, regardless of adjudication, a crime in any jurisdiction.	(nn) $250 to $1,000 administrative fine and suspension to revocation	(nn) $1,000 to $5,000 administrative fine and suspension to revocation
(oo) Section 455.227(1)(u), F.S. Termination from a treatment program for impaired practitioners as described in Section 456.076 for failure to comply, without good cause, with the terms of the monitoring or treatment contract entered into by the licensee or failing to successfully complete a drug or alcohol treatment program	(oo) $250 to $1,000 administrative fine and suspension to revocation	(oo) $1,000 to $5,000 administrative fine and suspension to revocation

SUMMARY OF IMPORTANT POINTS

- Seven steps comprise the complaint process:
    1. A complaint (an alleged violation of a law or rule) is filed with the DBPR.
    2. If the complaint is legally sufficient, the DBPR conducts an investigation and notifies the licensee-respondent. The complaint and the information obtained during the investigation are kept confidential until ten days after probable cause has been found to exist. The DBPR's investigative report is forwarded to the probable cause panel. In rare situations deemed to be too serious to allow the licensee to continue to practice real estate while the complaint process proceeds, the DBPR secretary may issue a summary (emergency) suspension.
    3. The probable cause panel consists of two FREC members. The probable cause panel makes a determination as to whether probable cause exists.
    4. If probable cause is found, the DBPR issues a formal (administrative) complaint. An Election of Rights is mailed with the complaint to the licensee. The licensee has 21 days to (1) not dispute the allegations of fact and request an informal hearing, (2) dispute the allegations of fact and request a formal hearing, or (3) not dispute the allegations of fact and waive the right to be heard. The licensee-respondent may enter into a stipulation (an agreement as to the facts of the case and the penalty reached between the attorneys for the DRE and the licensee).
    5. If there are no disputed facts, the Commission (probable cause panel members are excused) decides the case and imposes the penalty in an informal hearing held during a regular FREC meeting. If the licensee-respondent requested a formal hearing or if the respondent disputes the allegations, the case is heard by a Florida administrative law judge in a formal hearing. The administrative law judge prepares a recommended order.
    6. The FREC imposes the final order (members of the probable cause panel do not participate). The final order becomes effective 30 days after it has been entered.
    7. The licensee-respondent may appeal the final order.
- Administrative, civil, and criminal penalties that may be imposed for violations of real estate license law.
- The FREC may impose administrative penalties for violations of law or rules and regulations. A citation is issued for violations that are of no substantial threat to the public. Such citations carry fines ranging from $100 to $500. The DBPR may issue a notice of noncompliance as a first response to a minor violation. More serious offenses are punishable by fines of up to $5,000 for each violation of Chapters 455 and 475 and/or a suspension of up to 10 years. In extreme cases, the FREC may revoke a license.
- Revocation of a license is permanent with two exceptions. An applicant may not reapply for a sales associate license for five years if:
    1. a licensee has filed for renewal but did not comply with the continuing or post-licensing education requirement prior to the expiration date on the license; or
    2. an applicant submitted an application for licensure that contained false or fraudulent information.

- Failing to provide accurate and current rental information for a fee is a misdemeanor of the first degree, punishable in a court of law by a fine of up to $1,000 and/or by imprisonment of up to one year.
- All other violations of license law are misdemeanors of the second degree, punishable by a fine of up to $500 and/or by imprisonment of up to 60 days.
- Unlicensed practice of real estate for compensation is a felony of the third degree. The penalty is a fine of up to $5,000 and/or up to five years in jail.
- The real estate recovery fund is a separate account used to reimburse people who have suffered monetary damages as a result of license law violations by a licensee. Claims are limited to $50,000 per transaction and no more than $150,000 against one licensee involving multiple transactions. The license is automatically suspended upon payment from the fund until the fund is reimbursed (EDO exception).

REVIEW QUESTIONS

1. The probable cause panel is composed of
   a. a total of two members.
   b. at least one professional member.
   c. one consumer member, if available.
   d. All of the above

2. A person is eligible to seek recovery from the Real Estate Recovery Fund under which circumstance?
   a. He or she has received an uncollectable final judgment against a licensee in any action where the cause of action was based on a real estate brokerage transaction, unless specifically precluded.
   b. He or she is a licensed broker who acted as the agent in the transaction that is the subject of the claim.
   c. His or her claim is based on a real estate transaction in which the broker did not hold a valid, current, and active license at the time of the transaction.
   d. He or she has obtained a judgment against a real estate corporation.

3. Which action would cause a license to be revoked without prejudice?
   a. A licensee accepted an earnest money deposit on a property he knew was encumbered by an undisclosed lien.
   b. The broker obtained his license by means of fraud, misrepresentation, or concealment.
   c. A sales associate received her license as a result of an administrative error by the DBPR.
   d. For the referral of real estate business, a licensee shared a commission with a person (not a party to the transaction) who did not have a real estate license.

4. Which violation of real estate law is a misdemeanor of the first degree?
   a. False advertising
   b. Charging a fee for an out-of-date and inaccurate rental list
   c. Commingling of escrow funds
   d. Failure to retain brokerage relationship disclosure notices

5. What body must prepare and submit a recommended order of findings of fact and conclusions of law in a complaint case?
   a. Court of law
   b. Administrative law judge
   c. Probable cause panel
   d. DBPR

6. Any final order issued by the DBPR Secretary or a legally appointed designee resulting from circumstances that pose an immediate danger to the public's health, safety, or welfare is called a
   a. petition for review.
   b. stay of enforcement.
   c. summary suspension.
   d. license revocation.
7. Under which circumstance is the DBPR authorized to investigate a signed complaint filed against a licensee?
   a. If the alleged complaint is legally sufficient
   b. Only if the claimant has been harmed by the licensee's actions
   c. Only if the alleged violation was committed in the state of Florida
   d. Only if all of the above conditions have been met
8. Neglecting to correct omissions or errors on a license application that the DBPR returns to the applicant for correction is considered grounds for
   a. suspension of the applicant's rights.
   b. denial of the application without prejudice.
   c. revocation of the application.
   d. administrative revocation.
9. A broker has been found guilty of misrepresentation and fraudulent dealings in a real estate transaction. The buyer obtains a final judgment against a broker in the amount of $15,000 monetary damages, plus $5,000 attorney's fees and $2,000 court costs. The Florida Real Estate Commission is authorized to reimburse this buyer what amount from the Real Estate Recovery Fund?
   a. $15,000
   b. $17,000
   c. $22,000
   d. $25,000
10. When payment from the Real Estate Recovery Fund is made to satisfy a claim against a licensee, and the claim was not the result of the broker following an EDO, the Commission's action against the licensee must be
    a. citation.
    b. probation.
    c. suspension.
    d. emergency suspension.
11. Which type(s) of penalties may be imposed for real estate license law violations?
    a. Civil penalties only
    b. Administrative penalties only
    c. Civil and administrative penalties only
    d. Criminal, civil, and administrative penalties
12. The collective amount to be paid from the Real Estate Recovery Fund as a result of any one real estate transaction cannot exceed how much?
    a. $25,000
    b. $50,000
    c. $75,000
    d. $150,000

13. The decision as to whether probable cause exists is made by a majority vote of the
    a. Commission.
    b. administrative law judge.
    c. probable cause panel.
    d. Commission or the Department, as appropriate.

14. If a broker's license is suspended, the licenses of all the sales associates and broker associates working for that broker are
    a. denied.
    b. revoked.
    c. suspended.
    d. placed in involuntary inactive status.

15. The FREC does NOT have the power to impose which disciplinary penalty?
    a. Probation
    b. Imprisonment
    c. Administrative fine
    d. Denial of a license application

CASE STUDY PART 1

GETTING STARTED IN THE REAL ESTATE BROKERAGE BUSINESS

Department of Business and Professional Regulation, Florida Real Estate Commission	vs.	Wayne Wagie

Recommended Order: This case was heard in Miami on May 1, 2002, before Administrative Law Judge Robert E. Meale, Division of Administrative Hearings. The parties were represented by:

For Petitioner: Juana Carstarphen Watkins,
Senior Attorney, DBPR
For Respondent: Wayne Wagie, pro se

This matter arises from Petitioner's Administrative Complaint against Respondent Wayne Wagie.

Findings of Fact: Mr. Wagie, a licensed real estate broker, was the qualifying broker of Express Realty and Investments, Inc. Ms. Hanse was the office manager of Express Realty.

Express Realty served as an escrow agent in a contract dated May 9, 1999. For the closing, Express Realty issued two checks payable to the closing agent, totaling $19,169.08, and drawn on its escrow account. The checks were dated July 15, 1999, and were signed by Ms. Hanse. The bank failed to pay these checks due to insufficient funds.

The DBPR attempted to audit Express Realty. The investigator could not obtain relevant records from Ms. Hanse or Respondent concerning the real estate transaction for which Express Realty had issued escrow checks with insufficient funds.

On August 23, 1999, the Florida Real Estate Commission issued a citation to Respondent for failure to give the required disclosure or notice in a real estate transaction. Respondent paid the citation approximately four months after it had been served on him.

Soon after the citation was paid, the Petitioner received another complaint concerning a contract for sale and purchase of real property. In this transaction, Ms. Hanse represented herself to be a licensed real estate broker, showed the property to prospects, and accepted $5,000 in escrow on behalf of Express Realty.

Discussion Questions:

1. Which subsections of Chapter 475, F.S. were violated, and what were the violations?
2. What are the time periods for objecting to a citation and payment of a citation issued by the FREC?
3. Can a broker be held accountable for the actions of an unlicensed employee of the brokerage firm?

WEB LINK

Web Link: **http://www.doah.state.fl.us/internet/** (See case number 02-000138PL)

PART TWO

VALUING REAL PROPERTY

CHAPTER

6 OVERVIEW OF REAL ESTATE VALUATION

KEY TERMS

anticipation
appraisal
assemblage
assessed value
conformity
cost
demand
DUST
external diseconomies
external economies
federally related transaction
function of an appraisal
going-concern value
highest and best use
increasing and decreasing returns
insurable value
investment value
liquidation value
market value
overimprovement
plottage
price
progression
purpose of an appraisal
real estate–related financial transaction
reconciliation
regression
salvage value
scarcity
situs
substitution
supply
transaction value
transferability
USPAP
utility
value
value in use

OVERVIEW

This chapter explains state certification and licensure of appraisers and introduces the *Uniform Standards of Professional Appraisal Practice* (USPAP). The various types of value are discussed, and basic appraisal principles are described. This chapter does not focus on how to "conduct" an appraisal—rather on how to "analyze" an appraisal report. The chapter concludes with a discussion of the steps involved in the appraisal process.

Once you have completed this chapter, you should be able to:

- define a federally related transaction;
- recognize which appraisal assignments must be performed by state certified or licensed appraisers;
- describe when real estate licensees must comply with the USPAP;
- distinguish among the terms *price*, *cost*, and *value*;

- distinguish among the different types of value;
- distinguish among the various appraisal principles;
- distinguish between highest and best use as though vacant, and highest and best use as improved;
- describe the steps involved in the appraisal process; and
- distinguish among the different types of appraisal reports.

INTRODUCTION TO APPRAISAL

Certification and Licensure

Chapter 475, Part I, pertains to real estate brokers, sales associates, and schools. Under Part I, appraising is included in the definition of real estate services that brokers may perform (see Section 475.01, F.S.). Therefore, licensed real estate brokers and sales associates can perform appraisals for compensation. They may *not*, however, represent themselves as certified or licensed appraisers unless they hold such certifications or licenses. Real estate brokers may conduct appraisals of real property that do not require a state-certified or licensed appraiser (see below), provided they abide by the *Uniform Standards of Professional Appraisal Practice (USPAP)*.

Part II of the statute pertains to real estate appraisers and sets forth the requirements for licensed and certified appraisers according to federal statute. The Florida Real Estate Appraisal Board (FREAB) is charged with enforcing Chapter 475, Part II. The FREAB functions very similarly to the Florida Real Estate Commission (FREC). Both quasi-judicial bodies follow the same procedures for disciplining licensees.

The rules of the FREAB are codified in Chapter 61J1 of *the Florida Administrative Code*. (FREC rules are found in Chapter 61J2 of the Code.) The Department of Business and Professional Regulation (DBPR) licenses and certifies appraisers. The Division of Real Estate (DRE) provides support services to the FREC and to the FREAB.

Appraisal Basics

An **appraisal** is a supported, defended estimate of value of property rights *as of a given date*. The date of the estimate of value is important because value changes over time. For example, a condominium's estimated value will likely not be the same today and two years ago. The appraiser estimates the value of property (legal) rights associated with a parcel of real estate. For example, the estimated value of a subject property may differ depending on whether the appraiser is estimating the value of a life estate versus a fee simple estate.

The **purpose of an appraisal** is to estimate a *specific type of defined value*. There are many types of value and the value estimate will differ based on the type of value selected. For example, the estimated value will differ depending on whether the purpose of the appraisal is to estimate insurable value or market value. If insurable value is used, only the structure (not the land) is estimated for fire insurance coverage. However, estimating market value considers the legal rights associated with the value of the structure and the land. It is important that the appraiser indicate which type of value was used and define the specific type of value.

The **function of an appraisal** relates to how the client intends to use the appraisal. Appraisals are used, for example, to make buying and selling decisions. An appraisal might be used by a client who is a prospective buyer seeking a reasonable purchase price. Perhaps an appraisal will be used by a client to establish the value of a residential property at the time a divorce was finalized. And in another case, the appraisal will be used to establish the maximum loan amount for a mortgage loan application. It is very important to understand how an appraisal is to be used. The function of an appraisal guides the type of value to be estimated, the effective date of the appraisal, and so forth.

Comparative market analysis. Real estate brokers and sales associates typically prepare comparative market analyses (CMAs) to establish listing or offering prices. Comparative market analyses employ many of the techniques used in the appraisal process. However, a CMA focuses on the selling or asking *price*, whereas an appraisal focuses on the valuation. Chapter 475, F.S., mandates that real estate licensees who perform comparative market analyses of real estate in the ordinary course of business may *not* refer to or represent the CMAs as appraisals. A real estate licensee who prepares a CMA is not required to comply with the USPAP. Because most brokers are involved in listing and selling real estate, an entire chapter has been devoted to developing CMAs (see chapter 8).

Broker's price opinion. A broker's price opinion (BPO) is a written opinion of the value of real property. Florida real estate licensees are allowed to prepare and charge for BPOs provided the BPO is not labeled as an appraisal. If a sales associate or broker-associate performs a BPO, the compensation must be paid to the broker and not directly to the sales associate or broker-associate who prepared the BPO. A real estate licensee who performs a BPO is not required to comply with the USPAP. If a valuation assignment involves a federally related transaction, an appraisal must be conducted by a licensed or certified appraiser.

Federal Regulation

Title XI of the Financial Institutions Reform, Recovery, and Enforcement Act of 1989 (FIRREA) brought the appraisal industry under federal oversight and mandated states to license and certify appraisers.

The Appraiser Qualifications Board (AQB) of The Appraisal Foundation establishes the qualifications for state-certified and licensed appraisers. Qualification criteria include appraiser education and appraisal experience. Appraisal reports involving a federally related transaction must be prepared by a state-certified or licensed appraiser. A **federally related transaction** is any *real estate-related financial transaction* that a federal financial institutions regulatory agency (FFIRA) has either contracted for, or regulates, and requires the services of an appraiser. There are five federal financial regulatory agencies—the Office of Thrift Supervision (OTS), the Office of the Comptroller of the Currency (OCC), the Board of Governors of the Federal Reserve System (FRB), the Federal Deposit Corporation (FDIC), and the National Credit Union Administration (CUA).

A **real estate-related financial transaction** is any transaction involving the:

1. sale, lease, purchase, investment in or exchange of real property, including interests in property, or the financing thereof; or
2. refinancing of real property or interests in real property; or
3. use of real property or interests in property as security for a loan or investment, including mortgage-backed securities.

DISCIPLINARY GUIDELINES

475.25(1)(t). Violated the Uniform Standards of Professional Appraisal Practice as defined in s. 475.611, F.S.

First violation: $250 to $1,000 administrative fine and 30-day suspension to revocation

Second and subsequent violations: $1,000 to $5,000 administrative fine and suspension to revocation

Reference: 61J2-24.001, F.A.C.

Appraisals for real estate-related financial transactions require a state-certified or licensed appraiser unless the transaction has been specifically exempted from the requirement. A state-certified or licensed appraiser is *not* required if the transaction value is $250,000 or less (exceptions to this are discussed below). What is meant by the **transaction value** varies from assignment to assignment depending on the intended use of the appraisal. In most appraisal assignments, the transaction value is the loan amount. However, the transaction value in some situations is the market value. For example, if the assignment involves estimating the value of a foreclosed property, the transaction value is the market value. The specified value threshold of $250,000 is referred to as the *de minimis* requirement.

Real estate licensees are cautioned that just because a transaction is not a federally related transaction, it does not mean that real estate licensees are allowed to provide the appraisal services. FHA and VA transactions and appraisals for loans sold to Fannie Mae and Freddie Mac are not federally related transactions. However, Fannie Mae, Freddie Mac, HUD, and the VA require the use of state-certified or licensed appraisers for all loans with which these entities are involved, regardless of the amount of the loan.

It is a violation of federal law for a financial institution to seek, obtain, or compensate a person who the institution knows is not a state-certified or licensed appraiser for the performance of an appraisal associated with a federally related transaction. Furthermore, it is a violation of federal law for the Federal National Mortgage Association (Fannie Mae) or the Federal Home Loan Mortgage Corporation (Freddie Mac) to knowingly contract for the performance of an appraisal by a person who is not a state-certified or licensed appraiser in connection with a real estate-related financial transaction.

All appraisals for federally related transactions must be in writing and conform to the *Uniform Standards of Professional Appraisal Practice* (USPAP). Florida law goes further to require that *all appraisals* (regardless of whether the assignment involves a federally related transaction) performed by real estate appraisers *and* real estate licensees conform to USPAP. Real estate licensees must be familiar with the standards. Failure to do so may subject the licensee to discipline. Florida real estate licensees who are not state-certified or licensed appraisers and who perform appraisal assignments are cautioned to get a statement in writing from the client that the appraisal is not associated with a federally related transaction and does not require the services of a state-certified or licensed appraiser before accepting the assignment.

FIRREA formally recognizes The Appraisal Foundation as the source within the appraisal profession for the promotion of professional standards of behavior and appraiser qualification. Headquartered in Washington, D.C., the nonprofit Foundation accomplishes its goals through the work of its two independent boards:

- **Appraiser Qualifications Board (AQB).** The AQB establishes the qualifications for state licensing, certification, and recertification of appraisers. FIRREA mandates that all state-certified appraisers must meet the minimum education, experience, and examination requirements promulgated by the AQB.
- **Appraisal Standards Board (ASB).** The ASB sets forth the rules for developing an appraisal and reporting its results. In addition, it promotes the use, understanding, and enforcement of the *Uniform Standards of Professional Appraisal Practice* (USPAP). The ASB develops, interprets, and amends USPAP on behalf of the appraisal industry.

FIRREA also specifically recognizes USPAP as the accepted standard for real estate appraisal activity for federally related transactions. Today, it is considered the accepted standard for valuing all real property, personal property, business opportunities, and mass appraisal (the valuing of a group of properties). **USPAP** is a set of guidelines (standards of practice) to follow when providing appraisal services. USPAP is organized into ten standards. Standard 1 concerns the development of a real property appraisal. Standard 2 focuses on the reporting of a real property assignment. Standard 3 is concerned with reviewing an existing appraisal report. The remaining standards focus on consulting, mass appraisal, and personal property appraisal.

USPAP sets forth four rules:

1. **Competency rule.** An appraiser must be competent to perform the appraisal assignment, acquire the necessary competency to perform the assignment, or decline (withdraw) from the assignment.
2. **Ethics rule.** The ethics rule concerns conduct, management, confidentiality, and record keeping. An appraiser must perform assignments with impartiality, objectivity, and independence, and without accommodation of personal interest. An appraiser must not accept an appraisal assignment that is contingent on reporting a predetermined opinion of value. The confidential nature of the appraiser-client relationship must be protected. A work file must be prepared for each appraisal assignment.
3. **Scope of work.** In every appraisal assignment, the appraiser must identify the problem to be solved, perform the scope of work necessary to produce credible results, and disclose the scope of work involved.
4. **Jurisdictional exception.** If the state or federal constitution, legislative law (statute) or court-made law (case law), or administrative rule precludes compliance with a specific portion of USPAP in an appraisal assignment, only that specific portion of USPAP is void for the particular assignment.

Real estate brokers who appraise real estate must comply with USPAP. (CMAs need not conform to USPAP, nor may they be referred to as appraisals.) Chapter 475, F.S., empowers the Commission to discipline brokers and sales associates who violate any of the standards or any other provisions of USPAP.

To learn more about FIRREA, download a compilation of Title XI of FIRREA, as amended at: **http://www.appraisalfoundation.org/s_appraisal/bin.asp?SID=1&DID=197&CID=14&VID=2&DOC=File.PDF.**

The AQB has established the following classifications of appraisers:

Registered Trainee Appraiser. An individual who is registered with the DBPR and may only perform appraisal services under the direct supervision of a licensed or certified appraiser. Registered trainee appraisers may only accept appraisal assignments from their supervisory appraiser.

Licensed Appraiser. An individual licensed to issue appraisal reports for noncomplex one-family to four-family residential units having transaction values of less than $1 million and complex one-family to four-family residential units having transaction values of less than $250,000. The OCC considers a complex one-family to four-family residential property appraisal to be one in which the property itself, the form of ownership, or the market conditions are atypical. Examples of atypical factors may include the age of improvements, architectural style, size of improvements, lot size, neighborhood land use, potential environmental hazard liability, and leasehold interest. (*Note*: although the AQB and most states recognize the licensed appraiser category, the DBPR no longer issues licenses for this classification.)

Certified Residential Appraiser. An individual certified to issue appraisal reports for residential real property of one to four residential units, without regard to transaction value or complexity.

Certified General Appraiser. An individual certified to issue appraisal reports for any type of real property.

The AQB is responsible for setting minimum qualifications for real property appraisers. The requirements include qualifying education, experience, continuing education, and examination. These minimum qualifications are explained in the *Real Property Appraiser Qualification Criteria*.

Appraisal experience must have been obtained after January 30, 1989, and it must be USPAP compliant to qualify for credit. Certified residential and certified general appraisal applicants must complete a college course requirement:

- **Certified Residential.** Associate degree or higher in any field of study; or, in lieu of the degree, 21 semester credit hours of college credit courses; the required hours include specific core curriculum courses and hours mandated by the AQB.
- **Certified General.** Bachelors degree or higher in any field of study; or, in lieu of the degree, 30 semester credit hours of college credit courses; the required hours include specific core curriculum courses and hours mandated by the AQB.

Effective January 1, 2015, certified residential appraisers and certified general appraisers must have a bachelor's degree or higher in any field from an accredited college or university. In addition to the college degree or college-level course requirement, appraiser applicants must complete prelicense appraisal education. Table 6.1 summarizes the education and experience requirements for certified residential and certified general appraisers.

WEB LINK

For information regarding The Appraisal Foundation, the Appraiser Qualifications Board (AQB), the Appraisal Standards Board (ASB), and qualification criteria, visit The Appraisal Foundation's Web site at **www.appraisalfoundation.org**.

TABLE 6.1 ■ Education and Experience Requirements for Appraisers

Category	Appraisal Education Requirement*	Experience	College Degree or Coursework	State License Exam
Trainee	100** classroom hours (post-licensing education is also required)	None	No	No
Certified Residential	200 classroom hours	2,500 hours or more obtained over 24 months***	After January 1, 2015, a Bachelor's degree or higher (in any field) from an accredited college or university.	Yes
Certified General	300 classroom hours	3,000 hours or more obtained over 30 months***	After January 1, 2015, a Bachelor's degree or higher (in any field) from an accredited college or university.	Yes

* At least 15 hours of the classroom instruction must focus on the USPAP.

** Although the AQB minimum classroom hour requirement for the Trainee classification is 75 classroom hours, Florida Statutes mandates 100 classroom hours for the Trainee classification.

*** Refer to Rule 61J1-6.001, F.A.C. for information regarding the types of acceptable experience.

WEB LINK

Download the Student Appraiser Guide at **http://www.appraisalfoundation.org**. Select "Become An Appraiser," then "Qualifications for Becoming an Appraiser" to access the download.

Price, Cost, and Value

Fundamental to appraisal theory is distinguishing among the concepts of price, cost, and value. **Price** represents the dollars or other accepted currency that a particular buyer agrees to pay and a particular seller agrees to accept under the specific circumstances surrounding a transaction. Price (or transaction price) refers to the amount of money actually paid in a transaction. What a particular buyer and seller agree to, however, does not necessarily imply what other consumers will agree to. Individual motivations and the particular conditions surrounding a sale affect what specific buyers and sellers agree to.

Cost is the total dollar expenditure for land, labor, materials, overhead, and entrepreneurial profit required to bring a property into existence. Cost, as used in appraisal theory, applies to production—not exchange. Cost is *not* synonymous with value. Sellers frequently think that when they sell their property they should be able to recoup the cost of improvements. However, the marketplace does not value the improvements based on their original cost. Assume, for example, that a gourmet cook has remodeled his kitchen with a convection oven, a built-in microwave, solid oak custom cabinets, and a climate-controlled wine cellar. The remodeled kitchen may have *cost* $90,000. However, the typical buyer in the marketplace may *value* the upgraded kitchen for only a fraction of its cost.

Value, as of a certain time, represents the monetary worth of goods (property) and services to buyers and sellers. Value is conceptual in nature and is influenced by economic forces such as supply and demand. Appraisers are charged with the task of estimating the value typical buyers most likely will place on property.

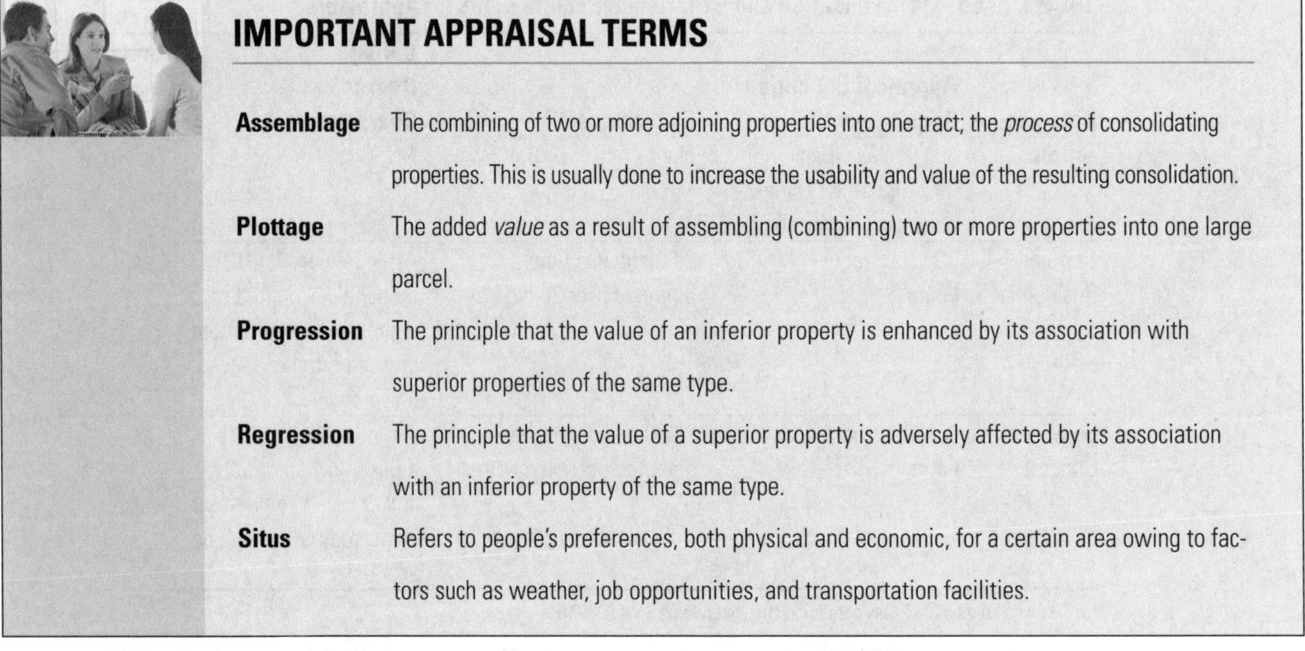

IMPORTANT APPRAISAL TERMS

Assemblage The combining of two or more adjoining properties into one tract; the *process* of consolidating properties. This is usually done to increase the usability and value of the resulting consolidation.

Plottage The added *value* as a result of assembling (combining) two or more properties into one large parcel.

Progression The principle that the value of an inferior property is enhanced by its association with superior properties of the same type.

Regression The principle that the value of a superior property is adversely affected by its association with an inferior property of the same type.

Situs Refers to people's preferences, both physical and economic, for a certain area owing to factors such as weather, job opportunities, and transportation facilities.

Practice Problem

A property owner purchases a lot and builds a house for $270,000. Ten years later, the owner is thinking of selling the property and has the house appraised. The property is appraised at $525,000. Shortly before putting the property on the market, the owner's son graduates from law school and lands a position with a firm in the owner's hometown. The property owner decides to help the young lawyer and his family by selling the house to them for $450,000. What is the cost, price, and value of this home?

(The solution to the Practice Problem is at the end of this chapter on page 166.)

VALUE DEFINITIONS FOR REAL PROPERTY APPRAISAL

Characteristics of Value

Many types of value exist, and each leads to a different value estimate. However, there are four *characteristics of value* (also referred to as *elements of economic value*) that apply to all types of value. A useful mnemonic is **DUST**.

TO REMEMBER

Characteristics of Value (DUST)

D Demand
U Utility
S Scarcity
T Transferability

- **Demand.** In economics, demand is more than a desire or need. Demand also implies the available means to obtain what is desired. The need or desire combined with the economic (financial ability to purchase) creates effective demand.
- **Utility.** To be valuable, goods or services must be useful and able to fill a need. In real estate, utility means the ability to provide useful services and benefits to an owner or tenant.
- **Scarcity.** The availability of goods or services in relation to present or anticipated demand determines scarcity. If the supply exceeds demand, there is less scarcity, and the value falls. If demand exceeds supply, more scarcity is created, and value increases. For example, when the number of available apartment units in an area exceeds the demand, apartment units are relatively less scarce, and landlords must reduce rents or lose tenants. When apartments are scarce, landlords can increase rents, and the excess demand will fill any resulting vacancies.
- **Transferability.** The legal ability to convey title and possession of goods creates *transferability*. This is an unusually important factor in real estate. Value cannot exist in cases where rights in land and the use of property cannot be transferred.

When all four characteristics of value are present, property has value that can be estimated by an appraiser.

Types of Value

Each type of value will result in a different dollar figure. USPAP requires that all appraisal reports indicate and define the type of value that was estimated. The types of value real estate brokers most frequently encounter are discussed below.

Assessed value. The value established for property tax purposes, **assessed value** is calculated in relation to a market value base. However, assessed value typically does not equal market value.

Going-concern value. The value of an operating business enterprise, **going-concern value** includes the enterprise's goodwill, that is, the intangible asset associated with the business's reputation, recognition of its name and franchise, and customer loyalty.

Insurable value. Often **insurable value** is estimated for insurance coverage purposes. It is based on replacement cost, taking into consideration insurance exclusions.

Investment value. The value of an investment to a particular investor based on requirements regarding rate of return, management involvement, risk, and other factors is called **investment value**.

Liquidation value. **Liquidation value** is the amount a property most likely will bring at a forced or hurried sale. It is sometimes used in valuing foreclosed properties and properties subject to tax liens.

Salvage value. The amount that part or all of a property's improvements can be sold for at the end of its economic life, taking into consideration the cost of removing the improvements from the land, is called **salvage value**.

Value in use. The value of a property based on a specified use that may not represent the property's maximum use (highest and best use) is its **value in use**. For example, Florida's Greenbelt Law (Chapter 193, F.S.) requires county property appraisers to base the assessed value of agricultural property solely on the land's current use, even though the property may be ripe for commercial development. Additionally, the IRS allows an estate's executor to value the property in the decedent's estate that is devoted to farming or is used in a closely held business based on the property's actual use rather than on its fair market value (see IRS Publication 448: "Federal Estate and Gift Tax"). Licensees are cautioned that an appraisal based on value in use may have no relationship to the property's market potential.

Market value. The consensus of the interactions of many buyers and sellers in a particular market, **market value** is the type of value appraisers most often are concerned with. Many recognized definitions of market value exist. USPAP cautions a person performing an appraisal that may be subject to litigation to seek the exact legal definition of market value in the jurisdiction where the person is offering services. If the appraisal involves a federally related transaction, FIRREA requires the following definition of market value:

> *The most probable price which a property should bring in a competitive and open market under all conditions requisite to a fair sale, the buyer and seller each acting prudently and knowledgeably, and assuming the price is not affected by undue stimulus. Implicit in this definition is the consummation of a sale as of a specified date and the passing of title from seller to buyer under conditions whereby:*

- buyer and seller are typically motivated;
- both parties are well informed and well advised, and acting in what they consider their best interests;
- a reasonable time is allowed for exposure in the open market;
- payment is made in terms of cash in U.S. dollars or in terms of comparable financial arrangements; and
- the price represents the normal consideration for the property sold unaffected by special or creative financing or sales concessions granted by anyone associated with the sale.

PRINCIPLES OF VALUE

To understand the dynamics of valuation theory, one must consider the many forces that shape people's attitudes and beliefs about value. Appraisal principles are the theories that attempt to explain the rationale behind market behavior. Appraisal literature identifies as many as 15 appraisal principles. Seven of the principles are discussed in this chapter to provide an overview of the economic forces that shape value.

Supply and Demand

All price and value forces have their effect through supply and demand.

Supply is the amount and type of real estate available for sale or rent at different price levels in a given real estate market. Typically, more of an item is supplied at a higher price and less at a lower price. Therefore, the supply of an item at a given price and time in a particular market indicates the item's relative scarcity. Factors that affect supply include the following:

Amount of available housing stock. To estimate current housing market inventory, appraisers and analysts study vacancy and absorption rates, as well as losses in existing stock and conversions of properties to nonresidential uses. The total inventory for a market is described by location, type, size, and age.

New development and new construction. New construction is related directly to the availability of construction loans and short-term financing. As money becomes increasingly available and less expensive, more homes are built, expanding the available supply of housing.

Decrease in the price of resources. A decrease in the price of resources (land, labor, capital, and entrepreneurial profit) used to produce a good increases the supplier's profit and therefore encourages production of more units.

The more abundant something is, the lower its price tends to be. Thus, an increase in the supply of an item or a decrease in the demand for an item tends to reduce price. Generally, the supply of housing stock is slow to adjust to changes in price levels because the time needed to find a suitable location and acquire the necessary permits and development approvals before construction is considerably lengthy. Because it is difficult to increase the supply of real property for a specific use in the short run, real estate values are affected strongly by current consumer demand.

Demand is the total quantity of a good that consumers are willing and able to purchase at various prices over a given period of time. Determinants of demand include the following:

Number of potential consumers. Over the past 25 years, the population's median age has increased, while average household size has decreased. Furthermore, the proportion of single Americans in the population, including divorced and widowed individuals, has increased. The 78 million baby boomers born between 1946 and 1966 account for one-third of the U.S. population and are projected to continue to provide a steady supply of homebuyers for years to come.

Consumer preferences and lifestyles. The influx of women to the workforce has influenced housing design, creating a desire for homes with minimal maintenance and a focus on convenience. Affluent, two-income households with disposable incomes demand amenities.

Employment rates, income, and expectations concerning future prices and income. The population's employment and income levels affect the affordability of residential property. Demand supported by purchasing power, or *effective demand*, is the type of demand people consider when purchasing homes.

Anticipation

The principle of **anticipation** is based on the premise that expectation of future benefits creates value. This is the underlying theory of the income capitalization approach to value—the anticipated (projected) income that a property will produce during the coming year is capitalized into present value. The value of residential property is based on the perceived benefits from the amenities and quality of lifestyle. A property's value as of a certain point in time is not based on its original cost (cost of production) or sale price history, but on what consumers consider its value to be, based on perceived future benefits. Appraisers therefore must be aware of consumer preferences and their anticipation of the future.

Substitution

The principle of **substitution** holds that when several goods or services offering similar benefits are available, consumers tend toward the one with the lowest price. Therefore, property values tend to be set when consumers acquire equally desirable substitute properties. Value then may be estimated from prices paid for these similar properties. This is the premise of all three approaches to value (see also chapter 7):

1. The sales comparison approach is based on the theory that a knowledgeable purchaser would pay no more for a property than the cost of acquiring an acceptable substitute property.
2. The cost-depreciation approach is based on the theory that a knowledgeable purchaser would pay no more for a property than the cost of acquiring an equally desirable site, combined with building an acceptable substitute structure.
3. The income capitalization approach is based on the theory that a property tends to be related to its competitive position among alternative (substitute) investment choices producing equivalent investment returns and risk.

Increasing and Decreasing Returns

The principle of **increasing and decreasing returns** states that when one or more factors of production are increased while others are held constant, output (in terms of physical units, dollar return, or other benefits) may increase up to a certain point. However, beyond some point, each additional unit of consumption adds less and less to satisfaction or total utility.

At some point, if a homeowner puts too many improvements into a home, the homeowner will not recover the capital invested. The home is said to be *overimproved*. An **overimprovement** occurs when an owner invests more money in a structure than the owner can reasonably expect to recapture. Appraisers adjust for overimprovements in the cost approach by deducting functional obsolescence from the cost of improvements. The relationship between cost and value-added also is important in the sales comparison approach, when determining the amount of dollar adjustments between comparable properties and a subject property. As long as money spent on improvements (for example, additional square feet or bedrooms) produces a proportionate increase in income or value, the law of increasing returns is in effect.

Conformity

The principle of **conformity** suggests that property values are maximized when architectural homogeneity and uniformity of land use occur in a neighborhood. In both residential and nonresidential markets, significant departure from the typical architectural style, size, and amenities of the surrounding area often leads to an adverse market reaction. Consider, for example, a retirement subdivision composed of approximately one hundred 1,000-square-foot to 1,200-square-foot ranch-style homes with white tile roofs. A single geodesic-domed residence sits among the other homes. Absurd, you may think, but such examples do exist. Properties that deviate greatly from the market norm are not accepted, and their values are reduced, compared with other more conforming properties. Therefore, from the appraiser's viewpoint, a major concern is whether improvements are typical for the neighborhood.

External Economies and Diseconomies

Factors that result from market forces external to a property can have a positive or negative impact on value. Because real estate is fixed in its location, it is subject to many external influences. **External economies** result from positive external factors that enhance property values, such as infrastructure to a site (roads, bridges, sewer, and water), police and fire protection, and so forth. When comparing two neighborhoods, an appraiser may have to consider, for example, the market effect of a natural gas line to one of the neighborhoods. Even when the gas line is not connected to a particular home, if hookup is available, the typical consumer may place value on the natural gas's availability. Similarly, a local city government's decision to target a portion of the city for revitalization, providing low-interest loans for redevelopment, positively affects the property values within the targeted area.

External diseconomies have a negative impact on value. External diseconomies result when the actions of people external to a property impose costs on others, such as the cleanup cost of pollution, neighborhood crime, and so forth. External influences affecting value can be found at national, regional, city, and neighborhood levels.

Highest and Best Use

The principle of highest and best use states that the values of sites and properties are maximized when the real estate is used most efficiently. **Highest and best use** is the probable and legal use of real property that is physically possible, defendable, and financially feasible and that results in the highest value. An appraiser must consider two types of highest and best use: (1) highest and best use of a site as though vacant and (2) highest and best use of the property as improved. USPAP requires the appraiser to consider the effect of the real property's highest and best use and to recognize that land is appraised as though vacant and available for development to its highest and best use and the appraisal of improvements is based on their actual contribution to the site.

The highest and best use of the site as though vacant is the legal (permissible) use of the site that would produce the greatest value. It is a site's "potential" highest and best use that determines its value. Highest and best use of a site as though vacant asks the question—if the site is (or were) vacant, what type of structure or other improvement should be erected? When a site has existing improvements, its highest and best use of the site as though vacant may differ from the existing use. Assume, for example, that a site is improved with a 20-year-old single-family home. The land is zoned for professional offices, and the properties on either side of the subject property are improved with professional office suites. If the subject site were vacant, the use that would generate the highest return to the site likely would be a professional office building. It is not economically feasible to demolish the existing residence, however, unless and until the vacant land value in its highest and best use exceeds the total value of the property in its current use.

To select a single highest and best use among alternative income-producing uses, an appraiser analyzes each use in terms of its potential rate of return and perceived income stability. Assume that an appraiser evaluates a vacant site zoned for a commercial strip unit. Developed properties in the surrounding vicinity indicate that the site could be developed as either a small retail center of specialty shops or commercial office suites. To determine which use is the site's highest and best use, the appraiser estimates the development costs, projected net operating income, and overall rate of return under each alternative use, taking into account income stability from each. (See Figure 6.1.)

In this case, specialty retail is the highest and best use because it results in the greater residual land value ($140,900) and requires the smaller outlay of development monies ($450,000). Note that various uses usually result in differing overall capitalization rates, which the appraiser derives by analyzing competing properties.

The highest and best use of a property as improved pertains to how the property with existing improvements should be used, rather than what use should be implemented for a vacant site. Highest and best use as improved therefore concerns whether the existing improvements should be maintained in their current state or whether they should be altered in some way to make them more valuable. In most cases, the existing improvements should continue to occupy the site, even though they may not maximize fully the site's potential. When conducting a highest and best use as improved analysis, an appraiser considers various alternative uses for an existing structure, some of which may require modifications to the improvements. The appraiser also must consider demolition of the existing structure and new construction. This alternative, however, typically is economically feasible only when the structure is nearing the end of its economic life.

To determine the highest and best use of an improved property, an appraiser estimates the total acquisition costs of obtaining each alternative use and the income projected from each use. Operating expenses are deducted to derive estimated net operating income (NOI) for each use. The appraiser then divides the NOI by the total cost of acquisition and alterations to derive the rate of return. The use that produces the highest rate of return is the highest and best use of the property as improved. When considering demolition, the appraiser estimates the net income to be earned from the new improvements and the rate of return on the total costs of demolition and new construction.

FIGURE 6.1 ■ Highest and Best Use as though Vacant

	Specialty Retail	Office Suites
Projected net operating income (NOI)	$65,000	$70,000
Overall capitalization rate	÷ 11%	÷ 10%
Total value	$590,900	$700,000
Development costs	–450,000	–600,000
Residual land value	$140,900	$100,000

For example, assume that an appraiser has been asked to evaluate a large five-bedroom, 40-year-old house located two blocks from a major state university. The neighborhood at one time was well kept and occupied by college faculty. Over the years, however, most of the homes have been rented to college students. Today, less than ten percent of the homes are owner-occupied. The appraiser estimates that the property can be acquired for $100,000. Analysis of market rents in the area indicates that the structure could generate $600 in monthly rent as a single-family home. An alternative use would be to rent the five bedrooms to college students, who would share the common living room and kitchen facilities. The appraiser estimates that market rent based on the shared-living plan would generate $900 per month ($180 per bedroom). Another alternative would be to demolish the house and build a new four-unit apartment building. The estimated market rent for college apartments is $550 per month, or $2,200 per month for the four-unit structure.

Figure 6.2 indicates that at this time, the highest and best use of the property as improved is a shared-living arrangement. Note that the new apartment unit would produce the greatest NOI. However, the larger net operating income does not offset the cost of demolition and new construction. Expenses of $1,000 have been estimated for the shared-living use to cover lawn maintenance and miscellaneous expenses not associated with the single-family rental use. Estimated expenses of $4,000 for the new apartments takes into consideration higher maintenance costs of individual kitchens and mechanical systems for each apartment and higher property management fees. Also note that a collection loss of 10 percent was estimated for this market. The rate of vacancy and collection loss is market-derived, and with a student rental population, it tends to be higher than it is for other markets due to greater turnover (graduation and transfers) and vacancies (summer term, for example).

THE APPRAISAL PROCESS

The systematic procedure referred to as the *appraisal process* is used to conduct property valuations. The procedure is similar to the scientific method—it requires analyzing the problem step by step, collecting and selecting appropriate market data, applying various valuation methodologies, and forming a conclusion and recommendation.

FIGURE 6.2 ■ Highest and Best Use as Improved

Costs	Single-Family	Shared-Living	New Apartments
Acquisition	$100,000	$100,000	$100,000
Demolition and construction	+ 0	+ 0	+ 250,000
Total cost	$100,000	$100,000	$350,000
Annual gross income	$7,200	$10,800	$26,400
Vacancy and collection loss (10%)	− 720	− 1,080	− 2,640
Effective gross income	$6,480	$ 9,720	$23,760
Expenses	− 0	− 1,000	− 4,000
Net operating income (NOI)	$6,480	$ 8,720	$19,760
Rate of return (NOI ÷ Total Cost)	6.5%	8.7%	5.6%

STEPS IN THE APPRAISAL PROCESS

1. Define the problem.
2. Preliminary analysis—select and collect data.
3. Analyze highest and best use.
4. Estimate land value.
5. Apply the three approaches to value.
6. Reconcile the value indications into a final value estimate.
7. Report the value.

Step One: Define the Problem

The first step in the appraisal process requires the appraiser to identify the subject property by either street address or a more precise legal description. The appraiser also must identify the property rights to be valued. An **appraisal** is a valuation of the property rights of ownership to a parcel of real property. The value associated with a leasehold interest or a life estate in a condominium unit, for example, differs from the fee simple estate interest in the same condominium unit. It also is possible that the valuation concerns only a fractional interest in the real estate, such as the subsurface rights. Therefore, the property rights to be valued are critical to the value conclusion.

USPAP requires the appraiser to indicate the date of the report (usually the signature or inspection date) and the value estimate's effective date. The effective date establishes the context for the value estimate. For example, an appraisal for inheritance tax matters may require a retrospective appraisal—that is, a value estimate before the date of the report. An appraisal for the proposed development of a shopping center requires a prospective appraisal—that is, a value estimate effective after the date of the report. The effective date of a residential property appraisal usually is the date of inspection, at which time the appraiser measures the structure and observes its condition. The appraiser also must indicate and define in the report the type of value to be estimated. Knowing how the appraisal will be used enables the appraiser to determine what type of report is sufficient. For example, is a standard form report required? Appraisals for one to four residential units involved in a federally related transaction must use the Uniform Residential Appraisal Report—URAR form. Finally, the appraiser must include any limiting conditions to which the appraisal is subject.

Step Two: Preliminary Analysis—Select and Collect Data

This step requires the appraiser to collect data and analyze the general environment and market trends affecting the subject property. External factors such as economic, social, governmental, and environmental trends are considered at the national, regional, and local levels. Economic indicators such as interest rates, effective purchasing power, construction costs, and available housing stock also are analyzed. Finally, information at the regional and community levels, such as population characteristics, price levels, employment opportunities, and economic base, are studied.

This stage also involves collecting preliminary data concerning the subject property, including the identity of the owners of record, type of ownership, assessed value of the property and amount of property taxes, identification of any easements or encroachments of record, and zoning classification. If the appraiser uses the cost-depreciation approach, current cost figures and market evidence of depreciation and obsolescence are collected. If the sales comparison approach applies, the appraiser collects data regarding sales of comparable properties. If the appraiser uses the income capitalization approach, current and historical income and expense data for the subject property and other similar properties are analyzed. The appraiser derives market capitalization rates by analyzing the transaction and income-expense data of similar properties.

Step Three: Analyze Highest and Best Use

In this step, the highest and best use as though vacant and the highest and best use as improved are identified. The comparables' highest and best use (as though vacant and as improved) should be the same as the subject property's highest and best use.

Step Four: Estimate Land Value

Many situations require the site and improvements to be valued separately. Florida statute requires separate site valuations for ad valorem tax purposes. IRS regulations require the cost of investment property to be allocated between the improvements and the site for calculation of depreciation allowance. The cost-depreciation approach to value entails a separate estimate for the site. Furthermore, Fannie Mae, Freddie Mac, the Department of Veterans Affairs (VA), and HUD/FHA (Federal Housing Administration) require separate site valuations even if the cost-depreciation approach is not used in the analysis.

Step Five: Apply the Three Approaches to Value

USPAP requires that certified and licensed appraisers attempt to use all three approaches to estimate value if enough market data are available. If the appraiser does not use an approach in the analysis, the appraiser must justify its omission. The cost-depreciation approach is most appropriate when the site value is well-substantiated, the improvements are new or nearly new and represent the highest and best use of the site, and the improvements do not suffer from substantial depreciation. The sales comparison approach usually provides the best indication of market value of residential property. The income capitalization approach applies to income-producing property.

Step Six: Reconcile the Value Indications and Final Value Estimate

Reconciliation is the process of evaluating and weighing each value indication obtained from the various approaches to value. An appraisal report usually contains three indicated values (one from each approach), and the appraiser reconciles these into a final estimate of value. The reconciliation process requires that the appraiser consider each approach's relative applicability and the source of the data collected in each approach. The appraiser must evaluate the data's reliability, choose the approach(es) that best applies to the specific appraisal problem, and select from among the alternative indications the value that best represents the defined value used in the assignment.

Assume that an appraiser has applied all three approaches to the appraisal of a two-year-old single-family home located in a neighborhood where the appraiser was able to locate five comparable sales. The appraiser believes that the data used in the sales comparison approach are most reliable because all sales were recent (within 12 months), the same builder constructed all of the comparables, very few adjustments for physical features were made, and all of the sales were located in the same subdivision (a location adjustment was not needed). The appraiser also relied heavily on the cost-depreciation approach because the home was nearly new and therefore was the property's highest and best use exhibiting almost no depreciation or obsolescence, and because the developer supplied reliable cost figures. The appraiser was able to apply the income approach because rental data were obtained on two homes in the same neighborhood. However, the appraiser gave this approach the least weight because the rental data were limited; about 95 percent of the homes in the neighborhood were owner-occupied. Figure 6.3 summarizes the appraiser's final reconciliation of the three approaches.

The appraiser could have given all of the weight to the sales comparison approach. The decision is subjective, based primarily on the reliability of the data collected and the purpose of the appraisal. In most cases, an appraiser uses reconciliation to blend varying estimates of value from different approaches and comparables into a final estimate of value.

Step Seven: Report the Value

The last step in the appraisal process is to prepare the appraisal report. As discussed below, this report can be an oral report (although such a report usually is not appropriate), a form report (such as the URAR form), or a narrative report. The appraiser and the client should agree on the type of report at the time the appraiser accepts the assignment.

TYPES OF APPRAISAL REPORTS AND REPORTING FORMATS

Appraisers may choose from three reporting formats to communicate appraisals: oral reports, form reports, and narrative reports.

Oral reports. Oral reports generally are reserved for situations involving expert testimony. An oral report should include the property description, assumptions, conditions, and reasoning on which the appraiser bases the value conclusion. (Appraisals involving federally related transactions must be written.)

FIGURE 6.3 ■ Final Reconciliation

Approach	Indicated Value		Weight		Weighted Value
Sales comparison	$160,000	×	55%	=	$ 88,000
Cost-depreciation	155,000	×	35%	=	54,250
Income capitalization	150,000	×	10%	=	+ 15,000
Final estimate of value					$157,250

Form reports. Financial institutions typically require standardized form reports. A standardized form provides a financial institution's appraisers with a quick and efficient way to communicate their work. Review appraisers and loan officers can follow and verify the information in a form report easily. Also, purchasers of mortgages in the secondary market (Fannie Mae, Freddie Mac, etc.) require that a standardized form be used. A form report requires the same appraisal methodology and supporting data as does a narrative report.

Narrative reports. Narrative reports are written reports that do not use standardized forms. USPAP recognizes three reporting options, characterized primarily by the scope and detail of presentation within the reports: self-contained reports, summary reports, and restricted reports.

Self-contained reports. Self-contained reports are detailed narrative reports that address each issue in depth and include complete descriptions of the data, reasoning, and analyses used in a valuation process. A self-contained appraisal report supplies all relevant information; no reference to the appraiser's work file is needed.

Summary reports. Narrative summary reports include some, but not all, of the descriptive information involved in a valuation process; that is, they summarize the data and analyses used. For example, a six-page market analysis section in a self-contained report may compare to a four-paragraph summation of external factors at the national, regional, community, and neighborhood levels in a summary report.

Restricted reports. Narrative restricted reports simply state appraisers' conclusions. Generally, they do not include any of the descriptive information supporting the valuation process. Restricted reports are meant to be used only by the clients—anyone else using the reports is considered an "unintended" user.

SUMMARY OF IMPORTANT POINTS

- An *appraisal* is an estimate or opinion of value of property rights as a specific date based on supportable evidence.
- Appraisers and real estate licensees who conduct real estate appraisals are required to comply with the *Uniform Standards of Professional Appraisal Practice* (USPAP) developed by the Appraisal Standards Board of the Appraisal Foundation. Appraisal reports involving a federally related transaction must be prepared by a state-certified or licensed appraiser.
- A comparative market analysis (CMA) is used to assist sellers with establishing an asking price or to assist a buyer with establishing an offering price. A CMA is not an appraisal.
- A *broker's price opinion* (BPO) is a written opinion of the value of real property. Florida real estate licensees are allowed to prepare and charge for BPOs provided the BPO is not labeled as an appraisal. If a valuation assignment involves a federally related transaction, an appraisal must be conducted by a licensed or certified appraiser.
- *Value* is determined by what consumers are willing to pay in the marketplace. *Price* refers to the amount of money actually paid. *Cost* is the total expenditure to create the improvement.
- To have value, goods and services must possess four traits: (1) demand, (2) utility, (3) scarcity, and (4) transferability.

- The type of value most frequently estimated is market value. *Market value* is the most probable price that a property should bring in a competitive and open market under all conditions requisite to a fair sale, with the buyer and seller each acting prudently and knowledgeably, and assuming the price is not affected by undue stimulus.
- *Supply* is the amount and type of real estate available for sale or rent at different price levels in a given real estate market.
- *Demand* is the total quantity of a good that consumers are willing and able to purchase at various price levels over a given period of time.
- The principle of anticipation is based on the premise that expectation of future benefits creates value.
- The principle of substitution holds that when several goods or services offering similar benefits are available, consumers tend toward the one with the lowest price.
- An *overimprovement* occurs when an owner invests more money in a structure than the owner can reasonable expect to recapture.
- The principle of conformity suggests that property values are maximized when architectural homogeneity and uniformity of land use occur in a neighborhood.
- External economies result from positive external forces that enhance property values. External diseconomies have a negative impact on value.
- *Highest and best use* is the most profitable use of a property. It is the probable and legal use of real property that is physically possible, defendable, and financially feasible.
- *Assemblage* is the combining of two or more adjoining properties into one tract. *Plottage* is the added value resulting from combining (assembling) two or more properties into one large parcel.
- *Progression* is the principle that the value of an inferior property is enhanced by its association with superior properties of the same type. *Regression* is the principle that the value of a superior property is adversely affected by its association with an inferior property of the same type.
- *Situs* refers to people's preferences, both physical and economic, for a certain area owing to factors such as weather, job opportunities, and transportation facilities.
- *Reconciliation* is the process of evaluating and weighing each value indication obtained from the various approaches to value.
- The steps in the appraisal process are (1) define the problem; (2) preliminary analysis; (3) highest and best use analysis; (4) estimate land value; (5) apply the three approaches to value; (6) reconcile; and (7) report the value estimate.
- Appraisers choose from three reporting formats to communicate appraisals: (1) oral reports, (2) form reports, and (3) narrative reports.

Practice Problem Solution

(The Practice Problem is located on page 154.)

The cost is the amount paid to purchase the lot and build the house: $270,000.

The price is the transaction price paid by the son: $450,000.

The value is the market value based on an appraisal: $525,000.

REVIEW QUESTIONS

1. A real estate licensee may accept which appraisal assignment?
   a. An assignment to appraise a residential condominium unit for the purpose of refinancing through Bank of America, N.A.
   b. An assignment to appraise a retail store for Florida Teachers' Credit Union
   c. An assignment to appraise a single-family home to be used by a couple applying for an FHA mortgage through a branch office of First USA Bank, N.A.
   d. An assignment to appraise a duplex for an attorney's client concerning estate liquidation

2. A professional office building was sold to an investor for $830,000. The $830,000 is best described as the property's
   a. market value.
   b. price.
   c. cost.
   d. going concern value.

3. A type of value based on a property's current use that does not take into consideration the property's highest and best use is referred to as
   a. assessed value.
   b. investment value.
   c. value in use.
   d. interim use.

4. When a homeowner, a single head of household, recently was laid off, she decided she must sell her home. A buyer purchased her home three weeks later, contingent on the homeowner agreeing to pay the buyer's closing costs. An appraiser collecting data for comparable sales may decide that the sale of the home does not reflect market value because
   a. the homeowner was a single head of household.
   b. payment was not made in cash.
   c. there is no indication as to whether the buyer was aware of the homeowner's unemployment.
   d. the price may have been affected by undue stimuli.

5. Determinants of demand do NOT include
   a. number and household composition of consumers.
   b. employment levels and average income.
   c. available housing stock.
   d. consumer preferences and lifestyles.

6. Which statement is MOST applicable to the principle of substitution as it applies to the cost-depreciation approach?
   a. If consumers expect the price of building materials to increase, they are more likely to purchase an existing home and remodel.
   b. An entrepreneur considers purchasing a property that has been used as a small cafe versus purchasing a nearby vacant lot and building a new cafe.
   c. An investor weighs the desirability of three investment properties and compares the projected net operating income from each of the properties.
   d. Two equally desirable homes are for sale on the same block in a subdivision. A prospective buyer makes an offer on one of the homes based on the lower of the two asking prices.

7. A home is located in a subdivision of three-bedroom and four-bedroom homes that typically feature two-car garages and screened-in porches. One of the homeowners adds a concrete in-ground pool, encloses the porch, and adds a third bath. The appraisal principle that MOST applies to this situation is
   a. increasing and decreasing returns.
   b. supply and demand.
   c. economies and diseconomies.
   d. substitution.

8. A car dealership is located on a heavily traveled street. Nearby are three car dealerships for other car manufacturers, as well as several auto body shops and auto repair shops. The value of the car dealership (business and real property) is MOST influenced by
   a. conformity.
   b. external economies.
   c. external diseconomies.
   d. increasing and decreasing returns.

9. The process of determining what type of structure should be built on a site ready for development is referred to as
   a. investment value.
   b. the principle of substitution.
   c. highest and best use as though vacant.
   d. highest and best use as improved.

10. The process of giving weight to the value derived from each of the three approaches is referred to as
    a. simple averaging.
    b. reconciliation.
    c. highest and best use analysis.
    d. validation.

11. A standardized appraisal report used for loan purposes is referred to as a
    a. narrative report.
    b. federally related transaction.
    c. form report.
    d. self-contained report.

Use the information below to answer questions 12 through 16:

An appraiser is evaluating a vacant site zoned for professional offices. The market analysis indicates that the property could be developed as either a dental clinic or a building of smaller professional office suites. The appraiser has projected annual net operating income for the clinic at $98,500 and for the office suites at $75,000. The market-derived capitalization rate for the two uses is 11 percent. The appraiser estimates development costs at $650,000 for the dental office and $475,000 for the office suites.

12. The capitalized value (rounded to nearest hundred) of the dental clinic is
    a. $98,500.
    b. $245,500.
    c. $650,000.
    d. $895,500.

13. The capitalized value (rounded to nearest hundred) of the professional office suites is
    a. $75,000.
    b. $450,000.
    c. $681,800.
    d. $825,000.

14. The residual land value (rounded to the nearest hundred) of the dental clinic is
    a. $98,500.
    b. $147,000.
    c. $245,500.
    d. $797,000.

15. The residual land value (rounded to nearest hundred) of the professional office suites is
    a. $206,800.
    b. $245,500.
    c. $681,800.
    d. $895,500.

16. The highest and best use of the site as though vacant is
    a. the dental clinic.
    b. the professional office suites.
    c. any use that produces the highest NOI.
    d. None of the above

CHAPTER

7 SALES COMPARISON, COST DEPRECIATION, AND INCOME APPROACHES

KEY TERMS

accrued depreciation
arm's-length transaction
cash equivalency
contract rent
curable
economic life
effective age
effective gross income (EGI)
external obsolescence
final adjusted sale price
fixed expense
fixture
functional obsolescence
gross income multiplier (GIM)
gross rent multiplier (GRM)
heterogeneous
incurable
market abstraction
market conditions-adjusted normal sale price
market rent
net operating income (NOI)
normal sale price
personal property
physical deterioration
potential gross income (PGI)
replacement cost
reproduction cost
reserve for replacements
successive sales analysis
trade fixture
vacancy and collection loss
variable expense

OVERVIEW

This chapter explains the procedures used in the three approaches to value and their underlying theories. Appraisers use three variations of the sales comparison approach: direct sales comparison, direct sales comparison using statistical inference, and regression analysis. Direct sales comparison, the most common variation of the sales comparison approach, requires a small sample of comparable sales (three or four typically) and produces a single estimate of value. This approach relies heavily on appraiser judgment. Direct sales comparison is the traditional methodology that prevails in appraisal practice and therefore is the focus of this chapter. The chapter also explains the cost-depreciation and income capitalization approaches.

Once you have completed this chapter, you should be able to:

- describe the assumptions underlying the sales comparison approach;
- calculate the various adjustments necessary under the sales comparison approach;
- distinguish between fixtures and trade fixtures;

- construct a sales comparison adjustment grid using the proper sequence of adjustments;
- distinguish among normal sale price, market conditions-adjusted normal sale price, and final adjusted sale price;
- list the steps in the cost-depreciation approach;
- distinguish between reproduction cost and replacement cost;
- describe the three methods for estimating cost;
- distinguish among the types of accrued depreciation;
- calculate an accrued depreciation adjustment using the lump-sum age-life method;
- define effective age and economic life;
- perform a GRM analysis;
- distinguish among potential gross income, effective gross income, and net operating income;
- distinguish among the three types of operating expenses;
- develop a reconstructed operating statement;
- calculate a market-derived capitalization rate; and
- calculate value using the income approach formula.

SALES COMPARISON APPROACH

The sales comparison approach to value is based on the premise that a property's value can be inferred from the transaction prices of similar properties, called *comparables*. This approach is founded on two underlying assumptions: (1) market price is valid evidence of market value, and (2) a well-informed buyer will not pay more for a property than the price of equally desirable substitute properties (the principle of substitution).

If we were interested in knowing the market value of IBM stock, we would investigate the opening and closing prices per share and the number of shares traded on that particular day. The price at which shares of IBM stock are traded on a given day indicates the stock's market value at that point in time. We qualify our value estimate to a given point in time because anyone who observes the stock market knows that stock prices change continually. Because one share of IBM common stock is identical to every other share of the same stock, it is said to be a *homogeneous* product. Furthermore, because many shares of identical stock are traded freely in a centralized market (a stock exchange), the traded price is also the stock's current value.

In the real estate market, we are interested in the transaction prices of real property. As with shares of stock, real estate values change over time, so our estimate of value is always as of a certain date, referred to as the *effective date*. However, the real estate market is far from perfect. Each property is unique—or **heterogeneous**—and real estate is traded infrequently. Consequently, we must compare a given property of interest, the subject property, with comparable properties that are not identical to the property of interest. This results in the need to adjust the transaction prices of traded properties to approximate the subject property's price. To make matters even more difficult, because of the limited market, an appraiser must rely on a small sample of traded properties to make value estimates as compared with the millions of shares of stock traded on a stock exchange.

The process of estimating the value of real property using direct sales comparison involves finding market transactions of properties comparable to the subject property. To be considered comparable, the transactions must involve transfer of the same property rights (or legal estate) as the subject property and they must have the same highest and best use. Also, the transactions must be the result of arm's-length bargaining. In an **arm's-length transaction** the parties deal from equal bargaining positions, they act in their own best interests, and they are not subject to each other's control or influence, as in transactions between family members. The appraiser adjusts the transaction prices of the comparables for differences from the subject property to arrive at an estimate of value for the subject.

Elements of Comparison

Factors requiring adjustment, known as *elements of comparison*, comprise both transactional characteristics and property characteristics. Each element of comparison is explained below. The section begins with a discussion of transactional characteristics and concludes with property characteristics.

Financing terms. The financing a buyer and seller agree to may influence the price paid for real estate. If a comparable transaction involved atypical financing, the appraiser may need to adjust the comparable's sale price to reflect normal financing terms for the market. However, if the appraiser determines that the atypical financing terms did not cause the comparable's sale price to differ from those produced under normal financing terms, the value adjustment equals zero. If atypical financing affects the purchase price at all, it usually drives the price upward. The resulting transaction price is the sum of two values—the value of the real property and the value of the special financing. It is the appraiser's task to estimate the value of the atypical financing and adjust the transaction price downward to reflect what the comparable would have sold for with normal financing.

Nonmarket financing generally involves one of four scenarios, as discussed below.

1. Mortgage assumption. In times of rising mortgage interest rates, it may benefit a buyer to assume the loan originally issued to the seller. In such a case, the buyer may be willing to pay a premium for the home in exchange for assuming the below-market interest rate loan.

2. Seller financing. A seller may be willing to finance all or a portion of the purchase price at a below-market interest rate.

3. Contract for deed. A seller may allow a buyer to purchase the property by making periodic payments. The seller accepts a down payment from the buyer and finances the rest of the purchase price. (A contract for deed also is known as an *installment sale contract* or a *land contract*.)

4. Wraparound loan. During periods of high interest rates, a buyer may be able to preserve an existing, low-interest loan by borrowing the outstanding amount plus an additional amount from the seller or a third party. The wraparound mortgage encompasses the existing mortgage, and a new mortgage "wraps" around it. Most lenders today use an alienation clause or a due-on-sale clause that prevents a seller and buyer from using this financing technique (see chapter 12).

In recent years, mortgage interest rates have been attractively low and stable, making the need for a financing adjustment less likely. However, even in times of low interest rates, a buyer may seek special financing concessions, such as seller financing, for example, due to a past bankruptcy, or seller assistance with the cost of discount points.

USPAP 2010–2011 STANDARDS RULE 1-2(c)

In developing a real property appraisal, an appraiser must identify the type and definition of *value* and if the value opinion is market value, ascertain whether the value is the most probable price:

- in terms of cash; or
- in terms of financial arrangements equivalent to cash; or
- in other precisely defined terms; and
- if an opinion of value is to be based on non-market financing or financing with unusual conditions or incentives, the terms of such financing must be clearly identified and the appraiser's opinion of their contribution to or negative influence on value must be developed by analysis of relevant market data.

Adjusting for financing. An appraiser may use several methods to estimate the effect of atypical financing. Theoretically, **market abstraction** works best. It involves locating several transactions of similar properties, some of which involved normal market financing and others that involved the type of nonmarket financing exhibited by the comparable sale. The appraiser must adjust each transaction price to reflect the others *except* for financing differences (also referred to as *paired data analysis*); any remaining price difference is attributed to the atypical financing. Some obvious limitations to applying this approach exist. Several recent sales of properties similar to the subject property and to the comparables involving both typical and atypical financing must be available. Also, the type of nonmarket financing must match the atypical financing of the comparable requiring adjustment. Finally, the abstracted adjustment is limited to the specific market from which it is derived.

A method known as **cash equivalency** calculates the present value of streams of cash inflows or outflows by discounting them at appropriate interest rates. The resulting values are cash equivalent prices. The value of the financing adjustment is measured as the present value of the difference between the mortgage payment on the favorably financed note and the mortgage payment that would have been required had the rate been the current market interest rate. The easiest and least controversial cash equivalency adjustment involves seller-paid points. Typically, seller-paid points are deducted from the transaction price to yield the cash equivalent price. Appraisers, however, always must consider how seller-paid points actually affected the market values of properties in a specific market. They must make certain that cash equivalency adjustments reflect market perceptions.

Conditions of sale. An appraiser must verify with one of the parties to a transaction the conditions under which the transaction occurred to determine whether it was an arm's-length transaction or whether the parties to the transaction did not have relatively equal bargaining power. Sales between family members or business partners and transactions concluded under abnormal pressure (for example, foreclosures) violate important assumptions regarding market value (see chapter 6). Because very little market evidence exists about how such conditions affect prices, appraisers avoid using these types of transactions as comparables.

Market conditions. When using past sales of comparable properties to make inferences about value in today's market, an appraiser must consider the market conditions under which a transaction occurred. The question of concern is this—Would the transaction prices paid for comparable properties, if sold in today's market, differ from the prices actually paid? An adjustment for market conditions is required if, since the time the comparable sales were transacted, property values in a given market have either appreciated or depreciated. The most common reason an appraiser cites for adjusting for market conditions is to compensate for inflation or deflation. However, even in stable economic times, market conditions may change due to investors' perceptions of the market, forces of supply and demand, tax law revisions, building moratoriums, changing local economies and diseconomies, and so forth.

An adjustment for market conditions is justified only if the market conditions in a particular market have changed over time. An adjustment is not necessary if market conditions have remained stable, even if considerable time has elapsed. Changes in market conditions usually are measured as a percentage of previous prices. If a property's physical characteristics remain unchanged, analyzing two or more sales of the same property over a period of time indicates the percentage of price change. This technique, known as **successive sales analysis**, involves locating properties in the same neighborhood (market) as the subject property that have sold recently (within the last few years) two or more times.

The repeat sales can vary in physical characteristics from the subject property. The most important element is that the sales occurred in the same marketplace. Therefore, location is the critical determinant of comparability for successive sales analysis. An appraiser should attempt to analyze several sets of sales to arrive at an appropriate adjustment for market conditions. An adjustment supported by just one set of sales is not reliable.

Assume, for example, that you have located three successive sales in the same neighborhood as the subject property. Record the initial selling price, the resale transaction price, and the number of months between the initial sale and resale for each property:

Property	Initial Price	Months Between Sales	Resale Price
A	$167,000	28	$182,900
B	158,500	26	172,200
C	160,000	22	174,000

You can obtain the percentage change of value by dividing the resale price by the initial price. Then calculate a monthly rate of change using the following formula:

Market Conditions Adjustment

	Resale price
minus	Initial sale price
equals	Difference in prices
divided by	Initial sale price
equals	Percentage change
divided by	Number of months between sales
equals	Monthly rate of change

Applying the formula to the text box above, the monthly rate of change for Property A is calculated as follows:

$182,900 resale price − $167,000 initial price = $15,900 difference in prices
$15,900 difference ÷ $167,000 initial price = .0952096 percentage change
.0952096 percentage change ÷ 28 months = .0034 monthly rate of change
(Rounded to fourth decimal place)

Apply the formula to Properties B and C to calculate their monthly rate of change. Compare your results to the table below:

Property	Resale Price	Initial Price	Difference in Price	Months Between Sales	Percentage Change	Monthly Rate of Change
A	$182,900	$167,000	$15,900	28	.0952096	.0034*
B	$172,200	$158,500	$13,700	26	.0864353	.0033
C	$174,000	$160,000	$14,000	22	.0875	.0040

*Rounded to the fourth decimal place

The average monthly rate of change is .0036 (.0034 + .0033 + .0040 = .0107 ÷ 3 = .0036), or just over one-third of 1 percent (.36 percent) per month. The average monthly rate of appreciation for property in this neighborhood is .36 percent per month. The monthly rate of change can be applied to past sale prices of comparable properties to determine the prices they should bring under current market conditions. Assume a comparable sold for $179,000 six months ago. To calculate the adjusted sale price for market conditions, multiply the transaction price by .0036 times six months:

$179,000 × (.0036 × 6 months) = .0216
$179,000 × .0216 = $3,866 adjustment for market conditions (rounded to nearest dollar)
$179,000 + $3,866 = $182,866

Successive sales analysis is valid, provided change occurs at a constant rate. However, markets often have cyclical or seasonal patterns. In an annual market, there may be a short period of time with erratic activity, but the average for the year does not identify the short-term fluctuation. For example, last year's average increase in values for condominiums

USPAP 2010–2011 STANDARDS RULE 1-2(e)

Appraisers must identify the characteristics of the property that are relevant to the type and definition of value and intended use of the appraisal, including:

- its location and physical, legal, and economic attributes;
- the real property interest to be valued;
- any personal property, trade fixtures, or intangible items that are not real property but are included in the appraisal;
- any known easements, restrictions, encumbrances, leases, covenants, contracts, special assessments; and
- whether the subject property is a factional interest, physical segment, or partial holding.

in Port Charlotte may be six percent. However, closer scrutiny reveals that all of the appreciation occurred in the first quarter of the year, when northern buyers were prevalent (supply and demand forces at work). Therefore, to assume a one-half percent rate of change per month would be faulty because an adjustment for market conditions would be based on the calendar quarter in which the sale took place.

Personal property. When a comparable transaction includes personal property that is not common to the subject property, the comparable's price must be adjusted by the personal property's value. Any tangible items not permanently attached to real estate are classified as **personal property**. Condominiums located in coastal and southern Florida sometimes are purchased completely furnished. In such a situation, the value of the personal property, or *chattel*, is estimated, then subtracted from the comparable's transaction price.

An appraiser must consider whether an item is personal property or a fixture to determine whether to include it in the real estate's value. **Fixtures** are items that originally were personal property, but have been permanently attached to or made part of real property. Because a fixture is real property, its contribution to value is included in the value estimate. Also, any personal property to be included in the value estimate should be identified and described in the appraisal. The appraiser also must distinguish between fixtures and trade fixtures. A **trade fixture** is an article a commercial tenant attaches as a necessary part of the tenant's trade or business. It remains personal property regardless of how the article is affixed. USPAP cautions that an appraiser may require additional expertise in personal property or business appraisal to allocate the overall value to the various components. Separate valuation of trade fixtures is required when they are significant to the overall value estimate.

Location. A property's location is judged in relation to comparable properties. In a previous survey conducted by the National Association of REALTORS®, prospective homebuyers identified proximity to employment, schools, shopping, and recreation as among the most important locational factors that influenced their selections. Other important locational considerations include the compatibility of land use and the quality of homes in the surrounding area (principle of conformity) and a sufficient buffer from external diseconomies, such as crime and highway noise. Proximity to noxious odors, air traffic patterns, and hazardous waste sites can have a significant negative impact on property value. When homebuyers compare neighborhoods, the availability and quality of governmental services such as fire and police protection are important, as is the availability of municipal services such as public waste systems, natural gas, storm sewers, street lighting, and so forth. When describing a subject property's location, an appraiser should note the condition and quality of surrounding properties, the availability of utilities and transportation, and the proximity to external economies and diseconomies.

If a comparable property is located in the same neighborhood as the subject property, it is likely that a location adjustment is not needed. It is possible, however, that the subject property and the comparable property do not share an equally desirable location within the same neighborhood. For example, one may be on the outer perimeter of the neighborhood, where it is exposed to negative influences, such as proximity to a busy street. When a comparable is located in a different neighborhood, the appraiser must conduct a thorough analysis to determine whether the differences between the two neighborhoods affect the comparable's sale price. The appraiser compares transaction prices of properties in the subject neighborhood with transaction prices of properties in the comparable neighborhood. It is recommended that the appraiser estimate locational adjustments by comparing recently sold properties that are similar in physical characteristics, but have different locational characteristics. This procedure uses a technique referred to as *paired data analysis*.

Assume, for example, that the subject property is located in the Milestone subdivision, developed by Robertson Development Company. Milestone is convenient to an elementary school, grocery stores, and other support services. The subdivision has an active neighborhood association, and the homes are well-maintained. Milestone is buffered by a strip of environmentally protected land. The Clear Creek subdivision, also developed by Robertson Development Company, is very similar in character to the subject neighborhood. However, Clear Creek is not as convenient to schools and shopping and it does not abut a natural habitat, making it more susceptible to road noise. The appraiser identifies pairs of very similar homes located in the subject property's neighborhood and in the comparable neighborhood. The appraiser compares home prices in the subject neighborhood with home prices in the comparable neighborhood to determine what price differential, if any, is associated with the different location. Because the same company built the homes in both subdivisions, the appraiser found comparable properties that are very similar in terms of quality of construction, floor plans, square footage, and so forth. Therefore, any price differential can be attributed to the different location.

The appraiser uses the following procedure to estimate the price differential.

Step one. Locate a home in the comparable property's neighborhood that is similar to the subject property. This is referred to as a *matched pair*. The appraiser must adjust for any differences in physical characteristics so that the two properties differ only in terms of location.

Step two. Locate at least one additional matched pair. Adjustments based on a single matched pair are not reliable.

Step three. Calculate the difference in transaction prices between the properties identified in the two locations. For example:

Property	Milestone	Clear Creek	Price Difference
Matched pair A	$175,000	$162,000	$13,000
Matched pair B	178,500	165,000	13,500

Step four. To calculate the percentage difference for each pair, divide the price difference by the smaller of the sale prices:

Property	Price Difference		Smaller Sale Price		Percentage Difference
Matched pair A	$13,000	÷	$162,000	=	8.02%*
Matched pair B	13,500	÷	165,000	=	8.18

*Rounded to second decimal place

Step five. Calculate the average price difference by averaging the two percentage differences:

$$(8.02\% + 8.18\%) \div 2 = 8.10\%$$

The appraiser concludes that a home in Milestone sells for about an eight percent premium as compared with a home in Clear Creek.

Physical characteristics. Physical characteristics that may require an adjustment include age and condition of the improvements, size (square footage) of the improvements, number and size of rooms; type and quality of construction; age and condition of mechanical systems; age and condition of the roof; functional utility; architectural design; amenities such as fireplaces, spas, and pools; and the site's physical characteristics, including size, shape, topography, and quality of landscaping. An appraiser should attempt to locate comparable transactions of properties similar to the subject property in terms of physical characteristics. Particularly desirable are comparables that agree with the subject property in terms of size, number of rooms, and age. The appraiser should derive any adjustments for physical characteristics from market evidence. The appraiser gives each significant physical difference a positive or negative dollar value or assigns it a relative percentage adjustment. Any adjustment is a value difference—it is not based on cost.

The preferred method of estimating adjustments is to extract the adjustment amount from the market using matched pairs. *Matched pairs analysis* involves selecting pairs of sales in the market, one with the item for which the appraiser seeks the adjustment and the other without the item. The theory is that if a single characteristic is the only difference between two sales, the difference in the two transaction prices can be attributed to the isolated property characteristic.

Assume the subject property is a four-bedroom, two-bath, two-car garage, split-plan home with an in-ground concrete pool. The homeowners enlarged the fourth bedroom to make a spacious home office. The home is situated on a corner lot. The appraiser has located two comparable sales in the same subdivision, both situated on interior lots. The comparables share the same floor plan, so they are similar in terms of physical characteristics. One of the comparable properties has an in-ground pool; the other does not. To extract the value of the pool, the appraiser deducts the smaller sale price from the larger one:

Property	Sale Price
Property A: 4-br, 2-ba, 2-car with pool, interior lot	$150,000
Property B: 4-br, 2-ba, 2-car without pool, interior lot	135,000

By subtracting the $135,000 sale price from $150,000, the appraiser attributes the $15,000 difference to the pool's value. It may have *cost* $20,000 to install the pool; however, market evidence indicates that buyers in this marketplace are willing to pay only $15,000 for the amenity.

Assume that the appraiser locates a third comparable transaction in the same neighborhood. It also has a pool and is located one block from the subject property on a corner lot. By comparing this property (let's call it Property C) with Property A, the appraiser isolates the value difference for the corner lot:

Property	Sale Price
Property C: 4-br, 2-ba, 2-car with pool, corner lot	$157,000
Property A: 4-br, 2-ba, 2-car with pool, interior lot	150,000

The appraiser extracts the value difference for the corner lot by using property A as the base sale. The premium (adjustment) is $7,000 for the corner lot.

To derive an adjustment for the additional square footage in the subject's fourth bedroom that the homeowners use as an office, the appraiser locates comparable property D in the same neighborhood. It is similar to property B except that it has an extra 300 square feet of living area:

Property	Sale Price
Property D: 4-br, 2-ba, 2-car without pool, 2,300 sq. ft. int. lot	$153,000
Property B: 4-br, 2-ba, 2-car without pool, 2,000 sq. ft. int. lot	135,000

The price difference for square footage is $18,000 divided by 300 square feet, or $60 per square foot. The appraiser uses this unit of comparison to make size adjustments. When projecting price adjustments for size, the appraiser must consider the principle of decreasing returns. The contribution of added square footage tends to be smaller than the contribution of the previous footage. Value increases as size increases to a point, but eventually the structure becomes overimproved in relation to its surroundings. Therefore, the appraiser takes into consideration the square-foot adjustment in relation to the surroundings.

Methods of Adjustment

An appraiser adjusts a comparable's transaction price toward the subject property. For example, if the subject property has a swimming pool, but a comparable does not, the appraiser increases the comparable's transaction price to reflect the pool's value. The appraiser adjusts the comparable's transaction price to simulate what it would have sold for in the marketplace if the property had been identical to the subject property. Adjustments can be made as percentages of sale price or as dollar value adjustments. Generally, dollar adjustments are preferred because they are easier to trace to market extraction. Adjustments for market conditions, however, almost always are described in percentage terms, such as six percent appreciation per year. The appraiser applies percentages to the comparable property's transaction price to derive a dollar adjustment. The sequence used to make multiple adjustments should be logical. In fact, the Appraisal Institute developed a sequence of adjustments that is generally accepted throughout the appraisal industry.

The appraiser makes any necessary adjustments for financing and conditions of sale (e.g., arm's-length bargaining, time on market before contract, etc.) first to determine a **normal sale price**. This is the price the property would have sold for *at the time of the transaction* if the transaction had been consistent with the market (e.g., typical days on the market, typical market financing, etc.). Financing adjustments and conditions of sale reflect transactional characteristics of comparable properties that differ from the subject property. The appraiser makes these adjustments before adjusting for market conditions, location, and physical characteristics. For example, if the appraiser makes a financing adjustment, the appraiser must refer to the financing conditions obtained at the time the transaction occurred. Therefore, the appraiser adjusts for financing and conditions of sale before adjusting for market conditions (change in value since date of sale) so that the adjustment for market conditions is applied to the correct value base.

The appraiser applies the adjustment for market conditions to the normal sale price to derive a **market conditions-adjusted normal sale price**—that is, the price the comparable likely would sell for in *today's market*. The market conditions-adjusted normal sale price becomes the value base for adjustments for location and physical characteristics because these adjustments reflect today's value. The **final adjusted sale price** therefore represents the price that the comparable property likely would sell for in today's market if it were exactly like the subject property.

The entire sequence of adjustments and the adjusted sale prices should be summarized in an adjustment grid like the one shown in Figure 7.1. The transaction price is entered first, then any adjustments for financing terms and conditions of sale are made to derive a normal sale price. Assume that property E involved seller-paid points; therefore, a down-

FIGURE 7.1 ■ Adjustment Grid

Element of Comparison	A	B	C	D	E	Subject
Transaction price	$150,000	$135,000	$157,000	$153,000	$160,000	Unknown
Financing terms	Market	Market	Market	Market	– $1,500	Market
Conditions of sale	Normal	Normal	Normal	Normal	Normal	Normal
Normal sale price	$150,000	$135,000	$157,000	$153,000	$158,500	
Market conditions	Equal	Equal	Equal	Equal	+ 3%	Today
Market conditions—Adjusted normal sale price	$150,000	$135,000	$157,000	$153,000	$163,255	
Location	Milestone	Milestone	Milestone	Milestone	+ 8%	Milestone
Physical characteristics:						
Square feet of living area	+$12,000	+$12,000	+$12,000	– $6,000	–$12,000	2,200 sq. ft.
Lot	+$7,000	+$7,000	Corner	+$7,000	+ $7,000	Corner
Pool	Pool	+$15,000	Pool	+$15,000	Pool	Pool
Final adjusted sale price	$169,000	$169,000	$169,000	$169,000	$171,315	

ward adjustment of $1,500 (cost of the points) was subtracted from the transaction price to derive a normal sale price of $158,500. Market conditions adjustments almost always are expressed as percentages of change in value since the time the transactions took place. The entries indicate that a market conditions adjustment was needed only for property E because all of the other properties were recent sales and reflect current market conditions. The appraiser has determined that properties have appreciated three percent since property E was sold. Therefore, the appraiser multiplies the normal sale price of $158,500 by 1.03 to derive the market conditions-adjusted normal sale price of $163,255.

Comparables A through D all were located in the Milestone subdivision, so a location adjustment was not required. Property E was located in the Clear Creek subdivision, so an upward adjustment of 8 percent was made to account for the less desirable location.

Adjustments for physical conditions were made to each comparable sale's market conditions-adjusted normal sale price to derive the final adjusted sale price. Property A required a +$7,000 adjustment because it was situated on an interior lot. It also was adjusted upward $12,000 for the difference in square footage (200 square feet × $60/sq. ft. = $12,000). Property B did not have a pool; therefore, it was adjusted upward by $15,000. It also required a +$7,000 adjustment for the lot and a +$12,000 adjustment for square footage. Property C required a single +$12,000 adjustment for square footage. Property D was adjusted +$15,000 for the absence of a pool, +$7,000 because it was situated on an interior lot and –$6,000 because it has 100 more square feet of living area than the subject property (100 square feet × $60/sq. ft. = $6,000). Finally, property E was adjusted upward by $7,000 for the interior lot and downward by $12,000 for extra square footage.

The results of the analysis provide strong market evidence that the subject property's value, based on the sales comparison approach, is $169,000. Property E's final adjusted sale price is somewhat higher. However, due to adjustments for financing, market conditions, and location, the appraiser likely would conclude that this sale is not very reliable market evidence compared with the other market transactions.

The final value estimate is not always a simple average. In reality, it is difficult to locate comparables that fit the mold for matched pairs, so the appraiser must use statistical models and inferences. Usually the final adjusted sale prices vary; the appraiser must reconcile them into a final estimate of value.

COST-DEPRECIATION APPROACH

The cost-depreciation approach is based on the theory that a knowledgeable purchaser will not pay more for a property than the cost of acquiring a similar site and constructing an acceptable substitute structure. Imagine a five-year-old single-family home located in the Milestone subdivision. A buyer admires the house so much that she has the exact same one built on the vacant lot next door. The two homes are identical in terms of square footage, floor plan, and building materials.

A single exception exists: one is brand new. The cost to build the new duplicate home is termed *reproduction cost*. But wouldn't the new home have greater market value than the five-year-old twin? The older home will suffer some loss in value due to physical deterioration and obsolescence: the roof shingles are five years old; all of the appliances and mechanical equipment have endured five years of use; and the carpet shows signs of wear. Therefore, the appraiser must estimate the value associated with the difference in age between the two homes.

COST-DEPRECIATION APPROACH

"The approach is especially persuasive when the site value is well supported and the improvements are new or suffer only minor accrued depreciation and, therefore, approximate the highest and best use of the site as though vacant."

Appraisal Institute, *The Appraisal of Real Estate,* 11th edition, p. 338.

Conceptually, the cost approach is a variation of the sales comparison approach: the subject property is compared to a new duplicate of itself. All of the elements of comparison are held constant, with the single exception of age, which is measured in terms of accrued depreciation. The underlying assumption is that the cost to reproduce a structure new, less any loss in value due to the subject property's actual age, plus site value, produces a valid estimate of market value.

Applicability of the Approach

The applicability of each approach to value is related to the availability of market data and reliability of the estimates. Many reliable sources of cost data exist. However, estimates of accrued depreciation tend to be less reliable for older structures. Thus, the cost-depreciation approach is most reliable for new or proposed construction and newer structures. It also is valuable when appraising owner-occupied residential properties located in an area characterized by very little market activity. Market activity is a must in obtaining reliable market data for the sales comparison approach. Furthermore, if the subject property is located in an area exclusively owner occupied, it makes the income approach less applicable.

An appraiser uses the cost approach to estimate the value of properties that are not exchanged frequently in the market, such as special-purpose properties. The approach is applicable for insurance appraisals because the approach requires land and improvements to be valued separately. Appraisals for accounting purposes use the cost approach to estimate depreciation for income tax purposes.

Steps in the Cost-Depreciation Approach

The steps involved in the cost approach are presented below. Each step is discussed in more detail later in the chapter.

Step one. Estimate the current reproduction (or replacement) cost of the improvements as of the appraisal date. Estimated costs include direct (hard) costs, indirect (soft) costs, and entrepreneurial profit.

Step two. Estimate the amount of depreciation from all causes (physical deterioration, functional obsolescence, and external obsolescence), and deduct it from the reproduction (or replacement) cost.

Step three. Estimate the value of the site and nonstructural site improvements assuming the site is vacant and will be put to its highest and best use.

Step four. To derive the property's estimated value, add the estimated value of the site, including site improvements, to the depreciated cost of the structural improvements.

Reproduction or Replacement Cost

Earlier, the cost to build a duplicate of the five-year-old home in the Milestone subdivision was referred to as *reproduction cost*. More specifically, **reproduction cost** is the dollar amount that would be required to build a structure that is an exact duplicate of the structure being appraised. It includes the current cost of older construction methodologies and functionally deficient systems. Reproduction cost usually is required for condemnation appraisals, and Fannie Mae and Freddie Mac require the use of reproduction cost on the Uniform Residential Appraisal Report (URAR) form.

Replacement cost is the dollar amount that would be required to construct improvements of equal utility to those being appraised, although not the exact physical duplicates. The appraiser estimates the cost of new improvements using modern design, materials, and technology. The major distinction between reproduction and replacement cost is that reproduction cost is defined in terms of a physical duplicate of the improvements, and replacement cost is defined in terms of utility equal to the subject improvements. Replacement cost assumes today's building technology. Therefore, many of the adjustments for functional obsolescence required when the appraiser uses reproduction cost are eliminated when using replacement cost. From the appraiser's viewpoint, using replacement cost avoids the need to make time-consuming cost estimates of obsolete components found in older construction. Appraisers also argue that market participants think in terms of utility rather than cost when rating quality and design.

Estimating Cost

Reproduction and replacement cost estimates are categorized into three types of costs: (1) direct (hard) costs, (2) indirect (soft) costs, and (3) entrepreneurial profit. Direct costs include materials, labor, and sub-contractor's and general contractor's overhead. Indirect costs include other costs associated with development, such as architectural and engineering fees, building permit fees, impact fees, and interest on construction financing. Entrepreneurial profit usually is estimated separately as a percentage of direct and indirect costs.

Sources of cost data include local builders and contractors and published cost services. The appraiser may use benchmark structures, such as the cost to reproduce a standard one-story house, to establish the base cost, then make adjustments to reflect differences between the benchmark structures and the subject property. Cost services provide cost information based on benchmark structures, as well as cost data for individual structural components and equipment.

Appraisers use three methods to estimate building costs. They are presented below from the most detailed to the least detailed.

1. Quantity survey method. This method involves a detailed inventory of all labor, materials, products, and indirect costs, plus the builder's profit, required to reproduce a building. The appraiser multiplies the number of items in the inventory by the cost per item. For example, in a single-family home with three baths, the appraiser multiplies the cost of one commode by three, the cost of one bathtub by three, and so on. If 1,000 lineal feet of 2 × 6s are required at $.50 per foot, the total cost would be $500.

2. Unit-in-place method. The appraiser calculates the cost of materials and labor for each component of a structure, such as the driveway, parking area, roof, foundation, walls, and floors. For example, the appraiser obtains the unit-in-place cost for a square of roofing (100 square feet), then multiplies by the number of units in the entire roof. Each separate component is treated in the same way. Adding the costs of installed equipment and fixtures and builder's profit results in the structure's total reproduction cost.

3. Comparative-unit method (or square-foot or cubic-foot method). The appraiser multiplies the cost per square foot or cubic foot of a recently built comparable structure (or benchmark structure) by the number of square feet in the subject property. In practice, the comparative-unit method is the most widely used method to estimate cost, primarily because the secondary mortgage market requires its use on the URAR form. The appraiser applies the method by referring to published cost manuals. In fact, reliance on these manuals to estimate reproduction cost dominates the appraisal industry today. Residential cost manuals contain benchmark structures for numerous categories of quality, such as low, fair, average, good, very good, and excellent quality.

The appraiser compares the subject property with the descriptions of quality (factors such as basic shape of the building, type of roof and interior walls, and typical features and equipment) to determine the appropriate benchmark structure. The manuals provide illustrations of homes to help the appraiser choose the appropriate quality of construction. Once the construction quality is selected, the appraiser refers to square-foot costs based on number of stories (e.g. one-story or two-story construction) and masonry or stud-framed construction. The appraiser calculates a base cost for the structure by multiplying the square feet of living area by the cost per square foot. The appraiser then adjusts for foundation (mild Florida climate, for example, usually involves a negative adjustment because of lower floor insulation R-value standards), roof covering, flooring, garage, porches, and so forth. Once the appraiser has totaled all of the calculations, a multiplier is applied to reflect local building costs. Figure 7.2 provides an example of an estimate of reproduction cost using the comparative-unit method.

Estimating Depreciation

Recall the five-year-old single-family home located in the Milestone subdivision. It is identical to the new home next door in terms of floor plan, square footage, and building materials. It is reasonable to assume, however, that the two homes do not have identical market values. Most consumers would penalize the five-year-old home somewhat for its age. The difference between the home's reproduction (or replacement) cost new and the perceived market value of the home today is referred to as **accrued depreciation**. The home's reproduction cost is an estimate of the improvement value as if it were new. Deducting the accrued depreciation enables the appraiser to estimate the improvement's market value. (The appraiser must also consider the site value.) Accrued depreciation links reproduction cost and market value.

Generally, accrued depreciation is associated with a structure's age. As a building grows older, it loses value due to exposure to the sun and rain and general use. However, not all depreciation is associated with age. A brand-new structure may suffer functional

FIGURE 7.2 ■ Estimation of Reproduction Cost Using the Comparative-Unit Method

	Square Feet	Cost per Square Foot	Total
Base building cost	2,052	$51.47	$105,616
Square foot adjustments:	2,052	– 2.09	– 4,289
Foundation (concrete slab)			
Flooring:			
75% carpet	1,539	2.91	4,478
15% vinyl	308	3.19	983
10% tile	205	7.72	1,583
Heating and cooling:			
Heat pump	2,052	1.37	2,811
Garage:	485	18.17	8,812
Ceiling finished	485	3.16	1,533
Enclosed porch:			
Ceiling	320	2.34	749
Concrete slab	320	3.49	1,117
Roof	320	7.44	2,381
Lump-sum adjustments:			
Built-in appliances:			
Oven			790
Fan and hood			285
Dishwasher			570
Garbage disposal			215
Total			**$127,634**
Local multiplier			**× .86**
Total reproduction cost of building improvements			**$109,765**

obsolescence due to inefficient design. Also, a new home may be penalized because it is near a busy street. Depreciation in a structure can be attributed to three major causes:

1. Physical deterioration. This type of depreciation includes ordinary wear and tear caused by use, lack of maintenance, exposure to the elements, and physical damage. Brittle roof shingles and a worn-out central air-conditioning compressor are examples of depreciation caused by **physical deterioration**. If correction of a defect results in as much added value as the cost to correct, the defect is said to be *curable*. An *incurable* defect is one in which the cost of curing the defect is greater than the value added by the cure.

2. Functional obsolescence. Anything that is inferior due to operational inadequacies, poor design, or changing tastes and preferences (for example, a poor traffic pattern, an outmoded design, too few bathrooms, or lack of closet space) is classified as **functional obsolescence**, which may be either curable or incurable. An overimprovement also is considered to be functional obsolescence.

3. External obsolescence. Any loss of value due to influences originating outside the property's boundaries (for example, an expressway adjacent to a residential subdivision, an industrial plant close to a residential neighborhood, or general deterioration of the neighborhood) normally is beyond the property owner's control; therefore, **external obsolescence** is considered to be incurable. External obsolescence is divided between the land and the improvements. Only that portion allocated to the improvements is deducted in the cost-depreciation approach.

Appraisers use three methods to estimate accrued depreciation. They are arranged below from the most detailed to the most simplistic.

1. Breakdown method. The breakdown method, used primarily to appraise investment real estate and older single-family structures, involves analyzing each category of depreciation separately.

2. Market extraction method. The market extraction method involves studying the sales of comparable properties that have depreciated to a similar degree as the subject property. The appraiser derives a depreciation estimate by analyzing the difference between reproduction cost new and the comparables' market values.

3. Lump-sum age-life method. The vast majority of residential appraisals that employ the cost-depreciation approach use the lump-sum age-life method to estimate accrued depreciation. The method is easy to use because it estimates a single value for accrued depreciation. It is appropriate for relatively new homes that do not suffer from significant functional and external obsolescence. The lump-sum method is based on a ratio of a property's effective age to its economic life. The appraiser multiplies the ratio by the reproduction cost new to derive accrued depreciation. The formula follows:

Accrued Depreciation

	Effective age
divided by	Economic life
multiplied by	Reproduction (or replacement) cost new
equals	Accrued depreciation

Effective age is the age indicated by a structure's condition and utility. Chronologically, the home in the Milestone subdivision is five years old. Its effective age, however, could be greater than, less than, or equal to five years. The effective age is affected by the type and quality of construction, the building materials chosen, and the presence or absence of maintenance and modernization over time. No precise methodology exists for deriving effective age. It is approximated by taking into consideration the improvements' current condition.

A structure's total **economic life** (or *useful life*) is the total estimated time in years that an improvement is expected to contribute to the property's value. Appraisers often use cost-estimating services as a source of information regarding total economic life. *The Residential Cost Handbook*, by Marshall and Swift Company, for example, estimates the economic life (referred to as *typical life expectancy*) for residential homes in good condition to be about 60 years. For investment properties, appraisers often use IRS guidelines as a source of information.

To estimate the accrued depreciation of the home in the Milestone subdivision, use the formula cited above. Assume the appraiser estimated the home's effective age to be four years after taking into consideration the home's current condition. Therefore:

(4 years effective age ÷ 60 years economic life) × $112,000 reproduction cost new = $7,466.67 accrued depreciation

An alternative way to perform this calculation is to first divide the reproduction cost by the economic life. The result is the annual depreciation. Multiply the annual depreciation by the effective age to derive the total accrued depreciation:

$112,000 reproduction cost new ÷ 60 years economic life = $1,866.66 annual depreciation × 4 years effective age = $7,466.67 accrued depreciation

Alternate Formula to Calculate Accrued Depreciation

	Reproduction cost new
divided by	Total economic life
equals	Annual depreciation
multiplied by	Effective age
equals	Accrued depreciation

The reproduction cost new of the home in Milestone is about $112,000. However, the home's market value is about $104,533 ($112,000 – $7,467), plus land value.

The lump-sum age-life method of calculating depreciation assumes that a structure depreciates at a constant rate. The lump-sum age-life method is sometimes referred to as *straight-line depreciation*. Depreciation, however, does not necessarily occur at a constant rate. Also, because the approach lumps all three categories of depreciation into a single adjustment, it implies that functional and external obsolescence are related to a structure's age. As a home ages, it is more likely that mechanical and building components will suffer from functional obsolescence. Older homes also tend to be more susceptible to external obsolescence (typically caused by proximity to external diseconomies). Under such conditions, it may be necessary to analyze the three types of depreciation separately. An appraiser should use the lump-sum age-life approach only when the property does not suffer significantly from functional and external obsolescence and when the structure is relatively new.

INCOME-CAPITALIZATION APPROACH

When the primary benefit of real estate ownership comes in the form of monthly or annual income, the income capitalization approach is a valid way to estimate value. The approach uses three types of ratios: (1) the gross income multiplier (GIM), (2) the gross rent multiplier (GRM), and (3) the overall capitalization rate (OAR). The appraiser uses direct capitalization to convert an estimate of a single year's expected income, either by dividing the net operating income estimate by an appropriate rate (OAR) or by multiplying the gross income by an appropriate multiplier (GIM or GRM). The appraiser also may use discounted cash flow models based on forecasts of the expected cash flows from a property for a specified period of years. This chapter is confined to discussion of the gross income multiplier, the gross rent multiplier, and the overall capitalization rate.

Gross Income Multiplier (GIM) and Gross Rent Multiplier (GRM)

The **gross income multiplier (GIM)** is the ratio between a property's gross annual income and its selling price. For example, if an income-producing property earns an annual gross income of $50,000 and sells for $450,000, it has sold at a GIM of 9 ($450,000 ÷ $50,000 = 9). In other words, the property sold for nine times its gross income. By studying the relationship of gross income to sale price of several income-producing properties of the same type in a given marketplace, an appraiser can calculate a market-derived income multiplier. The appraiser then applies the multiplier to the subject property's estimated market rent to determine its value.

Appraisers sometimes use a **gross rent multiplier (GRM)**. A GRM is the ratio between a property's gross monthly rental income and the sale price of the property. Gross rent multiplier refers to rent only and excludes any miscellaneous income a property generates, whereas the term *gross income multiplier* is more generalizable because it includes all income generated from a property. Because investors and real estate professionals sometimes use the terms *GIM* and *GRM* interchangeably, it is important that the appraiser define in the appraisal report which multiplier was used.

Investors typically value income-producing properties on the basis of the properties' income potential. GIM analysis and GRM analysis are appropriate when properties are purchased and sold on the basis of gross income. GIM analysis is usually reliable for valuing small commercial units and warehouses. GRM analysis is usually reliable for valuing rental houses and multifamily properties of up to 16 or 20 units. GIM analysis and GRM analysis requires an active market to produce reliable multipliers. Therefore, the approaches tend to be better for valuing smaller income-producing properties because they are more numerous, sell more frequently, and are more homogeneous than larger income-producing properties.

To derive a GIM or a GRM from market data, the appraiser must locate sales of comparable properties that generated rental income at the time of sale. The properties must be comparable to the subject property and to one another in terms of physical, locational, and investment characteristics. The comparable sales must exhibit gross incomes and operating expenses proportional to those of the subject property. If the proportion of gross income and operating expenses varies among the properties, gross income is not a reliable and consistent basis for setting prices. The comparable sales also must be traded in the same marketplace as the subject property. The same community and neighborhood forces must influence the subject property and the comparable sales.

Steps in the gross rent multiplier analysis. GRM analysis requires three steps: (1) estimate the subject property's market monthly rent, (2) estimate a market-derived GRM by analyzing comparable market transactions, and (3) multiply the subject property's market rent by the market-derived GRM. The same three steps apply to the GIM analysis. However, when using the gross income multiplier analysis, total gross annual income is used instead of gross monthly rental income.

Step one. To estimate the subject property's market rent, the appraiser must locate comparable rentals in the subject property's market area. The appraiser analyzes each rental and adjusts the comparable's rent to reflect the subject property's characteristics. The rental rates should represent verified arm's-length rental arrangements. The appraiser adjusts the comparables' rentals to obtain an indicated market rent for the subject property. This indicated rental rate is developed the same way that sale prices are inferred from comparable sale transactions under the sales comparison approach. Figure 7.3 presents three comparables (five or six are recommended), adjusted to reflect the subject property's characteristics. The adjusted rents indicate a market rent for the subject property of between $1,210 and $1,255 per month, or an average market rent of $1,233 per month ($1,235 + $1,255 + $1,210 ÷ 3 = $1,233.33).

Step two. This step requires the appraiser to analyze market transactions of comparable properties to develop a market-derived gross rent multiplier. The appraiser must locate properties comparable to the subject that sold recently and were rented at the time of sale. The comparables should be reasonably similar to the subject property with respect to size and must meet the requirements of comparability, proportionality of operating expenses, and identical community and neighborhood forces. Also, the sales must be open-market transactions, and the conditions of sale should be verified. Figure 7.4 presents the calculation of a market GRM using the gross monthly income and sale price information of five transactions.

The average of the GRMs (105.8 + 108.3 + 106.8 + 106.1 + 103.8 = 530.8; 530.8 ÷ 5) is 106.16, or 106.2 rounded. The transactions used to develop a market GRM are not necessarily the comparables used to derive market rent.

Step three. The final step in GRM analysis is to multiply the subject property's estimated market rent by the market-derived GRM to obtain the subject property's indicated value. Using the information in Figures 7.3 and 7.4, the appraiser multiplies the subject property's market rent of $1,233 by the market-derived GRM of 106.2. The result is an estimated market value of $130,944.60, rounded to $131,000.

FIGURE 7.3 ■ Market Rent Adjustment Grid

Element of Comparison	A	B	C	Subject
Monthly Rent	$1,215	$1,395	$1,320	
Bathrooms	Same	2.5	2.5	2.0
	0	– $60	– $60	
Covered parking	No	Yes	Yes	No
	0	– $50	– $50	
Screened porch	No	Yes	No	No
	0	– $30	0	
Washer/Dryer	No	Yes	Yes	Yes
supplied	+ $20	0	0	
Net adjustment	+ $20	– $140	– $110	
Indicated rent	**$1,235**	**$1,255**	**$1,210**	

Overall Capitalization

Overall capitalization develops an estimated value based on the present worth of future income from the subject property. Mathematically, the income capitalization approach is based on the relationship between value, income, and rate of return. The appraiser estimates the property's gross income, deducts a suitable amount for vacancy and collection loss, and estimates the expenses associated with operating the property to derive net operating income. The net income stream is converted into a lump-sum present value using the capitalization process. This method of capitalization is related mathematically to gross income multiplier analysis because cap rates are the reciprocals of multipliers. The rates the appraiser uses for capitalization are derived from market evidence by studying the rates of return for similar properties.

Steps in the income-capitalization approach. Overall capitalization requires six steps, as detailed below.

Step one. In the first step of the income capitalization approach the appraiser estimates the potential gross income. **Potential gross income (PGI)** is the maximum income a property would produce during a one-year period if it were totally rented or leased at the prevailing market rate. The appraiser should obtain the current rental rates (contract rent) for the subject property's units by examining the leases. **Contract rent** is the rent the tenants pay currently. The appraiser also analyzes data on past and current rental rates of similar properties and uses this information along with contract rent information to establish the fair market rent. **Market rent** is the rent the property would command if it were leased today at the prevailing rate. If the subject property is rented for less than market rent, the appraiser uses market rent to capitalize value.

Step two. This step requires the appraiser to estimate the typical vacancy and collection loss. **Vacancy and collection loss** is an allowance for reductions in potential gross income due to vacancies and uncollected rent. The allowance is calculated as a percentage of potential gross income. When estimating an allowance, the appraiser should analyze the local market, taking into consideration the type and physical characteristics of the property, the quality of the tenants, and local supply and demand factors.

Step three. Next, to arrive at the effective gross income, the appraiser subtracts vacancy and collection loss from PGI, then adds any miscellaneous income the property produces. **Effective gross income (EGI)** is the anticipated income from the operation of a property less the vacancy and collection loss allowance plus miscellaneous income.

FIGURE 7.4 ■ Calculation of Market GRM

Sale	Sale Price	÷	Monthly Rent	=	GRM
1	$127,000		$1,200		105.8
2	130,000		1,200		108.3
3	133,500		1,250		106.8
4	137,930		1,300		106.1
5	135,000		1,300		103.8

Step four. To derive the net operating income, the appraiser estimates the annual operating expenses and subtracts them from the EGI. **Net operating income (NOI)** is the income remaining after all relevant operating expenses have been subtracted. The appraiser should obtain information regarding the subject property's operating expenses from the owner's ledgers or another reliable source. Operating expenses used in the income capitalization process are forecasts of anticipated expenses. Therefore, they should not be based solely on past expense history. The appraiser studies comparable investment properties' expenses to determine the appropriateness of expense projections.

Operating expenses are classified into three types: (1) fixed expenses, (2) variable expenses, and (3) reserve for replacements.

Fixed expenses are operating expenses that generally do not fluctuate with occupancy and must be paid whether or not the property is occupied. Fixed expenses include real property tax and building insurance. The appraiser should consult the property appraiser's records to determine the property tax assessment and millage rate, then compare this information with that of comparable properties to evaluate tax burden ratios and assess the likelihood of possible future property tax increases or decreases. The appraiser also should consider the amount of insurance coverage prudent management would secure at a competitive local rate.

Variable expenses are operating expenses that vary with the level of occupancy. Variable expenses include management, utilities, maintenance and repair, and so forth. Even if the property owner manages the property, the appraiser should estimate a management expense. Management expense typically is expressed as a percentage of EGI, based on typical local rates the appraiser obtains from property management companies. Utility expenses are projected on a year-round basis using past charges and current expectations. The appraiser should review leases to see whether tenants reimburse the owner for utilities and whether the tenants' utilities are individually metered. A large maintenance expense incurred only every few years, such as exterior painting, should be prorated over the normal cycle.

Reserve for replacements is a reserve allowance that provides for the periodic replacement of short-lived components, such as the roof and mechanical equipment. Reserve for replacements is not really an expense because the money is held in reserve until sometime in the future, when the roof is reshingled or the mechanical equipment is replaced. Reserve for replacements is classified as an expense because the money will be expended in the future.

The appraiser estimates the annual reserve for each short-lived item by prorating the replacement cost over the item's expected useful life. For example, if the roof shingles are expected to last 15 years and the replacement cost is $12,000, the annual reserve allowance is $800 ($12,000 ÷ 15 years).

Reserve for replacements is treated as an expense for the purpose of calculating the net operating income. This is done to eliminate large differences in the NOI from year to year that can be directly attributable to cash outlays. If the entire expense of replacing the roof were to be taken into account for purposes of determining NOI in year 15, the NOI would be decreased by $12,000 in that year. Obviously, this would result in a much lower appraised value (remember NOI is used to estimate value) than if the NOI were reduced for this expense by only $800. Thus, treating reserve for replacements as an operating expense provides a much more accurate picture of the day to day operating expenses needed to maintain the property and results in a more realistic appraised value. However, because the reserves are not an actual expense in the year they are set aside, they must be added back into the NOI when calculating taxable income (chapter 14).

FIGURE 7.5 ■ Reconstructed Operating Statement

Stoufer Office Complex

Suite	Rent	×	Square Feet	=	Annual Rent
A	$13.44		3,400		$45,696.00
B	13.79		1,392		19,195.68
C	12.75		1,363		17,378.25
D	13.00		3,100		40,300.00
E	13.00		4,346		56,498.00
Total potential gross income (PGI)					$179,067.93
Less: vacancy and collection loss (5%)					–8,953.40
Effective gross income (EGI)					$170,114.53
Operating expenses:					
Real estate tax			$28,450		
Electricity			12,060		
Water and sewer			5,000		
Monthly elevator service			1,125		
Housekeeping			6,100		
Landscaping/maintenance			8,800		
Sanitation			2,900		
Reserve for replacement			6,000		
Management (5% of EGI)			8,507		
Total operating expenses					–$78,942
Net operating income					$91,172.53

An investment property's estimated revenues and expenses are summarized in a statement of income and expenses suitable for appraisal, referred to as a *reconstructed operating statement*. Business or personal expenses ordinarily are not considered to be operating expenses. Expenses such as mortgage payments, federal income tax, and depreciation deduction allowances for income tax purposes are not included in the reconstructed operating statement. Figure 7.5 presents an example of a reconstructed operating statement.

Step five. Now the appraiser analyzes comparable investment properties to derive an appropriate capitalization rate for the subject property. Often, the best source of data is the appraisals of other investment properties because the income data (NOI) have been projected. The appraiser simply divides the comparable's NOI by its market value to derive a capitalization rate. A market rate can be developed by averaging the derived

FIGURE 7.6 ■ Market-Derived Capitalization Rate

Sale	NOI	÷	Market Value	=	Rate
1	$95,180		$924,500		.103*
2	87,350		875,000		.100
3	90,870		865,425		.105
Average market-derived capitalization rate for area					.103 *or* .10 rounded

* Rounded to third decimal place

capitalization rates from two or three comparable investment properties. Refer to Figure 7.6 for an example of a market-derived capitalization rate.

NOI ÷ Market value = Capitalization rate

Step six. Finally, the appraiser divides the subject property's NOI by the market-derived capitalization rate to obtain the capitalized value. For example, using the NOI derived in Figure 7.5 and the capitalization rate estimated in Figure 7.6, the estimated value of the property is $911,730:

NOI ÷ Capitalization rate = Value
$91,173 ÷.10 = $911,730

SUMMARY OF IMPORTANT POINTS

- The sales comparison approach is based on the premise that the value of the subject property can be estimated by reviewing recent sales similar to the subject property and comparing those properties with the subject property.
- In an arm's-length transaction, the parties deal from equal bargaining positions.
- Cash equivalency, used to adjust for nonmarket financing, calculates the present value of streams of cash inflows or outflows by discounting the inflows or outflows at appropriate interest rates.
- A *fixture* is an item that originally was personal property but has been permanently attached to or made part of real property.
- A *trade fixture* is an article a commercial tenant attaches as a necessary part of the tenant's trade or business.
- When a transaction price has been adjusted for financing and conditions of sale, the resulting price is the normal sale price. The *normal sale price* is the price a property would have sold for at the time of the transaction if the transaction had been consistent with the market.
- The market conditions-adjusted normal sale price is derived by applying an adjustment for market conditions to the normal sale price.
- The final adjusted sale price is derived by making adjustments for location and physical characteristics to the market conditions-adjusted normal sale price.

- The cost-depreciation approach is based on the theory that a knowledgeable purchaser will not pay more for a property than the cost of acquiring a similar site and constructing an acceptable substitute structure.
- *Reproduction cost* is the cost to build a structure that is an exact duplicate of the property being appraised.
- *Replacement cost* is the cost to construct improvements of equal utility to those being appraised, although not the exact physical duplicate.
- The three methods used to estimate building costs are quantity survey method, unit-in-place method, and comparative-unit method.
- *Effective age* is the age indicated by a structure's condition and utility.
- *Economic life* is the total estimated number of years that an improvement is expected to contribute to the property's value.
- Accrued depreciation is composed of physical deterioration, functional obsolescence, and external obsolescence.
- The most common way to estimate accrued depreciation is referred to as the lump-sum age-life method, which applies a ratio of effective age and economic life to the structure's reproduction cost new.
- The *gross rent multiplier* (GRM) is the ratio between a property's gross monthly rent and its selling price. The *gross income multiplier* (GIM) is the ratio between the property's gross annual income and its selling price.
- The *income capitalization approach* develops an estimated value based on the present worth of future income from the subject property. The approach capitalizes net operating income into value.
- *Potential gross income* (PGI) is the total annual income a property would produce if it were fully rented and no collection losses were incurred. *Effective gross income* (EGI) is calculated by subtracting vacancy and collection losses from the PGI. *Net operating income* (NOI) is the income remaining after subtracting operating expenses from EGI.
- The three categories of operating expenses are (1) fixed, (2) variable, and (3) reserve for replacements.

REVIEW QUESTIONS

1. A home was sold for $118,500. The buyer secured a conventional mortgage. However, because he did not have enough cash to pay the discount points, the seller paid $3,000 of the buyer's points at closing. Which statement regarding financing adjustments is TRUE of this situation?
   a. An adjustment for financing is not required because the buyer obtained a conventional mortgage.
   b. The appraiser should add $3,000 to the comparable's transaction price.
   c. The appraiser should subtract $3,000 from the comparable's transaction price.
   d. The appraiser should add $3,000 to the subject property's market value.

Use the following information to answer questions 2 through 4.

The subject property is a four-bedroom, two-bath, two-car-garage home in the Dogwood Terrace subdivision.

2. Comp A, a three-bedroom, two-bath home with a screened-in porch, sold for $116,000. The appraiser values the porch at $2,500 and estimates the bedroom adjustment at $10,000. What is comp A's adjusted sale price?
   a. $113,500
   b. $123,500
   c. $126,000
   d. $128,500

3. Comp B sold for $118,900. It has a fireplace and professional landscaping and is 120 square feet smaller than the subject property. Calculate the adjustment for square footage at $60 per square foot. The fireplace adjustment is $1,500, and landscaping is valued at $2,000. What is comp B's adjusted sale price?
   a. $118,900
   b. $122,600
   c. $126,100
   d. $129,600

4. Comp C is located in Magnolia Terrace, which is not as convenient to shopping and schools as Dogwood Terrace. Therefore, the appraiser estimates a five percent adjustment for location. The appraiser also has determined that the comparable has a sprinkler system and superior landscaping valued at $3,500. The transaction price was $115,000. What is comp C's adjusted sale price?
   a. $105,750
   b. $117,250
   c. $120,750
   d. $124,250

Use the information below to answer questions 5 through 8.

You have located two successive sales in the same neighborhood as the subject property. The initial sale price and resale price are shown below, along with the number of months between the initial sale and the resale.

Property	Initial Price	Months Between Sales	Resale Price
A	$78,700	12	$83,500
B	81,250	16	86,900

5. What is property A's monthly rate of change?
   a. .0051
   b. .0610
   c. .0884
   d. .1061

6. What is property B's monthly rate of change?
   a. .0034
   b. .0043
   c. .0668
   d. .0695

7. What is the average monthly rate of change (rounded) based on the two monthly rates of change you obtained in questions 5 and 6?
   a. .43 percent
   b. .47 percent
   c. .52 percent
   d. .53 percent

8. A comparable sold for $82,000 18 months ago. Based on the average monthly rate of change from question 7, what is the comparable's market conditions-adjusted normal sale price?
   a. $88,584.18
   b. $88,937.20
   c. $90,024.04
   d. $90,185.38

9. When an appraiser adjusts for conditions of sale and nonmarket financing, the resulting figure is referred to as the
   a. appraised value.
   b. adjusted transaction price.
   c. normal sale price.
   d. market conditions-adjusted normal sale price.

10. The cost-depreciation approach MOST likely is considered to be very important in which situation?
    a. The subject property is a ten-year-old apartment complex in an active rental market.
    b. The subject property is a vacant site ready for development.
    c. The subject property is a single-family home in an established neighborhood with an active resale market.
    d. The subject property is a new home in a developing subdivision.

11. The method of estimating building costs that typically relies on published cost manuals for a cost per square foot, then adjusts for local building costs, is
    a. market extraction.
    b. unit-in-place.
    c. comparative unit.
    d. quantity survey.

12. A structure's reproduction cost new is $175,000. The home is 15 years old and has an effective age of 10 years. Assuming a total economic life of 60 years, what is the accrued depreciation (rounded) using the lump-sum age-life method? (Round to the nearest dollar.)
    a. $14,583
    b. $29,167
    c. $43,750
    d. $45,517

Use the information below to answer questions 13 through 15.

A multifamily unit consists of 20 two-bedroom apartments that rent for $700 per month and 15 three-bedroom apartments that rent for $825 per month. The vacancy and collection loss is estimated to be six percent. Management is five percent of effective gross income.

13. What is the potential gross income?
    a. $26,375
    b. $162,500
    c. $316,500
    d. $330,500

14. What is the vacancy and collection loss allowance?
    a. $9,750
    b. $18,990
    c. $19,830
    d. $20,750

15. What is the management expense (rounded)?
    a. $11,897
    b. $12,375
    c. $14,876
    d. $15,825

CHAPTER 8

COMPARATIVE MARKET ANALYSIS

KEY TERMS

comparative market analysis (CMA)

curb appeal

gross living area (GLA)

OVERVIEW

This chapter begins with a discussion of the differences and similarities between an appraisal and a **comparative market analysis (CMA)**. This chapter will show the sources of information required to prepare CMA. Because the licensee should use only similar properties in the analysis, a section of this chapter shows the common elements of comparison and discusses how to adjust for differences. The chapter finishes with a CMA case study.

Once you have completed this chapter, you should be able to:

- describe at least five differences between an appraisal and a CMA;
- explain the three major sections of a typical CMA report;
- remember the information used for preparing a CMA;
- suggest the best sources of information needed for a CMA;
- discuss the major elements of comparison between the comparable property and the subject property;
- correctly calculate the square footage of a building; and
- prepare a CMA that would allow a seller or buyer to understand values in the neighborhood.

INTRODUCTION

In the normal course of business, licensees are called upon to prepare a comparative market analysis for the seller or buyer as a means to help them make informed decisions on pricing a property. The estimate is an opinion of value, also called a broker's price opinion, and may not be called an appraisal. A broker may charge a fee for making a broker's price opinion.

While the CMA closely follows the methods used in the comparable sales approach to appraising, it is not an appraisal. Some of the differences between an appraisal and a CMA are:

- an appraisal uses the three approaches to value: cost, market, and income. The typical CMA provides a limited market data approach.
- appraisers usually make detailed analyses of the dollar adjustments necessary to reflect the differences in property characteristics. The CMA may include some adjustments for major differences, but very often just shows raw data on prices.
- most appraisal reports provide a specific market value in dollars. A CMA usually results in a range of values, not just one value.
- appraisal reports are concerned with prices actually paid for properties. CMAs also use properties currently on the market and those that did not sell.
- an appraiser should not be involved in the property transaction for personal gain. A licensee may be involved in a transaction as the listing or selling agent, and may prepare a CMA in order to assist the seller in establishing a listing price, or if working with the buyer, to assist the buyer in establishing an offering price.

The CMA is most effective when prepared for pricing residential properties up to four units or for residential building lots in a subdivision. It is usually not appropriate for commercial income properties.

Many licensees inspect the property before preparing a CMA. This reduces the chances for a surprise at the time of presentation. Some licensees feel that a pre-presentation visit, while helpful, is not time effective. Licensees must make their own judgments as to which method will provide the best results.

PREPARATION OF A COMPARATIVE MARKET ANALYSIS

Categories of Comparables

A CMA shows three major categories of properties: *sold within the previous 12 months*, *currently on the market*, and *listings that expired during the previous 12 months*.

Sold within the previous 12 months. A review of properties that have sold within the previous 12 months shows sellers and buyers the property's most likely appraisal value. If there are some unusually high or low prices in the study, licensees should try to see if there are good reasons for the variance. The most recent sales are the most reliable, especially in a changing market.

Currently on the market. Prices of properties currently on the market show sellers their competition. Since buyers will normally select the property with the best price, the seller should price the property appropriately. The seller should be made aware that the asking prices are typically higher than the selling prices.

For the best results in marketing the property, the seller should price the property just below the competition and just above recent sales.

Expired during the previous 12 months. It is a common occurrence when listed properties do not sell. Usually, the price was too high, considering the characteristics of the property. Reviewing this section of the CMA shows the seller that buyers resist overpriced listings. It also becomes clear to licensees that taking an overpriced listing is usually a waste of time.

Obtaining information about comparable properties that will be used in the report is usually easier if the property is in a recorded subdivision with many sales. Getting information takes longer if the property is in a rural area, because comparable properties are harder to find. The best sources for such information include:

- MLS® records;
- company files;
- public records; and
- other licensees.

MLS® records are the most convenient and comprehensive method of obtaining information about listings and sales. MLS® computer records may be searched by address, subdivision, size, price, or any other features that might show comparable properties. The major limitation with MLS® data is that it usually only includes properties listed by a REALTOR®, and does not include properties sold by an owner.

Company files usually have more information than the other sources, but they show only those properties listed or sold by the company.

Public records show all recorded sales data, and are used to supplement the data. Most county property appraisers and clerks in Florida now have online databases. These records, however, show only basic details and offer very little information about the property features.

Other licensees are a good source of information on properties not normally listed in MLS®, such as commercial, industrial, or agricultural properties, or those in rural areas that don't have a formal sharing service.

Common Elements of Comparison

A CMA is useful for sellers and buyers only if it fairly reflects the interaction of supply and demand for a specific property. For that reason, it is important that all properties used in the report be similar to the subject property in size, age, amenities, and location. Adjustments should be made for important differences such as swimming pools, condition, style, and other items. There are many amenities that must be considered when making a comparison. (See Table 8.1.)

Location. Location is so important that only in unusual circumstances should the licensee use a property outside the neighborhood as a comparable. Even within the same neighborhood, location may result in significant differences in value. For example, a house next to a busy street normally has a lower value than a house in the subdivision's interior.

Size and shape of lot. A level site usually is more valuable than a sloping site. Bigger is usually better, and a rectangular lot often is more desirable than a pie-shaped lot.

Landscaping. The licensee should evaluate trees and other greenery as to maturity and quality. The enhanced **curb appeal** of a well-landscaped home adds.

TABLE 8.1 ■ Information Needed to Prepare a Comparative Market Analysis

Before starting on the analysis, the licensee will find it helpful to have the following information:

Information Necessary	Source(s)
Owners' names and address	Owner, public records, city directory
Property description	Owner's deed, public records
Lot size (frontage and depth)	Owner's survey, recorded plat maps
Number and size of rooms and total square footage	Inspection and measurement
Building's construction and age	Inspection, owner, tax appraiser's office
Information relative to the neighborhood (schools, churches, transportation)	Inspection, owner
Current taxes	Owner's tax bill, tax appraiser's office
Amount of existing financing	Owner's records, mortgage status letter sent by licensee
Utilities and average payments	Owner's records, utility company records
Appliances to be included in the transaction	Owner
Personal property and fixtures included in the sale	Owner
Zoning classification (especially important for vacant land)	City/county planning department
Environmental hazards	Owner

Construction quality. Variations in construction quality may result in significant differences in property value. In some cases, the difference may be so great that the sold property should not be used as a comparable.

Style. Generally, a home's style should conform to that of other homes in the neighborhood. Substantial differences may result if the licensee uses the average square-foot prices of ranch homes to estimate a two-story home's value when the best comparable is another two-story home.

Design. Design features are important if some homes in an area have floor plans that are not functional or that are not accepted by the market. These are not good comparables for a home with a functional floor plan.

Age. In some established subdivisions, building sites are still available. If the licensee is preparing the CMA for a 20-year-old home, the licensee should avoid using a new home as a comparable sale.

Square feet of gross living area. All homes shown on the CMA should be comparable in size. Making dollar adjustments for small differences in size is relatively simple. However, the licensee should not compare a 2,500-square-foot home with a 1,500-square-foot home. Also, below-grade floor space is not considered **gross living area (GLA)** for most appraisals. It has less value than a home built above-grade. The licensee must be careful to use only comparable properties. If the licensee must make a square-foot adjustment, the licensee should not also adjust for number of bedrooms or for a family room, for example. This may lead to a double adjustment for two items that really represent the same thing.

It is important that the licensee measure the home accurately. Using builder plans or tax appraisal figures sometimes causes costly errors. Gross living area normally is calculated by taking exterior measurements, eliminating the garage, porches, and any workshops.

Number of rooms. The total room count should not include the foyer, bathrooms, or basement. If a comparable property has four bedrooms and the subject has only three, the square-foot adjustment probably will account for any difference. However, if one of the properties is a two-bedroom home in a neighborhood of three-bedroom and four-bedroom homes, an additional adjustment may be necessary. The number of bathrooms can have a significant impact on value, particularly when one of the properties has only one bathroom.

Kitchen. The market resists a kitchen with inadequate counter and storage space. Also, poorly maintained counters and cabinet finish may cause a kitchen to appear outdated, compared with others in the neighborhood. The age and condition of appliances also affect value.

Other space. A screened-in porch or Florida room adds value even though it is not counted in gross living area. The licensee should adjust for this difference.

Condition. The licensee should make adjustments if the subject property needs repairs that the homeowner refuses to make.

Garage. The licensee should make adjustments when the subject's garage or carport size differs from comparable properties' garages or carports.

Other improvements. The licensee should evaluate swimming pools, decks, patios, storage sheds, and other site improvements if they differ from comparable properties' improvements, making appropriate adjustments.

Adjusting for Differences

It would be ideal if all the comparable properties were identical to the subject property, but that situation rarely occurs. Therefore, the licensee may need to adjust for major differences so that the CMA does not mislead, however, making too many adjustments for less significant items also may mislead and could give the appearance that the licensee is trying to "back in" to a predetermined value.

All adjustments are made to the comparable property. They may be remembered using the acronym CIA-CBS:

If the **C**omparable is **I**nferior, **A**dd

If the **C**omparable is **B**etter, **S**ubtract

After the licensee makes adjustments, each category of property (for sale now, sold, expired) should be reconciled. While an appraiser usually reports a single dollar amount as the value, a real estate licensee often prefers to give a range of values. This allows the seller to list the property somewhat higher than the sold properties.

Computer-Generated CMAs

Several excellent software programs organize the data the licensee collects into an attractive presentation. Many MLS® service providers also offer built-in or optional software that allows REALTOR® members to download the comparable information directly into a listing presentation package. The fact that a computer generates the information does not in itself make the analysis more correct. The licensee should select only those properties comparable to the subject property.

Attachments to CMA

Photos of comparable properties along with a plat map of the neighborhood make the CMA easier to understand. A photograph of the home is a gift the owner may remember for a long time.

CASE STUDY—COMPARATIVE MARKET ANALYSIS

The following case study will illustrate the process a licensee uses to prepare a comparative market analysis. The licensee first must gather information necessary for a complete picture of the market in the neighborhood, including sales, listed properties, and expired listings. The next step is to enter the information in the appropriate section of the form. The licensee must analyze the differences between the comparable property sales and the subject property, estimate the contribution value of the differences, and make appropriate adjustments. Each sale can then be properly compared with the subject in a way that is understandable to the property owner.

Gathering Information

The licensee first must collect information about the subject property. This is best accomplished by discussions with the owner and inspection of the property. Then, the licensee should get information about property sales, usually through the property appraiser's records and MLS® records.

Getting information from the owner. You have just received a request from Wendall Kaski to discuss listing his family's home. You ask for and receive some basic information:

- Full names of all persons on the deed
  Wendall J. Kaski and Sara Cook Kaski, HW
- Property address
  1810 Mayfair Road, Oakville, Florida
- Owner's home and office phone number
  850-555-3496; 850-555-3487
- Number of bedrooms and baths in the home
  Four bedrooms, two baths
- Description of extras in the home
  Two-car garage, screened-in porch
- Convenient time for an appointment (If you decide to do a prepresentation inspection of the property, you will need two appointments—one to inspect the property and one to present the CMA.)
  7:20 this evening for an inspection of the property

FIGURE 8.1 ■ Calculate the Square Footage of Gross Living Area (See solution on following page.)

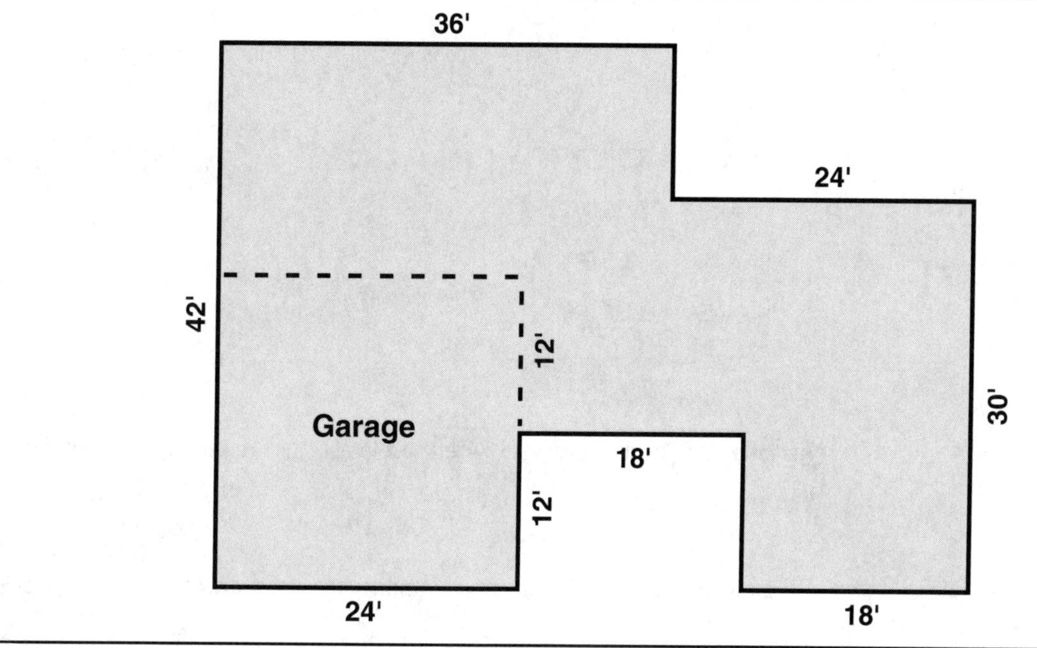

Gathering information from the online tax rolls through the MLS® system. The tax rolls for Leon County show the following information for the property:

Legal description:	Lot 29, Block C, Astoria Park, Unit 4—Oak County
Property tax appraisal:	$65,300
Annual taxes (including the homestead exemption):	$877
Year built:	1977
Base area:	1,420 square feet
Total area:	1,985 square feet (includes garage)
Last sale:	1977
Last sale price:	$37,100
Mortgage:	Colonial Mortgage Company

Because the tax appraiser's measurements are not always correct, you will measure the exterior of the Kaskis' home and prepare a sketch. (See Figure 8.1.) You will calculate the square footage and use your figures in the CMA, *not* those shown by the tax appraiser. See Figure 8.2 for solution to the square footage.

A search of the tax records shows seven sales in the subdivision within the previous year, ranging from $68,000 to $78,000. Six of the seven sales were reported in the MLS®, which gives more information on which to base comparisons. The sales are shown in the first section of the CMA. (See Figure 8.3.)

EXAMPLE OF MEAN, MEDIAN, AND MODE CALCULATIONS

Assume there are five sales in a neighborhood that sold for the following prices:

House 1	$245,000
House 2	$275,000
House 3	$275,000
House 4	$325,000
House 5	$450,000
TOTAL	$1,570,000

The **mean** is $314,000, calculated by getting a total of the five sale prices and dividing the result by 5. $1,570,000 ÷ 5 = $314,000.

The **median** is $275,000. It is the result of putting the group in ascending or descending price order and finding the middle number. In case there are an even number of sales, there are two middle numbers, so it is the mean of those two numbers.

The **mode** is $275,000, the price that occurs most often.

FIGURE 8.2 ■ Calculate the Square Footage of Gross Living Area – Solution

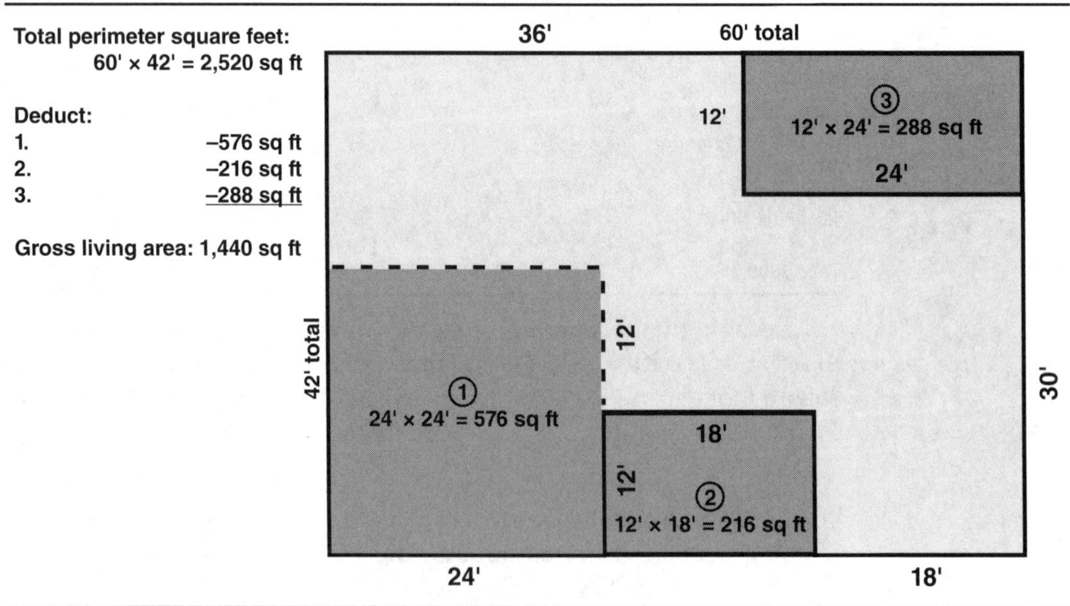

FIGURE 8.3 ■ Comparative Market Analysis Problem

Comparative Market Analysis Problem

Prepared for: Wendall J. and Sara Cook Kaski
Property address: 1810 Mayfair Road, Tallahassee, FL
Date: June 8, 20___
Description: **Your property** has _____ square feet with a two-car garage. Similar properties are shown below.

Properties sold within the previous 12 months

Property Address	Sale Price	List Price	Days on Market	Living Area	Features	Estimated Adjustment	Adjusted Sale Price	Comments
1806 Mayfair Road	$78,300	$81,500	145	1,540	Pool, larger			
1831 Mayfair Road	74,200	77,000	130	1,540	Larger			
1830 Wales Drive	70,000	71,000	103	1,440	Same			
2513 Doric Drive	71,500	73,000	113	1,440	Fireplace			
2489 Salmon Drive	67,500	71,000	93	1,440	1-car garage			
2517 Doric Drive	70,500	70,500	113	1,440	Same			
1845 Mayfair Road	71,500	?	?	1,540	Sold for-sale-by-owner			

Percent sales price/list price ________% Median $ __________

Properties currently on the market

Property Address	List Price	Days on Market	Living Area	Features	Estimated Adjustment	As Adjusted	Comments
2505 Colleen Drive	$80,000	60 est.	1,540	Pool, larger			
2410 Ionic Drive	73,000	30 est.	1,440	Same			
2402 Gothic Drive	70,500	60 est.	1,340	Fireplace, 1-car garage, smaller			
1800 Salmon Drive	72,500	140 est.	1,440	Same			

* = **most comparable** Median $ __________

Properties that were listed, but failed to sell during the previous 12 months

Property Address	List Price	Days on Market	Living Area	Features	Estimated Adjustment	As Adjusted	Comments
1705 Salmon Drive	75,000	180 ?	1,440				
2512 Colleen Drive	84,500	270 ?	1,540	Pool, larger			
1818 Doric Drive	74,000	120 ?	1,440	1-car garage			

Median $ __________

This information is believed to be accurate, but is not warranted.

The suggested marketing range is $ ___________ to $ ___________

Four properties currently listed for sale in the MLS® are shown in the second section of the CMA. Three listings that expired within the last 12 months are listed in the third section.

Analysis of amounts contributed by amenities. Over time, in reviewing data on sold properties, we can estimate what a pool, a garage, an extra bedroom, or a fireplace contributes to value. The matched pair analysis compares similar houses with and without a particular feature. The difference in price tends to indicate what the feature contributes in value. For instance, look at sales 1 and 2 in Figure 8.3. The only difference between the properties is a pool. Based on this limited test and a comparison of the prices, a pool seems to add about $4,000 to value.

For the purpose of this CMA, we will assume that properties sold in the neighborhood show the following value contributions:

- The contribution of a pool is $4,000.
- The contribution of a fireplace is $1,000.
- The contribution of an extra garage stall (two cars, rather than one) is $2,000.
- The contribution of extra living space is $40 per square foot.

Note that in Figure 8.3, after each major section of the report, we have room for you to enter the median sales or list price. There are three such measures, mean, median, and mode. The mean is the average. Add up the prices and divide by the number of properties. The median is the middle price in the group. The mode is the price that occurs most often. We use the median because, unlike the average, it removes the effects of an unusually high or low price. These concepts are explained below.

The CMA has been completed, with the exception of the adjustments shown above. Compare the subject property with each comparable property, and adjust the comparable property's price. Then complete the analysis and estimate the market range for the property.

SUMMARY OF IMPORTANT POINTS

- A real estate licensee, in the normal course of business, often prepares a comparative market analysis (CMA) to give an opinion of value.
- The CMA, while not an appraisal, uses the same methods of comparison.
- CMAs are most useful when used for single-family homes and multifamily residences up to four units.
- The CMA form has three major sections: (1) properties sold within the previous 12 months; (2) properties currently on the market; and (3) properties listed during the previous 12 months that did not sell.
- Information needed for preparation of a CMA may be found in MLS® records, company files, and public records.
- Important elements of comparison include location, age, size, condition, and other improvements.
- The licensee should adjust for major differences so that the CMA is not misleading.
- When adjusting comparable sales, use the CIA/CBS approach. If the comparable is inferior, add. If the comparable is better, subtract.

REVIEW QUESTIONS

1. A broker prepares a CMA and gives a broker's price opinion when taking a listing. The broker may
   a. legally refer to the opinion as an appraisal, provided he does not charge for the service.
   b. transmit a broker's price opinion unless he is also a licensed or certified appraiser.
   c. give a broker's price opinion, but may not refer to the opinion as an appraisal. A broker's price opinion is more appropriate because of his involvement in the transaction.
   d. not charge a fee for a broker's price opinion.

2. When a licensee prepares a CMA for a property she intends to list, the conclusions she draws from the CMA are called her broker's price opinion or
   a. appraised value.
   b. opinion of value.
   c. assessed value.
   d. replacement value.

3. Which statement about the differences between an appraisal and a CMA is FALSE?
   a. A CMA often provides the parties with a range of values rather than a specific value.
   b. While an appraisal is concerned primarily with properties sold, a CMA gives weight to properties currently on the market and those that did not sell.
   c. An appraisal provides the client with a range of values, while a CMA gives a specific value.
   d. An appraisal uses three approaches to value, when appropriate, while a CMA uses only one.

4. For the BEST marketing results, a seller should price the property just below
   a. expired listings and just above properties currently for sale.
   b. sold listings and just above properties currently for sale.
   c. properties currently for sale and just above sold properties.
   d. sold properties and just above properties currently for sale.

5. Concerning elements of comparison, which is TRUE?
   a. Location adjustments should not be made if both properties are in the same neighborhood.
   b. Differences in construction quality may disqualify a property for use as a comparable.
   c. Room counts should include living room, kitchen, dining room, bedrooms, and foyer.
   d. It is appropriate to use a ranch house as a comparable for a two-story house.

6. The BEST place(s) to find a property's legal description is (are)
   a. the owner's deed.
   b. utility company records.
   c. public records of deed recordings.
   d. Both A and C

7. The major sections of a CMA are
   a. sold, expired, withdrawn.
   b. price, location, size.
   c. sold, purchased, for sale.
   d. sold, for sale, expired.

8. Which statement regarding CMA preparation is FALSE?
   a. If the houses are comparable, it is common to use sales from different neighborhoods.
   b. Rectangular lots usually are more desirable than pie-shaped lots.
   c. A house next to a busy street normally has a lower value than one on a quiet street.
   d. A 2,500-square-foot home should not be compared with a 1,500-square-foot home.

9. A broker is preparing a CMA. The subject property has a pool, which contributes $4,000 to value. The comparable does not. The adjustment is
   a. + $4,000 to the subject.
   b. + $4,000 to the comparable.
   c. – $4,000 to the subject.
   d. – $4,000 to the comparable.

Use the information below to answer questions 10 and 11.

House A sold for $90,000 and has 1,800 square feet with a pool, but no fireplace. House B sold for $87,000 and has 1,800 square feet with a fireplace, but no pool. House C sold for $85,000 and has 1,800 square feet with no pool or fireplace. House D sold for $95,000 and has 1,900 square feet with a fireplace, but no pool. The subject property has 1,900 square feet, a fireplace, and a pool.

10. A licensee would find the value a pool contributes by comparing houses
    a. A and B.
    b. A and C.
    c. C and D.
    d. B and C.

11. A licensee would find the value a fireplace contributes by comparing houses
    a. A and B.
    b. A and C.
    c. B and C.
    d. D and B.

12. If an adjustment is made for square-foot differences between a subject property and a comparable property, the adjustment that usually results in double counting is one for
    a. a swimming pool.
    b. an extra bedroom.
    c. condition.
    d. location.

13. Which of the following is counted as gross living area?
    a. Screened-in patio
    b. Garage
    c. Below-grade floor space
    d. Foyer entry

14. A home measures 40 feet by 55 feet, which includes a 22-foot by 26-foot garage. What is the home's gross living area?
    a. 2,200 square feet
    b. 1,628 square feet
    c. 1,500 square feet
    d. 572 square feet

15. The acronym CIA-CBS would be used when a licensee was
    a. estimating the range of values for a property.
    b. making adjustments to the sale price of a comparable property.
    c. evaluating the curb appeal of a house.
    d. measuring a house.

CHAPTER 9

BASIC BUSINESS APPRAISAL

KEY TERMS

accrual basis accounting
balance sheet
book value
cash basis accounting
current ratio
debt-to-worth ratio
FIFO
GAAP
going-concern value
goodwill
income statement
intangible asset
inventory turnover ratio
LIFO
liquidation value
net-profit-to-owner-capital ratio
quick ratio
valuation account

OVERVIEW

A business appraisal serves many purposes and may require different approaches. Business owners and buyers of businesses sometimes don't understand why the market value estimated by the appraiser doesn't match the book value shown by the accounting records. This chapter will discuss those issues and show how certain accounting practices can distort value estimates. Ratio analysis is described, as well as adjusted financial statements. Finally, the chapter describes how an appraiser applies the approaches of value to the business.

Once you have completed this chapter, you should be able to:

- describe the characteristics of the legal entities a business appraiser may encounter;
- list at least five reasons for a business appraisal;
- list the five steps in the business appraisal process;
- describe at least three specific problem areas in a financial statement that may distort the firm's true economic value;
- explain the differences between cash basis accounting and accrual basis accounting;
- calculate the important financial ratios; and
- list and describe the four approaches to estimating business value.

FUNDAMENTALS OF BUSINESS APPRAISAL

One of the categories Chapter 475, F.S., defines as *real estate* is "any interest in business enterprises or business opportunities." Persons who appraise businesses must either hold a real estate license or be a certified appraiser. A broker who is involved in listing or selling the property normally would prepare a CMA, not an appraisal.

Similarities to Real Estate Appraisal

Business appraisers, like real estate appraisers, usually are employed to estimate the market value of the property being appraised. Many of the techniques used in that process are similar to real estate appraisal, particularly with respect to the income capitalization and cost approaches.

Because the nature of a business operation has many more variables than a parcel of vacant land or an income property, a business appraiser must have specialized training. The appraiser must understand financial statements, inventory valuation, and the valuation of intangible assets like franchises, copyrights, and goodwill.

Business Appraisal Definitions

A business appraisal is a supported and defended estimate of the value of a business or of certain assets of a business. Usually, the value estimate assumes that the business is in operation at the time of the appraisal and that the operation is likely to continue. Such an estimate is called **going-concern value**. Also, business appraisers often are asked to provide an estimate of **liquidation value**.

Reasons for a Business Appraisal

Sellers, buyers, banks, and family members are all persons who may request business appraisals for some of the reasons discussed below.

Contemplated sale or purchase of a business. An appraisal helps assure sellers or buyers that they are entering into a transaction that is economically sound.

Allocation of value to specific assets. A business owner who wishes to sell part of the business may know that some of the assets taken separately are worth more than the business as a going concern. A business appraisal helps the owner value the components of the business.

Financial reporting purposes. Often, a business owner must provide personal financial statements to a financial institution. A business appraisal provides the bank with an objective valuation of the business.

Mergers and acquisitions. A person overseeing a business merger or an acquisition normally requests an independent appraisal of the business to be acquired. If payment will be made in the acquiring company's stock, the owners of the company being acquired will want to know the value of the shares being received.

Liquidation of a business. A business's liquidation value is the value of business assets sold separately from the business itself. If it is a forced sale, the proceeds normally are less than if the company could carry out the sale in a more reasonable time period.

Divorce. Parties to a divorce who are attempting to agree on a financial settlement usually need to know the value of business property one or both spouses own. A business appraisal provides these figures.

Estate and inheritance taxation. Estate taxes are an important consideration for a deceased individual's personal representatives and family members. Market value of the business is necessary to calculate estate taxes. Also, the basis of property received as inheritance usually is its fair market value at the time of death. Many business appraisals are made for estate tax purposes.

Condemnation proceedings. A business appraiser may be required to estimate loss in value when a government takes part or all of a business's real property in an eminent domain proceeding. The appraiser may be called on to testify in a condemnation proceeding.

Determination of insurable value. Every small-business owner should make sure there is enough insurance to cover the business's tangible assets adequately. A total loss could result in the company's inability to continue operations. Even a partial loss may require the owner to make a substantial copayment under coinsurance clauses. A business appraisal helps eliminate problems associated with under-insuring.

The Business Appraisal Process

1. Define the problem. In this preliminary step of the business appraisal process, an appraiser must:

- identify the business and the interests to be valued, whether it is a complete business appraisal, a partner's interest, or a specific asset group;
- understand the appraisal's purpose;
- determine the type of value to be estimated (market, insurance, liquidation, etc.); and
- identify the appraisal's effective date. In some cases, this may be a date in the past (retrospective), perhaps for estate tax purposes. A valuation may be *prospective* if the appraiser estimates the value for some time in the near future, such as the opening of a new retail store.

2. Make a preliminary analysis, then select and collect the data. During the preliminary analysis, the appraiser reviews the factors affecting the particular business enterprise. Basic documents required include income statements and balance sheets for at least five years. The appraiser should interview the business owners and managers to understand the business thoroughly. The appraiser should collect market data for the products or services the firm offers, either from the Internet, published materials, or personal interviews.

3. Analyze the data. Often, the appraiser must adjust financial statements to better analyze the business. Once the appraiser has completed this, income statements and financial ratios are developed. The data is then compared with that of similar firms in the industry.

4. Prepare a final estimate of value. The final estimate of the business's value is the product of all the steps in the process and the appraiser's careful selection and analysis of the data, as well as the appraiser's experience, skill, and good judgment.

5. Prepare the appraisal report. The appraisal report should be presented in a way that does not mislead, contains enough information for the reader to understand it properly, and discloses any unusual assumptions or limiting conditions that may affect the business's value. A complete appraisal report includes the following information:

- Summary and conclusions
- Purpose of the appraisal (estate taxes, business sale, etc.)
- Definition of the value estimated (insurance, cost, market, etc.)
- Description of the subject business
- Appraisal's effective date
- Description of the appraisal process
- Summary of facts derived from the data collected
- Statement of the conclusions the appraiser reached after analyzing the data
- Assumptions and limiting conditions
- Supporting data, maps, financial statements, and other exhibits

UNDERSTANDING AND USING FINANCIAL STATEMENTS

Overview of Financial Statements

The appraisal process used to value business property is similar in many ways to the process used to value income property. Investors value both types of property based on the property's earnings, cash flows, and projected future incomes. However, there are also substantial differences in the appraisal processes.

When appraising a business, the appraiser faces some issues that usually are not encountered when appraising real property. Every business, despite similarities to other businesses, has many more variables than an income property. The appraisal of a 40-unit apartment building, for example, usually is much more straightforward than the appraisal of a small manufacturing firm. The apartment property's product is rental units, which may be compared easily with other properties. The manufacturing firm, on the other hand, may have many products, patents, competitors, customers, machines, and accounting methods.

The business appraiser is concerned primarily with two financial statements: the balance sheet and the income statement. The **balance sheet** shows the company's financial position at an exact moment in time, while the **income statement** reflects the company's profitability over a previous accounting period.

Problems with Accounting Principles

A business's financial statements usually are prepared and presented using generally accepted accounting principles **(GAAP)**. While these principles have been formulated primarily to standardize performance reporting, they may distort the firm's true value. Some of the problems a business appraiser may encounter are described below.

Estimates are necessary. The business owner or accountant estimates items like uncollectible receivables and income taxes. The business appraiser may adjust those estimates, sometimes based on the benefit of hindsight or the experience of competing firms.

FIGURE 9.1 ■ Sam's Mini-Markets

Beginning in 1971, Sam Shelton acquired property for ten stores in different parts of Orlando for $200,000 and built a 2,500-square-foot concrete block building on each site. The buildings and equipment cost a total of $400,000. The buildings are now fully depreciated. The analysis below shows the properties' book value versus their market value.

	Reported on Financial Statements	Current Market Value
Land and buildings	$ 600,000	
Less depreciation	– 400,000	
	$ 200,000	$1,250,000

Sam's accountant states the book value. Sam's business appraiser estimates the current market value.

Assets are reported at cost. An asset's **book value** is its original cost less depreciation. The business appraiser should restate the value of the asset to market value, not historical cost. An example would be a company with ten mini-markets. If the store locations were purchased years ago and are valued at historical cost, the appraisal would grossly underestimate their current market value. Therefore, the appraiser must make an adjustment to reflect current value.

Valuation accounts do not reflect value. Depreciation and amortization are called **valuation accounts**, although this is a misnomer. They usually allow recovery of an asset's cost over its estimated life, and do not accurately portray the asset's economic depreciation. Some businesses use a conservative approach for financial reports with shorter asset lives, while other companies are quite liberal. Using the example of Sam's Mini-Markets in Figure 9.1, assume that the concrete block buildings cost $40,000 each when they were constructed, but now are totally depreciated so that only the land value still shows on the books. The appraisal report should reflect the current value of land and buildings.

Certain assets or liabilities may be missing. Intangible assets such as licenses, copyrights, and goodwill often are omitted from the asset side of the balance sheet, especially if these items did not involve a cash outlay. However, there may be added value to an appliance store that has the franchise to sell a particular brand of dishwasher, for example. Or a company may have a patent on a machinery design that cost little or nothing, but adds a great deal to the company's profitability. Also, balance sheets may not reflect liabilities like pending lawsuits and long-term leases. (See Figure 9.2.)

FIGURE 9.2 ■ Jill's Machinery and Supply, Inc.

In 1984, Jill Harris designed a drill press that cut the time for manufacturing lawnmower engines in half. Jill paid an attorney to secure a patent, which cost $1,000. Today, the cost is fully amortized. She manufactures and sells the drill press to many small-engine companies. Without the patent, her business could not compete with larger companies in the field. Jill has been offered $300,000 for licensing rights to the product.

	Reported on Financial Statements	Current Market Value
Cost of patent	$1,000	
Less amortization	–1,000	
	$ 0	$300,000

Jill's accountant states the book value. Jill's business appraiser estimates the current market value.

Cash versus accrual accounting. The appraiser must make sure to compare firms using consistent accounting methods. Closely held firms often use **cash basis accounting**, which recognizes income when it actually is received and expenses when they actually are paid. **Accrual basis accounting** recognizes income when the sale is made, rather than when the cash is collected, and expenses are recognized when incurred rather than when paid. An example of the different results from using cash basis or accrual basis accounting on the financial reports is shown in Figure 9.3.

Inventory costing methods. In times of changing prices, the method used to charge the cost of sales may have a significant effect on earnings. First-in, first-out **(FIFO)** usually generates a higher reported profit for firms in times of rising prices. Last-in, first-out **(LIFO)** is more conservative. The *average method* results in a profit figure between the two. *Specific identification* identifies the exact piece of merchandise sold with its actual cost.

An easier way to visualize the different costing methods might be seen with a grocery store's refrigerated milk display. Assume prices are rising. While rotation of the stock to sell the older product first is very important, it is not part of this consideration.

- **FIFO:** If, when the milk comes from the producer, the store clerk loads the new shipment into the back of the case, customers take the milk from the front. If cost labels are attached to the jugs, the older milk will be charged at the old (cheaper) cost.
- **LIFO:** If a clerk puts the new milk in the front of the case, however, the customer will take that first. The newer milk will be charged at the newer (more expensive) cost.
- **Average:** If the clerk mixes them all up and the jugs are not labeled, the store will not know what the cost of each item is, so it could take the beginning cost, the latest cost, less the ending inventory, then apply an average. That would be somewhere in the middle of the first two methods.
- **Specific identification:** If the clerk puts a cost label on each jug, then mixes them up, the actual cost of each milk jug that is sold will be known.

FIGURE 9.3 ■ Abraham's Meat Supply, Inc.

Abraham's Meat Supply has been a staple of the Miami restaurant supply industry for 40 years. Abraham Metzer has operated the family business since inheriting it from his father in 1976. He continues to report the results of operations on a cash basis, while most similar companies report on the accrual basis. The business appraiser totals accounts receivable of $300,000 at year end, which are added to sales. There are accounts payable of $130,000 for suppliers (added to the cost of sales) and $20,000 for operating expenses. Because the valuation will be based on comparison of sales with other firms, the business appraiser makes the following adjustments:

	Reported on Cash Basis	Reported on Accrual Basis
Sales	$1,800,000	$2,100,000
Less cost of sales	– 780,000	– 910,000
Gross profit	$1,020,000	$1,190,000
Less operating expenses	– 725,000	– 745,000
Net operating income	$ 295,000	$ 445,000

If the business is valued at five times its earnings, the *added* value realized by using the accrual basis is $750,000 ($150,000 difference times five).

An example of the different results from using FIFO or LIFO accounting on the financial reports is shown in Figure 9.4.

Research and development accounting differences. Many conservative companies treat research and development costs as an expense. Other firms capitalize the expense and amortize it over several years. The differences affect both the income statement and the balance sheet valuation accounts.

Analyzing Financial Statements

The preceding discussion illustrates the need for a careful analysis of the business and its financial statements. While the business appraiser is not expected to be an accountant, it must be determined whether the financial statements present the firm's economic position fairly. Therefore, the appraiser should construct a historical series of financial statements, calculate financial ratios, and investigate unusual items.

Construct a historical series of financial statements. The first step in analyzing the financial statements is collecting the income statements and balance sheets for five years, if possible. The appraiser should review the statements to see that they are comparable in format from year to year. If the format or presentation differs, the appraiser should rearrange the presentations to make them as similar as possible.

Calculate financial ratios over time. Because of size differences, ratios allow for a better analysis than do raw data such as sales or net profit. A ratio study also may highlight parts of the statements that don't reflect the company's true economic position accurately. Some of the most important ratios are the current ratio, quick ratio, inventory turnover ratio, debt-to-worth ratio, and net-profit-to-owner-capital ratio.

FIGURE 9.4 ■ John's Armoire Store

John Sedgewick runs the largest armoire store in Tampa and maintains an inventory of more than 400 types of cabinets used as closets, entertainment centers, and pantries. He purchases most of them in Mexico and has them shipped to the United States. At the beginning of last year, John bought 500 armoires at $400 each, including freight, but his costs have been rising rapidly. In June he bought 500 armoires at $700 each. He sold 600 units last year for $600,000. John shows cost of goods sold based on FIFO. Most other stores of this nature use LIFO. The business appraiser makes the following analysis:

	Reported on FIFO Basis	Reported on LIFO Basis
Sales of 600 units	$600,000	$600,000
Less cost of sales:		
FIFO 500 @ $400, 100 @ $700	–270,000	
LIFO 500 @ $700, 100 @ $400		–390,000
Gross profit	$330,000	$210,000
Less operating expenses	–175,000	–175,000
Net operating income	$155,000	$ 35,000

If the business is valued at five times its earnings, the difference in value John realizes by using the FIFO inventory costing method is $600,000 ($120,000 difference times five)

Current ratio. The business appraiser calculates **current ratio** by dividing current assets by current liabilities. Current assets are cash or anything that can be converted into cash in one year. Current liabilities are any payments due within one year. The ratio is a common measure of the firm's ability to meet its obligations. Using the audited statement (first column) shown in Figure 9.5, the current ratio would be 2.8 ($310,000 ÷ $110,000).

Quick ratio. The **quick ratio** is a more conservative measure of the company's ability to meet short-term debts. The appraiser divides current assets (without inventory) by current liabilities. Using the audited statement (first column) shown in Figure 9.5, the quick ratio would be 2.4 ($310,000 – $50,000 ÷ $110,000).

Inventory turnover ratio. The **inventory turnover ratio** allows the business appraiser to view the efficiency with which the company manages its inventories. A large part of many businesses' capital is tied up in inventory. Overstocks on slow-selling items indicate that the appraiser may have to adjust inventory values downward. A year-to-year analysis may show serious problems developing. The appraiser calculates the ratio by dividing the

FIGURE 9.5 ■ Actual, Adjusted, and Market Balance Sheets

VALUE BUSINESS FURNITURE MANUFACTURING, INC.
Actual, Adjusted, and Market Balance Sheets
For the year ended December 31, 20__

	Audited Statement	Adjusted Statement	Market Values
ASSETS			
Cash	$ 40,000	$ 40,000	$ 40,000
Accounts receivable (net)	220,000	220,000	185,000[1]
Inventories	50,000	50,000	25,000[2]
Total current assets	$310,000	$310,000	$250,000
Plant and equipment (net)	400,000	400,000	700,000[3]
Company boat (net)	26,000[1]	0	26,000
License fee	14,000[2]	0	0
Total assets	$750,000	$710,000	$976,000
LIABILITIES			
Accounts payable	$ 45,000	$ 45,000	$ 45,000
Notes payable	40,000	40,000	40,000
Income taxes payable	25,000	25,000	25,000
Total current liabilities	$110,000	$110,000	$110,000
Notes payable (long-term)	75,000	75,000	75,000
Total liabilities	$185,000	$185,000	$185,000
CAPITAL			
Common stock	$280,000	$280,000	$280,000
Retained earnings	285,000	245,000	511,000
Total capital	$565,000	$525,000	$791,000
Total liabilities and capital	$750,000	$710,000	$976,000

[1,2] Audited Statement column (see **Preparing Financial Statements for Valuation Purposes, Adjusted balance sheet** on page 222)
[1,2,3] Market Values column (see **Preparing Financial Statements for Valuation Purposes, Market value balance sheet** on page 222)

firm's cost of goods sold by the ending inventory. The inventory turnover ratio for Value Business Furniture is 2.4. To solve, get the cost of goods sold using the audited statement (first column) shown in Figure 9.6, and divide it by the ending inventory in Figure 9.5 ($120,000 ÷ $50,000).

Debt-to-worth ratio. The appraiser calculates the **debt-to-worth ratio** by dividing the company's liabilities by its tangible net worth. The higher the ratio, the greater the financial leverage (and risk). Using the audited statement (first column) shown in Figure 9.5, the debt-to-worth ratio would be .327 ($185,000 ÷ $565,000).

Net-profit-to-owner-capital ratio. The **net-profit-to-owner-capital ratio** is much like the equity dividend rate for an investment property. It shows the one-year return to the investor on the capital. The formula is net profit divided by total capital. The net-profit-to-owner-capital ratio is .22, indicating a 22 percent return. To solve, get the net profit using the audited statement (first column) shown in Figure 9.6, and divide it by the total capital in Figure 9.5 ($125,000 ÷ $565,000).

Investigate unusual items and results. The third step in analyzing financial statements is to review unusual items. A horizontal (year-to-year) review of each line item in the income statement might show significant unexplained changes. The ratio analyses also may point out some questionable areas. Armed with this information, the appraiser should investigate the items by interviewing company officers to determine whether adjustments are necessary. Some examples of unusual items include:

- increases in miscellaneous income, which might raise questions about the source of and reasons for the income and whether it may be expected to continue;
- unusual receivables (often the offsetting entry to miscellaneous income), which must be investigated as to their collectibility; and
- a slowing inventory turnover ratio, which might suggest that the company is developing problems with overstocks on slowing product lines. This should flag the inventory valuation for the appraiser.

FIGURE 9.6 ■ Actual and Adjusted Income Statements

VALUE BUSINESS FURNITURE MANUFACTURING, INC.

Actual and Adjusted Income Statements
For the year ended December 31, 20__

Income	Audited Statement	Adjusted Statement	Pro Forma Statement
Furniture sales	$440,000	$440,000	$470,000
Less: cost of goods sold	–120,000	–120,000	–128,000
Gross profit	$320,000	$320,000	$342,000
General and administrative expense	–195,000	–152,000[1,2]	–167,000
Net profit	$125,000	$168,000	$175,000

[1,2] Adjusted Statement column (see **Preparing Financial Statements for Valuation Purposes, Adjusted income statement** on page 222)

Preparing Financial Statements for Valuation Purposes

After the appraiser has analyzed the financial statements and made any necessary adjustments, the financial statements that will help generate a good estimate of the business's value are ready to be prepared. These statements include the adjusted balance sheet, market value balance sheet, adjusted income statement, and pro forma income statement.

Adjusted balance sheet. Figure 9.5 provides an adjusted balance sheet for Value Business Furniture Manufacturing, Inc. Column one is the company's statement, as provided to the appraiser. Column two shows the balance sheet, as adjusted by the appraiser for two items. The numbered paragraphs correspond to the numbers in the figure.

1. The company owns a small cabin cruiser costing $26,000 that it uses for business entertainment. Because this asset is outside the company's normal business operations and would distort comparisons with other firms in the industry, it has been deleted.
2. Last year, the company paid $14,000 for the right to use a brand name from a company that is no longer in the business. The item has been deleted, and is of no value.

Market value balance sheet (Figure 9.5). The appraiser prepares this statement to present the firm's value fairly when items are stated at market value rather than original cost. Three items have been adjusted:

1. An account receivable for $35,000 from Bargain Office Equipment Sales, Inc., has been written off because the business filed for bankruptcy protection after the statements were completed.
2. One of the company's products, a computer workstation, was designed for a 14-inch monitor. Because most new PCs come with a 21-inch or 23-inch monitor, the $50,000 cost of that inventory product has been written down by $25,000.
3. The fair market value of the company's factory and equipment is $700,000. The original cost, less depreciation, was $400,000.

Adjusted income statement (Figure 9.6). The business appraiser prepares an adjusted income statement to make comparisons with other companies in the same industry. Items that would distort those comparisons are excluded. Two items are excluded from the income statement for Value Business Furniture Manufacturing, Inc., shown in Figure 9.6:

1. Boat operating costs of $12,000 have been removed from the statement.
2. The company pays its officers salaries substantially higher than those paid in the industry in general, primarily because the officers are family members. The amounts paid are adjusted downward by $31,000 to reflect competitive salaries.

Pro forma income statement (Figure 9.6). The adjusted income statement is the starting point for preparation of the pro forma statement. The pro forma income statement is the appraiser's best estimate of income and expenses for the next year or two at most.

The pro forma income statement is most important when using the income method.

VALUATION METHODS

The methods used to value business properties are very similar to those used to value real estate: sales comparison, cost-depreciation, and income capitalization. Another method, the liquidation value approach, is most applicable to valuation of a business.

FIGURE 9.7 ■ Comparable Sales of Furniture Manufacturing Firms

Comparable Sale	Selling Price	Annual Sales	Annual Net Income	Selling Price/ Annual Sales	Selling Price/ Annual NOI
Company 1	$840,000	$500,000	$207,400	1.68	4.05
Company 2	800,000	470,000	186,000	1.70	4.30
Company 3	650,000	380,000	162,500	1.71	4.00
Company 4	960,000	550,000	218,200	1.75	4.40
Average of the four sales			1.71		4.19
Pro forma annual sales and annual net operating income			× $470,000		× $175,000
Indicated value range			from $803,700	to	$733,250

Sales comparison approach. The appraiser using this approach to business valuation bases the subject business's value on the sale prices of similar businesses. Ideally, the appraiser has appraised these businesses so that there is enough data to make the best comparison. The appraiser examines each comparable sale to determine the relationship between gross income and the price the business sold for, as well as net income and the sale price. Once these relationships are calculated, the appraiser applies them to the subject property's gross and net incomes to estimate its value. Figure 9.7 shows the process of valuation for Value Business Furniture Manufacturing, Inc.

Cost-depreciation approach. The cost-depreciation approach to business valuation generally is the least effective in estimating value for a going concern because a business's market value depends more on sales and income than on the cost to reproduce its assets.

Income capitalization approach. Because the marketplace values net operating incomes and cash flows, the income capitalization approach is very important to the appraisal of a going concern. It should be noted that the sales comparison approach also relies on the pro forma net operating income to determine value. The major steps in the income capitalization approach follow:

1. Prepare a pro forma income statement that is typical for the business.
2. Select the capitalization rate that appropriately reflects the rates on similar businesses. Using the comparable sales shown in Figure 9.7, dividing the net income by the sale prices indicates an average capitalization rate of 23.9 percent.
3. Divide the net operating income by the capitalization rate. Value Business Furniture has a net operating income of $175,000. Divided by the .239 capitalization rate, the value indication is $732,200. Note that the values shown basically are the same in both approaches because the capitalization rate is the reciprocal of the income multiplier.

Liquidation value approach. A business's liquidation value is the anticipated proceeds from the sale of all its tangible assets less the firm's liabilities. Business appraisers apply this approach if a business is unlikely to continue operating, but sometimes it is used simply to provide the quick sale value of a firm's assets. This approach normally is the most conservative way to determine value. Financial institutions may be particularly concerned with liquidation value when lending to a new business or one that is unprofitable.

Valuation of Intangible Assets

Business appraisers encounter **intangible assets** in almost every appraisal; therefore, they must be familiar with the different types and understand the best ways to estimate their value. Not all intangible assets should be termed **goodwill**. Amortization of goodwill generally is not deductible for income tax purposes, while some other types of intangible assets may be amortized.

Business goodwill. Business goodwill may consist of a firm's reputation, quality of service, product quality, and residual advertising benefits. This goodwill usually is transferable to a new owner.

Personal goodwill. Personal goodwill consists of the owner's personal reputation and skills, as seen by customers, employees, and the public as a whole. This goodwill generally does not transfer when the owner sells the business.

Separable intangible assets. Franchises, licenses, copyrights, leasehold benefits, and trademarks are examples of separable intangible assets.

Methods of Valuation

If a business appraiser needs to state the values of tangible and intangible assets separately, the most common procedure is as follows:

1. Estimate the tangible assets' value.
2. Estimate the separable intangible assets' value.
3. Estimate the value of business and personal goodwill.

Appraisers use many techniques to value intangible assets. Two of the most common approaches follow.

Excess profits approach. In this approach, the appraiser first estimates the rate of return investors require, then applies that rate to the tangible assets' value. This provides the income attributable to those assets. After the appraiser deducts this income from total net operating income, any residual income belongs to the intangible assets. Applying the capitalization rate to the residual income results in the estimated value of the intangible assets.

Market residual approach. In the market residual approach, the appraiser first values the tangible assets, then deducts that amount from the business's total value. The difference is the intangible assets' value. The appraiser estimates the separable intangible assets' value by dividing the net income these assets generate by the capitalization rate. Any income remaining after the appraiser deducts tangible and separable intangible assets is the goodwill's value.

WEB LINK

For more information on Business Valuation, see: **http://www.bvresources.com/**
http://www.valuationresources.com/

TABLE 9.1 ■ Summary of Important Financial Ratios

The following table provides a good review of the financial ratios discussed in this chapter.

Ratio	Formula	Description
Current Ratio	Current assets ÷ Current Liabilities	Shows the firm's ability to pay its bills.
Quick Ratio	Current Assets – Inventories ÷ Current Liabilities	Sometimes called the "acid test ratio."
Inventory Turnover Ratio	Cost of Goods Sold ÷ Ending Inventory	Often shows when inventory levels are getting too high.
Debt-to-Worth Ratio	Liabilities ÷ Net Worth	If liabilities are high compared to net worth, the company is highly leveraged (and has more risk).
Net Profit-to-Capital Ratio	Net Profit ÷ Total Capital	Shows the return on the owners' capital.

SUMMARY OF IMPORTANT POINTS

- Business appraisers must be licensed, either as brokers or as certified appraisers.
- Business brokers may make appraisals provided the property is not part of a federally related transaction.
- A broker who prepares an appraisal must conform with the *Uniform Standards of Professional Appraisal Practice.*
- Business appraisers usually have specialized training in accounting, finance, and the valuation of intangible assets.
- Most businesses are appraised as going concerns, using the three traditional approaches to value; however, if a business is unlikely to succeed, the liquidation approach to value would be used.
- The business appraisal process is very similar to real estate appraising.
- Business appraisers usually must adjust financial statements to reflect market value.
- Some of the difficulties appraisers encounter when business owners use generally accepted accounting principles (GAAP) are:
  - assets are reported at cost, not market value;
  - depreciation accounts distort values;
  - some assets may not be reported;
  - accrual basis accounting may yield significantly different results than cash basis accounting; and
  - inventory costing using FIFO gives different results than costing using LIFO.
- Some of the most important business appraisal ratios are the current ratio, quick ratio, and debt-to-worth ratio.
- The pro forma income statement is important when using the comparable sales and income capitalization approaches to value.

REVIEW QUESTIONS

1. A woman inherited a substantial food service business when her father died. What would be the BEST action for her to take for estate tax purposes, and to establish her cost basis in the business to calculate gain if she should later sell it?
   a. Hire a new manager
   b. Order an appraisal that estimates the market value of the business as of the date of her father's death
   c. Close the business immediately
   d. Sell the business within six months of the date of her father's death

2. A broker is appraising a restaurant chain with 12 restaurants built about ten years ago. Which is TRUE of the broker's review of the business's financial statements?
   a. The locations are separable intangible assets and must be appraised using the residual method.
   b. The LIFO site location valuation method is the least conservative method to use.
   c. The balance sheet shows the locations at the original cost less depreciation, so they probably must be adjusted upward to reflect current market values.
   d. Book value is the proper valuation for the restaurant sites.

3. What is the MOST conservative ratio that helps determine whether a company can meet its financial obligations in the near future?
   a. Liquidation
   b. Quick
   c. Current
   d. Debt-to-worth

4. If the losses of a business are so great that the appraiser questions whether the business can continue, what is the MOST appropriate approach to value?
   a. Liquidation value
   b. Cost-depreciation
   c. Income capitalization
   d. Comparable sales

5. A review of a manufacturing company balance sheet shows: Cash $80,000; Accounts Receivable $175,000; Inventories $124,000; Accounts Payable $78,000; Owners' Capital $301,000. What is the current ratio?
   a. 1.00
   b. 2.91
   c. 3.27
   d. 4.86

6. Using the information in the previous question, what is the quick ratio?
   a. 3.27
   b. 2.91
   c. 2.27
   d. 1.00

7. What is the MOST likely use of a business appraisal prepared in October with a valuation date of January of the same year?
   a. Contemplated purchase of the business
   b. Liquidation of the business
   c. Divorce
   d. Estate taxes

8. Which statement is FALSE about generally accepted accounting principles?
   a. Assets are reported at cost.
   b. Valuation accounts reflect market values.
   c. Certain assets are missing.
   d. Differences in inventory costing methods occur.

9. An appliance store has experienced higher prices from manufacturers during the previous year, and has passed the increased prices on to the customers. Therefore, the MOST conservative accounting method for inventories would be
   a. FIFO (first-in, first-out).
   b. LIFO (last-in, first-out).
   c. average.
   d. FISH (first-in, still-here).

10. A photo supply company sells film, developers, and paper to photographers throughout the state. It uses cash basis accounting, and the income statement for the year shows sales of $500,000 and net operating income of $110,000. Because similar companies report on an accrual basis, a business appraiser adjusts the statements to the accrual basis for comparison. Accounts receivable are $90,000 and accounts payable are $30,000. Based on this information, the adjusted statements show sales of
    a. $530,000, net operating income of $200,000.
    b. $560,000, net operating income of $170,000.
    c. $590,000, net operating income of $170,000.
    d. $590,000, net operating income of $200,000.

11. A manufacturer has sales of $400,000 and net operating income of $75,000. Recent data show that comparable manufacturing companies typically are valued at two times their sales and ten times their net profits. What is the value range for the company?
    a. $150,000 to $400,000
    b. $150,000 to $4 million
    c. $400,000 to $600,000
    d. $750,000 to $800,000

12. When an appraiser reviews the data for comparable sales, she sees that a firm sold for $600,000. It reported sales of $300,000, gross profit of $145,000, and net operating income of $75,000. What was its capitalization rate?
    a. 12.5%
    b. 24.2%
    c. 25%
    d. 50%

13. Franchises, licenses, and copyrights are all examples of
    a. nonseparable intangible assets.
    b. goodwill.
    c. separable intangible assets.
    d. market residuals.

14. An appraiser's BEST estimate of the result of operations for one or two years in advance is called the
    a. adjusted balance sheet.
    b. pro forma balance sheet.
    c. audited income statement.
    d. pro forma income statement.

15. The major difference between the current ratio and the quick ratio is that
    a. capital is included when calculating the current ratio.
    b. the long-term portion of notes payable is used when calculating the quick ratio.
    c. inventories are excluded from current assets when calculating the current ratio.
    d. inventories are excluded from current assets when calculating the quick ratio.

CASE STUDY PART 2

VALUING REAL PROPERTY

Department of Business and Professional Regulation, Florida Real Estate Commission	*vs.*	*Sergio A. Becerra*

Recommended Order:

This case was heard in Miami before Administrative Law Judge Florence Snyder Rivas, Division of Administrative Hearings. The parties were represented by:

For Petitioner: Juana Carstarphen Watkins, Esquire, DBPR
For Respondent: Sergio A. Becerra, pro se

This matter arises from Petitioner's Administrative Complaint against Respondent Sergio A. Becerra.

Findings of Fact:

Respondent was a Florida state-certified residential real estate appraiser. Respondent registered his address with the DBPR as 5299 West 28th Avenue, Hialeah Gardens.

On February 2, Respondent developed and communicated an appraisal report for residential property located in Homestead, Florida. The Petitioner received a complaint concerning the appraisal three years later.

The Petitioner wrote the Respondent at his registered address. The letter was not returned. The Respondent's mother actually received the letter. At the time the letter was sent and received at Becerra's registered address, Becerra was living in Colorado.

The Respondent provided the DBPR with accurate address information three years after that. So, a state investigator arranged to meet Becerra at his new location. The Respondent no longer had the work file of the appraisal on the property. The Petitioner testified that the Respondent's conduct was hostile, suspicious, and secretive in his dealings with the investigator.

Respondent Becerra refused to answer questions regarding his practices concerning the development and maintenance of appraisal records. The investigator attempted to conduct a spot-audit of Becerra's books and records related to pending appraisals; however, Becerra refused to cooperate.

Discussion Questions:

1. Which subsections of Chapter 475, F.S. were violated, and what were the violations?
2. What are the time frames for notifying the DBPR of a change of address and a change of residency?
3. How long was the appraiser obligated to save the appraisal work file?

Web Link: **http://www.doah.state.fl.us/internet/** (See case number 03-0717/PL)

PART THREE

LISTING AND SELLING REAL PROPERTY

CHAPTER 10

BROKERAGE RELATIONSHIPS

KEY TERMS

agent
at arm's length
customer
designated sales associate
dual agent
fiduciary
general agent
no brokerage relationship
principal
residential sale
single agent
special agent
subagents
transaction broker
universal agent

OVERVIEW

This chapter begins with a general explanation of the law of agency and then details the various types of brokerage relationships practiced in Florida. The chapter also explains the licensee's duties and obligations to principals and customers.

Once you have completed this chapter, you should be able to:

- distinguish between the terms *general agent* and *special agent*;
- describe which legal provisions apply only to residential real estate transactions;
- describe the duties and disclosure requirements of a transaction broker;
- describe the duties and disclosure requirements that single agents have to their principals;
- define a *dual agent*;
- describe the purpose and requirements of the no brokerage relationship notice;
- list the no brokerage relationship duties;
- describe the process of transition from a single agent to a transaction broker;
- describe the requirements for *designated sales associates*; and
- identify the actions that will terminate a brokerage relationship.

LAW OF AGENCY

When a person delegates authority to someone to act on his or her behalf, an agency relationship has been created. Agency relationships fall within the body of law called *law of agency*.

There are two types of law that society looks to for guidance regarding agency relationships: common law and statutory law.

Common law (sometimes referred to as unwritten law) is law based on usage, general acceptance, and custom. It is judge-made law manifested in decrees and judgments of the courts (case law) as opposed to statutory law. Common law originated in England and was later incorporated into the U.S. legal system. Under the English common law, servants owed absolute loyalty to their masters. This absolute loyalty is one of the fundamental principles of the agency relationship. Agency law derives from common law.

Statutory law includes the statutes and rules enacted by legislatures and other governing bodies. In addition to the statutory laws of agency, real estate license law and the Florida Real Estate Commission (the FREC) rules directly affect and regulate the brokerage relationships among real estate licensees, buyers and sellers, and the public.

AGENCY RELATIONSHIPS IN GENERAL BUSINESS DEALINGS

In general, a person who delegates authority to another is referred to as the *principal*. A person who accepts the authority (and responsibilities, duties, and obligations associated with that authority) is referred to as the *agent*. An **agent** is the person entrusted with another's business. An agent is authorized to represent and act for the principal.

The agency relationship creates a *fiduciary relationship* with the principal. A *fiduciary* acts in a position of trust or confidence for another. The fiduciary owes complete allegiance to the principal. Agency relationships exist in many business transactions such as between an attorney (agent) and client (principal). An agency relationship may exist in certain real estate transactions. (This will be explained in detail in the next section of the chapter.)

A fiduciary relationship contrasts with the common public relationship that exists in normal trading transactions where people with adverse interests deal **at arm's length** with each other. People dealing at arm's length conduct negotiations on their own behalf without trusting the other's fairness or integrity and without being subject to the other's control or influence. In such cases, the legal doctrine of *caveat emptor* (let the buyer beware) applies.

There are three types of agents characterized by the extent of authority delegated to an agent in general business dealings: (1) universal agent, (2) general agent, and (3) special agent.

A **universal agent** is authorized by the principal to perform all acts that the principal can personally perform and that may be lawfully delegated to another. An attorney who manages the trust agreement of a mentally disabled adult is a universal agent for that client (the principal). Duties of the attorney-agent would include, for example, overseeing the principal's financial affairs, medical care, employment opportunities, and living arrangements.

A **general agent** is authorized by the principal to perform acts associated with the continued operations of a particular job or a certain business of the principal. A property manager, for example, acts as a general agent if authorized to show and rent apartments, collect rents, supervise maintenance and upkeep of the property, handle tenant relations, and perform bookkeeping duties. A sales associate is a general agent of the employing broker.

A **special agent** is authorized by the principal to handle only a specific business transaction or to perform only a specific act. If you hire a certified public accountant (CPA) to prepare your tax return and, if necessary, to answer any inquiries from the IRS concerning the tax return, the CPA is acting as a special agent for you (the principal). A real estate licensee may act as a special agent with buyers or sellers. This occurs when the buyer or seller and the brokerage firm enter into a single agent relationship. The broker agrees to represent the buyer or seller with regard to a single business transaction. Not all real estate brokers act as agents of buyers and sellers. (See Single Agent Relationship on page 238.)

BROKERAGE RELATIONSHIPS IN FLORIDA

Historically, there has been confusion among buyers and sellers regarding what role real estate licensees have in real estate negotiations. Sellers assumed that real estate licensees represented their interests because sellers traditionally paid the commission. However, the payment of commission or the promise of compensation alone is not what determines whether a brokerage relationship exists. A brokerage relationship can be accidently (inadvertently) created by a licensee's actions and words. For example, referring to a prospective purchaser as "my buyer" or "my client" may imply that the licensee is representing the buyer when in actuality the brokerage is representing the seller. Because of this confusion, the Florida legislature passed the Brokerage Relationship Disclosure Act. The Brokerage Relationship Disclosure Act is intended to inform and educate the public regarding the types of authority (brokerage relationships) that can be granted to a broker and the duties brokers have in each type of brokerage relationship.

Brokerage Relationship Options

Licensees have three basic options in all real estate transactions concerning the role the real estate brokerage firm will assume for buyers and sellers:

1. The brokerage firm may work as a *transaction broker* for the buyer and/or the seller.
2. The brokerage firm may work as a *single agent* of either the buyer or the seller (but *not* for both buyer and seller in the same transaction).
3. The parties may agree that the brokerage firm will not represent the buyer or the seller at all. This situation is referred to as *no brokerage relationship*. The brokerage firm simply facilitates the transaction.

In Florida, a real estate licensee may enter into a brokerage relationship either as a transaction broker or as a single agent with prospective buyers and sellers. Alternatively, the customer may desire not to be represented in any capacity by the brokerage firm. For example, property owners who have found buyers for their own homes (for-sale-by-owners, also referred to as FSBOs) may want a knowledgeable real estate firm to handle the paperwork regarding the transaction. However, a FSBO seller may not need or desire the broker to represent or negotiate on the seller's behalf. In such cases, FSBOs may elect no brokerage relationship with the brokerage firm.

It is illegal in Florida for a real estate licensee to operate as a dual agent. The term **dual agent** means a broker who represents as a fiduciary both the prospective buyer and the prospective seller in a real estate transaction. When a broker represents a buyer or a seller as a **fiduciary**, the broker is in a relationship of trust and confidence between the broker as agent and the seller as principal or the buyer as principal. A fiduciary relationship is created when a real estate broker accepts employment as a single agent of the seller or the buyer. In an agency relationship, the broker owes fiduciary duties to the principal. Florida real estate license law prohibits a broker from creating a fiduciary relationship with both the buyer and the seller.

Residential Transactions

Chapter 475 mandates certain duties and obligations in each type of brokerage relationship. These duties and obligations apply to *all* real estate transactions. However, written disclosures are required only when dealing in residential real estate transactions.

A **residential sale** is defined as the sale of improved residential property of four or fewer units, the sale of unimproved residential property intended for use as four or fewer units, or the sale of agricultural property of ten or fewer acres. Furthermore, the disclosure requirements do *not* apply to:

- nonresidential transactions;
- the rental or leasing of real property, unless an option to purchase all or a portion of the property improved with four or fewer residential units is given;
- auctions;
- appraisals; and
- dispositions of any interest in business enterprises or business opportunities, except for property with four or fewer residential units.

(Note: Licensees are no longer required to give customers a written disclosure when a transaction broker relationship is chosen.)

Transaction Broker Relationship

Under Florida law, it is *presumed* that all licensees are operating as transaction brokers unless a single agent or no brokerage relationship is established, in writing, with the customer. A **transaction broker** is a broker who provides limited representation to a buyer, a seller, or both in a real estate transaction, but who does *not* represent either party in a fiduciary capacity or as a single agent. In this relationship, the seller (or the buyer) is considered to be a customer of the real estate broker and *not* a principal. In a transaction broker relationship the buyer or seller (customer) is not responsible for the acts of a licensee.

Chapter 475 defines **customer** to mean a member of the public who is or may be a buyer or a seller of real property and may or may not be represented by a real estate licensee in an authorized brokerage relationship. Therefore, the seller (or the buyer) who chooses limited representation is a customer under the transaction broker relationship. A licensee may enter into a transaction broker relationship with both parties (buyer and seller) in a real estate transaction. The seven duties of the transaction broker in this limited form of representation are as follows:

1. Deal honestly and fairly. Licensees owe a duty of good faith and honesty to customers. A broker's customers are entitled to rely on any material statement related to a real estate transaction that is made by a licensee.

2. Account for all funds. The broker must account for all funds entrusted to him or her with regard to a real estate transaction. Such holdings are considered trust funds or escrow funds. Money and valuables entrusted to a broker must be kept separate from the broker's funds. The broker is not entitled to any trust or escrow funds until the transaction is concluded at a title closing. Brokers are required to keep complete records of all transactions and funds as well as to make available to the Department of Business and Professional Regulation (DBPR) such books, accounts, and records as will enable the DBPR to determine whether the broker is in compliance with Chapter 475.

3. Use skill, care, and diligence in the transaction. The broker, for example, must keep informed of current zoning and other developments that may affect the value of the property and must use diligence in facilitating the transaction.

4. Disclose all known facts that materially affect the value of residential real property and are not readily observable to the buyer. Licensees have a duty to disclose to buyers all known facts that materially affect the value of residential property. For example, a licensee is obligated to inform the buyer if there are cracks in the tile floor under the wall-to-wall carpeting caused from the foundation settling.

Questions sometimes arise regarding whether certain information concerning the seller or previous occupants of a property must be disclosed to prospective buyers. Federal fair housing law and the Florida statutes specifically mandate that the fact that an occupant of real property is infected or has been infected with human immunodeficiency virus (HIV) or diagnosed with acquired immune deficiency syndrome is *not* a material fact in a real estate transaction. This is personal medical information and must not be disclosed without prior authorization. Furthermore, Florida statute mandates the fact that a property was, or was at any time suspected to have been, the site of a homicide, suicide, or death is *not* a material fact that must be disclosed in a real estate transaction. A cause of action will not arise against a property owner or a real estate licensee for failure to disclose any of the information or events listed above.

5. Present all offers and counteroffers in a timely manner. Unless a party has previously directed the licensee otherwise in writing, the licensee must present *all oral and written offers* and counteroffers in a timely manner even if a valid contract exists.

6. Exercise limited confidentiality, unless waived in writing by a party. This limited confidentiality will prevent disclosure that the seller will accept a price less than the asking or listed price; that the buyer will pay a price greater than the price submitted in a written offer; of the motivation of any party for selling or buying property; that a seller or buyer will agree to financing terms other than those offered; or of any other information requested by a party to remain confidential.

7. Perform any additional duties that are mutually agreed to with a party. A real estate licensee must be careful not to accept duties beyond the scope of limited representation. To do so might create an unintended fiduciary relationship with a customer. For example, a transaction broker may not promise complete allegiance to a customer because to do so could be interpreted by a court of law to have created a fiduciary relationship.

In a transaction broker relationship, the parties to a real estate transaction are giving up their rights to the undivided loyalty of a licensee. This aspect of *limited representation* allows a licensee to facilitate a real estate transaction by assisting both the buyer and the seller. However, a licensee will not work to represent one party to the detriment of the other party when acting as a transaction broker to both parties. Real estate licensees are no longer required to give customers a written transaction broker notice. However, licensees must still fulfill the duties of a transaction broker when that form of representation is selected. The seven duties listed above apply to all real estate transactions (residential and otherwise) when the parties have agreed to a transaction broker relationship. (See Table 10.1, Brokerage Relationship Duties.)

Single Agent Relationship

A seller (or a buyer) may want to be represented by a real estate broker. In this case, the real estate broker is a single agent who represents the seller as a fiduciary in selling the home or the buyer in finding a home. The Florida real estate license law defines a **single agent** as a broker who represents, as a fiduciary, the buyer or the seller, but *not both*, in the same transaction. In a single agent relationship, the seller (or the buyer) is the principal and the real estate broker is the agent. The term **principal** is used to mean the party with whom a real estate licensee has entered into a single agent relationship.

Subagents are persons authorized to assist and represent the agent. A subagent has the same duties as the agent. A broker's sales associates are general agents of the broker and subagents of the broker's principals. For example, in a single agent relationship, the broker is an agent of the principal. The broker's sales associates and broker associates are subagents of the broker's principals. Sales associates and broker associates owe the same fiduciary obligations to the broker's principals as does their broker. (*Note:* This is true regardless of whether the associates, for tax purposes, are employees or independent contractors of the broker.)

The nine duties a real estate licensee owes to a buyer or seller who engage the real estate brokerage as a single agent are as follows:

1. Deal honestly and fairly. (See page 237, for explanation.)

2. Loyalty. The agent as fiduciary in a real estate transaction must avoid any situation that might breach the duty of undivided loyalty to the principal. The overriding rule is that a broker may not adopt an attitude that is adverse to the interests of the principal or act for himself or herself or some other person whose interests are contrary to those of the principal. Loyalty (faithfulness) requires the broker to always place the principal's interests above those of other persons with whom the broker deals. Courts have ruled (case law) that for brokers to be loyal to their principals, they cannot exercise duties in such a manner as to profit themselves or anyone else at the expense of the principal. The duty of loyalty includes, for example:

- obtaining the most favorable price and terms for the principal;
- acting on behalf of the principal;
- not acting for parties with adverse interest in the same transaction;
- never concealing the identity of the purchaser to induce the principal to sell;

- disclosing to the principal if the agent becomes personally interested in the principal's property; and
- never advancing the agent's or another person's interest at the expense of the principal.

3. Confidentiality. Much of the information a broker gains while employed by the principal is confidential. An agent cannot reveal to a third party, without the principal's permission, personal or private information that might lessen the principal's bargaining position. For example, a licensee cannot tell a buyer that a seller is forced to sell owing to poor health or loss of a job without the principal's permission. Brokers cannot divulge confidential information learned during the course of the single agency even after the transaction is concluded and the agent-principal relationship is ended. A broker is never free to use confidential information to the disadvantage of or reveal any harmful or unfavorable information about a former principal.

4. Obedience. An agent is obligated to act in good faith according to the principal's lawful instructions. The broker-agent is at all times obligated to act in conformity with the principal's instructions as long as those instructions are legal and relevant to the contractual relationship. If a broker feels that carrying out the principal's legal directions will harm the principal, then the broker must promptly inform the principal of all known facts along with the broker's opinion. However, if the principal will not change the instructions, the broker must either carry them out or withdraw from the relationship.

Brokers may not violate the law. For example, if a principal instructs a listing broker not to show the property or sell to a member of a particular minority or ethnic group, the broker cannot obey the principal's instructions because doing so would violate the law. In such an instance, the broker must inform the principal that to restrict certain groups of people from seeing or purchasing a listed property is a violation of the fair housing laws.

5. Full disclosure. It is a broker-agent's duty to keep the principal fully informed at all times of all the facts or information that might affect the transaction or the value of the property. An agent is obligated to disclose facts regarding a property's true worth. Agents may be held responsible for material facts they should have known and communicated to their principal but did not. Also, broker-agents must inform their seller principals, for example, of the buyer's financial condition, the status of the earnest money deposit, or if a personal relationship exists between the agent and the buyer. All material facts must be revealed to the principal even if the disclosure of such facts might cause the transaction to fail.

Full, fair, and prompt disclosure also includes notifying the principal if the broker is personally interested in buying the listed property. In such an event, the broker must clearly terminate the agent-principal relationship and inform the principal of all facts regarding the property that the broker has learned while in an agent's capacity. Otherwise, the broker could buy from the principal and subsequently sell at a higher price and keep the profit ("overage," "secret profit," or "secret commission"). To do so could be construed as fraud, misrepresentation, concealment, and/or dishonest dealing and could expose the broker to liability to both seller and buyer for the full amount of the secret profit. It might further give rise to disciplinary proceedings against the licensee.

6. Account for all funds. (See page 237 for explanation.)

7. Skill, care, and diligence in the transaction. A broker's obligations extend beyond merely selling a listing or locating a suitable property for a buyer. A real estate broker holds himself or herself out to the public as specially qualified by reason of experience,

TABLE 10.1 ■ Brokerage Relationship Duties

Duty	No Brokerage	Transaction	Single Agent
Deal honestly and fairly	✔	✔	✔
Disclose all known facts that affect value of residential property	✔	✔	✔
Account for all funds	✔	✔	✔
Use skill, care, and diligence		✔	✔
Present all offers and counteroffers		✔	✔
Exercise limited confidentiality		✔	
Perform additional duties that are mutually agreed to		✔	
Confidentiality			✔
Obedience			✔
Loyalty			✔
Disclosure (full)			✔

ability, and knowledge. If a broker's principal is a buyer, then the broker should attempt to obtain the property at the lowest price possible. If the broker's principal is a seller, then the broker should try to get the seller the most favorable price. This includes researching a property thoroughly to advise the seller of a reasonable listing price. Brokers should discuss with their principals any anticipated tax consequences and advise them to seek expert tax advice when appropriate. The duty of using skill, care, and diligence does not end with the signing of a contract. It continues via numerous services by the agent until the transaction is closed. If an agent does not perform with the required degree of skill, care, and diligence, the agent becomes liable to the principal for the damages the principal may have sustained and may be disciplined by the FREC.

8. Present all offers and counteroffers in a timely manner. (See page 237 for explanation.)

9. Disclose all known facts that materially affect the value of residential real property and are not readily observable to the buyer. (See page 237 for explanation.)

The nine duties listed above apply to all real estate transactions (residential and otherwise) when the parties have agreed to a single agent relationship.

No Brokerage Relationship

The seller (or the buyer) can choose not to be represented by a real estate broker. In such a situation, the broker would simply facilitate the sale (or the purchase) of real property without entering into either a single agent relationship or transaction broker relationship. A broker working in a **no brokerage relationship** capacity with a seller can enter into a listing agreement with that seller and be paid a commission. Similarly, a brokerage firm working in a no brokerage relationship capacity can work with a buyer. Florida law does not require that prospective buyers and sellers be represented. A real estate licensee working in a no brokerage relationship capacity with a buyer or a seller has the following three duties:

1. **Deal honestly and fairly.**
2. **Disclose all known facts that materially affect the value of residential real property that are not readily observable to the buyer.**
3. **Account for all funds entrusted to the licensee.**

BROKERAGE RELATIONSHIP LIMITATIONS

- If the brokerage firm has a transaction broker relationship with the seller, the brokerage firm can also work with the buyer, in the same transaction, as a transaction broker or in no brokerage relationship. The brokerage firm cannot represent the buyer as a single agent if the firm has a transaction broker relationship with the seller.
- If the brokerage firm is representing the seller as a single agent, the brokerage firm can work with the buyer, in the same transaction, in no brokerage relationship. The brokerage firm cannot represent the buyer as a single agent or work with the buyer as a transaction broker if the firm is also representing the seller as a single agent.

The brokerage relationship limitations described above apply, even if the buyer and seller are working with different sales associates in the same brokerage firm.

Disclosure Requirements

The duties of the chosen relationship must be fully described and disclosed in writing to a buyer or the seller, either as a separate and distinct disclosure document or included as part of another document, such as a listing agreement or buyer broker agreement. If the disclosure document is incorporated into a listing or buyer broker agreement, a signature line must be inserted immediately following the disclosure information. It is not sufficient to only have a signature line at the bottom of the listing or buyer broker agreement. The single agent disclosure must be made before, or at the time of, entering into a listing agreement or an agreement for representation, or before the showing of property, whichever occurs first. The no brokerage relationship notice must be disclosed in writing before the showing of property.

When incorporated into other documents, the required disclosure notice must be of the same size as, or larger type than, other provisions of the document and must be conspicuous in its placement to advise customers (or principals in a single agent relationship) of the brokerage duties. The first sentence must be printed in uppercase and bold type. The list of duties must be presented on the disclosure in the same order as listed in the statute. The disclosure notice may include information concerning the real estate brokerage such as the company name and logo, address, phone number, e-mail address, and so forth.

Although the disclosure notice provides for the customer's (principal's) signature, the signature is *not* mandatory (except for the transition to transaction broker notice and the designated sales associate notice discussed later in this chapter). If a customer or principal desires to proceed with the relationship but refuses to sign or initial the disclosure document, the licensee should include a copy of the disclosure in the file with a note indicating the date the disclosure was presented and that the buyer or the seller refused to sign the document. Under Florida law, it is presumed that all licensees are operating as transaction brokers unless another brokerage relationship is established. Therefore, there is no requirement to give a written transaction broker disclosure notice to the buyer and/or the seller.

Exceptions to Disclosure Requirements

Certain interactions a licensee has with buyers and sellers do not constitute a brokerage relationship. These situations are described in the real estate license law. When a licensee has an encounter with a buyer or seller under these specific situations, the licensee is *not* required to give a prospective buyer or a prospective seller a disclosure notice. The six situations that do not create a brokerage relationship are as follows:

1. When the licensee knows that a single agent or a transaction broker represents a prospective seller or a prospective buyer
2. At a bona fide "open house" or model home showing that does not involve eliciting: confidential information; the execution of a contractual offer or an agreement for representation; or negotiations concerning price, terms, or conditions of potential sale
3. During unanticipated casual encounters between a licensee and a prospective seller or a prospective buyer that do not involve eliciting confidential information; the execution of a contractual offer or an agreement for representation; or negotiations concerning price, terms, or conditions of a potential sale
4. When responding to general factual questions from a prospective seller or a prospective buyer concerning properties that have been advertised for sale
5. Situations in which a licensee's communications with a prospective buyer or a prospective seller are limited to providing either written or oral communication that is general, factual information about the qualifications, background, and services of the licensee or the licensee's brokerage firm
6. When an owner is selling new residential units built by the owner and the circumstances or setting should reasonably inform the potential buyer that the owner's employee or single agent is acting on behalf of the owner, whether because of the location of the sales office or because of office signage or placards or identification badges worn by the owner's employee or single agent.

If during any of the situations described above, a member of the public begins to provide confidential information or begins to negotiate concerning price, terms, and so forth, the licensee would at that point present the person with the appropriate disclosure notice depending on the circumstances and desire of the parties.

Practical Examples of Duty to Disclose

Michael was transferred to Seattle, so he wanted to sell his Florida residence. Harbor Realty entered into a single agent relationship with Michael. Harbor Realty later transitioned to a transaction broker relationship with Michael. Sales associate Merissa was working with Michael on behalf of Harbor Realty. Michael told Merissa that the air conditioner compressor would run for about an hour and then overheat and stop running. Merissa knew that Michael was anxious to sell, so she did not mention the air conditioner compressor to the buyer.

Practice Problem 1

Does the fact that Michael had a transaction broker relationship with Harbor Realty excuse nondisclosure of the air conditioner compressor's condition?

Practice Problem 2

Can the sales associate be disciplined for failing to inform the buyer that the compressor would overheat?

Practice Problem 3

Can Merissa's broker be held accountable for not disclosing the air conditioner compressor's condition to the buyer?

The solutions to the Practice Problems are located at the end of the chapter.

Transition to Another Relationship

A licensee may change from one brokerage relationship to another as long as the buyer or the seller, or both, give consent before the change occurs. For example, a single agent relationship may be changed to a transaction broker relationship at any time during the relationship between the agent and principal, provided the agent first obtains the principal's written consent to the change in relationship. To gain the principal's written consent to a change in relationship, the buyer or seller (or both) *must* either sign or initial the consent to transition to transaction broker notice set forth in Chapter 475. Note that this disclosure notice requires the buyer's or seller's signature (or initials) before the licensee may change from one brokerage relationship to another. If the principal refuses to sign or initial the consent to transition notice, the broker must continue to act as a single agent.

Assume that a brokerage firm represents Seller Rebecca as a single agent. Buyer Mike enters the brokerage firm with the purpose of finding a home to purchase. Buyer Mike is not working with any other real estate company. Buyer Mike indicates that he wants the real estate firm to represent him in the real estate negotiations and to work solely in his best interest. Therefore, Buyer Mike has indicated to the licensee that he desires single agent representation. The licensee must give Buyer Mike the single agent notice before entering into a buyer agency agreement or before showing Mike any property.

Because Buyer Mike has entered into a single agent relationship with the brokerage firm, the sales associate cannot show Seller Rebecca's home to the buyer. This is because a broker cannot be a single agent of the buyer *and* a single agent of the seller in the same transaction. This is true even if Rebecca and Mike use different sales associates with the same company because the single agent agreement is with the brokerage firm. If a real estate broker represents both parties in a transaction in a fiduciary capacity, an illegal *dual agent* relationship is created. Because the seller and the buyer have each entered into single agent relationships with the brokerage firm, they must both give written consent to transition (change) to transaction broker relationships in order for Buyer Mike to be shown Seller Rebecca's home. This is the purpose of allowing a licensee to transition from one agency status to another.

The consent to transition to transaction broker notice includes wording regarding the principal's permission to allow the single agent to transition to a transaction broker. The notice also includes a list of the duties that a transaction broker owes to the customer. The consent to transition to transaction broker notice can either be a separate document or be included as part of another document, for example, in the listing agreement. Refer to page 241 for information concerning the required format of the disclosure notice. (See Figure 10.3, Consent to Transition to Transaction Broker, on page 248.)

A licensee may also transition from a transaction broker relationship to a single agent relationship. Furthermore, a licensee may transition from any one of the brokerage relationships to another relationship. However, there is no specific disclosure language provided in the Florida license law for these situations. The licensee will have to accomplish the transition in a manner sufficient to withstand civil challenge under the common law.

Designated Sales Associates

In a nonresidential real estate transaction where the buyer and seller each have assets of $1 million or more, the broker at the request of the buyer and seller may designate two sales associates to act as single agents for the buyer and seller in the same transaction. The two sales associates in such an arrangement are referred to as **designated sales associates**. Note that in a residential transaction this would be an illegal dual agency.

In this arrangement, the broker serves as an adviser to each designated sales associate—not to the buyer or the seller. The broker serves as a neutral party helping to facilitate the process without giving guidance or representation to the parties in the transaction. The designated sales associates have the duties of a single agent and must give the buyer and the seller a special designated sales associate disclosure notice. The buyer and seller *must* sign the disclosure notice stating that their assets meet the threshold and requesting that the broker use the designated sales associate form of representation. A transition notice is not required.

Record Keeping

Florida law requires brokers to retain agreements that engage the services of a broker. Brokers must retain brokerage relationship disclosure documents and buyer broker agreements for five years for all residential transactions that result in a written contract to purchase and sell real property and all nonresidential transactions that use designated sales associates. This requirement includes files of properties that may have failed to close. If a transaction fails to close, the licensee should retain the brokerage relationship disclosure documents with the purchase and sale contract, escrow documentation, and other documents associated with the property, and place them in the "dead" (failed to close) file. The documents may be stored in a digitized format. The Commission may discipline a licensee for failure to abide by any provision in Section 475.278, F.S., including the duties owed to customers and principals, disclosure requirements, and record-keeping requirements set forth in law.

Terminating a Brokerage Relationship

Generally speaking, a transaction broker relationship or a single agent relationship is terminated when the objectives have been accomplished according to the terms of the contract that created the brokerage relationship and notice is given to the other party. A principal is justified in revoking a single agent relationship with the broker if the broker-agent breaches any of the fiduciary duties.

A brokerage relationship between a principal (or a customer) and a broker may be terminated for any one of the following reasons:

- Fulfillment of the brokerage relationship's purpose (for example, finding a ready, willing, and able buyer)
- Mutual agreement to terminate the brokerage relationship
- Expiration of the terms of the agreement (If no term is specified, the courts have ruled that a brokerage relationship may be terminated after a "reasonable" time.)
- Broker renounces the single agent relationship by giving notice to the principal or the broker renounces the transaction broker relationship by giving notice to the customer
- Principal revokes a single agent relationship or the customer revokes a transaction broker relationship, by giving notice. (In this case, the principal or the customer may be liable for damages, such as advertising expenses, incurred by revoking the brokerage relationship prior to the termination date of the listing contract or exclusive buyer contract.)
- Death of a seller's broker or the seller before the broker finds a ready, willing, and able buyer
- Death of the buyer's broker or the buyer before the broker finds a suitable property for the buyer
- Destruction of the property or condemnation by eminent domain
- Bankruptcy of the principal or the customer

SUMMARY OF IMPORTANT POINTS

- A person who delegates authority to another is the *principal*. A person who accepts the authority is the *agent*. An agent is authorized to represent and act for the principal. The agency relationship creates a *fiduciary* relationship with the principal. A fiduciary acts in a position of trust or confidence with the principal.
- In all real estate transactions, there are three options concerning the role the real estate brokerage firm will assume: (1) transaction broker for the buyer and/or the seller, (2) single agent of either the buyer or the seller, and (3) no brokerage relationship.
- Licensees may not operate as dual agents. A dual agent is a broker who represents both the buyer and the seller as a fiduciary.
- The duties and obligations in each type of brokerage relationship apply to all real estate transactions.

FIGURE 10.1 ■ Single Agent Disclosure Form

SINGLE AGENT NOTICE

FLORIDA LAW REQUIRES THAT REAL ESTATE LICENSEES OPERATING AS SINGLE AGENTS DISCLOSE TO BUYERS AND SELLERS THEIR DUTIES.

As a single agent, (insert name of Real Estate Entity and its Associates) owe to you the following duties:

1. Dealing honestly and fairly;
2. Loyalty;
3. Confidentiality;
4. Obedience;
5. Full disclosure;
6. Accounting for all funds;
7. Skill, care, and diligence in the transaction;
8. Presenting all offers and counteroffers in a timely manner, unless a party has previously directed the licensee otherwise in writing; and
9. Disclosing all known facts that materially affect the value of residential real property and are not readily observable.

______________________________ ________________

Signature (Seller or Buyer) Date

______________________________ ________________

Signature Date

- A written disclosure is required for residential transactions when a single agent relationship or a no brokerage relationship is chosen. The single agency disclosure must be made before, or at the time of, entering into a listing agreement or an agreement for representation, or before the showing of property, whichever occurs first. The no brokerage relationship disclosure must be made before the showing of property.
- A *residential sale* is defined as the sale of improved residential property of four or fewer units, the sale of unimproved residential property intended for use as four or fewer units, or the sale of agricultural property of ten or fewer acres.
- Under Florida Law, it is presumed that all licensees are operating as transaction brokers unless another brokerage relationship is chosen. A transaction broker provides limited representation to a buyer, a seller, or both, but does not represent either in a fiduciary capacity or as a single agent.
- License law mandates that a real estate broker working in a no brokerage relationship capacity has three duties: (1) deal honest and fairly, (2) disclose all known facts that materially affect the value of residential real property that are not readily observable to the buyer, and (3) account for all funds entrusted to the licensee.
- License law mandates that a real estate broker working as a transaction broker has the duties required in a no brokerage relationship plus four additional duties: (1) use skill, care, and diligence; (2) present all offers and counteroffers; (3) exercise limited confidentiality; and (4) perform additional duties that are mutually agreed to.

FIGURE 10.2 ■ No Brokerage Relationship Disclosure Form

NO BROKERAGE RELATIONSHIP NOTICE

FLORIDA LAW REQUIRES THAT REAL ESTATE LICENSEES WHO HAVE NO BROKERAGE RELATIONSHIP WITH A POTENTIAL SELLER OR BUYER DISCLOSE THEIR DUTIES TO SELLERS AND BUYERS.

As a real estate licensee who has no brokerage relationship with you, (insert name of Real Estate Entity and its Associates) owe to you the following duties:

1. Dealing honestly and fairly;
2. Disclosing all known facts that materially affect the value of residential real property which are not readily observable to the buyer; and
3. Accounting for all funds entrusted to the licensee.

_______________________________ _______________

Signature (Seller or Buyer) Date

_______________________________ _______________

Signature Date

- F.S. 475 mandates that a real estate broker working as a single agent has the duties required in a no brokerage relationship plus the first two additional duties required in a transaction broker relationship. Four duties apply exclusively to a broker working as a single agent: (1) confidentiality, (2) obedience, (3) loyalty, and (4) full disclosure.
- A real estate broker may change from a single agent relationship to a transaction broker relationship only with the express written permission of the principal. The principal must sign or initial the Consent to Transition to Transaction Broker disclosure before the change can occur.
- Brokers must retain brokerage relationship disclosure documents for five years for all residential transactions that result in a written contract to purchase and sell real property and all nonresidential transactions that utilize designated sales associates.
- In a nonresidential transaction and where the buyer and the seller each have assets of $1 million or more, the broker, at the request of the buyer and the seller, may designate two sales associates to be *designated sales associates*. In such situations, one sales associate acts as a single agent for the buyer and the other sales associate acts as a single agent for the seller. The broker is not considered a dual agent but rather a neutral party advising the designated sales associates to help facilitate the process. The buyer and seller must sign the Designated Sales Associate disclosure listing the duties of a single agent and affirming that the buyer and seller each have assets of at least $1 million.

FIGURE 10.3 ■ Consent to Transition to Transaction Broker

CONSENT TO TRANSITION TO TRANSACTION BROKER

FLORIDA LAW ALLOWS REAL ESTATE LICENSEES WHO REPRESENT A BUYER OR SELLER AS A SINGLE AGENT TO CHANGE FROM A SINGLE AGENT RELATIONSHIP TO A TRANSACTION BROKERAGE RELATIONSHIP IN ORDER FOR THE LICENSEE TO ASSIST BOTH PARTIES IN A REAL ESTATE TRANSACTION BY PROVIDING A LIMITED FORM OF REPRESENTATION TO BOTH THE BUYER AND THE SELLER. THIS CHANGE IN RELATIONSHIP CANNOT OCCUR WITHOUT YOUR PRIOR WRITTEN CONSENT.

As a transaction broker, (insert name of Real Estate Firm and its Associates) provides to you a limited form of representation that includes the following duties:

1. Dealing honestly and fairly;
2. Accounting for all funds;
3. Using skill, care, and diligence in the transaction;
4. Disclosing all known facts that materially affect the value of residential real property and are not readily observable to the buyer;
5. Presenting all offers and counteroffers in a timely manner, unless a party has previously directed the licensee otherwise in writing;
6. Limited confidentiality, unless waived in writing by a party. This limited confidentiality will prevent disclosure that the seller will accept a price less than the asking or listed price, that the buyer will pay a price greater than the price submitted in a written offer, of the motivation of any party for selling or buying property, that a seller or buyer will agree to financing terms other than those offered, or of any other information requested by a party to remain confidential; and
7. Any additional duties that are entered into by this or by separate written agreement.

Limited representation means that a buyer or seller is not responsible for the acts of the licensee. Additionally, parties are giving up their rights to the undivided loyalty of the licensee. This aspect of limited representation allows a licensee to facilitate a real estate transaction by assisting both the buyer and the seller, but a licensee will not work to represent one party to the detriment of the other party when acting as a transaction broker to both parties.

I agree that my agent may assume the role and duties of a transaction broker. (Must be initialed or signed.)

I have assets of one million dollars or more. I request that (insert name of Real Estate Firm) use the designated sales associate form of representation.

______________________________ ________________
Signature (Seller or Buyer) Date

______________________________ ________________
Signature Date

Practical Examples of Duty to Disclose

(Practice Problems are located on page 243.)

Practice Problem 1 Solution

No, transaction broker relationship duties include the duty to disclose all known facts that affect value of residential property. The fact that a transaction broker relationship existed did not relieve Harbor Realty from the duty to disclose the air conditioner compressor's condition.

Practice Problem 2 Solution

Yes, Merissa can be charged with Section 475.278, F.S.; failure to disclose facts that materially affect the value of property.

Practice Problem 3 Solution

Yes, the brokerage relationship is between Harbor Realty and the buyer. The broker for Harbor Realty, in addition to the sales associate, can be disciplined for not disclosing the air conditioner compressor's condition.

REVIEW QUESTIONS

1. Which disclosure notice must be given before a single agent can change to a transaction broker?
   a. No brokerage relationship
   b. Single agent
   c. Consent to transition to transaction broker
   d. Transaction broker

2. Steven is so cautious that he refuses to sign all disclosure documents. Your office policy is to include a note in his file indicating the time, date, place, and circumstance under which you made the disclosure that Steven refused to sign. You may NOT work with Steven under which circumstance?
   a. List Steven's home as a single agent
   b. Provide limited representation to Steven in locating a new home
   c. Provide real estate services to Steven in a no brokerage relationship
   d. Change from a single agent to a transaction broker to show Steven's home to an in-house buyer

3. The brokerage relationship disclosure requirements in Chapter 475 apply to the
   a. sale of a 20-unit apartment complex.
   b. sale of a condominium unit.
   c. residential lease agreement in a duplex.
   d. sale of a bookstore business and real property.

4. Which statement BEST describes the duty of loyalty in a single agent relationship?
   a. The broker must act in the best interest of the principal.
   b. The broker must disclose all latent defects to prospective buyers.
   c. The broker is held to a standard of care that requires knowledge concerning the land and physical characteristics of the property.
   d. The broker must be able to account for all funds received on behalf of the principal.

5. A real estate broker who works in a limited capacity for both the buyer and the seller in the same transaction is
   a. a dual agent.
   b. a transaction broker.
   c. bound to fiduciary duties to both the buyer and the seller.
   d. a single agent of both the buyer and the seller.

6. A buyer has entered into a buyer broker agreement with a real estate company. The agreement included the transaction broker notice. The licensee added the duties of loyalty and full disclosure to the agreement.
   a. Licensees may not modify the transaction broker notice.
   b. The licensee may add any additional duties, provided both parties agree to the new duties.
   c. The duties of loyalty and full disclosure are duties associated with a single agent relationship and may subject the licensee to liability.
   d. The buyer must initial each additional duty to indicate consent.

7. A licensee of ABC Realty must give the no brokerage relationship notice to
   a. a buyer who has a single agent relationship with XYZ Realty.
   b. every prospective buyer and prospective seller in all cases.
   c. a for-sale-by-owner (FSBO) seller before showing the FSBO home to a buyer customer of ABC Realty.
   d. every prospective buyer who walks through an open house listed by ABC Realty.

8. Broker Murl is an agent of the seller. The seller has disclosed to Murl that the ceramic tile is loose in the dining room because the cement did not adhere to the tile. The loose tile is not readily visible because it is covered with an area rug to protect the seller's toddler. Murl has satisfied his legal obligation if he tells the buyer
   a. that the floor appears to be in good condition.
   b. that ceramic tiles in the dining room are loose.
   c. that the buyer can order an inspection at his own expense if he is concerned about the floor.
   d. nothing unless he is asked specifically about the tile floor's condition.

9. A transaction broker has all of the duties listed below EXCEPT
   a. limited confidentiality.
   b. to use skill, care, and diligence.
   c. to disclose all known facts that materially affect the value of residential real property and are not readily observable to the buyer.
   d. obedience.

10. A brokerage relationship is terminated under which circumstance?
    a. The broker agent gives notice renouncing the brokerage relationship
    b. The purchase and sale contract is signed
    c. At the will of either party without notice
    d. When an offer is accepted

11. A seller lists her home for $116,900. The seller tells the sales associate that she needs to get at least $112,000 for the home. Following Sunday's open house, the sales associate receives two offers on the home. The first offer for $116,900 is contingent on the sellers taking back a $10,000 second mortgage. The second offer is for $112,000, with the buyer to secure her own financing. The sales associate should
    a. seek his broker's advice regarding which offer to present.
    b. present the full-price offer to the seller.
    c. present the second offer to the seller.
    d. present both offers, explaining the details of each to the seller.

12. In the common public relationship that exists in a typical real estate transaction, buyers and sellers are said to be dealing
    a. in a fiduciary capacity.
    b. at arm's length with each other.
    c. in an agency status with each other.
    d. under the doctrine of ethical confidentiality.

13. If a principal gives the broker instructions that will result in loss or harm to the principal, the broker
    a. is justified in not carrying out such instructions.
    b. should carry out such instructions without question.
    c. should carry out only that portion of the instructions that will not cause loss or harm to the principal.
    d. should inform the principal of possible harm inherent in the instructions, and then either do as instructed or withdraw from the relationship.

14. A broker's obligations to consumers with whom the brokerage firm has no brokerage relationship include the duty of
    a. full disclosure.
    b. accounting for all funds.
    c. loyalty.
    d. limited confidentiality.

15. Designated sales associates are best described as
    a. single agents for the buyer and the seller in nonresidential transactions where the buyer and the seller meet certain asset thresholds.
    b. the sales associates designated to represent the buyer and the seller in a transaction broker relationship.
    c. undisclosed dual agents.
    d. the sales associates in charge of the required brokerage disclosure forms for the brokerage office.

CHAPTER 11

CONTRACTS

KEY TERMS

agreement for deed
compensatory damages
contingency
contract
contract for sale and purchase
earnest money deposit
effect a sale
exclusive agency listing
exclusive-right-of-sale listing
Florida REALTORS®/ Florida Bar Contract for Sale and Purchase
find a property
find a purchaser
homeowners' association
inheritability
joint tenancy
lease option contract
lease purchase agreement
legal description
liquidated damages
net listing
open listing
option contract
owner in severalty
postdated check
prequalification
probate
procuring cause
radon gas
rescission on breach
right of first refusal
sale contract
sole owner
sole and separate owner
special assessment
specific performance
statute of frauds
stigmatized property
survivability
tenancy by the entireties
tenancy in common
time is of the essence
undivided interest

OVERVIEW

Contracts are agreements between two or more parties to do or not to do a specific thing. Because contracts are essential to real estate transactions, licensees must understand contract law in general as well as each specific type of contract. This chapter describes how to gather the required information for contracts. Other issues related to selling real property also are covered, including escrow deposits, as is the licensee's duty to disclose facts that may affect a property's value.

Once you have completed this chapter, you should be able to:

- describe the characteristics of the three major types of listings;
- describe at least three statutory requirements for listing agreements;
- distinguish between a listing broker's employment to *find a purchaser* and to *effect a sale*;

- list the four types of legal contracts the licensee may prepare;
- list four documents that the licensee can use to gather information for preparing a contract;
- describe the differences between a tenancy by the entireties, a joint tenancy, and a tenancy in common;
- specify what steps are desirable to protect the parties if the buyer takes occupancy either before or after the closing date;
- describe the differences between an option contract and a right of first refusal;
- describe the effects of the *Johnson v. Davis* Supreme Court ruling on real estate practice in Florida; and
- define the differences between a lease option agreement and a lease purchase agreement.

ENTITLEMENT TO COMMISSION

To be entitled to a commission, a real estate broker must have an employment contract. The contract could be a listing agreement with a seller or an employment agreement with a buyer.

Listing Agreements with Sellers

A listing agreement is an employment contract between an owner and a real estate broker. The listing broker may be a single agent representing the seller or a transaction broker with limited representation, or the broker may have no official brokerage relationship with the seller. Listing brokers and sales associates do not have the authority to sell or convey listed properties or to accept or reject offers to purchase unless they have power of attorney to do so. Brokers use three basic types of listing agreements in Florida: open listings, exclusive agency listings, and exclusive-right-of-sale listings. Licensees sometimes use net listings with any of the three types of listings, but generally avoid them.

Open listing. An **open listing** allows a broker to attempt to find a buyer for the property. The listing often is given to many brokers, and the broker who brings a ready, willing, and able buyer with an offer accepted by the seller or the broker who effects the sale receives a commission. An open listing is a unilateral contract because only the seller is obligated to perform. The broker does not promise to perform and is not required to advertise or otherwise market the property. While open listings on commercial and agricultural properties are not unusual, most residential brokers insist on exclusive-right-of-sale listings.

Either party may terminate an open listing at will. Without formal notification of termination, an open listing ends after a reasonable time. A seller need not notify the broker if another broker or the owner sells the property.

Exclusive agency listing. An **exclusive agency listing** allows the seller to sell without owing the broker a commission. It benefits the broker more than an open listing. All other brokers must work through the listing broker. The listing broker is entitled to a commission if any brokerage firm sells the property and normally agrees to split that commission with the cooperating broker.

A broker who has an exclusive agency may require the seller to agree not to advertise the property at a lower price than the broker's listed price, or place a sign on the property.

A broker's prospect may try to go around the broker, resulting in **procuring cause** disputes between the seller and the broker.

In most procuring cause disputes in open listings and exclusive agency listings, the buying prospect has not told the seller that a broker first presented the property. The owner sells the property at a lower price, believing no commission is due. The broker, however, wants to be paid and claims a commission from the seller. The broker could help reduce the chances of this happening by suggesting to the seller that any sale contract include the following words:

> *This property is listed with a broker under an agreement that the broker will be paid a commission for procuring a buyer for the property. Buyer warrants to the seller that he or she has not been shown or made aware of this property by any real estate broker or sales associate. Buyer agrees that if information to the contrary is proven by a broker claiming a commission, the buyer will reimburse the seller for commissions due to said real estate broker, as well as legal fees.*

The buyer who attempts to go around the broker to get a better price will refuse to sign such a statement. This should give the seller notice that the broker may be due a commission.

Exclusive-right-of-sale listing. With an **exclusive-right-of-sale listing**, a seller lists property with only one broker. The seller agrees to pay that broker a commission if the property is sold during the listing period, no matter who sells the property. Exclusive-right-of-sale listings are the most widely used type of listing. The obvious advantage to the broker is the guarantee of compensation if the property is sold. The owner also benefits because the broker works harder and spends more time and money marketing the property.

Only exclusive-right-of-sale and exclusive agency listings may be placed into the multiple listing service (MLS®). Because no single broker controls open listings, they may not be entered into the system.

Net listing. A **net listing** is created when an owner states a minimum acceptable amount and a broker agrees to market the property at a higher price. Any excess over the owner's required amount pays the broker's commission. However, if the broker brings in an offer much higher than the owner's minimum, the broker may not be entitled to receive more than a customary commission to prevent "unjust enrichment." A disadvantage of a net listing is that a broker actually may work for nothing if the owner accepts an offer at or below the minimum. While legal in Florida, net listings create many problems and are illegal in some states. Licensees should avoid using them.

As an example of a net listing, assume a seller tells her broker, "I want $100,000 net to me. I'll pay closing costs, but add your six percent commission to my net price." What should be the broker's price?

If the broker says, "$106,000," that would be incorrect. The correct amount would be $106,382.98, calculated by dividing the net price by 100 percent less commission rate ($100,000 ÷ .94 = $106,382.98).

Written documents. Not all listing agreements are written. The statute of frauds does not apply to real estate listing contracts unless the term is for more than one year. Oral listing agreements are enforceable in Florida if there is substantial evidence of their existence. Even an implied listing is enforceable with enough evidence that the seller knew and approved of the broker's efforts to sell the property.

Whatever the type of listing, the broker always should insist on a written document to prevent misunderstandings and to prove, if necessary, the existence and terms of the agreement.

Rules concerning listing agreements. A written listing agreement must have a definite expiration date and may not be renewed automatically. It must include a sufficient property identification, show the price and terms the seller will accept, and indicate the amount of the broker's commission. Both the owner and the broker (or the broker's authorized representative) must sign the agreement, and the broker must give the owner a copy within 24 hours.

Listing Agreements with Buyers

Listing agreements between sellers and brokers have been, and continue to be, the most common employment agreements in real estate. Residential buyer agreements are less common. Commercial brokers have long used buyer listing agreements, sometimes called *agreements to find real property*, and the number of residential brokers using these agreements is increasing. A broker who has entered into an employment agreement with a buyer may be a single agent or a transaction broker or have no official brokerage relationship with the buyer.

Buyers often resist signing an exclusive buyer's agreement, and many licensees don't ask for the agreement. A buyer who agrees to pay the broker a commission, reduced by any amount the seller pays, might request, for example, that the broker show for-sale-by-owner properties and foreclosure properties. A broker whose commission is not protected might avoid showing such properties, which often are excellent bargains.

Entitlement to commission. Many owners have only a vague understanding of real estate terms like *exclusive-right-of-sale*, *exclusive agency*, or *procuring cause*. In the complex world of real estate, misunderstandings and lawsuits between brokers and buyers and sellers are not uncommon. Courts at various levels have shown clearly that when brokers perform as agreed, they are entitled to compensation.

For example, an owner entered into an exclusive-right-of-sale listing agreement with a broker. The broker sold part of the property, and the owner later sold several different parcels of the property to neighbors. The broker sued for a commission on the parcels the owner sold. The owner contended that he had not understood the listing contract completely and that the broker was not the procuring cause of the sale. The trial court agreed, but the verdict was overturned later on appeal. The appeals court held that because the owner was not prevented from reading the listing contract before signing it, and because the broker did not suggest that the seller not read it, the owner was bound by the contract.

Another case involved a broker who brought a buyer to the seller, but did not take part in the parties' negotiations. The parties maintained that because the broker was not involved in the negotiations, he was not the procuring cause of the sale. An appeals court held for the broker because he brought the property to the buyer's attention.

To reduce the chance of misunderstandings and lawsuits, licensees, after suggesting that the seller read the listing contract, should explain the important parts of the agreement to the seller.

Procuring cause. A seller employs a broker either to find a purchaser or to effect a sale. If required to **find a purchaser**, the broker is entitled to a commission when the seller is presented with an offer from a ready, willing, and able buyer at the list price or any other terms acceptable to the seller. The issue is not as clear when a buyer employs the broker to **find a property**. Has the broker performed (by finding the right property)? Most authorities would say that it is only when the buyer contracts to purchase it.

If the seller's broker is employed to **effect a sale**, the broker must bring an offer from a buyer who closes the transaction. "No closing, no commission" is the common expression.

Many court decisions have minimized the distinctions between the two approaches. For example, in an *effect-a-sale* listing, if the broker produces a buyer who is ready, willing, and able to meet all of the seller's requirements and the seller arbitrarily refuses the contract, the seller owes the full commission whether or not the transaction is closed.

PURCHASE AND SALE CONTRACTS

Unauthorized Practice of Law

Real estate brokers may prepare listing agreements, sale contracts, option contracts, and lease agreements (on the Supreme Court-approved form) in the course of their business. Real estate licensees should recommend that a buyer or seller have an attorney draw an option contract or, to reduce liability, licensees should use standardized option contract forms. If an advertisement states that, for a fee, a licensee would complete or review contracts for persons not buying through the licensee, that licensee would be practicing law.

Licensees should not prepare legal documents such as deeds, mortgages, and promissory notes. Activities of this nature may result in charges of practicing law, leading to disciplinary action and liability for damages in a civil suit.

Both the licensee who prepares a contract and the licensee's employer are responsible for mistakes in the agreement. If errors, omissions, or ambiguities exist regarding material terms, the courts will not go outside the contents of the contract to decide intent. The licensee who prepared the contract may not explain an intent not shown in the contract's contents. If a contract is vague and unenforceable, the result could be no transaction at all, loss of commission, and a possible civil lawsuit against the licensee.

A licensee should be careful when drafting a lengthy special clause for a sale contract. If the clause later proves to be defective, the licensee may be liable to the parties for damages. If a licensee is not absolutely certain how to word a special clause, it is best to consult an experienced real estate attorney. Many typical special clauses are available in forms developed by the Florida REALTORS®, local boards or associations of REALTORS®, and private brokerage firms. Applicable clauses are checked, and the special clause page is then attached to the contract.

Statute of Frauds

Many years ago, wealthy persons occasionally paid witnesses to falsely testify in court that a seller had agreed to sell their property. Many landowners were victimized and forced to sell their properties at below-market prices because of the practice. The English statute of frauds was enacted in 1677 to correct this and other similar abuses. In Florida, an agreement to sell or the actual sale of any interest in real property is subject to the **statute of frauds**, and to be enforceable, it must be in writing and signed by all parties bound by the contract. Also, an agreement or a promise that cannot be performed by both parties within one year after the contract date must be evidenced by a written document. Listing contracts for one year or less are not covered by the statute of frauds. Electronic signatures are legally valid. (See next section.)

Two exceptions to the statute of frauds exist:

1. *Executed contracts*. Performance of the promise made proves the contract existed; therefore, the function of the statute of frauds has been accomplished, and a written form is not required. An example would be a seller who deeds property to a buyer completing a "hand shake" agreement.
2. *Partial performance*. Usually, the statute of frauds does not apply to partially performed contracts if two conditions have been met: (1) partial or full payment has been made; and (2) the buyer has either taken physical possession of or made improvements to the subject property. For example, if a buyer makes a $1,000 payment toward the purchase of a home, then moves into the home, the function of the statute has been accomplished. The payment and possession are regarded as evidence that a valid contract exists.

ELECTRONIC SIGNATURES IN THE GLOBAL AND NATIONAL COMMERCE ACT

Eliminating Legal Barriers to Electronic Commerce

Before the ESIGN law, many state laws required certain contracts to be written on paper and signed with pen-and-ink signatures.

Electronically signed contracts are now legally enforceable. The law defines an electronic signature as "an electronic sound, symbol, or process, attached to or logically associated with a contract." The law simply removes the requirement that certain contracts and other records be written and signed on *paper*. Of course, the parties are still free to decide whether or not to enter into an electronic contract, and may insist on a written contract.

DOCUMENTS NECESSARY TO PREPARE THE CONTRACT

A licensee must have complete information about a property before writing a contract. If the selling sales associate is not also the listing sales associate, most of the necessary information may be found in the listing data provided in the MLS®. If not, the listing agent should be contacted for the information. Collecting the information required to complete a contract is an important task. Usually, the listing sales associate gathers the information when taking the listing. The licensee also should ask for the documents the owners received when they closed on the purchase of the property. Once the licensee gathers all of the information necessary, it must be verified for accuracy. Some important documents the licensee needs are described below.

Deed. The licensee should take the owner's name and address and the property's legal description from a deed, title insurance policy, or survey. The deed also shows the property interest the owners hold (fee simple, life estate, etc.), as well as any encumbrances on the property. Licensees should be aware that MLS® data, property appraiser information, and even listing agreements have been wrong on occasion. All of the property owners must sign the purchase and sale contract.

Survey. A survey shows encroachments, easements, and violations of setback requirements. The licensee also may wish to verify the legal description as shown on the seller's deed and title insurance policy.

Mortgage. If the seller says the loan is current and the seller has not made prepayments, the licensee usually can calculate the remaining principal balance on the loan. On a financial calculator, enter the beginning balance (as present value), interest rate, payment amount, and number of payments made, then solve for the future value. The licensee also may use loan progress financial tables. The licensee should send a status, or estoppel, letter to the lender requesting the loan status and advising the lender of the seller's intent to pay off the mortgage (many lenders require at least 30 days' notice).

Zoning, zoning variances, and nonconforming uses. The licensee should ask the seller about the property's status with respect to zoning and land uses. The licensee also should get a warranty from the owner declaring that the owner is not aware of any violations of zoning or restrictive covenants. This usually is included as part of most sellers' property disclosure forms.

PROVISIONS OF REAL ESTATE CONTRACTS

A real estate **sale contract**, sometimes called a **contract for sale and purchase**, is a written agreement for the transfer of real property from seller to buyer, with both signing the document. The contract developed by the Florida REALTORS® and the Florida Bar—the **Florida REALTORS®/Florida Bar Contract for Sale and Purchase**—is widely used in Florida.

These forms are designed for specific types of transactions. The Florida REALTORS®/Florida Bar Contract for Sale and Purchase is intended for use in routine transactions involving the sale of single-family dwellings or unimproved real property. It is designed as a bilateral contract that expresses the intent of the parties to a transaction. The Florida REALTORS®/Florida Bar contract is *not* suitable for any of the following types of transactions:

- Business purchase or sale contract
- Construction or improvements contract
- Contract for deed (installment contract, agreement for deed)
- Exchange agreement (contract for exchange of real property)
- Lease with option to buy
- Option contract (to be described later in this chapter)
- Unique or complex transactions

If a vacant site other than a single-family vacant lot is being purchased, special wording should be included in the contract concerning the property's suitability for its intended use compared with the area's land-use plan. If the buyer has any doubt about a permitted land use, he or she should be given a reasonable time after contracting (a **contingency**) to ensure that the use intended for the property is legally permissible.

Contract date. The date of a real estate contract for enforcement purposes is the date when the last of the parties signed or initialed the agreement. The contract specifies many dates for performance. In most contracts, a clause is included saying, "**Time is of the essence.**" This single-sentence clause has important legal consequences. Any party's failure to perform the promises made within the contract time limits is a default by the nonperforming party. This default could result in loss of deposit or other monetary damages and a right of cancellation by the other party. Licensees must pay special attention to dates and times, and:

- use realistic times;
- make certain that the times complement and are consistent with the times in other blank spaces; and
- set up calendar deadlines in the office to monitor the parties' performance once they have signed the sale contract.

Parties

Seller. Each seller's name should be shown as it is on the deed, including the seller's marital status. The prior title insurance policy also contains this information.

If a home is on the property, the licensee should obtain the signatures of spouses of the joint owners. If a house is on the property and the property is owned individually by a married person, the licensee should include the spouse's name on the contract and obtain the signatures of both husband and wife because the title company will require the spouse's signature on the deed to avoid possible future litigation about homestead rights.

If the property is owned jointly, all owners must sign the contract.

Buyer. Each buyer's name should be shown in the contract as the buyer wants the deed to be drawn. Also, each buyer shown on the contract must sign the contract. If a buyer later wants to take title in another manner and the contract permits it, the licensee should obtain an appropriate assignment or amendment to the contract. If the seller is a corporation, a partnership, or another entity, the buyer should have legal advice. Buyers also can buy property as sole owners, tenants in common, joint tenants, or tenants by the entireties.

Sole owner. A **sole owner**, sometimes called an **owner in severalty**, can be single, unmarried, divorced, or widowed. At the owner's death, the property is inheritable, either by will or, if intestate, by descent. A **sole and separate owner** is a married person who owns property in her own name while implying the spouse is alive. If the property is a homestead and the owner is survived by a spouse and lineal descendants, the surviving spouse gets a life estate and the lineal descendants are remaindermen. If there are no lineal descendants, the spouse receives a fee simple estate to the homestead.

Joint tenancy with right of survivorship versus tenancy in common. The principal difference between joint tenancy and tenancy in common has to do with survivability (joint) versus inheritability (common). Both are ownerships by two or more persons with **undivided interests**, which means that no individual can identify a particular portion of the property.

A **joint tenancy** with right of survivorship has the characteristic of **survivability**. If one party dies, the other owns the property immediately, and the property does not become part of the decedent's estate.

A **tenancy in common** has the characteristic of **inheritability**. If one owner dies, that share is distributed according to the will or, if no will exists, according to state laws. **Pro-**

bate laws have been established to take control of an estate, paying all rightful debts of the decedent before the estate is distributed to the heirs.

Tenancy by the entireties. A **tenancy by the entireties** is ownership by husband and wife, treated as one owner. This is important, because judgment debts of only one of the parties do not result in a valid lien against the marital property. Survivability is a characteristic of this form of ownership. That is, if one spouse dies, the other owns the property immediately. Unlike a joint tenancy, one partner may not sell his or her share; both must convey their interests simultaneously. Licensees should not automatically assume that a married couple will take title as tenants by the entireties. Many couples buy as tenants in common, particularly if both spouses have children by previous marriages. This allows each party to will interest to their own children. If the couple had purchased using a tenancy by the entireties, the surviving spouse would be entitled to the entire property and probably would will it to his or her children.

It may be considered practicing law to advise buyers about which tenancy to use when taking title to real property. The best advice licensees can give is: "See your attorney."

Property Description

The property's **legal description** is an essential element of the contract. A defective legal description can render the contract unenforceable. If a survey shows that the property is not as represented in the contract, the buyer may attempt to cancel the contract. For example, if the contract shows the parcel contains 20 acres and a survey later shows 16 acres, this could give the buyer the right either to cancel the contract or to renegotiate the purchase price.

The legal description must be written so that a surveyor can find the property based on that description. If that test fails, the contract may voided. County tax rolls have errors and abbreviated descriptions that could be legally insufficient, and MLS® listing sheets may repeat errors made by others. To be certain the legal description is correct, licensees should refer to copies of deeds, title insurance policies, and surveys.

Sometimes, a licensee will not have a complete legal description at the time of contract. This often occurs when a parcel of land will be split. If the question cannot be resolved before the contract's execution, the contract may be made contingent on the results of a survey. The contract should indicate that the legal description will be amended to conform to the survey.

A platted subdivision description should include the county name, subdivision name, lot and block number, and plat book and page number where the subdivision was recorded. An unplatted property description should include the county name, the legal description from a survey or prior deed, and a reference to section, township, and range.

The licensee also should enter the street address, city, and zip code into the contract. This may help clarify an insufficient legal description.

Personal Property

Although it represents a minor portion of the purchase price, personal property being purchased by the buyer may be regarded as a material term of the contract. Inaccurate, incomplete, or insufficient descriptions of the personal property to be transferred can render the contract unenforceable.

In the typical house transaction, the licensee prepares and attaches to the contract a detailed inventory of all personal property included in the sale, with defects disclosed, if applicable. The list should include all kitchen equipment and appliances, whether or not built in, and other equipment and appliances, such as outside television antennas and satellite dishes, pool equipment, lawn furniture, and other easily removable fixtures. The licensee should quantify items where applicable.

The Florida Department of Revenue has made several rulings on the sales tax liability of personal property included in the sale of real property. Personal property itemized in the contract with a separately stated price for each is subject to sales tax. However, a sale contract that simply lists the property, such as a "refrigerator, range, and washer/dryer," etc., is a nontaxable sale. Many contracts also include wording like "the attached inventory of personal property is being left as a convenience to the parties."

Purchase Price

The preprinted contract calls for a fixed purchase price to be expressed in monetary terms. If the purchase price depends on a survey, the calculation method should be stated in a contract addendum. For example, if the property is unplatted acreage that needs a survey and the parties agree on a price per acre, the licensee should multiply that price per acre by the number of acres a survey shows. Whenever an addendum is used, it should contain the original contract's date, the parties' complete names, and a complete legal description. It also must be dated and signed by the parties.

The method of payment includes the deposit, any financing on the property, and the cash due from the buyer at closing. The total of the amounts in these lines must equal the purchase price, or the error may invalidate the contract.

Earnest Money Deposit

Licensees must present all offers, with or without a good-faith deposit. If an offer is presented without a good-faith deposit, the seller usually counteroffers for a substantial earnest money deposit to help ensure that the buyer performs. The buyer is not legally required to give an **earnest money deposit** on a real estate contract. A recent appeals court case affirmed that a promise to buy and a promise to sell are enough consideration to create a valid contract for the sale of real property.

Inserting the amount and wording in the earnest money blank. The licensee should enter the amount of the deposit and the name of the party who will hold the deposit. The escrow agent should sign the receipt for the funds. For many years, the practice has been that the office that works with the buyer holds the deposit until closing. This practice is beginning to change as brokers search for new ways to reduce business risk.

No escrow account. There is no legal requirement that a broker maintain an escrow account. Increasingly, brokers—particularly in smaller offices—ask the closing agent to hold the buyer's deposit. If so, the buyer's check is made payable to the closing agent, and the closing agent's name is shown in the contract. If a broker does not have an escrow account, bookkeeping and reconciliation requirements can be avoided. It also reduces the risk of disciplinary action and it eliminates the broker's reporting and resolution responsibilities in case of conflicting demands between the buyer and the seller. Most title companies that hold a deposit require a court order before disbursement to one party unless the parties can work out their differences through mediation.

Form of funds. A buyer usually gives the broker a check payable to the escrow agent. The contract is subject to the check's collection. A buyer may pay the deposit in cash. The broker must report the transaction to the IRS on Form 8300 if the total amount of cash in one transaction exceeds $10,000.

A third-party check is made by a person other than the person presenting the check. It may be payable to the escrow agent or to the buyer, who then endorses it and gives it to the broker. Collection on these checks is more difficult if they are dishonored.

Subsequent additional earnest money. If the deposit will be made in two installments, the contract provides a space to enter the amount of additional deposit required. Often, this is done for persons who need to transfer funds from their savings to checking accounts or for out-of-town buyers. The amount of the additional deposit and the time limit to make that deposit should be inserted in the contract. If the buyer defaults by failing to make the additional deposit, the contract usually allows the seller to recover not only the initial deposit but also any unpaid deposit.

Notes as earnest money. Occasionally, a buyer does not have enough funds to give the broker a substantial earnest money deposit. This often occurs with zero-down-payment VA financing when the seller agrees to pay closing costs. In this case, the seller probably should request a promissory note from the buyer as earnest money. The broker should have the note made payable to the seller, but the broker holds the note. If the buyer defaults, the broker, after complying with conflicting demands requirements, gives the note to the seller for collection. Brokers may not accept promissory notes as earnest money without a seller's approval.

Old earnest money for a new contract. Many offers to buy do not result in a contract, but the broker already may have the earnest money. The deposit can be used for another transaction, but the broker should ensure that the escrow account records provide a good audit trail. Of course, if an escrow dispute arises over the first contract, the broker may not count those funds as earnest money for another purchase until the dispute is resolved by one of the statutory escape procedures.

When a licensee is the buyer. DBPR auditors sometimes discover that licensees who buy properties show they have made an earnest money deposit on the contract but do not actually place the funds in their escrow accounts. The most common reason given is that the deposits are less than the real estate commissions due the licensees. FREC rules are clear on this matter. A licensee's failure to deposit the earnest money in the escrow account within three business days is a serious violation.

Time for Acceptance of Offer and Counteroffers

A buyer who makes an offer on real property sets a time limit for the seller's acceptance and written communication back to the buyer, after which the offer is terminated. The time limit should be established considering the buyer's urgency and the time necessary to deliver offers and counteroffers. Letters, faxes, and telegraph deliveries are accepted as legally enforceable documents. A licensee who faxes an accepted contract to the offeror should call to confirm that the party received the fax. Also, the licensee should note in the file the fax's date and time, the recipient's fax number, and the fact that receipt was confirmed. The effective date of the contract is the date when the last of the buyer or the seller has signed or initialed the offer or counteroffer.

Closing Date

The closing date is not a legal requirement of sale contracts. If no closing date is shown on a contract and the parties cannot agree to one, the courts set a reasonable time. The licensee should enter the closing date into the contract. Once the date has been set, however, all parties must adhere to it if the words *time is of the essence* are included in the contract. Either party's failure to close on the agreed date causes a default.

The closing date should be set for a reasonable time after any conditions have been satisfied and the title evidence is delivered.

Proration of Expenses and Income

Property expenses and income are prorated between the parties. The seller normally reimburses the buyer for taxes during the time the seller occupied the property. Insurance usually is not prorated. If the mortgage is assumed, interest for the month normally is paid in arrears, and the seller pays the buyer for the time used. If the property is rented, the seller must pay the buyer the rent for the balance of the month. The buyer normally pays for the closing day.

Occupancy and Possession

Most contracts allow the buyer to occupy the property on the closing day. Occasionally, the seller requests to remain in the property after closing, resulting in the buyer's delayed possession. If the seller will remain in the property, a separate residential lease agreement should be made as an addendum to the contract.

A buyer often needs to occupy a property before the closing. While this is not recommended, the parties to the contract may agree to the early possession. In this case, the buyer should inspect the property carefully, then agree to take the property in its present condition at the time of occupancy. A separate lease describing the date of occupancy, rent to be paid, and other terms should be made as an addendum to the contract.

If tenants occupy the property, the tenants' identities should be described in a special clause, along with a brief description of the rental terms. The contract should require the seller to furnish estoppel letters from the tenants acknowledging the lease terms, security deposit amounts, and any advance rents. The letters, along with copies of all written leases, should be delivered to the buyer not less than 15 days before closing.

If the buyer takes early occupancy or if the seller remains in possession following closing, the parties should make certain to acquire proper fire, casualty, and liability insurance. When the party in possession is not the owner, homeowner's insurance does not provide appropriate coverage, particularly for the tenant's personal property.

Financing

Time limit for loan application and loan commitment. Licensees should have current information on available interest rates, points, and the time requirements for processing applications. It is important that the financing contingency clause describe a mortgage that the buyer can obtain. Also, the time limit given to obtain a firm commitment from a lender should be realistic and liberal. The licensee should have a reasonable idea of the time local institutions require to process loan applications. Some licensees enter 15 days as the time limit for loan approval when the market requires 30. This may result in a voidable contract if the lender cannot perform as quickly as needed. Having the loan approval date closer to the closing date may be better.

Buyer financial statement for seller to review. If the seller will finance the property for the buyer, the seller usually requests a financial statement from the buyer, as well as a credit report. The licensee, when presenting the buyer's financial statement, should give the seller a written disclosure that the buyer or the buyer's accountant prepared the financial statement and that the licensee takes no responsibility for its accuracy.

Buyer preapproval for the loan. A licensee should be able to show there is a reasonable certainty that the buyer is financially able to purchase the property. The licensee saves time and energy by recommending that the buyer be **preapproved** by a lender. In this process, the lender gets the buyer's financial data, checks the buyer's credit rating, and tells the buyer how much can be borrowed. When presenting an offer to the seller, the buyer who has been preapproved is in a stronger negotiating position than a buyer who has not.

Owner occupied as principal residence. If the contract depends on the buyer qualifying for a high loan-to-value ratio loan (more than 80 percent), the licensee may want to insert in the contract language about the buyer agreeing to be an owner-occupant of the property. If not for this clause, the buyer later might refuse to occupy the property, the lender might reject the loan, and the buyer might be entitled to a refund of the deposit.

Conditional on buyer obtaining a loan. Most contracts have a financing contingency that allows buyers to get back the earnest money if they cannot get the loan described in the contract. The clause was designed to prevent surprises to buyers who contract for properties in good faith. Sometimes, however, a buyer tries to get out of any obligations under the contract by taking actions that cause the lender to reject the loan. An example may be a buyer who tells the lender he has purchased a new truck, making his debt ratio too high, or a married couple who claims to be filing for divorce. Some sellers insert the following wording to prevent abuses of this contingency:

> *Buyer agrees that any action buyer initiates after loan application that causes the lender to reject the loan application constitutes a default by buyer.*

Specify loan documents buyer must execute. Some licensees specify the loan documents a buyer must sign both at the time of loan application and at closing. Others use general language stating that a buyer agrees to sign all loan documents a lender requires.

Specify Financing Terms

Cash sale. A cash sale has no financing contingency. The buyer agrees to close and pay cash at closing. If a buyer does not have the required cash to close and must get a mortgage, the licensee should inform the seller of this fact. The buyer risks losing the deposit and paying damages if for any reason financing cannot be found.

Seller to carry first mortgage. If the seller will finance the property, the contract must resolve several issues:

- The parties must agree on whether the mortgage will have a due-on-sale clause or whether it will be assumable by subsequent buyers. If it is to be assumable, the parties then agree on whether subsequent buyers must qualify financially.

- If the seller does not want the loan to remain outstanding for many years, it can be set up with a payment schedule based on a 15-year or 30-year loan, with the unpaid loan balance coming due in five years. This is called a *balloon payment*.
- The seller should consider requiring tax and insurance reserves if the loan is greater than 80 percent of the property's value. This protects the seller from tax liens or an expired insurance policy.
- The mortgage documents should contain a clause that says judgment liens or unpaid tax liens placed on the property constitute a default in the mortgage, allowing the mortgagee to call the entire loan due and payable.
- An additional protection for the seller is to have the mortgagor pledge the property's rents toward payment of the mortgage. In case of default, the mortgagee then asks the court to appoint a receiver to collect the rents for the account.
- A cross-defaulting clause in the special clauses should be included so that a default on any senior lien automatically causes a default on the second mortgage.

Some contracts with purchase-money mortgages contain unusual provisions, such as a wraparound mortgage, a partial release clause, or a subordination clause. The licensee should attach the suggested mortgage form to the contract as an exhibit. Where the purchase-money mortgage is beyond the scope of the description in the preprinted form, the licensee should suggest that the parties employ an attorney to draft the mortgage. The contract should avoid abbreviated descriptions of what the parties intend. For example, a clause like "Seller will take back a standard purchase-money wraparound mortgage" is ambiguous and could lead to disputes.

New conventional first mortgage. The contract may be contingent on the buyers obtaining a specific type of loan to purchase the property. The contract should stipulate that the loan interest rate not exceed a stated amount and should include the loan-to-value ratio and the loan term. Some lenders allow the borrower to get an 80 percent loan-to-value ratio loan with an additional purchase-money mortgage to be held by the seller. This saves the borrower the cost of private mortgage insurance.

Straight (nonamortized) second mortgage. Another creative financing method is a nonamortizing second mortgage. The buyer pays interest only until the loan comes due at some time in the future.

New VA loan. While VA mortgages are not limited by law, lenders are protected adequately only if a loan is no greater than $417,000. A buyer who wants to borrow more may have to pay 25 percent of the excess in cash. The contract should show whether the buyer or seller will pay loan discount fees or closing costs.

The VA escape clause must be included in the contract. That is, if the VA appraisal comes in lower than the purchase price, the contract is voidable at the buyer's option. The buyer is entitled to a full refund of the earnest money deposit. The buyer does, however, have the right to complete the purchase.

New FHA loan. If the buyer uses Federal Housing Administration (FHA) financing, the party paying the loan closing costs should be informed about, and agree to pay, the up-front mortgage insurance premium (UFMIP). FHA and VA appraisers sometimes identify repairs that must be made to the property before the mortgage is closed. The contract should establish which party will pay for such repairs (normally, the seller does).

Adjustable-rate loans. If the financing is an adjustable-rate mortgage, the contract should reflect that and indicate the principal amount of the loan and the beginning interest rate.

Loan assumptions. The licensee should ensure that the stated balance of the mortgage to be assumed is accurate. While the contract form might allow minor variations between the actual balance of the existing mortgage and the amount stated, any material differences could give the buyer a right of cancellation. An estoppel letter from the mortgagee shows the balance, the interest rate, and under what conditions, if any, the mortgage can be assumed.

Some older FHA and VA mortgages can be assumed without lender consent. Licensees should explain the financial exposure the seller may have if not released from liability when the loan is assumed.

Most mortgages, if they can be assumed at all, require that a buyer qualify financially. If the lender consents, the seller is released from liability. Occasionally, the loan's interest rate changes. The licensee must understand the conditions under which the loan can be assumed.

Evidence of Title

Time to examine title. The buyer has a reasonable time to examine the abstract (usually 30 days) or title commitment (usually 5 to 10 days) after receiving the document.

The seller must convey marketable title subject to the liens and encumbrances the parties agree to in the contract. The buyer or the buyer's attorney must notify the seller in writing of any defects within the period of time specified in the contract.

Type of Deed to be Delivered

If a sale contract does not specify the type of deed the seller must give, Florida law requires that the seller convey the property by a statutory warranty deed. Two witnesses must sign the deed, which must be in recordable form, acknowledged, and with documentary stamps attached.

Default and Dispute Resolution

If one party breaches the contract, the injured party has several remedies:

Liquidated damages. The most common remedy available to a seller when a buyer defaults is entitlement to the earnest money deposit. This is an example of **liquidated damages**. The broker may not disburse the funds without the parties' written agreement, except according to Chapter 475. If forfeited, the earnest money deposit goes to the seller unless the listing agreement provided for the deposit to be split between the seller and the broker.

Rescission on breach. The party who has been injured by the breach may sue for a **rescission on breach**. If the seller defaults, the buyer is entitled to a return of the earnest money deposit and damages. Thus, the contract is rescinded.

Compensatory damages. The party who has been injured by the breach may sue for **compensatory damages**. A seller might sue for compensatory damages if the earnest money deposit was insufficient. A buyer might ask for damages if the seller defaults. If a property has been misrepresented, the buyer could accept the property and sue for damages or refuse the property and sue.

Specific performance. A suit for **specific performance** asks the court to enforce the contract as written. For example, if a seller refuses to sign the deed, the court may require that the seller close the transaction as promised.

Other Issues Regarding Sale Contracts

Special assessment. A **special assessment** is a lien the government places on property for work done that theoretically increases the property's value. For example, if a dirt road is paved, the value of the properties on that road is assumed to increase by at least the amount of the assessment. The value increase probably is effective when the improvement is complete. Consequently, a seller usually must pay the lien if the improvement is completed (certified and confirmed by the governmental agency) by the date of closing. The buyer is expected to assume pending liens unless the work is substantially completed on the contract's effective date.

Licensee acting as buyer or seller. Licensees often buy and sell real estate for their own accounts. Those who buy their own listings probably have the greatest exposure to charges of misrepresentation. Obviously, such licensees work in their own interest and no longer can act as a single agent for the other party to the transaction. Simply making a transition to transaction broker, however, is a poor choice because of the self-interest involved and the licensee's duty to treat both parties to the transaction equally. The licensee must relate to the seller any information known about the property and disclose that the seller is no longer represented by the licensee. The seller should acknowledge this disclosure, preferably in the contract.

Licensees buying from another person should disclose their license status and provide a no brokerage relationship notice. The other party should acknowledge this disclosure, preferably in the contract, as a protection from later claims of misrepresentation. Once disclosure has been made, the licensee legally may accept a commission in the transaction.

Contingent on sale of buyer's property. Often, a person whose home currently is for sale looks for another home to purchase. Sometimes, the person finds the right home before the old one has been sold and wants to reserve the replacement home. This often is accomplished by making the contract contingent on the sale of the buyer's current home. In this case, the contract should identify the buyer's home and include a time limit for the sale. Many times, sellers require that the buyer's home be listed at market value with a brokerage firm and be listed in the MLS®.

This may not benefit the seller, who is put in the position of evaluating the chances of the buyer's home selling. Usually, the seller wants to continue marketing the property, giving the initial buyer a right of first refusal. The contract would allow the seller to give notice to the first buyer if the seller receives another acceptable offer. The first buyer then would have, perhaps, 24 to 48 hours to decide whether to remove the contingency. If the buyer removes the contingency without having sold the home, the contract should also require that the buyer remove the financing contingency. If this were not done, and if the buyer's house remained unsold, the buyer might not be able to qualify for the new loan and would have a way to get out of the contract.

Right of first refusal. Sometimes, a **right of first refusal** is used in circumstances other than the one described above. For instance, a seller may require a contract from the buyer giving the seller the right of first refusal if the property is later placed on the market and sold to another party. A Florida appeals court recently voided a right of first refusal that was binding on the owner, her heirs, and assigns. The owner had died, and the court ruled that the right expired after the owner's death.

Contingent on property inspection. Licensees can reduce their liability by suggesting that each buyer include in the contract their desire to have the property inspected by a qualified professional. The contract should be made contingent on the buyer's approval of the inspection results. A contingency of this nature should give the buyer enough time to have the property inspected, but should establish a time limit, such as ten days.

Conditional on spouse's approval. Often, a buyer visits from another city to find a suitable home. If successful, the buyer wants to tie up the property until the spouse can travel to see it. The request is reasonable because otherwise the trip could be wasted if the property were sold to another party just before the spouse arrived. This is, in effect, a free option, so a contingency of this nature should include a short but reasonable time limit.

Signing and acknowledgment. No law requires that a contract be witnessed or acknowledged. Preprinted forms used in Florida rarely provide witness signature lines or space for notaries to acknowledge the documents. In fact, acknowledgment may indicate the buyer's intent to record the sales contract, an action the seller should resist. Recording a sale contract encumbers the property title, and may make it difficult to resell the property quickly if a problem occurs with the contract.

Number of copies needed. When an offer is prepared, the buyer signs it, then the selling sales associate makes enough copies for the seller, the listing agent, and the seller's attorney, if applicable. When the licensee presents the contract to the seller, copies that can be written on should be given to the seller. If the seller decides to make a counteroffer, the original contract is presented, with the changes made, for initials and signatures.

DISCLOSURE

Psychologically Impacted or Stigmatized Properties

Properties that have been the scenes of murders or suicides or are alleged to be haunted are **stigmatized properties**. In fact, buyers have sued real estate sales associates and brokers because the sales associates didn't disclose the property's history.

A recent change to Chapter 689 (Conveyances of Land and Declarations of Trust) settled the matter; disclosure is not required.

> *"The fact that a property was, or was at any time suspected to have been, the site of a homicide, suicide, or death is not a material fact that must be disclosed in a real estate transaction. A cause of action shall not arise against an owner of real property, his or her agent, an agent of a transferee of real property, or a person licensed under Chapter 475 for the failure to disclose to the transferee that the property was or was suspected to have been the site of a homicide, suicide, or death or that an occupant of the property was infected with human immunodeficiency virus or diagnosed with acquired immune deficiency syndrome." [689.25(1)(b)]*

Occupant Infected with HIV or AIDS

Section 760.50 F.S., prohibits discrimination based on acquired immune deficiency syndrome (AIDS) and human immunodeficiency virus (HIV). Under the statute, any person with or perceived as having AIDS or HIV is entitled to every protection available to people with disabilities. A person may not discriminate against an otherwise qualified individual in housing because the individual is, or is regarded as being, infected with AIDS or HIV.

Homeowners' Association Disclosure

If a purchaser of residential property is required to become a member in a **homeowners' association**, a Homeowners' Association Disclosure (see Figure 11.1) must be given to the buyer. Each contract entered into for the sale of property governed by covenants subject to disclosure required by this section must contain in conspicuous type a clause that states:

> *If the disclosure summary required by Section 689.26, Florida Statutes, has not been provided to the prospective purchaser before executing this contract for sale, this contract is voidable by buyer by delivering to seller or seller's agent written notice of the buyer's intention to cancel within 3 days after receipt of the disclosure summary or prior to closing, whichever occurs first. Any purported waiver of this voidability right has no effect. Buyer's right to void this contract shall terminate at closing.*

A contract that does not conform to this requirement is voidable at the option of the purchaser prior to closing.

This section does not apply to any association regulated under Condominiums (Chapter 718), Cooperatives (Chapter 719), Vacation and Time-Sharing (Chapter 721), or Mobile Home Park Lots (Chapter 723), or to subdividers registered under the Land Sales Act (Chapter 498). It also does not apply if disclosure regarding the association is otherwise made in connection with the requirements of those chapters.

Ad Valorem Tax Disclosure (Chapter 689, F.S.)

The Save Our Homes Amendment to the Florida Constitution limits the annual increases in the assessed value of a homestead property. The assessment can increase annually by three percent or the percentage of increase in the Consumer Price Index, whichever is less. When the property is sold, it is reassessed at full market value. Recent "hot markets" in Florida have resulted in high appreciation rates, so many buyers are shocked when their first tax bill is much higher than they expected.

Before the buyer signs a contract to purchase, Florida real estate licensees must give a property tax disclosure that includes the following wording:

Property Tax Disclosure Summary

BUYER SHOULD NOT RELY ON THE SELLER'S CURRENT PROPERTY TAXES AS THE AMOUNT OF PROPERTY TAXES THAT THE BUYER MAY BE OBLIGATED TO PAY IN THE YEAR SUBSEQUENT TO PURCHASE. A CHANGE OF OWNERSHIP OR PROPERTY IMPROVEMENTS TRIGGERS REASSESSMENTS OF THE PROPERTY THAT COULD RESULT IN HIGHER PROPERTY TAXES. IF YOU HAVE ANY QUESTIONS CONCERNING VALUATION, CONTACT THE COUNTY PROPERTY APPRAISER'S OFFICE FOR INFORMATION.

FIGURE 11.1 ■ Homeowners' Association/Community Disclosure

HOMEOWNERS' ASSOCIATION/COMMUNITY DISCLOSURE

IF THE DISCLOSURE SUMMARY REQUIRED BY SECTION 720.401, FLORIDA STATUTES, HAS NOT BEEN PROVIDED TO THE PROSPECTIVE PURCHASER BEFORE EXECUTING THIS CONTRACT FOR SALE, THIS CONTRACT IS VOIDABLE BY BUYER BY DELIVERING TO SELLER OR SELLER'S AGENT OR REPRESENTATIVE WRITTEN NOTICE OF THE BUYER'S INTENTION TO CANCEL WITHIN 3 DAYS AFTER RECEIPT OF THE DISCLOSURE SUMMARY OR PRIOR TO CLOSING, WHICHEVER OCCURS FIRST. ANY PURPORTED WAIVER OF THIS VOIDABILITY RIGHT HAS NO EFFECT. BUYER'S RIGHT TO VOID THIS CONTRACT SHALL TERMINATE AT CLOSING.

Disclosure Summary

For ____

(name of community)

1. As a purchaser of property in this community, you will be obligated to be a member of a homeowners' association.
2. There have been or will be recorded restrictive covenants governing the use and occupancy of properties in this community.
3. You will be obligated to pay assessments to the association. Assessments may be subject to periodic change. If applicable, the current amount is $______________ per __________. You will also be obligated to pay any special assessments imposed by the association. Such special assessments may be subject to change. If applicable, the current amount is $____________ per ____________.
4. You may be obligated to pay special assessments to the respective municipality, county, or special district. All assessments are subject to periodic change.
5. Your failure to pay special assessments or assessments levied by a mandatory homeowners' association could result in a lien on your property.
6. There may be an obligation to pay rent or land use fees for recreational or other commonly used facilities as an obligation of membership in the homeowners' association. If applicable, the current amount is $____________ per ____________.
7. The developer may have the right to amend the restrictive covenants without the approval of the association membership or the approval of the parcel owners.
8. The statements contained in this disclosure form are only summary in nature, and, as a prospective purchaser, you should refer to the covenants and the association governing documents before purchasing property.
9. These documents are either matters of public record and can be obtained from the record office in the county where the property is located, or are not recorded and can be obtained from the developer.

____

Date

____

Purchaser

____

Purchaser

Radon Gas

Many authorities believe radon gas is the second leading cause of lung cancer in the United States. **Radon gas** occurs when radioactive materials in the soil break down. The gas seeps into buildings through the foundations. As building insulation techniques improve, the gas accumulates and becomes a health hazard. Licensees must attach a radon gas disclosure statement to every contract. The law does not require that a test be conducted. If the buyer wants a test, the contract should be contingent on acceptable gas levels. Acceptable test results generally are set at a measurement of less than four picocuries per liter of air.

Duty of Seller To Disclose

In the case of *Johnson v. Davis*, the Florida Supreme Court held that the seller had a duty to inform the buyer of the residential property about any known property defects that materially affected the property's value. Chapter 475, F.S., holds licensees to the same standard. If a licensee sells a property and knows the roof leaks, for example, the licensee must disclose this fact to the buyer.

In another recent case, *Dorton v. Jensen*, the court interpreted *Johnson v. Davis* by assessing subjectively how the disclosure would have affected the buyer's decision to buy, no matter whether the property's value was affected materially. This could expand the application to include situations where the defect may not have a material effect on value.

Lead-based paint disclosure. The Federal Residential Lead-Based Paint Hazard Reduction Act applies to residential buildings built before 1978.

The law requires that the seller, landlord, or licensee provide the following before a buyer signs a contract:

- Lead hazard information pamphlet
- Disclosure of the presence of any known lead-based paint or lead-based paint hazard
- Ten-day period to conduct an inspection

The lead warning statement shown in Figure 11.2 must be attached to the contract.

Transaction Fees

Because many consumers make decisions on brokerage relationships partly based on the amount of fees charged, disclosure of such fees should be made before a seller signs a listing agreement or before showing property to a buyer. Disclosure of the fee just before the buyer signs the sales contract is too late.

In October 2001, HUD published a statement of policy that does not automatically make transaction fees a violation of RESPA but sets guidelines that must be followed. Brokers who charge transaction fees should be very cautious. There are now significant limitations on the amounts of such transaction fees as well as a defined test, which must be satisfied in order to avoid a violation of RESPA.

The National Association of REALTORS® in a review of the HUD Statement of Policy, recommended to members that brokers who charge a transaction fee adhere to the following guidelines:

- The fee may not be excessive and must bear a direct relationship to the additional services or functions performed by the real estate broker.
- The fee must be for actual services rendered.
- A real estate broker *may not* charge or collect a transaction fee that is simply an add-on to the transaction with the consumer and has no direct relationship to

FIGURE 11.2 ■ Lead-Based Paint Hazard Notice

LEAD-BASED PAINT HAZARD DISCLOSURE STATEMENT

Every purchaser of any interest in residential real property on which a residential dwelling was built prior to 1978 is notified that such property may present exposure to lead from lead-based paint that may place young children at risk of developing lead poisoning. Lead poisoning in young children may produce permanent neurological damage, including learning disabilities, reduced intelligence quotient, behavioral problems, and impaired memory. Lead poisoning also poses a particular risk to pregnant women. The seller of any interest in residential real property is required to provide the buyer with any information on lead-based paint hazards from risk assessments or inspections in the seller's possession and notify the buyer of any known lead-based paint hazards. A risk assessment or inspection for possible lead-based paint hazards is recommended prior to purchase.

____________________ Signed   ________________ Date

work performed. In accordance with HUD's Statement of Policy, the charging and collection of administrative fees where no work or services are provided, or where such work or services are nominal in nature or duplicative, are violations of RESPA.

- The charging and collection of such fees must be fully disclosed to the consumer. The best practice is to disclose in the listing agreement that the commission will be, for example "6% + $250" so that the amounts show on one line in the HUD-1 form at closing. If they are on different lines, the licensee may have to justify the fees and show that substantial work was done.

Other Disclosures

Energy-efficiency brochure. The Florida Building Energy Efficiency Rating Act requires that buyers receive a brochure with information on the option for getting an energy-efficiency rating on the building. The brochure must be given before the buyer signs the contract. The Act also created a uniform rating system for new and existing residential, commercial, and public buildings.

WEB LINK

Download and print a copy of the brochure at **http://energygauge.com/FlaRes/info-brochure.pdf.**

Building code violations. Sellers who have been cited for a building code violation, or have a citation pending, must disclose the fact in writing to buyers prior to closing a sale. The disclosure must:

- state the existence and nature of the violation and proceedings;
- provide a copy of the pleadings, notices, and other materials received by the seller; and
- state the buyer's agreement to be liable for correcting the code violation.

Within five days after transfer of the property, the seller must give notice to the code enforcement agency of the name and address of the new owner, and provide copies of the disclosure notices given to the buyer.

A seller who violates this provision is guilty of fraud. Real estate licensees should be certain that sellers are aware of this disclosure requirement. [125.69(2)(d)]

Licensees should provide certain other disclosures, some of which are more fully covered elsewhere in this text:

- Brokerage relationships (Chapter 10)
- Known facts that materially affect the value of residential property (Chapter 10)
- Radon gas (Chapter 17)
- Lead-based paint (Chapter 17)

OTHER CONTRACTS

Lease Purchase Agreement

A **lease purchase agreement** is a lease that binds the parties to a sale contract. Two separate documents should be used: a Supreme Court-approved lease agreement and a contract for sale and purchase. A lease purchase agreement should be distinguished from a **lease option contract**, which gives a tenant the option, but does not obligate the tenant to purchase.

Option Contract

An **option contract** is a contract between a property owner (optionor) and a prospective buyer (optionee) in which the optionee, for a consideration, has the right (not the obligation) to purchase or lease the property at a specified price during a designated period. To be enforceable in Florida, an option must contain all of the essential elements of a contract.

When first formed, an option contract is unilateral. The optionor is obligated to sell if the optionee gives proper notice, but the optionee is not obligated to purchase and may allow the option to expire.

Options frequently are used to give a developer or buyer time to resolve problems related to financing, zoning, title, or feasibility before committing to purchase or lease. Options also are useful instruments when assembling several parcels of land.

Besides the required information in an option contract, other provisions may be included. For example, the contract normally contains a statement of the method of notice required to exercise the option. Also, there should be some provision concerning the option money (the consideration) if the option is not exercised. And unless the contract terms expressly prohibit it, an option normally is assignable.

Chapter 475.43, F.S., states in part: "All contracts, options, or other devices not based upon a substantial consideration, or that are otherwise employed to permit an unlicensed person to sell, lease, or let real estate, the beneficial title to which has not, in good faith, passed to such party for a substantial consideration, are hereby declared void and ineffective in all cases, suits, or proceedings . . ." Obviously, the state legislature recognized a way by which an unlicensed person could use an option contract to act as a broker and thereby get around the license law.

Option contracts often are designed with less care and attention than necessary. The licensee must remember that an option contract is converted into a sale contract when the option is exercised. However, if the option doesn't include all the terms material to the transaction and leaves some terms or decisions for future agreement, the option contract normally is not enforceable. For example, if the option calls for a purchase-money mortgage as part of the method of payment and does not include the interest rate or the mortgage duration, courts normally would refuse to enforce the contract. It is clear that licensees may fill in the blanks on approved option forms, but there is still some debate among attorneys about whether a licensee can actually "draw" an option contract. Because of the complexity of the issues and the potential liability involved, licensees should recommend that the parties have the option drawn by a real estate attorney.

Agreement for Deed

An **agreement for deed** sometimes is called a *contract for deed*, a *land contract*, or an *installment contract*. A licensee may not prepare an agreement for deed because it is more like a mortgage than a sale contract. Recently, a licensee was disciplined for culpable negligence (fined $1,000 and suspended for three months) for preparing an agreement for deed. Agreements for deed are discussed more fully in Chapter 12.

SUMMARY OF IMPORTANT POINTS

- Contracts are agreements between two or more parties to do or abstain from doing something.
- Licensees can prepare listing contracts, sale contracts, form option contracts, and Supreme Court-approved lease agreements.
- Preparation of any other legal document is considered an unauthorized practice of law.
- The statute of frauds requires that contracts for the sale of real property be in writing and signed.
- The three listing agreements used in Florida include open listings, exclusive agency listings, and exclusive-right-of-sale listings.
    - An open listing is given to many brokers, and only the broker who sells the property is entitled to be paid.
    - An exclusive agency listing gives the listing to only one broker, but the owner reserves the right to sell the property without paying a commission.
    - An exclusive-right-of-sale listing guarantees the broker compensation no matter who sells the property.
- A written listing agreement must have an expiration date and cannot be renewed automatically.
- A copy of the signed listing agreement must be given to the owner within 24 hours.
- A broker may be employed to find a purchaser or to effect a sale. If the listing requires the broker to find a purchaser, the broker has performed upon finding a ready, willing, and able buyer who agrees to purchase at the listed price or any terms acceptable to the seller. If required to effect a sale, the broker is due a commission only if the property transaction closes.

- The licensee should show the complete legal names of the buyer and seller, as well as their marital status, on the contract.
- The licensee should take the seller's name and the property's legal description from a deed or title insurance policy.
- A form contract designed for residential property should not be used for business sales, new construction, exchanges, or contracts for deed.
- The law does not require a buyer to make an earnest money deposit, but a deposit is recommended. Brokers are not legally required to maintain an escrow account.
- A seller must approve the acceptance of a postdated check as earnest money.
- It is not a good practice to let a buyer take possession of the property before closing. If this cannot be avoided, the buyer and seller should enter into a lease agreement, allowing the seller to recover possession of the property more quickly if the buyer defaults.
- In case of breach of contract, the injured party has the right to collect liquidated damages, usually the earnest money deposit, or to sue for cancellation of the contract, for specific performance, or for compensatory damages.
- If the licensee buys property and the contract shows an earnest money deposit, the licensee must deposit the required earnest money into the broker's escrow account.
- Licensees need not disclose that a homicide, suicide, or death occurred in a property. It is illegal for licensees to disclose information that discriminates against persons with HIV or AIDS.
- *Johnson v. Davis* is a court case that required the sellers to disclose facts that may materially affect the residential property's value. Chapter 475, F. S., sets forth the duty of such disclosure for all licensees.
- An option contract gives the optionee the right, but not the obligation, to purchase property at a specified price and specified terms for a specific period of time.
- Option contracts must have substantial valuable consideration and may not be used as a way to circumvent the real estate license law.
- Agreements for deed are financing devices for the sale of properties. Title normally is not transferred until all agreements have been satisfied. Licensees may not prepare contracts for deed.

REVIEW QUESTIONS

1. The Florida REALTORS®/Florida Bar Contract for Sale and Purchase is LEAST suitable for transactions involving the sale of a(n)
   a. single-family home.
   b. condominium dwelling unit.
   c. unimproved property.
   d. business.

2. A purchase contract included the words, "Time is of the essence." Another clause required the buyer to make and complete a mortgage application within ten days of the contract's effective date. Because he needed to get copies of his tax returns from his accountant, the buyer did not apply until the 12th day. Based on this information, the buyer
   a. may cancel the contract for nonperformance.
   b. has defaulted and may lose his earnest money deposit.
   c. is not in default because he had good-faith reason for the late application.
   d. has committed a misdemeanor.

3. One of the BEST sources for verifying information about an owner's correct legal name and a property's legal description is
   a. MLS® data.
   b. a copy of the deed.
   c. the previous sale contract.
   d. the appraisal report.

4. A buyer agreed to buy a small rental home and made a $2,000 good-faith deposit. The parties intended to put the agreement in writing later, but failed to do so. With the seller's permission, the buyer painted the house. The seller subsequently got a higher offer and refused to sell, claiming it was because the real estate contract was not written. If the case goes to court, what is the MOST likely result?
   a. The court probably would decide that the seller need not honor the contract because contracts for the sale of real property must be in writing and signed.
   b. The buyer probably would have won if she had taken occupancy to the property before closing. Because that did not happen, the seller would win.
   c. Because the buyer gave the seller the money, then painted the house, the court probably would enforce the oral contract.
   d. The court probably would rule that the contract violated the statute of limitations and would void the agreement.

5. Which statement about a real estate option contract is FALSE?
   a. It is an enforceable agreement binding only the optionee.
   b. It must be written.
   c. Only the optionor is bound.
   d. It must contain all the essential elements of a contract.

6. A person has attempted to get a real estate license, but could not pass her state exam. She began buying options on properties for token considerations, then advertising and selling the properties for a profit. One owner gives her an option on property at a price of $100,000. She sells and assigns the option to another person for $30,000, but the owner refuses to honor the option. In this situation, which statement is TRUE?
   a. The owner must honor the option.
   b. The owner may sell for $130,000, but must pay a commission.
   c. The owner need not honor the option; substantial valuable consideration did not exist.
   d. The person could be disciplined by the FREC.

7. The minimum description requirement in a contract for a platted subdivision does NOT include
   a. lot and block number.
   b. the number of acres in the parcel.
   c. plat book and page number of recorded plats.
   d. the county in which the property is located.

8. Which factor(s) would cause a broker the MOST problems in an exclusive agency listing agreement?
   a. For-Sale-by-Owner sign on the property giving the seller's phone number
   b. Fact that the broker will not get paid if any other broker sells the property
   c. Advertising by the owner at a price lower than the broker is quoting
   d. Both A and C

9. Which type of listing makes the listing broker automatically the procuring cause of the sale?
   a. Exclusive-right-of-sale
   b. Exclusive agency
   c. Open
   d. Self-renewing

10. A broker completes the blanks on a six-month option agreement for a buyer on a property on Circle Drive. The buyer puts up $5,000 in option money. Because the buyer is not sure what owner financing terms should be, the broker writes, "Owner financing, to be agreed on when this option is exercised." Three months later, the buyer notifies the seller of her intent to close and meets with the seller to agree on the financing terms. The seller wants a higher interest rate and a shorter loan term than the buyer will accept. In this situation,
    a. the buyer can sue, and the court will force the seller to a lower interest rate.
    b. the option was too vague and will not be enforced.
    c. the seller can sue the buyer and force her to close at the higher interest rate.
    d. the parties must seek binding arbitration.

11. The effective date of the Florida REALTORS®/Florida Bar contract is the date
    a. the buyer signs the contract and gives the earnest money deposit.
    b. the seller signs the contract.
    c. of closing.
    d. on which the buyer or seller last signs the offer or counteroffer.

12. A man owns a homesteaded property built in 1989. He recently married, but his wife is not on the deed. He and his wife want a larger home, so he contacts a broker to sell his home. The broker soon finds a buyer. What must the broker include in the contract to ensure that title will be transferred properly?
    a. The husband's marital status and the fact that he is the sole and separate owner
    b. Both names and both signatures
    c. Fact that the husband is married, but owns the property without his spouse
    d. Lead-based paint hazard disclosure statement

13. Survivability is a characteristic of a
    a. tenancy at will.
    b. joint tenancy.
    c. tenancy in common.
    d. tenancy for years.

14. Which statement concerning a buyer's earnest money deposit is FALSE?
    a. If the broker deposits the check within three business days, the broker is not responsible if the check is dishonored.
    b. If the total amount of cash given in the transaction is more than $10,000, the broker must report the receipt of the cash to the IRS.
    c. A broker may not legally accept a postdated check as an earnest money deposit.
    d. While a postdated check is not illegal, the broker must note clearly on the deposit receipt that the check is postdated, and the broker must get the seller's approval before the contract is signed.

15. Which statement is FALSE concerning a licensee who buys property for himself?
    a. The seller should be given a No Brokerage Relationship Notice.
    b. The fact that the buyer is a real estate licensee and does not represent the seller should be included in the contract.
    c. If the contract shows an earnest money deposit, the licensee need not deposit that money into the broker's escrow account if the licensee's share of the commission is greater than the escrow deposit.
    d. If the contract shows an earnest money deposit, the licensee must actually deposit that money into the broker's escrow account.

16. The legal description entered on a contract for sale and purchase
    a. is usually not necessary if the property address is given in its place.
    b. should be taken directly from the county tax appraiser's database.
    c. must be written so that a surveyor can locate the property boundaries.
    d. is not an essential element of the agreement.

17. How should personal property that is being purchased by the buyer be noted in the contract?
    a. Itemize personal property separately with a value for each item.
    b. Do not mention the personal property in the contract to avoid sales tax.
    c. Note on the contract that the sale includes personal property as agreed to by the parties.
    d. List each item, noting any applicable defects, and attach to the contract.

18. If a contract does NOT set a closing date
    a. either party may void the contract.
    b. the parties have a reasonable time for closing.
    c. the contract is void for lack of an essential contract requirement.
    d. all of the above may occur.

19. A buyer has contracted for a unique oceanfront home he has wanted to own for years. If the seller subsequently defaults by refusing to convey title to the buyer, the MOST likely action the buyer will pursue is a suit for
    a. compensatory damages.
    b. liquidated damages.
    c. specific performance.
    d. cancellation.

20. If a buyer signs an offer to purchase property contingent on first selling her current home, the seller's agent should NOT suggest that the
    a. buyer be required to give an earnest money deposit.
    b. buyer be required in the contract to list her home in the multiple-listing service.
    c. seller take the property off the market.
    d. seller keep her property on the market and give the buyer a 24-hour right of first refusal.

CHAPTER 12

FINANCING REAL ESTATE

KEY TERMS

acceleration clause
adjustable-rate mortgage
annual cap
annual percentage rate (APR)
automated underwriting
balloon payment
blanket mortgage
buydown
certificate of reasonable value (CRV)
certificate of title
conditional commitment
conforming loan
contract for deed
cosigner
credit scoring
due-on-sale clause
entitlement
equity kicker
exculpatory clause
firm commitment
foreclosure
fully amortized mortgage
funding fee
graduated-payment mortgage
home equity loan
Homeowners Protection Act of 1998
housing expense ratio
index
initial investment
kickback
lien theory
lifetime cap
loan constant
margin
mortgage insurance premium (MIP)
mortgagee
mortgage participation
mortgagor
nonconforming loan
novation
package mortgage
partially amortized mortgage
participation mortgage
prepayment clause
prepayment penalty clause
priority
private mortgage insurance (PMI)
purchase-money mortgage
receivership clause
reduction option mortgage
redemption (equity of)
reverse annuity mortgage
sale and leaseback
secured note
subordinate
subordination clause
term mortgage
time-sharing
title theory
total obligations ratio
unsecured note

OVERVIEW

The economic turmoil of the last few years have caused a great deal of hardship to builders, real estate licensees, and homeowners. As the recovery takes hold, brokers and sales associates who continue their professional education will be rewarded.

A licensee must have a good working knowledge of financing to provide the best service for customers. This chapter describes the instruments used in a mortgage loan and the rights of lenders and borrowers. Understanding the benefits and drawbacks of the different types of mortgage loans available for residential buyers helps licensees market properties more effectively. Several alternative financing approaches are discussed, such as contracts for deed, wraparound loans, and sale-leaseback. Because federal regulation affects lending practices, the Equal Credit Opportunity Act, the Truth-in-Lending Act, and the Real Estate Settlement Procedures Act are included. The last part of the chapter describes the process of loan application and processing and how automated software is dramatically changing the way lenders work.

Once you have completed this chapter, you should be able to:

- describe the difference between a note and a mortgage;
- explain the benefits of having the first recorded lien on a property;
- describe the differences between a term loan, a partially amortized loan, and a fully amortizing loan;
- list three possible scenarios that could cause loss for a consumer buying property with a contract for deed;
- explain why the APR disclosure for a 30-year loan may understate the lender's yield;
- list at least five requirements of the Real Estate Settlement Procedures Act;
- calculate the minimum qualifying ratios for conventional and FHA mortgages; and
- estimate the approximate yield to the lender when the lender charges discount points.

Troubling Times

Beginning in 2007, the housing market began to deflate, causing a meltdown in the real estate industry and the financial markets. Large banks, hedge funds, and investment firms had losses of a magnitude never imagined, eroding their capital bases and requiring a federal rescue from a systemic failure.

In September 2008, Fannie Mae and Freddie Mac were in critical financial condition, and were placed under the conservatorship of the Federal Housing Finance Agency, one of the most sweeping government interventions in private financial markets in many years.

Lenders, Congress, the administration, and scholars have a lot to evaluate in making proposals to prevent a future financial crisis. Real estate professionals who understand the new financial rules will be ready when the markets recover.

MORTGAGES, NOTES, AND THE RIGHTS AND OBLIGATIONS OF THE PARTIES

This section describes promissory notes and mortgages and the specific clauses found in each type of document. It also covers mortgage lenders' and borrowers' rights and duties.

Promissory Note

A promissory note is a promise to pay a sum of money in the future. After the borrower (maker) signs the note, it is a legally enforceable instrument. A note without a mortgage is an **unsecured note**. A **secured note** contains wording referring to a security interest in personal property, or to a mortgage on real property. A note must state the amount of the debt, the interest rate, the amount and time of each payment, and the loan term.

A note requires only the borrower's signature. If another person signs the note's face, that person becomes a **cosigner** and is personally liable for repaying the debt. For this reason, notes are not witnessed or acknowledged.

Mortgage

A mortgage is a pledge of real property to secure a note. If the note maker defaults on the promise, the lender has a right to have the property sold and to use the proceeds to pay the debt. The parties to a mortgage are the **mortgagor** (borrower) and the **mortgagee** (lender). All mortgages must have a note, but not all notes are secured by mortgages.

Essential elements of a mortgage. A mortgage must contain the borrower's and the lender's legal names, and must be signed by the borrower. It must include the property's legal description and convey a security interest in that property. The mortgage must reference the promissory note. The Fannie Mae/Freddie Mac mortgage form uses these words:

> *Borrower owes Lender the principal sum of $__________. This debt is evidenced by Borrower's note dated the same date as this Security Instrument (Note), which provides for monthly payments, with the full debt, if not paid earlier, due and payable on ____________ __________________________.*

Three mortgage clauses especially important to borrowers include the acceleration clause, the prepayment clause, and the due-on-sale clause.

The **acceleration clause** allows the lender to call due the remaining loan balance if the borrower defaults. Without this clause, the lender could sue for only the delinquent payments. Most mortgages, once accelerated, force payment of the total principal. Fannie Mae and Freddie Mac use a standard mortgage instrument in which the acceleration clause applies only if the property goes to foreclosure. The mortgage allows the borrower to reinstate simply by paying the delinquent payments and costs. This reinstatement privilege does not apply if the acceleration occurred because of a due-on-sale clause.

A **due-on-sale clause** is a specific type of acceleration clause. If the property is sold, the lender may require immediate payment of the loan, effectively preventing the buyer from assuming the loan. Years ago, before the clause was used commonly, sellers could let buyers assume their mortgages. If the buyers defaulted, the sellers were liable for the debts when the properties were foreclosed. The due-on-sale clause therefore protects not only the lender, but also the original borrower. In the late 1980s, FHA and VA policies changed to require that buyers qualify financially before they can assume the sellers' mortgages. After a new buyer has been qualified, the seller is released from liability on the loan. This process is known as a *full substitution of borrowers*, or a **novation**.

An **exculpatory clause** is a mortgage provision that requires the lender to look only to the property in case the borrower defaults. For example, John bought a condominium last year for $600,000 and financed the purchase with a mortgage of $540,000. When this year the market value dropped to $450,000, John abandoned the property. If the mortgage had an exculpatory clause, he would lose his $60,000 down payment but could not be held personally liable. While exculpatory clauses are sometimes used in commercial mortgages, they are not commonly used in residential mortgages.

A **prepayment clause** gives the borrower specific permission to pay the debt ahead of schedule. VA, FHA, Fannie Mae, and Freddie Mac mortgages allow prepayments. A **prepayment penalty clause** requires that the borrower pay a predetermined fee to pay off the loan early. Many second mortgage companies include penalty provisions in their loans because the lenders want the high interest rates to remain in force. Chapter 696, F.S., states that "any note which is silent as to the right of the obligor to prepay the note in advance of the stated maturity date may be prepaid in full by the obligor or her or his successor in interest without penalty."

A **receivership clause** is used in income property mortgages. The lender requires the borrower to execute an "assignment of leases and rents," which would be used if the borrower is in default. If this clause were not in the mortgage, the borrower could collect the rents and spend them without paying the required mortgage payments ("milking" the property). The lender under this clause would petition the courts to have all the rents collected from the tenants by a court-appointed receiver who will manage the property.

A **subordination clause** is used when a builder buys a site from a developer who finances the purchase. While the mortgage is in senior position, the clause allows the builder to get a first mortgage for a construction loan, and the developers mortgage will drop to second place. It is very attractive to builders because they don't have to pay off the original loan and it reduces their cash requirements. The developer, because of the willingness to subordinate, sells more home sites.

Mortgage theory. Two types of mortgage theory exist. In states using **title theory**, a mortgage transfers the property to the lender (mortgage deed) or a third-party trustee (deed of trust) until the loan is repaid. Under modified common law, if the borrower defaults, the lender could take possession of the property. However, most title theory states now require foreclosure proceedings before the borrowers lose their rights.

Most states, including Florida, use the **lien theory**. That is, the borrower owns the property, and the lender has a lien. If the borrower defaults, the lender forecloses on the mortgage lien. The clerk of the court sells the property at a public sale to satisfy the debt.

Mortgage priorities. The **priority** order of liens is critical to lenders. In Florida, property taxes and special assessments come before all other liens. Other liens generally are ranked by their chronological order of recording. Most institutional lenders require that their liens be in first position, with only property taxes and special assessments having higher priority liens.

EXAMPLE: The benefits of higher priority:

Coral Federal Savings Bank has a first mortgage on a residence for $102,000. AAAbest Mortgage has a second mortgage for $35,000. The property owner is having financial problems and does not pay his credit card company, which later records a court judgment of $10,000. When the owner defaults on his mortgage, Coral Federal forecloses. The property is sold at public auction for $130,000. The proceeds are distributed as follows:

Auction price	$130,000
Less:	
Governmental expense of sale	– 475
First mortgage, including $3,000 for collection costs	–105,000
Balance remaining	$ 24,525

The $24,525 balance pays part of the AAAbest mortgage. All liens on the property are discharged, meaning that AAAbest loses $10,475 and the credit card company loses $10,000. Coral Federal was paid in full because it held a first mortgage. The buyer receives the property free of liens except for the ad valorem taxes.

Rights of Mortgage Lenders

Foreclosure is the legal action used after a mortgagor defaults on a note secured by a mortgage on real property. The property is sold at public auction, taking away the mortgagor's rights in the property. When the property is sold, the original mortgage lien and any lower priority liens are extinguished.

Right to foreclose. **Foreclosure** is a process that has been at the top of the news stories in recent years. For example, in September 2012, more than 28,000 mortgage foreclosures were filed in Florida. 41 percent of all sub-prime loans in the Miami area were in some process of foreclosure as of March 2012. Other areas of the state are also under great pressure.

Section 45.031, F.S., concerns judicial sales procedure applicable to the sale of real or personal property under an order or judgment. The property owner and lienholders of lower priority are defendants in the action. Junior lienholders usually join in the lawsuit to ensure that they are paid from any surplus funds from a sale. Once a judgment for foreclosure has been made, the court directs the clerk to sell the property at public sale, usually between 20 and 35 days later. The notice of sale is published once a week for two consecutive weeks in a newspaper published in the county where the sale will be held. The notice must contain a description of the property, the time and place of sale, a statement that the sale will be made pursuant to the final judgment, case number, and name of the clerk handling the case.

The average foreclosure time, from the initial *lis pendens* recording until the lender owns the property, is 861 days in Florida, according to *RealtyTrac.com*.

The successful high bidder must post a deposit and pay the balance of the purchase price within the prescribed time. After the property's sale, the clerk files a certificate of sale. If no objections to the sale are filed within ten days, the successful bidder gets a **certificate of title** to the property, which the clerk records. When the mortgage is foreclosed, if the sale proceeds exceed the amount owed to the foreclosure plaintiff plus costs, the junior liens (by chronological recording order) will be paid, and after the proceeds of the sale are used up any remaining junior lienors will get nothing. Lenders that are not paid in full may request a deficiency judgment. If granted, the judgment becomes a lien on other property the borrower may own in any county where the judgment was recorded.

Right to transfer (assign) the mortgage. Mortgagees have the right to transfer their interests in a mortgage; that practice is universal. Most fixed-rate mortgages are sold immediately in the secondary mortgage market, giving the original lenders the cash to make more loans. The lenders earn an origination fee and often continue to service the mortgages, collecting payments and earning additional fees. While the origination fee usually does not cover the costs of making a loan, a lender's profit comes mainly from servicing fees.

Rights of Borrowers

Right of possession. The borrower has a right of possession that may not be taken away except by foreclosure.

Equity of redemption. The right of **redemption** allows a borrower to prevent a foreclosure sale by paying the entire balance due to the lender. This is true whether the right is not included or is prohibited in a mortgage. Because a sale of property at foreclosure is final, the equity of redemption ends at the time of the sale.

CONVENTIONAL, FHA, AND VA MORTGAGE LOANS

Conventional Mortgage Loans Conventional mortgage loans are neither government insured (FHA) nor government guaranteed (VA). Conventional loans usually are less complicated to obtain than FHA or VA loans, but have higher qualifying requirements. Interest rates on conventional loans generally are about ¼ of one percent lower than FHA loans and don't require an initial mortgage insurance premium.

Fannie Mae and Freddie Mac requirements for purchasing loans in the secondary market have broad impact among lending institutions. Each year, Fannie Mae and Freddie Mac establish the maximum home loan mortgage limit.

WEB LINK

For more information on Fannie Mae and Freddie Mac, see **www.fanniemae.com** and **www.freddiemac.com.**

Calculation of mortgage payment. Brokers normally use financial calculators to calculate mortgage payments. The financial calculator has five basic financial function keys. In order to calculate the payment, the broker would enter the number of payments (N), the interest rate applicable to each payment (%I), the balance of the loan (PV), then solve for the payment (PMT).

EXAMPLE: Assume that the broker wants to determine the payment for a 30-year, $200,000 mortgage at four percent annual interest with monthly payments. The broker enters the amounts given, then solves for the payment, PMT, as shown below.

N	%I	PV	PMT	FV
360	.333333	200,000	954.83	0

Where:

N	=	number of monthly periods in loan term (30 years × 12 months)
%I	=	market interest rate (4 percent ÷ 12 months)
PMT	=	monthly mortgage payment (press to calculate)
PV	=	present value (loan amount)
FV	=	future value: input zero when calculating the payment, because the value of the loan will be zero at the end of the term

Some brokers use financial tables to calculate the mortgage payment. Table 12.1 shows a table of monthly mortgage payment factors. Each factor in the table is known as a **loan**

constant, sometimes shown as *k* in mortgage formulas. The loan constant is the percentage of the mortgage paid periodically for principal and interest.

Assume that a buyer obtains a 30-year loan for $100,000 at a 5 percent interest rate, paid monthly. When you follow the 5 percent row across to the 30-year column, you get a monthly constant of .0053682. Multiply that by the $100,000 loan amount and the monthly payment for principal and interest is $536.82.

WEB LINK

For a quick mortgage payment calculator including PITI, see **www.mortgage-calc.com/.**

Assumption of conventional mortgages. A fixed-rate conventional mortgage usually is not assumable by a buyer of the property. The mortgage most lenders use is the Fannie Mae/Freddie Mac Uniform Instrument. Paragraph 17 of that mortgage form states that a lender may call due the loan if any interest in the property is sold or transferred. An adjustable-rate conventional mortgage generally is assumable if the buyer qualifies for the loan.

Private mortgage insurance (PMI). Private mortgage insurance protects the lender against financial loss if a borrower stops making mortgage payments. Fannie Mae's statistics show that low-down-payment loans have a much higher rate of delinquencies. Most lenders require that a borrower pay for mortgage insurance if the loan-to-value ratio is greater than 80 percent. Typically, mortgage insurance pays up to 25 percent of the mortgage if there is a loss when a borrower defaults. For example, if the loss on a $200,000 mortgage is $60,000, the mortgage insuror will pay $50,000 ($200,000 × .25) and the lender must absorb the remaining $10,000 loss.

Homeowners Protection Act

The **Homeowners Protection Act of 1998** set rules both for automatic termination and for borrower cancellation of PMI on home mortgages. These rules do not apply to government-insured FHA and VA loans or to loans with lender-paid PMI.

For home mortgages signed on or after July 29, 1999, PMI must, with certain exceptions, be terminated *automatically* when the borrower has achieved 22 percent equity in the home based on the *original property value*, if the mortgage payments are current. PMI also can be canceled, when the borrower *requests it*—also with certain exceptions—when the borrower achieves 20 percent equity in the home based on the original property value, if the mortgage payments are current.

There are three exceptions for which the PMI may continue:

1. If the loan is "high-risk"
2. If the borrower has not been current on the payments within the year prior to the time for termination or cancellation
3. If the borrower has other liens on the property

Conforming vs. Nonconforming Loans

Fannie Mae and Freddie Mac are the two largest secondary market corporations that purchase conforming closed loans from mortgage lenders. **Conforming loans** meet all Fannie Mae and Freddie Mac requirements for underwriting, appraising, and forms usage. Conforming loans also must conform to the maximum loan amounts that Fannie Mae and Freddie Mac may purchase. Jumbos are mortgages with loan amounts exceeding the

TABLE 12.1 ■ Monthly Mortgage Payment Factor Table

Multiply the mortgage principal by the factor to calculate the mortgage payment.

Interest Rate	10 Years	15 Years	20 Years	25 Years	30 Years
5.00%	0.0106066	0.0079079	0.0065996	0.0058459	0.0053682
5.25%	0.0107292	0.0080388	0.0067384	0.0059925	0.0055220
5.50%	0.0108526	0.0081708	0.0068789	0.0061409	0.0056779
5.75%	0.0109769	0.0083041	0.0070208	0.0062911	0.0058357
6.00%	0.0111021	0.0084386	0.0071643	0.0064430	0.0059955
6.25%	0.0112280	0.0085742	0.0073093	0.0065967	0.0061572
6.50%	0.0113548	0.0087111	0.0074557	0.0067521	0.0063207
6.75%	0.0114824	0.0088491	0.0076036	0.0069091	0.0064860
7.00%	0.0116108	0.0089883	0.0077530	0.0070678	0.0066530
7.25%	0.0117401	0.0091286	0.0079038	0.0072281	0.0068218
7.50%	0.0118702	0.0092701	0.0080559	0.0073899	0.0069921
7.75%	0.0120011	0.0094128	0.0082095	0.0075533	0.0071641
8.00%	0.0121328	0.0095565	0.0083644	0.0077182	0.0073376
8.25%	0.0122653	0.0097014	0.0085207	0.0078845	0.0075127
8.50%	0.0123986	0.0098474	0.0086782	0.0080523	0.0076891
8.75%	0.0125327	0.0099945	0.0088371	0.0082214	0.0078670
9.00%	0.0126676	0.0101427	0.0089973	0.0083920	0.0080462
9.25%	0.0128033	0.0102919	0.0091587	0.0085638	0.0082268
9.50%	0.0129398	0.0104422	0.0093213	0.0087370	0.0084085
9.75%	0.0130770	0.0105936	0.0094852	0.0089114	0.0085915
10.00%	0.0132151	0.0107461	0.0096502	0.0090870	0.0087757
10.25%	0.0133539	0.0108995	0.0098164	0.0092638	0.0089610
10.50%	0.0134935	0.0110540	0.0099838	0.0094418	0.0091474
10.75%	0.0136339	0.0112095	0.0101523	0.0096209	0.0093348
11.00%	0.0137750	0.0113660	0.0103219	0.0098011	0.0095232
11.25%	0.0139169	0.0115234	0.0104926	0.0099824	0.0097126
11.50%	0.0140595	0.0116819	0.0106643	0.0101647	0.0099029
11.75%	0.0142029	0.0118413	0.0108371	0.0103480	0.0100941

current Fannie Mae/Freddie Mac limit. Every year, new loan limits are announced for one-family to four-family loans that Fannie Mae and Freddie Mac may purchase.

Nonconforming loans do not meet these standards. They often are kept in a lender's portfolio rather than sold. They usually have higher interest rates.

Government Insured or Guaranteed Mortgage Loans

FHA-insured mortgage loans. Before the Great Depression, most lenders required a 50 percent down payment on a home. This put home ownership out of the reach of most Americans. Builders and lenders agreed that the key to stimulating home ownership was lowering down payment requirements without increasing lenders' risk. The National

Housing Act of 1934 created the Federal Housing Administration (FHA), a government insurance agency, to meet this need.

With an FHA-insured loan, a borrower can buy a home with a lower down payment than other mortgages. The borrower is required to pay a **mortgage insurance premium (MIP)**. The insurance protects the lender in case the borrower stops making payments. The insurance program currently requires an up-front mortgage insurance premium (UFMIP) and an annual premium divided between the monthly payments.

FHA 203(b) residential loan. The most common FHA loan for homebuyers is the FHA 203(b) residential loan. A homebuyer can get a fixed-rate mortgage on a one-family to four-family home with a down payment of 3.5 percent of the lesser of the purchase price or appraisal. The FHA calls the down payment an **initial investment.**

The FHA has established maximum mortgage amounts it will insure based on housing costs in different areas. The FHA makes loans in even $50 increments. If a calculated amount is not an even $50, it is rounded to the next lower $50 increment.

EXAMPLE: Hank wishes to purchase a new home for $140,000. The home appraises for $140,000. If allowable closing costs are $2,400, the acquisition cost is $142,400. Using the 3.5 percent down payment requirement, the loan amount is calculated as shown below:

Price + closing costs	$142,400
Down payment of 3.5% ($4,984 rounded up to the next highest $50 increment)	– $5,000
Mortgage	= $137,400

The FHA does not regulate interest rates; rates are set by lenders based on the market. Borrowers may reduce the interest rate by prepaying interest as points. Theoretically, the payment of one discount point should lower the quoted rate of a 30-year mortgage by 1/8 of 1 percent. For example, if FHA rates are 4 percent, the payment of four points should reduce the buyer's interest rate to 3½ percent. The FHA requires that the borrower set up an escrow account with the lender and pay 1/12 of the annual taxes and insurance.

WEB LINK

For more information on FHA loans, see **www.hud.gov/index.html**.

Assumption of FHA Loans

FHA loans made before December 1, 1986, are freely assumable with no buyer qualification. Because interest rates before that date were higher than today's rates, assuming these loans usually is not feasible. Unless released from liability, the seller remains liable for five years after the transfer.

FHA loans made between December 1, 1986, and December 14, 1989, can be assumed only if a buyer qualifies. When the buyer is approved, the seller is released from liability. Investors may assume these loans. FHA loans made after December 14, 1989, stopped allowing investors to assume the mortgages.

Other FHA loan programs. The Section 234(c) program, which is similar to the Section 203(b) program, insures condominium mortgages. Section 245 insures graduated-payment mortgages for buyers who expect their incomes to increase in the next five to ten years.

The monthly payments in the early years of these negative amortization loans do not cover the interest, and this unpaid interest is added to the loans' principal balances. Monthly payments of principal and interest increase each year for up to ten years, depending on which one of five graduated-payment plans the buyers select. Plan III, which requires a payment increase of 7.5 percent annually for the first five years, then levels out, is still the most common. The down payment is higher because the loan balance increases for the first few years and could erode the borrower's equity in the property.

Direct endorsement program for lenders. Direct endorsement makes it easier and quicker for people to buy homes because it allows their lenders to approve the mortgage insurance applications rather than submit the paperwork to the FHA. Most single-family FHA mortgage lending is done through direct endorsement, which enables an FHA-insured mortgage to be closed as quickly as other mortgages.

Department of Veterans Affairs (VA) Loan

Mortgage companies, savings associations, and banks all make VA loans. Most VA loans do not require a down payment. The VA's partial guarantee on a loan **(entitlement)** protects the lender against loss if the borrower does not make payments. It is intended to encourage lenders to offer veterans loans with more favorable terms. The amount of guarantee depends on the loan amount and whether the veteran has already used some of the entitlement. With the current maximum guarantee of $104,250, a veteran who hasn't used any of the benefit can obtain a VA loan of up to $417,000, depending on the borrower's income level and the property's appraised value. The DVA has the authority to make loans to veterans in areas where mortgage lenders are not available.

Mortgage guarantee concept. The VA has the authority to guarantee the construction and purchase of homes. The following table outlines VA loan eligibility:

Loan Amount	*Guaranteed Amount*
$0 to $45,000	50% of the loan amount
$45,001 to $144,000	Minimum $22,500
	Maximum is 40% of the loan amount up to $36,000
More than $144,000	Up to $104,250 or 25% of the loan amount

Most lenders require that a combination of the guarantee entitlement and any cash down payment must equal at least 25 percent of the property's reasonable value or sale price, whichever is less. Because the maximum VA guarantee is $104,250, the maximum loan most lenders will make with no down payment is $417,000 ($104,250 ÷ .25). Unlike the FHA, the VA imposes no maximum loan requirement. Therefore, a lender might agree to make a higher loan if the veteran paid 25 percent of the amount exceeding $417,000 as an extra down payment.

Eligibility and loan guarantee entitlement. Eligible veterans, surviving spouses of eligible veterans, and members of the armed forces on active duty all can apply for VA loans.

A veteran who has already obtained a VA loan may have remaining entitlement to use for another VA loan. The entitlement was much lower in years past and has been increased over time by changes in the law.

A veteran can have a previously used entitlement restored to purchase another home with a VA loan if the veteran:

- has sold the property purchased with the prior VA loan and has repaid the loan in full;
- buys the other home, qualifies to assume the VA loan, and substitutes entitlement for the same amount of entitlement the veteran seller used originally; or
- has repaid the prior VA loan in full, but has not disposed of the property purchased with that loan.

Interest rates. Individual lenders set the interest rates on VA-guaranteed loans. Because the rates are negotiable, a buyer or seller may pay points to a lender to reduce the interest rate. The amount paid in points may not be added to the loan amount.

Certificate of reasonable value (CRV). The **certificate of reasonable value (CRV)** is based on an appraiser's estimate of the value of the property to be purchased. The loan amount may not exceed the CRV.

Closing costs and VA funding fee. Lenders may charge reasonable closing costs, but may not include these costs in a loan (except when the loan is for refinancing). A veteran purchaser or the seller may pay the following costs, or they may share them:

- VA appraisal
- Credit report
- Loan origination fee (usually one percent of the loan)
- Discount points
- Title search and title insurance
- Recording fees
- State and local transfer taxes, if applicable
- Survey
- Funding fee

No commissions, brokerage fees, or buyer broker fees may be charged to the veteran buyer.

All but certain exempt veterans (those receiving VA disability compensation, those who are rated by VA as eligible to receive compensation as a result of pre-discharge disability examination and rating, and unmarried surviving spouses of veterans who died in service or as a result of a service-connected disability) must pay a **funding fee** to the VA. A down payment of five percent or more reduces the fee. For every VA home loan, the funding fee may be paid in cash or included in the loan.

Assumption and release of liability. VA loans made before March 1, 1988, are assumable to veterans or nonveterans without buyer qualification, but the sellers remain liable. For VA loans made after that date, buyers must qualify to assume the loans, and the sellers then are released from liability.

WEB LINK

For more information on VA loans, see **www.benefits.va.gov/homeloans/.**

Rural Housing Services Administration

The Rural Housing Services Administration is part of the U.S. Department of Agriculture. It offers direct loans to farmers and rural communities for farms, homes, and businesses. The agency originates new loans, insures loans, and guarantees loans other lenders make.

WEB LINK

For more information on Rural Housing Services Administration, see **www.rurdev.usda.gov/rhs.**

MORTGAGES BY METHOD OF PAYMENT

Three classifications of mortgages are based on the way borrowers make payments: term mortgages, partially amortized mortgages, or fully amortized mortgages.

Term mortgages. A **term mortgage**, sometimes called a *straight-term mortgage*, is a loan in which the borrower pays only interest, with the principal coming due at the end of the term. Term loans are common in development and construction.

Interest-only mortgages. During the real estate boom, many buyers borrowed funds for their home purchase with interest-only mortgages. Because these loans are very risky, they are rarely granted to homebuyers today. The interest on an interest-only mortgage is calculated by multiplying the loan amount by the interest rate, then dividing the result by 12. A $500,000 mortgage at 5 percent would have annual interest of $25,000 and a monthly interest payment of $2,083.33. The payment on a traditional 30-year amortized mortgage would be $2,684.11, a difference of $600.78. As the loan is paid, the interest portion of each payment will go down, and the principal portion will go up. At the end of 30 years, the borrower with an interest-only mortgage still owes $500,000. The borrower with a traditional mortgage has a house that is free and clear. The only way for the first borrower to do as well is to invest the $600.78 into a mutual fund or other device, such as a certificate of deposit (CD), each month and receive at least 5 percent interest. Unfortunately, many people don't have the financial discipline to make that investment, and risk-free investments with a five percent return are hard to find.

Partially amortized mortgages. A loan that includes both principal and interest, but that comes due before the loan is fully paid, is called a **partially amortized mortgage**. For example, assume a seller finances the buyer's purchase for $50,000 with a 30-year term loan at 9 percent interest, due and payable in five years. Payments are $402.31 per month; however, the loan requires a **balloon payment** of $47,940.07 at the end of the fifth year.

Fully amortized mortgages. A **fully amortized mortgage** is paid off by periodic installments of interest and principal. The amount of each payment remains constant during the life of the loan. Interest is the largest part of the payment in the loan's early years. As the loan period progresses, the interest in each payment decreases and the principal portion increases.

MORTGAGES BY PAYMENT OR YIELD VARIABILITY

Adjustable-rate mortgage (ARM). **Adjustable-rate mortgages** are alternatives to the traditional fixed-rate mortgage during high interest rate periods. In recent years, mortgage rates have been low and stable, and ARMs are less of a factor in the market. ARMs remain an alternative for persons who intend to own their properties for a relatively short time.

The interest rate in an adjustable-rate mortgage changes periodically; one-year, three-year, and five-year adjustment programs are available. The rate is determined by adding a **margin** to a recognized **index**. The index changes; the margin remains constant for the life of the loan. The most common indices include the one-year constant-maturity Treasury (CMT) securities, the Cost of Funds Index (COFI), and the London Interbank Offered Rate (LIBOR). Interest rate changes for conventional loans usually are limited to two percent per year **(annual caps)** and six percent over the lives of the loans **(lifetime caps)**. FHA ARMs have caps of one percent annually and five percent lifetime.

Payment-option mortgage. Payment-option mortgages were another innovation of the go-go markets during 2003–2006. This "pick-a-pay" loan allows the borrower to choose a payment rate that can be lower than required to amortize the loan and can even turn into a negative-amortization loan. While most amortizing loans have a regular reduction of the principal balance, "negative-am" loans feature a principal balance that increases. These loans are a problem for many borrowers (and for the lenders who must foreclose). This type of loan all but disappeared in the aftermath of the financial crash.

Graduated-payment mortgage (GPM). In a **graduated-payment mortgage**, the monthly payments in the loan's early years do not cover the accrued interest. This unpaid interest is added to the principal balance, which makes it a negative amortization loan.

Reduction option mortgage. A **reduction option mortgage** benefits the borrower if interest rates decline. Under this plan, the borrower has an option to refinance at a lower interest rate. The borrower and the lender agree on an option period, typically for four years beginning in the loan's second year. The lender agrees that the borrower, by paying a fee, can refinance at the current interest rate at the time. The borrower pays a higher initial interest rate as consideration for this option.

Early payment mortgage. An early payment mortgage is not a special program; it is a regular mortgage that the borrower prepays systematically. One common way to pay a 30-year loan in half the time is by making a monthly payment and adding the principal amount scheduled for the next month. (See Figure 12.1.)

Borrowers can use many other ways to prepay a loan. Examples are shown in Figure 12.2.

Because interest is tax deductible, the after-tax savings would be less dramatic than shown. Also, making the higher payments involves an opportunity cost, because the difference in payments might be invested to receive interest.

15-year mortgage. Fifteen-year mortgages have become popular with many borrowers. The difference between a 15-year mortgage and an early payment mortgage is that while the borrower *must* make the higher payments on the 15-year mortgage, early payments on the 30-year loan are optional. The 15-year mortgage offers several advantages: the interest rate is lower, the loan is paid off sooner, and interest savings are substantial. The principal disadvantage is the higher required payment, which could cause a default if the borrower has a financial emergency.

Buydowns. When interest rates are high, many builders offer to buy down the rates for borrowers by prepaying some interest. A typical builder program is a 3-2-1 **buydown.** Assume that interest rates are at 10 percent. The builder pays a lump sum to the lender, and the lender allows the borrower to pay seven percent interest in the first year, eight percent interest in the second year, and nine percent interest in the third year. In the fourth year, the rate stabilizes at ten percent. The lender qualifies the buyer at the seven percent rate.

FIGURE 12.1 ■ Early Payment Mortgage

A borrower wishes to save interest by prepaying the mortgage systematically. The borrower's partial amortization schedule for a 4 percent, 30-year, $100,000 mortgage is shown below.

Month	Beginning Balance	Payment	Principal	Interest	Ending Balance
January	$100,000.00	$477.42	$144.09	$333.33	$99,855.91
February	$99,855.91	$477.42	$144.57	$332.85	$99,711.34
March	$99,711.34	$477.42	$145.05	$332.37	$99,566.29
April	$99,566.29	$477.42	$145.53	$331.89	$99,420.76
May	$99,420.76	$477.42	$146.02	$331.40	$99,274.74
June	$99,274.74	$477.42	$146.50	$330.92	$99,128.24
July	$99,128.24	$477.42	$146.99	$330.43	$98,981.25

In January, the borrower adds the principal amount scheduled for the February payment, $144.57, to the regular payment of $477.42, making a payment to the lender of $621.99 The ending balance of the loan is then $99,711.34, as if the borrower made two payments. In February, the borrower adds the principal amount scheduled for the April payment, $145.53, to the regular payment of $477.42, making a payment to the lender of $622.95. The loan's ending balance is then $99,420.76, as if the borrower paid the loan through April. The real payment schedule is shown below.

Month	Beginning Balance	Payment	Principal	Interest	Ending Balance
Jan	$100,000.00	$621.99	$288.66	$333.33	$99,711.34
Feb	99,711.35	622.95	290.58	332.37	99,420.76

Can you calculate the payment the borrower will make in March?

Continuing this program, the borrower would make increasingly higher payments each month and would pay off the loan in 15 years.

For example, assume a buyer has income of $4,000 per month. Under FNMA guidelines, he can pay 28 percent PITI (principal, interest, taxes, insurance), or $1,120. Assuming taxes and insurance are $250, $870 remains for principal and interest. The buyer would qualify for a 10 percent loan of approximately $99,000. With the buydown, the buyer would qualify for a loan of approximately $130,800. However, as the rates increase to 10 percent, the buyer and the lender are at risk if the buyer's monthly income does not increase equally.

FIGURE 12.2 ■ Traditional $100,000, 4%, 30-Year Mortgage Versus Early Payment Systems

	Payment	Interest Paid	Interest Saved
Traditional 30-year mortgage	$477.42	$71,871	$ 0
Add $25 per month to payment	502.42	64,794	7,077
Add $100 per month to payment	577.42	49,552	22,319
15-year mortgage (interest rate = 3.5 percent)	739.68	33,142	38,729
Biweekly mortgage (Regular payment $477.42 ÷ 2 × 26 payments/yr.)	238.71	60,652	11,219

MORTGAGES BY PURPOSE

Purchase-money mortgage. By strict definition, a **purchase-money mortgage** is any mortgage that finances a property's purchase. More commonly, however, a seller accepts a purchase-money mortgage as part of the purchase price of real property. Purchase-money mortgages often are used in land transactions when a seller owns property free and clear and agrees to finance the land for a developer. The buyer gets easier financing, and the seller generally gets a higher interest rate than is available from other investments.

Purchase-money mortgages also are used in residential transactions when a borrower gets a new loan (or assumes an existing mortgage) and asks the seller to help finance the down payment. For example, assume that Jack wants to purchase a $200,000 home using a non-qualifying assumable VA loan with a current balance of $120,000. Jack has $50,000 to use as a down payment and asks the seller to finance the balance. The seller agrees to take back a purchase-money mortgage for $30,000, and the sale is closed. The seller's lien is behind the VA loan, but the buyer's 40 percent equity position reduces the chance of default.

Participation mortgage. A **participation mortgage** allows the lender to participate in an investment property's equity return, protecting the lender from inflation. Such participation sometimes is called an **equity kicker**. The lender makes a fixed-rate loan with the possibility of contingent interest. The amount of contingent interest could be a percentage of gross or net income, a percentage of periodic reappraisals, or a percentage of sales proceeds. The participation mortgage is not common because investors resist equity participation.

A *shared appreciation mortgage (SAM)* is a type of participation mortgage used in residential transactions. Under a typical plan, the lender would give the borrower a below-market interest rate in return for a 40 percent share in the property's increased value at the end of five years. An appraisal would establish the value, and the lender's share of the increase would be added to the principal balance of the loan, with the payments increased so that the mortgage will be paid off by maturity.

A **mortgage participation**, while it sounds similar, is unrelated. A mortgage participation occurs when a developer wants to borrow on a very large project, and the lender does not want to invest a large percentage of its loan portfolio. For example, assume a developer wants to build a $400 million theme park between Orlando and Clermont and proposes it to a lending institution. The loan may be an attractive investment, but the size may be too large for the lender, which may contact other lenders to participate in the loan. The investor signs a note and mortgage to the consortium, and the lead lender services the loan.

Blanket mortgage. A **blanket mortgage** covers more than one parcel of property. The most common type of blanket mortgage is a land development loan, in which the developer plats a large tract of land into smaller parcels, giving the lender a blanket mortgage on the entire tract.

The mortgage would need to include a partial release clause so the developer can give marketable title to the property when a buyer pays cash. A licensee cannot sell a parcel of land that is encumbered by a blanket mortgage unless the parcel can be released for payment of an amount less than that remaining due from the purchaser after the sale.

When a parcel is sold, the developer sends the lender a predetermined payment so that the lender releases the parcel from the mortgage.

EXAMPLE: Broker Patti represents Brett Wilson, who owns a 100-acre tract of land in west Gadsden County. (See Figure 12.3.) The property is priced at appraisal: $4,000 per acre. A developer submits an offer to purchase the property at the asking price if the seller agrees to hold owner financing with 10 percent down. The developer wants to build roads and sell five-acre to seven-acre tracts as Ponderosa Ranchettes. Brett wants his interests protected in case the developer defaults.

Patti recommends that Brett see an attorney, then makes the following suggestions:

- "The amount of your mortgage will be $360,000—that's $3,600 per acre. You should have the developer pay 110 percent ($3,960) of the pro rata amount for each release."
- "If you let the developer sell anywhere in the 100 acres and release the parcel, you may have a problem if you have to foreclose. The land will look like a checkerboard when you get it back. And certainly, you'll get all the low area back." Patti draws five tracts running perpendicular to the highway and letters them A through E. Each has 20 acres. "Let's require that the developer release each complete tract starting with tract A, moving west toward tract E. That way, if he defaults, you still will have a good piece of property."
- "You want to be sure that you do not sell and release the most valuable property first. That's why I have made the tracts perpendicular to the highway."

Brett's attorney approves the suggestions.

Reverse annuity mortgage. Many elderly persons on fixed incomes have substantial equity in their homes, but cannot qualify for conventional loans. A **reverse annuity mortgage** allows an elderly homeowner to use money that need not be paid back until the homeowner leaves the house or the house is sold (by the owner or the estate after the owner's death). Draws are treated as tax-free advances. The loans often are called *home equity conversion loans* (HECM). A reverse mortgage is a nonrecourse loan, meaning the amount owed to the lender never can exceed the house's value. A lender recovers its principal, plus interest, when the home is sold. The remaining proceeds from the sale of the home goes to the homeowner or to the deceased's survivors. If the sale proceeds do not cover the amount owed, the lender calls on the loan insurer to pay the shortage.

FIGURE 12.3 ■ Future Home of Ponderosa Ranchettes

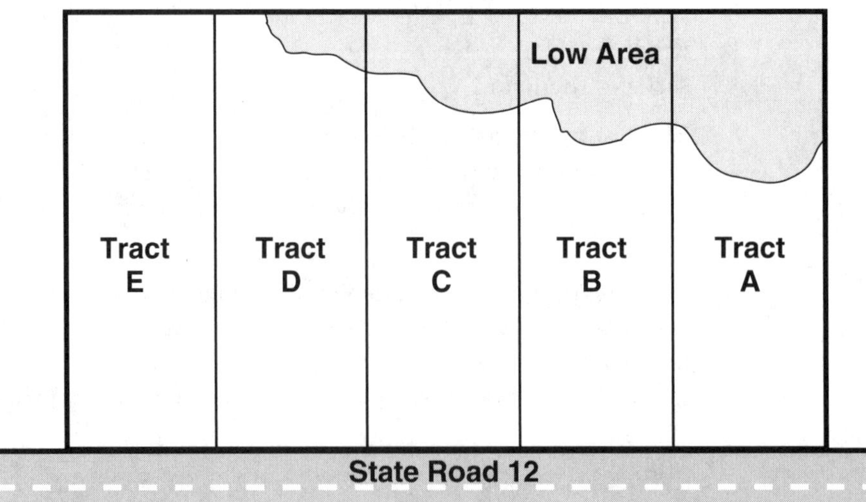

Conventional lenders make reverse annuity mortgages, which the FHA sometimes insures. The Federal Housing Administration, which is part of HUD, collects insurance premiums from the borrowers to provide this coverage.

The size of a reverse mortgage loan is based on the borrower's age, the interest rate, and the home's value. The borrower must be at least 62 years old. The older the borrower, the larger the percentage of the home's value that can be borrowed. For example, a Miami couple, 71 and 69 years old, respectively, could borrow up to 153,000 on a $250,000 home in a single lump sum, or get a monthly payment of $945 for as long as they live in the home.

Under this program, the amount a person may borrow is capped by the maximum FHA mortgage limit for the area, which varies depending on local housing costs. As a result, owners of higher priced homes cannot borrow any more than owners of homes valued at the FHA limit.

HUD's reverse mortgage program collects funds from the insurance premiums the FHA charges to borrowers. Each borrower pays a two percent up-front premium plus ½ percent on the loan balance each year. These amounts usually are added to the borrower's principal balance.

Figure 12.4 shows the growth in the number of reverse mortgages.

Package mortgage. A **package mortgage** includes the real property and personal property in a home. Many vacation homes are sold furnished, and lenders agree to accept as collateral the personal property along with the real property. This practice helps the cash flow of a buyer who otherwise would not have enough cash left after the closing to buy furniture or appliances.

Home equity loan. **Home equity loans** allow owners access to funds at better interest rates than most other consumer loans. Banks often agree to pay all closing costs. The interest rates, which vary, usually are tied to the prime rate plus a margin, and federal law defines their upper limit. The interest on most home equity loans is tax deductible for persons who itemize expenses, which makes this type of loan more attractive than other types of consumer credit.

A home equity loan usually is a second mortgage that allows the borrower to take out a lump sum or to access a line of credit by check or bank credit cards. Generally, the loan amount is limited to 80 percent of a property's value.

For example, assume Anne owns a home valued at $124,000. She has an existing mortgage of $72,500 and wants to get a home equity loan. If the bank's limit is 80 percent of value, how much will it lend her? The bank will lend 80 percent of value, less other mortgages, so $124,000 times .80 equals $99,200. If Anne owes $72,500 on her first mortgage, the bank will lend her $26,700 ($99,200 – $72,500) on a home equity loan.

OTHER TECHNIQUES USED IN FINANCING REAL ESTATE

Investors use techniques other than mortgage loans to finance real property. These methods include time-sharing, contracts for deed, sale-leasebacks and wraparound mortgages.

FIGURE 12.4 ■ Number of Reverse Mortgages by Year

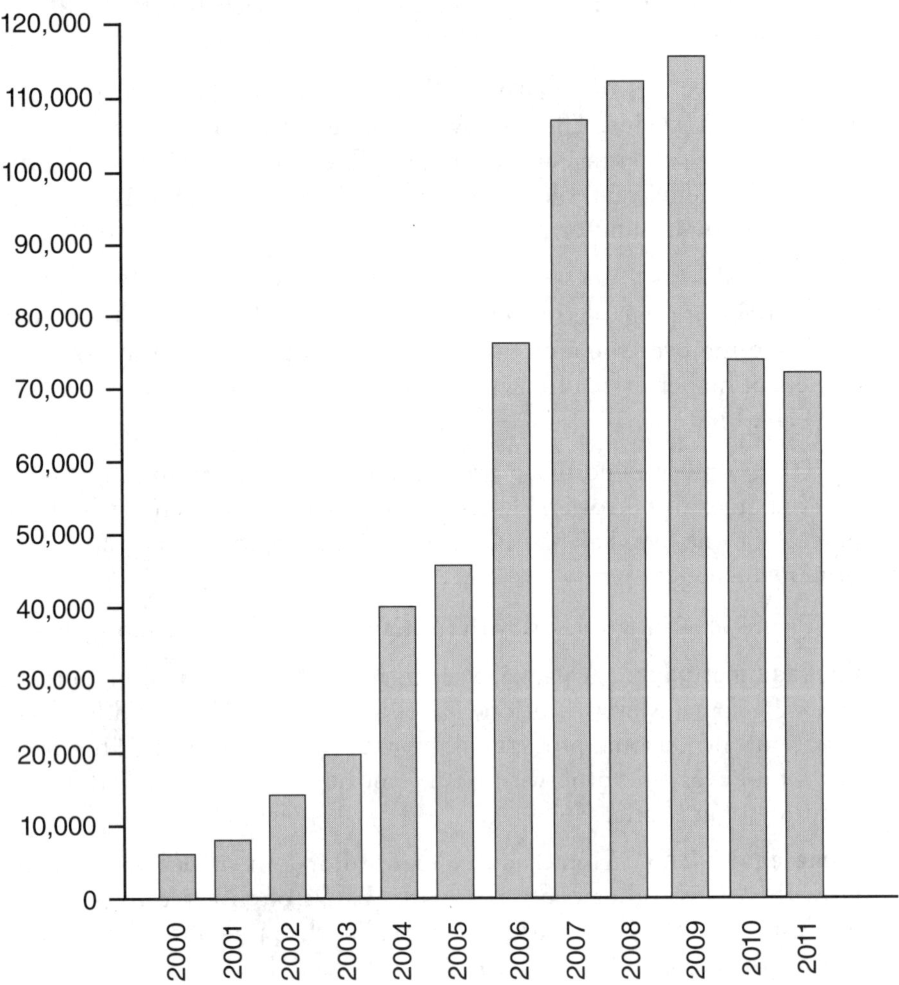

Source: CFPB analysis of FHA data

Time-Sharing

Many persons who take one-week or two-week vacations cannot afford to buy vacation homes on their own. Sometimes friends and family pool their money to buy a beach house, then share it on a pro rata basis. Time-share developers make that concept available to those who otherwise could not buy. A typical **timesharing** plan divides a vacation condominium into 52 weekly shares. Buyers may purchase one or more weeks of ownership. The price varies depending on the time of the year, the property's amenities, the apartment's size, and location within the building.

The Florida Real Estate Time-Share Act, Chapter 721, F.S., applies to all time-sharing plans with more than seven time-share periods over at least three years. Parts of the act also apply to time-share properties outside Florida that are marketed in Florida. In addition, the act regulates time-share resales. Unlicensed employees of a time-share developer may sell time-share periods, but must be paid strictly by salary. Sales personnel must have current, active real estate licenses to be paid commissions.

A developer must disclose pertinent facts about a property to each potential purchaser in an offering statement. The statement must establish the time-share's duration, the amount the buyer owes, the form of ownership, and the ten-day cancellation period. Management for the project must be in place before the first sale of a time-share interest.

Time-share ownership is one of two types: interval ownership or right-to-use. Interval ownership allows the buyer to receive a recordable deed. Subsequently, the buyer can sell or rent the property. Right-to-use time sharing is temporary, lasting from 40 to 99 years. After that time, the property reverts to the developer.

Sellers must make the following disclosures to purchasers of new time-share units:

- "You may cancel this contract without any penalty or obligation within ten days from the date you sign this contract or within ten days after you receive the public offering statement, whichever is later. If you decide to cancel this contract, you must notify the developer in writing of your intent to cancel. Your notice of cancellation will be effective on the date you send it to [name of developer] at [address of developer]. Any attempt to obtain a waiver of your cancellation right is unlawful. While you may execute all closing documents in advance, closing (as evidenced by delivery of the deed or another document) before your ten-day cancellation period expires is prohibited."
- "The purchase of a time-share period should be based on its value as a vacation experience or as a place to spend leisure time and should not be considered for the purpose of acquiring an appreciating investment or with an expectation that you will resell the time-share period."

Disclosures and the wording required in contracts for listing and selling resale time-share units are described in detail in FREC Rule 61J2-23.001 and 61J2-23.002. Disclosures required on listing contracts describe the broker's duties and compensation as well as a statement that the broker does not guarantee a sale. Sale contracts must disclose the amount of the current assessment for common expenses, the fact that the assessment may be increased from time to time, and whether the assessment includes ad valorem taxes. If ad valorem taxes are not included in the assessment, the amount of taxes must be shown. Further disclosure informs the buyer of the personal liability and penalties for failure to pay the assessment.

WEB LINK

The DBPR has many resources related to the Florida Timeshare Act at **http://www.state.fl.us/dbpr/lsc/timeshare/links.shtml.**

Contract for Deed

A **contract for deed** is used most often as a way to finance the acquisition of vacant property for home sites. The buyer enters into a contract with the seller in which the buyer agrees to make periodic payments and the seller agrees to give the buyer a deed when the buyer has made all of these payments. The buyer may take possession at the time the contract is signed. Licensees always should advise buyers to seek an attorney's advice and assistance in preparation of the document.

In the past, if the buyer defaulted on the agreement by failing to make payments, the buyer was forced off the property with no payment for any equity the buyer may have built up. The Florida legislature corrected this abuse so that now when a contract is recorded, the seller has legal title and the buyer gets equitable title to the property. In case of default, the buyer's equitable rights must be foreclosed. The land is sold at auction, with the proceeds paying taxes first, then the contract's unpaid balance. Any excess belongs to the buyer.

Licensees should be extremely careful when dealing with properties to be sold under a contract for deed. Sometimes a developer's property has a blanket mortgage with no release provisions, so even if the buyer pays all cash for a home site, the developer cannot give an unencumbered deed. This is the reason the developer uses a contract for deed. Licensees violate the law if they sell property encumbered by a blanket mortgage that cannot be released for a payment less than the amount the buyer owes.

Many times, a seller wishes to avoid recording a contract for deed so there will be no cloud on the title if the seller cancels the contract and dispossesses the buyer. The buyer should insist that the contract be recorded. This allows homestead exemption for property taxes. More important, it gives constructive notice of the buyer's rights in the property so that judgments or other liens against the seller will be subordinate to the buyer's rights.

Sale and Leaseback

Many businesses use **sale and leaseback** financing to give the companies more leverage. Assume that Discount Linens, Inc., wants to open a new store in Clearwater. If the company owns the property, it may tie up as much as 20 percent of its equity capital. Instead, the company may prefer to build the store, then sell the property to an investor, such as an insurance company, then enter into a long-term lease (25 to 99 years is typical). Discount Linens, Inc. gets 100 percent or greater financing on the property. The company may deduct the entire amount of any lease payment for taxes, and no mortgage shows as a liability on the company's balance sheet, which helps improve financial ratios.

CONSUMER FINANCIAL PROTECTION BUREAU

The Consumer Financial Protection Bureau (CFPB) was created under the Dodd-Frank Wall Street Reform and Consumer Protection Act of 2010 and is the new "800-pound gorilla" regulator of consumer credit, banking, and mortgage lending. The official start date of the CFPB was July 21, 2011.

The agency is an independent unit located inside and funded by the United States Federal Reserve; it is affiliated with the U.S. Treasury Department. It writes and enforces bank rules, conducts bank examinations, monitors and reports on markets, and collects and tracks consumer complaints.

The CFPB consolidated employees and responsibilities from several federal regulatory bodies, including the Federal Reserve, the Federal Trade Commission, the Federal Deposit Insurance Corporation, and the Department of Housing and Urban Development. The agency inherited regulatory power over many credit statutes, including but not limited to the following:

- Equal Credit Opportunity Act
- Truth in Lending Act
- Real Estate Settlement Procedures Act
- Home Mortgage Disclosure Act
- S.A.F.E. Mortgage Licensing Act – Federal Registration of Residential Mortgage Loan Originators

- S.A.F.E. Mortgage Licensing Act – State Compliance and Bureau Registration System
- Land Registration (Federal Interstate Land Sales Disclosure Act)
- Fair Credit Reporting

WEB LINK

For more information, visit the Consumer Financial Protection Bureau Web site at **www.consumerfinance.gov/.**

Equal Credit Opportunity Act (ECOA)

The Equal Credit Opportunity Act (ECOA) prohibits discrimination in any aspect of a credit transaction based on any of the following:

- Race
- Color
- Religion
- Sex
- National origin
- Marital status
- Age (provided the applicant has the capacity to contract)
- Applicant's receipt of income derived from any public assistance program
- Applicant's exercise, in good faith, of any right under the Consumer Credit Protection Act, the umbrella statute that includes ECOA

WEB LINK

The Federal Trade Commission has more information about the ECOA at **http://www.consumer.ftc.gov/articles/0347-your-equal-credit-opportunity-rights.**

Truth-in-Lending Act and Regulation Z

The purpose of the Truth-in-Lending Act (also called the Consumer Credit Protection Act) and Regulation Z is to provide uniform disclosure of credit costs to help consumers better compare loan programs. Among other things, a truth-in-lending disclosure provides information the consumer can use to learn the true cost of credit, expressed as an **annual percentage rate (APR)**. (See Figure 12.5.)

The note interest rate, any points or origination costs, and most lender imposed fees, such as underwriting and processing fees, all are used in the APR formula. The law requires lenders to use a standardized formula and imposes penalties for errors. Any costs of obtaining a loan must be shown.

Some disclosures, however, may lead a consumer to make poor choices. For example, on a fixed-rate loan, the formula assumes that the borrower will hold the loan full term (30 years, 15 years, etc.). With an ARM, the assumption is that the interest rate the borrower pays will increase from the start rate to the index plus margin rate, then remain stable for the loan term. Unless these assumptions actually hold true, disclosures often understate the true APR. (See Figure 12.6.)

FIGURE 12.5 ■ Real Estate Licensees and the Truth-in-Lending Act

The Truth-in-Lending Act also applies to real estate licensees who advertise credit terms to be granted by an institutional lender. When a licensee advertises certain information, called "triggers," the licensee must disclose all the components of the financing.

For example, any of the following information in a real estate ad is a "trigger":

- The amount or percentage of the down payment ("5% down"; "$4,000 down")
- The amount or percentage of any payment ("payments $896.54 monthly")
- The number of payments or the period of repayment ("15- or 30-year mortgages available")
- The amount of any finance charges ("Less than $1,800 interest in year one")

Any "trigger" requires the licensee to disclose the following information:

- The amount or percentage of the down payment, which would normally show the purchase price, the down payment, and the amount financed
- The terms of repayment, which would normally show the payment amount and the number of payments required
- The annual percentage rate, using that term or the abbreviation "APR," taking into account the amount of the loan, the timing of the payments, the finance charge, and the note rate

Some statements about credit are too general to trigger additional disclosures. Examples of statements that are permitted include:

"No down payment"

"Easy terms"

"Biweekly payments"

The law also made bait-and-switch advertising a federal offense. For instance, if a builder advertises a seven percent APR loan, with the builder paying all closing costs, the builder must do as advertised.

Regulation Z applies to residential mortgage lending, not to commercial loans.

WEB LINK

The Office of the Comptroller of the Currency has more information about the Truth-in-Lending Act at: **http://www.occ.gov/publications/publications-by-type/comptrollers-handbook/index-comptrollers-handbook.html.**

FIGURE 12.6 ■ When the APR Disclosure Doesn't Tell the Whole Story

Harold is considering purchasing a home in Jacksonville. The interest rate quoted is 7 percent if he agrees to pay three points. Assuming no other costs, this makes the APR about 7⅜ percent. With no points, the loan interest rate is 7⅜ percent, also. When Harold asks Arthur, his transaction broker, whether he should pay the points, Arthur asks, "How long do you plan to live in the property?" Harold answers, "About three years."

Arthur sees that if Harold takes the 7 percent loan, he must amortize the 3 points over the period of ownership. This results in an additional 1 percent per year over the note rate (3 percent ÷ 3 years = 1 percent). Adding that to the note rate of 7 percent, the real APR, with the points, is 8 percent. Arthur suggests that Harold take the 7⅜ percent loan and pay no points.

REAL ESTATE SETTLEMENT PROCEDURES ACT

The Real Estate Settlement Procedures Act (RESPA) was designed to help consumers shop more effectively for settlement services and to eliminate kickbacks and referral fees that increase unnecessarily the costs of closing a loan transaction. A lender must follow RESPA guidelines when it makes a loan on a one to four-family residential property. This includes most purchase loans, assumptions, refinances, property improvement loans, and equity lines of credit. HUD's Office of Consumer and Regulatory Affairs, Interstate Land Sales/RESPA Division enforces the Act.

Disclosures at the time of loan application. When a borrower applies for a mortgage loan, the mortgage broker or lender must give the borrower the following:

- a special information booklet, called "Buying Your Home—Settlement Costs and Helpful Information," that contains consumer information regarding various real estate settlement services (required for purchase transactions only);
- a mortgage servicing disclosure statement, which discloses to the borrower whether the lender intends to service the loan or transfer it to another lender; and
- a good-faith estimate (GFE) of settlement costs, which lists the charges the buyer likely will pay at settlement. Beginning in 2010, the GFE was changed from two to three pages, and includes certain tolerances for accuracy. Some of the items on the "estimate" may not increase; others may not increase more than 10 percent. There is concern among many lenders that the new GFE is inferior to the one it replaced. Two very important items are missing from the form:
    - Only the principal and interest portion of the mortgage payment is shown, not the total monthly mortgage payment (including taxes and insurance).
    - Total settlement costs are shown, but not the total cash needed to close.

    Many lenders are filling in the gaps by giving borrowers a worksheet to provide the information. Interestingly, the worksheets are very similar to the old GFEs. A sample GFE is shown in Figure 12.7.

If the borrower doesn't receive these documents at the time of application for the mortgage, the lender must mail them within three business days of receiving the loan application. If the lender turns down the loan within three days, however, RESPA does not require the lender to provide these documents.

Disclosures before settlement (closing). An affiliated business arrangement (AFBA) disclosure is required whenever a settlement service provider involved in a RESPA-covered transaction refers the consumer to a provider in which the referring party has an ownership interest.

Disclosures at settlement. The HUD-1 Settlement Statement provides an accounting for the buyers' and sellers' funds at the closing of the transaction. A borrower may request to see the HUD-1 statement one day before the actual settlement. The settlement agent then must give the borrower a completed HUD-1 Settlement Statement based on information the agent has at that time. In 2010, an additional page was added to the HUD-1 comparing the actual settlement charges to the charges estimated by the lender on the GFE. A blank copy of the new HUD-1 is shown in Figure 13.4.

The Initial Escrow Statement itemizes the estimated taxes, insurance premiums, and other charges expected to be paid from the escrow account during a loan's first 12 months.

It lists the escrow payment amount and any required cushion. Although the statement usually is given at settlement, the lender has 45 days from settlement to deliver it.

Disclosures after settlement. Every year, loan servicers must deliver to borrowers an Annual Escrow Statement. The statement shows all escrow account payments during the year. A borrower is notified of any shortages or surpluses in the account and of action being taken to correct the situation.

A Servicing Transfer Statement is required if a loan servicer sells or assigns the servicing rights to a borrower's loan. Generally, the loan servicer must notify the borrower 15 days before the transfer's effective date. The notice must include the new servicer's name, address, and telephone numbers, as well as the date the borrower should begin making payments to the new servicer.

Limits on escrow accounts. RESPA prohibits a lender from charging excessive amounts for an escrow account. Each month, the lender may require the borrower to pay into the escrow account no more than $\frac{1}{12}$ of the total of all disbursements payable during the year, plus an amount necessary to cover any shortage in the account. In addition, the lender may require a reserve not to exceed an amount equal to $\frac{1}{6}$ of the total disbursements for the year.

The lender must perform an escrow account analysis once during the year and notify the borrower of any shortage. An excess of $50 or more must be returned to the borrower.

RESPA prohibitions. RESPA prohibits certain practices that increase the cost of settlement services. No person may give or accept anything of value **(kickback)** for referrals of settlement service business associated with a federally related mortgage loan. Neither may a person give or accept any part of a charge for services that are not performed. Real estate brokers may, under the law, accept referral fees from other real estate brokers. Homesellers may not require homebuyers to purchase title insurance from a particular company.

WEB LINK

The Department of Housing Development has more information about RESPA, including the statute, at: **http://www.hud.gov/offices/hsg/sfh/res/respa_hm.cfm.**

RESIDENTIAL LOAN UNDERWRITING

Initial Interview and Loan Application

A prospective buyer should shop carefully for the right lender. Rates are important, but the lender's reputation for good service also is critical. Once the lender has been chosen, the buyer should arrange to be approved for the loan.

A preapproval is not issued by the lender until the information provided by the applicant has been verified and the lender has reviewed the credit report. The lender will verify income by looking at W-2 forms or recent pay stubs and will check that the borrower has enough funds to close by reviewing bank statements.

Some licensees want the prospective buyer to be fully approved. That's a step further than preapproval. Not only have the income and funds available been verified, but the loan has been approved by one of the automated underwriting systems, such as Fannie Mae's *Desktop Underwriter*. This gives a seller the strongest evidence that a buyer is ready, willing, and *able* to close the transaction.

FIGURE 12.7 ■ Good Faith Estimate

OMB Approval No. 2502-0265

Good Faith Estimate (GFE)

Name of Originator Borrowers Friend Mortgage Company	Borrower John Borwer and Sandy Borwer, a married couple
Originator Address 3500 NE Parkway Miami, FL 33146	Property Address 1854 West Newhouse Court Miami, FL 33165
Originator Phone Number 305-555-9087	
Originator Email Sally.Linder@BorrowersFriendmortgage.com	Date of GFE February 18, 201_

Purpose

This GFE gives you an estimate of your settlement charges and loan terms if you are approved for this loan. For more information, see HUD's *Special Information Booklet* on settlement charges, your *Truth-in-Lending Disclosures,* and other consumer information at www.hud.gov/respa. If you decide you would like to proceed with this loan, contact us.

Shopping for your loan

Only you can shop for the best loan for you. Compare this GFE with other loan offers, so you can find the best loan. Use the shopping chart on page 3 to compare all the offers you receive.

Important dates

1. The interest rate for this GFE is available through March 18, 201_ at 4:00 pm. After this time, the interest rate, some of your loan Origination Charges, and the monthly payment shown below can change until you lock your interest rate.
2. This estimate for all other settlement charges is available through March 18, 201_
3. After you lock your interest rate, you must go to settlement within 30 days (your rate lock period) to receive the locked interest rate.
4. You must lock the interest rate at least 15 days before settlement.

Summary of your loan

Your initial loan amount is	$ 200,000.00
Your loan term is	30 years
Your initial interest rate is	4.5 %
Your initial monthly amount owed for principal, interest, and any mortgage insurance is	$ 1,013.37 per month
Can your interest rate rise?	☒ No ☐ Yes, it can rise to a maximum of %. The first change will be in
Even if you make payments on time, can your loan balance rise?	☒ No ☐ Yes, it can rise to a maximum of $
Even if you make payments on time, can your monthly amount owed for principal, interest, and any mortgage insurance rise?	☒ No ☐ Yes, the first increase can be in and the monthly amount owed can rise to $. The maximum it can ever rise to is $.
Does your loan have a prepayment penalty?	☒ No ☐ Yes, your maximum prepayment penalty is $.
Does your loan have a balloon payment?	☒ No ☐ Yes, you have a balloon payment of $ due in years.

Escrow account information

Some lenders require an escrow account to hold funds for paying property taxes or other property-related charges in addition to your monthly amount owed of $ 1,013.37 .
Do we require you to have an escrow account for your loan?
☐ No, you do not have an escrow account. You must pay these charges directly when due.
☒ Yes, you have an escrow account. It may or may not cover all of these charges. Ask us.

Summary of your settlement charges

A	Your Adjusted Origination Charges (See page 2.)	$2,160.00
B	Your Charges for All Other Settlement Services (See page 2.)	$4,722.86
A + B	Total Estimated Settlement Charges	$ 6,882.86

FIGURE 12.7 ■ Good Faith Estimate (continued)

Understanding your estimated settlement charges

Your Adjusted Origination Charges

1. **Our origination charge** This charge is for getting this loan for you.	$2,000.00
2. **Your credit or charge (points) for the specific interest rate chosen** ☐ The credit or charge for the interest rate of [ ] % is included in "Our origination charge." (See item 1 above.) ☐ You receive a credit of $ [ ] for this interest rate of [ ] %. This credit **reduces** your settlement charges. ☒ You pay a charge of $ [2,000.00] for this interest rate of [4.5] %. This charge (points) **increases** your total settlement charges. The tradeoff table on page 3 shows that you can change your total settlement charges by choosing a different interest rate for this loan.	$2,000.00
A Your Adjusted Origination Charges	$ 4,000.00

Some of these charges can change at settlement. See the top of page 3 for more information.

Your Charges for All Other Settlement Services

3. **Required services that we select** These charges are for services we require to complete your settlement. We will choose the providers of these services. *Service* — *Charge* Appraisal/Credit Report — POC/$55.00 Amortization Schedule — $25.00 Courier Fee — $20.00	$100.00
4. **Title services and lender's title insurance** This charge includes the services of a title or settlement agent, for example, and title insurance to protect the lender, if required.	$700.00
5. **Owner's title insurance** You may purchase an owner's title insurance policy to protect your interest in the property.	$850.00
6. **Required services that you can shop for** These charges are for other services that are required to complete your settlement. We can identify providers of these services or you can shop for them yourself. Our estimates for providing these services are below. *Service* — *Charge* Survey — 350	$350.00
7. **Government recording charges** These charges are for state and local fees to record your loan and title documents.	$52.50
8. **Transfer taxes** These charges are for state and local fees on mortgages and home sales.	$1,100.00
9. **Initial deposit for your escrow account** This charge is held in an escrow account to pay future recurring charges on your property and includes ☒ all property taxes, ☒ all insurance, and ☐ other [Mortgage Insuran].	$2,630.00
10. **Daily interest charges** This charge is for the daily interest on your loan from the day of your settlement until the first day of the next month or the first day of your normal mortgage payment cycle. This amount is $ [24.66] per day for [17] days (if your settlement is [5/15/201_]).	$419.18
11. **Homeowner's insurance** This charge is for the insurance you must buy for the property to protect from a loss, such as fire. *Policy* — *Charge* Insurses-all, Inc. — $2,050.00	$2,050.00
B Your Charges for All Other Settlement Services	$ 8,251.68
A + B Total Estimated Settlement Charges	$ 12,251.68

Good Faith Estimate (HUD-GFE) 2

FIGURE 12.7 ■ Good Faith Estimate (continued)

Instructions

Understanding which charges can change at settlement

This GFE estimates your settlement charges. At your settlement, you will receive a HUD-1, a form that lists your actual costs. Compare the charges on the HUD-1 with the charges on this GFE. Charges can change if you select your own provider and do not use the companies we identify. (See below for details.)

These charges **cannot increase** at settlement:	The total of these charges **can increase up to 10%** at settlement:	These charges **can change** at settlement:
▪ Our origination charge ▪ Your credit or charge (points) for the specific interest rate chosen *(after you lock in your interest rate)* ▪ Your adjusted origination charges *(after you lock in your interest rate)* ▪ Transfer taxes	▪ Required services that we select ▪ Title services and lender's title insurance *(if we select them or you use companies we identify)* ▪ Owner's title insurance *(if you use companies we identify)* ▪ Required services that you can shop for *(if you use companies we identify)* ▪ Government recording charges	▪ Required services that you can shop for (if you do not use companies we identify) ▪ Title services and lender's title insurance (if you do not use companies we identify) ▪ Owner's title insurance (if you do not use companies we identify) ▪ Initial deposit for your escrow account ▪ Daily interest charges ▪ Homeowner's insurance

Using the tradeoff table

In this GFE, we offered you this loan with a particular interest rate and estimated settlement charges. However:

- If you want to choose this same loan with **lower settlement charges,** then you will have a **higher interest rate.**
- If you want to choose this same loan with a **lower interest rate,** then you will have **higher settlement charges.**

If you would like to choose an available option, you must ask us for a new GFE.

Loan originators have the option to complete this table. Please ask for additional information if the table is not completed.

	The loan in this GFE	The same loan with lower settlement charges	The same loan with a lower interest rate
Your initial loan amount	$ 200,000.00	$ 200,000.00	$ 200,000.00
Your initial interest rate [1]	4.5 %	5 %	5.5 %
Your initial monthly amount owed	$ 1,013.37	$ 1,073.64	$ 1,135.58
Change in the monthly amount owed from this GFE	No change	You will pay $ 60.27 **more** every month	You will pay $ 122.21 **less** every month
Change in the amount you will pay at settlement with this interest rate	No change	Your settlement charges will be **reduced** by $ 2,000.00	Your settlement charges will **increase** by $ 4,000.00
How much your total estimated settlement charges will be	$ 12,251.68	$ 10,251.68	$ 8,251.68

[1]For an adjustable rate loan, the comparisons above are for the initial interest rate before adjustments are made.

Using the shopping chart

Use this chart to compare GFEs from different loan originators. Fill in the information by using a different column for each GFE you receive. By comparing loan offers, you can shop for the best loan.

	This loan	Loan 2	Loan 3	Loan 4
Loan originator name	Brwrs Friend M			
Initial loan amount	$200,000.00			
Loan term	30 Years			
Initial interest rate	4.5%			
Initial monthly amount owed	$1,013.37			
Rate lock period	30 Days			
Can interest rate rise?	No			
Can loan balance rise?	No			
Can monthly amount owed rise?	No			
Prepayment penalty?	No			
Balloon payment?	No			
Total Estimated Settlement Charges	$12,251.68			

If your loan is sold in the future

Some lenders may sell your loan after settlement. Any fees lenders receive in the future cannot change the loan you receive or the charges you paid at settlement.

When the buyer contracts to buy a home, the next step is to apply for the mortgage. Figure 12.8 shows a list of items the buyer should bring to the application appointment. The licensee may want to provide such a list as part of the sale package.

Real estate loan processing begins when the lender completes a standardized loan application form based on information the buyer provides. All loan applications are designed to show a borrower's financial ability to meet a loan agreement's basic obligations.

Credit history. When the loan application is complete, the loan processor requests the borrower's credit report from a credit-reporting service. The credit report shows the borrower's willingness to pay debt on time, and the lender reviews it carefully.

The credit report is prepared after a thorough check with the creditors indicated on the loan application. The public records are researched for judgments or lawsuits pending against the applicant. When the investigation is completed, the credit search company sends the loan processor a confidential report of its findings.

This report usually states the applicant's age, address and status as a tenant or an owner, the length of residency at the current address, a brief employment history, and a credit profile, both past and present.

The credit profile itemizes the status of current and past accounts, usually identified by industry, such as banks, department and specialty stores, and finance companies. In addition, it shows the quality and dates of the payments made and their regularity or delinquency, as well as any outstanding balances. This payment history is the most important part of the entire report because it reveals how well the applicant has managed debt over time. Loan processors know that a person's history in meeting financial obligations likely forecasts future behavior. As a result, the lender pays strict attention to the credit report's last section, which shows the applicant's attitude toward debt and payment pattern.

Many credit reports now show a credit score. **Credit scoring** uses statistical samples to predict how likely it is that a borrower will pay back a loan. To develop a model, the lender selects a large random sample of its borrowers, analyzing characteristics that relate to creditworthiness. Each of the characteristics is assigned a weight based on how strong a predictor it is. Credit scores treat each person objectively because the same standards apply to everyone. Credit scores are blind to demographic or cultural differences among people.

The most commonly used credit score today is known as a "FICO" score, named after the company that developed it, Fair, Isaac & Co. FICO scores range from 500 to 850. The lower the score, the greater the risk of default. A person with a FICO score of 725, for example, should be able to get a mortgage at a much lower interest rate than a person who has a score of 510. The FICO Web site calculator shows the individual could save more than $75,000 in interest over 30 years on a $100,000 loan.

According to FICO, a person's credit score uses the following factors:

- 35 percent of the score is determined by *payment histories* on credit accounts, with recent history weighted a bit more heavily than the distant past;
- 30 percent is based upon the amount of *debt outstanding* with all creditors;
- 15 percent is produced on the basis of *how long the borrower has been a credit user* (a longer history is better if there have always been timely payments);
- 10 percent is composed of very *recent history* and whether or not the borrower has been actively seeking (and getting) loans or credit lines in the past months;
- 10 percent is calculated from the *mix of credit held*, including the *amount of new credit* the borrower has taken on. This factor reviews the number of accounts, the length of

FIGURE 12.8 ■ Items to Bring to a Mortgage Application Appointment

When You Apply for Your Mortgage . . .
by John W. Simmons, Broker

Thanks for using our real estate firm to find your new home. To help you apply for your mortgage loan, we have prepared this list of items the lender needs.

Name of mortgage lender ________________________________ Phone ____________
Address____
Date of application_________ Time________ Loan officer ____________________

Bring your sales contract, with all addendums, and a receipt for your deposit if it is not included on the contract as well as the following personal information:

1. **Addresses** for the past two years, along with names and addresses of landlords or financial institutions to which you made your housing payments
2. **Employers** for the past two years complete with addresses
3. **Bank accounts**—names and addresses and account numbers
4. **Shares of stock owned**—company names, number of shares, and value
5. **Life insurance**—face value, beneficiaries, and cash surrender value
6. **Real estate** owned—property address, market values, outstanding mortgage balances (if any) and mortgage company names, addresses, and account numbers
7. If you have **sold a home** in the previous two years, a copy of the closing statement and a copy of the recorded deed
8. **Automobiles**—makes, models, present values, amounts owed and lender names, addresses, and account numbers
9. **Household furniture and personal items,** including an estimate of their replacement value
10. **Other valuable assets or retirement accounts**
11. **Current liabilities**—creditor names, addresses and account numbers, monthly payments, and present balances
12. **Bank cards**—names and addresses of issuing banks, account numbers, monthly payments, and present balances
13. **Child care** expense amount
14. **Child support payments or alimony**—amount and duration
15. **Insurance payments**—amounts for hospital, car, and life
16. **Social Security numbers** of all borrowers
17. **Commissions or bonuses,** including the previous two years' tax returns, along with W-2 or 1099 forms
18. **Self-employed** profit and loss statements, balance sheets, and tax returns for the previous three years
19. **VA loan applicants** need either Form DD-214 *or* a Certificate of Eligibility
20. **Checkbook** to pay for the application fee, appraisal, and credit report. This amount varies based on the type of loan
21. **Pay stubs** for the previous 30 days and W-2 forms for the past two years
22. **Canceled rent checks** for the previous 12 months, if you rent
23. **Final divorce settlement,** if divorced
24. **Sale agreement** on your current home, if you are selling
25. **Current mortgage information,** if you have a mortgage

I appreciate the opportunity to be of assistance in this transaction.

____ Phone ____________
John W. Simmons, Broker

the accounts, recent requests for credit report, and the length of time since the credit request was made by potential buyers. Note that if people check their scores by going directly to the credit reporting agency, it will not affect the score.

How to increase a personal credit score. Increasing one's personal credit score is a long-term process. Some of the most important steps to a better credit score include:

- Pay bills on time. Late payments and collections can have a serious impact on the FICO score.
- Do not apply for credit frequently. Having a large number of inquiries shown on your credit report can lower the score.
- Reduce credit-card balances. Persons who are "maxed out" will find their scores decline.
- Be certain to obtain enough credit to establish a credit history. Not having sufficient credit can negatively impact the score.

Freddie Mac has found that borrowers with credit scores above 660 are likely to repay the mortgage, and underwriters can do a basic review of the file for completeness. For applicants with scores between 620 and 660, the underwriter is required to do a comprehensive review. A very cautious review would be made for persons with credit scores below 620, who would probably end up paying higher interest rates.

Verifying and analyzing the income. The loan analyst evaluates the quality of the applicant's income. The applicant's employer is asked for an opinion of job stability and possible advancement. Applicants whose employment records show frequent shifts in job situations that result in upward mobility each time are given full consideration. Lenders are, however, wary of applicants who drift from one job classification to another and cannot seem to establish themselves in any specific type of work.

After the deposit and employment verifications are returned with acceptable information and a favorable credit report is obtained, the lending officer evaluates thoroughly the data collected before continuing with the loan process.

Not only is the regular salary of a family's primary wage earner basic to the analysis, but a spouse's full income usually is accepted. Extra sources of income also may be included in the analysis if circumstances warrant it. Bonuses are accepted as income only if they are received regularly. If commissions are a large part of an applicant's income base, the applicant's earnings history is evaluated as to the stability of this income as a regular source for an extended time. Overtime wages are not included in the analysis unless they have been and are expected to be earned consistently. Pensions, interest, and dividends are treated as full income.

A second job is accepted as part of the regular monthly income if it can be established that the job has existed for at least two years and is likely to continue. Child support income also can be included in monthly income, but only if it is the result of a court order and has a proven track record. Government entitlement funds also are considered.

Income/expense ratios. Ratios conventional lenders use depend on the amount of the buyer's equity and credit score. The two primary guidelines are the **housing expense ratio** and the **total obligations ratio**. The formulas for determining both follow:

Housing expense ratio = Monthly housing expenses ÷ Monthly gross income
Total obligations ratio = Total monthly obligations ÷ Monthly gross income

For example, assume John and Jill are purchasing a new home with monthly PITI payments of $1,200. They have other obligations of $420. Their combined income is $4,600 per month. What are their ratios?

Housing expense ratio:	$1,200 ÷ $4,600 = 26%
Total obligations ratio:	$1,620 ÷ $4,600 = 35.2%

For conventional loans, the suggested ratios are 28 percent of gross income for housing expenses and 36 percent of gross income for total obligations. FHA loans allow a 31 percent housing expense ratio and a 43 percent total obligations ratio. The VA requires a 41 percent total obligations ratio and subtracts the obligations from the gross income. The remainder must exceed the requirement the VA publishes in the Table of Residual Incomes. These ratios are general guidelines, and circumstances may allow somewhat higher ratios for individual borrowers.

Property Analysis

The lender on a residential loan looks primarily to the borrower's income and willingness to pay. Real estate lenders know, however, that life is filled with events beyond a person's control. Death can take away a family's primary source of income abruptly. Poor economic conditions can have serious financial impact. Mistakes in personal or business decisions can result in bankruptcies, damaging or destroying credit in the process. To reduce the risk of loss from these uncertainties, real estate lenders look to the value of the collateral as the basic underlying assurance for recovery of their investments in default situations. An appraisal, a title examination, and a survey help lenders make that evaluation.

Appraisal. A lender uses the value of property pledged for collateral to set the mortgage loan amount. A borrower's cash equity in a property has a direct bearing on the soundness of the loan. A borrower who makes a large down payment is less likely to have a mortgage default than a borrower who has a small amount at risk. As the loan-to-value ratio increases, so does the lender's risk. If a lender agrees to lend 95 percent of a property's value, the lender wants to be certain of two things—first, that the market value is correct, and second, that the borrower has five percent equity in the property. Consequently, the lender will agree to lend 95 percent of the value estimated in a certified appraisal *or* 95 percent of the sale price, whichever is less.

Title examination. The assurance of good title is as essential to a loan's approval as are the borrower's credit and the collateral's value. After a preliminary evaluation of the borrower's application, the loan processor orders a title report on the property. A title report consists of three components: a survey (as discussed below), a physical inspection of the property, and a search of the public records.

In Florida, institutional lenders normally require the borrower to pay for a title insurance policy, often called an ALTA (American Land Title Association) policy. ALTA policies are issued for the loan amount and cover many unusual risks, including forgeries, incompetency of parties, legal status of parties, and surveying errors. Special endorsements to the policy cover additional risks such as protection against any unrecorded easements or liens, rights of parties in possession of the subject property, mining claims, water rights, and other negotiated special items pertinent to the property involved.

Survey. As part of title work, lenders require property surveys. Although many properties are part of subdivisions engineered and described by licensed and registered surveyors and engineers, some owners have enlarged their homes or made additions to the improvements since the original surveys. These might violate setback restrictions in the local zoning laws. Some properties have been subdivided, while others now have encroachment problems.

Problems in a survey cause a cloud on the title. The loan processing stops until this cloud is cleared to the lender's satisfaction. Such a cloud could be an unsatisfied construction lien, an income tax lien, a property tax lien, an easement infraction, an encroachment, or a zoning violation. Sometimes, a seller's name is not correct on the deed, an error exists in the legal description, or the deed has a faulty acknowledgment or lacks the appropriate signatures. Because of the complexities in a real estate transaction, there are many possibilities for faults to appear in a title search and property survey.

Loan Analysis

The loan-to-value ratio is a measure of a loan's riskiness. As the ratio increases toward 100 percent, the lender's risk increases substantially. The loan-to-value ratio is calculated by dividing the loan amount by the property's value.

Interest rate and discount points. When the lender gives a prospective borrower a rate quote, the borrower is often undecided about whether to pay discount points. Discount points can be considered prepaid interest that will reduce the interest rate on the note. In effect, a borrower has a "menu" of interest rates based on the amount paid as discount points. Figure 12.9 shows a sample market quote for a 30-year fixed-rate loan. Fluctuations in the market cause differences from day to day in the differential of discount points and yield.

From the example, it's obvious that a person who intended to occupy the property for three years should avoid paying points because it would take almost six years to break even. In some cases, a borrower should ask the lender to raise the interest rate, not only to avoid discount points but also to avoid paying an origination fee.

If a person expected to remain in the property for the full 30-year period, and would not be refinancing or making an early loan payoff, the savings could be worth paying points. At line five, for instance, the borrower breaks even at 69 months. The difference in payments of $33.23 for the remaining 291 months would total $9,670, well worth paying the points.

Of course, the better way to analyze points is by considering the time value of money. Using the 5.5% rate on line five, the borrower pays $2,300 in *today's* dollars (that could be invested to return some interest), to get a savings sometime in the *future*. A financial calculator approach shows a longer payback period:

Financial Calculator Keystrokes to Find Payback Period for $2,300 Points with a 6% Yield

%I	PMT	PV	FV	Solve for: N
.5	33.23	2,300	0	86 months

Where:

%I	=	*monthly* market interest rate 6% ÷ 12 months = .5
PMT	=	savings per monthly payment
PV	=	dollars paid in points
FV	=	input zero for this problem

Solve for:

N	=	number of months to pay back points

FIGURE 12.9 ■ Comparison of Rates and Discount Points

Based on a $100,000 30-year Fixed-Rate Mortgage

A. Interest Rate	B. Discount Points	C. Principal and Interest Payment	D. Payment Difference from 6% Rate	E. Amount Paid in Discount Points	F. Months at Lower Rate for Points Payback (E ÷ D)
1. 6.000	0	$599.55	--	$0.00	0
2. 5.875	0.5	$591.54	$8.01	$500	62.4
3. 5.750	1.2	$583.57	$15.98	$1,200	75.1
4. 5.625	1.7	$575.66	$23.89	$1,700	71.2
5. 5.500	2.3	$567.79	$31.76	$2,300	72.4

Loan term. Shorter loan terms generally result in lower interest rates because lenders have less risk from inflation. For instance, the interest rate on a 15-year loan is often quoted ½ of 1 percent lower than that of a 30-year loan.

Availability of mortgage insurance. Bank regulation generally prohibits lenders from making loans where they are at risk for more than 80 percent of a property's value. If a borrower wants a loan greater than 80 percent of value, the borrower must qualify for mortgage insurance (or a VA guarantee). The mortgage insurer's acceptance of the borrower is a critical step in the loan process. FHA insurance requires an up-front premium plus a monthly premium. In recent years, private mortgage insurance usually charges an annual premium, paid monthly.

Loan fees and calculations. APR calculations use points or origination costs and most lender-imposed fees, such as underwriting and processing fees. Chapter 13 describes many closing costs charged on a new loan.

Underwriting decision and loan commitment. A lender may make a **conditional commitment** to a borrower so that the closing process can continue without delay. For example, a conditional commitment might be subject to the borrower's employment or credit verification being returned without any surprises or to the requirement that the appraisal equal at least the purchase price.

A **firm commitment** is issued by a lender that, having received everything necessary to evaluate the loan, contracts to fund the loan. No other information is required from the borrower.

Automated underwriting. The computer is revolutionizing the lending industry. One of the most important steps to help speed the loan process and reduce costs is **automated underwriting**. For instance, Fannie Mae's *Desktop Underwriter* offers streamlined documentation and verification requirements and an enhanced automated system to assess property value. This allows lenders to give borrowers credit and appraisal decisions at the time of application. The software quickly evaluates credit risks and suggests ways that the process can go more smoothly.

For example, if a borrower wanting an 80 percent loan presents employment information and a W-2 form, the software pulls up the credit report immediately. If the credit score is high, it offers an immediate appraisal using data generated by thousands of Fannie Mae appraisal reports in the files. An exterior property inspection may be all that is necessary, avoiding the need for a full appraisal report. This saves the consumer money and reduces delays. The software also suggests more suitable loan programs based on the applicant's financial data.

A good loan officer can "tweak" (not misrepresent) the figures. For example, if a person is too high on the debt ratio and has applied for a 15-year fixed mortgage, the automated underwriting system may not give an approval. Tweaking the loan, such as setting a payment based on a 20-year loan term, may result in an approval when the loan officer submits it to the computer a second time. If it doesn't work, the loan officer may try a 25-year loan term and resubmit.

Underwriting loans currently is much different than in the 1990s. Then the automated underwriting systems worked out all the debt ratios and told the underwriter what to verify. No more. Today, if the system says the borrower needs three months of bank statements, two recent pay stubs, and last year's tax return, all the underwriter has to do is check to see that they are in the file.

Once *Desktop Underwriter* has evaluated the risk and approves the loan, Fannie Mae must purchase the loan.

SUMMARY OF IMPORTANT POINTS

- The note is a promise to repay the amount borrowed, while the mortgage is security for the note.
- If the note is not paid, the creditor may file suit to have the property sold to pay the debt.
- The most important types of mortgages are FHA-insured, VA-guaranteed, and conventional.
- FHA and VA loans have lower qualifying ratios, making such loans more readily available to consumers.
- Term mortgages require a borrower to pay interest only, with the principal due at the end of the loan term.
- Partially amortized mortgages require a balloon payment at the end of the term, while fully amortized mortgages have equal level payments for the life of the loan.
- An adjustable-rate mortgage (ARM) has a variable interest rate based on an index. A lender's margin is added to the index to determine the rate of interest charged to the borrower. The rate changes when the index changes, but annual caps restrict the amount of annual change allowed.
- Traditional fixed-rate mortgages have the same payment for the entire term of the loan.
- A purchase-money mortgage is seller financing.
- A blanket mortgage covers more than one property parcel.
- A reverse annuity mortgage is one in which the lender makes a payment to elderly homeowners based on their equity in the property.
- The Equal Credit Opportunity Act prohibits lender discrimination.
- The Consumer Financial Protection Bureau (CFPB) is the primary regulator of consumer credit, banking, and mortgage lending.

- The Truth in Lending Act requires lenders to disclose to the consumer the effective annual percentage rate of interest.
- The Real Estate Settlement Procedures Act protects consumers by requiring lenders to fully disclose the costs of closing a transaction.
- The borrower's income shows the ability to pay and the credit report shows the borrower's attitude toward paying debt on time.
- After qualifying the borrower, the lender will qualify the property: An appraisal determines that the property value is adequate; a title report ensures that the mortgage lien is safe; and a survey ensures that there are no encroachments or easements that will affect the lien.

REVIEW QUESTIONS

1. A bank makes a loan to a borrower, who signs a note, thanks the loan officer, and leaves with the money. The bank has made a(n)
   a. mistake.
   b. secured loan.
   c. unsecured loan.
   d. mortgage loan.

2. A borrower stopped making payments on his mortgage six months ago. What clause in the mortgage allows the lender to call the entire amount due to prepare for foreclosure?
   a. Due-on-sale
   b. Exculpatory
   c. Acceleration
   d. Penalty

3. What does RESPA NOT require to be furnished to the borrower by the lender at the time of loan application (or within three days of the loan application)?
   a. The annual percentage rate of effective interest on the loan
   b. A good-faith estimate of settlement costs
   c. A special information booklet called "Settlement Costs and You"
   d. A Mortgage Servicing Disclosure statement

4. A title insurance company offers to pay a real estate sales associate $50 for each RESPA closing referred to the company. This is
   a. legal if the buyer approves.
   b. illegal under Regulation Z of the Truth in Lending Act.
   c. prohibited under RESPA requirements.
   d. legal under the Florida legislation allowing such payments.

5. A homebuyer is shopping for a new $200,000 mortgage. He expects to live in his new home for about four years. He can get a 30-year, 6.25 percent fixed-rate mortgage with principal and interest payments of $1,231.43 with no points. He can also get a 5.875 percent mortgage loan (payments of $1,183.08) with three points. How many months will it take the homebuyer to break even on the points if he takes the lower interest rate loan, using simple arithmetic?
   a. 60
   b. 100
   c. 124
   d. 127

6. A person wishes to buy a home priced at $100,000 with an FHA mortgage. His closing costs are $2,000. The loan limit in his area is $154,896. What is his down payment?
   a. $2,290
   b. $3,337.50
   c. $3,600
   d. $4,600

7. Many lenders can approve FHA loans without submitting the applications to the FHA for review. This quick process is called
   a. automated underwriting.
   b. CRV.
   c. conditional underwriting.
   d. direct endorsement.

8. A lender probably would make a VA loan for more than $417,000 to a qualified veteran if the veteran
   a. has good credit.
   b. served in the Persian Gulf war.
   c. used his DD-214 to apply for a higher entitlement.
   d. paid 25 percent of the amount exceeding $417,000 as a down payment.

9. A buyer is purchasing a $425,000 home with an 80 percent mortgage. The monthly loan constant from a mortgage payment table at 6.25 percent for 30 years is 0.00616. The monthly payment of principal and interest will be
   a. $1,856.71.
   b. $1,967.54.
   c. $2,094.40.
   d. $2,616.80.

10. A loan designed to have negative amortization is what type of mortgage?
    a. Adjustable-rate
    b. Partially amortized
    c. Graduated payment
    d. Blanket

11. An owner's home is appraised at $145,000. Value for ad valorem taxes is $135,000. His existing FHA mortgage has a balance of $64,315. He applies for a home equity loan, and the lender explains that the maximum loan-to-value ratio for all loans is 80 percent. How much can he borrow?
    a. $43,685
    b. $51,685
    c. $64,548
    d. $108,000

12. A woman purchased property under a contract for deed. When she signed the papers with the seller, the document was not witnessed or notarized. When she later tried to record, the contract was rejected because it had not been acknowledged. What is her financial exposure?
    a. She can't get homestead exemption.
    b. The seller could resell the property to another person, and she would lose the property.
    c. Any judgment liens recorded against the seller also would encumber her property.
    d. All of the above

13. How does a retail chain store benefit from a sale-leaseback transaction?
    a. Its financial ratios are improved because no mortgage is listed in the liabilities section.
    b. It can deduct the full lease payment for federal income tax purposes.
    c. It can cash out, getting 100 percent (or more) of the property's value.
    d. All of the above

14. A man is moving to Miami, but expects to be transferred by his company in three years. When applying for a $200,000, 30-year mortgage on his new home, he is given an option by the lender for a 6% loan with no points or 5.875% with two points. Which statement is TRUE?
    a. He should pay the points and take the lower rate.
    b. He should not pay points and should take the 6% rate.
    c. He should pay the points, but take a 15-year mortgage.
    d. He should seek another lender who has a fixed plan without such options.

15. Which statement is TRUE of RESPA loan transactions?
    a. The lender has five days to give a good-faith estimate of settlement costs.
    b. The lender must provide the HUD-1 form within one day after the loan application.
    c. The lender must deliver to the borrower an annual escrow statement at least once per year.
    d. The lender may not transfer the loan to another servicer.

16. A borrower with a very high credit score MOST likely will
    a. be required to make at least a 20 percent down payment.
    b. get the best credit terms and the fastest loan processing.
    c. be turned down for the loan.
    d. encounter financial trouble.

17. A homebuyer applies for a loan that requires monthly PITI payments of $800. His income is $3,000, and he has other obligations of $400. He applies for a conventional loan that will be sold to Fannie Mae. Based on this information, he
    a. probably will be turned down; his housing expense ratio is too high.
    b. probably will be turned down; his total obligations ratio is too high.
    c. probably will be turned down; both ratios are too high.
    d. qualifies for the loan.

18. Which statement is TRUE of loan risk and underwriting?
    a. Risk decreases as the loan-to-value ratio increases.
    b. A 50 percent loan is risky for the lender.
    c. A lender will lend the greater of the purchase price or the appraised value.
    d. None of the above is true.

19. Fannie Mae's current yield requirement is 6 percent. A homebuyer wants to get a 5¾ percent loan. How can she do it?
    a. Have at least a B+ credit rating
    b. Pay one discount point
    c. Pay two discount points
    d. Pay four discount points

20. Fannie Mae must purchase a mortgage from a lender if the
    a. mortgage has been accepted for private mortgage insurance.
    b. lender issued a firm commitment to the borrower.
    c. lender uses Fannie Mae's *Desktop Underwriter*, which shows that the loan meets Fannie Mae's requirements.
    d. borrower is disabled.

CHAPTER 13

CLOSING REAL ESTATE TRANSACTIONS

KEY TERMS

365-day method
30-day month method
composite closing statement
documentary stamp taxes
good-faith estimate
HUD-1 Settlement Statement
intangible taxes

OVERVIEW

The closing of a real estate transaction is the final step in the process of title transfer that began when the contract for purchase and sale was written. A broker often finds that a checklist helps organize the many details required for a smooth closing. While the title closing agent handles many of the closing duties, including the preparation of closing statements, the broker must ensure that the statements conform to the agreement between the seller, the buyer, and the buyer's lender.

The HUD-1 Settlement Statement must be used for mortgage loans covered by the Real Estate Settlement Procedures Act. This chapter describes the closing process and helps the broker understand prorations and the HUD-1 Settlement Statement.

Once you have completed this chapter, you should be able to:

- describe the tasks the broker must complete that lead to a successful closing;
- explain the major objectives of a preclosing inspection;
- list the three disclosures that a lender should make at the time of loan application;
- describe the major sections of the HUD-1 Settlement Statement;
- describe the process used in prorating taxes, homeowners' association dues, and prepaid rents; and
- prepare a HUD-1 Settlement Statement.

FIGURE 13.1 ■ Property Sale Information Sheet

Property Address: ______________________________

Seller: ______________________ Buyer: ______________________
Contract Date: ______________________ Closing Date (Est.): ______________________

SELLER	**BUYER**
Listing Broker: ______________	**Selling Broker:** ______________
Phone: __________ Fax: __________	Phone: __________ Fax: __________
Listing sales associate: ______________	Selling sales associate: ______________
Home Ph.: __________ Office Ph.: __________	Home Ph.: __________ Office Ph.: __________
Mobile Ph.: ______________	Mobile Ph.: ______________
Seller: ______________	**Buyer:** ______________
Old address: ______________	Present address: ______________
New address: ______________	City, State, Zip ______________
City, State, Zip ______________	Current Home Ph. __________ Ofc.: __________
Current Home Ph.: __________ Ofc.: __________	Will buyer occupy new home? ______
Existing mortgage for Payoff (P)	New Mortgage Lender: ______________
Assumption (A)	Type (Fixed; ARM: FHA, VA, Conv.): ______________
1st Mortgage holder: ______________	LTV Ratio: ________% Interest Rate: __% Yrs: ______
2nd Mortgage holder: ______________	
Seller's Attorney: ______________	Buyer's Attorney: ______________
Ph.: ______________	Ph.: ______________

Lender: ______________________ **Loan Officer:** ______________________

Title Company: ______________________ **Closing Agent:** ______________________

Appraiser: ______________________

Date Scheduled to Close: ______________________

Service Providers:

Pest inspection: ______________ Ph.: ______________
Home inspection: ______________ Ph.: ______________
Roof inspection: ______________ Ph.: ______________
Contractor: ______________ Ph.: ______________
Surveyor: ______________ Ph.: ______________

Buyer's Insurance Company: ______________________________

Agent: ______________________ Phone: ______________________

Property status: ❑ Occupied by seller ❑ Occupied by tenant ❑ Vacant

Key to property for inspection: ❑ At listing office ❑ In lockbox at property ❑ Call seller for appointment

THE BROKER'S ROLE IN CLOSING

Buyers and sellers expect their sales associates to professionally monitor and coordinate all details of their closings. Most lenders and title closing agents prepare documents very carefully, but a licensee must review the documents to ensure that they are correct. A transaction that goes smoothly from contract to closing reflects well on the firm as well as the sales associate. It is likely to result in additional business for the licensee.

PRELIMINARY STEPS TO A CLOSING

A real estate licensee's duties include skill, care, and diligence in every aspect of a real estate transaction—including the closing. The best way to organize the work flow for an efficient closing is to use a written plan. Checklists can be a key component of this plan. Figure 13.1 provides a handy reference form that lists information about the buyer, seller, cooperating broker, and lender, as well as other service providers.

Another form that helps organize the closing is the closing progress chart shown in Figure 13.2. Blanks are provided for each side of the transaction (listing and selling) to establish each agent's responsibilities. A discussion of these responsibilities follows.

Notice of "under contract" to MLS. A duty of the listing agent, this notice alerts all parties that a contract is pending.

Binder deposited in bank. FREC rules require that the buyer's good-faith deposit be placed in the bank no later than three business days after receipt of the funds.

Deliver required condominium documents (if the subject property is a condominium resale). Because the buyer has a three day right to cancel after receiving all the documents, these should be given to the buyer as soon as possible after the contract is signed. The buyer should sign a receipt for the condominium documents so the time will begin to run.

Additional deposit received, if required. If the contract requires the buyer to give additional funds as a good-faith deposit, the licensee must ensure that the funds are received and deposited as required.

Loan application made by buyer. The buyer's failure to comply with the contract terms is a default, and the seller must be notified. Both the listing and selling licensees should monitor compliance.

Contingencies cleared in writing. The licensee must ensure that action is taken to clear the contingencies as soon as possible. Some normal contingencies include a home inspection, a soil test, a roof inspection, and financing.

Appraisal. The licensee must be certain that the appraiser has access to the property.

Loan approval. Most contracts require a loan commitment within a specified number of days from the contract date. The licensee must provide any information or documents the lender requests.

Title insurance ordered by lender or sales associate. Usually the party paying for the title insurance chooses the title closing agent from the lender's approved list. Many title companies prefer to begin title work even before loan approval is obtained, but the licensee should ensure that there will be no charge if the closing does not occur.

FIGURE 13.2 ■ Closing Progress Chart

Property Address: ____________________

Seller: Buyer:

Listing Sales Associate				Closing Progress Chart	Selling Sales Associate			
#	Sched Date	Actual Date	X	Closing duties	DONE	X	Sched. Date	Actual Date
1				"Sale pending" sign on listing				
2				Notice of under contract to MLS				
3				Binder deposited in bank $__________				
4				Additional binder received, if required. $ __________				
5				Loan application made by buyer				
6				Contingencies cleared in writing:				
7				Home inspection by: __________				
8				Soil test from: __________				
9				Roof inspection by: __________				
10				Other (describe): __________				
11				Appraisal by: __________				
12				Loan approval from: __________				
13				Title insurance ordered from: __________				
14				Pest inspection ordered (after loan approval) from:				
15				Report received and delivered to buyer				
16				Report received and delivered to lender				
17				Treatment ordered, if required				
18				Structure inspection ordered, if necessary				
19				Work completed and approved				
20				Required repairs ordered				
21				Required repairs completed				
22				Survey ordered (After loan approval)				
23				Survey completed. Results. . .				
24				Encroachments, survey problems cleared				
25				Buyer to get hazard insurance				
26				Insurance policy to title closing agent				
27				Buyer/seller contacted for closing appointment				
28				Pre-closing inspection				
29				Closing papers reviewed with buyer/seller one day prior				
30				Buyer given figure for certified check for closing				
31				Binder check prepared to take to closing				
32				Closing date				
33				Signed closing papers received by sales associate				
34				**Post-closing duties**				
35				Commission check to broker				
36				Sign/lockbox picked up from property				
37				Buyer/seller letter of thanks				
38				Follow-up visit to buyer/seller				
39				Notice of closed sale to MLS				

FIGURE 13.2 ■ Closing Progress Chart (Continued)

Note: If comments on any line of the chart are necessary, place an "X" in the appropriate place, then enter the comments here:

Date	Line #	Comments on Closing Progress Chart

Wood-destroying organisms inspection ordered. A copy of the inspection report should be delivered to the seller, buyer, lender, and title closing agent. If treatment or repairs are required, agents working with the buyer and seller should communicate and agree on the details. If a structural inspection is needed, a licensed contractor should be engaged to examine the property and estimate repair costs.

Required repairs ordered. The appraisal could show the need for a new roof, or the buyer may have made the contract contingent on the seller replacing a swimming pool vinyl liner. As soon as loan approval is obtained, the seller or buyer should order the work. The appropriate party should inspect the work to be sure that it has been done properly.

Survey ordered. The lender or the title closing agent orders the survey after loan approval. In case of survey problems such as encroachments, the licensee must act quickly to help clear the problem. If a new loan is required, the survey must contain the borrower's name, the lender's name, and the title insurance underwriter's name.

Buyer hazard insurance. The buyer should contact an insurance agent early in the transaction to be sure the closing is not delayed. If a hurricane or tropical storm is in the "box" (see Figure 13.3), insurance companies stop issung new policies until the danger has passed.

Hazard insurance policy to closing agent. The sales associate must monitor the transaction to be certain that the insurance policy is delivered to the title closing agent.

Buyer/seller contacted for closing appointment. Soon after loan approval, the sales associates should coordinate a closing time with the buyer, seller, lender, and title closing agent.

Preclosing inspection. The buyer should make a preclosing walkthrough inspection. The sales associate should not conduct the inspection because of the liability involved. The inspection ensures that:

- the property is ready for occupancy;
- the property was not damaged by the seller's moveout;
- personal property the seller is required to leave remains on the property;

FIGURE 13.3 ■ Areas of Tropical Storms and Hurricanes that Cause Insurance Delays

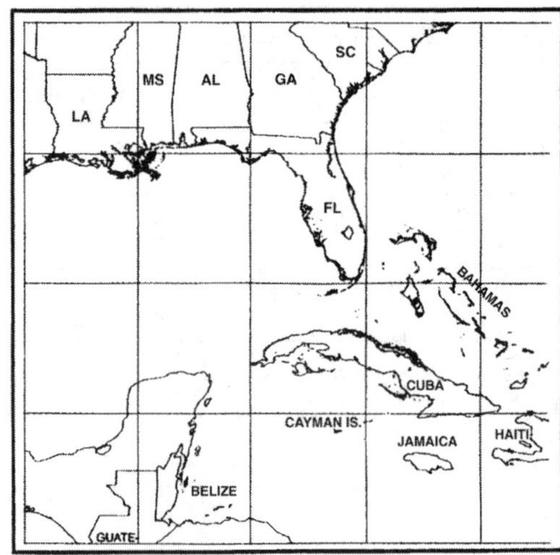

- all required repairs and maintenance have been completed; and
- the property has been maintained in the condition as it existed at the time of contract.

Closing papers reviewed with the buyer or seller one day before closing. The licensee must monitor all phases of the closing and carefully review the closing statements. When possible, the licensee should deliver copies of all documents to the buyer or seller or to his or her attorney. The sales associate should review the closing statements to ensure that all items are correct, and be able to explain each item to the buyer or seller at the appointment. The sales associate working with the buyer should compare the closing statement to the lender's **good-faith estimate**. The sales associate working with the seller should compare the figures to those the seller received on the net proceeds form. The next section covers closing statements in detail. The buyer's attorney will want to review the following applicable documents:

- Mortgage loan documents
- Deed
- Land-use restrictive covenants
- Title insurance binder, commitment, and exceptions
- Satisfaction of existing liens
- Condominium and home association documents
- Existing leases

Buyer given figure for certified check for closing. The licensee should provide the buyer with this amount as soon as possible to allow the buyer time to get to the bank to secure a certified check for the necessary funds.

Earnest-money check prepared for closing. The sales associate should get the earnest-money check from the broker, clip it to the closing file folder, and take it to the closing.

At the closing. The licensee should be completely attentive to every part of the closing. Professionalism is the key to putting buyers or sellers at ease when they are dealing with what may be their largest single asset.

Signed closing papers received by sales associate. The sales associate should be sure the office file is fully documented. This includes any walkthrough clearance papers the buyer signs for the seller, closing statements all parties sign, and copies of the survey and wood-destroying organism reports. If disbursement is made at closing, the sales associate also receives the commission check at this time.

Postclosing duties. The sales associate should return the closing file to the office for processing, send a letter of thanks to the customer, and arrange to visit the customer to make sure everything is satisfactory.

IRS reporting requirements. The Foreign Investment in Real Property Tax Act requires a buyer of property owned by a foreign investor to withhold tax equal to 10 percent of the amount realized on the sale. The tax may be withheld by the title closing agent as a service and must be deposited with the IRS within 30 days. Among other exemptions, the sale of a personal residence is exempt if the amount realized does not exceed $300,000.

Also, the closing agent reports residential sales and exchanges on Form 1099-S. A transaction is not reported if the seller gives written assurance that the full amount of the gain is tax free.

PRORATING PROCEDURES

Items Typically Prorated Between Buyer and Seller

In every closing, income and expenses associated with the ownership of the property must be prorated between buyer and seller. In most cases, the **365-day method** is used to prorate annual expenses. The annual cost is divided by 365 days to get a daily rate, which is multiplied by the number of days involved to get the amount due. Sometimes there are monthly or quarterly amounts that must be prorated, in which case the dollars are divided by the number of days in the period. When calculating prorations using the **30-day month method**, the annual cost is divided by 12 months, then by 30 days to get the daily rate. This rate is multiplied by the number of days involved to get the amount due.

Proration calculations should be based on the last day of seller ownership. The day of closing is charged to the buyer. By negotiation or custom in an area, the day of closing may be charged to the seller.

The most common items prorated on a closing statement are property taxes, homeowners' association dues, and rents and security deposits the seller collects in advance. A discussion of each follows.

Prorating property taxes. Property taxes, paid in arrears, are the buyer's responsibility at year end. For this reason, the seller must compensate the buyer for the seller's share of the taxes. The only exception occurs when a closing takes place at the end of the year and the seller already has paid the taxes.

If we assume that the closing date is June 12 and that property taxes are $3,224, the proration is calculated as follows:

Beginning	**Closing Date**	End
January 1	June 12	December 31

Seller owns during this period	Buyer will own for this period
162 days	203 days

Number of days from January 1 through June 11:

January	31
February	28
March	31
April	30
May	31
June	11
Total	162

Daily rate $3,224 ÷ 365 days = $8.83288 per day
Daily rate $8.83288 × 162 days = $1,430.93

Proration exercise. Calculate the following property tax prorations:

Closing Date	*Taxes*	*Amount*	*Debit to*
June 10	$2,567	$	❑ Buyer ❑ Seller
November 13	$4,260 (Paid 11/3)	$	❑ Buyer ❑ Seller
February 8	$1,892.56	$	❑ Buyer ❑ Seller

Prorating association dues. Homeowners' associations collect dues from owners, usually in advance. Sometimes these dues are collected monthly, but most often are paid annually. Condominium association dues are paid in advance and are usually collected monthly.

For annual payment dues. If we assume a June 12 closing date with annual dues of $450, we assume the seller has paid the annual bill, so the buyer owes the seller for the unexpired portion. The proration is calculated as follows:

Beginning	**Closing Date**	End
January 1	June 12	December 31

Seller	Buyer
162 Days	203 days

Number of days from June 11 through December 31:

June	19
July	31
August	31
September	30
October	31
November	30
December	31
Total	203

Daily rate $450 ÷ 365 = 1.23288 per day
Daily rate 1.23288 × 203 days = $250.27

In situations where dues are paid in arrears, multiply the daily rate by the number of days used by the seller. Seller must pay the buyer.

For monthly payment dues. If we assume a June 12 closing date with monthly condo dues of $587, the seller has paid for the full month, so the buyer must pay the seller for the 19 days that are unexpired. The proration is calculated as follows:

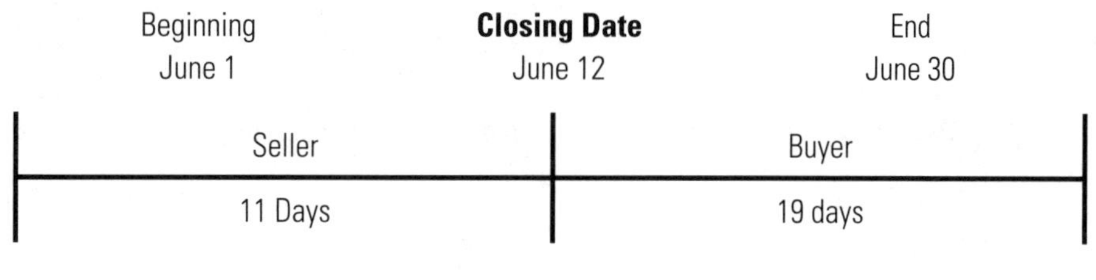

Daily rate $587 ÷ 30 = 19.56667 per day
Daily rate 19.56667 × 19 days = $371.77

Prorating rent. Prepaid rent is prorated for income property. The seller collects the rent and should compensate the buyer for the rent for the period after the closing. The buyer also should be credited for the security deposits collected by the seller and any additional advance rent.

If we assume a closing date of June 12, with a duplex rented for $700 on each side and rents collected on June 1 by the seller, the proration is calculated as follows:

Beginning June 1 | **Closing Date** June 12 | End June 30

Seller — 11 days | Buyer — 19 days

Rent of $700 × 2 units = $1,400
Daily rate $1,400 ÷ 30 days = $46.66667
Daily rate $46.66667 × 19 days = $886.67

Proration exercise. Please calculate the following rent prorations:

Closing Date	Rent Collected	Proration	Debit to	
May 10	$4,750	$	❑ Buyer	❑ Seller
November 13	$ 750	$	❑ Buyer	❑ Seller
February 8	$2,300	$	❑ Buyer	❑ Seller

Security deposits or advance rents the seller collected are credited to the buyer in full at closing.

Prorating hazard insurance. Because it is rare for a buyer to assume an existing policy, this text does not cover insurance prorations. The buyer should purchase a new policy, and the seller should cancel the existing policy and request a refund.

Documentary stamp taxes and intangible taxes. **Documentary stamp taxes** are collected on the deed and the note. The seller normally pays for stamps on the deed, and the buyer pays for stamps on the note.

The deed stamps are based on the sale price, and are $.70 per $100 or fraction thereof. (That means that the price must be rounded to the next highest $100 before the calculation is made.) For example, if a property sells for $260,001, the documentary stamp taxes would be calculated as follows:

$$\$260{,}001 \div 100 = 2{,}600 \text{ hundreds plus a fraction, rounded to } 2{,}601$$

$$2{,}601 \times \$.70 = \$1{,}820.70$$

Deed stamps exercise. Please calculate the following documentary stamp taxes:

Sale Price	Documentary Stamp Tax
$420,000	$
$128,210	$
$242,500	$

The note stamps are based on the mortgage amount, and are $.35 per $100 or fraction thereof. (That means that the mortgage amount must be rounded to the next highest $100 before the calculation is made.) For example, if the amount of a new mortgage note is $208,535, the documentary stamp taxes would be calculated as follows:

$$\$208{,}535 \div 100 = 2{,}085 \text{ hundreds plus a fraction, rounded to } 2{,}086$$

$$2{,}086 \times \$.35 = \$730.10$$

Note stamps exercise. Please calculate the following documentary stamp taxes:

Mortgage Amount	Documentary Stamp Tax
$436,000	$
$141,202	$
$316,500	$

Stamp taxes on a note are collected only on new debt. That would include a new mortgage loan, an assumption, or a novation on an existing loan whereby the buyer assumes the obligation. They are not collected in a situation where a buyer purchases a property "subject to" an existing mortgage (because the buyer has not assumed the obligation).

Intangible taxes are based on mortgage amounts for new loans only, and are .002 of the loan amount. The loan amount is not rounded. For example, if a property sells for $260,000 with a new mortgage for $208,535, the intangible taxes would be calculated as follows:

$$\$208{,}535 \times .002 = \$417.07$$

Intangible tax exercise. Please calculate the following intangible taxes:

Mortgage Amount	Intangible Tax
$436,000	$
$141,202	$
$316,500	$

PREPARATION OF THE CLOSING STATEMENT

The Contract for Sale

The closing statement is, in effect, the purchase and sale contract reduced to numbers. Problems encountered at closings often are the direct result of poorly written contracts. If a contract is not clear about which party must pay a certain closing cost, the closing agent must allocate the cost based on local custom.

Parts of the RESPA Settlement Statement (HUD-1)

The **HUD-1 Settlement Statement** provides an itemized listing of the funds payable at closing. Closing agents must prepare the HUD-1 form for the parties to a federally related residential mortgage loan. The form has become the standard and is used in nearly all residential closings, whether or not required. Each item in the statement is assigned a separate number within a standardized numbering system. Figure 13.4 provides a blank HUD-1 statement.

Effective January 1, 2010, the HUD-1 statement has three pages. Page 1 shows the parties, the property description, the lender, the settlement agent, and a summary of the borrower's and seller's transactions. Page 2 (Section L) itemizes the settlement charges for each party, such as the broker's commission, loan closing costs, prepaid items, escrow account setup, title charges, and recording charges. The total expenses for each party on page 2 are transferred to page 1. When explaining the statement to the buyer and seller, the closing agents start at page 2, then go to page 1. The new page 3 compares the amounts on the HUD-1 statement to the lender's good faith estimate (GFE).

The following is an example of how a HUD-1 Settlement Statement goes together: Wendy Putnam Smith has entered into a purchase contract for a home located at 6798 Stonegate Road, Sunnyland, FL. The seller is Cecil L. Harrolsen, the lender is Tri-State National Bank, and the settlement agent is Dean Title Co. Wendy will finance the purchase price of $140,000 with a new 80 percent conventional mortgage at 7.5 percent interest. There is no requirement for mortgage insurance or for escrowing reserves. The seller's mortgage payoff is $112,549 at the date of closing. Wendy and Cecil privately agreed that Wendy would purchase Cecil's washer, dryer, and refrigerator for $428, which they have asked to be shown on the closing statement. The broker's 7 percent commission does not include the personal property. The closing date of October 14 belongs to the buyer. While this closing statement shows the insurance premium being collected at closing, licensees should be aware that many lenders want the policy prepaid before the closing.

Other items included in the closing are shown in the next section.

HUD-1

Line #	*Item*	*Amount*
101, 401	Purchase price	$140,000.00
102, 402	Purchase of appliances	428.00
201	Earnest-money deposit	5,000.00
202	Principal amount of new loan **(Price times loan-to-value ratio: $140,000 × .80 = $112,000)**	112,000.00
504	Payoff of first mortgage loan	112,549.00
	Buyer's loan closing costs:	
801	Origination charge—1% of the loan amount **(Loan amount times the percentage: $112,000 × .01 = $1,120)**	1,120.00
802	Loan discount—2 points **(Loan amount times points: $112,000 × .02 = 2,240)**	2,240.00
804	Appraisal fee	POC*
805	Credit report	POC*
806	Tax service fee	69.00
808	Processor incentive	62.00
Prorations:		
211, 511	Property taxes for the year (paid in arrears)—$2,782 **(Annual taxes divided by 365 days times number of seller days: $2,782 ÷ 365 = $7.62192 per day; $7.62192 × 286 seller days = $2,179.87)**	$2,179.87
213, 513	Homeowners' association dues for the year (paid in *arrears*)—$240 **(Annual dues divided by 365 days times number of seller days: $240 ÷ 365 = $.65753 per day; $.65753 × 286 seller days = $188.05)**	188.05
Prepaid items:		
901	Prepaid interest on new mortgage **(Loan amount times interest rate divided by 365 times number of days remaining in month of closing, counting the day of closing: $112,000 × .075 = $8,400: $8,400 ÷ 365 = $23.01370 per day; $23.01370 × 18 days = $414.25)**	$414.25
903	Hazard insurance premium	1,140.00
Buyer's expenses:		
1102	Settlement or closing fee to Dean Title Co.	$100.00
1103	Owner's title insurance	925.00
1104	Lender's title insurance	350.00
1105	Florida 9 endorsement	72.00
1106	ALTA 8.1 endorsement	25.00
1202	Recording fee—deed	26.00

HUD-1 (Continued)

Line #	*Item*	*Amount*
1202	Recording fee—mortgage	28.50
1204	Documentary stamp tax on note	392.00
	(Loan amount divided by 100; round to next whole number; multiply by $.35: $112,000 ÷ 100 = $1,120; $1,120 × .35 = $392)	
1205	Intangible taxes on mortgage	224.00
	(Loan amount times .002: $112,000 × .002 = $224)	
1302	Survey	300.00
1303	Pest inspection	75.00
Seller's expenses:		
701, 703	Commission paid to Tillie Evans Realty @ 7%	$9,800.00
	(Sale price times commission rate: $140,000 × .07 = $9,800)	
1202	Satisfaction (release) recording fee	6.00
1204	Documentary stamp tax on deed	980.00
	(Sale price divided by 100; round to next higher whole number; multiply by $.70: $140,000 ÷ 100 = $1,400; $1,400 × .70 = $980)	
1304	Courier fee	20.00
1400	Enter total from line 1400 for borrower at line 103 on page 1; enter total for seller at line 502 on page 1	

*POC on the statement means "paid outside closing."

Based on the information given, complete the blank HUD-1 statement in Figure 13.4.

The HUD-1 Settlement Statement is not prepared by the broker. The title closing agent is the party responsible for preparation of the statement. However, the broker is expected to know where to locate various charges and payments on the statement and to be able to answer questions from the buyer or seller about the statement.

The preparation of the HUD-1 Settlement Statement in the previous section provided the knowledge to know where to find specific charges and credits on the statement. The next section will include several closing statement cases. You will be expected to correctly answer eight questions on each of the cases.

Now, answer the following questions without looking back at the HUD-1 form:

1. How much is the buyer's new mortgage and where does it show on the HUD-1?
   a. $140,000; on page 1 on the borrower's side and the seller's side
   b. $140,000; on page 2 on the borrower's side and the seller's side
   c. $112,000; on page 1 on the borrower's side only
   d. $112,000; on page 1 on the borrower's side and the seller's side

2. How much are the government transfer taxes for the buyer and the seller and where does this information appear on the HUD-1?
   a. Seller $784; Buyer $616; page 2
   b. Seller $980; Buyer $616; page 2
   c. Seller $980; Buyer $1,008; page 2
   d. Seller $784; Buyer $392; page 1

FIGURE 13.4 ■ HUD-1 Settlement Statement

OMB Approval No. 2502-0265

A. Settlement Statement (HUD-1)

B. Type of Loan

1. ☐ FHA 2. ☐ RHS 3. ☐ Conv. Unins. 4. ☐ VA 5. ☐ Conv. Ins.	6. File Number:	7. Loan Number:	8. Mortgage Insurance Case Number:

C. Note: This form is furnished to give you a statement of actual settlement costs. Amounts paid to and by the settlement agent are shown. Items marked "(p.o.c.)" were paid outside the closing; they are shown here for informational purposes and are not included in the totals.

D. Name & Address of Borrower:	E. Name & Address of Seller:	F. Name & Address of Lender:
G. Property Location:	H. Settlement Agent:	I. Settlement Date:
	Place of Settlement:	

J. Summary of Borrower's Transaction		K. Summary of Seller's Transaction	
100. Gross Amount Due from Borrower		**400. Gross Amount Due to Seller**	
101. Contract sales price		401. Contract sales price	
102. Personal property		402. Personal property	
103. Settlement charges to borrower (line 1400)		403.	
104.		404.	
105.		405.	
Adjustment for items paid by seller in advance		**Adjustments for items paid by seller in advance**	
106. City/town taxes to		406. City/town taxes to	
107. County taxes to		407. County taxes to	
108. Assessments to		408. Assessments to	
109.		409.	
110.		410.	
111.		411.	
112.		412.	
120. Gross Amount Due from Borrower		**420. Gross Amount Due to Seller**	
200. Amounts Paid by or in Behalf of Borrower		**500. Reductions In Amount Due to Seller**	
201. Deposit or earnest money		501. Excess deposit (see instructions)	
202. Principal amount of new loan(s)		502. Settlement charges to seller (line 1400)	
203. Existing loan(s) taken subject to		503. Existing loan(s) taken subject to	
204.		504. Payoff of first mortgage loan	
205.		505. Payoff of second mortgage loan	
206.		506.	
207.		507.	
208.		508.	
209.		509.	
Adjustments for items unpaid by seller		**Adjustments for items unpaid by seller**	
210. City/town taxes to		510. City/town taxes to	
211. County taxes to		511. County taxes to	
212. Assessments to		512. Assessments to	
213.		513.	
214.		514.	
215.		515.	
216.		516.	
217.		517.	
218.		518.	
219.		519.	
220. Total Paid by/for Seller		**520. Total Reduction Amount Due Seller**	
300. Cash at Settlement from/to Borrower		**600. Cash at Settlement to/from Seller**	
301. Gross amount due from borrower (line 120)		601. Gross amount due to seller (line 420)	
302. Less amounts paid by/for borrower (line 220)	( )	602. Less reductions in amount due seller (line 520)	( )
303. Cash ☐ From ☐ To Borrower		**603. Cash ☐ To ☐ From Seller**	

The Public Reporting Burden for this collection of information is estimated at 35 minutes per response for collecting, reviewing, and reporting the data. This agency may not collect this information, and you are not required to complete this form, unless it displays a currently valid OMB control number. No confidentiality is assured; this disclosure is mandatory. This is designed to provide the parties to a RESPA covered transaction with information during the settlement process.

Previous editions are obsolete | Page 1 of 3 | HUD-1

FIGURE 13.4 ■ HUD-1 Settlement Statement (Continued)

L. Settlement Charges			
700. Total Real Estate Broker Fees		Paid From Borrower's Funds at Settlement	Paid From Seller's Funds at Settlement
Division of commission (line 700) as follows:			
701. $ to			
702. $ to			
703. Commission paid at settlement			
704.			
800. Items Payable in Connection with Loan			
801. Our origination charge $	(from GFE #1)		
802. Your credit or charge (points) for the specific interest rate chosen $	(from GFE #2)		
803. Your adjusted origination charges	(from GFE A)		
804. Appraisal fee to	(from GFE #3)		
805. Credit report to	(from GFE #3)		
806. Tax service to	(from GFE #3)		
807. Flood certification	(from GFE #3)		
808.			
900. Items Required by Lender to Be Paid in Advance			
901. Daily interest charges from to @ $ /day	(from GFE #10)		
902. Mortgage insurance premium for months to	(from GFE #3)		
903. Homeowner's insurance for years to	(from GFE #11)		
904.			
1000. Reserves Deposited with Lender			
1001. Initial deposit for your escrow account	(from GFE #9)		
1002. Homeowner's insurance months @ $ per month $			
1003. Mortgage insurance months @ $ per month $			
1004. Property taxes months @ $ per month $			
1005. months @ $ per month $			
1006. months @ $ per month $			
1007. Aggregate Adjustment –$			
1100. Title Charges			
1101. Title services and lender's title insurance	(from GFE #4)		
1102. Settlement or closing fee $			
1103. Owner's title insurance	(from GFE #5)		
1104. Lender's title insurance $			
1105. Lender's title policy limit $			
1106. Owner's title policy limit $			
1107. Agent's portion of the total title insurance premium $			
1108. Underwriter's portion of the total title insurance premium $			
1200. Government Recording and Transfer Charges			
1201. Government recording charges	(from GFE #7)		
1202. Deed $ Mortgage $ Releases $			
1203. Transfer taxes	(from GFE #8)		
1204. City/County tax/stamps Deed $ Mortgage $			
1205. State tax/stamps Deed $ Mortgage $			
1206.			
1300. Additional Settlement Charges			
1301. Required services that you can shop for	(from GFE #6)		
1302. $			
1303. $			
1304.			
1305.			
1400. Total Settlement Charges (enter on lines 103, Section J and 502, Section K)			

Previous editions are obsolete Page 2 of 3 HUD-1

FIGURE 13.4 ■ HUD-1 Settlement Statement (Continued)

Comparison of Good Faith Estimate (GFE) and HUD-1 Charges		Good Faith Estimate	HUD-1
Charges That Cannot Increase	**HUD-1 Line Number**		
Our origination charge	# 801		
Your credit or charge (points) for the specific interest rate chosen	# 802		
Your adjusted origination charges	# 803		
Transfer taxes	#1203		

Charges That in Total Cannot Increase More Than 10%		Good Faith Estimate	HUD-1
Government recording charges	# 1201		
	#		
	#		
	#		
	#		
	#		
	#		
	#		
	Total		
	Increase between GFE and HUD-1 Charges	$ or	%

Charges That Can Change		Good Faith Estimate	HUD-1
Initial deposit for your escrow account	#1001		
Daily interest charges	# 901 $ /day		
Homeowner's insurance	# 903		
	#		
	#		
	#		

Loan Terms

Your initial loan amount is	$
Your loan term is	years
Your initial interest rate is	%
Your initial monthly amount owed for principal, interest, and and any mortgage insurance is	$ includes ☐ Principal ☐ Interest ☐ Mortgage Insurance
Can your interest rate rise?	☐ No. ☐ Yes, it can rise to a maximum of %. The first change will be on and can change again every after . Every change date, your interest rate can increase or decrease by %. Over the life of the loan, your interest rate is guaranteed to never be **lower** than % or **higher** than %.
Even if you make payments on time, can your loan balance rise?	☐ No. ☐ Yes, it can rise to a maximum of $.
Even if you make payments on time, can your monthly amount owed for principal, interest, and mortgage insurance rise?	☐ No. ☐ Yes, the first increase can be on and the monthly amount owed can rise to $. The maximum it can ever rise to is $.
Does your loan have a prepayment penalty?	☐ No. ☐ Yes, your maximum prepayment penalty is $.
Does your loan have a balloon payment?	☐ No. ☐ Yes, you have a balloon payment of $ due in years on .
Total monthly amount owed including escrow account payments	☐ You do not have a monthly escrow payment for items, such as property taxes and homeowner's insurance. You must pay these items directly yourself. ☐ You have an additional monthly escrow payment of $ that results in a total initial monthly amount owed of $. This includes principal, interest, any mortgage insurance and any items checked below: ☐ Property taxes ☐ Homeowner's insurance ☐ Flood insurance ☐ ☐ ☐

Note: If you have any questions about the Settlement Charges and Loan Terms listed on this form, please contact your lender.

Previous editions are obsolete Page 3 of 3 HUD-1

3. The binder deposit on the HUD-1 is
   a. $5,000 debit to the seller; page 1
   b. $5,000 credit to the buyer; page 1
   c. $5,000 debit to the seller; page 2
   d. $5,000 debit to the buyer; page 2

4. Where is the sales price placed on the HUD-1?
   a. Debit to the seller only; page 1
   b. Credit to the buyer, debit to the seller; page 1
   c. Debit to the buyer, credit to the seller; page 1
   d. Credit to the seller only; page 2

5. What is the proration for taxes, and where does this information appear on the HUD-1?
   a. $2,187.49 debit to the seller, credit to the buyer; page 2
   b. $2,187.49 debit to the buyer, credit to the seller; page 1
   c. $2,179.87 debit to the seller, credit to the buyer; page 1
   d. $602.13 credit to the buyer only; page 1

Look over the HUD-1 Settlement Statement again. The expenses are on page 2. The total of the expenses for each party at the bottom of page 2 are then carried forward to page 1. The buyers' expenses are shown toward the top of the buyers' side because the expenses will add to the amount the buyers owe. The sellers' expenses are shown farther down the page on the sellers' side, because the expenses are subtracted from the sellers' proceeds.

To visualize the effect of page 1 a little better, draw a horizontal line just above lines 120 and 420. Any numbers above the line will add to the amount due from or to the respective parties. Numbers below the line will deduct from those amounts.

For testing purposes:

- You should be able to calculate prorations for taxes, rent, and association fees.
- You must determine which party will be debited or a credited.
- You should know where the entry for items like purchase price, mortgage amounts, prorations, and expenses are shown on the statement *without having the statement available for reference.*

Closing Statement Case Study Number 1

Jack and Susan Wilder, husband and wife, are purchasing a home located at 1021 94th Court, Jacksonville, FL 32217. The seller is Ellen Smith. The sale price is $178,000. The Wilders will give the broker an earnest money deposit of $6,000. The closing date of April 15 belongs to the buyer. The Wilders will finance the purchase with a new 80 percent loan-to-value mortgage. Property taxes for the year are estimated to be $3,618 and will be prorated using the 365-day method. Other information about this transaction follows.

Buyer Wilder's expenses are as follows:

- Attorney's fee 330.00
- Title insurance 1,240.00
- Recording fee—deed 6.00

- Recording fee—mortgage 19.50
- Documentary stamp tax on note (calculate) ________
- Intangible taxes on new mortgage (calculate) ________
- WDO inspection 225.00
- Survey 400.00

Seller Smith's expenses are as follows:

- Brokerage commission at 6% 10,680.00
- Documentary stamp tax on deed (calculate) ________

Based on this information, please answer the following questions:

1. Where is the sales price placed on the HUD-1?
   a. Debit to the seller, credit to the buyer; page 1
   b. Credit to the seller, debit to the buyer; page 1
   c. Debit to the seller only; page 1
   d. Credit to the seller only; page 2

2. How much are the government transfer taxes for the buyer and the seller and where does this information appear on the HUD-1?
   a. Seller $1,246; Buyer $498.40; page 2
   b. Seller $1,246; Buyer $783.20; page 2
   c. Seller $1,246; Buyer $996.80; page 2
   d. Seller $623; Buyer $1,246; page 1

3. The binder deposit on the HUD-1 statement is
   a. $6,000 Debit to the seller; page 2
   b. $6,000 Credit to the buyer; page 1
   c. $6,000 Debit to the seller; page 1
   d. $6,000 Debit to the buyer; page 2

4. How much is the buyer's new mortgage and where does it show on the HUD-1?
   a. $142,400; on page 1 on the borrower's side only
   b. $142,400; on page 2 on the borrower's side and the seller's side
   c. $178,000; on page 1 on the borrower's side only
   d. $178,000; on page 1 on the borrower's side and the seller's side

5. What is the proration for taxes, and where does this information appear on the HUD-1?
   a. $1,030.88 debit to the seller, credit to the buyer; page 2
   b. $2,187.49 debit to the buyer, credit to the seller; page 1
   c. $1,030.88 debit to the seller, credit to the buyer; page 1
   d. $2,587.12 credit to the buyer, debit to the seller; page 1

Closing Statement Case Study Number 2

Using the following information, answer questions 1 through 5.

Selling Price	$200,000.00
Binder deposit	10,000.00
New 75 percent first mortgage	?
Payoff of existing first mortgage	$47,893.43
Prorations:	
City and county taxes	2,275.00
Annual association dues paid by seller January 1	650.00
Buyer's expenses:	
Title insurance	650.00
Recording deed	6.00
Appropriate taxes on note and mortgage	?
Attorney's fee	300.00
Seller's expenses:	
Brokerage fee	6%
Appropriate stamp taxes on deed	?
Attorney's fee	250.00

The seller is Stinson. The buyer is Flaherty. The closing date is July 20. Day of closing is charged to the buyer. Use the 365-day method for calculating prorations.

1. What is the proration for association fees and where will it show in the HUD-1 statement?
   a. $356.16 credit seller, debit buyer; page 2
   b. $356.16 credit buyer, debit seller; page 1
   c. $293.84 debit seller, credit buyer; page 1
   d. $293.84 credit seller, debit buyer; page 1

2. What is the brokerage fee and where does it appear on the HUD-1 statement?
   a. $12,000 seller and buyer; page 1
   b. $12,000 seller; page 1
   c. $12,000 seller; page 2
   d. $12,000 buyer; page 2

3. What are the total government taxes for note, mortgage, and transfer and where is this information found on the HUD-1 statement?
   a. $2,750; page 2
   b. $2,225; page 1
   c. $2,225; page 2
   d. $825; page 2

4. Where is the title insurance shown in the HUD-1 statement?
   a. Seller; page 1
   b. Buyer; page 1
   c. Buyer; page 2
   d. Seller and buyer; page 2

5. What is the tax proration and where does it show on the HUD-1 statement?
   a. $1,240.35 debit seller, credit buyer; page 2
   b. $1,246.58 debit seller, credit buyer; page 2
   c. $1,246.58 debit seller, credit buyer; page 1
   d. $1,252.81 debit seller, credit buyer; page 2

Closing Statement Case Study Number 3

Using the following information, answer questions 1 through 5.

Ms. Harrison is buying a rental house from Mr. Johnson. The purchase price is $224,000. Ms. Harrison gave the broker a good-faith deposit of $4,000. The broker has the listing on the property, and her commission is 7 percent.

Ms. Harrison will finance the purchase with a new 60 percent loan-to-value mortgage. Payoff of current loan including principal and interest is $142,356.35.

The closing date is August 17, with the day of closing belonging to the buyer. Mr. Johnson had rented the property on June 1 for $1,400 per month, and had collected the first and last month's rent, along with a security deposit of $300. The rental payments are current. City and county taxes are $1,947.09. Property tax proration should be made using the 365-day method. Mr. Johnson will furnish a warranty deed with required stamps attached.

Ms. Harrison has agreed to pay the documentary stamps on the new loan, and to pay for title insurance costing $550. The cost to record the deed is $7, paid by the buyer. Buyer's attorney fees are $75, and the seller will pay $60 for his attorney to review the documents.

1. What is the proration for property taxes and where will they show on the HUD-1 statement?
   a. $1,216.26 debit seller, credit buyer; page 2
   b. $1,216.26 credit seller, debit buyer; page 1
   c. $1,221.60 debit seller, credit buyer; page 1
   d. $1,216.26 debit seller, credit buyer; page 1

2. What are the documentary stamp taxes and intangible taxes on this transaction and where will they be found on the HUD-1 statement?
   a. $1,568.00 seller, $739.20 buyer; page 2
   b. $739.20 buyer, $1,568 seller; page 1
   c. $1,568 seller, $1,836.80 buyer; page 2
   d. $701.60 buyer, $1,568 seller; page 2

3. What is the amount of the new mortgage and where will it show on the HUD-1 statement?
   a. $134,400, debit seller, credit buyer; page 1
   b. $134,400 debit seller; page 1
   c. $134,400 credit buyer; page 1
   d. $134,400 credit seller, debit buyer; page 1

4. How much is the rent and security deposit debit and credit, and where will it appear on the HUD-1 statement?
   a. $2,522.58, credit buyer, debit seller; page 1
   b. $2,522.58, debit seller, credit buyer; page 1
   c. $2,577.42, credit seller only; page 1
   d. $2,377.42, debit seller, credit buyer; page 1

5. How will the payoff of the existing loan be shown in the HUD-1 statement?
   a. Debit seller, credit buyer; page 1
   b. Credit seller only; page 1
   c. Debit seller only; page 1
   d. Credit seller, debit buyer; page 1

Closing Statement Case Study Number 4

Using the following information, answer questions 1 through 5.

Mr. Hunt is selling his rental house to Mr. Skau for $325,000, with a $10,000 earnest money deposit given to the broker. Mr. Skau will finance the purchase with a 70 percent first mortgage. The transaction will close on October 16 with the day of closing charged to the sellers.

The house is rented for $1,900, with the rent due on the first day of the month. Each tenant has paid a security deposit equal to one month rent. The rent proration should be calculated using the actual number of days in the month.

Mr. Hunt will pay the brokerage commission of 7 percent and the documentary stamp tax on the deed. Mr. Skau will pay title insurance of $1,965, the $400 survey cost, recording fees of $68.50, required state taxes on the loans, and a hazard insurance premium of $3,210.

Property taxes of $4,012 for the year will be prorated between the parties using the 365-day method.

1. How is the insurance premium handled on the HUD-1 statement?
   a. Debit seller, credit buyer; page 2
   b. Credit seller; page 2
   c. Debit seller; page 2
   d. Debit buyer; page 2

2. What is the balance of the new mortgage and how will it be shown on the HUD-1 statement?
   a. $227,500; credit buyer, debit seller; page 1
   b. $260,000; debit buyer only; page 1
   c. $227,500; credit buyer only; page 1
   d. $227,500; credit buyer only; page 2

3. What is the tax proration, and how will it show on the HUD-1 statement?
   a. $3,176.62 debit buyer, credit seller; page 2
   b. $3,176.62 credit buyer, debit seller; page 1
   c. $835.38 credit buyer, debit seller; page 1
   d. $3,297.53 debit seller, credit buyer; page 2

4. What is the brokerage commission and how will it be shown on the HUD-1 statement?
   a. $22,750 debit to buyer; page 1
   b. $22,750 debit to seller; page 2
   c. $19,500 debit to seller; page 2
   d. $7,000 debit to buyer; page 1

5. Where is the total amount due from the buyer shown on the HUD-1 statement?
   a. On the buyer's side at the top of page 1
   b. On the buyer's side at the bottom of page 2
   c. On the buyer's side at the bottom of page 1
   d. On the buyer's side at the top of page 2

SUMMARY OF IMPORTANT POINTS

- A licensee is expected to monitor all details of a transaction's closing. In fact, a licensee has numerous tasks to accomplish between the contract date and the closing date.
- A checklist is one of the best ways to ensure that the licensee completes all tasks.
- Buyers and sellers expect the licensee to have reviewed all closing documents for completeness and accuracy. The broker is expected to have a complete understanding of closing statements and to be able to answer questions from the buyer or the seller.
- The IRS requires a buyer of property owned by a foreign investor to withhold 10 percent of the purchase price of the amount realized on the sale, and to deposit the sum with the IRS within 30 days. The sale of a personal residence is exempt if the amount realized is not greater than $300,000.
- A debit to a party is a charge to the party, increasing the amount due from the buyer and reducing the amount due to the seller. A credit benefits the party, reducing the amount due from the buyer and increasing the amount due to the seller.
- Property taxes are normally paid in arrears and are usually prorated using the 365-day method.
- Homeowners' association fees are normally paid in advance, and monthly fees are prorated based on the number of days in the month. Annual dues are prorated using the 365-day method. Because the seller paid the dues in advance, the buyer owes the seller for the unexpired portion of the dues.
- Rent is usually paid in advance. Because the seller collected the full month, the seller owes the buyer for the amount of days left in the month.
- Documentary stamp taxes on the deed are usually paid by the seller and are $.70 per hundred or fraction thereof of the purchase price.
- Documentary stamp taxes on the note are usually paid by the borrower and are $.35 per hundred or fraction thereof of the loan amount.
- Intangible taxes on the note are usually paid by the borrower, and are .002 of the note amount.
- The HUD-1 Settlement Statement is used in nearly every residential transaction, and has three pages.
  - Page 1 includes the purchase price, mortgages, prorations, the total of expenses, as well as the total amount due from buyer and the total amount due to seller.
  - Page 2 lists expenses in the buyer or the seller column as appropriate. The total is entered on page 1.
  - Page 3 compares the actual costs of the borrower with the costs quoted in the Good-Faith Estimate (GFE).

REVIEW QUESTIONS

1. If a homebuyer contracts to purchase a home and makes a $1,000 check payable to the broker's trust account as an earnest money deposit, then
   a. the broker must deposit it in his escrow account within three business days.
   b. it reduces the amount due to the seller at closing by $1,000.
   c. it reduces the amount due from the buyer at closing by $1,000.
   d. both A and C are true.

2. As a cost of obtaining a real estate loan, one point equals one percent of the
   a. purchase price.
   b. title insurance premium.
   c. appraised value.
   d. loan amount.

3. A homebuyer has purchased a new home for $435,000. She is financing the purchase with a new 80 percent mortgage and will pay cash for the balance. What is the total of the documentary stamp taxes and intangible taxes on the financing, and where will they appear on the HUD-1 statement?
   a. $1,914 debit buyer only; page 2
   b. $1,914 credit buyer only; page 2
   c. $4,959, debit buyer, credit seller; page 1
   d. $4,959 debit buyer only; page 1

4. The HUD-1 Settlement Statement
   a. must be used in all real estate transactions in Florida.
   b. or a composite closing statement may be used in a federally related transaction.
   c. consists of two pages: the buyer's statement and the seller's statement.
   d. is used in nearly all residential closings, whether or not it is required.

5. In the HUD-1 Settlement Statement
   a. the broker's commission is shown on the front page.
   b. the seller's expenses are shown on page two.
   c. prorations of taxes are shown on page two.
   d. the amount due from the buyer is shown on page two.

6. If the closing is on September 8 and property taxes are $3,890, how will the property taxes be prorated and how will they appear on the HUD-1 statement?
   a. $2,664.38 credit seller, debit buyer; page 2
   b. $2,664.38 debit seller, credit buyer; page 1
   c. $2,675.04 credit buyer, debit seller, page 1
   d. $2,664.38 debit seller only; page 1

7. What is correct about homeowner's insurance coverage on an existing home?
   a. The buyer normally assumes the seller's policy and pays the seller for the unexpired portion.
   b. The lender requires the buyer to pay one full year's premium in advance.
   c. If the loan-to-value ratio is less than 80 percent, the lender requires the buyer to pay one full year's premium in advance, then 1⁄12 of the premium monthly.
   d. Arranging to purchase a policy within two days of closing is prudent on the part of the buyer.

8. The closing agent must provide Form 1099-S to the seller of a residence at closing
   a. in all cases.
   b. only when the property's sale price is greater than $300,000.
   c. if the seller is an alien resident of the United States.
   d. unless the seller provides a written assurance that the full amount of the gain is tax free.

Using the information below, prepare prorations as needed and answer questions 9–15 on how the transaction would appear on the HUD-1 Settlement Statement.

Purchase price of rental property	$275,000.00
Brokerage commission—paid by seller	7%
Binder deposit given to broker	12,000.00
Closing date—September 15 (charge to the *buyer*)	
Prorating method—365-day	
Buyer will finance purchase with a new 80 percent mortgage	?
City and county property taxes paid in arrears	4,795.25
Homeowners' association fees paid in advance for the year	575.00
Rent paid by tenant to seller in advance for month	2,200.00
Security deposit paid by tenant to seller in advance	2,000.00
State taxes:	
Documentary stamps on deed—seller will pay	?
Documentary stamps on note—buyer will pay	?
Intangible taxes—Buyer will pay	?
Buyers' attorney fees	475.00
Title insurance—seller and buyer will split cost equally	3,425.00
Recording fees—buyer to pay	64.00

9. How is the first mortgage shown?
   a. $220,000 debit buyer only; page 1
   b. $220,000 credit buyer only; page 1
   c. $220,000 debit seller, credit buyer; page 1
   d. $275,000 credit buyer only; page 2

10. How is the brokerage fee handled?
   a. $19,250 credit seller only; page 1
   b. $19,250 debit seller only; page 2
   c. $19,250 debit seller, credit buyer; page 2
   d. $16,500 debit seller only; page 2

11. How is the binder deposit shown?
    a. \$12,000 debit seller, credit buyer; page 1
    b. \$12,000 credit buyer only; page 1
    c. \$12,000 debit buyer only; page 1
    d. \$12,000 debit seller, credit buyer; page 1

12. How is the title insurance handled?
    a. \$1,712.50 credit buyer only; page 1
    b. \$1,712.50 credit buyer, debit seller; page 1
    c. \$1,712.50 credit buyer only; page 1
    d. \$1,712.50 debit buyer, debit seller; page 2

13. What is the proration for property taxes?
    a. \$3,376.38 debit seller only; page 1
    b. \$3,376.38 debit seller, credit buyer; page 1
    c. \$3,376.38 debit buyer only; page 2
    d. \$3,389.52 debit seller, credit buyer; page 1

14. What are the documentary stamp taxes and intangible taxes on the deed and mortgage?
    a. Debit seller \$1,925, credit buyer \$1,925; page 1
    b. Debit seller \$1,925, debit buyer \$1,210; page 2
    c. Credit seller \$1,925, credit buyer \$1,210; page 1
    d. Debit seller \$1,925, debit buyer \$1,980; page 1

15. How is the proration of homeowner fees handled?
    a. Credit seller, debit buyer \$170.14; page 1
    b. Debit seller, credit buyer \$404.86; page 1
    c. Debit seller, credit buyer \$170.14; page 1
    d. Credit seller, debit buyer \$404.86; page 1

CHAPTER

14 FEDERAL INCOME TAX LAWS AFFECTING REAL ESTATE

KEY TERMS

active participant
after-tax cash flow
boot
capital gain
dealer
depreciation
home acquisition loan
home equity loan
home office
installment sale
investment interest
like-kind exchange
long-term gain
nonpassive income
passive income
qualified intermediary
reversion from sale
Roth IRA
short-term gain
standard deduction
tax credit
tax deduction
vacation homes

OVERVIEW

Buyers and sellers look to real estate professionals to explain how income taxes affect ownership of personal homes and investment properties. While licensees are not expected to be tax experts, the duty of skill, care, and diligence requires a basic understanding of this important subject. This chapter begins by covering the deductibility of homeowner expenses such as taxes and interest. The material discusses the rules permitting the use of IRA accounts for home investments, as well as the tax deductions for vacation homes and home offices. It also describes the rules for avoiding taxes on the gain from the sale of a personal home.

The next section of the chapter deals with taxes on investment property and explains how to calculate taxable income from an investment property. The chapter also covers the important issue of deducting an investment's tax losses from the investor's other income.

The next section describes how to estimate the taxes due from the sale of an investment property. The last section of the chapter discusses installment sales and tax-deferred exchanges. Buyers and sellers should be advised to seek tax advice from an attorney or an accountant.

Once you have completed this chapter, you should be able to:

- list the two principal tax deductions available to homeowners;
- list the two types of home loans that qualify for a homeowner's interest deduction;

- itemize the five requirements for deducting buyer-paid points;
- explain how to use an IRA to contribute to the down payment and acquisition costs of a new home;
- list the requirements for excluding tax on the gain from the sale of a principal home;
- itemize the steps required to calculate taxable income from an investment property's operations;
- describe the process used to allocate a property's acquisition costs between land and improvements;
- calculate the annual depreciation for both residential income properties and nonresidential income properties; and
- list two methods for deferring taxes on the disposition of investment property.

AMERICAN TAXPAYER RELIEF ACT OF 2012

The American Taxpayer Relief Act of 2012 signed into law in 2013, extended many of the tax cuts made in 2001, 2003, and 2009.

Taxpayers earning $400,000 ($450,000 for joint filers) will pay higher rates; 39.6 percent (up from 35 percent) on ordinary income, and 20 percent on capital gains and qualified dividends (up from 15 percent). The itemized deduction and the personal exemption phase-out will be reinstated for married persons filing jointly with incomes above $300,000.

The law permanently extended the Bush tax cuts for individuals with taxable income under $400,000 ($450,000 for joint filers), including the 15 percent rate on capital gains and qualified dividends.

The law extended the $5 million estate and gift tax exemption (indexed for inflation), and increased the top tax rate on estates to 40 percent.

INCOME TAX TREATMENT—PRINCIPAL AND SECOND HOMES

Home ownership is one of the most important factors in the growth of our economy and the stability of our political system. The tax code is an additional incentive for families to purchase their own homes. Part of that encouragement comes as tax deductions for interest and property taxes. Tax savings from the deductions may result in a lower net house payment. Families can keep all or most of the gain when they sell their homes.

Interest Deduction

Licensees are sometimes asked whether interest on a personal home is a deductible expense for income taxes. The answer is, "maybe." Owners who purchased homes after October 13, 1987, may deduct all or part of the interest they paid on up to two homes. Two types of home loans qualify for the interest deduction: home acquisition mortgages and home equity mortgages.

Home acquisition loans. **Home acquisition loans** are used to buy, construct, or improve homes. Up to $1 million in debt qualifies for a home mortgage interest deduction ($500,000

FIGURE 14.1 ■ Interest Deduction on a Home Equity Loan

Arthur owns a home he bought in 1982 for $150,000 with a $140,000 mortgage. This year, the value of his home was $204,000, and the mortgage balance was $112,000. Arthur may deduct the interest on a home equity loan of up to $92,000 ($204,000 – $112,000).

If the value of his home had been $225,000, he could have deducted the interest on a home equity loan of up to the $100,000 maximum.

if the owner is married, filing separately). The IRS defines a residence as *any* structure that provides basic living accommodation, such as sleeping, cooking, and toilet facilities. This may or may not be real estate and might include a beach condominium, mobile home, motor home, or yacht.

Home equity loans. **Home equity loans** are used for any other purpose. Qualifying home equity debt is limited to the *lesser* of the following:

- $100,000 ($50,000 if married, filing separately) *or*
- the fair market values of the principal home and one second home, *less* acquisition debt and any pre-1987 mortgage debt. (See Figure 14.1.)

Interest on personal loans is not deductible and usually has higher interest rates. In spite of this, many taxpayers make prepayments on their mortgages before paying off personal loans, a questionable financial strategy. Generally, nondeductible, higher interest loans should be paid first.

The mortgage loan must be recorded, or the interest may not be deducted.

EXAMPLE: John and Mary wished to purchase a home. John's parents had $300,000 in several six percent bank CDs. John suggested that they lend him $100,000 so he could purchase the home, and he agreed to repay them with interest at nine percent. His parents made the loan, and John made monthly payments. At the end of each year, John referred to his amortization schedule and deducted the interest portion of the payments. A random IRS audit revealed that the mortgage had not been recorded. The IRS disallowed John's $28,231 in deductions for the previous three years and charged a penalty plus interest.

Before October 13, 1987, there was no limit to the loan amount that qualified for the interest deduction. After that date, however, interest on only $1 million in loans can be deducted.

If an individual borrows more than the allowed limit on a mortgage, the interest *may* be deductible as **investment interest**. The loan proceeds, however, must be segregated and used specifically for investment purposes, rather than for personal use. The deduction is limited to investment income.

Home construction mortgages. Interest may be deductible from the time construction begins and for 24 months following if, at completion, the home is used as a principal home or a second home. The loan amount is subject to the $1 million ceiling.

Home improvement loans. These loans are treated as acquisition debt subject to the $1 million ceiling, but only for the amount of actual improvements that can be capitalized. Interest on debt incurred to repair a property is not included.

Refinanced loans. The owner may deduct interest as follows:

- If the loan is for the same amount or for less than an old loan, there is no tax effect.
- If the funds are used to buy, build, or improve a home, it is acquisition debt, subject to the $1 million limit.
- If the funds are used for any other purpose, it is home equity debt, subject to the $100,000 limit for deductibility.

Other types of loans. On a graduated-payment mortgage, the interest usually is higher than the actual payment, resulting in negative amortization. A cash-basis taxpayer may deduct only interest actually paid. The lender identifies this amount in the year-end tax statement.

An institution that pays a borrower monthly payments or a lump sum makes a reverse mortgage. The borrower pays principal and interest when selling the home. No deduction is allowed until interest actually is paid.

An institution offering a lower fixed-rate loan in addition to a share of the equity increase after, for example, five years makes a shared appreciation mortgage. The lender's share is added to the loan, but it is *not* interest. Interest the borrower pays on the increased loan is deductible.

Points. One point equals one percent of the loan. Points are, in effect, prepaid interest. When a loan is used for the acquisition or improvement of a personal home, points are deductible in the year paid as interest if the:

- personal residence secures the loan;
- charging of points is an established business practice in the area;
- amount of points doesn't exceed the typical charges for points in the area;
- amount of points is based on a percentage of the loan and described on the closing statement as "points," "origination fee," or "loan discount"; and
- borrower pays the points directly to the lender, not to a mortgage broker.

Deductibility of points. The following four considerations should be remembered about the deductibility of points:

1. Points are deductible in the year paid only if the loan is for the purchase of a principal residence.
2. Deductions for points paid for a second home, investment property, or refinancing must be spread out over the life of the loan.
3. Points paid are not deductible if they are higher than usual for the area.
4. Points paid by the seller are deductible by the buyer as interest. The amount must be deducted from the home's cost basis. The seller may treat the points as a

FIGURE 14.2 ■ Amounts of Points Deduction is Limited

Jerry is in a high tax bracket, which he expects will be substantially lower when he retires. He can get a 7½ percent loan on his new property from his banker, but arranges instead to pay 32 points to reduce the interest rate to 3½ percent. He deducts the points in the year paid.

Because of the unusually large interest deduction, the IRS flags the return. In the subsequent audit, the IRS disallows the deduction because the amount of points exceeded the typical charges for the area. Jerry must write off the excess points over the life of the loan.

selling expense. Points paid to refinance the property are not fully deductible the year paid. Instead, they are capitalized and can be written off over the period of the loan.

Prepayment penalties. Penalties a lender levies for an early loan payoff are deductible as interest in the year paid. Delinquency penalties, however, generally are not. The IRS says that the charge compensates the lender for the extra work to be done in the collection process, rather than covering the use of the money.

Property Tax Deduction

A homeowner may deduct ad valorem taxes in the year paid. When taxes are required as part of the monthly mortgage payment, the taxes are deductible in the year the lender actually hands them over to the tax collector.

The Standard Deduction

Many taxpayers who have only a few deductions find it saves them more money to use the **standard deduction**. In 2012, the standard deduction for a married couple filing jointly was $11,900. This amount is adjusted annually for inflation. If a couple itemized their taxes, interest, and medical expenses, for example, and they totaled $9,800, using the standard deduction would save the couple more on their taxes.

Therefore, it makes sense that for interest and property taxes to offer significant tax savings, the deductions must exceed the standard deduction. (See Figure 14.3.)

The IRA deduction for down payment. First-time homebuyers can use up to $10,000 of their IRA savings for a down payment or related expenses. A "first-time" buyer is a person who had no ownership interest in a principal home for the previous two years. It also may be used for a child, grandchild, or ancestor. The income tax effects depend on which type of IRA the money comes from, traditional or Roth.

Traditional IRA. The traditional IRA allows a taxpayer to deduct the qualifying amount of contributions each year. Earnings in the fund are tax deferred, and at age 59½, the taxpayer may withdraw funds. These distributions are taxable. Early withdrawals are taxable immediately and generally incur a 10 percent penalty. Funds of up to $10,000 withdrawn for first-time home purchase expenses are taxable, but the account holder pays no penalty.

FIGURE 14.3 ■ Itemizing versus the Standard Deduction

John and Helen purchased a home for $160,000, partly because they wanted the tax deductions for interest and property taxes. The statement from the lender showed that interest for 2007 was $7,653 and property taxes were $2,057. Their other deductions totaled $400. Did they have a tax savings?

No. The total deductions, when itemized, were $10,110. The standard deduction was $10,700. They received no tax benefit from taxes and interest. John and Helen would have a tax savings only if their itemized expenses were greater than the standard deduction.

Roth IRA. Contributions to a Roth IRA, which became available in 1998, are not deductible, but the earnings are tax free. Distributions that meet both of the following requirements can be made tax free and with no penalties:

- The account holder does not take a distribution for five years after the first contribution is made, *and*
- The taxpayer is age 59½ or older or is disabled, the account owner dies, or the distribution is used for first-time homebuyer expenses.

SPECIAL RULES

Special rules apply for tax deductions on vacation homes and for persons who deduct expenses for home offices.

Vacation Homes

Persons who own **vacation homes** as their second homes can deduct interest up to the limits described earlier and all property taxes. If a property is rented for less than 15 days in a tax year, the rental income is not reported, and normal homeowner deductions for taxes and interest apply. When that unit is rented for 15 or more days, the rules change. The owner must specify the number of days of personal use and the number of days the unit is rented at fair market value. If the number of personal use days does not exceed 14, the unit is taxed as an income property (see the next section). However, if the owner or any family members use the property for more than 14 days or more than 10 percent of the days the home was rented, the unit is treated as a residence. Expenses can be deducted only to the extent of rental income. (See Figure 14.4.)

Office in Home

Persons who operate businesses from their homes often deduct expenses such as insurance, repairs, utilities, and depreciation. Simply doing business from home does not qualify a person for the deductions, however. **Home office** deductions are a very controversial area of the tax law, and the IRS has set rigid requirements to prevent abuses. A taxpayer must

FIGURE 14.4 ■ Vacation Rentals with Personal Use

Sandra and Robert own a home on St. George Island. Robert is preparing the tax return. His records show 12 personal use days and 100 fair-value-rental days. Rental income for the year was $11,800. Expenses were $14,900, including interest, taxes, management fee, maintenance, and depreciation.

Robert carefully avoided using the unit more than 14 days for tax purposes. However, his use exceeded 10 percent of the rental days (12 ÷ 100 = 12%), so it is treated as a residence anyway. He may deduct only $11,800 of his expenses, the amount of his rental income.

FIGURE 14.5 ■ Can You Deduct the Business Use of Your Home Expenses?

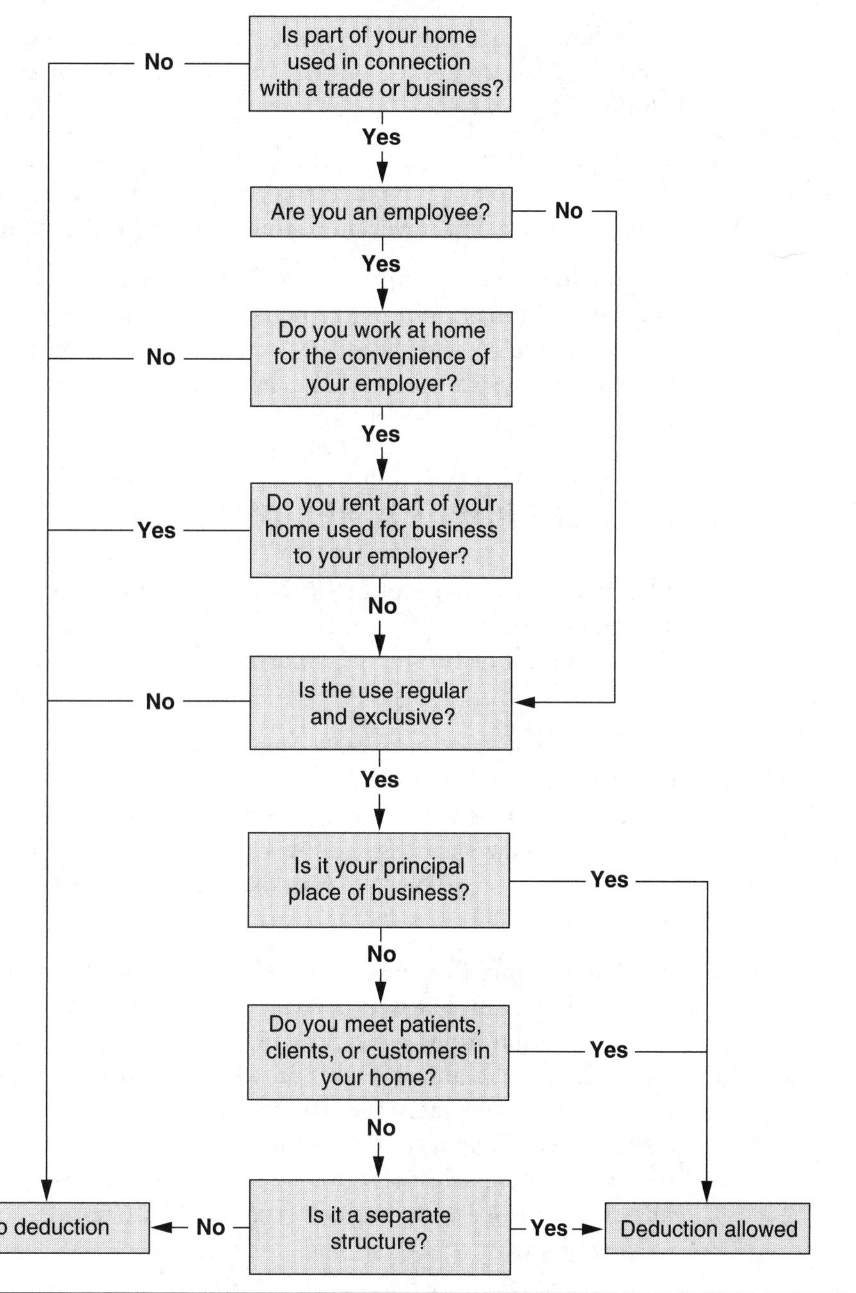

Source: IRS Publication 587—Business Use of Your Home

prove that he or she uses the home area for which a deduction is claimed *exclusively* and on a *regular basis* either as:

- a place of business to meet or deal with customers in the normal course of your business; or
- one's principal place of business, meaning the taxpayer spends most working hours there and derives most of the business income from the home office. For

example, a plumber's home office deduction was disallowed because he spent most of his time at customers' homes repairing their plumbing.

A home office meets the principal place of business rule if the taxpayer uses it to conduct administrative work and no other fixed location exists where the taxpayer carries out administrative work.

A specific area must be *exclusively* office space, with no personal activities in that space. If the home office meets all tests, the taxpayer may deduct a pro rata share of the home expenses, but never more than the business income.

Employees of a company or real estate sales associates rarely, if ever, qualify for home office deductions if they are provided office space at work. Also, a sales associate's income is attributable to outside selling activities rather than the activities in the home office. Another issue is the need for the broker to register the office as a branch location with the DBPR if customers visit the home.

SALE OF PRINCIPAL RESIDENCE

The Taxpayer Relief Act of 1997 made substantial tax savings available to homeowners. The rules allow a single filer to exclude tax on up to $250,000 of the gain from the sale of the filer's principal residence. Married couples filing jointly may exclude up to $500,000. (See Figure 14.6.)

To exclude gain, a taxpayer must both own and use the home as a principal residence for two of the five years before the sale. The ownership and use periods need not be continuous. The two years may consist of 24 full months or 730 days. Short absences, such as for a summer vacation, count as periods of use, but longer breaks, such as a one-year sabbatical, do not. The taxpayer also must not have excluded gain on another home sold during the two years before the current sale.

The Internal Revenue Service has established "temporary" regulations on the subject of excluding gain, but with a reduced maximum amount, when the seller does not satisfy one of the time rules. The tax law provides an exception to the two-year rules for use, ownership, and claimed exclusion when the primary reason for the sale is health, change in place of employment, or, to the extent provided in IRS regulations, "unforeseen circumstances." Taxpayers may establish by the facts and circumstances of their situations that their home sales were for one of these reasons. To make things easier, the IRS has identified various "safe harbors" that will automatically establish that the sale is for one of these reasons.

FIGURE 14.6 ■ Avoiding Tax on Sale of a Home

Harold and Deidra have owned their Orlando residence for 18 years. Harold has just turned 55 and has retired. Their dream is to make a trip to the far east, then explore the United States. Broker Jim prepares a CMA on their property, indicating that, after expenses, they may have a $475,000 gain. Harold fears that the taxes on the sale will be more than his cash proceeds.

Jim explains that the law allows them to avoid paying any taxes on up to $500,000 of any gain. "That savings is enough for you to take a long vacation to Australia and Hong Kong later," he says.

Home sale related to change in employment. The temporary regulations provide that a home sale will be considered related to a change in employment if a qualified person's new place of work is at least 50 miles farther from the old home than the old workplace was from that home. This is the same distance rule that applies for the moving expense deduction. The employment change must occur during the taxpayer's ownership and use of the home as a residence. A qualified person is the taxpayer, the taxpayer's spouse, a co-owner of the home, or a member of the taxpayer's household.

Home sale related to health. A sale will be considered because of health if the primary reason is related to a disease, illness, or injury of a qualified person. If a physician recommends a change in residence for health reasons, that will suffice. In addition to the persons listed above, a person qualified for health reasons includes certain close relatives, so that sales related to caring for sick family members will qualify.

Home sale based on "unforeseen circumstances." A sale will be considered as occurring primarily because of unforeseen circumstances if any of these events occur during the taxpayer's period of use and ownership of the residence:

- Death
- Divorce or legal separation
- Becoming eligible for unemployment compensation
- A change in employment that leaves the taxpayer unable to pay the mortgage or reasonable basic living expenses
- Multiple births resulting from the same pregnancy
- Damage to the residence resulting from a natural or man-made disaster or an act of war or terrorism
- Condemnation, seizure, or other involuntary conversion of the property

Any of the first five situations listed must involve the taxpayer, spouse, co-owner, or a member of the taxpayer's household to qualify. The regulations also give the IRS Commissioner the discretion to determine other circumstances as unforeseen.

For qualifying sellers, the maximum exclusion amount is limited to the percentage of the two years that the person fulfilled the requirements. Thus, a qualifying seller who owns and occupies a home for one year (half of two years), and who has not excluded gain on another home in that time, may exclude half the regular maximum amount, or up to $125,000 of gain ($250,000 for most joint returns). The proportion may be figured in days or months.

Loss on the sale of a personal home is not deductible.

EXCLUSION FROM TAXATION OF MORTGAGE DEBT FORGIVENESS

The Mortgage Forgiveness Debt Relief Act created a window of time during which homeowners pay no taxes for mortgage debt forgiveness. Previously, if a lender forgave all or part of a mortgage, the borrower was considered to have received income that was taxable. Under the law, a taxpayer may exclude up to $2 million of income from the debt on a principal residence that is forgiven during the years 2007 through 2013. This includes mortgage debt reduced in a mortgage refinance as well as debt forgiven in a foreclosure.

The rule applies only to acquisition indebtedness, which would be funds for the purchase or improvement of the home. Home equity loans not used for improvements do not receive the benefit.

The lender who forgives a mortgage must send the taxpayer a Form 1099C or 1099A that should show the fair market value of the home and the amount of the loan. The difference would normally be the income received. If audited, the taxpayer will have to document that funds were spent for the purchase or improvement of the home.

INCOME TAX TREATMENT—REAL ESTATE INVESTMENT OPERATIONS

Net operating income, before-tax cash flow, and after-tax cash flow. Appraisers are interested primarily in an investment property's net operating income. This was discussed in detail in Chapter 7. Financial institutions want assurance that an investment can pay the annual debt service and leave enough before-tax cash flow to provide a cushion. Although the investor is interested in these two amounts, probably the most important total to the investor in evaluating the real return is the financial statement's bottom line, known as **after-tax cash flow**. This is the result of either subtracting income taxes paid from before-tax cash flows or adding income tax savings that can be used as a shelter against other income. The complete financial statement for an income property is shown in Figure 14.7.

Determining Taxable Income

Calculating the taxable income from operations starts at net operating income. Then the reserve for replacements is added, and interest and depreciation for the year are deducted, as is amortization of loan costs. (See Figure 14.8.)

Reserve for replacements. The reserve for replacements spreads large, infrequent expenses such as roof replacement equally among each year's financial statements. Appraisers and investors use it to stabilize the net operating income necessary to capitalize value. The reserve is similar to depreciation in that it provides for the wearing out of different components of the property. Congress has mandated arbitrary recovery periods for the improvements and allows a tax deduction for depreciation. The reserve is not tax deductible; it must be added back to the net operating income if it has been deducted in the operating expenses.

Interest. Interest paid on income property is tax deductible; principal payments are not. A taxpayer can determine interest paid by referring to an amortization schedule or by using a

FIGURE 14.7 ■ Income Property Financial Statement

	POTENTIAL GROSS INCOME	PGI
less	Vacancy and collection loss	– V
plus	Other income	+ OI
equals	**Effective gross income**	**= EGI**
less	Operating expenses	– OE
equals	**Net operating income**	**= NOI**
less	Annual debt service	– ADS
equals	**Before-tax cash flow**	**= BTCF**
plus or minus	Federal income taxes	+/– FIT
equals	**After-tax cash flow**	**= ATCF**

FIGURE 14.8 ■ Calculating Taxable Income for Investment Property

	NET OPERATING INCOME
plus	Reserve for replacements
less	Interest
less	Depreciation
less	Amortization of loan costs
equals	Taxable income (loss)

financial calculator. Interest paid during construction of investment real estate is not deductible in the year it is paid; it is capitalized and becomes part of the building's cost.

Depreciation. Real estate income properties that have definite life spans, such as buildings, can be depreciated. Land, which has an indeterminate life span, cannot be depreciated. The cost of an investment property must be allocated between land and building using a defensible ratio. (See Figure 14.9.) Many taxpayers refer to an appraisal of the property, while others use the tax appraiser's building ratio. Once the building ratio has been determined, the ratio is applied not only to the purchase price, but also to the property's acquisition costs, such as survey, title insurance, and appraisal expenses.

Depreciation, also called *cost recovery*, is based on an arbitrary recovery period. Residential income property, with the dwelling units producing at least 80 percent of the income, has a straight-line recovery period of 27½ years. Nonresidential income property has a recovery period of 39 years. Therefore, the depreciation for Janice's office building in Figure 14.10 would be $8,482.05 per year ($330,800 ÷ 39 years).

Depreciation is a tax deduction that does not require a cash payment; principal payments are cash payments that are not deductible. A quick way to assess the tax-sheltering aspects of an income property's cash flow is to measure the depreciation exceeding the principal payments on the mortgage. This excess is the amount of cash flow that is sheltered.

FIGURE 14.9 ■ Janice's Office Building: Allocating Acquisition Costs to Building and Land

Janice buys an office building for $400,000. She pays $2,000 for an appraisal, $700 for a survey, $9,000 for her broker's commission, and $1,800 for title insurance. The appraisal indicated that the total property value was $400,000: the building's value is $320,000, and land is $80,000. What is the depreciable basis of Janice's office building?

	Purchase price of property	$400,000
plus	Appraisal	+2,000
plus	Survey	+ 700
plus	Broker commission	+9,000
plus	Title insurance	+1,800
equals	Total acquisition costs	$413,500
times	Building ratio	× .80
equals	Depreciable basis	$330,800

FIGURE 14.10 ■ Janice's Office Building: Calculating Taxable Income for an Investment Property

Janice's office building shows $40,000 in net income during the second year of operation. A $3,000 reserve for replacement is included in the operating expenses. Depreciation is $8,482.05. Interest for the year was $23,858.07. Janice's taxable income is calculated as follows:

	Net operating income	$40,000.00
plus	Reserves for replacement	+ 3,000.00
less	Interest	–23,858.07
less	Depreciation	– 8,482.05
equals	Taxable income	$10,659.88

In many situations, personal property is part of the purchase price, allowing a separate allocation to items such as furniture and appliances. Most real estate-related personal property has a seven-year recovery period. Because of the shorter cost recovery period, personal property qualifies for bigger depreciation deductions.

The depreciation deduction for a property's first and last years of ownership is based on the midmonth convention. That is, when the property is acquired or sold, whatever the date, cost recovery is calculated from the middle of the month. For example, assume an investor, a calendar year taxpayer, bought his property on March 1. While he would like to take depreciation for ten full months of the year, the IRS allows depreciation for only half of March, giving him 9½ of 12 months.

Taxes from Operations

Taxable income from rental properties may be offset by losses from the investor's other rental properties. The amount remaining is taxed at the taxpayer's income tax rate.

Losses. While most investment properties show some taxable income, occasionally a property has negative taxable income (a tax loss). The investor can use the loss to reduce the taxable (not the nonpassive) income of other real estate investment properties the investor owns.

Rental income and losses are automatically treated as **passive income** unless they are earned or incurred by a person who makes a living in real estate. If a net loss results from all passive activities, the loss generally cannot offset **nonpassive income**, such as wages, salaries, dividends, or interest. One exemption from the rule covers owners who participate in their properties' management decisions. An **active participant** whose adjusted gross income is less than $100,000 may deduct up to $25,000 of the passive losses from nonpassive income, such as salaries. The deduction, reduced by fifty cents for each additional dollar earned, is suspended when adjusted gross income reaches $150,000. Limited partners are not active participants; therefore, they do not qualify for the allowance.

If an investor sustains losses that are greater than what can be deducted currently from other passive income, the investor may use the losses to offset passive income in the future. The investor also may use the losses to reduce the gain when the property is sold.

Full-time real estate professionals, such as builders, developers, investors, property managers, real estate brokers, and sales associates, may deduct the entire operating loss from any other income, including nonpassive income. To deduct losses in full, a real estate professional must devote more than 50 percent of personal services and at least 750 hours to all real property businesses in which the professional participates materially. With a married couple, only one spouse must meet the requirement.

Tax classifications of investment. For tax purposes, four principal classifications of real property exist: personal residence, for sale to customers, trade or business, and investment.

1. Personal residence. Taxes on personal homes were discussed at the beginning of this chapter. In summary, qualified interest and taxes are deductible, and all or part of the gain on the sale of a home may be excluded from taxation.

2. For sale to customers. When owners of real estate hold their properties as inventories, such as homebuilders or subdivision developers, they are classified as dealers. Dealers in real estate may not deduct depreciation; may not defer recognition of gain, either by exchange or the installment plan; and may not have gain taxed at lower capital gains rates.

3. Trade or business. Real estate held for use in a taxpayer's trade or business, such as an office building, a manufacturing plant, or a retail store, receives the most favorable tax treatment. All of the investment's operating expenses are deductible, including depreciation. Operating losses are fully deductible against other income. Capital gains may be deferred by exchange or the installment sale method. Capital losses are deductible.

4. Investment. Real property held for investment is treated as a passive investment, which limits the use of tax losses to shelter other nonpassive income. The taxpayer may deduct depreciation at his or her own tax rate. At the time of sale, the taxpayer must pay taxes on all depreciation taken at the 25 percent rate, but this usually is lower than the rate at which the depreciation was deducted originally. Capital gains are taxed at lower rates than ordinary income. Up to $3,000 on net capital losses may be deducted annually, with the balance carried forward to future years until it is depleted.

Investor's tax status. The way a property is owned affects how it is taxed. For example, a corporation pays taxes on its income at corporate income tax rates. When shareholders receive their returns from the corporation as dividends, they must pay taxes on the dividends. If the business had been organized as a partnership, a real estate investment trust, an S corporation, a tenant in common, or an individual, taxes are paid only once, at the individual level.

Figure 14.10 shows how the taxable income is calculated for Janice's office building. Figure 14.11 shows how the taxes are calculated from the taxable income, then deducted from before-tax cash flow to get the after-tax cash flow.

FIGURE 14.11 ■ Janice's Office Building: Calculating After-Tax Cash Flow for an Investment Property

If Janice's marginal tax rate is 28 percent, she pays $2,984.77 ($10,659.88 × .28) in income taxes for this property. This figure is subtracted from before-tax cash flow in order to show after-tax cash flow:

	Net operating income	$40,000.00
less	Annual debt service	–25,785.38
equals	Before-tax cash flow	$14,214.62
less	Income taxes	–2,984.77
equals	After-tax cash flow	$11,229.85

TAX INCENTIVES FOR LOW-INCOME HOUSING

Low-income housing has long been a priority for government policymakers, who offer developers tax credits to encourage them to build or rehabilitate low-income housing. The requirements to qualify are complex and the availabilities of credits are limited, but those developers who do their homework can increase their investment returns substantially. A **tax credit** is a 100 percent direct reduction in taxes. It is about three times better than a tax deduction, as the following example shows.

A person who earns $100,000 in taxable income pays taxes on the last dollars of income at 28 percent. A $10,000 ***tax deduction*** *would save $2,800 in taxes ($10,000 × 28%). A tax credit of $10,000 would save the full $10,000.*

The low-income housing tax credit program works as follows:

- An owner-developer who builds or rehabilitates low-income housing is entitled to a nine percent credit of the qualified cost each year for ten years. The costs must exceed $2,000 per unit.
- If the construction is subsidized by the federal government or tax-exempt bonds, the credit is reduced to four percent per year.
- If an existing property that has not been used as low-income housing for the previous ten years is converted to low-income housing, the credit is four percent per year.
- Target requirement: (1) At least 20 percent of the units must be occupied by tenants with incomes of 50 percent or less of the area's median income *or* (2) at least 40 percent of the units must be occupied by tenants with incomes of 60 percent or less of the area's median income. The incomes are adjusted for family size.

These credits offset taxes on both passive and active income. However, if the taxpayer's rental properties show a taxable loss, the credits are limited. In effect, the combination of credits and tax losses cannot result in more than the equivalent of a $25,000 loss.

The total tax credit available is calculated based on a state's population. The credit is $1.25 per resident. In Florida, that limits the total credits to around $17 million.

SALE OF INVESTMENT REAL ESTATE

Determination of Gain or Loss

Figure 14.12 provides an example of calculating gain or loss. The 1997 Taxpayer Relief Act and amendments made in 1998 reward long-term investors with lower tax rates, but make the calculation more complicated.

Taxation of Gain or Loss

When a capital asset (such as real property) is sold, the owner may have a **capital gain** or a capital loss. The tax due on the gain depends on the length of time the property was held. There are two types of capital gains treatments: short-term and long-term.

An owner has **short-term gain** if the property has been held for one year or less. Short-term gain is taxable at the taxpayer's rate.

FIGURE 14.12 ■ Janice's Office Building: Calculating Gain or Loss for an Investment Property as Shown on Schedule D

After five years, Janice sells her building for $700,000. Selling costs were $38,000. She made capital improvements totaling $75,000. She has taken depreciation of $42,410.26 during her years of ownership. Based on this information, Janice calculates gain as follows:

1.	Amount realized or total selling price		$700,000
2.	*less* Selling expenses		– 38,000
3.	*equals* Net selling price		$662,000
4.	Cost or other unadjusted basis	$413,500	
5.	*plus* Improvements and certain legal fees	+ 75,000	
6.	Total		$488,500
7.	Gain or loss		$173,500

If we assume that Janice makes less than $400,000 in ordinary income, her gain is taxed at 15 percent. The depreciation taken during the five-year period is taxed at 25 percent. (See Figure 14.13.)

An owner has **long-term gain** if the property has been held for more than one year. The maximum tax rate on long-term gains is 15 percent for taxpayers earning less than $400,000 ($450,000 for joint filers) and 20 percent for taxpayers making more than those amounts. If the taxpayer's overall ordinary tax rate is in the 10 or 15 percent tax brackets, then their capital gains rate is zero.

The portion of gain that comes from the depreciation taken during the holding period is subject to taxes at a 25 percent rate. (See Figure 14.13.)

An investor may deduct up to $3,000 in net losses on investment real property, with the balance carried forward to future periods. For example, if Janice sells one of her properties and incurs a $7,000 loss, she may deduct $3,000 this year, $3,000 next year, and

FIGURE 14.13 ■ Janice's Office Building: Calculating Taxes on Gain From Sale of an Investment Property

Janice calculates the gain on the sale of her property to be $173,500. Because her ordinary income is less than $400,000, this gain is taxed at 15 percent; the depreciation is taxed at 25 percent. Janice calculates her taxes on the gain as follows:

1.	Capital gain		$173,500.00
2.	*times* Maximum tax rate		× 15%
3.	*equals* Tax on gain		$26,025.00
4.	Depreciation	$42,410.26	
5.	*times* Tax rate	× 25%	
6.	*equals* Tax on depreciation		$10,602.57
7.	Total tax on sale—*3 plus 6*		$36,627.57

The unamortized balance of loan costs may be written off as interest.

$1,000 the year after that. If, however, she has a $5,000 capital gain next year, she can offset the remaining $4,000 against that gain.

After-tax reversion. Reversion from sale is another term for *proceeds from the sale*. The balance of Janice's mortgage is now $276,821.82. The calculation for Janice's after-tax proceeds from sale is shown in Figure 14.14.

METHODS OF DEFERRING TAXES UPON DISPOSITION (SPECIAL RULES)

Most investors should consider the advantages in deferring or avoiding payment of taxes on the disposition of property. Three principal methods accomplish this objective: installment sales, like-kind exchanges, and distribution at death.

Installment Sales

The **installment sale** method of reporting offers several advantages:

- If property is sold on the installment sale basis by a taxpayer in a high tax bracket who is close to retirement, the retiree may be able to pay taxes on the gain at a lower tax rate in later years. This is particularly effective if the gain on sale is a short-term gain.
- The installment sale method allows for better planning, because the entire amount to be received is spread out over many years rather than coming in one lump sum.
- Interest rates on owner financing often are more attractive than other investments of comparable risk.

In an installment sale of depreciable property, the investor reports any depreciation recapture as income in the year of sale. The recaptured depreciation is deducted from the gross profit before the investor calculates the gross profit percentage.

If an installment mortgage on a sale of property for more than $150,000 is pledged as security for a loan, the net loan proceeds are treated as a payment on the installment obligation and are immediately taxable.

Installment sale reporting is automatic when owner financing is involved, but the seller may elect to pay taxes on the entire gain in the year of sale. Losses may not be deferred under the installment sale method. An example of installment basis reporting is shown in Figure 14.15.

FIGURE 14.14 ■ Janice's Office Building: Calculating the After-Tax Equity Reversion (Proceeds from the Sale)

	Sale price	$700,000.00
less	Costs of sale	– 38,000.00
less	Payoff of mortgage	–276,821.82
less	Income taxes	– 36,627.57
equals	After-tax equity reversion	$348,550.61

FIGURE 14.15 ■ Installment Sale Reporting Example

In 1980, Harry purchased a tract containing 150 acres for $700,000. This year, he agrees to sell it to an investor for $1.5 million with a 20 percent down payment. Harry will hold a 15-year mortgage at 10 percent. His selling costs are $104,000. To calculate how much of each principal payment is taxable as gain, Harry takes the following steps:

To calculate realized gain:

1. Sale price (contract price)	$1,500,000
2. *less* Selling costs	–104,000
3. *equals* Net sale price	1,396,000
4. *less* Adjusted basis	–700,000
5. *equals* Gross profit	$696,000

To calculate the gross profit percentage:

6. Realized gain ÷ contract price (5 ÷ 1)

$696,000 ÷ $1,500,000 = 46.4%

46.4 percent of each payment other than interest represents gain on the sale and is taxable. The taxable portion of the $300,000 down payment (20 percent) is $139,200 (46.4 percent of $300,000).

Like-Kind Exchanges

In a **like-kind exchange**, real estate held for investment or for productive use in a trade or business may be exchanged for other real estate of the same character, called *like-kind property*. Realized gain on the disposition may be deferred until the owner disposes of the new property. Like-kind property that may be exchanged includes any of the following:

- Residential income-producing property
- Commercial property
- Industrial property
- Vacant land held for investment (except dealer property)
- Leaseholds for 30 years or more
- Hotels and motels

Tax-deferred exchanges of real property are not available for dealers or for personal homes. A two-party like-kind property exchange does not qualify if the parties are related, if either party sells the property voluntarily within two years of the exchange, or if one property is outside the United States.

While the capital gains rates are very attractive for investors, the like-kind exchange is the method of choice to dispose of investment property. It allows the investor to acquire more or larger properties without using any of the capital to pay taxes. (See Figure 14.16 for an example of a tax-deferred exchange.)

Often, one party must pay the other cash or personal property to balance the equities. This **boot** is taxable to the party receiving it. In other cases, the mortgage on the property

FIGURE 14.16 ■ Example of a Tax-Deferred Exchange

Wilson has a piece of property that Jones wants, but Wilson wants to do a tax-deferred exchange. Jones does not have a property that Wilson wants, but agrees that he will buy a property selected by Wilson, then transfer it to him to complete the exchange. Wilson finds a property he likes. Jones buys it, then transfers it to Wilson. If Jones does not complete the acquisition and transfer to Wilson, Jones must pay Wilson the price in cash.

given up is more than the mortgage on the property received. This net mortgage relief also is taxable boot. If neither party receives boot, neither needs to recognize any gain, or pay any taxes on the disposition.

A direct barter of properties is difficult. For example, John may have property he wants to dispose of and may find another property he wants instead. The problem is, that owner may not want John's property. Because of this problem, the three-way or multi-party exchange was a technique designed to solve the difficulties of a two-way swap. Unfortunately, these exchanges have lots of problems also. When one or more of the parties fail to cooperate with the exchange, or one of the needed transactions fails, the entire exchange fails. Multi-party exchanges, at best, are difficult and risky.

The Deferred Exchange

Section 1031 of the tax code allows traders to set up an exchange for properties not yet available. The replacement property must be identified within 45 days of the initial transfer, and title to the replacement property must be transferred within 180 days or before the tax return due date (including extensions), whichever is sooner.

The exchange is handled by a qualified intermediary who simplifies the transaction. (See Figure 14.17.) A **qualified intermediary** is an unrelated party who, for a fee, facilitates a deferred exchange. The intermediary may not be an employee of an owner, or a person who has acted as an owner's professional adviser, such as an attorney, an accountant, an investment broker, or a real estate agent.

While some qualified intermediaries take title to the replacement property, then transfer it to the owner, this arrangement probably is not as good as having direct deeds from owner to buyer. First, Florida's documentary stamp tax can be a significant expense in a transaction, and paying it twice serves no purpose. Second, if the intermediary were to have any judgments or other liens recorded against him or her, any properties acquired, even if held for five minutes before the transfer out, would be encumbered. Third, envi-

FIGURE 14.17 ■ Example of a Tax-Deferred Exchange Using a Qualified Intermediary

Wilson has a piece of property and wants to arrange a tax-deferred exchange. He lists the property with his broker and gets an offer from Jones, which he accepts. Wilson contacts a qualified intermediary, who agrees to complete all the paperwork for a fee. Wilson assigns his contract to the intermediary. The intermediary suggests that Wilson start looking for another property immediately. Wilson's broker finds a listed property and negotiates a contract. Wilson assigns his purchase contract to the intermediary. The intermediary ensures that the necessary paperwork is completed and attends the closings.

FIGURE 14.18 ■ Example of Distribution to Heirs

Larry Hamilton owned vacant land he acquired in 1952 for $22,000. The property's fair market value when Larry died was $330,000. If Larry had sold it before his death, taxes on the gain would have totaled about $60,000. Larry's son, William, inherited the property and sold it two years later for a net price of $340,000. William's gain was $10,000, and he paid capital gains taxes of $2,000.

ronmental laws may impose toxic waste cleanup liability on anyone in the chain of title, which includes the qualified intermediary.

An important IRS opinion recently endorsed what is commonly called a reverse exchange. While most exchanges are done on a delayed basis, under a reverse or "parking" exchange, an unrelated third party, such as a qualified intermediary, acquires and warehouses the replacement property until the investor sells the original property.

Among other requirements, the exchange must be completed within 180 days. While reverse exchanges have no special tax benefits, they do offer investors an option they might otherwise lose because of timing. Persons interested in using this safe harbor method should contact their CPA for information on all the requirements.

Distribution to Heirs

Another way to shelter income against the capital gains tax is to continue to own investment property until death. (See Figure 14.18.) At that time, the owner's heirs acquire the property, and their basis, for tax purposes, is the property's market value at the time of the decedent's death.

For the years 2011 and 2012, there is a lifetime exclusion of $5 million. The tax rate for estates over $5 million is 35 percent. Estate taxes are complex, and owners of large estates should employ qualified estate planners.

WEB LINK

Web Link: **www.irs.gov/**

SUMMARY OF IMPORTANT POINTS

- The two principal tax deductions available to homeowners are interest and property taxes.
- If a homeowner occupies a residence for two years, he may exclude up to $250,000 ($500,000 for married couples filing jointly) on the gain from the home's sale.
- Taking the standard deduction rather than itemizing expenses on a tax return may be more advantageous, depending on whether the standard deduction is greater than the itemized expenses.
- Points paid on financing the purchase of a home, whether by the buyer or the seller, may be deducted.

- A homebuyer who has not owned a residence for the previous two years can use up to $10,000 of an IRA to make the down payment and pay acquisition costs on a home.
- Expenses for a vacation home, if the owner uses the home more than 14 days per year or the home is rented out more than 10 percent of the time, are deductible only to the extent of rental income.
- A person who wishes to deduct expenses for an in-home office is subject to very strict guidelines.
- An investor may deduct interest and depreciation from a rental property's net operating income.
- Reserves for replacement are not deductible.
- The first step in calculating depreciation is to allocate acquisition costs between land and improvements.
  - Only improvements may be depreciated.
  - Residential income property may be depreciated straight-line using a 27½-year life.
  - Nonresidential improvements may be depreciated straight-line using a 39-year life.
- If an investment property shows an operating loss, the investor's ability to deduct the loss from the nonpassive income depends on the investor's situation. If the investor earns more than $150,000 in income, she may not deduct any of the loss, but can use it in future years against passive income or at the time of sale. An active participant earning less than $100,000 may deduct up to $25,000 of the loss from other nonpassive income.
- A real estate professional may deduct the entire loss from other nonpassive income.
- Long-term gains on the sale of investment property have a maximum 15 percent tax rate for taxpayers earning less than $400,000 ($450,000 for joint filers) and 20 percent for taxpayers making more than those amounts. Any depreciation taken during the holding period is recaptured and taxed at 25 percent.
- If all sales, when taken together, show a loss, a maximum of $3,000 in net losses is deductible annually.
- An installment sale allows the investor to pay taxes on the gain as the payments are received, rather than paying in the year of sale.
- A like-kind exchange allows the investor to defer paying taxes on the gain until the new property is sold. Boot is taxable property received that is not like-kind.
- Distribution to heirs is another way to defer taxes from a property's disposition.

REVIEW QUESTIONS

1. Which statement is FALSE about interest deductions on a personal residence?
   a. Interest on a motor home used as a second home is not deductible.
   b. Interest on up to $1 million in home acquisition debt on two homes can be deducted.
   c. Qualifying home equity debt is limited to a maximum of $100,000.
   d. The mortgage loan must be recorded or the interest cannot be deducted.

2. An owner bought his home for $124,000 in 1986, financed with a $116,000 mortgage. This year, the value of the home is $178,000, and his mortgage balance is $97,000. How much can he borrow on a home equity loan if he wants all the interest to be deductible?
   a. $27,000
   b. $54,000
   c. $62,000
   d. $81,000

3. Points are NOT deductible by a buyer in the year of purchase if
   a. the seller pays for the points.
   b. points are the same or less than the typical charges for points in the area.
   c. the points are paid for the purchase of investment property.
   d. the points are paid for the purchase of the buyer's personal residence.

4. A married couple bought a home in Scenic Heights. When William began to do their tax return, the deductions were $5,280 for interest, $800 for property taxes, and $600 for Florida sales taxes. The couple's top tax rate is 25 percent. How much in tax savings did this couple realize from the home purchase?
   a. $0
   b. $1,478
   c. $1,702
   d. $1,870

5. Deductible expenses of an income property do NOT include
   a. ad valorem taxes and maintenance.
   b. depreciation and amortization of loan costs.
   c. reserves for replacements and principal payments.
   d. interest payments on debt exceeding $1 million.

6. A man purchased his home in Clearwater in 1995. He sold it this year for $840,000, a gain of $300,000, then purchased a new home within 24 months for $500,000. The man
   a. owes taxes on the difference between $840,000 and $500,000. The new home's price had to be equal to or greater than the older home's adjusted sale price.
   b. must pay capital gains taxes on $50,000 of the gain.
   c. may exclude the entire gain, up to $500,000.
   d. may roll over the gain into a new residence as a like-kind exchange.

7. A job change required that a couple sell their home one year after its purchase. They had a $20,000 gain on the sale, but did not buy a new home for 30 months. The couple
   a. is entitled to exclude one-half ($10,000) of the gain.
   b. is entitled to one-half the $500,000 exclusion ($250,000); the entire gain is excluded.
   c. must pay taxes on the entire gain because they did not remain in the property for the required two years.
   d. must pay taxes on the entire gain because they did not buy another home within 24 months, as required.

8. An office building shows net operating income of $75,000. Operating expenses were $28,000, including reserve for replacements of $6,800. Interest was $49,200, and depreciation was $15,200. What was this property's taxable income?
   a. –$17,400
   b. $10,600
   c. $17,400
   d. $59,800

9. A woman's income this year was $94,000. She owns an apartment building, which generated a negative taxable income of $34,500, and an office building, which showed taxable income of $6,200. If she is an active participant in the management of both buildings, she may
   a. offset the $6,200 taxable income against her other buildings' taxable loss, deduct $25,000 of the remaining loss against her active income, and use the balance against the gain on the sale of the building later or against any other passive income she has.
   b. deduct $25,000 from her active income. She must save the rest and use it to offset the gain on the sale of the same property.
   c. deduct none of the loss because the loss is passive.
   d. deduct all of the loss from her active income because her income is less than $100,000.

10. A homebuilder has built too many homes and ends up with seven properties on the market for more than a year. He sells two for a combined profit of $60,000 and finances them himself. He keeps the others for sale. He
    a. can deduct interest and depreciation on the homes and receive capital gains treatment on the profits.
    b. can deduct depreciation, but does not receive capital gains treatment.
    c. cannot deduct depreciation, nor does he receive capital gains treatment, but he may recognize the profit on the installment basis.
    d. cannot deduct depreciation, nor does he receive capital gains treatment, and he must pay taxes on the profit in the year of sale.

11. A taxpayer in the 27 percent bracket owns an apartment building that she purchased four years ago. Her personal income from her salary for the year is $218,000. Her operating expenses over that period have been $94,540, including a reserve of $8,512 and depreciation of $14,682. NOI is $124,683. Her adjusted property basis is $184,650 after she reduces the original price by depreciation. When she sells the building for $294,000, how are her gain and depreciation taxed?
    a. Gain of $109,350 is taxed at 15 percent; depreciation of $14,682 is taxed at 10 percent
    b. Gain of $109,350 is taxed at 15 percent; depreciation of $14,682 is taxed at 25 percent
    c. Gain of $94,668 is taxed at 15 percent; depreciation of $14,682 is taxed at 25 percent
    d. Entire gain is taxed at 15 percent; no tax is due for depreciation

12. An investor sells four properties this year, all of which he had held for more than 12 months. Two had a gain, one for $24,240 and the other for $47,495. The other two had losses of $7,000 and $9,800. The investor
    a. may deduct a total of $3,000 of the losses from the gains, so taxable gain is $68,735. The gains are taxable at a maximum 20 percent tax rate.
    b. can use the $3,000 of *each* loss to reduce the gains, so taxable gain is $65,735.
    c. must pay taxes on $71,735 in gains.
    d. can deduct the total losses of $16,800 from the total gains of $71,735. Taxable gain is $54,935.

13. Owner 1 owns a duplex and a building site. Owner 2 is willing to exchange a small office building, which is a little more valuable than the total of Owner 1's properties. Owner 1 exchanges the property and pays Owner 2 $20,000 in cash. Which is correct?
    a. Owner 1 must pay capital gains taxes on the difference in value she paid in boot.
    b. Owner 2 must pay capital gains taxes on the amount she received in boot.
    c. The transaction is tax deferred for both parties.
    d. Because no qualified intermediary was involved, the fair market value less costs is taxable to each owner.

14. An owner purchased a vacant land in West Palm Beach in 1967 for $84,000. The value of the property when he died this year was $450,000; it was the bulk of his estate. His nephew, who inherited the property, sold it for $450,000, paying 10 percent in closing costs. The nephew's marginal tax rate is 31 percent. What are his taxes on the sale?
    a. $0
    b. $64,200
    c. $81,000
    d. $99,510

CASE STUDY PART 3

LISTING AND SELLING REAL PROPERTY

Department of Business and Professional Regulation, Florida Real Estate Commission	*vs.*	*Mary Prudhoe*
Recommended Order:	This case was heard in Orlando on September 12, [year 3], before Administrative Law Judge W. L. Richardson, Division of Administrative Hearings. The parties were represented by: For Petitioner: Bruce W. Carpenter, Esquire, DBPR For Respondent: Joseph H. Campbell.	
Findings of Fact:	This matter arises from Petitioner's Administrative Complaint against Respondent Mary Prudhoe. On August 6, [year 1], Dr. and Mrs. Richard M. Sanctions (the "Sanctions") entered into a Contract for Sale and Purchase of their residence. The contract listed Respondent as the agent for Atlas Enterprises, Ltd. (the "Buyer"). The next day, Respondent executed a single agency disclosure form stating that Respondent was the agent for the Sanctions as sellers. Respondent also presented an addendum to the Contract making it contingent upon a home inspection satisfactory to the Buyer. The home inspection indicated repairs were required, and the Sanctions made the repairs. The Sanctions entered into a contract for the purchase of a replacement residence. The Sanctions placed $10,000 in escrow for the purchase of the replacement residence. Respondent requested an extension of the closing on behalf of the Buyer but did not give the Sanctions a reason for the requested extension. The Sanctions refused to extend the closing without a reason and demanded the funds in escrow. Respondent refunded the escrow of $5,000 to the Buyer. The Sanctions forfeited the $10,000 they had placed in escrow on the replacement residence because they were unable to close without the sale proceeds for the sale of their residence. On October 26, 1999, Petitioner filed an administrative complaint against Respondent alleging that Respondent committed a breach of trust in a real estate transaction. Respondent timely requested an administrative hearing.	

Discussion Questions:

1. Which subsections of Chapter 475, F.S. were violated, and what were the violations?
2. Did Respondent commit a breach of trust in the real estate transaction?
3. What course of actions should Respondent have followed?

WEB LINK

Web Link: **http://www.doah.state.fl.us/internet/**

PART FOUR

SPECIALTIES

CHAPTER

15 INVESTMENT REAL ESTATE

KEY TERMS

assemblage
base rent
discounted cash flow analysis
dynamic risk
effective interest rate
escalator lease
expansion option
expense stop
gross lease
gross leasable area
HVAC
index lease
internal rate of return (IRR)
marketability
net leasable area
net lease
net-net-net lease
net present value (NPV)
note rate
overage lease
percentage lease
plottage
pro forma statement
renewal option
rent concession
return on equity (ROE)
return on investment (ROI)
sales threshold
sensitivity analysis
static risk
step-up lease
tenant improvement allowance
triple-net lease

OVERVIEW

A broker who sells real estate investment property must be able to communicate factual information to principals and customers so they can make informed decisions. The broker should be able to clearly present a property's physical characteristics, regulatory requirements, lease terms, operating expenses, financing, and cash flows. The broker must understand a customer's financial abilities and goals to find the right property for the investor. By understanding the principles of investment analysis, brokers reduce their liability and satisfy their customers' needs.

This chapter describes some of the steps investment brokers use to evaluate income property, including:

- matching an investor with the right property;
- evaluating the sites and improvements of income properties;
- determining the type of lease terms most appropriate for property;

- evaluating different financing alternatives; and
- analyzing the financial aspects of an investment using ratios and discounted cash flow methods.

Once you have completed this chapter, you should be able to:

- list the characteristics that affect an investment site's value;
- list at least eight structural components of an income property building and the types of problems a broker might observe;
- distinguish between the terms *gross leasable area* and *net leasable area*;
- describe the difference between a percentage lease and a net lease;
- calculate the additional rent required from financing a tenant improvement;
- describe the difference between simple interest and add-on interest;
- itemize three methods an investor can use to reduce the annual debt service on a mortgage;
- describe the priorities of leases compared with mortgages on the same property;
- list at least six problem areas that a broker must scrutinize when reviewing an owner's operating statement;
- construct an annual operating statement for an income property;
- calculate the appropriate financial and investment ratios used to evaluate a one-year statement;
- describe the process used to estimate the after-tax equity reversion;
- calculate the present value of a series of unequal cash flows;
- calculate an investment's net present value;
- describe the differences between net present value and internal rate of return;
- list at least six types of risk; and
- list at least six categories of information that a broker should understand about an investor.

Matching Investment Properties with Investor Needs

Before presenting a property to an investor, a broker should know as much as possible about the investor's needs and the property characteristics that best fit those needs.

The investor's needs. An interview with the investor identifies important information that the broker needs to match the investor to the right property. A list of some information the broker should discuss with the investor follows:

- What does the investor have now? Include cash, mutual funds, and equity in a personal residence and investment properties.
- What are the investor's liabilities, such as debts on installment financing, automobiles, alimony, child support, and mortgages?
- Does the investor face any contingent liabilities? The investor may need cash in the future for retirement income, college education for children, a daughter's wedding, or care for an elderly parent.
- What is the investor's risk profile? This sometimes depends on the investor's age and assets. Young investors often take greater risks for higher returns, while

investors near retirement are more careful. Also, persons with few assets to lose generally take greater risks.

- What is the investor's earning potential? An investor whose earnings substantially exceed current living needs has additional funds for savings and investment.
- Is the investor a good manager? Owners who can manage their own properties competently can save significant management fees.
- What are the investor's goals? Understanding specific investment goals allows the broker to make better choices when presenting properties for the investor's consideration.

Property characteristics. Once the broker has counseled the investor, the broker is ready to locate and present a property that fits the investor's assets, goals, and abilities. When measuring the property characteristics, the broker must consider the investment's return, its risk, its liquidity, tax factors, the amount of time required of the investor, and the investor's objectives. A discussion of each follows.

Return. The return on the capital investment is an important consideration. Obviously, an investor currently receiving a 10 percent after-tax return on a mutual fund will be unwilling to invest in a real estate property yielding 9 percent. The broker must understand the investor's return requirements before presenting a property.

Risk. The broker must analyze a venture's risk. A risk-averse investor probably would not be interested in acquiring a vacant site to construct a strip shopping center but may be more comfortable with a fully occupied property.

Liquidity. Liquidity means "Can I get my money back quickly without taking a loss?" Real estate tends to have low liquidity compared with securities or savings accounts. Investment properties are complex and often take substantial time for analysis and negotiation. Even if a buyer can be found quickly for an investment property, closings take time. In short, it is time consuming to dispose of an income property for current cash needs, and an emergency may require the investor to sell the property at a loss.

Marketability. Marketability describes the ability of real estate to be bought and sold. If there is an active marketplace for a property, it has good marketability. Marketability is similar to liquidity, except that liquidity implies that the full value of the property is realized at the sale, whereas marketability simply indicates that the property can be bought and sold easily.

Tax factors. Income tax consequences can affect the return on a property. An investor in a low tax bracket receives fewer tax benefits from an investment than does an investor who pays taxes at the top rate.

Time required. Management requirements are not as great a burden for a person who works a normal work week and manages a duplex, but a physician who works 70 hours weekly may resist purchasing any property requiring significant management time.

Objectives. Indirect effects on an investor's ego, experience, or reputation influence what type of property the investor will consider. For instance, prestige buildings, which often show mediocre returns, may appeal to the investor with a high ego drive. The respected minister of a large church probably will not want to own a property in poor condition that rents to migrant farm workers for fear of being perceived as being a slumlord.

SITE DESCRIPTION

The investment broker must analyze carefully the physical characteristics of each property that seems to meet the investor's needs.

The major components of an income property are land and improvements. Land that is ready for a specific purpose is called a *site*. A site's value is affected by the use of the sites around it, by its ability to serve either existing or potential income uses, and by its highest and best use.

The broker must understand the impact of a site's physical features, its locational attributes, the restrictions on its use, and its economic usefulness:

- Physical features include the site's size and shape, topography, drainage, soil condition, and environmental conditions. If the property is located in a FEMA flood hazard area, the site's value is affected adversely.
- Access, road frontage, and visibility are important locational attributes. Surrounding property uses also are an important consideration.
- Legal restrictions, such as zoning, building permits, easements, and restrictive covenants, affect the property's use. The broker must disclose to the investor if a property has a nonconforming (grandfathered) use. If the building were damaged or destroyed later, a new building would have to meet all code requirements, and it is likely that the site's former use could not continue.
- Community acceptance of the proposed use of the property is important and should be reviewed early in the analysis. Failure to gain community acceptance may make the use politically unacceptable to regulators. Many developers have spent substantial sums in planning only to have the proposed development blocked.
- The property's economic usefulness is affected by the land available for a particular use. Sometimes, **assemblage** of more than one parcel is required. **Plottage** is the increase in value if the value of the two as a whole is greater than the sum of the values of each taken separately. A site may have excess land that is not required for the use.

STRUCTURAL CHARACTERISTICS OF INCOME PROPERTY BUILDINGS

While a commercial investment broker is not expected to be a structural engineer or contractor, the broker must understand the basic structural components of income property buildings. These improvements include the following:

Type and condition of roof. The roof is the structure and the roof cover. The structure comprises the joists, trusses or rafters, bracing and ties, and roof decking. The cover consists of gutters, gravel stops, and skylights. Types of covers include tar and gravel (built-up roof), shingles, wood shakes, tile, slate, composition shingles, barrel and other concrete tiles, copper, and steel. The broker should recommend that a qualified roofing contractor examine the roof.

Type and condition of HVAC system. HVAC stands for *heating, ventilation, and air-conditioning*. This broad category of items includes boilers, pumps, cooling systems, piping, ducts, and registers. Basic heating and cooling systems consist of heat pumps, space heaters, hot water, chilled water, and gas and electric forced air systems. As systems age, the maintenance problems increase.

Nature and capacity of electrical systems. This category includes the service distribution, panel box, light fixtures, and receptacles. Copper wiring is preferred. Many properties built in the 1960s and 1970s have aluminum wiring that later was found to be a fire hazard. Older systems may need replacement to provide service to the heavy appliances, air-conditioning, and electronic devices used in today's apartments and offices.

Nature and capacity of telephone service. New lines may be necessary. In newer office buildings, many tenants demand fiber-optic cables for faster Internet connections.

Nature and condition of elevators. Elevators in older buildings are expensive to replace, and many owners prefer renovation. The equipment must be checked for maintenance, safety, and proper operation.

Insulation level. Many properties built before the 1980s are not well-insulated, resulting in high utility costs. There is no quick way to learn whether an older property has adequate insulation. If an inspection under the roof or over the ceiling of the top floor reveals no insulation, it is also likely that none exists in the walls. Many older public buildings were insulated and fireproofed with asbestos, a dangerous substance banned in the late 1970s. The trend today is to treat the asbestos in place by encapsulating it with an adhesive or enclosing it with an airtight barrier. While these methods are expensive, they are less costly than removing the material.

Utilities. Utilities are a major operating expense for many income properties. Apartment properties usually have separate electric and gas meters for each unit. Office buildings and retail properties need flexibility in unit sizes, but should have separate metering for each tenant when possible. Expense passthroughs on cost-of-electricity increases help reduce the owner's risk. Shopping centers usually require tenants to pay their own utilities.

Adequacy of storm drainage system. The system should be compared with current city or county requirements. If the property was built when an older regulation was in force, remodeling or enlargement may demand new building permits, requiring the owner to pay high impact fees or to build expensive run-off holding ponds.

Condition of appliances and special equipment. In dwelling units, this includes the age of refrigerators, water heaters, ovens and ranges, and smoke detectors.

Condition and needs of drives and parking areas. Paved areas should be free of holes, large cracks, and weed growth. Paint striping should be fresh.

Survey of land and buildings. The broker must measure carefully the structure's square footage (or cubic footage if it is a warehouse or an industrial property). Because value projections often depend on a property's size, inaccurate measurements may result in significant valuation errors. This also applies to individual dwelling units in an apartment building and individual spaces in an office building because rental rates often are based on a unit's square footage. A building's efficiency also is an important consideration in its profitability. A building that is 20 percent hallways and lobby is 80 percent efficient.

A property survey also reveals any encroachments or easements. An encroachment from another property may require legal action to cure. If a building encroaches on another property, it may be very expensive to cure. Easements give others the right to use or cross the property and may restrict the investor's ability to build a structure or fence.

LEASES AND LEASE TERMINOLOGY

A lease is a contract between the owner (lessor) and the occupant (lessee). The general requirements for a valid lease are the same as those for an enforceable contract. The parties must be legally competent and have a meeting of the minds. The agreement must be for a legal purpose, and there must be consideration. Leases for more than one year must be written and signed to be enforceable.

Rental Rates

Investors use many methods to establish lease rates. The rental rate for dwelling units normally is set for each unit rather than being priced on a square-foot basis. Commercial and office properties' rental rates typically are quoted as dollars per square foot of leased space. The area's measurement may be based on gross leasable area or net leasable (usable) area. **Gross leasable area** is all the area inside the tenants' space, including bathrooms and sometimes common hallways. **Net leasable area** normally includes only the area the tenants use.

Base rents in office or commercial buildings normally allow use of all common areas, such as parking, lobby, elevators, and bathrooms. Often, the number of parking spaces is limited. Maintenance of the common areas usually is included in the base rent. Shopping centers and other commercial buildings often add a common area maintenance fee to the base rent based on the space a tenant occupies.

The dollar amount of the lease payments should be shown in the lease rather than a price per square foot. This decreases the chance for a later dispute over the measurement.

Types of Leases

The six types of leases discussed in this chapter include gross leases, percentage leases, net leases, escalator leases, index leases, and step-up leases.

Gross lease. A **gross lease** requires the tenant to pay a gross rent, with the landlord paying taxes, maintenance, and insurance. This type of lease is most commonly used with dwelling units.

Percentage lease. Sometimes called **overage leases, percentage leases** are often used for retail tenants. A minimum (base) rent is charged, plus a percentage of the tenant's gross sales over a predetermined threshold. For example, if a tenant's base rent is $50,000 annually and the percentage is four percent, the sales threshold would be $1.25 million ($50,000 ÷ .04). If the store's sales for the year are $1.65 million, it has exceeded the threshold by $400,000. The additional rent would be $16,000 ($400,000 × .04), and the total rent would be $66,000.

This is often attractive to the tenant because the overage rent is a variable expense, and is usually not a hardship because any sales amount greater than the **sales threshold** also generates greater profits to the business. Landlords prefer the percentage lease because as the sales volume grows (either by increased business or by inflation), the landlord shares in the increase.

The base rent is set by comparison of rental rates for competing properties. The percentage rent is usually based on guides published by real estate management organizations.

Stores with high sales volumes and low profit margins (such as grocery stores) would usually pay lower percentage rates than stores with lower sales.

The owner's duties in monitoring the required percentage payment include defining the term *gross sales*, auditing the sales reports, and establishing the method of payment.

Net lease. The term *gross lease* suggests that the owner is responsible for paying all expenses associated with the property, while a **net lease**, sometimes called a **net-net-net lease** or **triple-net lease**, implies that the tenant is responsible for taxes, maintenance, and property insurance. Because owners seem to interpret these terms differently, the property manager must be certain that the lease specifically reflects each party's responsibilities.

Escalator lease. Office buildings and retail properties often have medium-term to long-term lease agreements with their tenants. Because of this, an owner wants some protection from increasing expenses during a lease term. The owner often gets this protection by negotiating an **expense stop** or expense passthrough. In an **escalator lease**, the owner and the tenant determine a base amount for expenses, such as taxes, utilities, insurance, and maintenance. The owner's obligation to pay expenses exceeding the base amount "stops" and passes through to the tenant.

Index lease. An **index lease** requires changes in the rent payment based on some published index, such as the Consumer Price Index. Assume that the consumer price index is 100, and the rent is $20,000 per year. If the following year the index rises to 105, it has risen five percent. The rent would also rise by five percent ($1,000), so the new rent would be $21,000.

Step-up lease. Sometimes called a *graduated lease*, a **step-up lease** has rent increases built into the schedule of rents. For example, a step-up lease could require rent of $8,000 in the first year, $8,300 in the second year, and $8,650 in year three.

Rent concessions. Depending on market conditions, the property manager may offer **rent concessions** to be competitive. Such a concession might be a rent reduction or temporary free rent. A rent reduction is less desirable because at renewal time, renegotiating an amount satisfactory to the owner may be more difficult. On the other hand, one or two months' free rent does not affect the monthly rent in the lease. The concession often is delayed until later in the lease period—for instance, in the 6th month, then again in the 12th month.

Tenant Improvement Allowances

Tenants often require alterations or improvements before they take occupancy. While painting and cleaning is typical for residential tenants, the renovations for office, commercial, and industrial properties tend to be much more extensive and costly. The owner of one of these buildings normally is expected to furnish a standard number of electric outlets and lights, walls, and windows, and the tenant may be required to pay for partitioning or additional plumbing. Tenant requirements also vary by type of business. A dentist's or doctor's office requires more renovation work than a real estate office. A manufacturing plant may require more than a storage and distribution warehouse. A bank branch costs more than a clothing retailer to renovate. And many businesses will not rent space that does not conform to Americans with Disabilities Act (ADA) requirements to provide accessibility to employees and customers.

Retail and industrial space tends to be rented as a basic building with a heating and air-conditioning system. The tenant usually pays for all improvements. In office buildings,

FIGURE 15.1 ■ Tenant Improvement Allowance

The manager of a small office building has calculated that annual net rents must be at least $15 per square foot to provide a fair return to the owner. QuickSell Realty, Inc., offers to sign a three-year lease for 2,000 square feet if the landlord will make specified renovations. The manager estimates that the improvements will cost $4,500. The owner is, in effect, financing the improvements for the tenant. The manager calculates the amortization of $4,500 at 10 percent for three years to be $145.20 per month, as shown below.

Using a financial calculator, input the following values and solve for the monthly payment:

N	%I	PMT	PV	FV
36	.83333	145.20	4,500	0

Where:

N	=	number of monthly periods in loan term (three years × 12 months)
%I	=	market interest rate (10% ÷ 12 months)
PMT	=	monthly mortgage payment (solve for payment)
PV	=	loan amount
FV	=	input zero when solving for present value

A comparison of the rent necessary to meet the landlord's required return is shown as if the tenant paid for the improvements up front versus the landlord paying for the work.

		If Tenant Pays for Improvements	If Landlord Pays for Improvements
	Required net rent/square ft.	$ 15	$ 15
times	Number of square ft.	× 2,000	× 2,000
equals	Minimum annual rent	$30,000	$ 30,000
divided by	12 months	÷ 12	÷ 12
equals	Minimum monthly rent	2,500	2,500
plus	Improvement cost amortization	0	+ 145.20
equals	Monthly rent from tenant	$ 2,500	$2,645.20

the tenant generally pays for extra partitioning and redecorating. The owner should be aware of how the improvement allowances affect the property's net income. In reality, the owner must receive enough in additional rent to pay for the improvements. One approach to calculating **tenant improvement allowance** is shown in Figure 15.1.

Improvement allowances requested by tenants who are renewing their leases must be considered in light of market conditions, the costs of the allowances, and the tenants' stability and rent payment histories.

Options

Many leases give the tenants options to renew their leases or options to expand.

Renewal option. The right to extend the lease term under specified conditions is called a **renewal option**. Because the option benefits the tenant, it usually requires an increase in the rent, perhaps based on a predetermined percentage or on an index, such as the Consumer Price Index.

Expansion option. The guarantee that the tenant (usually a growing commercial company) may lease additional adjacent space in the property after a certain period is called an **expansion option**. If the owner provides this option, the owner may not rent the adjacent space on a long-term basis. Therefore, most owners would rather use a right of first refusal.

MORTGAGES

Most buyers finance the purchase of income property with a new mortgage loan. A buyer should analyze the basic terms of a mortgage, particularly the interest rate, the amortization period, and possible balloon payments. Because investors tend to favor high current cash flows over greater equity in later years, reducing the mortgage payment is an important goal.

Interest rate and computation. Income property is a riskier loan than an owner-occupied home, so lenders charge higher interest rates. ARMs reduce the risk of inflation to lenders, so their interest rates tend to be lower. An investor who believes that inflation and interest rates will remain stable may choose an ARM.

Lenders charge higher interest rates on long-term mortgages because of the risk of inflation. Therefore, a borrower might get a lower rate if the loan is for seven to ten years, rather than 25 years. The payment on this type of loan usually is calculated as if the loan

FIGURE 15.2 ■ Simple versus Add-on Interest

Comparison between Simple Interest and Add-on Interest
$100,000 for Ten Years at Ten Percent Interest

Simple interest

A $100,000 loan at 10 percent interest for ten years requires monthly payments of $1,321.51. The lender's yield is 10 percent.

Using a financial calculator, input the following values and solve for the monthly payment:

N	%I	PMT	PV	FV
120	.8333	1,321.51	100,000	0

Where:

N	=	number of monthly periods in loan term (10 years × 12 months)
%I	=	market interest rate (10% ÷ 12 months)
PMT	=	monthly mortgage payment (solve for payment)
PV	=	loan amount
FV	=	input zero when solving for present value

Add-on interest

The principal of $100,000 is multiplied by the interest rate to get $10,000 per year. This figure is multiplied by the number of years, so the total interest is $100,000. The total interest plus the beginning principal equals $200,000. Divided by 120 payments, this equals a monthly payment of $1,666.67. The yield to the lender on this loan is 15.9 percent.

FIGURE 15.3 ■ Amortization Term

Comparison of Equity Return Rates for Partially Amortized Mortgage Compared to a Fully Amortized Mortgage

Jack Blanton is preparing an investment analysis for an income property he has listed. The property shows NOI of $60,000, and its value is $550,000. Jack calls several lenders and learns that they will make a $412,500, 25-year loan at an interest rate of nine percent, or a 10-year loan amortized over 25 years at 8.25 percent. The equity is $137,500 (25 percent of $550,000). Jack calculates the mortgage payments by using a financial calculator, as follows:

25-year mortgage:

N	%I	PMT	PV	FV
300	.750	3,461.68	412,500	0

10-year balloon mortgage amortized over 25 years:

N	%I	PMT	PV	FV
300	.6875	3,252.36	412,500	0

Where:

N	=	number of monthly periods in loan term
%I	=	market interest rate
PMT	=	monthly mortgage payment (solve for payment)
PV	=	loan amount
FV	=	input zero when solving for present value

		25-year mortgage	10-year balloon mortgage
	Net operating income	$60,000.00	$60,000.00
	Mortgage payment times 12 months	–41,540.16	–39,028.32
less	Before-tax cash flow (BTCF)	$18,459.84	$20,971.68
equals	Equity dividend rate (BTCF ÷ Equity)	13.4%	$15.2%

period were 25 years, but the unpaid loan balance is due in a balloon at the end of the tenth year. Other loans offer shorter terms with balloon payments, with lenders having the option to adjust the rate. The approach has risks, however, if market conditions make refinancing difficult when the balloon payment is due.

When getting quotes for interest rates, an investor also needs to know how the lenders define the interest. Most common is simple interest, calculated on the outstanding balance. Most real property mortgages use simple interest. Occasionally, personal property (refrigerators, ranges, etc.) is financed with add-on interest. In this approach, the interest is calculated on the total amount of the loan, then added to the balance before the lender determines the monthly payment. While both types of loans may have the same **note rate**, the **effective interest rate** for the add-on plan is much higher. (See Figure 15.2.)

Amortization term. The loan term affects the mortgage payment amount and thus the before-tax cash flows. A mortgage amortized over a short term reduces cash flows and the investor's current return. (See Figure 15.3.)

Other terms affecting the payment. Other terms that affect the monthly mortgage payment include loan participation and negative amortization. Many times, a commercial lender will agree to a lower interest rate if it can participate in any of a property's increases in income. The owner makes a constant payment over the life of the loan, plus an additional payment based on the property's performance. An owner takes this option if it's believed a low inflation rate will continue.

A negative amortization loan increases current cash flows to the borrower, but because the mortgage payments do not cover the required interest, the difference is added to the loan.

Recourse provisions. Most mortgages include a provision prohibiting transfer of the property without the lender's consent. If the lender allows a transfer, the seller must understand the situations under which he will remain liable for the obligation. If the buyer buys *subject to* the mortgage, the seller is totally liable. If the buyer *assumes and agrees to pay* the obligation, both parties are liable, and the lender may collect from either one or both. If the buyer agrees to an assumption with *novation*, the seller is removed from liability and the buyer takes sole responsibility.

Prepayment clauses. Prepayment mortgage clauses describe the conditions required for paying the mortgage earlier than scheduled. Many lenders do not charge a penalty for prepayment. A lender generally cannot enforce both a due-on-sale clause and a prepayment penalty, but it may charge a prepayment penalty when a loan is paid through refinancing proceeds. The investor should determine the lender's prepayment policies in advance.

Legal priority of leases versus mortgages. The principal mortgage lender usually requires that the mortgage have priority over all liens other than taxes and assessments. Recording a lease establishes priority for liens recorded afterward. If a tenant leases property that has a prior mortgage lien, the lender may foreclose the lease rights. During the late 1980s, when office building vacancies averaged 25 percent, many buildings were foreclosed. Tenants who believed they had valid long-term leases at very low rates became month-to-month tenants. A tenant's only protection is to have the lender's agreement to subordinate the mortgage to the lease—an agreement most lenders refuse to give.

Owners should be aware that refinancing properties with existing leases may be a problem because of the priority of the leases. Each lease agreement should contain a provision that the tenant agrees to subordinate to any new financing on the property.

Importance of an estoppel letter for existing mortgages. Occasionally, it is still possible to purchase investment property using the existing financing. An estoppel letter gives the buyer assurance of the mortgagee's agreement to the transfer of ownership, the interest rate and mortgage term, the principal balance, and the date of the last payment.

INVESTMENT ANALYSIS

An investment property broker also must understand investors' needs and the ways they make their investment decisions.

The creation of investment pro forma statements. The first step in preparing a **pro forma statement** is to estimate potential gross income based on the rents for comparable properties. Vacancy and collection losses are deducted, and other income is added, to get the effective gross income. Operating expenses must be estimated based on the owner's records and the analyst's forecast of future costs. The analyst must estimate an appropriate vacancy rate based on competing properties in the market.

While an appraiser is concerned primarily with capitalizing net operating income, the investor and the lender usually are more interested in cash flows before and after taxes.

After estimating the net operating income, the investor must determine which financing will provide the best return, consistent with acceptable risks. (The methods of calculating annual debt service were discussed in Chapter 12.) The investor deducts annual debt service from net operating income to determine before-tax cash flow.

Calculating income taxes from operations was discussed in Chapter 14. The investor deducts estimated income taxes from before-tax cash flows to get after-tax cash flows.

Verification and adjustment of data provided by the owner. The most important part of a financial analysis is gathering complete and accurate data. The owner's records are the primary source of information, but sometimes those records can mislead an investor. Some problems with the owner's statements are discussed below.

Deferred maintenance. It is important that the investor inspect the property thoroughly to learn whether expenses have been understated because necessary maintenance on the building or equipment was not done.

Capital improvements. The property may need a new roof, an exercise room, or an addition to a parking garage to stay competitive.

Understated reserve for replacements. The investor should calculate the reserve necessary to replace building components, and should fund the reserve adequately by reducing the purchase price to reflect the amounts needed.

Rent concessions. The investor must determine whether rent concessions have been given to maintain acceptable occupancy rates and whether these concessions must be continued to maintain occupancy levels. An investor should review the leases completely and obtain an affidavit from the seller that there are no agreements with the tenants that are not shown on the leases.

No management fees. Often, the owner is the manager and does not include management fees in the financial statements. The investor should include an appropriate management fee in the pro forma statement.

Short-term tenants. Sometimes, a property owner packs the property with tenants on short-term leases. The buyer should consider how many tenants will stay in the property after the purchase.

Advance rent discounts. Occasionally, an owner needing cash flow discounts future rents for an advance payment of several months. Tenant estoppel letters should reduce surprises to the buyer.

Tenants' own appliances. An owner may give a rent credit to tenants in older properties who use their own refrigerators and other appliances. The buyer may need to purchase these items after the tenant moves. Tenant estoppel letters should reveal this problem.

The investor should analyze the financial statements carefully. Another prudent step is to ask tenants to sign estoppel letters verifying rents, security deposits, next rent payment dates, special rent concessions, and appliance ownership.

The use of reserves for replacements in after-tax calculations. Reserves for replacements normally are included as operating expenses in financial statements. An owner must replace the carpeting, roof, appliances, and other items in a matter of years. For example, if an apartment property will need new carpeting in five years, and the owner expects to pay $50,000 to replace it, the owner adds $10,000 per year to the reserves. This stabilizes the net operating income by making annual charges rather than a large charge in five years. It also represents more fairly the property's current expenses as the carpeting is used up. Appraisers use replacement reserves to stabilize net operating income when they capitalize income to value.

Some disagreement exists in the industry, however, about whether to add back the reserve when calculating after-tax cash flow. Some investment authorities add back the reserve because it is not allowed as a tax deduction and because no actual cash outlay was paid until the replacement was made. Other experts believe that because the property is being used up, much the same as depleting inventory in a manufacturing plant, the reserve is a current cost that should *not* be added back to after-tax cash flow. This approach is more conservative and results in a lower cash flow. Naturally, different perceptions of property value could result from the two approaches.

Assume that two brokers working for two prospective buyers evaluate the same property, each using a different method for the reserve. If each buyer required the same rate of return, the buyer using the method that adds back the reserve would, theoretically, pay more for the property.

Each approach has persuasive arguments. Because no established standard exists for whether reserves for replacements should be included in the financial statements, a broker should note clearly the method used to prepare an analysis. When comparing alternative properties' rates of return, an investor should be certain that the reserves have been handled consistently in all the analyses. This text takes a more conservative approach and does not add back the reserve when calculating after-tax cash flow.

The next section shows the process of investment analysis for a small office building as it might be prepared by a commercial investment broker.

CASE STUDY—TIMBERLANE OFFICE SUITES

Timberlane Office Suites, located on the near northeast side of Tallahassee, can be marketed as a prestige location with no vacancies. A national credit bureau rents 1,200 square feet; a law firm occupies 1,000 square feet; an insurance agent has 1,600 square feet; and a real estate broker rents 1,800 square feet. Each space is metered separately for power. The rental rate is $15 per square foot. The building is well-maintained, and the entire project has a feeling of success.

The building value is 80 percent of the total, based on the tax rolls. The owner has provided financial statements that do not include either a reserve for replacements or a management fee. The investor's broker prepares a pro forma statement. Although the property currently has no vacancies, the broker uses a six percent vacancy rate and a management fee of five percent. Other adjustments reflecting current expense rates are noted.

The property is priced at its appraisal value of $475,000, and the seller has agreed to pay loan closing costs. The buyer makes less than $400,000 in ordinary income, and is in the 28 percent marginal tax rate. Based on the buyer's risk profile, the broker makes the analysis using a 25-year mortgage at the current rate of eight percent with a 25 percent down payment. The broker calculates the mortgage payment using a financial calculator, as follows:

N	%I	PMT	PV	FV
300	.6667	2,749.60	356,250	0

Where:

N	=	number of monthly periods in loan term (25 years × 12 months)
%I	=	market interest rate (8% ÷ 12 months)
PMT	=	monthly mortgage payment (solve for payment)
PV	=	loan amount
FV	=	input zero when solving for present value

Figure 15.4 shows the first year's annual operating statement using the owner's figures, except where noted.

FIGURE 15.4 ■ Annual Property Operating Statement

Property:	Timberlane Office Suites		Price:	$475,000
Location:	1815 Timberlane Road, Tallahassee, FL 32308		Loans:	$356,250
Prepared by:	Richard Sanders, Broker		Equity:	$118,750

	Item	%	Amount	Comments
PGI	Potential gross income	100%	84,000	5,600 sq. ft. @ $15 per sq. ft.
– V	Vacancy	6.0%	–5,040	Use 6%, although no current vacancy
+OI	Other income		1,500	From vending machines
EGI	Effective gross income	100%	80,460	
	Operating expenses:			
	Accounting and legal		950	Increased $200 from owner's records
	Advertising		300	
	Insurance		1,605	Increased $140 from owner's records
	Management fee	6.0%	4,828	Not included in owner's figures
	Payroll		0	
	Property taxes		7,600	Increased $800 from owner's records
	Repairs and maintenance		1,000	
	Janitorial, lawn, pest control, trash		5,455	Increased $420 from owner's records
	Supplies		300	
	Utilities		2,400	Increased $350 from owner's records
	Miscellaneous		505	
	Reserve for replacements	4.0%	3,218	Not included in owner's figures
–OE	Total operating expenses	35.0%	28,161	
NOI	Net Operating Income	65.0%	52,299	
–ADS	Annual debt service		–32,995	$356,250 @ 8% 25 years = 2,749.60/mo
BTCF	Before-tax cash flow		19,304	
–Taxes	Federal income tax expense		–4,884	See Figure 15.5
ATCF	After-tax cash flow		14,420	

The figures above are an estimate and are not guaranteed.

FIGURE 15.5 ■ Calculation of Taxes on Timberlane Suites

	Net operating income	$52,299
plus	Reserve for replacements	+ 3,218
less	Interest	−28,331
less	Depreciation ($380,000 ÷ 39 years)	− 9,744
equals	Taxable income	17,442
times	Marginal tax rate	× 28%
	Taxes (or savings) to table above	$ 4,884

Financial and Investment Ratios

Financial statement ratios offer the investor an opportunity to compare the subject property's operating results with other similar properties. These ratios are based on the pro forma operating statement for a typical year.

Debt service coverage ratio. This ratio of net operating income to annual debt service is a lender requirement. The ratio is based on the perceived riskiness of the projected NOI. In the Timberlane Suites study, assume that a lender requires NOI to be at least 1.4 times greater than the annual debt service. It is calculated as follows:

Net operating income ÷ Annual debt service = Debt service coverage ratio

$52,299 ÷ $32,995 = 1.59

Therefore, the coverage is more favorable than the lender requires.

Operating expense ratio. This ratio is calculated by dividing operating expenses by effective gross income. Testing the numbers provides useful comparison with similar properties. For Timberlane Suites, the ratio is calculated as follows:

Operating expenses ÷ Effective gross income = Operating expense ratio

$28,161 ÷ $80,460 = 35%

Price per square foot. The price per square foot is a common yardstick used to select preliminary properties. An investor may compare this price with the cost to construct a similar building on the site. Price per square foot is calculated for Timberlane as follows:

Price ÷ Number of sq. ft. = Price per sq. ft.

$475,000 ÷ 5,600 sq. ft. = $84.82 per sq. ft.

A check of similar office buildings that have sold recently shows that the subject property falls within the range of $78 to $86 per square foot.

Rent per square foot. This figure commonly is used to shop competitive properties. When comparing one building's rent per square foot with another's, the broker must be certain that the services the owners provide are comparable. Rent per square foot is calculated for Timberlane as follows:

Potential gross income ÷ Number of sq. ft. = Rent per sq. ft.

$84,000 ÷ 5,600 sq. ft. = $15 per sq. ft.

Expenses per square foot. This measurement of a building's costs, when used with comparable properties, helps an investor evaluate an owner's financial statements for accuracy. Expenses per square foot are calculated for Timberlane as follows:

Operating expenses ÷ Number of sq. ft. = Expenses per sq. ft.

$28,161 ÷ 5,600 sq. ft. = $5.03 per sq. ft.

Net operating income per square foot. NOI per square foot is another useful measurement for comparable properties. It is calculated for Timberlane as follows:

Net operating income ÷ Number of sq. ft. = NOI per sq. ft.

$52,999 ÷ 5,600 sq. ft. = $9.46 per sq. ft.

Cash break-even ratio. For investors concerned with cash flows, the break-even ratio is very important. It is the percentage of potential gross income that an investor must collect to break even. If all units are alike, the break-even ratio is the occupancy rate required to break even. It is calculated for Timberlane as follows:

Operating expenses – reserves + annual debt service ÷ Potential gross income = Cash break-even ratio

$28,161 – $3,218 + $32,995 ÷ $84,000 = 69%

Margin of safety. The margin of safety is directly related to the cash break-even ratio. While the cash break-even ratio gives a sense of the occupancy level required to break even, the margin of safety shows the other side of the equation, the vacancy ratio. The calculation is one minus the cash break-even ratio:

1 – .69 = 31%

Overall capitalization rate (OAR). The capitalization rate also is called **return on investment (ROI).** It would be the investor's return if he paid no mortgage on the property. The OAR includes both debt and equity and helps an investor value income property. Students will recognize I ÷ R × V as the solution aid. The OAR is calculated for Timberlane as follows:

Net operating income ÷ Value = Rate

$52,299 ÷ $475,000 = 11%

Equity dividend rate. This rate of **return on equity (ROE)** sometimes is called the *cash on cash return*. Investors use the equity dividend rate most frequently in their initial investment analysis. The rate is calculated for Timberlane as follows:

Before-tax cash flow ÷ Equity = Equity dividend rate

$19,304 ÷ $118,750 = 16.3%

Loan constant. The loan constant (k) is the constant annual percentage of the original loan amount required as principal and interest payments. Calculated by dividing the annual debt service by the original mortgage principal, the loan constant for Timberlane follows:

Annual debt service ÷ Original mortgage balance = Mortgage constant

$32,995 ÷ $356,250 = .0926

The mortgage constant is related directly to the interest rate and the mortgage term. An increase in the interest rate causes the constant to increase. A longer loan term causes it to decrease. Normally, an investor wants the lowest loan constant possible to decrease loan payments and increase cash flow. If the loan constant is less than the capitalization rate, positive leverage exists and the equity dividend rate is higher than the capitalization rate. If the loan constant is greater than the capitalization rate, the equity dividend rate is affected adversely.

If the annual constant on the debt service is less than the overall rate of return (OAR), the result is positive leverage. In Timberlane Suites, any loan with a loan constant of less than 11 percent (the capitalization rate) increases the investor's return. Notice that the equity dividend rate is higher than the capitalization rate—positive leverage at work. The buyer has a capitalization rate of 11 percent and a loan constant (*k*) of 9.26 percent. This has increased the equity dividend rate to 16.3 percent.

Loan-to-value ratio over time. The loan-to-value ratio shows the percentage of value a lender agrees to lend. It is calculated for Timberlane as follows:

Mortgage amount ÷ Price = Loan-to-value ratio

$356,250 ÷ $475,000 = 75%

As time progresses, the lender's position improves, value increases, and the loan is reduced by amortization. The loan-to-value ratio therefore declines, and the lender's safety margin increases. For example, at the end of the fifth year, based on a three percent appreciation rate, Timberlane's property value is $550,655, as shown below:

N	%I	PMT	PV	FV
5	3	0	475,000	550,655

Where:

N	=	number of years property is held
%I	=	interest rate
PMT	=	input zero because the owner makes no payments
PV	=	beginning value
FV	=	solve for future value

The mortgage balance will be reduced to $328,726, as shown in the calculations below. The loan-to-value ratio will be 59.7 percent.

N	%I	PMT	PV	FV
60	.6667	–2,749.60	356,250	328,726

Where:

N	=	number of monthly periods for which the owner has made payments (5 years × 12 months)
%I	=	monthly interest rate (8% ÷ 12 months)
PMT	=	monthly mortgage payment (given in problem) (Note: This is a negative number.)
PV	=	beginning loan amount
FV	=	solve for future value of the mortgage

Practical Application of the Ratios

These ratios should be used not just to report a property's status but as important keys in evaluation. A careful investor uses the ratios to help determine the price to be paid based on income and cash flow.

The following format, which helps in this evaluation process, uses two calculations. The first estimates the amount of the mortgage loan that is available; the second determines how much down payment the investor is willing to make. When the two results are added, the investor knows the price that will bring the required return.

Estimating the amount of available financing based on lender standards. To determine the financing, the investor needs to know the lender's requirements for the debt service coverage ratio, and also must calculate the mortgage loan constant (*k*) based on current lending rates. Dividing the NOI by the required debt coverage ratio shows the allowed annual debt service. Dividing this figure by the loan constant results in the available loan amount.

Assume that the mortgage market will give the buyer of a commercial building a 25-year loan at an eight percent interest rate. The monthly payment factor is .00772, and the annual factor (constant) is .09261. With a net operating income of $70,000, a required debt coverage ratio of 1.4 and an annual loan constant of .09261, the annual debt service can be $50,000 and the maximum loan would be $539,898, as shown below:

1. Net operating income ÷ Debt coverage ratio = Annual debt service

   ($70,000 ÷ 1.4 = $50,000)

2. Annual debt service ÷ Mortgage loan constant = Mortgage loan amount

   ($50,000 ÷ .09261 = $539,898)

Calculating the down payment based on the investor's return standards. The next step is to calculate the maximum down payment. Once the mortgage amount is determined, the investor subtracts the annual debt service from the net operating income to get before-tax cash flow. If the investor divides this number by the required equity dividend rate, the result is the down payment the investor is willing to make.

In the same example, we have estimated that the debt service the lender will allow is $50,000. The net operating income is $70,000. The investor deducts the debt service of $50,000 to yield the $20,000 cash flow. If the investor's required return is 11 percent, the down payment would be $181,818, as calculated below.

1. Net operating income – Debt service = Before-tax cash flow

   ($70,000 – $50,000 = $20,000)

2. Before-tax cash flow ÷ Required rate of return = Down payment

   ($20,000 ÷ .11 = $181,818)

Calculating the purchase price. After completing the previous steps, the investor simply adds the results of both steps to determine the purchase price. For the example, the calculation follows:

	Mortgage amount available from lender	$539,898
plus	down payment from buyer	+181,818
equals	purchase price offered	$721,716

FIGURE 15.6 ■ Calculating the Purchase Price for an Investment Property

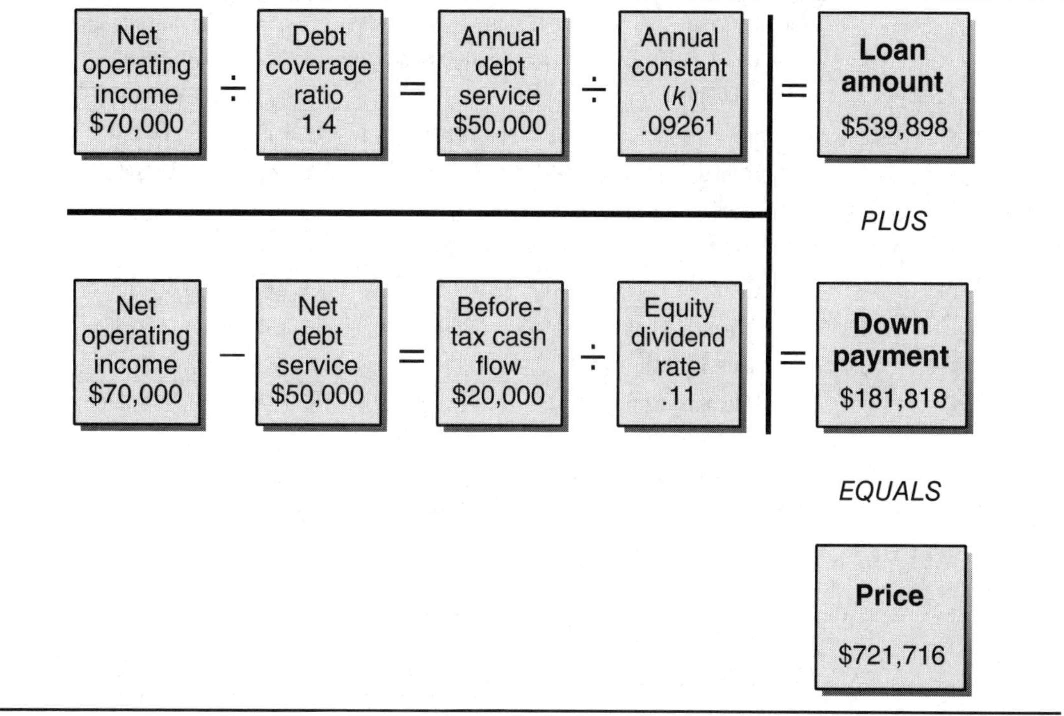

Figure 15.6 summarizes the process.

Because the loan amount is less than 75 percent loan to value, it should be acceptable to the lender. This is a powerful technique for valuing income property.

Five-Year Cash Flow Analysis

After completing the one-year statement, the broker is ready to complete a cash flow report for the expected holding period of the property. For brevity, this study uses a five-year holding period, but most investors hold their properties longer.

For purposes of this study (see Figure 15.7), assume that effective gross income for Timberlane increases three percent annually, while total operating expenses, including reserves, increase by four percent. This analysis is quite detailed. It may be done with a calculator, but using a computer spreadsheet program makes the process much quicker once the investor has designed the initial template. Ready-made software templates also are available.

Broker Sanders now estimates the cash proceeds from the sale of the property. The most important estimate, the selling price, can be calculated by several methods, including multiplying the purchase price by a realistic appreciation rate or capitalizing the estimated net income at the end of the period.

FIGURE 15.7 ■ Cash Flow Analysis Worksheet

Property name:	Timberlane Office Suites	Purchase price:	$475,000
Prepared by:	Richard Sanders, Broker	Loan amount:	$356,250
Date prepared:	4/14/20xx	Down payment:	$118,750

	Year 1	Year 2	Year 3	Year 4	Year 5
1. Potential gross income	$84,000	$86,520	$89,116	$91,789	$94,543
2. Vacancy and collection losses	–5,040	–5,191	–5,347	–5,507	–5,673
3. Other income	1,500	1,545	1,591	1,639	1,688
4. Effective gross income (plus 3%/yr.)	80,460	82,874	85,360	87,921	90,558
5. Operating expenses (plus 4%/yr.)	–28,161	–29,287	–30,459	–31,677	–32,944
6. Net operating income	52,299	53,587	54,901	56,244	57,614
7. Annual debt service	–32,995	–32,995	–32,995	–32,995	–32,995
8. Cash flow before taxes	19,304	20,592	21,906	23,249	24,619
9. Income tax savings (expense) see line 18	–4,884	–5,389	–5,912	–6,454	–7,016
10. Cash flow after taxes	14,420	15,203	15,994	16,795	17,603

Calculation of Tax Liability

	Year 1	Year 2	Year 3	Year 4	Year 5
11. Net operating income	$52,299	$53,587	$54,901	$56,244	$57,614
12. Add: reserves for replacement	3,218	3,347	3,481	3,620	3,765
13. Interest	–28,331	–27,944	–27,525	–27,071	–26,579
14. Loan point amortization	0	0	0	0	0
15. Depreciation	–9,744	–9,744	–9,744	–9,744	–9,744
16. Taxable income (loss)	17,442	19,246	21,113	23,049	25,056
17. Marginal tax rate	28%	28%	28%	28%	28%
18. Tax liability to line 9	4,884	5,389	5,912	6,454	7,016

The figures above are estimates, not guarantees.

If broker Sanders assumes a three percent annual appreciation rate, the value at the end of year five would be $550,655, calculated as follows.

N	%I	PMT	PV	FV
5	3	0	475,000	550,655

Where:

N = number of years the owner holds the property
%I = interest rate
PMT = input zero because the owner makes no payments
PV = beginning value
FV = solve for future value

If broker Sanders uses a capitalization rate of 11 percent and capitalizes the NOI for year six, anticipated to be $59,000, the value at the end of year five would be $536,363, calculated as follows:

$$\text{Year 6—estimated NOI} \div \text{Capitalization rate} = \text{Selling price}$$
$$\$59{,}000 \div .11 = \$536{,}363$$

He uses the more conservative method and estimates the sale price to be $536,000. If the selling costs are eight percent, he calculates the after-tax proceeds from the sale as shown in Figure 15.8.

Present Value of a Series of Cash Flows

Ratio analysis versus discounted cash flow analysis. While ratio analyses such as equity dividend rates and capitalization rates are important measurements of a property's productivity, they are lacking in three important areas: changing cash flows over time, the time value of money, and the cash proceeds from the sale of the property.

FIGURE 15.8 ■ After-Tax Equity Reversion (Proceeds from Sale)

Property name:	Timberlane Office Suites	Sale price:	$536,000
Prepared by:	Richard Sanders, Broker	Loan balance:	$328,725
Date prepared:	4/14/20xx	Equity:	$207,275

Line #	**Description**		
	To calculate taxes at time of sale:		
1.	Sale price (estimated by capitalization of NOI)		$536,000
2.	*less* Selling costs (6%)		– 32,160
3.	*equals* Amount realized		$503,840
	less basis:		
4.	Original cost	$475,000	
5.	*plus* Capital improvements	0	
6.	*less* Depreciation	– 48,720	
7.	*equals* Adjusted basis		$426,280
8.	*equals* Gain (loss) on sale		$ 77,560
9.	*less* Depreciation (line 6)		– 48,720
10.	*equals* Gain, not including depreciation		$ 28,840
11.	*times* Capital gains tax rate		× 15%
12.	*equals* Income taxes on gain		$ 4,326
13.	*plus* Depreciation tax (line 6) $48,720 × 25%		+ 12,180
14.	Total income tax on sale		$ 16,506
Calculate after-tax equity reversion:			
15.	Sale price:		$536,000
16.	*less* Selling costs		– 34,560
17.	*less* Income taxes		– 16,506
18.	*less* Mortgage balance		–328,725
19.	*equals* After-tax equity reversion		$156,209

Another shortcoming of the ratio analysis is the investor's difficulty in weighting the importance of the different ratios. Should the decision be based primarily on the cash break-even rate or on the equity dividend rate? Should the investor assign an arbitrary weight to each, such as eight possible points for capitalization rate, ten for equity dividend rate, and five for debt coverage?

Discounted cash flow analysis is an important analytical technique used to evaluate income properties. Specifically, the analysis of **net present value (NPV)** and **internal rate of return (IRR)** address the shortcomings inherent in more traditional techniques in the following ways:

- It takes into account the anticipated changes in cash flows over the property's holding period.
- It adjusts the value of cash flow based on when the investor receives the cash flow and accounts for the time value of money. A dollar earned today and invested at 10 percent will be worth $1.10 next year. Conversely, $1.10 due in one year is not worth that today. Its present value is $1.
- It discounts the net proceeds from the future sale of the property, accounting not only for appreciation but also for mortgage amortization.

It provides a decision-making tool for selecting among competing investments. The investment with the highest NPV is the best choice.

An investor usually calculates NPV and IRR using a financial calculator or a computer spreadsheet program. When neither of these is available, the analyst may use financial tables to make the calculations. In the following table, the present value factor for a 12 percent rate is taken from financial tables for the calculation:

Year	*After-Tax Cash Flows*	*Present Value Factor*	*Present Value*
1	14,420	× .892857	$12,875
2	15,203	× .797194	12,120
3	15,994	× .711780	11,384
4	16,795	× .635518	10,674
5	17,603 + 156,209	× .567427	$98,626
	Total present values		$145,679

Using a financial calculator, input the following values and solve for the present value of each year:

End of Year 1

N	%I	PMT	PV	FV
1	12	0	12,875	14,420

End of Year 2

N	%I	PMT	PV	FV
2	12	0	12,120	15,203

End of Year 3

N	%I	PMT	PV	FV
3	12	0	11,384	15,994

End of Year 4

N	%I	PMT	PV	FV
4	12	0	10,674	16,795

End of Year 5

N	%I	PMT	PV	FV
5	12	0	98,626	173,812

Note: Some financial calculators have shortcuts to this method. Each year's cash flow may be entered, as well as the initial investment and the required interest rate. It is then quite simple to calculate the internal rate of return and the net present value.

Where:

N	=	year in which owner will receive cash flow
%I	=	required interest rate
PMT	=	input zero for this problem
PV	=	solve for present value of the future cash flow
FV	=	cash flow expected for the year

The above calculation indicates an investor could make a down payment of up to $145,679 when purchasing the property to get a 12 percent rate of return. As shown earlier, the cash investment for Timberlane Suites was $118,750. The difference, $26,929, is the property's *net* present value. Therefore, net present value is the present value less the initial investment. If the NPV is positive, the investor receives a higher rate than the required 12 percent. If the NPV is negative, the return is unsatisfactory and the investor rejects the property.

Using the factor tables, the analyst continues increasing the factor (discount rate) until the present values have been reduced to the down payment (zero NPV). When the present value of the cash flows equal the down payment, the rate is the property's internal rate of return. For Timberlane Suites, the exercise shows that the IRR, after tax, is 17.7 percent.

The IRR also can be calculated using before-tax results, but alternative investments usually are compared after taxes to make the best decision. For example, if an investor with a 28 percent tax rate is considering an investment in Timberlane Suites versus a mutual fund that has been returning 18 percent after taxes, the investor might lean toward the mutual fund because of the time investment the real estate requires. However, the only proper way to compare returns is after taxes, as the following table shows:

	Timberlane Suites	*Mutual Fund*
Before taxes	n/a	18.00%
less Taxes @ 28%	–n/a	–5.04%
After taxes	17.1%	12.96%

What might have been a difficult decision before comparing the investments fairly now seems clear. The real estate works best in this case, even allowing a premium on the return for risk and time.

Risk Analysis

Investors use several levels of risk analysis, including a one-year study of debt coverage and cash break-even ratios. Advanced risk analysis includes discounted cash flow studies using the most likely outcome and sensitivity analysis.

The major risk ratios are the debt coverage ratio and the cash break-even ratio. Each must be studied in light of the property type being analyzed. Lenders often adjust NOI projections as well as anticipated vacancy rates and reserves for replacements. A higher debt coverage ratio may be required based on a lender's evaluation of the investment's risk. For example, a lender may accept a debt coverage ratio of 1.25 if the owner has long-term leases with creditworthy tenants, but require a 1.5 ratio for a developer of a speculative strip shopping center.

Lenders also use the cash break-even ratio as an underwriting criterion. The higher the cash break-even ratio, the higher the risk. While a lender may accept an 82 percent cash break-even ratio for an occupied office building, that ratio would be too high for a motel, which is likely to have lower occupancy rates.

Sensitivity analysis. The five-year cash flow worksheet for Timberlane Office Suites was based on the most likely case scenario. It assumed a three percent annual increase in gross income, a four percent increase in operating expenses, a six percent vacancy throughout the holding period, and a sale price based on an 11 percent capitalization rate of the NOI, which increases two percent annually. While the arithmetic in the calculations may be correct, the investor has no certainty that the underlying assumptions are valid.

Sensitivity analysis is a technique that measures anticipated returns using best case, worst case, and most likely case scenarios. For instance, if the Timberlane assumptions are incorrect and income increases by five percent annually, vacancies are only three percent, and operating costs increase only three percent, the returns will be enhanced significantly. Conversely, if income increases by only 1 percent, expenses increase by five percent, and vacancies grow to 10 percent, the NOI would drop by about $15,000 in year five. The cash break-even ratio would have increased to about 85 percent, and the debt coverage ratio would be lower. Lenders and investors must analyze risk carefully using sensitivity analysis and other techniques.

Types of Risk

Investors must evaluate risks carefully and seek ways to reduce the risks. Risks to an investor include business risk, financial risk, capital risk, regulatory risk, and inflation risk.

Business risk. Business risk assumes that the property will not achieve the investor's required rate of return on capital because of unforeseen changes in capital requirements, gross income, vacancies, operating expenses, and property value at the time of sale. Two types of business risk include static risk and dynamic risk. **Static risk** is associated with fire, storm, flood, theft, or liability from accidents. Usually, the investor can buy insurance to cover the risk. **Dynamic risk** concerns changes in the economy, supply and demand conditions, tax codes, and so forth. The investor cannot insure against these significant risks, which can be mitigated only by careful due diligence before purchase and continuing analysis during ownership. The investor expects a higher return to compensate for dynamic risk.

Financial risk. Mortgage financing increases the investor's risk. Obviously, an investor who pays all cash for a property has greater safety than an investor who has a very low debt coverage ratio. To reduce financial risk, the investor may attempt to reduce the loan constant by a longer amortization period, lower interest rate, or lower mortgage amount.

Capital risk. If the investor cannot secure additional financing when needed, either from bank loans or equity funds, the property will have a high capital risk (sometimes called *external financial risk*). This happened in 2010 when liquidity in the capital markets made borrowing more difficult. When money is easy and interest rates are low, capital risk is reduced.

Regulatory risk. Regulatory risk is a category of dynamic risk. Laws affecting the use or taxation of a property can affect its cash flows and value at sale severely. One example is the Tax Reform Act of 1986, which reduced tax-sheltering aspects of income properties. Florida's Growth Management Act also has an important impact on certain properties' values.

Inflation risk. Inflation has a major impact on investors and properties. There are winners and losers. Winners tend to be borrowers, real estate investors, and the IRS. Losers are those on fixed incomes as well as lenders and taxpayers. While most properties experience high rates of appreciation, interest rates increase to a point where builders and developers cannot start new projects. The resulting shortage of space fuels the price increases. Income property owners must make certain that cash flows increase at least as fast as inflation because investors require higher rates of return.

Using the Timberlane example, the fifth year NOI was capitalized at an 11 percent rate. If inflation during the five years has increased from three percent to 12 percent, investors probably would want an additional nine percent (to 19 percent) return to maintain the same "real" rate.

SUMMARY OF IMPORTANT POINTS

- Investment real estate brokers must seek additional education to serve investors' needs adequately.
- A broker must understand the term "due diligence" and be alert for obvious flaws in a building's structure.

- A knowledge of lease terminology helps to ensure that all parties understand clearly how rents are established, whether by square foot of gross rentable area or net rentable area.
- In an **escalator lease**, a base amount for expenses, such as taxes, utilities, insurance, and maintenance, is determined. Any expenses exceeding the base amount passes through to the tenant.
- An **index lease** increases the rent payment based on some published index, such as the Consumer Price Index.
- A **net lease** implies that the tenant is responsible for taxes, maintenance, and property insurance.
- A **gross lease** suggests that the owner is responsible for paying all expenses associated with the property.
- The broker should understand the appropriate situations for percentage leases.
- Owners' interests may be protected from uncontrolled cost increases when they use net leases or expense stops.
- Sometimes, rent concessions or tenant improvement allowances attract quality tenants and therefore are appropriate.
- The broker must be aware of current trends and requirements in mortgage lending.
- The broker should be familiar with prepayment clause language, the legal priority of leases versus mortgages, and the importance of an estoppel letter for an existing mortgage.
- The investment broker must be capable of preparing pro forma financial statements for a property that reflect not only the owner's records but also any necessary expenses the owner's records do not show. After compiling the statements, the broker prepares a ratio analysis of the property that indicates its level of risk and returns.
- Ratio calculations:

  Debt service coverage ratio. Net operating income ÷ Annual debt service = Debt service coverage ratio
  Operating expense ratio. Operating expenses ÷ Effective gross income = Operating expense ratio
  Price per square foot. Price ÷ Number of sq. ft. = Price per sq. ft.
  Rent per square foot. Potential gross income ÷ Number of sq. ft. = Rent per sq. ft.
  Expenses per square foot. Operating expenses ÷ Number of sq. ft. = Expenses per sq. ft.
  Net operating income per square foot. Net operating income ÷ Number of sq. ft. = NOI per sq. ft.
  Cash break-even ratio. Operating expenses – Reserves + Annual debt service ÷ Potential gross income = Cash break-even ratio
  Margin of safety. The calculation is one minus the cash break-even ratio: 1 – .69 = 31%
  Overall capitalization rate (OAR). Net operating income ÷ Value = Rate
  Equity dividend rate. Before-tax cash flow ÷ Equity = Equity dividend rate
  Loan constant. Annual debt service ÷ Original mortgage balance = Mortgage constant

- Discounted cash flow methods of income property analysis give the investor strict decision-making criteria.
- Net present value and internal rate of return are two measures that provide the best estimates of a property's return over the holding period.
- After the broker has completed the preliminary studies, and if the property is still under consideration, the broker prepares a risk analysis using techniques such as sensitivity analysis.
- **Static risk** is associated with fire, storm, flood, theft, or liability from accidents. The investor can buy insurance to cover the risk.
- **Dynamic risk** concerns changes in the economy, supply and demand conditions, tax codes. Because this risk can't be insured, it is mitigated by analysis and a higher required return.
- The broker must learn as much as possible about the investor's situation to be able to match the investor with the right property.

REVIEW QUESTIONS

1. An investor purchased an apartment building for $1,200,000 encumbered by a 7 percent mortgage with a balance of $845,000. Net operating income was $142,500. Monthly mortgage payments are $5,972.28, and depreciation in the first year was $32,800. The investor's equity dividend rate for this property is
   a. 10.7 percent.
   b. 14.2 percent.
   c. 18.1 percent.
   d. 20.0 percent.

2. A property has net operating income of $134,000. A buyer can finance the purchase of the property with a mortgage for $800,000, with annual payments of $57,500. If the investor wants a return of 12 percent on his equity, how much will that investor be willing to use as a down payment on this property?
   a. $217,600
   b. $637,500
   c. $716,932
   d. $1,116,667

3. If NOI is $78,600 and before-tax cash flow is $42,600 and an investor requires a 14 percent equity dividend rate, how much would the investor be willing to pay as a cash down payment?
   a. $5,964
   b. $11,004
   c. $304,286
   d. $561,429

4. A hair styling studio occupies space in a shopping mall. Its lease requires base rent of $2,400 per month plus six percent of gross sales over the predetermined threshold. Above what annual sales level would the store have to pay additional rent over the base rent?
   a. $600,000
   b. $480,000
   c. $244,000
   d. $28,800

5. An office building manager knows that the building requires a minimum rent of $14.80 per square foot annually to pay expenses, debt service, and the owner's 10 percent return. An insurance agency wishes to rent 5,300 square feet for four years if the landlord will make certain improvements in the property, including partitioning and electrical work. The manager gets an $8,048 bid for the cost of renovations. The going rate for financing this type of work is 11 percent. The factor table for 11 percent for four years shows a monthly constant of .025846. What monthly rent rate should the manager quote to the company?
   a. $208.00
   b. $6,704.33
   c. $6,744.68
   d. $86,488.00

6. Which is NOT a way to reduce a loan constant?
   a. Making a smaller down payment
   b. Increasing the loan term
   c. Reducing the interest rate by agreeing to a partially amortized mortgage
   d. Making the mortgage interest-only

7. Which is TRUE if the loan constant is higher than the capitalization rate?
   a. The result is positive leverage.
   b. The equity dividend rate will be higher than the capitalization rate.
   c. The capitalization rate will always exceed the cash break-even ratio.
   d. The equity dividend rate will be lower than the capitalization rate.

8. If an investor buys property and takes over the seller's payments
   a. the buyer is totally liable if the property was purchased subject to the mortgage.
   b. the seller is liable if there was a novation.
   c. both are jointly and severally liable if it was a simple assumption of the mortgage.
   d. both are jointly and severally liable if there was a novation.

9. A developer owned a building encumbered by a first mortgage. The developer could not lease enough space and defaulted. The bank subsequently foreclosed the mortgage. A tenant had leased 18,000 square feet for 20 years two months ago, and it recorded the lease for protection against liens. Which of the following statements is TRUE about the situation?
   a. The bank may foreclose, but must allow the tenant to stay at the same rent rate.
   b. If the tenant signed a subordination agreement with the developer agreeing to subordinate to the lender, the tenant has no rights. Otherwise, its lease is superior to the mortgage.
   c. The bank has priority, and if it includes the tenant as a defendant in the foreclosure suit, the tenant becomes a tenant at sufferance after the foreclosure.
   d. Because the tenant recorded the lease, legally the bank may collect any deficiency from the foreclosure sale from both the developer and the tenant.

Use the following information to answer questions 10 through 16.

A buyer of a 20-unit apartment building purchased for $880,000 rents each unit for $700 monthly. Vacancies are estimated at 7 percent. The annual operating expenses, including the reserve of $7,812, are $59,400. Annual debt service on the $660,000 mortgage is $66,464. Interest on the debt service for year one is $59,101. Depreciation is $25,454. The apartment building owner's tax rate is 31 percent.

10. What is the property's net operating income?
    a. $87,209
    b. $96,840
    c. $124,987
    d. $156,240

11. Assuming an 11 percent capitalization rate, what is the property value?
    a. $792,816
    b. $880,364
    c. $1,136,200
    d. $1,420,000

12. What is the before-tax cash flow?
    a. $30,376
    b. $59,400
    c. $66,464
    d. $96,840

13. What are the income taxes for the year?
    a. $3,245
    b. $4,768
    c. $6,230
    d. $8,595

14. What is the after-tax cash flow?
    a. $14,215
    b. $18,935
    c. $24,146
    d. $36,606

15. What is the annual loan constant?
    a. .0845
    b. .0900
    c. .0967
    d. .1007

16. The investor's leverage is
    a. positive.
    b. negative.
    c. neutral.
    d. negative only for the first two years; then it becomes positive.

17. An investor calculates the present value of a property's cash flow, discounted at his required return of 12 percent, to be $78,450. This means that the investor should
    a. purchase the property if the price is greater than that amount.
    b. not purchase the property if the price is greater than that amount.
    c. purchase the property if the cash investment is greater than that amount.
    d. not purchase the property if the cash investment is greater than that amount.

18. If NPV is negative, the
    a. investment is acceptable.
    b. investment is unacceptable.
    c. property has a cash loss.
    d. property cannot break even.

19. An investor can reduce which risk by buying insurance?
    a. Dynamic
    b. Static
    c. Capital
    d. Inflation

20. Which risk is mitigated by requiring a higher rate of return on investment?
    a. Dynamic
    b. Static
    c. Capital
    d. Inflation

CHAPTER 16

ZONING AND PLANNING, SUBDIVIDING OF LAND, AND SPECIAL ISSUES

KEY TERMS

concurrency
dedication
development of regional impact (DRI)
Growth Management Act
hardship
impact fees
nonconforming use
planned unit development (PUD)
property report
special exception
special flood hazard areas (SFHA)
subdivision plat map
subdivision regulations
variance
wetlands
zoning
zoning board of adjustment
zoning ordinances

OVERVIEW

This chapter begins with an overview of the evolution of zoning and planning laws in Florida. Nonconforming uses, special exceptions, and variances are explained. Other zoning-related matters are discussed, including flood zones, planned unit developments, and subdivision regulations. The provisions of the Interstate Land Sales Full Disclosure Act are presented. The chapter concludes with a brief discussion of the federal Clean Water Act of 1997 and the Coastal Zone Management Act.

Once you have completed this chapter, you should be able to:

- describe the major provisions of the Growth Management Act;
- know when a development of regional impact review is needed;
- understand the concurrency provision's purpose;
- distinguish among variance, special exception, and nonconforming use;
- describe the characteristics of a planned unit development;
- distinguish between zoning and subdivision regulations;
- explain the use of impact fees and dedication of land;

- explain the antifraud and registration provisions of the Interstate Land Sales Full Disclosure Act; and
- briefly describe the purpose of the Clean Water Act of 1997 and the Coastal Zone Management Act.

THE EVOLUTION OF LAND USE PLANNING IN FLORIDA

Very little organized planning existed for urban growth in the early 1900s. A few notable exceptions include the towns of Palm Beach, Naples, Hollywood, and Vero Beach, which were planned in the 1920s and 1930s. In 1939, Florida was the last of the 48 states to adopt its version of the Standard Zoning Enabling Act, which gave cities (not counties) the authority to zone. The law, permissive in nature, became Chapter 176, F.S.

The Florida Planning and Zoning Association supported a bill to authorize cities *and* counties to plan, zone, and exercise regulatory functions. Beginning in 1951, versions of the bill were introduced in every Florida legislative session until it finally passed 18 years later in 1969. The legislation became Chapter 163, Part II, F.S. The law, permissive in nature, gave cities and counties enabling authority to plan, zone, regulate subdivision of land, and enact and enforce construction codes.

Florida adopted a new state constitution in 1968. Article 8 of the constitution gave broad powers of home rule to municipalities. In 1973, the legislature passed the municipal Home Rule Powers Act to implement Article 8. Cities were authorized to exercise municipal powers, except where expressly prohibited by law. The act also repealed Chapter 176, F.S. In 1972, the Florida legislature passed the Environmental Land and Water Management Act, which became Chapter 380, F.S. The law established areas of critical state concern and adopted statewide guidelines and standards to be used in determining whether particular developments must undergo development of regional impact review. **Development of regional impact (DRI)** is defined under Section 380.06, F.S., to mean any development that, because of its character, magnitude, or location, would have a substantial effect on the health, safety, or welfare of citizens of more than one county. The law is significant because the state declared an active role in the planning and development process.

The Local Government Comprehensive Planning Act was adopted in 1975 and became part of Chapter 163, F.S. The act was revolutionary because it set forth mandatory planning for all units of local government having land-use regulatory powers. It also established components of the comprehensive plan. In 1985, the Florida legislature adopted the Local Government Comprehensive Planning and Land Development Regulation Act, also referred to as the **Growth Management Act**. Almost all of the language of the 1975 act was retained. The act also repealed the 1969, Chapter 163, Part II, language. The 1985 act and later amendments were enacted to ensure that local governments conduct planning programs and manage their current and future growth. Local governments must show that they have set reasonable standards and have adequately planned for and provided funding for the impact of growth. The act includes a **concurrency** provision that mandates that infrastructure, such as water and waste treatment facilities needed to support additional development be in place concurrent with the development and that local governments discourage urban sprawl in their comprehensive plans.

ZONING REGULATIONS

Zoning is a municipality's regulation of structures and land uses in designated areas. **Zoning ordinances** are local laws that implement the comprehensive plan. Local government exercises police power by regulating and controlling the use of land and structures within designated land-use districts or zones. Each zone is assigned a specific land-use classification. Unless an exception is granted, only the assigned land use is allowed in a particular zone to protect against uses that might reduce the value of neighboring properties. Zoning ordinances regulate the following:

- Permissible uses for each parcel of land
- Lot size
- Type of structures
- Building heights
- Setback requirements (the space between lot lines and building lines)
- Density (the ratio of land area to structure area also known as *floor area ratio*—determined by dividing the total floor area of a building by the total land area of the site)

State law requires that the zoning code a local community adopts be consistent with its plan for development. The zoning districts are identified on a map according to the plan in order to maintain property values, matching designated use to the character of the land and discouraging urban sprawl. The three general zoning classifications (residential, commercial, and industrial) typically are divided further into subclassifications. The use within each subclassification is more narrowly defined, with separate zones for single-family homes on lots of one acre or more, single-family homes on half-acre lots, condominiums, apartments, and so forth.

Appeals and Exceptions to the Zoning Code

Owners of real estate may appeal enforcement of zoning restrictions in cases where strict compliance would cause undue hardship or reduce property values. To handle appeals and requests for relief, most zoning authorities have established a semijudicial body called the **Zoning Board of Adjustment**, or simply Board of Adjustment. The primary function of the Zoning Board of Adjustment is to provide property owners with some degree of relief from otherwise rigid zoning codes. The board must take all possible precautions to render objective, unbiased decisions because its quasi-judicial powers give it some of the characteristics of a court. Once the Zoning Board of Adjustment renders a decision, most zoning laws will allow a property owner only one additional avenue of appeal, litigation in the courts.

Nonconforming use. A legally **nonconforming use** is a use established before zoning or before the present zoning classification and as such is allowed to continue despite its nonconformance with the zoning code. The landowner cannot be ordered to discontinue the use immediately unless compensated for a taking. The methods used to correct a nonconforming use vary around the state. Most zoning authorities allow a time period long enough for the nonconforming property owner to recapture the investment in the property. After the designated period expires, the landowner must convert the property use to that use for which the area is zoned. As long as the time limit is reasonable, such ordinances have been upheld in court. Other communities allow a legal nonconforming use to continue until ownership changes. In still other areas, the nonconforming use is said to *run with the land*, not with the individual owner. In such cases, the nonconforming user may convey the land to another, and the buyer can continue the nonconforming use. The nonconforming owner may not enlarge the use. If the landowner discontinues the nonconforming use, the owner will not be allowed to resume the use in the future. If a nonconforming building is substantially destroyed by fire or other means, it must be rebuilt in compliance with the current zoning code.

Variance. A **variance** is permission obtained from the appropriate governmental authorities to deviate somewhat from the designations under the zoning code. A variance is generally a modest deviation from the zoning code requirements. A variance allows a property owner to vary from strict compliance with all or part of a zoning code because to comply would force an undue hardship on the property owner. Two conditions must be met before a property owner may be granted a variance from existing zoning requirements:

1. The property owner must show that a **hardship** exists or will be created by strict compliance with zoning requirements and that the owner did nothing to cause the hardship. Hardship has nothing to do with economic or personal hardship. It involves land use, and the hardship must relate to the property use.
2. The zoning board of adjustment must use the same established criteria to judge the validity of all requests for variances. This ensures fair and impartial treatment for each property owner requesting a variance.

Case law has established that no one has a right to a variance, so courts will not overturn the administrator's decision to deny a variance unless they deem the decision to be arbitrary.

Special exceptions. The Zoning Board of Adjustment is authorized to issue **special exceptions** for controlling the location of particular land uses. Special exceptions are used to control the location of particular land uses. It is common in zoning codes to omit certain uses from the zoning classifications. These uses are allowed by special permit only, which involves obtaining local zoning officials' approval. Hospitals, churches, schools, recreational facilities such as golf courses, and cemeteries are examples. The special exception process allows community officials to retain control over the location of such uses in those situations where they may be objectionable.

Federal Flood Insurance Program

Congress created the National Flood Insurance Program (NFIP) to help provide property owners with coverage against losses due to flooding. The NFIP offers flood insurance to homeowners, renters, and business owners if their community participates in the NFIP. Participating communities agree to adopt and enforce ordinances that meet or exceed FEMA requirements to reduce the risk of flooding. The Federal Emergency Management Agency (FEMA) administers the flood program. FEMA prepares flood maps for every city and county in the United States.

Flood insurance can be purchased for any property located in a community participating in the NFIP. Homes and buildings located in the 100-year flood plan, referred to as **special flood hazard areas (SFHA)**, financed with mortgage loans from federally regulated or insured lenders are required to have flood insurance (flood map zones A and V). SFHAs have a 1 percent or greater chance of flooding in any given year, which is equivalent to a 26 percent chance of flooding during a 30-year mortgage.

Planned Unit Development

A **planned unit development (PUD)** is a concept involving a development larger than a traditional subdivision, generally allowing mixed uses within the development and designed to provide a maximum amount of land for open space. PUDs have specific characteristics that set them apart from the usual neighborhood and subdivision developments:

- The density of dwelling units is higher than that allowed for conventional, single-family developments.
- Typically, many of the PUD's dwelling units are either apartments or town houses (multifamily).
- PUD dwelling units normally are clustered, with planned green spaces between the clusters.
- Most PUDs include residential areas, shopping areas, and professional offices.

Some zoning maps designate areas of the community as PUD zones, while other communities adopt a floating-zone concept in which a PUD becomes affixed to a particular land area when the developer presents an appropriate proposal for mixed use to the community officials. The developer usually needs community approval for the entire PUD at inception. The initial approval allows for the PUD and sanctions the development's overall concept. A PUD usually is constructed in phases over several years. As the developer plans each phase of the PUD, community approval is required for the specifics of the particular phase. In communities where the floating-zone concept prevails, the developer must obtain the planning board's approval along with a zoning change from the local governmental body.

Subdivision Regulations

Subdivision regulations are restrictions on the division of a parcel of land into two or more units. A subdivision requires the local planning board's prior approval. Zoning controls the land use. **Subdivision regulations** control the size and location of streets and sidewalks, the placement of sewer and water lines and mandated drainage facilities, and the location of parks and open spaces. When the subdivider presents a plat plan to the planning board, the board determines whether the streets, sewers, and other infrastructure meet the conditions necessary to maintain public health, safety, and welfare.

Subdivision regulations generally take the form of standards, specifications, and procedures for street signs, streetlights, fire hydrants, storm drains, sanitary sewers, curbs, gutters, and sidewalks. The regulations may require the developer to post a performance bond to ensure compliance with these rules. The final plat, or **subdivision plat map**, the developer submits illustrates in detail the improvements required under the subdivision rules. The subdivision plat map is recorded in the county where the property is located. Subdividers frequently pay **impact fees** to fund major, off-site infrastructure expansion that serves the community at large as well as the subdivision residents.

Approval of the developer's plat usually coincides with the community's agreement to accept title to all streets, streetlights, and so forth when they are completed. The developer agrees to comply with the various subdivision regulations and in return the community accepts a **dedication**, or return of title, of the infrastructure facilities, including roads, sewers, hydrants, and drainage structures.

Interstate Land Sales Full Disclosure Act

The Interstate Land Sales Full Disclosure Act is a federal law that regulates the sale or lease of land. The law is intended to prevent fraudulent marketing schemes through the mail or other means of interstate commerce that may occur when land is being sold without being seen by out-of-state buyers.

The Interstate Land Sales Full Disclosure Act is administered by the secretary of the Department of Housing and Urban Development (HUD) through its Office of Interstate Land Sales Registration. The law requires developers to register their developments with HUD and to disclose to prospective buyers important facts regarding the real estate. The law has two components:

1. *Antifraud provision.* Developers of 25 or more lots must provide each purchaser with a disclosure document referred to as a **property report**. The property report contains relevant information about the real estate and must be delivered to each purchaser before the signing of the contract. Purchasers who received the property report prior to signing the contract may cancel the contract within seven days. Purchasers who did not receive the property report before signing the contract may cancel the contract any time within two years from the date of signing.
2. *Registration requirement.* Land developers must register subdivisions of 100 or more lots with HUD.

FEDERAL LAWS REGARDING LAND USE

Clean Water Act. **Wetlands** have groundwater levels at or near the surface for much of the year or are covered by aquatic vegetation. Wetlands are important to the ecological system because they provide areas for storm waters to gather for their slow return to the groundwater and air. Wetlands are also the natural habitat for many plants and animals. The federal Clean Water Act created a permit system administered by the U.S. Army Corps of Engineers for most dredging and filling activities in wetlands connected with navigable waters. Before it issues a permit, the Corps must prepare an environmental impact statement (EIS) that studies the environmental factors associated with development. Landowners who fill wetland areas without first acquiring a permit can be ordered to remove the fill and restore the wetland.

Coastal Zone Management Act. The Coastal Zone Management Act (CZMA) is administered by the Environmental Protection Agency (EPA). CZMA encourages states (and native American tribes) to care for wetlands, floodplains, estuaries, beaches, dunes, barrier islands, and coral reefs (as well as the fish and wildlife using those habitats) found within its jurisdictions. States and native American tribes affected include areas bordering the Atlantic, Pacific, and Arctic Oceans, Gulf of Mexico, Long Island Sound, and Great Lakes. While most laws typically impose mandatory duties and responsibilities, compliance with this law is voluntary. To encourage participation, the CZMA makes federal financial assistance available to any coastal state or territory that is willing to assume the responsibility to develop and implement a comprehensive coastal management program.

In 1990, Congress reauthorized the CZMA. In this reauthorization, Congress identified *nonpoint source (NPS) pollution* as a major factor in pollution of coastal waters. NPS pollution is caused by rainfall or snowmelt moving over and through the ground. As the runoff moves, it picks up and carries away natural and human-made pollutants. These pollutants are eventually deposited into lakes, rivers, wetlands, coastal waters, and ground waters. Nonpoint source pollution includes excess fertilizer, herbicides, oil, grease, and toxic chemicals found on or in the soil. Congress recognized that effective solutions to nonpoint source pollution could be implemented at the state and local levels. Therefore, in the Coastal Zone Act Reauthorization Amendments of 1990 (CZARA), Congress called upon states with federally approved coastal zone management programs to develop and implement coastal nonpoint pollution control programs.

SUMMARY OF IMPORTANT POINTS

- The Environmental Land and Water Management Act identified areas of critical state concern and adopted statewide guidelines and standards to be used in determining whether developments must undergo development of regional impact reviews.
- The Growth Management Act requires cities and counties to prepare comprehensive land-use plans. The act also contains a concurrency provision that requires infrastructure to be in place concurrent with new development.
- A *comprehensive plan* is a statement of policies for the future physical development of a city, county, or region.
- A *zoning ordinance* is a local law that implements the comprehensive plan.
- Zoning boards of adjustment provide a process for appeal when property owners feel that existing zoning laws cause them undue hardship or reduce their property values.
- Subdivision regulations control the size and location of streets and sidewalks, the placement of sewer and water lines, and the location of parks and open spaces.
- Impact fees are used to fund major, off-site infrastructure expansion that serves the community at large as well as the subdivision residents.
- A *legally nonconforming use* is the permission to continue a use despite the current enacted zoning ordinance.
- Variances grant landowners permission to build or use land to relieve hardships the owners did not cause.
- Special exceptions help control the location of certain land uses not included in the zoning ordinance.
- A *planned unit development* is a concept involving a development larger than a traditional subdivision, generally allowing mixed uses within the development and designed to provide a maximum amount of land for open space.
- *Special flood hazard areas* (SFHAs) are designated in the 100-year flood plan and have a 1 percent or greater chance of flooding in any given year.
- Wetlands have groundwater levels at or near the surface for much of the year or are covered by aquatic vegetation.
- The Coastal Zone Management Act is a federal law designed to protect and preserve sensitive wetlands and coastal regions.
- The Clean Water Act created a permit system administered by the U.S. Army Corps of Engineers for dredging and filling activities in wetlands connected with navigable waters.

REVIEW QUESTIONS

1. A proposed area shopping mall is expected to affect the health, safety, and welfare of the citizens of a tri-county area. Which MOST likely will be required before development of the new shopping mall?
   a. Nonconforming use permit
   b. Flood insurance
   c. Registration with the DBPR as a subdivider
   d. Development of regional impact review

2. If a proposed new residential development of 10,000 homes may not begin construction until an expansion to the water treatment plant is completed, the legal authority to block or postpone development comes from the
   a. local zoning code.
   b. concurrency provision of the Growth Management Act.
   c. denial of a special exception.
   d. hardship rule.

3. Sunset Diner has been in business since 1990 in its present location. The restaurant is located in an area subsequently zoned residential. The diner may continue in business as a
   a. nonconforming illegal use.
   b. special exception.
   c. legally nonconforming use.
   d. variance from current zoning due to an economic hardship.

4. The city of Clearview does not classify any particular area within the community specifically for planned unit developments. However, the city does occasionally approve developers' requests for PUDs. This is BEST described as a
   a. floating-zone concept.
   b. fixed-zone concept.
   c. subdivision regulation.
   d. special-use permit.

5. A subdivision developer is charged $12,000 per home before construction to help fund the water treatment plant's expansion. This expense is referred to as a(n)
   a. use tax.
   b. impact fee.
   c. property tax.
   d. construction permit fee.

6. The size and location of streets and sidewalks and the placement of sewer and water lines are controlled by the
   a. zoning board of adjustment.
   b. zoning code.
   c. subdivision regulations.
   d. building code.

7. A land developer must register subdivisions of 100 or more lots with which agency?
   a. Florida Division of Land Sales
   b. Department of Housing and Urban Development
   c. The Securities and Exchange Commission
   d. Federal Trade Commission

8. A purchaser of a lot in a subdivision of 25 or more lots who signs a contract for purchase has the right to cancel the contract
   a. within the three-day cooling-off period.
   b. at any time before pledging a good-faith deposit.
   c. for a period of seven days following the date the contract was signed.
   d. for a period of 20 days after the developer receives the notice of cancellation.

9. Land areas that have groundwater levels at or near the surface much of the year are called
   a. floodplains.
   b. wetlands.
   c. coastal plains.
   d. subterranean.

10. The federal law that requires states to undertake coastal lands planning and to develop management programs that protect and develop these sensitive lands is the
    a. Growth Management Act.
    b. Coastal Protection Law.
    c. Coastal Zone Management Act.
    d. Comprehensive Planning and Land Development Regulation Act.

CHAPTER

17 ENVIRONMENTAL CONCERNS AFFECTING REAL ESTATE TRANSACTIONS

KEY TERMS

asbestos
CERCLA
environmental due diligence
environmental site assessment
innocent landowner defense
lead-based paint hazard
National Priorities List (NPL)
Phase I assessment
potentially responsible person (PRP)
radon gas

OVERVIEW

Real estate licensees must be alert to the possibility of environmental contamination on the properties they deal with. Potential environmental pollutants include asbestos insulation, underground storage tanks, chemical and petroleum spills, septic tank systems, and so forth. A site may be contaminated as a result of current or past site activities, unauthorized dumping, or disposal or migration of contaminants from adjacent or nearby properties. Selling property contaminated by hazardous substances has serious legal consequences.

The single most important environmental law affecting real estate transactions is the Comprehensive Environmental Response, Compensation, and Liability Act (CERCLA). This chapter explores the many aspects of CERCLA, including how to define the term *potentially responsible persons*, access to National Priorities List, and ordering an environmental site assessment. It also suggests ways to reduce liability, particularly when dealing in commercial and industrial properties. The chapter covers other environmental issues, including radon gas and lead-based paint, and explains requirements regarding disclosure.

Once you have completed this chapter, you should be able to:

- define *potentially responsible person;*
- list the criteria for the innocent landowner defense;
- understand the National Priorities List's purpose and use;
- define *environmental due diligence*;
- describe the information contained in a Phase I environmental assessment;
- describe the disclosure requirements for radon gas;

- describe the disclosure requirements for lead-based paint; and
- list the types of properties exempted from the lead-based paint requirements.

COMPREHENSIVE ENVIRONMENTAL RESPONSE, COMPENSATION, AND LIABILITY ACT (CERCLA)

Congress enacted **CERCLA** in 1980 to provide governmental authorities with the ability to respond to releases of hazardous substances from sites that endanger public health and the environment. CERCLA established prohibitions and requirements concerning closed and abandoned hazardous waste sites, provided for liability of persons responsible for releasing contamination at such sites, and established a trust fund for cleanup. In addition, CERCLA provided for the publication of the National Contingency Plan (NCP), which established guidelines and procedures for responding to the release or potential release of hazardous substances. CERCLA also provided for the publication of the National Priorities List of contaminated sites throughout the United States. The Environmental Protection Agency (EPA) is charged with implementing CERCLA.

CERCLA broadly defines those liable for cleanup to include any **potentially responsible person (PRP)**. PRPs include:

- present owners and operators of a contaminated site;
- persons who owned or operated a site at the time hazardous substances were located at the site;
- generators of hazardous substances found at a site; and
- persons who arranged to transport hazardous substances to a site.

Under the law, previous owners as well as current owners of a contaminated property are liable for the cost to clean up the hazardous wastes found on the property. A PRP does not have to participate in, or even know about, the disposal of a hazardous substance—merely being an owner or operator qualifies a person as a PRP and exposes the owner or operator to liability. Potentially responsible persons may include, for example, lessors who were unaware of activities occurring on a site or a lender that foreclosed on a defaulted mortgage, then participated in managing the property. The liability under CERCLA is either strict or joint and several. *Strict liability* means that the government need not show a PRP's fault, only that the persons fall within the definition of a PRP. *Joint and several liability* means that any one or more of a group of PRPs can be sued without including all of them, and those sued are responsible for the total response costs.

Superfund Amendments and Reauthorization Act (SARA)

CERCLA was amended in 1986 by the Superfund Amendments and Reauthorization Act (SARA). SARA increased the size of the cleanup Superfund. The Superfund trust is financed primarily through taxes imposed on petroleum companies and chemical manufacturers. The amendment also added an **innocent landowner defense**. Current owners could be responsible for cleanup costs when hazardous substances are discovered unless they can prove that they meet the requirements of the innocent landowner defense. To qualify, an owner must meet the following criteria:

- The landowner did not know that the property was contaminated at the time of purchase.

- Once the contamination was discovered, the landowner reacted responsibly.
- The owner made reasonable inquiries into the property's past uses *before* purchase to determine whether the property was contaminated.

The courts consider whether the purchaser possessed any special knowledge or experience; the relationship of the purchase price to the property's market value assuming no contamination; the availability of commonly known or reasonably ascertainable information about the property; the obviousness of the presence or likely presence of contamination (i.e., red flags); and qualified individuals' ability to detect the contamination by appropriate inspection. At a minimum, the purchaser should inspect the property visually, check government records concerning past ownership and property uses, and investigate further if the purchase price is obviously lower than the market price of comparable properties in the market area. A purchaser's ability to demonstrate reasonable inquiry before purchase may depend on whether the real estate agent was diligent in disclosing known information concerning the property. Real estate agents may be held liable for failing to disclose known environmental problems associated with a property being marketed or for negligently failing to disclose readily observable environmental contamination.

National Priorities List

To help the public obtain information regarding contaminated real property, CERCLA authorized the EPA to publish and maintain the **National Priorities List (NPL)**. The NPL's primary purpose is to serve as an information and management tool. The NPL identifies for the public those sites that appear to warrant remedial actions. The identification of sites for the NPL is intended primarily to guide the EPA in:

- determining which sites warrant further investigation to assess the nature and extent of the health and environmental risks associated with the sites;
- identifying what CERCLA-financed remedial actions may be appropriate;
- notifying the public of sites the EPA believes warrant further investigation; and
- notifying potentially responsible parties that the EPA may initiate CERCLA-financed remedial action.

The major effect of being placed on the NPL is that the site is eligible for Superfund monies to clean up the site. After removing the contamination, the EPA bills the identified PRPs for the cleanup costs. Regional EPA offices have information regarding the locations and statuses of contaminated properties. Florida real estate brokers can obtain reports of potentially contaminated properties in their market areas by contacting the regional EPA office located in Atlanta, Georgia. The NPL also is available on the Internet. The available information includes an assigned facility identification number, site name, address, county, copy of the site report, and mapping information regarding site location. Brokers should familiarize themselves with environmental hazards that exist in their market areas. A broker's inspection of real estate should include investigation of readily apparent environmental problems.

WEB LINK

To learn more about the National Priorities List (NPL) visit the Environmental Protection Agency Web site at **www.epa.gov/superfund**. Click on "About Superfund" for information concerning how sites are placed on the NPL. From the Superfund home page, click on "Basic or Advanced Query" located under the tools menu to locate hazardous waste sites in your local area. If you prefer, you can write to the EPA Region 4 Office, Sam Nunn Atlanta Federal Center, 61 Forsyth Street SW, Atlanta, GA 30303, or call (404) 562-9900 to obtain a copy of the NPL.

Environmental Due Diligence

It is often prudent for a broker to recommend that a buyer or seller hire an environmental consultant to identify and evaluate environmental risks associated with a parcel of land. The process of taking the appropriate steps to determine whether a site is contaminated is called **environmental due diligence**. To avoid liability for cleanup costs, lenders must exercise due diligence when making loans on real property. With regard to SARA's innocent landowner defense, the courts in many instances have defined "all appropriate inquiry into a property's environmental status prior to acquisition" to mean an environmental site assessment conducted by an environmental professional. Therefore, the most effective way to minimize exposure to environmental liability in real estate transactions is for the purchaser or other interested party to investigate for the potential presence of hazardous substances before purchasing, selling, leasing, financing, or foreclosing on a property. An **environmental site assessment** is a study designed to assess the likelihood that hazardous substances may be present on a property. Environmental assessments may go through as many as four phases; the extent and scope of each assessment varies with the particular site. In 1989, the Office of Thrift Supervision (OTS) released Bulletin TB-16 on environmental due diligence outlining the four phases of an environmental site assessment.

Phase I. This is primarily an investigative phase during which the due diligence work takes place. A **Phase I assessment** generally is undertaken to discover potential contamination or noncompliance with environmental laws and regulations. A typical Phase I report includes the activities described below:

- Historical study of the subject site's use and improvements
- Review of building, zoning, fire, and other local department records that contain information regarding the property
- Review of the EPA's National Priorities List
- Review of federal and state lists of registered underground storage tanks (USTs) and lists of leaking USTs
- Inspection of the site and improvements, with attention to the use of hazardous materials in the structure(s) or operating equipment
- Verification of whether present or past owners or tenants have stored, created, or discharged hazardous materials
- Review of whether appropriate procedures, safeguards, permits, and notices are in place
- Analysis of old aerial photographs to determine the construction or demolition of buildings and the existence of ponds and disposal areas on the property over time
- Review of building records and a visual inspection of the building(s) to determine whether asbestos-containing building materials are present
- Review of scientific reports to determine the potential levels of radon in the soil

Phase II. A Phase II assessment is performed if red flags are apparent or if they are discovered during the Phase I investigation. This phase involves field testing and analysis—for example, the testing of underground storage tanks for content and integrity.

Phase III. A Phase III assessment is much more detailed and consists of all the Phase I and Phase II activities in addition to complex soil, water, and air quality analysis. Phase III programs are site-specific and usually consist of remediation action plans subject to regulatory approval and supervision.

TABLE 17.1 ■ Reducing Liability

Reducing Liability
Sellers and licensees should avoid making representations about a property's environmental condition.
A listing agreement should state that the contract makes no warranties or representations as to the property's environmental condition that the contract does not express in writing.
Language requiring a seller to disclose any information known regarding the property's environmental condition can be added to the disclosure form; however, this seller's disclosure may not be enough to protect the broker.
Licensees should recommend environmental assessments whenever red flags appear; however, they must realize that such assessments reduce, but do not eliminate, uncertainty concerning environmental condition.
Provisions may be included in a purchase and sale agreement that allocate risk of environmental problems among the parties to the agreement or that make the sale conditional on a satisfactory environmental assessment.
A representation agreement with a buyer who seeks vacant land should state that the buyer must not rely on any representations the real estate licensee makes to determine the property's environmental condition.

Phase IV. The final phase is a management phase that designates parties or agencies to prevent any further contamination.

Reducing Liability

Real estate licensees must recognize potential environmental hazards in commercial, industrial, agricultural, and residential properties. To guard against the enormous risk of hazardous waste liability, contract and lease provisions should be worded to protect against environmental liabilities. Each commercial lease should include a provision prohibiting the use or storage of hazardous substances on the premises and requiring the lessee to comply with all environmental laws.

Whenever a property's environmental integrity is in question, the broker should recommend that the seller order an environmental assessment. If a potential environmental hazard is apparent or is discovered in a Phase I assessment, an attorney should draft the required disclosure. Furthermore, brokers should advise every buyer to obtain an environmental assessment before purchase to discover the extent of any existing contamination and to enable the buyer to qualify as an innocent landowner under CERCLA and the SARA amendment. This action may shift any potential liability away from the brokers. Refer to Table 17.1 for more ways to reduce liability.

BROWNFIELDS REVITALIZATION ACT

Brownfields are old industrial sites that may contain toxic wastes. The legislation provides states with financing to clean up polluted industrial sites. The legislation also shields purchasers and their lenders from liability for pre-existing contamination that they did not cause, providing the purchaser meets certain criteria.

EPA STATEMENT REGARDING TESTING

Do not rely on radon test results taken in other homes in the neighborhood to estimate the radon level in your home. Homes that are next to each other can have different indoor radon levels. While radon problems may be more common in some areas in the local community or state, any home may have a problem. Testing your home is the only way to find out what your radon level is.

Reference: *EPA's Home Buyer's and Seller's Guide to Radon*, United States Environmental Protection Agency, November 2006.

ASBESTOS

Asbestos is a mineral fiber that was used commonly until 1978 in a variety of building construction materials for insulation and as a fire retardant. These products include, for example, pipe insulation wrapping; furnace encasements; asbestos and cement shingles, siding, and roofing; resilient floor tiles; the backing on vinyl sheet flooring; and stove and oven door gaskets. Any products manufactured today that contain asbestos must be labeled clearly. Asbestos fibers become dangerous when they are disturbed or they are removed improperly, causing the fibers to become airborne. Inhaling microscopic asbestos fibers can result in respiratory diseases including lung scarring, lung cancer, and cancer of the chest cavity.

Not all asbestos-containing material poses a hazard. It is best not to disturb asbestos material that is in good condition. Generally, material in good condition does not release asbestos fibers. Care should be taken to prevent the material from being damaged, disturbed, or touched. The danger escalates when the fibers become fragile or exposed to the air. An alternative to removing the asbestos is to encapsulate (seal off) disintegrating asbestos. A Phase I environmental assessment should include an asbestos inspection in any structure built before 1978. The EPA recommends periodic inspection of known asbestos-containing material for signs of damage or deterioration. If an owner considers renovating or remodeling a structure containing asbestos materials, the owner should consult an asbestos specialist.

WEB LINK

To learn more about asbestos, visit the EPA's Asbestos home page at **www.epa.gov/asbestos/**. If you prefer you can call the National Asbestos Hotline at (800) 368-5888.

RADON

You cannot see, smell, or taste radon, yet it is all around us—even in the fresh air we breathe. Outdoors, radon is not a problem because the surrounding air and natural breezes allow the gas to dissipate into the atmosphere. However, when radon gas accumulates in high concentrations within buildings it is known to cause lung cancer. Well-insulated, energy-efficient homes especially tend to trap radon gas. Decaying uranium in the soil produces **radon gas**, which can seep into homes and accumulate. Radon typically moves up through the ground to the air above and into a home through cracks in the foundation, utility conduits, spaces around the plumbing, basement floors and walls, and crawl spaces.

FIGURE 17.1 ■ Required Radon Disclosure Language

"RADON GAS: Radon is a naturally occurring radioactive gas that, when it has accumulated in a building in sufficient quantities, may present health risks to persons who are exposed to it over time. Levels of radon that exceed federal and state guidelines have been found in buildings in Florida. Additional information regarding radon and radon testing may be obtained from your county health department."

Reference: Section 404.056(7), F.S.

The EPA estimates that about 1 out of every 15 homes in the United States contains elevated radon levels. Breathing the ambient air can introduce cancer-causing radioactive particles into the human respiratory system. As people breathe the radioactive particles, the particles become trapped in the lung's lining, causing lung damage that may lead to lung cancer over time. The Surgeon General warns that radon is the second leading cause of lung cancer (just behind cigarette smoking) in the United States today—and persons who smoke and live in homes with high radon levels are particularly at risk of getting lung cancer. An estimated 7,000 to 30,000 people die each year from lung cancer attributed to radon gas.

The concentration of radon in air is measured in units of picocuries per liter of air (pCi/L). The EPA reports that about .4 pCi/L of radon normally is found in the air outside. The average indoor radon level is estimated to be about 1.3 pCi/L. Congress has set a long-term goal that indoor radon levels be no more than outdoor levels. While this goal is not yet technologically achievable in all cases, most homes today can be reduced to 2 pCi/L or below. Testing is the only way to determine whether a home has an elevated radon level. The EPA recommends intervention if the radon level in a home is 4 pCi/L or higher.

Most homes can have their radon levels reduced to acceptable levels for about the same cost as common home improvements. A contractor's average cost to lower the radon level in a home is about $1,200, although it can range from $500 to about $2,500. Sealing cracks and other openings in the foundation is a basic part of most approaches to reducing radon levels. In other cases, the contractor uses a system with pipes and fans to reduce radon. Such a system, called *subslab depressurization*, does not require major changes to the home.

The EPA recommends that sellers test their homes before putting them on the market and, if necessary, lower the radon levels. Test results and information regarding any corrective measures can be positive selling points. Furthermore, radon tests require a minimum of 48 hours up to 90 days. Therefore, it may benefit a seller to test the home early and avoid a delay at closing. A buyer may choose to include a radon inspection contingency agreement in the real estate contract. Then if the radon exceeds a specified level (for example, 4 or more picocuries), the seller would have to take the appropriate steps to reduce the level or the purchaser could terminate the contract.

Florida Disclosure Requirements

Section 404.056(7), F.S., requires a mandatory radon disclosure at the time or before a person enters into a contract for sale and purchase or a rental agreement. Florida law does *not* require testing to determine radon levels before sale or lease. Figure 17.1 contains the required disclosure language. Neither does the law require that the notification be acknowledged by a signature. However, if the disclosure is made on a separate document, it is recommended that the broker secure the buyer's or lessee's signature.

WEB LINK

See the EPA's *Consumer Guide to Radon Reduction* at **http://www.epa.gov/radon/pubs/consguid.html.**

LEAD-BASED PAINT

It is estimated that 75 percent of the nation's housing stock built before 1978 (about 64 million dwellings) contain lead-based paint, and the vast majority of homes built before 1950 contain substantial amounts of lead-based paint. The federal government has determined that as many as 3 million children younger than age six in this country have low-level lead poisoning. The ingestion of household dust containing lead from deteriorating lead-based paint is the most common cause of lead poisoning in children. At low levels, lead poisoning in children causes intelligence quotient deficiencies, reading and learning disabilities, impaired hearing, reduced attention span, hyperactivity, and behavior problems.

Congress passed the Residential Lead-Based Paint Hazard Reduction Act, also known as *Title X*, in 1992. Section 1018 of the law directed the Department of Housing and Urban Development (HUD) and the EPA to require the disclosure of known information on lead-based paint and lead-based paint hazards before the sale or lease of most housing built before 1978. **Lead-based paint hazards** are any conditions that expose people to lead from lead-contaminated dust, lead-contaminated soil, or lead-contaminated paint that has deteriorated or is present in accessible surfaces, such as window sills. The law pertains only to housing built before 1978 because the Consumer Product Safety Commission banned the use of lead-based paint for residential use in that year. Section 1018 requires seller or lessor to:

- provide the purchaser or lessee with the lead hazard information pamphlet, "Protect Your Family from Lead in Your Home" (see Figure 17.2).
- disclose to the purchaser or lessee the presence of any known lead-based paint or lead-based paint hazards. The seller or lessor must disclose, based on actual knowledge, whether the property contains lead-based paint or lead-based paint hazards.
- provide all test results available to the seller or lessor. If any prior testing has been done, the seller or lessor must provide to the purchaser or lessee copies of all testing results and records. For a large multifamily property, the regulations require that even if the unit in question has not been tested, the lessor must disclose whether lead was found in other units in the building or complex. The lessor also must disclose whether any lead was found in common areas, such as hallways or playgrounds.
- allow the purchaser ten days (unless the parties agree on a different period of time) to conduct a risk assessment or an inspection for the presence of lead-based paint hazards.
- include the lead warning statement and acknowledgment in the sale or lease contract. A sale contract must include an attachment containing specific warning language (see Figure 17.3) on a separate sheet of paper and an acknowledgment that the purchaser has received all the relevant disclosure information. For the purchaser, the sheet also must include a section acknowledging that a ten-day opportunity to conduct a lead test was given to the purchaser, unless the parties

FIGURE 17.2 ■ EPA Lead Hazard Information Packet

FIGURE 17.2 ■ EPA Lead Hazard Information Packet (Continued)

Simple Steps To Protect Your Family From Lead Hazards

If you think your home has high levels of lead:

- Get your young children tested for lead, even if they seem healthy.
- Wash children's hands, bottles, pacifiers, and toys often.
- Make sure children eat healthy, low-fat foods.
- Get your home checked for lead hazards.
- Regularly clean floors, window sills, and other surfaces.
- Wipe soil off shoes before entering house.
- Talk to your landlord about fixing surfaces with peeling or chipping paint.
- Take precautions to avoid exposure to lead dust when remodeling or renovating (call 1-800-424-LEAD for guidelines).
- Don't use a belt-sander, propane torch, high temperature heat gun, scraper, or sandpaper on painted surfaces that may contain lead.
- Don't try to remove lead-based paint yourself.

Recycled/Recyclable
Printed with vegetable oil based inks on recycled paper (minimum 50% postconsumer) process chlorine free.

CASE IN POINT

A Washington, D.C.-area landlord was sentenced to incarceration for two years for obstructing an investigation by the Department of Housing and Urban Development and making false statements to federal officials. The landlord concealed from HUD officials his failure to notify tenants of the presence and hazards associated with lead-based paint. The case is the first-ever criminal prosecution in the United States related to failure to give lead hazard warnings that are required by the federal Lead Hazard Reduction Act of 1992. The landlord was also sentenced to pay a fine of $50,000 and ordered to provide all tenants with new notices about lead paint assessments performed by an independent contractor required under the terms of a plea agreement with prosecutors.

Reference: Department of Housing and Urban Development. "Compliance and Enforcement." http://www.hud.gov/offices/lead/compliance/index.cfm

agreed otherwise. Lease contracts must include, either as an attachment or within the contract, the same information as required in the sale contract, except the inspection rights do not apply.

For a sale transaction, disclosure must occur *before* the seller accepts the purchaser's written offer to purchase. If the potential purchaser makes an offer before receiving the requisite disclosures, the seller may not accept that offer until the disclosure activities are completed and the potential buyer has had an opportunity to review the information and consider whether to amend the offer before becoming obligated under the contract. For a lease transaction, the lessor must provide the information and complete the disclosure portion of the lease before the lessor accepts the lessee's offer. The lessor also must provide the lessee with an opportunity to review the disclosure information and amend the lease offer.

Whenever a seller or lessor enters into a contract with a real estate agent to sell or lease a residential property, the regulations require the licensee to make sure the seller or

FIGURE 17.3 ■ Required Warning Statement

"Every purchaser of any interest in residential real property on which a residential dwelling was built prior to 1978 is notified that such property may present exposure to lead from lead-based paint that may place young children at risk of developing lead poisoning. Lead poisoning in young children may produce permanent neurological damage, including learning disabilities, reduced intelligence quotient, behavioral problems, and impaired memory. Lead poisoning also poses a particular risk to pregnant women. The seller of any interest in residential real property is required to provide the buyer with any information on lead-based paint hazards from risk assessments or inspections in the seller's possession and notify the buyer of any known lead-based paint hazards. A risk assessment or inspection for possible lead-based paint hazards is recommended prior to purchase."

Reference: Residential Lead-Based Paint Hazard Reduction Act of 1992.

lessor complies with the regulations. The licensee must certify in writing that the licensee advised the seller or lessor of obligations under the law and that the licensee is aware of the duty to ensure that the seller or lessor complies with the disclosure requirements. The rules do *not* require the seller or landlord to test for or remove lead-based paint. Furthermore, noncompliance with the law does not invalidate the lease or sale contract. However, any seller, landlord, lessor, or real estate agent who knowingly violates the law is jointly and severally liable to the purchaser or lessee for triple damages. Such persons also may be subject to civil and criminal penalties. Table 17.2 summarizes the disclosure requirements.

The lead-based paint law does *not* apply to:

- housing built after 1977.
- commercial facilities (unless the facilities are part of a residential dwelling).
- zero-bedroom units, such as efficiencies, lofts, and dormitories.
- leases for 100 days or less when the tenants have no ability to renew or extend the leases. Month-to-month leases having no specified termination dates are *not* exempt, and the disclosures to these tenants must be made before the initial agreements. If a lease for 100 days or less is extended beyond the 100-day period allowed for exemption, the disclosures must be made before the extension occurs.
- designated housing for the elderly and the handicapped (unless children younger than age six live or are expected to live there).

TABLE 17.2 ■ Summary of Lead-Based Paint Disclosure Requirements

Seller Responsibilities

- Give the buyer the EPA pamphlet.
- Give the buyer ten days to test for lead, unless the parties agree on another period.
- Disclose all known lead-based paint and lead-based paint hazards in the dwelling and provide the buyer with all available test results.
- Include standard warning language as an attachment to the sale contract.

Landlord Responsibilities

- Give renters the EPA pamphlet.
- Note that the ten-day inspection period is not required in rental situations.
- Disclose all known lead-based paint and lead-based paint hazards in the dwelling and provide renters with all available test results.
- Include standard warning language in the lease or as an attachment.
- Complete and sign statements verifying completion of the requirements.
- Retain the signed acknowledgment for three years.

Real Estate Licensee Responsibilities

- Make certain that sellers and landlords are aware of their obligations. The licensee may photocopy the EPA pamphlet or order bulk quantities for use by the licensee's sellers and landlords.
- Ensure that sellers give buyers the ten days (or other days agreed to) to conduct an inspection.
- Ensure that sellers and landlords disclose the proper information to buyers and renters.
- Ensure that leases and sale contracts include proper disclosure language.
- Comply with the law even if sellers or landlords don't.
- Certify in writing that the licensee advised sellers and lessors of their obligations.

- rental housing that has been inspected by a certified inspector and found to be free of lead-based paint.
- foreclosure sales.
- renewals of existing leases in which the owner already has made the required disclosures and has obtained no new information since then.

WEB LINK

For more information on lead hazards, see the EPA's page containing posters and brochures at **http://www.epa.gov/lead/pubs/brochure.htm.**

SUMMARY OF IMPORTANT POINTS

- The Comprehensive Environmental Response, Compensation, and Liability Act (CERCLA) is administered by the Environmental Protection Agency (EPA). Key features of CERCLA are as follows:
  1. Established the Superfund to clean up hazardous waste sites and to respond to spills.
  2. Created the process for identifying potentially responsible persons (PRPs) and for ordering them to take responsibility for cleanup.
  3. Provided for the publication of the National Priorities List of contaminated and potentially contaminated sites.
- The Superfund Amendments and Reauthorization Act (SARA) created an innocent landowner immunity status. Key features of SARA are as follows:
  1. Establish criteria by which to judge whether a person or business could be exempted from liability.
  2. To claim the innocent landowner defense, the purchaser must meet a series of criteria, including making reasonable inquiries into the property's past uses before purchase.
- An environmental site assessment studies the likelihood that hazardous substances may be present on a property. If red flags signal a potential environmental concern, the broker should recommend that a Phase I assessment be conducted.
- Asbestos is a mineral fiber that was used before 1978 for its fireproofing and insulating qualities. It is a health hazard when fibers break down and are inhaled. Encapsulation can prevent asbestos fibers from becoming airborne.
- Florida statute requires a mandatory radon disclosure at the time or before a person enters into a contract for sale and purchase or a lease agreement. The law does not require testing to determine radon levels before the sale or lease.
- Before a person enters into a sale or lease of a dwelling built before 1978, the Residential Lead-Based Paint Hazard Reduction Act requires the disclosure of any lead-based paint and lead-based paint hazards known to exist. The seller or lessor also must provide the purchaser or lessee with a lead hazard information pamphlet and any existing lead test results. In a residential sale, the purchaser must be allowed ten days (or another period the parties agree to) to conduct a lead inspection.

REVIEW QUESTIONS

Use the information below to answer questions 1 through 3.

Ken owns and operates a used-car lot and auto repair shop. The business is located next to a vacant lot. The adjacent lot has a stream flowing through it that eventually spills into Paines Prairie State Preserve. Ken allows oil and other auto fluids to seep unchecked onto the adjacent property, then into the creek. Ken purchased the business two years ago. He claims that most of the trash, old car batteries, and discarded oil filters that line the borders of his property were there when he bought the business.

1. According to the Comprehensive Environmental Response, Compensation, and Liability Act, who is a potentially responsible person for the cleanup of the environmental contamination?
   a. The previous owner, who inappropriately discarded the auto parts on the property
   b. The current owner, Ken
   c. Both Ken and the previous owner
   d. Before anyone can be considered as potentially responsible, it must be determined who dumped the discarded auto parts on the property.

2. For Ken to qualify as an innocent landowner, he must prove that
   a. the discarded auto parts were visible on the site before he purchased the property.
   b. he tried to clean up the debris around his business.
   c. he reacted to the environmental contamination responsibly when he was made aware that auto fluids were seeping into the creek.
   d. he has conformed to city and county regulations concerning the operation of his auto repair business.

3. Ken is fed up with being harassed by government officials, so he decides to list his business for sale with your real estate company. Which statement is TRUE of this situation?
   a. You should recommend that Ken commission a Phase I environmental assessment and disclose the study's results to prospective buyers.
   b. You should instruct Ken to remove the discarded auto parts before he lists the property so that he will not have to disclose any potential environmental hazard associated with the auto parts.
   c. You should list the property as a transaction broker rather than as a single agent so that you are relieved of any liability associated with the environmental contamination.
   d. You should check the National Priorities List to see whether Ken's property is listed. If not, it is reasonable to assume that the auto fluid seepage is minor and need not be disclosed to buyers unless they specifically inquire about the discarded batteries and oil filters.

4. Which statement BEST describes the purpose of a Phase I environmental assessment?
   a. Detailed study to discover potential contamination or noncompliance with environmental laws and regulations
   b. Governmental report designed to identify potentially responsible persons and assess liability for cleanup costs
   c. Involved scientific study of water, soil, and air sample analyses for the purpose of designing a remediation action plan to eliminate known environmental contamination
   d. Report consisting of the property's identification number, location information, and government analysis that is in the public domain

5. Marty is a prospective renter of a unit in a large multifamily complex that your real estate company manages. Marty is an amateur photographer and states that she wants to convert the guest bathroom into a darkroom for developing her film. Which statement is TRUE of this situation?
   a. A clause should be included in the lease that Marty must dispose of all chemicals she uses properly and she must comply with all environmental laws.
   b. The broker should draft special lease provisions to protect against potential environmental hazards and include this language in the lease agreement to protect the owner.
   c. The tenant should be instructed to pour the discarded chemicals into a sealed jar or can and dispose of it in the trash.
   d. The tenant should be instructed to pour spent chemicals down the kitchen or bathroom sink, and then flush the pipes thoroughly with tap water for at least three minutes.

6. Which statement applies to the potential danger associated with asbestos if a structure was built before 1979?
   a. The broker should inspect the property thoroughly to determine whether asbestos-containing materials are present.
   b. The broker should recommend that a professional inspection be conducted to determine whether any asbestos-containing materials are present in the structure.
   c. The broker must include in all real estate contracts mandatory warning language concerning the health risk associated with inhaling asbestos fibers.
   d. All structures built prior to 1979 should be considered health hazards.

7. Which statement regarding radon gas is FALSE?
   a. Florida law requires a mandatory radon disclosure at the time or before a person enters into a contract for sale and purchase of real estate.
   b. Radon tests conducted in homes within a single neighborhood provide reliable estimates of whether the radon level is high in another home located within the same neighborhood.
   c. Florida law does not require mandatory testing to determine radon levels before a purchase.
   d. Radon gas does not pose a health hazard when breathing outdoor air.

8. Which statement is TRUE of the Residential Lead-Based Paint Hazard Reduction Act?
   a. Florida law requires mandatory testing for the presence of lead-based paint hazards.
   b. It applies only to residential dwellings built before 1950.
   c. Tenants of residential units have ten days to cancel the lease agreements if lead-based paint is found in the dwellings.
   d. Real estate agents must comply with the requirements of the law even if sellers or landlords don't.

9. If you are a landlord of a multifamily apartment complex built in 1971, which statement is TRUE?
   a. The property is exempt from the lead-based paint disclosure requirements because it was built after 1950.
   b. You must include mandatory warning language as a separate attachment to the lease.
   c. You must disclose the presence of lead-based paint or known lead-based paint hazards that exist only in the unit that is available for rent.
   d. You must give each tenant a copy of "Protect Your Family from Lead in Your Home."

10. You rent one-bedroom apartments to college students on month-to-month lease agreements that do not specify termination dates. The apartments were built in 1971. In this situation, which statement is TRUE regarding lead-based paint disclosure laws?
    a. You are exempt from the lead-based paint disclosure requirements because the leases are short term.
    b. College apartments are exempt from the lead-based paint disclosure requirements.
    c. As long as children younger than age six do not reside in the units, you are exempt from the disclosure requirements.
    d. You must meet the disclosure requirements before the initial lease agreement is entered into.

CHAPTER 18

PROPERTY MANAGEMENT

KEY TERMS

Americans with Disabilities Act
Civil Rights Act of 1866
community association
Fair Housing Act
fixed lease
Florida Landlord and Tenant Act
graduated lease
ground lease
index lease
steering
tenancy at sufferance
tenancy at will
tenancy for years
tester
three-day notice
writ of possession

OVERVIEW

This chapter begins with a discussion of the many opportunities available in property management. Most property managers must have a Florida real estate license with several important exemptions. Types of income properties as well as the many skills required of property managers are discussed. Regional, neighborhood, and property analyses are described. Because marketing the rental property is extremely important, the chapter includes a section on advertising and showing property. Discussions of tenant relations, security deposits, and rent collection policies are included, as is an explanation of the types of leases in general use. Maintenance programs, accounting, and communications with an owner are other important topics. The final portion of the chapter describes the laws important to property managers.

Once you have completed this chapter, you should be able to:

- understand the licensing requirements for property managers and list the exemptions from the requirements;
- understand the definition *of community association* and the employment situations that require a community association manager's license;
- list at least six skills required of a property manager;
- list the three types of analyses a manager must prepare to understand the market and the property;
- explain the important parts of the marketing process;

- list the major advertising media property managers use;
- describe the methods Chapter 475 requires to handle security deposits;
- understand which lease forms licensees may complete;
- list the three basic types of leases;
- list the four major types of property maintenance;
- know the requirements of civil rights and fair housing statutes;
- itemize the important sections of the Residential Landlord and Tenant Act; and
- list at least six environmental hazards that are important to property managers.

INTRODUCTION

Investors achieve higher profits when their properties are competently managed, and often hire professional property managers to do the job. Property managers operate, maintain, and increase the value of real estate investments. Community association managers manage condominiums, cooperatives, and planned communities through homeowners' associations. When owners lack the time or expertise needed for the management of their real estate investments or homeowners' associations, they hire a property manager or a community association manager.

Property managers collect rent and pay the mortgages, taxes, insurance premiums, payroll, and maintenance bills. They prepare financial statements for presentation to the owners. Property managers advertise the property and employ rental agents to find tenants. Community association managers collect association fees that help pay for things such as landscaping, clubhouse, and swimming pool maintenance.

Property managers contract with and monitor janitorial workers, landscapers, and other maintenance personnel. They resolve complaints from residents and tenants.

Property managers must comply with laws such as the Americans with Disabilities Act, the Federal Fair Housing Amendment Act, and local fair housing laws, and the local and state building codes.

Scope of Property Management

While location and design are important, the key to achieving an investor's profit objectives is good management. Property owners have many options when considering how to best manage their assets. They may choose to manage their own properties, hire in-house manager employees, employ licensed brokers as their property managers, or hire firms that specialize in property management.

Direct owner management. Many first-time investors manage their own properties in order to save money. Often, these investors don't have the specialized knowledge or experience necessary to manage their properties well. An investor's close personal and financial involvement often causes stress. This stress involves three areas: collection problems, maintenance complaints, and tenant damage to the property. If coping with the stress is difficult, the next step is for the investor either to hire an employee as property manager or to employ a broker to manage the property.

In-house management staff. Many organizations, such as hotel chains, shopping center developers, and condominium and apartment property owners, directly employ property managers. They prefer hiring and training their own people for better control and management. These employees may range in qualifications from resident managers and handymen to highly trained professional managers.

Broker management. Many buyers who purchase investment property through a brokerage firm ask the broker to manage the property. In some cases, the same sales associate who sold the property manages it, although this arrangement is rarely satisfactory. The trend is for full-service real estate companies to establish separate management divisions staffed by persons trained in property management.

Many real estate brokers point to the cash flows their property management divisions generate as the key to surviving real estate recessions. A division also may produce many leads for the sales division when tenants wish to buy their own properties or when an owner wishes to sell a property.

Property management firms. Some real estate brokerage firms specialize in property management and counseling but do not offer other types of brokerage services. The success of this type of operation is due to the strict focus on the management function, providing high levels of professional expertise in this complex field. Firms specializing only in management forgo the opportunity to list and sell the properties they manage.

Licensing Requirements and Exemptions

Activities requiring a real estate license. Leasing or renting real property for another person for compensation is a real estate service that requires a Florida real estate license, unless otherwise exempted.

Exemptions from the licensing requirement. The following persons are exempt from the licensing requirements:

- Owners, when renting or leasing their own properties
- Employees, agents, or independent contractors of corporations, partnerships, trusts, joint ventures, or other entities that rent or lease their own properties, provided the individuals are not paid commissions or other compensation on a transactional basis
- Salaried employees of an owner, or of a registered broker for an owner, of an apartment community who work in an on-site rental office in a leasing capacity
- Persons employed for salaries as managers of condominiums or cooperatives as a result of any activities or duties they have in relation to the renting of individual units within such complexes if rentals they arrange are for periods of no greater than one year
- Persons who rent or advertise for rent, for transient occupancy, any public lodging establishment licensed under Chapter 509, F.S.
- Persons renting mobile home lots or recreational vehicle lots in mobile home parks or travel parks

Unlawful activities of unlicensed salaried employees. Except for the exempt person who works in an on-site rental office, it is unlawful for unlicensed employees of a brokerage firm to show rental properties, write lease agreements, or provide other services that may be considered brokerage activities. Persons performing these activities must have Florida real estate licenses.

COMMUNITY ASSOCIATION MANAGER'S LICENSE

Persons fulfilling the duties of a community association manager of the above described association must be licensed if they perform the following duties for compensation:

- controlling or disbursing funds;
- preparing budgets or other financial documents;
- assisting in the notice or conduct of meetings and coordinating maintenance and other services for the association.

Reference: Section 468.431(2), F.S.

Community Association Management License

Florida Statute 468, Part VIII, entitled "Community Association Management," requires certain community association managers to obtain licenses from the Department of Business and Professional Regulation (DBPR).

A **community association** is defined as a "residential homeowners' association in which membership is a condition of ownership of a unit in a planned unit development, or of a lot for a home or a mobile home, or of a townhouse, villa, condominium, cooperative, or other residential unit that is part of a residential development and that is authorized to impose a fee which may become a lien on the parcel." Under this law, the term *community association* is further defined to include any association that is "greater than 10 units or has an annual budget in excess of $100,000."

A person who performs only clerical duties under a licensed association manager need not be licensed.

PROPERTY MANAGEMENT MARKETS

For this discussion, the field of property management is divided into two major classifications: residential and commercial property. Each type of property may be further subdivided and requires specialized knowledge and skills.

Residential Real Estate

Residential property management is a field that encompasses the management not only of single-family and multifamily homes, but also condominiums, cooperatives, and vacation rentals.

Single-family homes. The most popular form of residential property in the United States is a single-family home. Most individuals starting to build real estate investment portfolios purchase single-family homes because of the relatively small investment required. Single-family homes are more manageable for novice investors. As the number of properties an investor owns grows, it is often decided at some point to hire a professional management team.

Multifamily properties. Multifamily housing is a more efficient and cost-effective use of land in urban areas. The lower per-family cost of construction has resulted in this rapidly growing segment of the real estate market. Smaller properties are often owner managed, whereas most larger apartment properties are managed professionally.

Cooperatives and condominiums. Cooperative and condominium apartments usually are owner-occupied buildings governed by Boards of Directors the owners elected. These boards generally hire professional managers to oversee the properties. Many larger neighborhood homeowners' associations also find it necessary to employ professional managers. Managers of these associations usually must have community association manager's licenses.

Vacation rentals. Florida remains one of the world's principal tourist destinations. As a result, there are many opportunities to manage short-term vacation rental properties. Because the rental periods range from a few days to several months, this high tenant turnover requires that most firms have janitorial and maintenance personnel on staff. It also requires strong marketing and organizational skills. Individuals who manage transient rental properties, as defined in F.S. 509, are exempt from Chapter 475's license requirements.

Commercial Real Estate

Commercial real estate property management includes various types of properties, such as office buildings, shopping centers, parking garages, and chain stores. The two principal categories of commercial real estate are office property and retail property.

Office property. Managers are needed for small office buildings, garden developments, high-rise complexes, and office parks. The success of most office property is determined primarily by its location relative to the prospective workforce, transportation facilities, and other business services. Many major corporations occupy and manage their own real estate.

Retail property. Retail property includes freestanding buildings, shopping centers of all sizes, and specialty centers such as off-price and factory outlet centers. Larger shopping centers, because of their size and tenant diversity, challenge professional property manager's skills in many ways.

SKILLS REQUIRED OF A PROPERTY MANAGER

A professional property manager must understand the local real estate market. The manager also must be able to:

- employ, train, and supervise employees;
- understand and apply accounting principles as well as prepare and analyze operating reports;
- understand the operation of many building components, such as plumbing, electrical, and heating and air systems, and the maintenance required to keep them in good working order;

- maintain tenant relations in a manner that enhances the residents' goodwill while representing the owner's interests;
- understand and observe applicable laws, including the Florida Landlord and Tenant Act, the Florida real estate license law, and federal laws relating to fair housing and the Americans with Disabilities Act;
- establish a strong marketing program with advertising and brochures and prepare the property for showing;
- understand the basics of leasing space, including space planning, area design, and building layout;
- be aware of building and health codes and regulations for local, state, and national jurisdictions;
- know the principles of purchasing, including soliciting bids and establishing a system of work orders and purchase orders;
- understand the principles of appraising, finance, money markets, financial trends, and local market conditions;
- have a general knowledge of construction techniques; and
- be sensitive to environmental issues.

THE RENTAL PROCESS

Evaluating the Rental Market

A property manager must evaluate the market at the regional and neighborhood levels. When the analysis has been completed, the manager then must evaluate the subject property itself.

Regional market analysis. A regional market analysis is valuable in interpreting economic trends. The analysis should include demographic and economic information on the regional or metropolitan area in which the subject property is located. The regional analysis typically presents population statistics and trends, a list of major employers in the area, income and employment data, a description of transportation facilities, and supply and demand trends. It also should explore the city's economic base and prospects for the future in the area.

Neighborhood market analysis. A neighborhood market analysis helps the property manager determine the optimum rental prices the subject property can realize. The manager begins the analysis with a tour of the area. Equipped with local maps, area zoning ordinances, applicable building codes, and statistical data on the population, the property manager assesses four major factors in the market area, as discussed below.

1. Boundaries and land use. Before analyzing the neighborhood market, the property manager must determine the area's boundaries. Rivers, lakes, railroad tracks, parks, highways, or expressways may help define the borders.

2. Transportation. Transportation facilities and accesses are crucial to the success of residential property. Apartment dwellers in large cities may require a location close to public transportation. Traffic counts are important to owners of commercial sites. A lack of parking may cause substantially reduced cash flows for office buildings, retail properties, and apartments.

3. Economy. Brokers, appraisers, and local newspapers are sources of information for assessing the health of the neighborhood. Current rental rates for similar properties in the neighborhood are sound indicators of the neighborhood economy. When demand is greater than supply, rents are high. The manager obtains the most reliable rental rate information by shopping the competition.

4. Supply and demand. The occupancy rate for a particular type of property reflects the interaction of supply and demand at its current rental level. A high occupancy rate indicates a shortage of space and the possibility of rental increases. Low occupancy, as evidenced by many For Rent signs posted in the area, results in tenant requests for lower rents and other concessions.

The oversupply of space that results in low occupancy rates can be either technical or economic in nature. *Technical oversupply* occurs when available units outnumber potential tenants, while *economic oversupply* occurs when available space is priced beyond the purchasing power of potential tenants.

Neighborhood amenities and facilities. The property manager should note the number and location of parks, playgrounds, theaters, restaurants, schools, colleges, churches, and any other social or cultural organizations that will be attractive to potential tenants.

Property analysis. The property manager must inspect the subject property's exterior, interior, and equipment to collect the data necessary to estimate maintenance and operating costs for the next year.

An exterior inspection should alert the property manager to repairs that have been deferred under the previous owner or manager. Masonry, windows, eaves and trim, roofs, porches, grounds, parking areas, fire escapes, and any other common areas must be examined for poor maintenance.

During an inspection of the interior, the property manager should check entrances, halls, laundry rooms, heating and air-conditioning systems, and other interior areas. The manager should estimate redecorating or replacement expenses along with expenses for personnel required to satisfy the routine housekeeping and maintenance requirements for these areas.

A physical inventory of the interior and exterior also will reveal areas of deferred maintenance and durable obsolescence. It will help the property manager to determine whether the property complies with building, housing, and zoning codes.

The manager should compare the property with similar properties with respect to unit sizes, rental rates, vacancy rates, location, construction, age, special features, amenities, condition of premises, and size of building staff. Operating expenses for comparable properties can help the property manager develop both a rental schedule and an operating budget.

The manager then should be able to provide the owner with an estimate of any capital expenditures required to make the building competitive with similar properties in the area.

Marketing Rental Units

Well-presented property commands higher rental rates and experiences higher occupancy rates than similar property that is poorly marketed. The property manager determines marketing objectives primarily by the type of property, supply and demand, and available financial resources.

Type of property. Every type of property requires its own marketing plan. Residential tenants may look in the classified ads, but potential shopping center tenants rarely use that medium. New properties require much more intensive and expensive marketing efforts than those that are almost fully occupied.

Supply and demand. A stable market with high occupancy rates demands a less intense marketing program than a high-vacancy market. A property manager with a healthy property might advertise in ways that enhance the property's image. If vacancy rates are high, the message might shift to price reductions, free rent, or other concessions designed to rent the property more quickly.

Financial resources. The income a property generates often affects the dollars that owners will spend on marketing. Because cash flows are critical when vacancies are high, owners sometimes tell their property managers to cut costs, including advertising expenses. In fact, because higher occupancy rates usually return more dollars than the promotion costs, the best strategy is to increase the advertising effort.

Advertising Methods

The property manager has many options for property promotion. While the marketing methods depend on the factors discussed above, the most commonly used methods include signs, newspaper advertising, broadcast media, and direct mail. The licensee should review Chapter 475, F.S., and FREC rules to ensure that advertising is not misleading and that it identifies the firm properly to avoid charges of blind advertising.

Signs and billboards. The property manager should erect an appropriate sign identifying the management firm, the type of space for rent, and the phone number to call for information. For Rent signs often carry information about the space offered for rent and a number to call. If billboards are used, they should emphasize the same message other media carry. It is better to rent 12 billboards for one month than to rent one billboard for 12 months and risk losing the message.

Newspapers. To be effective, newspaper advertising must appeal to a specific tenant. It stresses the property's benefits, describes the location, states the price, and tells how to get more information. Classified advertising is the most common method for promotion of residential rental property. Display advertising often is used for new properties and prestige locations. It provides more visual impact and is more expensive.

Apartment guides. Apartment guides are full-color advertising magazines that are distributed free in grocery stores, motels, airports, and restaurants. Many property managers find these magazines to be as powerful as newspaper advertising for generating rental prospects.

Broadcast media. Radio and television advertising is expensive. It is seen and heard over a broad area by many who are not potential tenants. Therefore, the property manager must analyze carefully the advertising's cost per prospect. It works best for large, new, residential properties.

Direct mail. Where newspapers and broadcasting are the "shotgun" approaches to advertising, scattering the message to prospects and nonprospects alike, direct mail is the "rifle" approach. This promotion method, which focuses on potential prospects, is effective for industrial and commercial property owners. While it is expensive to design and mail brochures, a good mailing list makes the advertising cost-effective.

Image

Regardless of the advertising method, the property manager must make the message consistent in all media so it creates the image that will generate the most tenants. The image chosen for many residential properties focuses on architecture (Spanish, French, tropical), security (gated community), views (waterfront), or convenience.

Promotional Programs

Good public relations often enhances the marketing effort. It is important that property managers maintain good relationships with the press, the public, and the real estate community. Many managers volunteer to speak to school groups and various interest groups. Press releases about the property, the management company, or trends in the real estate market may help to enhance the company's or the property's image. To increase the chances of being published, the article must be newsworthy and objective and must not sound like advertising.

Showing the Property to Prospective Tenants

The previous section describes ways to generate interest among prospective tenants. Because of the expense involved in creating that interest, the property manager must ensure that the rental staff's actions result in each prospect becoming a tenant. The steps the manager must take to market the property include qualifying, creating interest and desire, and handling objections.

Qualifying. Every rental prospect, whether residential or commercial, should be asked to complete a lease application. This provides the customer's identity, the type of property desired, rental history, and financial status. Most property managers require authorization to order a credit report as part of the application process. A prospective tenant's poor credit rating usually results in future management problems. For this reason, the tenant's application should be declined. All applications should be handled the same way to avoid possible violations of fair housing laws.

The manager should learn each customer's needs, such as the amount of space or number of rooms, price range, parking requirements, and demographic information the customer requires. It also is important to determine the prospect's urgency to move.

The owner's needs are basic: the tenant must be compatible, stable, and financially able to fulfill the lease terms. Compatibility in an upscale shopping center means that the tenant fits with the retail mix. A strip shopping center manager ordinarily would not rent to a second dry cleaner.

Investigating the tenant's rental history may cause the property manager to decide that the business moves too frequently to justify paying for substantial remodeling costs to adapt the space to the tenant. And unless it has room to expand, a rapidly growing company also may be only a temporary tenant.

Creating interest and desire. Nothing is more important than showing the property effectively. The manager should comment on the excellent exterior appearance while describing the staff's attention to maintenance. The residential manager should not show too many units or the prospect will feel no urgency to make a timely decision. The manager

RECOMMENDED BROKER ACCOUNTING METHODS

While it is not required under the law, brokers should establish three property management escrow accounts to assist in bookkeeping and audit.

The first is a security deposit account. The second is an advance rent account. The third is a property rental account into which rents are deposited and from which bills are paid.

This system makes a FREC audit much more straightforward.

should demonstrate a unit's features, answer any questions the prospect has, and give the prospect time to inspect, measure, and evaluate the space.

Handling objections. Sometimes an objection indicates a customer need that the qualifying process did not identify and requires the manager to select another type of unit to suit the customer. However, if the manager knows that the property meets the prospect's needs, any objection raised may be simply a negotiating point. If the property manager reads this correctly, it also can be a closing tool. For example, the manager might ask, "Mr. Sims, is the condition of the carpeting all that is keeping you from moving in?" If the answer is yes, and if the manager is authorized to make such concessions, the manager should prepare an agreement to enter into a lease that includes carpet replacement. The agreement must be signed by both parties and accompanied by a good-faith deposit from the prospect. An attorney usually prepares the lease agreement itself unless it is a residential lease form that has been approved by the Florida Supreme Court.

Tenant Policies

Carefully developed tenant-oriented policies are necessary for the property's continued profitability. Solid tenant relationships encourage lease renewals, and a strong collection policy ensures prompt payment.

Tenant relations. Once the tenant signs a lease and takes occupancy, the manager's ability to maintain a good relationship will help keep the tenant. Poor communication causes many misunderstandings. A clearly written lease along with a brochure outlining policies, rules, and regulations helps reduce misunderstandings.

Tenant complaints and conflicts among tenants. The most common tenant complaint concerns maintenance service requests. The lease and policy brochure should reflect the division of duties between the manager and the tenant. Management must not treat the tenant request as if it is an annoyance, and it should provide prompt service if it is an owner responsibility. If the request is not a service the owner provides, but a tenant responsibility, the tenant should be told immediately.

Another common problem is tenant conflicts related to noise, parking, and sanitation. The manager must investigate and ensure that the offending tenant is made aware of and observes tenant policies.

FIGURE 18.1 ■ Demand Letter

Apartment Management Company, Inc.
Demand Letter

To: ____________________

You are hereby notified that you are indebted to me in the sum of $__________ for the rent and use of the premises at ______________________, Sunnydale, Sun County, Florida, now occupied by you, and that I demand payment of the rent or possession of the premises within three days (excluding Saturday, Sunday, and legal holidays) from the date of delivery of this notice, to-wit on before

____________________.

____

As agent for the owner
Apartment Management Company, Inc.
Sunnydale, Florida 33198

Delivery of this notice was by:
Personal delivery to tenant
Leaving at tenant residence

By: ________________________________ Date: ______________

Fees, security deposits, and rental collection. A residential lease often requires that the tenant pay various fees at the lease's inception. A common example is a nonrefundable pet fee. Such nonrefundable fees may be forwarded to the owner. Security deposits and the last month's rent, if collected, must be placed into an escrow account. These fees usually are not deposited into an interest-bearing account for two reasons:

1. The Florida Landlord and Tenant Act requires that the landlord pay a portion of the interest received to the tenant.
2. The requirements of Chapter 475, F.S., make accounting for such interest time-consuming for the broker.

A tenant should have no doubt that the manager considers late rent to be a default in the lease. While some management companies charge late fees for rents paid after the fifth of the month, nearly all post a **three-day notice** requiring either immediate payment or possession of the premises. (See Figure 18.1.) If the manager does not follow through, the tenant may infer that late rent payments are acceptable.

THE LEASE AGREEMENT

While employees of owners may complete the blanks on an owner lease form, real estate licensees may not complete any lease form unless it has been specifically approved by the Florida Supreme Court. Completion of any other form may leave the broker open to charges of "unauthorized practice of law."

Standard Lease Agreement Clauses

Most lease forms contain certain standard clauses. A discussion of some of those clauses follows.

Term and parties. This clause shows the beginning and ending dates and identifies the parties. The landlord should be certain that any party who is to be responsible for the performance under the lease is named. For instance, if three parties wish to rent the property, all three should be named.

Property rented. The address of the property as well as a list of each item of furniture and appliances should be included here. This is called "the premises."

Rent payments and charges. The amount of the rent and the frequency of payment is described. If the property is a transient rental unit that is rented for less than 180 days, Florida sales tax must be paid by the tenant.

Deposits, advance rent, and late charges. Security deposits, pet deposits, and advance rents are usually covered in a lease. Penalties for bad checks may include fees and the requirement that future payments be paid in cash or by money order.

Use of premises. This clause may describe restrictions on the property with respect to residential use, overnight guests, pets, and hazardous materials. It also prohibits the tenant from damaging the premises, making alterations, and causing disturbances.

Maintenance. The landlord usually is required to maintain the building in accordance with building, housing, and health codes, and to maintain the exterior structure and plumbing. Other maintenance responsibilities are assigned by negotiation. Usually, major maintenance is the landlord's responsibility unless the tenant specifically accepts responsibility in the lease, and *major* is defined as a dollar sum filled in the lease. For instance, some landlords agree to make repairs costing over $50, while repairs under $50 are the tenant's responsibility.

Utilities. This clause assigns responsibility for payment of the utilities.

Casualty damage. Usually, if the property is substantially damaged or destroyed, the tenant may vacate the premises. The tenant is not liable for further rent payments.

Default. If the landlord does not correct a lease violation, usually within seven days after notice from the tenant about the violation, the landlord is in default. If the landlord's failure to comply is due to causes beyond the landlord's control and the property is uninhabitable, the tenant is not liable for rent during that period. If the tenant stays in the property, the tenant is allowed to reduce the rent in proportion to the loss of use.

The tenant is normally in default if the tenant fails to pay rent when due and if the default continues for three days after notification from the landlord. The tenant can also be in default for damaging the premises or causing unreasonable disturbances. Other violations must be corrected within seven days after written notice from the landlord.

If the landlord accepts rent knowing the other party is in default or if the tenant pays rent knowing the other party is in default, the person waives the right to terminate the lease or bring suit for default. This does not prevent the party from doing so if there is a future default.

Remedies and defenses—Assignment and subleasing. The parties may decide on the tenant's right to sublease without the landlord's consent. If the space is subleased to another party by the original tenant, the original tenant remains liable in case of default by the tenant who subleased. The new tenant may be evicted by the landlord for failure to pay rent but is not personally liable, because no contract exists between the landlord and the new tenant.

Other clauses. Some of the other clauses in a lease include "time is of the essence," which requires that all dates be observed exactly.

Leases with an Option to Purchase

The broker must be careful when asked to prepare a lease with an option to purchase and should advise the parties to seek an attorney's assistance. The option contract should be prepared in the same detail as a sales contract because if the buyer wishes to exercise the option, it may be void if required details are missing.

Other Types of Leases

Many properties are subject to long-term **ground leases**, so that the owners of the improvements do not own the land. Ground leases often are used as another form of financing for developers, except that ground leases are almost always net leases, with the building owners paying all taxes and assessments on the properties. Very little property management is associated with ground leases, except for rent collection and enforcement.

Besides the three basic types of leases (gross lease, net lease, and percentage lease), the licensee should understand several other lease types. Each of the basic leases has a payment schedule that may be fixed, graduated, or indexed. A **fixed lease** has level payments. A **graduated lease** has prearranged rent increases at certain intervals. An **index lease** may be tied to a published index, such as the Consumer Price Index.

Proration of rents. Most property managers want all rental payments to come due on the first of each month for better control. If a tenant takes possession after the first of the month, this requires that the manager prorate the rent and charge only the amount due for the balance of the month.

Assignment, sublease, and subordination of space. Because the property manager wants to be certain that all tenants are qualified and compatible, assignment or sublease of space usually is prohibited unless the landlord approves the new tenant. The original tenant still is liable under the lease unless the landlord releases the tenant.

Types of occupancy. A **tenancy for years** is an agreement with a definite expiration date. A **tenancy at will** is an agreement allowing the tenant to occupy the property without an expiration date. Required notice of termination is based on the interval of rent payments. An occupancy with monthly payments requires 15 days' notice. A **tenancy at sufferance** occurs when the tenant remains in possession of the property after the tenant's rights expire. The landlord may demand immediate possession.

Maintenance

One of a property manager's principal functions is the establishment and operation of an effective property maintenance program. A complete program includes maintenance for:

- physical integrity (an inspection and maintenance schedule for the property's structural elements, such as exterior walls, roofs, and parking areas);

- functional performance (keeping equipment such as heating and air-conditioning units, plumbing and electrical systems, and appliances in good working order);
- housekeeping (keeping the property clean and well-maintained); and
- merchandising (the marketing tool that includes carpet replacement, landscaping, and decorating that makes the property desirable).

Maintenance personnel. The manager usually bases the decision on whether to have an in-house maintenance staff or to hire outside contractors on a cost analysis. Firms that manage many properties usually can justify hiring at least some general maintenance workers while continuing to employ independent companies to perform more specialized tasks. The state contractor's license law exempts real estate licensees, while acting as owners' agents, when they contract for repairs, maintenance, remodeling, or improvements if the total contract for labor, materials, and all other items is less than $5,000. A licensee must hire licensed contractors where such work requires it. If the contract amount is greater than $5,000, even if the work is divided, a general contractor is required.

Preventive maintenance inspections. Preventive maintenance is much more cost effective than emergency repairs. The manager must decide the type and frequency of maintenance inspections required to keep property components in top condition. Some areas must be checked daily or monthly, while others may be inspected less frequently. The manager should establish and follow rigorously an annual schedule of inspections and maintenance tasks.

Supervising security. Violent crime has become a major problem for every citizen, and the property manager who doesn't take the tenants' security seriously may face devastating losses from lawsuits. Managers of larger properties may choose to hire their own security personnel or contract with security firms. In Tallahassee, a property management firm was required to pay damages of $1.1 million because a tenant was injured by a burglar who crawled through an open window. The jury felt that the poorly maintained property invited the criminal act.

Accounting, Recordkeeping, and Insurance

Annual budget and operating statements. The property manager must prepare an annual operating budget that includes all anticipated income and expense items. Once the landlord approves the budget, it is the manager's responsibility to operate within the budget. The monthly property operating statement (see Figure 18.2), sometimes called a *property operating statement* or *statement of operations*, includes all rents, operating expenses, and debt service. The actual results of operations should be compared with both the budget and the same period for the prior year. The manager should explain variances from the budget and prior year in notes attached to the statement. This analysis allows the manager to manage by exception, concentrating primarily on those items that show large variances.

Record keeping. The property manager must ensure that all records are well-organized for quick access. Financial records should be retained permanently. Leases, tenant documents, and correspondence should be kept at least five years. Licenses should be posted or filed, as appropriate. Maintenance warranties should be retained during the warranty periods. Careful records must be maintained on all property operating and security deposit accounts in case of a DBPR audit.

FIGURE 18.2 ■ Monthly Operating Statement

Sunrise Cove Apartments
Operating Statement—August

	Current Month			Year to Date		
	Actual	**Budget**	**Variance**	**Actual**	**Budget**	**Variance**
Income						
Rent	$9,245.96	$9,400.00	$(154.04)	$74,216.82	$75,200.00	$ (983.18)
Vending	168.57	175.00	(6.43)	1,298.20	1,400.00	(101.80)
Total Income	$9,414.53	$9,575.00	$(160.47)	$75,515.02	$76,600.00	$(1,084.98)
Expenses						
Lawn Maintenance	$ 344.00	$ 344.00	$ 0.00	$ 2,752.00	$ 2,752.00	$ 0.00
Repairs and Maintenance	1,512.20	978.00	(534.20)	7,982.60	7,824.00	(158.60)
Advertising	278.43	290.00	11.57	2,402.16	2,320.00	(82.16)
Management fee	659.01	670.25	11.24	5,286.05	5,362.00	75.95
Utilities	287.00	300.00	13.00	2,316.00	2,400.00	84.00
Taxes	0.00	0.00	0.00	0.00	0.00	0.00
Insurance	0.00	0.00	0.00	2,540.00	2,498.00	(42.00)
Total Expenses	$3,080.64	$2,582.25	$(498.39)	$23,278.81	$23,156.00	$ (122.81)
Other payments						
Debt service	–$4,266.11	–$4,266.11	0.00	–$34,128.88	–$34,128.88	0.00
Capitalized expense	0.00	0.00	0.00	0.00	0.00	0.00
Cash flow	$2,067.78	$2,726.64	$(658.86)	$18,107.33	$19,315.12	$(1,207.79)
Check to owner	0.00	0.00		16,039.55	16,588.88	
Cash retained	$2,067.78	$2,726.24		$ 2,067.78	$ 2,726.24	

Notes to owner about operating statement—August
Actual income for the month was below budget because Apt. 16 was vacant for two weeks. Painting and repairs were $535 over budget because Apt. 16 required over $700 in painting and repairs. The tenant had been in the unit for five years and things had gotten a little shabby. All other expenses were close to budget. We've retained the owner's check this month and will do so as agreed for the following three months so that there are enough funds available to pay the estimated taxes of $7,560 in November. We have just about completed painting the doors and frames on all the units, and that will be paid next month, but we think it will be right on budget.

Risk Management and Insurance

One of the property manager's most important functions is reducing risk to the owner and the management company. The manager must identify the risks, avoid them, or control them with training and loss-reduction plans, and transfer as many of the risks as possible through insurance or other means.

Identifying the risks. Identifying risks begins with an inspection of the property and a review of tasks the staff performs. Contractors should be required to provide certificates of insurance. Many insurance companies offer loss control suggestions, and the manager should implement them when feasible.

Avoiding the risks. Avoiding the risks may require policies like no dogs on the property (or, at the least, no aggressive breeds, such as rottweilers or pit bulls). Hiring only contractors with workers' compensation insurance also avoids risk. Removing pool slides or diving boards reduces the chances of an accident.

Controlling the risks. Security patrols, additional lighting, and low shrubbery help control criminal activity. Adding stair rails, even on small walkway steps, controls risk. Maintenance personnel should wear safety glasses and back braces for lifting. In fact, insurance policies often provide discounts for these preventive measures.

Transferring the risks. The principal way to transfer the risk is to purchase insurance. Another way is to have hazardous work done by outside contractors who are insured against work-related risks. Such contracts should be made directly between the owner and the contractors to reduce the property manager's liability. Having each tenant sign an agreement to be responsible for the contents of his or her space and to hold the owner and manager harmless also transfers risk.

Property insurance. Because of the large sums of money at stake, the manager should discuss insurance options with the owner and get the owner's decision about which coverage to purchase. The property manager should not expose himself or herself to liability by acting as an insurance expert. The property manager should obtain insurance quotes for all-peril insurance coverage as well as commercial general liability insurance.

Other insurance the manager should purchase includes:

- loss of income insurance if units become vacant due to loss or damage;
- workers' compensation; and
- commercial automobile liability.

If a claim for accident or damage is made, the manager should notify the insurance carrier and follow up to ensure that the claim is handled properly.

Manager's risk management. The property manager should be named as an additional insured in the owner's general liability policy, and the manager should get a certificate of insurance from the company. The property manager should insure the manager's own workers with worker's compensation and general liability insurance. Also, the manager should insure office contents including computers and software. Employees should be bonded (dishonesty insurance) for any cash or property for which the manager is responsible. Errors and omissions insurance protects the manager from liability for mistakes or other oversights. The manager also should require in the management contract a clause stating that the owner indemnifies the manager against damages not caused by the manager's negligence or willful wrongdoing.

THE OWNER-MANAGER RELATIONSHIP

The property manager is normally a single agent for the owner and, while attempting to maintain the tenants' goodwill, must not forget the fiduciary duties to the owner. These duties include skill, care, and diligence; obedience; loyalty; disclosure of all known facts; accounting; and confidentiality. Managers may not suggest to tenants that they will represent the tenants' interests in negotiations or complaints. This would make the broker a dual agent, which could result in FREC disciplinary action as well as monetary damages from a lawsuit.

Professional management associations. Property managers have many opportunities to enhance their professional skills through education courses. Institutional investors often seek out persons to manage their properties who possess designations demonstrating that they have completed rigorous courses of study. The Institute of Real Estate Management (IREM) awards the prestigious Certified Property Manager (CPM), Accredited Resident Manager (ARM), and Accredited Management Organization (AMO) designations. All members of the Institute must subscribe to a strict code of ethical behavior.

Negotiating the Management Agreement

It is important that the owner and property manager put the full management agreement in writing and sign it.

Management agreement provisions. The management agreement should identify the parties to the contract and define their authority and responsibilities, indicate the duration of the agreement, and spell out the requirements for reporting the results of operations. It also should indicate how and when either party may terminate the agreement.

The agreement should describe the manager's authority to rent, operate, and manage the premises. The authority gives the manager power to advertise the property, sign leases for one year or less, collect rents, and terminate tenancies. The manager also is empowered to arrange for necessary repairs under an authorized dollar amount.

Because the statute of frauds requires that leases for periods longer than one year be in writing and signed by the parties to be enforceable, only the owner's signature is acceptable. Without a power of attorney, the property manager does not have the authority to sign such leases for the principal.

Compensation for management services. Compensation methods for property managers depend on the types of properties they manage, the property occupancy rates, and the amount of time and effort involved. A fixed fee is appropriate for association management, while a percentage of income generated is common on rental properties. A combination of the two is appropriate for new properties because of the initial high vacancy rates and for problem properties. Smaller properties often require as much time to manage as larger properties, so commission percentage rates tend to be higher.

Personal communications. A property manager who stays in touch with the owner reduces the chances for misunderstandings and enhances the bond between the parties. It is not enough for the owner to receive only a monthly check with an accounting. The manager should send a letter or call regularly to inform the owner about the current market and the manager's efforts.

Evaluating management performance. The owner of a rental property may evaluate the manager's performance by comparing the property operations with the budget and previous years. A personal inspection of the premises helps the owner determine that the property is maintained properly. The owner also should stay informed about general market conditions. Market knowledge puts a 15 percent vacancy rate into better perspective if competitive properties have 25 percent vacancy rates.

STAFFING AND EMPLOYEE RELATIONS

The property manager should employ persons who are efficient, versatile, customer-oriented, and loyal. Each staff member should be aware of required duties. The best way to accomplish this objective is to prepare written job descriptions. Often, because a management team is small, each job description is very broad. Larger teams tend to have more specialized job functions. Also, a job description should describe carefully the employee's limits of authority. Examples of positions within a larger management team include the:

- executive property manager, who supervises operations for all of the owner's properties, including budgeting, advertising, staffing, and communicating with the owner;
- resident manager, sometimes called the *property supervisor,* who is responsible for the activities of maintenance and leasing personnel, as well as tenant relations; and
- leasing agents, who are selected for their selling skills and their ability to turn visitors into tenants.

Recruiting, Training, and Retaining Qualified Personnel

The most important characteristic of a successful management team is the quality of its personnel. It is a primary function of the property manager to attract, train, and keep the best employees available.

The methods used to recruit staff depend on the job description and the property size. A resident manager for a 30-unit apartment building often can be recruited through newspaper classified ads, or may be a tenant in the building. Important qualifications include an attention to detail, a good attitude, and a genuine desire to maintain good tenant relationships. The property manager should train the resident manager to make sure all duties are understood. Close supervision may be necessary until the property manager is certain that the individual can perform effectively. A larger property requires personnel with more training and experience, and the property manager often comes from the rental staff of the same property or another property the firm manages. Clerical staff usually are recruited through employment services or newspaper advertising.

When a property manager hires an individual, the manager must make sure the person is trained in company policies and is completely familiar with the job duties. In-service training enhances the staff's professional growth.

Retaining good employees is important, not only from the standpoints of loyalty and continuity but also economics. Training new staff is time consuming and expensive. Employees must be treated with respect and must feel that the management appreciates them. Their compensation must be competitive with similar positions. Good work should be recognized and rewarded.

APPLICABLE FEDERAL AND STATE LAWS

The property manager must understand the laws that regulate the profession. This includes fair housing laws, the Americans with Disabilities Act, and the Florida Landlord and Tenant Act.

REQUIREMENTS FOR HANDLING TENANT SECURITY DEPOSITS AND ADVANCE RENTS

The owner may hold the funds in one of three ways:

1. Hold the money in a separate, non-interest-bearing account.
2. Hold the money in a separate, interest-bearing account and pay the tenant at least 75 percent of the average interest or a straight five percent, whichever the landlord elects.
3. Commingle the funds, provided the owner posts a surety bond with the clerk of the court for the total amount of security deposits and advance rent (or $50,000, whichever is less) and pays the tenant five percent simple interest. This option is available to an owner only, never to a broker.

The landlord must disclose to the tenant how the money is being held within 30 days of receiving the funds. Pet deposits and other nonrefundable deposits are not covered under these provisions.

These requirements do not apply to transient rentals by hotels or motels; nor do they apply in those instances in which the amount of rent or deposit is regulated by public housing authorities or federal housing programs.

Federal and State Fair Housing Laws

Fair housing laws are designed to give every citizen the right to live where he or she chooses without arbitrary rejection based on race, color, religion, or any other legally protected status.

Civil Rights Act of 1866. Under this act, any manner of racial discrimination is prohibited. While the Fair Housing Act may provide exemptions for private owners, the **Civil Rights Act of 1866** allows no exceptions for discrimination based on race.

Fair Housing Act (Title VIII of the Civil Rights Act of 1968). The application of this law to property managers is very broad. The **Fair Housing Act**, with its amendments, prohibits discrimination in housing based on race, color, religion, sex, national origin, handicap, or family status. A property manager may not, for discriminatory reasons:

- refuse to show, rent, or negotiate with a person for housing;
- discriminate in a lease's terms or conditions;
- engage in discriminatory advertising;
- falsely tell potential renters that a property is not available; or
- **steer** members of protected classes into buildings or areas that are occupied primarily by members of the same class (steering).

Testers ensure compliance with the law and gather evidence of violations. Such testing might involve a white couple and a minority couple asking to see an apartment. If the minority couple is told that no apartments are available, or they are shown a less desirable apartment, the offending manager can expect strong enforcement action to follow.

Americans with Disabilities Act. The **Americans with Disabilities Act** makes it unlawful to discriminate against persons with physical or mental impairments. Title I of the act prohibits discrimination in employment. The property manager should not ask a prospective employee to list conditions or diseases, prior hospitalizations, or the amount of time absent from work last year. The employer may be required to modify the facilities to make the work area accessible to employees with disabilities. Small businesses may be entitled to tax credits covering this expense.

Title III addresses disabled persons' accessibility to public accommodations, commercial buildings, and multifamily dwelling units. Public and common-use portions of dwellings must be readily accessible to and usable by all disabled persons. There also are required standards for doorway widths, heights of light switches, and grab bars in bathrooms, for example, for buildings built after this law's enactment.

The Florida Landlord and Tenant Act

Property managers in Florida must observe the requirements of the **Florida Landlord and Tenant Act**, Chapter 83, F.S., which has two major sections:

- Part I—nonresidential tenancies
- Part II—residential tenancies

The following discussion focuses on residential tenancies.

Landlord's statutory duties. The landlord must comply with applicable building, housing, and health codes, and keep the structure and plumbing in good repair. Unless otherwise agreed in writing, the landlord of a dwelling unit other than a single-family home or duplex must provide pest control, locks and keys, clean and safe common areas, garbage removal and receptacles, and facilities for heat, running water, and hot water. The landlord of a single-family home or duplex must provide working smoke detectors.

Tenant's statutory duties. The tenant must comply with all building, housing, and health codes; keep the premises clean and sanitary; remove garbage; use all equipment in a reasonable manner; and refrain from disturbing neighbors unreasonably.

Tenant remedies for breach by landlord. If the landlord does not comply with material provisions of the rental agreement within seven days after the tenant delivers a written notice of the noncompliance, the tenant may terminate the rental agreement.

When the tenant vacates the premises, the landlord must return the deposit within 15 days or notify the tenant within 30 days of the landlord's intent to claim part or all of the security deposit and the reason for this claim. If the landlord does not notify the tenant, the landlord forfeits the right to make a claim. Unless the tenant objects within 15 days the landlord deducts the amount of the claim and sends the balance of the deposit to the tenant.

Landlord's right to enter the premises during lease term. The tenant may not withhold consent unreasonably for the landlord to inspect the premises, make repairs, supply agreed-upon services, or show the apartment. The landlord may not abuse the right to enter to harass the tenant. The landlord may enter the dwelling unit at any time to preserve the premises. The landlord must give at least 12 hours' notice before entering for repairs, and the repairs must be made between 7:30 AM and 8:00 PM. If the tenant notifies the landlord of an extended absence, the landlord may enter only with the tenant's consent or to protect the premises.

CASE IN POINT

A sales associate, when asked, disclosed to an owner the race of the prospective tenants. Upon hearing this, the owner refused to rent to the tenants. The sales associate was suspended for two years and fined $1,000.

Reference: *Florida Realtor,* Florida REALTORS®, Volume 72, Number 4, April 1997.

Eviction requirements. If the tenant is late in paying rent, the landlord may not cut off utility services, change the locks, or remove outside doors, locks, roofs, or windows in an effort to force the tenant to move. Such actions leave the landlord liable for actual damages or three months' rent, whichever is greater.

If the tenant fails to pay rent after receiving a three-day notice, the landlord must give written notice to demand possession of the premises. If the tenant does not vacate the premises, the landlord must file a complaint to recover possession in county court. A landlord's agent may not take any action other than filing the initial complaint unless the agent is an attorney.

After receiving a final judgment against the tenant, the landlord must obtain a **writ of possession** to have the sheriff evict the tenant. Eviction begins 24 hours after the sheriff serves notice to the tenant.

The sheriff does not physically evict the tenant and is present only to ensure that the tenant does not interfere with the landlord's removal of the tenant's furniture and other belongings. Eviction can be an emotionally charged event, and the landlord should take precautions for personal safety during the process. After the personal property has been removed, the landlord should have the locks changed.

Environmental hazards. The property manager must understand typical environmental hazards and their effect on the property and its tenants. Those most relevant to property managers include asbestos, radon, and lead-based paint. These hazards are discussed in Chapter 17.

WEB LINK

For the complete text of Florida's Landlord and Tenant Act, and the Division of Consumer Services consumer brochure, go to the Division's Web site at **http://www.800helpfla.com/landlord_text.html.**

SUMMARY OF IMPORTANT POINTS

- While many property managers hold Florida real estate licenses, owners are exempt from that requirement, and employees of owners need not have a license so long as their compensation is by salary.
- Many brokers enter the property management field because it offers many benefits, one of which is stable income.
- Brokers manage residential properties, office and retail properties.
- In addition to rental properties, many property managers are employed as community association managers for condominiums and homeowners' associations.

- The qualifications for a property manager include not only the ability to work well with people but also knowledge of building systems, marketing skills, and sensitivity to environmental problems.
- The manager is expected to employ and train employees, prepare financial reports, and ensure that there are no violations of the fair housing laws.
- A property manager must analyze the market area as well as the property. A market analysis indicates the economic health of the area and the neighborhood, while the property analysis shows the owners the condition of the physical property, such as deferred maintenance.
- The advertising and promotion program might include billboards, newspapers, apartment guides, radio and television, and direct mail. The manager must evaluate each medium to determine the most effective method of promotion.
- Once the promotion has generated prospective tenants, the manager must be certain that the rental staff is well trained.
- The staff must understand how to create interest and desire and handle objections.
- Persons who wish to sign a lease must be qualified, and the staff must make a background check.
- The policies of the management company must be communicated to the tenant to reduce misunderstandings.
- The most common tenant complaint concerns maintenance service requests.
- Maintenance is provided for physical integrity, functional performance, housekeeping, and merchandising.
- Tenants should have no doubt that the collection policies will be enforced in the event their rent is late.
- Another important function of the manager is accounting and record keeping.
- The Florida Landlord and Tenant Act, as well as the Florida real estate license law, spells out requirements for holding and accounting for tenant deposits.
- Owners depend on the manager to control risk through insurance and other steps, such as prohibiting certain breeds of dogs.
- Many managers hire outside contractors who are licensed and insured to transfer some of the risk.

REVIEW QUESTIONS

1. When the owners moved to Atlanta for 18 months, they asked their neighbor to rent their home, send them all the bills, and "look after things." For this service, the neighbor was paid half of the first month's rent, then $25 per month. Which statement is TRUE of this situation?
   a. This practice is acceptable if the neighbor calls her compensation a fee, rather than a commission.
   b. Unless the neighbor has a real estate license, she must be an employee of the owner to make it legal.
   c. Both the owner and the neighbor have violated Chapter 475, F.S.
   d. This is a real estate service requiring the neighbor to be licensed as or registered with a broker.

2. An office center employs a manager a to manage the property, hire and train the office staff, and serve as its principal leasing agent. The new manager, who will be paid by salary, does not have a real estate license. This situation
   a. makes his leasing activities a violation of Chapter 475, F.S.
   b. requires that he hire a leasing agent to handle that portion of the management.
   c. allows him to lease the property, but does not permit him to write the lease agreements.
   d. does not prevent him from carrying out his duties.

3. A real estate broker owns two companies. One is a brokerage firm, and one handles short-term rentals. A competitor learns that the broker has been paying travel agents a 15 percent fee for sending her tenants for the short-term rental company, and it files a complaint with the DBPR. What is TRUE about this situation?
   a. Because this activity is exempt from the license requirement, the DBPR will determine that no violation has occurred, provided that no monies from this activity are deposited into the broker's escrow account.
   b. The broker has violated the law by paying unlicensed persons for referring customers.
   c. The broker may be disciplined by the FREC.
   d. Both B and C are true.

4. A broker introduces her unlicensed employee to prospective tenants who shows and rents the single-family homes and duplexes the broker manages. If her broker pays the employee a salary that is not tied to her rental activities
   a. the employee may legally perform the assigned activities.
   b. the employee has violated the law, but her employer has not.
   c. both the employee and her broker have violated Chapter 475.
   d. the broker has violated the law, but the employee has not.

5. There are 700 homes in a homes association that has the right to file a lien for nonpayment of unit assessments. The directors hire a manager for compiling the budget and preparing checks for the association's president to sign. The manager
   a. must acquire a real estate license.
   b. must acquire a community association manager's license.
   c. need not acquire a license.
   d. Both A and B are true.

6. A broker has just been hired to handle leasing for an apartments complex. Because the property is new, the broker is working to establish the optimum pricing for each apartment size. The study that would affect the decision MOST directly would be the
   a. regional market analysis.
   b. land-use study.
   c. property analysis.
   d. neighborhood market analysis.

7. A high-intensity marketing program MOST likely will be used with a
   a. property that has a 93 percent occupancy rate.
   b. large office occupied with six AAA tenants.
   c. new 400-unit apartment property.
   d. new industrial building with 5,000 square feet.

8. The manager of an industrial park has two buildings for lease. One of the MOST effective ways to reach potential tenants using the rifle approach is
   a. billboards.
   b. broadcast media.
   c. direct mail.
   d. display advertising.

9. The MOST common way to advertise residential apartments is
   a. direct mail.
   b. classified advertising.
   c. billboards.
   d. radio and television.

10. Which advertising strategy is ill-advised?
    a. Be certain the message is consistent in all media
    b. Ensure the advertising creates the image that will generate the most tenants
    c. Reduce spending on the advertising if revenues are lower than the budget
    d. Avoid use of classified advertising because it is currently considered to be a waste of advertising dollars

11. The MOST effective way to make sure tenants pay rents on a timely basis is to
    a. maintain good relationships with the tenants.
    b. require a lease application before agreeing to lease to a tenant.
    c. maintain good communications with the tenants.
    d. establish a strong collection policy that includes a three-day notice when the rent is late.

12. A broker manages an office center. He shows the properties, fills in the blanks in the owner-designed lease form, collects the first month's rent, and places it in his trust account. When the owner signs the lease, he writes a check from the escrow account to his general operating account as his commission, which is allowed under the terms of his management agreement. The broker
    a. has violated the law because of the way he handles the commission.
    b. has not violated the law.
    c. may not legally complete a lease form that is not Supreme Court–approved.
    d. should not place the first month's rent in a trust account.

13. A man has inherited a large freestanding office building. He has no property management experience. He does not want to worry about paying taxes or maintenance. If a large national company with excellent credit wishes to lease the building for 20 years, which type of lease would be BEST for his situation?
    a. Percentage lease
    b. Gross lease
    c. Net lease
    d. Tenancy at will

14. A tenant in a retail store has three more years on his lease. Because his business is barely breaking even, he subleases the store to another merchant. The landlord did not approve the sublease, but the lease agreement does not prohibit subleasing. What is TRUE about this situation?
    a. Unless the lease specifically allows subleasing, the tenant's action is illegal.
    b. While the action is not illegal, the tenant remains liable under the lease.
    c. The new tenant is personally liable to the landlord if the tenant defaults.
    d. The landlord may raise the rent immediately, and the new tenant is obligated to pay.

15. An individual owns a duplex that he manages personally. If he refuses to rent to a prospective tenant based on the person's race, which is TRUE?
    a. Because the Fair Housing Act excludes private homeowners, he has not violated the law.
    b. Because he did not use a broker for the rental, he has not violated the law.
    c. Because it was based on race, the act violates the Civil Rights Act of 1866.
    d. He has violated both the 1866 and 1968 Civil Rights Acts.

16. A resident manager of one of the largest apartment properties in Tampa was asked by a prospective tenant to locate her in an area of the property where lots of children lived so that her two children would have others to play with and so they would not disturb elderly tenants. The manager saw a win-win-win situation for her, his elderly tenants, and himself and placed her according to her wishes. Based on this information, which is TRUE?
    a. While this is an acceptable practice in property management, the manager actually could not have refused to rent to her because of the children.
    b. While the practice generally is frowned upon, government testers rarely enforce this part of the law.
    c. The manager's action is legal, provided it damages no party in the property.
    d. The manager's illegal act could result in heavy fines to the owner.

17. An owner of a property management company manages more than 1,500 apartments. She places an ad for a bookkeeper in the paper, and many people apply for the position. When she interviews, which question(s) should the owner avoid asking to protect against charges of discrimination?
    a. "How much time did you miss from work last year due to illness?"
    b. "That's an unusual last name. Is it Lebanese?"
    c. "Have you ever been in a hospital for treatment of a communicable disease?"
    d. The owner should avoid all of the above.

18. An owner of a rental home in Lake Worth has never kept a tenant's deposit without good cause and has a strong financial statement. Yesterday she received a check for \$3,100, representing \$1,000 for the first month's rent, \$1,000 for the last month's rent, \$1,000 as a security deposit, and \$100 for a nonrefundable pet fee. Assuming she does not buy a surety bond, she must deposit
    a. \$3,100 in a separate account until the end of the lease.
    b. \$2,000 in a separate account, representing \$1,000 for the first month's rent and \$1,000 as a security deposit.
    c. \$2,000 in a separate account, representing \$1,000 for the last month's rent and \$1,000 as a security deposit.
    d. only the security deposit into a separate account.

19. When tenants were late on their rent, the owner simply gave them a three-day notice, then set their personal property outside their apartments, turned off the water, and changed the locks. Collection problems were reduced substantially. Which is TRUE of this situation?
    a. The property owner is liable for any of his tenants' actual damages, including loss of their personal property.
    b. The practice is acceptable providing a tenant has been given at least three days' notice.
    c. The property owner is liable to the evicted tenants for at least three months' rent.
    d. Both A and C are true.

20. A way to avoid risk, as opposed to transferring or controlling risk, is to
    a. inspect the property.
    b. buy insurance.
    c. hire security personnel.
    d. remove diving boards from the pool.

CASE STUDY PART 4

SPECIALTIES

Department of Business and Professional Regulation, Florida Real Estate Commission vs. William A. Gold

Recommended Order: This case was heard in Pensacola on July 16, [year 2], before Administrative Law Judge H. C. Brewer, Division of Administrative Hearings. The parties were represented by:

For Petitioner: Bruce W. Carpenter, Esquire, DBPR

For Respondent: Samuel H. Abraham, Esquire

This matter arises on Petitioner's Administrative Complaint against Respondent William A. Gold.

Findings of Fact: The Respondent, at all times pertinent hereto, has been a licensed Florida real estate broker. The Petitioner's investigator, Sean Brower, conducted an office inspection and an audit of the Respondent's escrow accounts and the broker's trust accounts on April 2, [year 1].

The Respondent maintained an account entitled "Rental escrow account." An audit of that escrow account revealed a total trust account liability of $16,861.51. The reconciled bank balance, however, was for $4,001.82. This resulted in an apparent shortage of $12,858.69.

Mr. Brower was not of the opinion, and found no evidence, that the Respondent had taken and used any of the funds for his personal use. Rather, the shortage reflected, in essence, a situation where the brokerage had used certain owners' funds to cover other owners' expenses, when the owners with the expenses had accounts which did not contain sufficient funds to cover their own rental property management expenses. There was no intentional conversion of funds in the owners' distribution escrow account or in the security deposit escrow account for the Respondent's own use or for any improper use or use detrimental to any client's interest.

Respondent admitted in his testimony that a broker should not use funds from an escrow account to "loan money" to another owner but rather should use the a brokerage's own funds and that a monthly reconciliation statement review should identify any shortages for correction.

No damages were found to have occurred to clients of the firm.

Discussion Questions:

1. Which subsections of Chapter 475, F.S. were violated, and what were the violations?
2. Did the respondent commit a breach of trust in the real estate transaction?
3. Can an administrative penalty be imposed on a licensee if no damage results to a member of the public?

WEB LINK

Web Link: **http://www.doah.state.fl.us/internet/**

PRACTICE FINAL EXAM

This practice examination provides 100 multiple-choice questions intended to help you prepare for both the end-of-course examination and the state broker's examination. The authors recommend that you treat this exam as if it were your final examination: complete it at one sitting and limit your time to three hours. Because you may wish to review this exam several times before taking your state examination, we suggest that you do not write on the exam, but instead use the tear-out answer sheet at the back of the book.

1. Hazel's brokerage firm has an annual expense budget of $162,000 that includes her own salary. She wants to make $20,000 profit. If she has seven sales associates, what must each sales associate generate in company dollars for Hazel to achieve her goal?
   a. $14,000
   b. $23,143
   c. $26,000
   d. $34,200

2. Licensed personal assistants may
   a. be employed and paid commissions by sales associates.
   b. be employed by sales associates but must be paid commissions by the firm's broker.
   c. never be classified as independent contractors.
   d. perform real estate services that make only their employing sales associates financially liable, but not the firm's broker.

3. An organization is limited to 100 shareholders. It pays no taxes directly, and the owners pay taxes on their shares of the net income whether or not they receive dividends from the company. This entity is a(n)
   a. C corporation.
   b. limited partnership.
   c. quasi partnership.
   d. S corporation.

4. A business appraiser calculates a company's current ratio by
   a. multiplying assets by net worth.
   b. dividing current assets by current liabilities.
   c. dividing current liabilities by net worth.
   d. subtracting current liabilities from current assets.

5. Which type of ownership allows property to be inherited?
   a. Tenancy in severalty and tenancy in common
   b. Tenancy at will and joint tenancy
   c. Tenancy by the entireties and tenancy in common
   d. Tenancy by the entireties and joint tenancy

6. A buyer agreed to purchase a lot in Lakeland for $17,000. She gave the broker a good-faith deposit of $11,000 in cash and agreed to close the property within 60 days and pay the balance in cash. The sale was contingent on the buyer receiving acceptable soil tests from an engineering firm and determining that the land use allowed a mobile home. The broker
   a. should not have written a contingency contract for land use.
   b. violated Chapter 475, F.S. by accepting a cash deposit greater than $10,000.
   c. must place the deposit in his trust account by the end of the next business day.
   d. must report the transaction to the IRS on Form 8300.

7. When a broker receives an earnest money deposit from a buyer, the broker
   a. must deposit the funds into his escrow account by the end of the next business day.
   b. is responsible if the check is dishonored even if he made a timely deposit.
   c. may accept it in the form of a postdated check with the seller's approval.
   d. may never accept a postdated check because of their illegal status in Florida.

8. An owner agreed to sell his restaurant property. The buyer gave the broker an earnest money deposit of $4,000. One day before closing, the buyer told the broker she had found another property and would not be closing the transaction. The owner lost more than $12,000 because of the default. What remedy would BEST compensate him?
   a. Suit for rescission on breach
   b. Suit for compensatory damages
   c. Suit for liquidated damages
   d. Suit for interpleader

9. The FHA program that insures condominium mortgage loans is Section
   a. 203(b).
   b. 234(c).
   c. 235.
   d. 245.

10. A veteran can have his previously used entitlement restored to buy another home with a VA loan if he
   a. has had more than three VA loans in the past.
   b. agrees to make at least a 20 percent down payment on the new home.
   c. has paid off the previous loan.
   d. fought in World War II or in Korea.

11. Which is FALSE about adjustable-rate mortgages?
   a. The index changes periodically.
   b. The rate is calculated by adding the margin to the index.
   c. It is unpopular because it has negative amortization of the principal.
   d. The margin remains constant throughout the loan period.

12. What type of mortgage encumbers more than one parcel of property?
   a. Blanket
   b. Package
   c. Participation
   d. Purchase-money

13. A 57-year-old executive at an insurance company applies at a local bank for a mortgage loan on a new property she has contracted to buy. Her income is sufficient, the loan officer tells her, but because of her age the income is not likely to continue for as long as the mortgage loan. He suggests that she apply at her credit union instead. Based on this information, the loan officer
    a. has violated the Fair Housing Act.
    b. has violated the Equal Credit Opportunity Act.
    c. is guilty of redlining.
    d. has violated the Truth-in-Lending Act.

14. If the closing is on July 6, the prepaid interest on a new institutional mortgage covers a period of how many days and is charged to whom?
    a. 6 days; seller
    b. 6 days; buyer
    c. 26 days; buyer
    d. 57 days; buyer

15. The HUD-1 Settlement Statement
    a. must be used for all real estate transactions in Florida.
    b. need not be used in a federally related transaction.
    c. consists of two pages: the buyer's statement and the seller's statement.
    d. must be used for all real estate transactions covered under the RESPA requirements.

16. What does RESPA NOT require a lender to furnish to a borrower at the time of the loan application or within three days of loan application?
    a. Annual percentage rate of effective interest on the loan
    b. Good-faith estimate of settlement costs
    c. Special information booklet called "Settlement Costs and You"
    d. Mortgage servicing disclosure statement

17. A transaction closes on November 15. The seller has paid $1,816.25 in annual taxes. The day of closing is charged to the buyer. Using the 365-day method, what is the proration on the closing statement?
    a. Debit seller, credit buyer $233.87; page 1
    b. Credit seller, debit buyer $233.87; page 1
    c. Debit seller, credit buyer $1,582.38; page 1
    d. Debit seller $233.87, credit buyer $1,582.38; page 1

18. A title insurance company offers to pay a real estate sales associate $50 for each RESPA closing she refers to the company. This is
    a. legal if the buyer approves.
    b. illegal under Regulation Z of the Truth-in-Lending Act.
    c. prohibited under RESPA.
    d. legal until the Florida legislature enacts legislation prohibiting such payments.

19. An owner has a capital gain of $147,000 on the sale of her home. She has owned the property for three years. The sale price was $325,000. Costs of sale were $5,000, qualified fix-up costs were $1,000, and moving costs were $4,000. How much must she pay in capital gains taxes on this sale if her normal tax rate is 25 percent?
    a. $0
    b. $0 if within two years she buys and occupies another home with a price equal to or greater than the old residence's adjusted sale price
    c. $34,250
    d. $36,750

20. When an improved investment property is sold, the tax rate on depreciation that has been deducted previously generally is
    a. 15% for a 25% tax-rate taxpayer or 5% for a 15% tax-rate taxpayer.
    b. 25%.
    c. 28%.
    d. the same as the taxpayer's marginal tax rate.

21. An investor purchases an office building for $700,000. He pays $4,000 for an appraisal, $1,000 for a survey, $30,000 for his broker's commission, and $3,000 for title insurance. The appraisal indicated that the total property value was $700,000 and the land was worth $140,000. What is the allowed depreciation deduction per year?
    a. $14,358.97
    b. $15,138.46
    c. $18,923.08
    d. $21,469.09

22. Which type of real property does NOT allow the owner to deduct depreciation for federal tax purposes?
    a. A residential apartment building
    b. A commercial store operated as a trade or business
    c. The business office of a homebuilder
    d. A homebuilder's inventory of unsold homes

23. The maximum long-term capital gains on property sold by a taxpayer in the 25 percent bracket who earns less than $400,000 in ordinary income is
    a. 12 percent.
    b. 15 percent.
    c. 25 percent.
    d. 28 percent.

24. When completing an exchange of real property that conforms with Section 1031 of the Internal Revenue Code, the
    a. replacement property must be identified within 180 days of the initial transfer.
    b. properties must be exchanged simultaneously.
    c. title to the replacement property must be transferred within 180 days or before the tax due date plus any extensions.
    d. exchanger's broker may place the proceeds of the sale of the first property in escrow awaiting the transfer of the new property.

25. A ten-year lease requires the tenant to pay $4,000 per month as well as taxes, insurance, and maintenance on the building. What type of lease is this?
    a. Gross
    b. Net
    c. Participation
    d. Expense stop

26. A developer owns an office building in Fort Lauderdale that is encumbered by a mortgage. He leases 10,000 square feet to a tenant for ten years at a very attractive rate. Six months later, the bank forecloses on the mortgage and ends up as the property owner. What is the status of the tenant's lease?
    a. The bank is subject to the lease terms.
    b. The bank is subject to the lease for a maximum of one year after the foreclosure.
    c. The bank is subject to the lease for a maximum of six months after the foreclosure.
    d. The bank may terminate the tenant's lease.

27. Required maintenance on a property that the owner cannot or will not do is called
    a. deferred maintenance.
    b. reserve for replacements.
    c. nonpreventive maintenance.
    d. corrective maintenance.

28. An apartment owner wants to know the equity dividend rate, also called the *cash-on-cash return*. How is this ratio calculated?
    a. Before-tax cash flow divided by the owner's equity
    b. Owner's equity divided by the before-tax cash flow
    c. Net operating income divided by the value
    d. Annual debt service divided by the equity

29. Positive leverage results when
    a. the loan-to-value ratio is greater than the breakeven ratio.
    b. the owner borrows more than the property's value.
    c. if the annual constant on the debt service is less than the overall rate (OAR).
    d. the annual constant on the debt service is more than the overall rate (OAR).

30. The internal rate of return is the discount rate at which the present value of the cash flows equals the
    a. price of the property.
    b. initial investment (down payment).
    c. mortgage balance.
    d. annual debt service.

31. An owners' association is defined as a community association under Chapter 468, F.S., if it has more than how many units and an annual budget exceeding how much?
    a. 50; $50,000
    b. 10; $100,000
    c. 50; $150,000
    d. 100; $50,000

32. In a market with many vacancies
    a. "technical oversupply" means potential tenants outnumber units available.
    b. "economic oversupply" means units available outnumber potential tenants.
    c. economic oversupply occurs when available space is priced beyond the means of potential tenants.
    d. All of the above

33. What mortgage right allows a borrower to prevent a foreclosure by paying the entire balance due to the lender?
    a. Exculpatory
    b. Right of possession
    c. Novation
    d. Equity of redemption

34. The MOST common tenant complaint in apartment properties centers on
    a. rent rates.
    b. maintenance service requests.
    c. security deposit requirements.
    d. rent collection.

35. The Homeowners' Association Disclosure summary required under Section 720.401 was not provided to the prospective buyer before executing the purchase contract. What is the status of the contract?
    a. Void
    b. Canceled
    c. Valid and enforceable
    d. Voidable by the buyer

36. When preparing a lease agreement
    a. a broker may prepare only the residential lease forms approved by the National Association of REALTORS®.
    b. the property owner may personally fill in the blanks only on a form approved by the Florida Supreme Court.
    c. the property owner may personally prepare any lease form that she and the tenant agree on.
    d. a broker may use either a lease form prepared by an attorney or one that has been approved by the Florida Supreme Court.

37. Which statement is TRUE regarding for sale by owners (FSBOs)?
    a. Real estate licensees are exempt from all state and federal telemarketing laws with regard to prospecting for listings.
    b. Federal law allows real estate licensees to contact an FSBO seller if they have an actual buyer interested in the property.
    c. Federal telemarketing laws allow licensees to contact FSBO sellers to solicit listings if they have a yard sign.
    d. Calling an FSBO seller to solicit listings is punishable by a maximum fine of $1,000 per call.

38. An investor purchased an apartment building for $1,600,000 encumbered by a seven percent mortgage with a balance of $1,250,000. Net operating income was $178,500. Monthly mortgage payments are $8,053.77, and depreciation in the first year was $47,900. The equity dividend rate for this property is
   a. 12.7 percent.
   b. 13.2 percent.
   c. 19.3 percent.
   d. 23.4 percent.

39. A buyer of a new home for $695,000 is assuming the existing $240,325 mortgage. The owner is providing a new purchase money mortgage in the amount of $346,019, and the buyer will pay cash for the balance. What is total of the documentary stamp taxes and intangible taxes on the financing?
   a. $1,903.39
   b. $2,264.14
   c. $2,744.24
   d. $2,744.79

40. A buyer of a new home for $240,000 will have annual taxes of $5,200 and insurance for $1,200. She gets a new 90 percent conventional mortgage for 30 years at 7.25 percent. The monthly mortgage insurance premium is $110. The loan constant from a mortgage payment table is .0068218. Using this information, what will be the new homeowner's total monthly payments (PITI)?
   a. $1,473.51
   b. $2,046.84
   c. $2,116.84
   d. $2,280.56

41. A married Florida resident sales associate who wants to apply for a broker's license must
   a. complete and sign the irrevocable consent to service form.
   b. include a personal financial statement with the application.
   c. submit two passport quality photographs with the application.
   d. disclose her maiden name on the application, if her maiden name is different from the name on her license application.

42. A licensed Florida real estate sales associate is also an active member of The Florida Bar. She wants to become a broker. She is exempt from which requirement?
   a. 14-hour continuing education
   b. 45-hour postlicensing education
   c. Broker prelicense course
   d. State license exam

43. A licensed Florida real estate broker decides to move to Quebec, Canada. What must he do regarding his license?
   a. Place his broker license in voluntary inactive status.
   b. Discontinue performing real estate services in the state of Florida.
   c. Notify the Commission of his nonresident status within 60 days of the change in residency.
   d. Surrender his broker license to the DBPR.

44. A licensed real estate broker's real estate license expires on March 31 of every even-numbered year. On March 25, he mailed in his renewal application and fee. He registered to attend a continuing education course on March 30 and 31, but the class was canceled at the last minute. Which statement applies to this situation?
    a. The Commission will take no action against the broker because the class was canceled.
    b. If the broker is audited and the fact that the broker has not completed his education requirement is discovered, the Commission will discipline him.
    c. The broker will be required to pay a late fee only.
    d. The broker must report the school that canceled the course to the DRE to avoid being disciplined for failing to complete his education requirement.

45. A homeowner is planning to relocate to Oregon. She gives Quick Results Realty a listing to sell her home. Because she expects to be relocated to Oregon before the listed property is sold, she gives her trusted friend power of attorney for the purpose of executing the purchase and sale agreement on her behalf. Which statement is TRUE regarding the arrangement?
    a. This is not a violation of Florida real estate license law.
    b. For this to be legal, the homeowner must hold an active Florida real estate license.
    c. Both the homeowner and her friend are in violation of Florida real estate license law.
    d. Her friend is guilty of the unlicensed practice of real estate.

46. An active New York broker has held a license since 1990. She now lives in Jacksonville, Florida, and wants a Florida real estate broker's license. Which statement applies to this situation?
    a. She must first take and pass the sales associate course and licensure exam.
    b. She may apply for a Florida broker license under mutual recognition.
    c. She is required only to take and pass the state broker license exam.
    d. She must successfully complete the broker prelicense course and pass the state broker license examination.

47. Mike has recently passed the broker license exam. He plans to open his own real estate brokerage as a sole proprietorship. Mike intends to name his brokerage Mike's Complete Real Estate Services. Which statement is FALSE?
    a. Mike must hold an active broker license in order to deal with the public.
    b. Mike must register his trade name with the DBPR.
    c. Mike must register his trade name with the Florida Department of State.
    d. Mike must register his business address with the DBPR.

48. Jack and Jill form a general partnership real estate brokerage entity. Jill has an active broker license but Jack does not. Jill is killed in a car accident. Which statement is TRUE regarding this situation?
    a. The partnership is automatically dissolved.
    b. Because there is one remaining partner, Jack need not notify the DBPR.
    c. New brokerage business may continue without interruption.
    d. A new active broker must fill the vacancy within 14 calendar days and register with the DBPR.

49. Jack and Jill form a limited partnership to broker real estate. They are NOT required to
    a. file a certificate of limited partnership with the Department of State.
    b. include the words "Limited" or "Ltd." in the name.
    c. register the business entity with the DBPR.
    d. register all limited partners with the DBPR.

50. Which statement regarding corporations is FALSE?
    a. FREC rules prohibit a not-for-profit corporation from registering as a real estate brokerage entity.
    b. Corporations are dissolved by filing a dissolution of corporation with the Division of Corporations.
    c. Ownership in a corporation is transferred by the purchase and sale of stock.
    d. All of the officers and directors of a real estate brokerage corporation must be registered with the DBPR.

51. Able Realty Company is having an exterior entrance sign made for a new branch office location. What information need NOT be included on the entrance sign?
    a. The words "Branch Office"
    b. Able Realty Company
    c. Licensed (or Lic.) Real Estate Broker
    d. The broker's name

52. Which statement applies to real estate offices under the Americans with Disabilities Act?
    a. Brokers who lease office space are not required to modify the office space.
    b. Existing structures are not required to be modified under ADA guidelines unless an employee requires special accomodations.
    c. The real estate office is considered to be both a commercial facility and a public accommodation and as such must be accessible to persons with physical or mental disabilities.
    d. Real estate offices that have fewer than ten employees are exempt from ADA requirements.

53. Which statement applies to the situation where a classified advertisement includes the phrase "wheelchair ramp at front entrance"?
    a. The Fair Housing Act states that real estate advertisements should not contain explicit features such as "wheelchair ramp."
    b. The words "wheelchair ramp" are required by the Americans with Disabilities Act.
    c. The FREC rules prohibit singling out certain individuals.
    d. The Fair Housing Act allows advertisements to describe specific accessibility features that a property includes.

54. Which statement is FALSE concerning escrow or trust accounts?
    a. Escrow accounts are used to hold other people's monies, including earnest money deposits, advance rent, and security deposits.
    b. Brokers may deposit up to $5,000 of personal funds in a property management escrow account.
    c. Brokers who have an interest-bearing sales escrow account and a non-interest-bearing sales escrow account may keep up to $1,000 of personal funds in each account.
    d. The FREC rules require the word "escrow" or "trust" to appear in the name of the account.

55. A prospective buyer came into the listing company's real estate office on Monday morning and left with the receptionist a written offer accompanied by an earnest money check to purchase a vacant lot. Which statement is TRUE regarding this situation?
    a. The receptionist must turn the deposit over to the listing sales associate within one business day.
    b. Unlicensed receptionists are not allowed to accept escrow money.
    c. The broker must deposit the escrow check into the escrow account no later than the end of business on Thursday of the same week.
    d. The broker must deposit the escrow check into the escrow account no later than the end of business on Wednesday of the same week.

56. Which individual is required to hold a Florida real estate license?
    a. An individual who negotiates long-term lease agreements for commercial property.
    b. An employee of Forest Lawn who sells cemetery plots.
    c. An employee of Sand Pebble Mobile Home Park who is paid on a salary plus bonus structure to rent mobile home lots.
    d. The treasurer of Mississippi River Fuel Company who negotiates oil leases on behalf of the company and is paid on a salary basis only.

57. Which phrase BEST describes the term *escrow*?
    a. Money or other things of value held by the broker in trust for others
    b. Cash or checks held by an interested third party
    c. Uncollected funds held for safekeeping
    d. Broker's future commission held until the transaction is closed

58. A broker's bank statement indicates an ending balance for the previous month of $95,000. There are $2,000 of deposits in transit and $18,000 in checks outstanding. What is the adjusted bank balance?
    a. $71,000
    b. $75,000
    c. $79,000
    d. $111,000

59. During the last calendar month, a broker deposited three earnest money deposit checks totaling $25,000. The bank statement for that month reflects two outstanding checks totaling $5,000. (The balance was zero at the beginning of the month.) What is the broker's trust liability for the month?
    a. $5,000
    b. $20,000
    c. $25,000
    d. $30,000

60. A closing scheduled for last Friday did not occur because the buyer did not show up. The broker is still holding a $5,000 earnest money deposit for that sale in her escrow account. The broker has been unable to locate the buyer, and the seller has made no demands regarding the earnest money deposit. What should the broker do?
    a. Deliver the $5,000 to the seller as liquidated damages
    b. Notify the FREC that the broker has conflicting demands
    c. Continue to hold the money in escrow until the buyer can be located
    d. Notify the FREC that the broker has a good-faith doubt regarding the escrowed funds

61. What is the maximum allowable reimbursement from the recovery fund for financial losses suffered as a result of a licensee's unlawful acts?
    a. $25,000 per transaction, up to $50,000 for multiple transactions
    b. $50,000 per transaction, up to a maximum of $100,000 for multiple transactions
    c. $50,000 per transaction, up to a maximum of $150,000 for multiple transactions
    d. The actual amount of the judgment up to $1 million

62. The broker complied with an EDO but was sued by the seller. The seller was awarded a judgment against the broker. The seller has made a claim against the recovery fund. Which statement is TRUE regarding the real estate recovery fund?
    a. The broker is subject to automatic suspension of his real estate license until he has repaid the recovery claim in full.
    b. The Commission may sanction the broker administrative fines and other penalties associated with the recovery fund claim.
    c. The broker may avoid having to reimburse the recovery fund by filing bankruptcy.
    d. The Commission will take no action against the broker's license as a result of the claim against the recovery fund.

63. An administrative complaint was filed against a broker. The probable cause panel found reasonable grounds for prosecution. The broker has received a formal complaint. He disagrees with the violations alleged in the formal complaint. The broker
    a. may elect to have the Commission hear the case in an informal complaint.
    b. is entitled to have the case heard by an administrative law judge in a formal hearing.
    c. may request that a letter of guidance be issued to settle the matter administratively.
    d. should mail a letter to the DRE objecting to the formal complaint.

64. Which statement applies to notices of noncompliance?
    a. A notice of noncompliance typically involves a fine of $100 to $1,000 per offense.
    b. A notice of noncompliance is a type of civil penalty.
    c. The DBPR must issue a notice of noncompliance as a first response to a minor violation.
    d. A licensee must take action to correct the violation within 30 days.

65. The FREC does NOT have the authority to impose which penalty when a licensee violates Chapter 475 of the Florida Statues?
    a. Prison sentence
    b. Fine up to $5,000
    c. Letter of guidance
    d. Citation

66. Which statement concerning the USPAP applies to licensed real estate brokers?
    a. Real estate brokers are required to abide by the USPAP when preparing CMAs.
    b. Real estate brokers are exempt from the USPAP requirements.
    c. Real estate brokers who prepare real estate appraisals are required to comply with the USPAP.
    d. Real estate brokers are required to comply with the USPAP only if preparing an appraisal associated with a federally related transaction.

67. A broker is a buyer agent for a buyer. The buyer has hired the broker to conduct an appraisal on the property he is purchasing for the purpose of securing a mortgage from a local credit union. Which statement is TRUE regarding this situation?
   a. The broker must comply with the USPAP in order to conduct this appraisal.
   b. The broker must disclose in the appraisal that he was the agent in the transaction in order to conduct this appraisal.
   c. The broker is prohibited from being compensated for performing this appraisal assignment because he received compensation as the buyer agent.
   d. Because this is a federally related transaction, the appraisal must be conducted by a state certified or licensed appraiser.

68. Millpond Bread Company is for sale. The company makes high quality bread, enjoys a loyal customer base, and has little direct competition. Millpond Bread Company is being sold complete with its ovens, other specialized bread baking equipment, and bread recipes. The store is located in leased space. What type of value should the appraiser use to estimate the value of Millpond Bread Company?
   a. Liquidation value
   b. Going-concern value
   c. Package mortgage value
   d. Investment value

69. Which statement describes the principle of substitution as it applies to the cost-depreciation approach?
   a. The theory that a knowledgeable purchaser would pay no more for a property than the cost of acquiring an acceptable substitute property
   b. The theory that a knowledgeable purchaser would pay no more for a property than the cost of acquiring an equally desirable site, combined with building an acceptable substitute structure
   c. The theory that the value of a property tends to be related to its competitive position among substitute investment choices producing equivalent investment returns and risk
   d. The theory that value is created by expectation of future benefits

70. An appraiser is preparing an appraisal of an improved property. The property is located on a major street, and a 20-year-old concrete block strip development is situated on the property. The appraiser is considering whether it would be prudent to demolish the existing structure and build a new office complex. The appraiser is conducting a(n)
   a. highest and best use analysis as though vacant.
   b. external economies analysis.
   c. highest and best use analysis of the property as improved.
   d. principle of substitution analysis.

71. Which reporting option is NOT a narrative report according to USPAP guidelines?
   a. Form report
   b. Self-contained report
   c. Summary report
   d. Restricted report

72. After an appraiser has derived three separate indicated values using the various approaches to value, the appraiser then calculates a final estimate of value using
   a. regression analysis.
   b. simple averaging.
   c. reconciliation.
   d. probability analysis.

73. Which element of comparison is adjusted to derive a normal sale price using the sales comparison approach?
   a. Conditions of sale
   b. Market conditions
   c. Location
   d. Physical characteristics

74. The cost-depreciation approach is MOST applicable to which appraisal assignment?
   a. 20-year-old residential home in a fully developed subdivision
   b. Millpond Bread Company—real estate and business value
   c. 1-year-old duplex in an area of mixed use
   d. 5-year-old gasoline station on an exit of Interstate I-75

75. The subject property is a 4-bedroom, 3-bath home with a screened porch. Comp A's transaction price was $205,000. The appraiser made a $5,000 adjustment because Comp A does not have a screened porch, a $15,000 adjustment for an extra half-bath, and a $10,000 adjustment for superior condition. What is the final adjusted sale price of Comp A?
   a. $185,000
   b. $195,000
   c. $220,000
   d. $230,000

76. A successive sale was located in the subject property neighborhood. The initial sale price was $62,500, and 18 months later the property sold for $75,000. What is the monthly rate of change?
   a. .0111
   b. .0167
   c. .0667
   d. .0833

77. The reproduction cost new of a structure is $215,000 and the land value is $30,000. The structure is 9 years old and has an effective age of 7 years. Assuming a total economic life of 60 years, calculate the accrued depreciation using the lump-sum age-life method. (Round to the nearest dollar.)
   a. $15,000
   b. $25,083
   c. $28,583
   d. $32,250

78. Using the data presented below, calculate a market GRM. (Round final answer to one decimal place.)

Sale	Sale Price	Monthly Rent
1	$127,000	$1,250
2	$132,000	$1,300
3	$135,000	$1,350

a. 101.0
b. 101.5
c. 101.6
d. 101.7

79. Finders Realty Company represents a buyer as a transaction broker. To whom must the sales associate for Finders Realty give the no brokerage relationship notice?
a. To all sellers before showing property to the buyer
b. To every listing agent before showing the listed properties to the buyer
c. To all for-sale-by-owner (FSBO) sellers before showing a FSBO to the buyer
d. To every single agent seller represented by Finders Realty Company

80. The duties of a transaction broker do NOT include
a. accounting for all funds.
b. presenting all offers and counteroffers in a timely manner.
c. using skill, care, and diligence in the transaction.
d. confidentiality.

81. In order to transition from a single agent to a transaction broker, the broker must secure the buyer's or seller's signature on which document?
a. Single agent notice
b. Transaction broker notice
c. Consent to transition to transaction broker
d. No brokerage relationship notice

82. An executed contract for sale and purchase fails to close. What is the requirement regarding retention of the brokerage relationship documents associated with the transaction?
a. The broker is not required to retain the brokerage relationship documents.
b. The broker must secure a written release from both the buyer and the seller before destroying the brokerage relationship documents.
c. The broker must retain the brokerage relationship documents for a period of two years.
d. The broker must retain the file with the brokerage relationship documents for a period of five years.

83. If a licensee intends to give limited representation to a homeseller, which brokerage relationship disclosure(s) is (are) required?
a. Transaction broker notice
b. Both a no brokerage relationship notice and a transaction broker notice
c. Consent to transition to transaction broker notice
d. No disclosures are required.

84. If a broker knows that there is a structural defect that affects the value of residential property, the broker is obligated to disclose this information to the buyer
   a. only if the broker is a buyer's representative.
   b. only if the broker is a transaction broker for both parties.
   c. only if the broker is a single agent of the seller.
   d. regardless of the type of brokerage relationship that exists with the buyer and the seller.

85. Construction of a proposed residential development may not start until a new sewage treatment plant is completed. The legal authority to block or postpone development comes from the
   a. subdivision restrictions.
   b. Clean Water Act.
   c. concurrency provision of the Growth Management Act.
   d. police power under the Environmental Protection Agency.

86. A local gasoline station that has been in business since 1978 is in an area subsequently zoned for multifamily. The gas station is considered to be a
   a. special exception.
   b. legally nonconforming use.
   c. hardship exception.
   d. buffer zone.

87. Who would NOT be considered a potentially responsible person (PRP) under CERCLA?
   a. Present owners and operators of a contaminated site
   b. Past owners and operators that owned or operated the site at the time the hazardous substance came to be located at the site
   c. Persons who arranged for the transportation of the hazardous substance to the site
   d. A prospective buyer of a contaminated site who executed an offer to purchase

88. A landlord's responsibilities under the Lead-Based Paint requirements do NOT include
   a. giving renters the required EPA pamphlet.
   b. giving renters a 10-day inspection period to test for lead.
   c. disclosing all known lead-based paint hazards.
   d. securing completed and signed statements verifying completion of the lead-based paint requirements

89. Which statement BEST describes the purpose of a Phase I Environmental Assessment?
   a. A government report that lists potentially responsible persons and assesses liability for cleanup
   b. A report consisting of the property's identification number, location, and government analysis that is in the public domain
   c. A detailed assessment of the costs involved in cleaning up a contaminated site
   d. A detailed study to discover potential contamination or noncompliance with environmental laws

90. Which statement is FALSE concerning radon gas?
   a. Radon tests conducted in homes within a single neighborhood provide reliable estimates of whether radon gas is a potential hazard in neighboring properties.
   b. Florida law requires radon disclosure.
   c. Radon contamination poses a greater risk to smokers.
   d. Florida law does not require radon testing.

91. Real estate licensees must comply with the *Uniform Standards of Professional Appraisal Practice* (USPAP) when conducting which value estimates?
   a. Appraisals
   b. Broker price opinions
   c. Comparative market analyses
   d. Real estate licensees are exempt from the provisions of USPAP

92. What is found on the third page of the HUD-1 Settlement Statement?
   a. The total amount due from the buyer and the total amount due to the seller.
   b. A recap of the buyers' and sellers' expenses.
   c. A comparison of the buyers' costs with the Good Faith Estimate.
   d. The signature page for the buyer, seller, title closing agent, and broker.

Closing Statement Case Study

A home is sold for $398,000. The buyers gave their broker a $10,000 good-faith deposit. The buyers will finance the purchase with a new 75 percent loan-to-value mortgage loan.

Closing date is July 3 with the day of closing charged to the buyer. Property taxes are $8,412 and homeowners' association dues are $125 monthly and were paid in advance. Prorations should be made using the 365-day method.

The sellers will pay the 7 percent brokerage fee, the documentary stamp tax on the deed, and title insurance of $2,200.

The buyers will pay the appropriate state taxes on the note and mortgage, $66 in recording fees, and a survey cost of $475.

Based on this information, answer the following questions about how the transaction will be shown on the HUD-1 Settlement Statement.

93. How is the purchase price shown?
   a. $398,000 debit buyer only; page 1
   b. $398,000 debit seller, credit buyer; page 1
   c. $398,000 credit seller, debit buyer; page 1
   d. $398,000 credit buyer only; page 1

94. How is the new first mortgage shown?
   a. $298,500 debit buyer only; page 1
   b. $298,500 credit buyer only; page 1
   c. $298,500 debit seller, credit buyer; page 1
   d. $398,000 credit buyer only; page 1

95. How is the brokerage fee handled?
   a. $27,860 credit seller only; page 1
   b. $27,860 debit seller only, page 2
   c. $27,860 debit seller, credit buyer; page 2
   d. $23,880 debit seller only; page 2

96. How is the binder deposit shown?
   a. $10,000 credit seller, debit buyer; page 1
   b. $10,000 credit buyer only; page 1
   c. $10,000 debit buyer only; page 1
   d. $10,000 debit seller, credit buyer; page 1

97. How are the homeowners' fees prorated?
   a. $8.06 credit buyer only; page 1
   b. $8.06 credit buyer, debit seller; page 1
   c. $116.94 credit buyer only; page 1
   d. $116.94 debit buyer, credit seller; page 1

98. What is the proration for property taxes?
   a. $4,217.52 debit seller only; page 1
   b. $4,217.52 debit seller, credit buyer; page 1
   c. $4,217.52 debit buyer only; page 2
   d. $4,194.48 debit seller, credit buyer; page 1

99. What are the documentary stamp taxes and intangible taxes on the deed and mortgage?
   a. Debit seller $2,786, credit buyer $1,641.75; page 1
   b. Debit seller $2,786, debit buyer $1,641.75; page 1
   c. Credit seller $2,786, debit buyer $2,686.50; page 1
   d. Debit seller $2,786, debit buyer $1,641.75; page 2

100. Where are the totals of the buyers' and sellers' expenses shown?
   a. Page 1 only.
   b. Page 2 only.
   c. Pages 1 and 2.
   d. Pages 1, 2, and 3.

GLOSSARY

A

Abstract of title A condensed history of the recorded documents affecting title to real property.

Acceleration clause A mortgage clause that allows the lender to call the entire balance due and payable immediately in the event of a default by the borrower.

Accrual basis accounting A method of matching income and expenses to the period for which they are applicable, regardless of when they are received or paid.

Accrued depreciation The difference between the cost to reproduce the property (as of the appraisal date) and the property's current value as judged by its "competitive condition."

Active participant The status of an investor in rental income property resulting from the investor's involvement with the management decisions of the property. A taxpayer must be an active participant to deduct taxable losses from other income.

Adjustable-rate mortgage (ARM) A mortgage loan program that allows the lender to change the interest rate based on a published index that is beyond the lender's control.

After-tax cash flow The amount remaining after expenses, mortgage payment, and income taxes have been deducted from the gross income of an investment property.

Agent A representative; one who is authorized to act on behalf of another; a person entrusted with another's business.

Agreement for deed Sometimes called a *contract for deed,* a *land contract,* or an *installment contract.*

Americans with Disabilities Act (ADA) A federal statute designed to remove physical barriers that prevent equal access to public places, and to ensure that qualified persons have equal employment opportunities regardless of disability.

Annual cap Restricts the amount of annual rate change.

Annual percentage rate (APR) A calculation required under the Truth-in-Lending Act that discloses the annual cost of credit, including financing charges.

Anticipation Based on the premise that value is created by expectation of future benefit.

Appraisal A supported, defended estimate of value of property rights as of a given date.

Arbitration The act of having a third party render a binding decision in a dispute between two parties.

Arm's-length transaction A transaction in which the parties are dealing from equal bargaining positions.

Asbestos A mineral fiber that was commonly used prior to 1979 in a variety of building construction materials for insulation and as a fire retardant.

Assemblage The combination of two or more parcels of land into one tract.

Assessed value Worth established for each unit of real property for tax purposes by a county property appraiser.

Automated underwriting A method to process a loan application using computer software that often includes automatic credit reporting, property valuation data, ratio analysis, and other underwriting information.

B

Balance sheet A financial statement showing the assets, liabilities, and net worth of an individual or company. The total of the assets *balance,* or equal, the total of the liabilities and net worth.

Balloon payment The final payment due under a partially amortized mortgage that is larger than the periodic payments made during the term of the loan.

Base rent The minimum rent required in a lease. Used primarily with leases that allow for an additional rent, such as percentage leases.

Blanket mortgage Collateral for a promissory note that encumbers more than one parcel of property.

Blind advertising Advertising that fails to disclose the registered name of the brokerage firm.

Book value The amount shown for capital assets (equipment, real estate, etc.) on the books of a company, less depreciation taken for accounting purposes.

Boot Unlike property received in a real estate tax-deferred exchange that is taxable, such as cash or other personal property.

Business plan A long-range plan that includes an organization's objectives, goals, and strategies.

Buydown An advance interest payment (usually by a seller) to a lender so that a purchaser of the property has a lower initial interest rate.

Buyer's market A period in a real estate economy when the supply of properties for sale exceeds the demand for those properties, giving buyers a negotiating advantage.

C

Capital gain Profit made on the sale of a capital asset, such as real property.

Caps (annual, lifetime) The maximum interest rate change allowed on an adjustable-rate mortgage. The cap may be set for a single period or for the life of the loan.

Cash basis accounting A bookkeeping system that applies revenues to the period they were collected and expenses to the period they were paid, without regard for the period for which the item was applicable.

Cash equivalency The price of a property reduced to a present value cash sum that takes into account the value of financial terms and any noncash items or services included as part of the consideration.

CERCLA The Comprehensive Environmental Response, Compensation, and Liability Act enacted by Congress in 1980.

Certificate of reasonable value (CRV) A value used by the Department of Veteran's Affairs for guaranteeing a mortgage loan based on an appraisal by a VA-approved appraiser.

Chronology of recording A dated list of the public records related to a specific parcel of real property that establishes a priority of rights in the property.

Certificate of title A statement of opinion by an attorney or abstractor on the status of the title to a parcel of real property based on an examination of the public records.

Citation A statement of an alleged violation and the penalty to be imposed.

Civil Rights Act of 1866 A statute that prohibits discrimination based on race regarding the inheritance, purchase, lease, sale, holding, and conveying of real property.

CMA *See* comparative market analysis.

Commingle The illegal practice of mixing a buyer's, seller's, tenant's, or landlord's funds with the broker's own money or of mixing real estate brokerage escrow money with the broker's personal or business funds.

Commission override A method of calculating compensation for a supervisor or sales manager, usually a percentage of either the gross or net commission generated by a sales associate.

Community association A residential homeowners' association in which members own a residence in a development authorized to impose a fee that may become a lien on the parcel. Chapter 468, F.S., further defines it to include any association "greater than 10 units or with an annual budget over $100,000."

Company dollar The funds remaining after the costs of sales, such as commissions paid to sales associates, referral fees, and cooperating fees paid to other brokers, are deducted from gross commissions received by the company.

Comparative market analysis (CMA) A list of properties in an area similar to the subject property that are currently listed, have recently sold, or have failed to sell in a reasonable marketing period. It is the basis for a licensee's "opinion of value" to a buyer or seller.

Compensation Anything of value or a valuable consideration, directly or indirectly paid, promised or expected to be paid or received.

Compensatory damages Damages requested or awarded in a civil suit that reimburse the injured party for actual damages sustained.

Complaint An alleged violation of a law or rule.

Composite closing statement A real property settlement statement that itemizes each of the seller's, buyer's, and closing agent's part of the transaction, usually on one page.

Concurrency A provision that mandates that infrastructure, such as roads, and water and waste treatment facilities needed to support additional development be in place concurrent with development.

Conditional commitment A lender's agreement with a borrower allowing the closing process to continue without delay, subject to the lender's receipt of documents such as a borrower's employment or credit verifications, or the requirement that the appraisal be at least the amount of the purchase price.

Conflicting demands When parties to a contract are in disagreement regarding disbursement of escrowed funds.

Conforming loan A mortgage loan that meets all requirements of Fannie Mae and Freddie Mac, making it possible for the originating lender to sell the loan to those secondary market lenders.

Conformity Principle that property values are maximized when there is architectural homogeneity and uniformity of land use in a neighborhood.

Contingency A condition in a contract that, unless satisfied, may make the contract voidable by one or both of the parties.

Contract An agreement between two parties to do or abstain from doing some specific act.

Contract for deed An agreement between an owner and a buyer in which the owner agrees to deliver title to real property when all agreements, including payments, have been fulfilled.

Contract rent The rent currently being paid by the tenants.

Contract for sale and purchase A written agreement between a buyer and a seller for the transfer of title to real property.

Conversion Securities that the depositor intends to be converted into cash.

Corporate veil The imaginary shield shareholders obtain against personal liability by incorporating. Creditors of the corporation may look only to the assets of the corporation and not to the shareholders' personal assets.

Corporation A legal entity created by state statute, consisting of an association of one or more individuals.

Corporation sole An ecclesiastical or church organization headed by a bishop or other clerical official who has been empowered by the church to hold title to church property.

Cosigner A person who agrees, along with another party, to take responsibility for payment of a debt.

Cost The amount to produce or acquire something.

Credit scoring A method of reporting a person's credit standing with a numeric or letter grade used by lenders in setting interest rates, down payments, and credit limits.

Curb appeal The impression a buying or renting prospect receives, good or bad, upon seeing a property for the first time.

Current mailing address The current residential address which is used by a licensee or permit holder to receive mail through the U.S. Postal Service.

Current ratio Calculated by dividing current assets by current liabilities.

Customer A member of the public who is or may be a buyer or seller of real property and may or may not be represented by a real estate licensee in an authorized brokerage relationship.

D

Dealer A person who deals in real estate as a business, rather than an investor, such as a builder or land developer. Gains or losses are ordinary income or loss, and the dealer may not deduct depreciation.

Debt-to-worth ratio Calculated by dividing the company's liabilities by its tangible net worth.

Declaratory judgment A statutory remedy to establish the rights of the party when the rights are in doubt.

Dedication The transfer of privately owned lands to the public without compensation, with the intent that the land will be accepted and used for public purposes.

Demand (principle of supply and demand) The quantity of goods or services wanted by consumers.

Depreciation A loss in value for any reason. For tax purposes, depreciation is a deductible expense of an income property.

Designated sales associate A sales associate appointed by the broker to represent the interests of one party in a transaction when another sales associate in the firm represents the other party. The buyer and seller must have assets of $1 million and sign disclosures stating their assets meet the required threshold.

Development of regional impact (DRI) A large project affecting more than one county.

Discounted cash flow (DCF) analysis A generally accepted method for estimating the present value of investment property by discounting each year's cash flow by an appropriate interest rate. *See* internal rate of return (IRR) and net present value (NPV).

Documentary stamp taxes Collected on the deed and the note during closing of the real estate transaction.

Dual agent An agent representing both buyer and seller in a transaction (not legal in Florida).

Due-on-sale clause A covenant in a mortgage that requires the lender's approval before the property title is transferred. If a transfer is made without approval, the lender may accelerate the mortgage, calling it due and payable immediately.

DUST Acronym for the four characteristics of value: demand, utility, scarcity, and transferability.

Dynamic risk Concerns changes in the economy, supply and demand conditions, tax codes, and so forth.

E

Earnest money deposit Money or property put up by the buyer as good faith and as security for the performance of a real estate contract.

Economic life The period of time a property is expected to be profitable or productive.

Effect a sale A condition in a listing agreement requiring that a closing take place on a property before the commission is due the broker.

Effective age The age indicated by the condition and utility of a structure.

Effective gross income (EGI) The resulting amount when vacancy and collection losses are subtracted from potential gross income.

Effective interest rate The cost of borrowing money that includes not only the note interest rate but also lender's fees paid in advance.

Employer identification number (EIN) A unique number assigned by the federal government to an organization for use in reporting income taxes and employee payments. Similar to the Social Security number assigned to individuals.

Entitlement The amount of guarantee for a veteran's home purchase given to a lender by the Department of Veteran's Affairs. Lenders normally lend up to four times the amount of the entitlement.

Environmental due diligence The process of taking the appropriate steps to ascertain, whether a site is contaminated.

Environmental site assessment A study designed to assess the likelihood that hazardous substances may be present on a property.

Equity kicker A lender's participation in an investment property's equity return.

Escalator lease Lease agreement in which the owner and the tenant determine a base amount for expenses, such as taxes, utilities, insurance, and maintenance; the owner's obligation to pay expenses exceeding the base amount "stops" and passes through to the tenant.

Escrow account An account in a bank, title company, credit union, savings association, or trust company used solely for safekeeping customer funds and not for deposit of personal funds.

Escrow disbursement order (EDO) A course of action for determining the disposition of a contested deposit.

Exclusive agency listing An agreement given to a broker by a seller to pay the broker's commission if the property is sold by any broker, but reserving the seller's right to sell directly without owing a commission.

Exclusive-right-of-sale listing An agreement given to a broker by a seller to pay a commission to the broker if the property is sold during the listing period. The broker is legally the procuring cause of any sale.

Expansion option A landlord's guarantee that a tenant may lease adjacent space in a property if needed by the tenant at a specified time in the future.

Expense stop A landlord's cost control method in a lease that sets a limit on the amount of expenses such as taxes, insurance, utilities, etc. The tenant agrees to pay any expenses above the "stop" amount.

External diseconomies The result when the actions of people external to a property impose cost on others.

External economies Positive external factors that enhance property values.

External obsolescence Any loss of value due to influences originating outside the boundaries of the property.

F

Fair Housing Act A part of the Civil Rights Act of 1968 (Title VIII) that prohibits discrimination against persons based on race, color, religion, national origin, sex, handicap, or family status.

Federally related transactions Any real estate-related financial transaction that any of the major federal financial institution's regulatory agencies or any of its regulated institutions engages or contracts for and that requires the services of an appraiser.

Fictitious name Any name under which a person transacts business other than his or her legal name.

Fiduciary A person in a position of trust and confidence with respect to another person.

FIFO (first-in, first out) A method of accounting for the cost of sales that values the inventory sold at the oldest cost of the product. In a time of rising costs, it produces the highest reported profit of any of the inventory methods.

Final adjusted sale price The price that a comparable property would likely sell for in today's market if it were exactly like the subject property.

Find a property A buyer employs the broker to find a property.

Find a purchaser A condition in a listing agreement requiring the broker to produce a buyer who is ready, willing, and able to purchase a property at the listed price, or any other price agreeable to the seller. Until the broker has performed, no commission is due.

Firm commitment An agreement by a lender, usually after a complete evaluation of the loan application, to lend a specific sum of money to a borrower.

FIRREA The Financial Institutions Reform, Recovery and Enforcement Act of 1989.

First-degree misdemeanor An offense that under Chapter 775, F.S., carries a penalty of up to $1,000 fine and/or imprisonment for up to one year. Failing to provide accurate and current rental information for a fee is a misdemeanor of the first degree.

Fixed expense An expense that does not fluctuate proportionately to increases or decreases in income.

Fixtures Items that originally were personal property but have been permanently attached to or made part of real property.

Fixed lease A lease that has level payments.

Florida Landlord and Tenant Act A Florida statute (Chapter 83, F.S.) that regulates the rights and duties of owners and tenants of residential and commercial buildings.

Florida REALTORS®/Florida Bar Contract for Sale and Purchase A form developed by the Florida REALTORS® and The Florida Bar Association.

Foreclose (foreclosure) A legal process initiated by a lender in case of a mortgage default. It extinguishes the rights of others, including the owner and lien holders with a lower priority.

Formal complaint A detailed list of charges against the licensee that must be answered within the statutory time limit.

Formal hearing In the event that a formal complaint cannot be resolved at an informal hearing, the DBPR requests that the case be formally prosecuted under Chapter 120, F.S. before an administrative law judge.

Franchise The right to use a trade name as well as specific business operating procedures designed by the company that sells the franchise.

Fully amortized mortgage A type of loan paid off in equal monthly payments of principal and interest.

Function of an appraisal How the client intends to use the information contained in an appraisal report. The function of an appraisal guides the type of report that will be prepared for the client.

Functional obsolescence Anything that is inferior due to operational inadequacies, poor design, or changing tastes and preferences.

Funding fee A charge levied by the Department of Veteran's Affairs that contributes to the cost of operating the VA loan guarantee.

G

Generally accepted accounting principles (GAAP) A set of standard accounting methods accepted by the American Institute of Certified Public Accountants.

General agent Authorized by the principal to perform only acts related to a business or to employment of a particular nature.

General partnership An association of two or more persons for the purpose of jointly conducting a business, each being responsible for all the debts incurred in the conducting of that business, each having the power to bind the other(s) in transactions, and each being entitled to receive a share of the profits in the amount agreed upon by the parties.

Going-concern value The value of a firm that is operating. Going concern value is normally more than the value of a similar company no longer in business.

Good faith Describes a party's honest intent to transact business, free from any intent to defraud the other party, and each party's faithfulness to one's duty or obligations as set forth by contract.

Good-faith doubt When the closing or consummation date of the sale, lease, or other real estate transaction has passed, or one or more parties have expressed an intention not to close, and the broker has not received conflicting or identical instructions from all of the parties concerning how to disburse the escrowed funds.

Good-faith estimate A lender's disclosure required under RESPA showing a borrower all loan closing costs known to the lender at the time of application.

Goodwill The portion of the purchase price of a business entity that exceeds the net worth of the company as shown on the company's books and records.

Graduated commission A method of compensation based on a sales associate's level of production. When production reaches a certain point, the commission percentage increases.

Graduated lease A lease that has prearranged rent increases at certain intervals.

Graduated-payment mortgage A loan with payments that start low, and increase over the loan term. Any unpaid interest is added to the principal balance (negative amortization).

Gross income multiplier (GIM) The GIM is the ratio between a property's gross annual income and the sale price. The GIM includes all annual income generated from a property.

Gross leasable area The full amount of space in a building that can be leased, but that usually does not include the lobby, elevators, and stairwells unless one tenant leases the entire building.

Gross lease An agreement to occupy space that requires the landlord to pay for taxes, maintenance, and insurance.

Gross living area (GLA) Space above the grade level that is finished and occupied as part of the living area of a house, not including basements, screen porches or garages, etc.

Gross rent multiplier (GRM) The GRM is the ratio between a property's gross monthly rental income and the sale price of the property. The gross rent multiplier refers to rent only and excludes any miscellaneous income.

Ground lease A lease that is almost always a net lease, with the building owners paying all taxes and assessments on the propery.

Group license A term used to mean that a sales associate is registered with an owner-developer who owns properties in the name of various entities.

Growth Management Act The Local Government Comprehensive Planning and Land Development Regulation Act, adopted by the Florida Legislature in 1985.

H

Hardship As it relates to land use, a hardship occurs where, in the absence of a variance, no reasonable use can be made of the property. A hardship may be due to unique physical limitations of the property such as a steep slope or an irregular-shaped lot.

Heterogeneous Unique.

Highest and best use The probable and legal use of real property which is physically possible, defendable, financially feasible, and results in the highest value.

Home acquisition loan A mortgage loan used to purchase a residence.

Home equity loan A mortgage secured by a personal residence. It provides a line of credit available for draws when needed by the homeowner. It is sometimes used as a home improvement loan.

Home office A separate work space set up in a residence for business purposes.

Homeowners' association An association of which a purchaser of residential property may be required to become a member.

Homeowners' association disclosure A requirement that a broker must provide summary information about a homeowners' association, including whether there are restrictive covenants, any mandatory assessments, or the right to file a lien against property in the neighborhood for nonpayment of the assessment.

Homeowners' Protection Act of 1998 Established rules for automatic termination and borrower cancellation of PMI on home mortgages.

Hotelling A brokerage firm's strategy to reduce its office space by allowing sales associates to reserve a workstation for a desired time period.

Housing expense ratio A guideline used by lenders to evaluate a borrower's ability to make mortgage payments. It is calculated by dividing the mortgage payment (PITI) by the borrower's gross monthly income.

HUD-1 Settlement Statement The closing statement required to be used in all transactions covered under the Real Estate Settlement Procedures Act (RESPA).

HVAC Acronym for a building's heating, ventilation, and air-conditioning system.

I

Impact fees A municipal assessment against new residential, industrial, or commercial development projects to compensate for the added costs of public services generated by the new construction.

Income statement A statement of the income and expenses for a period of time, also called a *profit and loss statement* or *statement of operations*.

Increasing and decreasing returns When one or more factors of production are increased while others are held constant, output may increase at an increasing rate up to a certain point; however, beyond some point each additional unit of consumption adds less and less to satisfaction or total utility.

Independent contractor A person who is to achieve certain results without direction or control by another person on the methods used to accomplish the results. A real estate licensee who does not have taxes or Social Security contributions withheld from commission payments by the broker.

Index A percentage amount that fluctuates periodically and is the basis for determining interest rate changes on adjustable rate mortgages.

Index lease A lease that requires changes in the rent payment based on some published index, such as the Consumer Price Index.

Individual retirement account (IRA) A tax-deferred investment designed to encourage individuals to save and invest for their retirement

Informal hearing Opportunity for the formally charged licensee to present his or her case during a regular Commission meeting.

Inheritability The quality of an estate that allows the owner to designate the person to whom title of real property passes after death.

Initial investment Down payment, or original equity invested by a buyer of real property.

Initial license The first license issued to a licensee upon passing the state licensing examination.

Innocent landowner defense Certain criteria that relieves current property owners from the cleanup costs when hazardous substances are discovered.

Installment sale A transfer of property in which the owner finances the property for the buyer, receiving payments in future periods.

Institutional advertising Advertising designed to enhance consumer confidence in an organization.

Insurable value Estimated for insurance coverage purposes; based on replacement cost, taking into consideration insurance exclusions.

Intangible asset A right that results in a competitive advantage for an organization, such as a franchise or copyright.

Intangible taxes A state tax required before a mortgage is recorded. It is 2 mils (.002) of the mortgage amount.

Internal rate of return (IRR) A percentage yield that discounts all projected cash flows to a present value equal to the initial investment. *See* discounted cash flow (DCF) and net present value (NPV).

Interpleader A legal proceeding whereby the broker, having no financial interest in the disputed funds, deposits with the court the disputed escrow deposit so that the court can determine who is the rightful owner.

Inventory turnover ratio Calculated by dividing the firm's cost of goods sold by the ending inventory.

Investment interest The expense from interest resulting from the purchase or carrying costs on an income-producing property. It is deductible for tax purposes up to the amount of investment income.

Investment value The value of an investment to a particular investor based on his or her requirements regarding rate of return, management involvement, risk, and so forth.

Involuntary inactive The licensure status that results when a license is not renewed at the end of the license period prescribed by the DBPR.

J

Joint tenancy Real property ownership by two or more persons in which all parties have the same rights of possession, equal interests, purchased at the same time, are all on the same deed, and have the right of survivorship.

Joint (ad)venture Two or more parties in an arrangement confined to only one or a limited number of business deals.

K

Kickback A payment or receipt of money or other thing of value, for referring customers rather than for performing a service.

L

Lead-based paint disclosure A required notification to buyers or tenants of real property built before 1978, itemizing the dangers inherent in the paint used in that period.

Lead-based paint hazard Any condition that causes exposure to lead from lead-contaminated dust, soil, or paint that has deteriorated or is present on accessible surfaces such as window sills.

Lease option contract An agreement between a tenant and a landlord that gives the tenant the right, but not the obligation, to buy the property at a specific price and terms at some time in the future.

Lease purchase agreement An agreement between a tenant and a landlord requiring the parties to buy and sell the subject property at the end of the lease.

Legal description A description of real estate that allows a surveyor to locate the exact boundaries of the property.

Legally sufficient A complaint that contains facts indicating that a violation of the statute or FREC or DBPR rules has occurred.

License A written document issued by the DBPR that serves as prima facie evidence that the holder is allowed to perform real estate services for others for compensation.

Lien theory A legal practice that gives a mortgagor title to the property and gives the mortgagee (lender) a lien on the property until the mortgage is satisfied. *See* title theory.

Lifetime cap Restricts the amount of interest rate change over the life of the loan.

LIFO (last-in, first-out) A method of accounting for the cost of sales that values the inventory sold at the latest costs of the product. In a time of rising costs, it is the most conservative approach, and produces the lowest reported profit of any of the inventory methods.

Like-kind exchange An exchange of real property held for investment for another parcel of real property held for investment that qualifies for deferment of taxes from gain on the sale.

Limited liability company An alternative, hybrid business entity with the combined characteristics and benefits of both limited partnerships and S corporations.

Limited liability partnership A business entity that features protection from personal liability but with fewer legal restrictions compared to other business entities.

Limited partnership A business entity consisting of one or more general partners and one or more limited partners.

Limited representation Representation duties of a transaction broker limited in the areas of loyalty and disclosure.

Liquidated damages The amount of valuable consideration for a contract agreed by the parties to be just compensation in case of default.

Liquidation value The most likely price a property should bring in a quick sale. Sometimes called *quick sale value*.

Litigation A lawsuit; the act of carrying on a lawsuit; a case before a court of law.

Loan constant The percentage of the original loan amount that is paid for principal and interest.

Lockbox A small key safe attached to a property. Persons with access to the safe can remove a key to open the property. Used extensively by real estate professionals as a means for quick property access.

Long-term gain A gain on a capital asset that has been held for more than one year, resulting in a more favorable capital gains tax rate.

M

Margin The additional percentage added to the index on an adjustable-rate mortgage. While the index changes periodically, the margin remains the same for the entire loan period.

Marketability The ability of real estate to be bought and sold. If there is an active marketplace for a property, it has good marketability. Marketability is similar to liquidity, except that liquidity implies that the full value of the property is realized at the sale, whereas marketability simply indicates that the property can be bought and sold easily.

Market abstraction A method of estimating the effect of atypical financing that involves locating several transactions of similar properties, some of which that involved normal market financing and others that involved the type of non-market financing exhibited by the comparable sale.

Market conditions—adjusted normal sale price The result of applying the adjustment for market conditions to the normal sale price.

Market rent The rent that the property would command if it were leased today at the prevailing rate.

Market value The most probable price a property will bring from a fully informed buyer, willing but not compelled to buy, and the lowest price a fully informed seller will accept if not compelled to sell.

Mediation The act of having a third party attempt to reconcile a dispute between two parties.

Minor violation Violation of statutes and rules that the FREC deems not to endanger the public's health, safety, or welfare.

Moral turpitude An act of corruption, vileness, or moral depravity; a disgraceful action or deed.

Mortgagee The lender who holds a mortgage lien on real property for collateral.

Mortgage insurance premium (MIP) The amount paid by a borrower for insurance that protects the lender against loss in case of the borrower's subsequent default. Normally the FHA mortgage insurance is called MIP, and private mortgage insurance is called PMI.

Mortgage participation A large loan in which more than one lender participates. Sometimes occurs when one lender does not want to invest a large percentage of its loan portfolio.

Mortgagor The borrower who owes money on a mortgage loan. In Florida, the mortgagor owns the property.

Multiple licenses Licenses held by a broker in two or more real estate brokerage firms.

N

National priorities list (NPL) Identification of those sites that appear to warrant remedial action, from environmental damage.

Net leasable area The space in a building that is directly usable by a tenant and included in the calculation of rent. It does not include hallways, the lobby, elevators, or stairwells.

Net lease A lease that requires the tenant to pay for specified operating expenses of the building, such as taxes, maintenance, and insurance. This allows the landlord to effectively keep all of the rent paid by the tenant, because there are no other operating expenses.

Net listing An agreement by an owner giving a broker the right to sell real property. The owner specifies a required amount from the sale and the broker's compensation is any amount over the net amount. In Florida, the broker may keep only an amount equal to a customary commission.

Net operating income (NOI) The income remaining after subtracting all relevant operating expenses.

Net present value (NPV) The discounted value of projected cash flows minus the initial cash outlay. *See* discounted cash flow (DCF) and internal rate of return (IRR).

Net-profit-to-owner capital ratio Net profit divided by total capital.

Nolo contendere A pleading of no contest by a defendant; a plea in a criminal action not admitting guilt but subjecting the defendant to punishment as if it were a guilty plea.

Nominal interest rate The interest rate stated on the face of the promissory note. *See* annual percentage rate (APR).

Nonconforming loan A mortgage loan that does not meet the requirements for purchase by Fannie Mae or Freddie Mac.

Nonconforming use Continuing legal land use that is not in compliance with zoning ordinances.

Nonpassive income Income of an individual from salary, self-employment income, interest, dividends, or retirement income. Passive activity losses generally may not be deducted from nonpassive income. *See* passive income.

Noncompete clause Clauses that prohibit employees or sales associates from competing with the broker or working for any firm that competes with the broker after leaving the firm.

Normal sale price Result after adjusting the transaction price for financing and conditions of sale.

Note rate Interest rate on the note only.

Notice of noncompliance A statement of a minor initial violation.

Novation An assumption of a mortgage in which the buyer of the property qualifies financially with the mortgagee, who then releases the seller from liability on the note; a full substitution of borrowers.

O

Open listing A nonexclusive agreement in which a seller agrees to compensate a broker if the broker procures a sale of the property, but reserves the right to sell the property directly without paying a commission.

Opinion of value An estimate of a property's market value prepared by a licensee when listing or selling property. It is usually based on a comparative market analysis.

Option contract An agreement that allows one to buy, sell, or lease real property for specified terms within a specified period of time.

Ostensible partnership One or more parties cause a third party to be deceived into believing that a partnership exists when no such arrangement exists.

Owner in severalty *See* sole owner.

Overage lease A lease requiring a base rent plus an additional rent (overage) based on a variable figure such as sales or an index. *See* percentage lease.

Overimprovement An addition or change to property not in line with its highest and best use, or a betterment that exceeds that justified by local conditions.

P

Package mortgage A security agreement that includes both real property and personal property as collateral for a promissory note.

Partially amortized mortgage A loan agreement in which the payments during the term of the mortgage have not paid all the principal before the maturity date of the mortgage, requiring a balloon payment.

Participation mortgage A loan in which the lender is allowed to share in part of the income or sale proceeds of a property.

Passive income Income or losses from real estate rental property. Losses are not generally deductible from nonpassive income such as salaries, etc. *See* nonpassive income.

Percentage lease An occupancy agreement that requires the tenant to pay a base rent plus a percentage of sales. *See* overage lease.

Personal property Any tangible item not permanently attached to real estate.

Phase I assessment The investigative phase of an environmental site assessment where the due diligence work takes place.

Physical deterioration Ordinary wear and tear caused by use, lack of maintenance, exposure to the elements, and physical damage.

Plottage The increased value that may result from two or more parcels of property being combined into one larger parcel (assemblage).

Point of contact information Any means by which to contact the brokerage firm or individual licensee, including mailing address(es), physical street address(es), e-mail address(es), telephone number(s), or facsimile telephone number(s).

Planned unit development (PUD) A residential project with mixed land uses and high residential density.

Postdated check A check that has been dated by the maker for some date in the future, having the effect of making it a promissory note.

Potential gross income (PGI) The maximum income expected during a one-year period if the property were totally rented at the prevailing market rate.

Potentially responsible persons (PRP) Individuals whom CERCLA identifies as potentially liable for cleanup of hazardous sites.

Prepayment clause A mortgage provision that describes the conditions under which a borrower may pay off a mortgage.

Prepayment penalty clause Requires that the borrower pay a predetermined fee to pay off the loan early.

Prequalification The initial fact-finding meeting between a prospective borrower and a lending institution that helps the borrower to understand what loan amount the bank will be willing to give the borrower based on the borrower's financial information.

Price The amount of dollars that a buyer agrees to pay and a seller agrees to accept under the specific circumstances surrounding a transaction.

Prima facie evidence Requiring no further proof; acceptable on its face.

Principal The party employing the services of a real estate broker as a single agent.

Priority The chronological order of recorded documents that establishes the rights of persons in a property, such as how proceeds of a foreclosure sale will be distributed.

Private mortgage insurance (PMI) The amount paid by a borrower for insurance that protects the lender against loss in case of the borrower's subsequent default. Normally the FHA mortgage insurance is called MIP, and private mortgage insurance is called PMI.

Probable cause Reasonable grounds for prosecution.

Probate The process followed by the court in distributing the assets of a decedent's estate.

Procuring cause The person directly responsible for the sale of real property.

Pro forma statements Projected financial statements that are based on assumptions that may or may not be valid.

Purchase-money mortgage A mortgage used to acquire real property. Most commonly used to describe seller financing.

Purpose of an appraisal The purpose of an appraisal is to estimate value.

Q

Qualified intermediary A person competent to be a facilitator for a Section 1031 tax-deferred exchange.

Quick ratio Current assets (without inventory) divided by current liabilities.

R

Radon gas A colorless, odorless gas resulting from the breakdown of naturally occurring radioactive materials in the soil. Most authorities believe it to be a serious health hazard.

Real estate services Includes any real estate activity involving compensation for performing the service for another. The Florida real estate license law identifies eight real estate-related activities that require a Florida real estate license.

Real Estate Settlement Procedures Act (RESPA) A federal statute relating to fair disclosure of closing costs in a real estate transaction.

Real property An interest or estate in land and any interest in business enterprises or business opportunities, including any assignment, leasehold, subleasehold, or mineral right.

Recission on breach Remedy for breach of contract.

Recommended order A determination by an administrative law judge that includes findings and conclusions as well as other information required by law or agency rule to be in a final order.

Reconciliation The process of evaluating and weighing each value indication obtained from the various approaches to value.

Redemption (equity of) The mortgagor's right to pay off a mortgage loan balance to stop a foreclosure sale.

Reduction option mortgage The right given to a borrower to reduce the interest rate on a mortgage during a specified period by paying a fee.

Registered Placing real estate business entities on the official records of the DBPR.

Renewal option A tenant's right to renew a lease agreement at a specified rent rate.

Rent concession A reduction in rent, or alterations to the property by the landlord, to encourage a tenant to sign a lease.

Replacement cost The number of dollars that would be required to construct new improvements of equal utility to those being appraised, although not the exact physical duplicate.

Reproduction cost The number of dollars that would be required to construct a new structure that is an exact duplicate of the structure being appraised.

Reserve for replacements A noncash expense used for income property financial projections to account for major expenses expected to occur during the holding period for replacement of building components such as roof and air-conditioning systems.

Resident A person who has resided in Florida continuously for a period of four calendar months or more within the preceding year, regardless of whether the residence was a recreational vehicle, hotel, rental unit, or other temporary or permanent location.

Residential sales The sale of improved residential property of four units or fewer, the sale of unimproved residential property intended for use as four units or fewer, or the sale of agricultural property of 10 acres or less.

Return on investment (ROI) The investor's return if he or she paid no mortgage on the property.

Reverse annuity mortgage A mortgage that secures periodic payments to elderly persons who have borrowed on the equity in their homes. The mortgage must be repaid when the property is sold, or when the owner dies.

Reversion from sale The cash proceeds received from the sale of an investment property after income taxes have been paid.

Right of first refusal The right, but not the obligation, of a person to take the place of a buyer with the same terms agreed to by the seller and the buyer.

Roth IRA Type of IRA; contributions are not deductible, but earnings are tax-free.

S

Sale and leaseback A financing technique whereby the owner sells a property and then rents it back from the buyer for continued occupancy.

Sale contract An agreement between a buyer and a seller to transfer title to a parcel of real property.

Sales threshold A predetermined limit on tenants' rent when a percentage lease is used.

Salvage value The amount that part or all of a property's improvements can be sold for at the end of its economic life, taking into consideration the cost of removing the improvements from the land.

S corporation A corporation qualified under IRS guidelines to pass through expenses and income to the shareholders, which pays no taxes at the corporate level.

Second-degree misdemeanor A violation of Chapter 475, F.S., is at least a second-degree misdemeanor. Under Chapter 775, F.S., the penalty for a second-degree misdemeanor is a fine up to $500 and/or imprisonment for up to 60 days per offense.

Secured note A promissory note that is backed by a mortgage on property.

Seller's market Economic conditions in which listings sell quickly, and many sellers market their own properties.

Sensitivity analysis The process of estimating investment returns measuring the impact of different assumptions.

Short-term gain A capital gain on investment property held for one year or less, taxed at higher rates than those for long-term gains.

Single agent A broker who represents, as a fiduciary, either the buyer or seller but not both in the same transaction.

Sole and separate owner A person who owned a property jointly with a spouse but is now the only owner.

Sole owner The only person holding title to real property.

Sole proprietorship Dealing as an individual in business.

Special assessment A tax imposed on a parcel of property that has been improved by the government.

Special agent Authorized by the principal to handle only a specific business transaction or to perform only a specific act by the government.

Special exception An individual ruling in which a property owner is granted the right to a use otherwise contrary to law.

Specific (product) advertising Advertising designed to promote a particular property, as opposed to institutional advertising. Often called *product advertising*.

Specific performance A motion in a court suit in case of default on a sale contract that would require one of the parties to complete the contract as promised.

Standard deduction An amount specified by IRS to be deducted from gross income by persons who elect not to itemize expenses on their tax returns.

Static risk Risk associated with fire, storm, flood, theft, or liability from accidents.

Statute of frauds The requirement under common law, case law, and the statutes, requiring contracts for the sale of real property to be written and signed to be enforceable.

Steering Directing members of protected classes into buildings or areas that are occupied primarily by members of the same class.

Step-up lease Lease that has rent increases built into the schedule of rents.

Stigmatized property A property that is less desirable to buyers because of some occurrence on the property, such as a murder or suicide.

Stipulation A voluntary agreement between the DBPR and respondent (licensee).

Steering A discriminatory act in which a property manager steers members of protected classes into buildings or areas that are occupied primarily by members of the same class.

Subdivider A person who owns any interest in subdivided lands or who is engaged in the disposition of subdivided lands whether directly, indirectly, or through the services of an employee, agent, or independent contractor.

Subdivision Any contiguous land that is divided or proposed to be divided into 50 or more lots, parcels, units, or interests; or any land, whether contiguous or not, that is divided or proposed to be divided into 50 or more lots, parcels, units, or interests that are offered as part of a common promotional plan.

Subdivision plat map A plan of a tract of land subdivided into lots and showing required or planned amenities.

Subdivision regulations Control the size and location of streets and sidewalks, the placing of sewer and water lines and mandated drainage facilities, and the location of parks and open spaces.

Subordinate The act of a lender with high priority allowing another party to achieve a higher legal priority.

Subpoena A writ or order commanding the person named to appear and to testify in a legal proceeding.

Substitution An economic principle; no prudent buyer will pay more for a property than the cost of an equally desirable replacement property.

Successive sales analysis An appraisal technique used to adjust for market conditions that involves analyzing two or more of the same property over a period of time to derive the percentage of price change.

Summary suspension Emergency or immediate suspension of a license to protect the public.

Supply The quantity of goods or services offered for sale to consumers.

Survivability The quality of an estate with more than one owner giving immediate title to the party or parties who remain after one of the parties dies. Present in a joint tenancy and in a tenancy by the entireties.

T

Tax credit A direct reduction in the amount of taxes due.

Tax deduction An allowed cost or expense that reduces taxable income.

Telemarketing The use of the telephone as a marketing tool to solicit services directly to the public.

Telephone solicitation The initiation of a telephone call for the purpose of encouraging the purchase of, or investment in, property, goods, or services.

Tenancy at sufferance Continued occupancy by a tenant after lease expiration, without agreement from the landlord. The landlord does not need to give notice to require the tenant to move.

Tenancy at will A periodic tenancy that does not have a fixed term, and that requires specific notice to cancel the tenancy.

Tenancy by the entireties Undivided ownership of property by a married couple requiring both parties to sign any documents transferring an interest. The property passes immediately to the surviving party at the death of one of the spouses.

Tenancy for years A lease with a definite term of occupancy.

Tenancy in common An undivided interest in property held by two or more persons that passes to the heirs if one of the parties dies.

Tenant improvement allowance An amount given to a tenant to allow the tenant to renovate a property. Landlords often prefer to give an allowance rather than agree to do the work to reduce the risks in case the costs are greater than expected.

Term mortgage A mortgage that requires interest payments only, with the principal balance coming due in its entirety at maturity.

Testers Persons who visit a real estate sales office to determine that sales associates are not violating the fair housing laws.

30-day month method A method of prorating expenses and income on a closing statement that assumes 12 months of 30 days each. The annual cost of an item is divided first by 12 months to get a monthly rate, then the monthly rate is divided by 30 days to get a daily rate. The monthly rate is multiplied by the number of full months used, and the daily rate is multiplied by the number of days used in the month of closing.

Three-day notice A document from a landlord to a delinquent tenant demanding payment of the rent or possession of the premises within three days.

365-day method A method of prorating expenses and income on a closing statement that uses a 365-day year. The annual cost of an item is divided by 365 to get the daily rate, then the daily rate is multiplied by the number of days used.

Time is of the essence A clause in a sales contract that requires performance of the contract within the exact time limits specified in the agreement.

Time-sharing The right to occupy a property for a specific part of a year.

Title insurance A guarantee that the title insurance company will pay an owner or a mortgagee if title to property is later discovered to be defective.

Title theory A legal practice that gives a mortgagee (lender) title to the property and gives the mortgagor the right to occupy the property while not in default. When the mortgage is satisfied, a *reconveyance deed* is given to the borrower. *See* lien theory.

Total obligations ratio A guideline used by lenders evaluating the ability of a borrower to make mortgage payments. It is calculated by dividing the borrower's total obligations, including mortgage payment (PITI), by the borrower's gross monthly income.

Trade fixture An article that is attached by a commercial tenant as a necessary part of the tenant's trade or business.

Trade name A fictitious name that may be any name except the actual name or trade name of another FREC licensee or registrant.

Transaction broker A broker who provides limited representation to a buyer, a seller, or both in a real estate transaction, but does not represent either in a fiduciary capacity or as a single agent.

Transaction coordinator A person employed by a broker to handle the details of closings for the sales associates in a real estate firm.

Treble damages Triple damages.

Triple-net lease A lease that requires the tenant to pay not only rent but also taxes, maintenance, and insurance on the property.

Trust liability The total sum of all deposits received, pending, and being held by the broker at any point in time; it is other people's monies placed with the broker that corresponds to a specific real estate transaction.

U

Undivided interest No individual can identify his or her particular portion of the property.

Universal agent Authorized by the principal to perform all acts that the principal can personally perform and that may be lawfully delegated to another.

Unsecured note A promissory note without a mortgage, based strictly on the credit of the borrower.

USPAP The Uniform Standards of Professional Appraisal Practice; the accepted standard for real estate appraisal activity for federally related transactions.

V

Vacancy and collection loss An allowance for reductions in potential gross income attributable to vacancies and uncollected rent.

Vacation home Second homes that have income tax restrictions on the deductibility of expenses depending on the number of days rented during the year.

Valuation account An account set up in the books of a company to reflect current asset value. A common example of a valuation account is depreciation and amortization.

Value The worth of something.

Value in use The value of a property leased on a specified use that may not represent the property's maximum use (or highest and best use).

Variable expense Expenses that go up and down based on increases or decreases in sales or rental income.

Variance An exception to zoning regulations or ordinance granted to relieve a hardship.

Voluntary inactive The licensure status that results when a licensee has applied to the DBPR to be placed on inactive status.

W

Wetlands Land areas where groundwater is at or near the surface of the ground for enough of each year so as to produce a wetland plant community, such as swamps and marshes.

Writ of possession A court order allowing the landlord to evict a tenant.

Z

Zoning Classification of real property for various purposes; the government power to control and supervise the utilization of privately owned real property.

Zoning board of adjustment A semijudicial body whose primary function is to provide property owners with some degree of relief from otherwise rigid zoning codes.

INDEX

ANSWER SHEET

PRACTICE EXAM

Score: ____________________

Wrong Ways to mark answers:

RIGHT WAY to mark answers:

1	Ⓐ Ⓑ Ⓒ Ⓓ	**21**	Ⓐ Ⓑ Ⓒ Ⓓ	**41**	Ⓐ Ⓑ Ⓒ Ⓓ	**61**	Ⓐ Ⓑ Ⓒ Ⓓ	**81**	Ⓐ Ⓑ Ⓒ Ⓓ
2	Ⓐ Ⓑ Ⓒ Ⓓ	**22**	Ⓐ Ⓑ Ⓒ Ⓓ	**42**	Ⓐ Ⓑ Ⓒ Ⓓ	**62**	Ⓐ Ⓑ Ⓒ Ⓓ	**82**	Ⓐ Ⓑ Ⓒ Ⓓ
3	Ⓐ Ⓑ Ⓒ Ⓓ	**23**	Ⓐ Ⓑ Ⓒ Ⓓ	**43**	Ⓐ Ⓑ Ⓒ Ⓓ	**63**	Ⓐ Ⓑ Ⓒ Ⓓ	**83**	Ⓐ Ⓑ Ⓒ Ⓓ
4	Ⓐ Ⓑ Ⓒ Ⓓ	**24**	Ⓐ Ⓑ Ⓒ Ⓓ	**44**	Ⓐ Ⓑ Ⓒ Ⓓ	**64**	Ⓐ Ⓑ Ⓒ Ⓓ	**84**	Ⓐ Ⓑ Ⓒ Ⓓ
5	Ⓐ Ⓑ Ⓒ Ⓓ	**25**	Ⓐ Ⓑ Ⓒ Ⓓ	**45**	Ⓐ Ⓑ Ⓒ Ⓓ	**65**	Ⓐ Ⓑ Ⓒ Ⓓ	**85**	Ⓐ Ⓑ Ⓒ Ⓓ
6	Ⓐ Ⓑ Ⓒ Ⓓ	**26**	Ⓐ Ⓑ Ⓒ Ⓓ	**46**	Ⓐ Ⓑ Ⓒ Ⓓ	**66**	Ⓐ Ⓑ Ⓒ Ⓓ	**86**	Ⓐ Ⓑ Ⓒ Ⓓ
7	Ⓐ Ⓑ Ⓒ Ⓓ	**27**	Ⓐ Ⓑ Ⓒ Ⓓ	**47**	Ⓐ Ⓑ Ⓒ Ⓓ	**67**	Ⓐ Ⓑ Ⓒ Ⓓ	**87**	Ⓐ Ⓑ Ⓒ Ⓓ
8	Ⓐ Ⓑ Ⓒ Ⓓ	**28**	Ⓐ Ⓑ Ⓒ Ⓓ	**48**	Ⓐ Ⓑ Ⓒ Ⓓ	**68**	Ⓐ Ⓑ Ⓒ Ⓓ	**88**	Ⓐ Ⓑ Ⓒ Ⓓ
9	Ⓐ Ⓑ Ⓒ Ⓓ	**29**	Ⓐ Ⓑ Ⓒ Ⓓ	**49**	Ⓐ Ⓑ Ⓒ Ⓓ	**69**	Ⓐ Ⓑ Ⓒ Ⓓ	**89**	Ⓐ Ⓑ Ⓒ Ⓓ
10	Ⓐ Ⓑ Ⓒ Ⓓ	**30**	Ⓐ Ⓑ Ⓒ Ⓓ	**50**	Ⓐ Ⓑ Ⓒ Ⓓ	**70**	Ⓐ Ⓑ Ⓒ Ⓓ	**90**	Ⓐ Ⓑ Ⓒ Ⓓ
11	Ⓐ Ⓑ Ⓒ Ⓓ	**31**	Ⓐ Ⓑ Ⓒ Ⓓ	**51**	Ⓐ Ⓑ Ⓒ Ⓓ	**71**	Ⓐ Ⓑ Ⓒ Ⓓ	**91**	Ⓐ Ⓑ Ⓒ Ⓓ
12	Ⓐ Ⓑ Ⓒ Ⓓ	**32**	Ⓐ Ⓑ Ⓒ Ⓓ	**52**	Ⓐ Ⓑ Ⓒ Ⓓ	**72**	Ⓐ Ⓑ Ⓒ Ⓓ	**92**	Ⓐ Ⓑ Ⓒ Ⓓ
13	Ⓐ Ⓑ Ⓒ Ⓓ	**33**	Ⓐ Ⓑ Ⓒ Ⓓ	**53**	Ⓐ Ⓑ Ⓒ Ⓓ	**73**	Ⓐ Ⓑ Ⓒ Ⓓ	**93**	Ⓐ Ⓑ Ⓒ Ⓓ
14	Ⓐ Ⓑ Ⓒ Ⓓ	**34**	Ⓐ Ⓑ Ⓒ Ⓓ	**54**	Ⓐ Ⓑ Ⓒ Ⓓ	**74**	Ⓐ Ⓑ Ⓒ Ⓓ	**94**	Ⓐ Ⓑ Ⓒ Ⓓ
15	Ⓐ Ⓑ Ⓒ Ⓓ	**35**	Ⓐ Ⓑ Ⓒ Ⓓ	**55**	Ⓐ Ⓑ Ⓒ Ⓓ	**75**	Ⓐ Ⓑ Ⓒ Ⓓ	**95**	Ⓐ Ⓑ Ⓒ Ⓓ
16	Ⓐ Ⓑ Ⓒ Ⓓ	**36**	Ⓐ Ⓑ Ⓒ Ⓓ	**56**	Ⓐ Ⓑ Ⓒ Ⓓ	**76**	Ⓐ Ⓑ Ⓒ Ⓓ	**96**	Ⓐ Ⓑ Ⓒ Ⓓ
17	Ⓐ Ⓑ Ⓒ Ⓓ	**37**	Ⓐ Ⓑ Ⓒ Ⓓ	**57**	Ⓐ Ⓑ Ⓒ Ⓓ	**77**	Ⓐ Ⓑ Ⓒ Ⓓ	**97**	Ⓐ Ⓑ Ⓒ Ⓓ
18	Ⓐ Ⓑ Ⓒ Ⓓ	**38**	Ⓐ Ⓑ Ⓒ Ⓓ	**58**	Ⓐ Ⓑ Ⓒ Ⓓ	**78**	Ⓐ Ⓑ Ⓒ Ⓓ	**98**	Ⓐ Ⓑ Ⓒ Ⓓ
19	Ⓐ Ⓑ Ⓒ Ⓓ	**39**	Ⓐ Ⓑ Ⓒ Ⓓ	**59**	Ⓐ Ⓑ Ⓒ Ⓓ	**79**	Ⓐ Ⓑ Ⓒ Ⓓ	**99**	Ⓐ Ⓑ Ⓒ Ⓓ
20	Ⓐ Ⓑ Ⓒ Ⓓ	**40**	Ⓐ Ⓑ Ⓒ Ⓓ	**60**	Ⓐ Ⓑ Ⓒ Ⓓ	**80**	Ⓐ Ⓑ Ⓒ Ⓓ	**100**	Ⓐ Ⓑ Ⓒ Ⓓ

Notes

Notes

Notes

Notes

Notes

Notes